The Bluejackets' Manual

TWENTIETH EDITION

The
Bluejackets'
Manual

Revised by
Bill Bearden
and Bill Wedertz

United States Naval Institute
Annapolis, Maryland

Library of Congress Catalog Card Number: 3-1595
ISBN: 0-87021-111-0

Printed in the United States of America
Sixth printing with corrections, June 1981

This book is dedicated to all those sailors who held a steady helm in the past, those who are steering a straight course today, and those who will plot the Navy's path into the future.

THE UNITED STATES NAVY

GUARDIAN OF OUR COUNTRY

The United States Navy is responsible for maintaining control of the sea and is a ready force on watch at home and overseas, capable of strong action to preserve the peace or of instant offensive action to win in war.

It is upon the maintenance of this control that our country's glorious future depends; the United States Navy exists to make it so.

WE SERVE WITH HONOR

Tradition, valor, and victory are the Navy's heritage from the past. To these may be added dedication, discipline, and vigilance as the watchwords of the present and the future.

At home or on distant stations we serve with pride, confident in the respect of our country, our shipmates, and our families.

Our responsibilities sober us; our adversities strengthen us.

Service to God and Country is our special privilege. We serve with honor.

THE FUTURE OF THE NAVY

The Navy will always employ new weapons, new techniques, and greater power to protect and defend the United States on the sea, under the sea, and in the air.

Now and in the future, control of the sea gives the United States her greatest advantage for the maintenance of peace and for victory in war.

Mobility, surprise, dispersal, and offensive power are the keynotes of the new Navy. The roots of the Navy lie in a strong belief in the future, in continued dedication to our tasks, and in reflection on our heritage from the past.

Never have our opportunities and our responsibilities been greater.

Contents

Contents

Appendices

viii

Foreword

I can't think of any single book that has done so much to help young men and women become better sailors than *The Bluejackets' Manual*. Since 1902 it has become the definitive authority on naval matters, for everyone from the greenest recruit to the saltiest master chief.

Countless times in my career I have referred to *The Bluejackets' Manual* for information on subjects ranging from the Uniform Code of Military Justice, seamanship, military tradition and history, to ceremonial procedure. For those that need more in-depth information, thousands of words have been printed on each of these subjects, but the basic information contained in *The Bluejackets' Manual* is normally enough for any of us.

It is this "back to basics" approach that has made this book so much an integral part of a sailor's, particularly a new recruit's, life. This update of the 20th edition maintains the tradition started in 1902 and contains a wealth of naval and general military information that a sailor can use from the first day of "boot camp" to the day of retirement.

A sailor's life is not always an easy one, but the difficulty can be somewhat relieved by acquiring the knowledge necessary to be a good sailor. That knowledge can be found in these pages. I urge you to read *The Bluejackets' Manual* and use the information found herein. In doing so, you will make yourself a better sailor and make ours a better and stronger Navy.

Thomas S. Crow

Thomas S. Crow
Master Chief Petty Officer
of the Navy

Preface

When *The Bluejackets' Manual* first appeared in 1902, there were few sources of information available for the fledgling bluejacket. In the first *BJM*, LT Ridley McLean provided the first source of practical information for recruits, and the first handbook by which petty officers could endeavor to advance themselves.

Today there are literally thousands of different references: other textbooks, rate training manuals, technical manuals, etc. With this thought in mind, the 20th edition makes no pretense of being a comprehensive textbook. It is, however, a "back-to-basics" book that covers a lot of territory.

Graduation from boot camp does not mean an end to the usefulness of the 20th edition. Although the *BJM* is intended as a "Navy primer," this edition includes a great deal of information that will be of interest to career Navy men and women. It is thus a valuable reference book for all sailors.

Of particular interest is the addition of an extensive bibliography (Appendix J) which offers additional references, both official and unofficial, on hundreds of subjects. This should be especially useful to ship and station career counselors, retention teams, and other administrators, as well as to division officers and petty officers.

The 20th edition of *BJM* is a blend of the old Navy and new Navy. While the "old" is reflected in the Navy's time-honored customs and ceremonies, new material has been added in order to keep the *BJM* current with the technological advances and intricacies of today's Navy. The 20th has also been completely reillustrated with many never-before-published photos, taken by Navy photojournalists.

Acknowledgments

This newly revised edition of *The Bluejackets' Manual* is the product of considerable time and effort by more than 200 contributors. Assistance was sought from numerous ships, other seagoing commands and shore-based activities, as well as individual experts in all areas covered in *BJM*.

The majority of the customs, ceremonies, and traditions information and the naval history appendix is the result of the efforts of CDR Tyrone G. Martin, commanding officer of USS *Constitution*. Information on current ship and aircraft types came from Blanche Schneider, John C. Reilly, Jr., and Harland Foote; the Uniform Code of Military Justice—contained in Chapter 4—was prepared by Charlie West, of Baltimore, Maryland, a retired Army legal officer. P. E. Kiley provided the Security Program information.

Response from the fleet and force master chiefs was overwhelming. Of particular note was the assistance provided by MMCM(SS) Richard G. Slocum, Submarine Force, Pacific Fleet; NCCM Charles Griva, Commander-in-Chief, Pacific Fleet; and AVCM Harvey L. Murphy, Naval Reserve Headquarters.

Much of the material contained in Chapter 1 on recruit training was verified and updated by MMCM(SS) James H. (Rob) Roberts and MMCM Hal (Boots) Butcher, command master chiefs for RTC Orlando and RTC Great Lakes, respectively.

Other contributors included CUCM F.J. Bergeron, Naval Submarine Training Center, Pacific; SKCM Fred E. Stahl, Naval Technician Training Center, Meridian, Mississippi; and CTM1s Serio J. Rossi and Michael C. Carr and CTM3s Stephen L. Simpson and Allen J. Reynolds, all of the Naval Security Group Activity, Shaggs Island, Sonoma, Washington; Judy V. VanBenthuysen, CHINFO (OI-2252); and LT Roger Hull, YN1 Cathy Mason and Bunny Ellis, all of the Navy Recruiting Command's personnel office.

This edition would not have been possible without the tremendous across-the-board support from all departments and branches of the Naval Military Personnel Command. The continued support of everyone in the Master Chief Petty Officer of the Navy's office is greatly appreciated. They put us in touch with many of the experts—both within and outside the command—who assisted in updating this edition.

Other NMPC contributors who did their utmost to answer

Acknowl- our questions include RADM Harold G. Rich and his entire Pers-
edgments 6 staff, with special acknowledgements to LCDR Ronald B. Wils-
bach (Pers-6a2) and DMC Norman S. Butman (Pers-6b4). Other
help came from LCDR M.L. Franzia (Pers-242), Ben G. Lewis
(Pers-72A), YNC J. Wyatt (Pers-5232), and ENS Frank Simonds
(Pers-5132).

Some sound advice and constructive suggestions came from
members of the Naval Reserve. Of particular note were the con-
tributions of RMCM W.H. Smith, command master chief for the
Navy and Marine Corps Reserve Center, Orlando, Florida;
AVCM Sylvester Skaleski, command master chief for NAS Glen-
view, Illinois; YNCS J.F. Slusser, command senior chief for the
Naval Air Reserve Unit, North Island (San Diego), California; and
AKC F.N. Keener, command chief for the Naval Air Reserve Unit,
Point Mugu, California.

The photo illustrations for this edition are mostly the products
of the creative efforts of the Navy's photojournalist community.
All of the individual photo credits appear on page 577. The
photographic re-illustration of BJM could not have been accomplished without the untiring efforts of Bob Carlisle, CHINFO OI-
225, and the able assistance of his staffers, JO1 Evelyn Jutte,
Becky Walker, and Lyn Sundberg. The interest and support
received from PHC Milt Putnam, of the Atlantic Fleet Audio-Vi-
sual Command, and PH2 Dwain Patton, of CAMPUS Magazine
in Pensacola, was particularly helpful.

Special thanks go to Carol Swartz, Naval Institute editor of the
BJM, whose editorial guidance was invaluable. Considerable
time, attention to detail, and enthusiastic support came from
Peggy Oyler, Richard Carr, Steve Smith, Fred Higgins, Nush Gra-
bowski, Les and Gloria Gibbons, JO1 Mark Malinowski of
MCPON's office, NCC Bob Abbott, and NCCM Carl Jones, command master chief for the Chief of Naval Operations.

I. Welcome Aboard

1. Introduction to the Navy

Welcome Aboard! These words carry a world of significance. They mean that you have reached one of the biggest decisions a young person can make—you have volunteered to enlist in the United States Navy. By doing so, you have become a member of one of the most famous military services in the world, and have joined one of the biggest businesses in the United States. Not only have you proved your understanding of citizenship by offering your services to your country, but you also have taken the first step toward an exciting and rewarding career.

Today's Navy is a massive and complex organization—a far cry from the makeshift fleet that opposed the British in the Revolutionary War. At the beginning of March 1981, the Navy had 537,500 officers and enlisted personnel, 301,500 civilian employees, and an active operating force of 542 ships and 5,393 (active and "pipeline") aircraft. It will cost about $55.6 billion to operate the Navy this year; that's 32.2 percent of the entire U.S. defense budget or 7.7 percent of total federal spending.

The Navy plays a vital role in maintaining our national security; it protects us against our enemies in time of war, and supports our foreign policy in peacetime. Through its exercise of sea power, it ensures freedom of the seas, so that merchant ships can bring us the vital raw material we import from overseas—like petroleum, coffee, rubber, sugar, and aluminum. Sea power makes it possible for us to use the oceans when and where our national interests require it, and denies our enemies that same freedom.

First Enlistment

Your introduction to the Navy started at your home-town recruiting station, with interviews and processing by a trained petty officer. Your enlistment (often called a hitch or cruise) may be for four, five, or six years. (Four years is a normal hitch; five years is for those who are approved for training in one of 12 specific ratings; and six years is for those qualifying for nuclear, electronic, and submarine training.) If you enlisted for four years and are a high school graduate, you may have selected the Navy Occupational Specialty School Guarantee Program, which opens up a career in one of 50 specialty ratings in 12 fields; or you may have selected one of the 60 or more Navy technical schools.

Welcome Aboard   All recruits begin their naval careers at a Naval Training Center (NTC) in Great Lakes, Illinois; San Diego, California; or Orlando, Florida. Women are trained in Orlando; men may be sent to any of the three, with no assurance that it will be the one nearest home.

NAVAL TRAINING CENTER, GREAT LAKES
This center, located on Lake Michigan about 40 miles north of Chicago, was opened on 1 July 1911. During World War II, nearly a million men were trained at Great Lakes.

NAVAL TRAINING CENTER, SAN DIEGO
Located on San Diego Bay, this center was opened on 1 June 1923. San Diego is also homeport for many Pacific Fleet ships.

NAVAL TRAINING CENTER, ORLANDO
The Orlando center, about 50 miles west of the Kennedy Space Center, was opened 1 July 1968. All enlisted women—about 5,000 a year—receive training here.

4

Each Naval Training Center consists of three commands:
Administrative Command (AdCom) maintains buildings and grounds at the NTCs and provides housing, clothing, pay, and medical and dental care. AdCom also handles recreational and Navy Exchange facilities, communications, postal and transportation service, and police and fire protection.

Service School Command (SSC) consists of the schools that provide technical training for various ratings. These schools train petty officers from the fleet and recruits who have finished boot camp.

Recruit Training Command (RTC) is where you go first. The RTC puts you through the transition from civilian to military life with a very busy schedule of lectures and drills on the Navy's history, traditions, customs, and regulations. It also gives you instruction in basic military subjects.

The day of arrival at the center is called "receipt day," the day when your initial processing begins. The next day is "one-one day"—first week and first day of training; the rest of the first week consists of one-two day, one-three day, one-four day, and so on.

If you don't already have a social security number, you will be assigned one, and that number will be yours for the rest of your life. Memorize it, because almost every form you fill out in the Navy will require it.

Enlistment

First Weeks in the Navy

The procedure may vary from one training center to another, but in general it goes like this: Report in, turn in orders, and draw your bedding and bunk assignment for your first night "on board." That same day, or the next, you will begin training. You will also fill out forms: a bedding custody card, a stencil chit, a receipt for a chit book (to be used instead of money for purchases at the Navy Exchange), a safe-arrival card for your parents, a clothing requisition, a packing slip to send your personal gear home (the Navy pays the shipping costs), and others.

You might have your first meal while still in civilian clothes. Here is a typical menu:

Breakfast	Dinner	Supper
Hard or Soft Cooked Eggs	Spaghetti	Country-Style Chicken
Grilled Hot Cakes	Baked Lasagna	Chicken Gravy
Hot Maple Syrup	Lyonnaise Green Beans	Oven-Browned Potatoes
Beef Hash	Pepperoni Pizza	Buttered Green Peas
Broiled Ham Slices	Toasted Garlic Bread	Salad Bar
Pastry Bar	Chilled Peach Halves	Pineapple Pudding

Speed Line	Speed Line
Chilled Prunes	Chicken Noodle Soup
Chilled Fruit Juice	Hot Fish Sandwich
Assorted Dry Cereal	Salad Bar
Hot Oatmeal	Fruit Jello

And you'll get a haircut. The barbers won't scalp you; they'll leave something to comb—but you won't have much time to comb it. Later, at your first duty station, you will be allowed some choice in hair style, as long as it stays within the Navy's standards for grooming.

Your schedule will include the following:

COMPLETE MEDICAL EXAMINATION
The exam will cover eyes, teeth, heart, blood, urinalysis, X-rays, inoculation—the works. If you need dental work, it will be scheduled.

CHIT BOOK AND DITTY BAG ISSUE
You will be issued a chit book of coupons you can use to spend in the exchange, for toilet articles, sewing kit, shoeshine gear, notebook, stationery, postage stamps, and a pen and pencil. The total cost will be deducted from your pay.

5

INITIAL CLOTHING ISSUE

This includes enough uniform clothing to make you look like a sailor. Eventually you will receive a complete outfit, or seabag, worth hundreds of dollars, and a marking stencil for putting your name on every item.

Training Organization

Soon after you've reported in, you will be placed in a training unit (TU) and will meet the people you'll be with for the next several weeks. Then, during a formal commissioning ceremony, an officer will welcome you to the training center, give a brief talk on the history and mission of the Navy, assign your unit a training number, present a unit flag (guidon) bearing that number, and introduce your company commander (CC). (While traditionally known as CCs, they are sometimes called training unit supervisors (TUS), although this term is used mostly in written correspondence.)

COMPANY COMMANDER

Each training unit, about 84 recruits, is taken through training by its CC—an outstanding leading petty officer who is intimately familiar with instructional techniques, principles of leadership, and administrative procedures. The CC instructs you in military and physical drill and shows you how to keep yourself, your clothing, equipment, and barracks in smart, shipshape condition. While you're in RTC, as far as you're concerned your

Figure 1–1 The company commander, the most important person in the Navy for the recruit, takes the new sailor through training.

company commander is the most important person in the Navy. Your CC also went through recruit training some years ago and has many years of naval experience. Follow the example of your CC and you'll have a good start on a successful Navy career.

While you are at RTC, your CC is one person who is always available to answer questions and help you. The CC is the only person in the chain of command that you can talk to directly without first obtaining permission from someone else.

CHAIN OF COMMAND

The Navy is organized like a pyramid, with one man on top and many people (recruits) on the bottom. From highest to lowest, it runs like this:

Chief of Naval Operations (CNO)
Chief of Naval Education and Training (CNET)
Chief of Naval Technical Training (CNTECHTRA)
Commander NTC
Commanding Officer RTC
Executive Officer RTC
Brigade Commander
Regimental Commander
Battalion Commander
Company Commander
Recruits

You may start out at the bottom of the pyramid, but the Navy will spend a lot of time and money making you into the kind of sharp, well-trained sailor it needs.

Remember that everyone in the Navy began at the bottom, and senior officers were once recruits exactly like you. Everyone in the Navy is junior to someone; but since about 85,000 men and women enlist every year, there will already be at least a dozen other people junior to you before you finish reading this.

RECRUIT ORIENTATION

This is when you're taught the basics about the way the Navy does things. First you have to become familiar with salutes, uniforms, customs and ceremonies, Navy routine and time, and terminology. In training you'll spend many hours learning the details of these subjects, but this is what you need to know to start.

Salutes: You must salute all officers, men and women, when addressed by them or when meeting them. While you're in recruit training, you must also salute all senior petty officers wearing aiguilletes.

Uniforms: The uniform worn by a Navy person shows at a glance his rank or rating and thus his military authority. You must

Figure 1–2 A company commander teaches one of the basics of military service —a proper salute.

quickly learn to identify those officers and enlisted people that you see most often during training. Each officer wears a gold cap device made up of a shield, eagle, and crossed anchors. The number of gold stripes on the sleeves or shoulder boards shows the rank—three for commander, two and one-half for lieutenant commander, two for lieutenant, etc. (See chapter 3, Uniforms.)

Customs and ceremonies: The ceremony of "colors"—the raising and lowering of the United States flag—is performed twice a day. "The Star Spangled Banner" is played by the band, if there is one, and everyone within sight stops, faces the colors, and salutes—from the first note of the music or bugle call "attention," until the last note or the call "secure."

The most impressive ceremony at the RTC is graduation, when your company and others take part in a full parade, with band, color guard, and a special company carrying the flags of all 50 states. A senior officer reviews the companies, gives official recognition to outstanding recruits, and presents other awards.

Routine: The daily routine at the training center and elsewhere in the Navy appears in a bulletin called the plan of the day (POD). It issues the special orders for the day, gives the hours of meals, inspections, parades, and other events; names duty officers and duty petty officers; and even lists the titles and times of movies. You should read the POD every day.

Time: The Navy runs on a 24-hour day. When you go aboard ship you will see a clock with a 24-hour dial. Hours of the day are numbered from 1 to 24; at noon, instead of starting again with 1, the Navy goes on to 13. The hours, such as 8 A.M., or 7 P.M., are called 0800 (zero eight hundred) and 1900 (nineteen hundred). Never say "nineteen hundred hours." Hours and minutes in Navy time go like this: 10:45 A.M. is 1045 (ten forty-five), 9:30 P.M. is 2130 (twenty-one thirty).

Terminology: The Navy uses many different words for the same things you had at home. Beds are bunks, bathrooms are heads, floors are decks, walls are bulkheads, stairways are ladders, and drinking fountains are scuttlebutts. You go topside for upstairs; below for downstairs. The Navy also uses short abbreviations in place of long titles, such as these:

APO	Athletic petty officer
BI	Barracks inspection
CC	Company commander
CD	Competitive drill
DDPO	Division duty petty officer
DOT	Day of training
EPO	Educational petty officer
FFTU	Firefighting training unit
MAB	Military aptitude board
MD	Military drill
MDT	Military day of training
MED	Medical evaluation division
MTDPO	Military training duty petty officer
MTO	Military training officer
MTSA	Military training special assistant
NQS	Non-qualified swimmer
PI	Personnel inspection
RCPO	Recruit chief petty officer
RFAT	Recruit final achievement test
RIF	Recruit in-processing facility
ROD	Rate-grade title of the day
RPOD	Recruit plan-of-the-day
STD	Special training division
TOD	Term of the day
TTO	Technical training officer
TU	Training unit

Back to School

Recruit training will keep you busier than you've ever been, with a daily schedule of a dozen 40-minute instruction periods, five days a week, and a 10-minute break between the periods.

DAILY ROUTINE
0530	Reveille
0545	Breakfast (to 0730)
0615	Morning muster, field day
0730	Commence instruction periods
0755	First call
0800	Colors, sick call
1100	Noon meal (to 1330)

1300   Sick call
1650   Evening meal (to 1900)
1720   Recreation and athletic events, cafeteria, telephone center open to 2000
          First call to colors 5 minutes prior to sunset
          Sunset—colors
1800   Free period, study (to 2000)
2000   Field day (to 2100)
2100   Shower
2130   Taps, bed check

SATURDAY ROUTINE
0530   Reveille
0545   Breakfast (to 0730)
0755   First call
0800   Colors, sick call
0830   Athletic events as scheduled
1100   Noon meal (to 1330)
1300   Sick call, free period
1650   Supper (to 1900)
1730   Recreation and athletic events, cafeteria, telephone center open until 2000
          First call to colors 5 minutes prior to sunset
          Sunset—colors
1800   Free period (to 2000)
2000   Field day (to 2100)
2100   Shower
2130   Taps, bed check

10

Figure 1–3 "A place for everything and everything in its place" makes sense when you're aboard ship, where clothing space is at a premium, and ashore.

Instruction covers four general areas: naval and military training, technical training, administrative, and processing. Subjects include:

Accident prevention	Leave, liberty, and conduct ashore
Advancement program	Lookout training
Aircraft familiarization	Marlinespike seamanship
Career incentives/medical benefits	Military drill
Chain of command	3-M system
Classification	Navy mission and organization
Code of conduct/Geneva Convention	NBC warfare/defense
Cultural adjustments	Officer recognition
Decision-making and time management	Operational security
Deck equipment	Ordnance and weapons
Damage control	Paint and preservation
Education benefits	Personal hygiene
Enlisted service record	Physical conditioning
Financial responsibility	Rates and ratings
Firefighting	Security information
First aid	Ship familiarization
General orders	Small boats
Hand salute and greetings	Survival at sea
History of the Navy	Telephone talkers
Honors and ceremonies	Uniform Code of Military Justice
Inspections	Watch, quarter, and station bill
Leave and earning statement/pay	Watchstanding

ID card: The Armed Forces of the United States Identification Card—ID card for short—identifies you as a member of the armed forces. It is not a pass; it remains government property while you have it, and must be returned when you're discharged. Altering it, damaging it, counterfeiting it, or using it in an unauthorized manner—such as lending your card to someone, or borrowing another person's card—can result in disciplinary action.

Active-duty personnel are issued green ID cards; inactive-duty personnel get a red card; retired personnel get a blue one. An active-duty card shows your name, social security number, photograph, and the date your enlistment expires. Carry your card at all times. It also serves as your Geneva Convention Card, relative to the treatment of prisoners of war.

Cards of those in paygrades E-1 to E-3 are marked "non-petty officer." Cards for E-4s to E-9s carry the identification PO3, PO2,

PO1, CPO, SCPO, or MCPO, as appropriate. If you lose your card, you will have to sign a statement telling the circumstances of the loss.

Special requests: If your request is reasonable, it will probably be granted. Requests are normally made by means of the special request/authorization form (NAVPERS Form 1336/3—often called a request chit) which covers special liberty, leave, special pay, commuted rations, and most other requests not specifically provided for otherwise.

NAVAL AND MILITARY TRAINING

This involves a lot more than learning to march. Military drill will teach you the importance of instant response to orders and the absolute necessity for teamwork. You will see the significance of this later—on the flight deck of an aircraft carrier, in the control tower aboard a naval air station, or in the nerve center of a nuclear submarine. Few jobs in the Navy are completely independent; you must depend upon your shipmates, and they on you.

Training in this area also includes instruction in folding and stowing clothing, barracks sanitation, watchstanding, and the general orders. You'll also study the Navy organizational structure, mission, and regulations. All hands in the Navy, no matter what their specialty, must have the same basic knowledge, and be able to perform the same military duties.

TECHNICAL TRAINING

Technical training begins at the training center and continues throughout your tour in the Navy. At RTC you will have training sessions covering seamanship, firefighting, NBC (nuclear, biological, and chemical) defense, weapons and ordnance, ships and aircraft, maintenance, and rating duties. You will also study general subjects such as uniforms, salutes, history, discipline and justice, and pay and allowances.

ADMINISTRATIVE AND PROCESSING

These periods enable you to have final classification interviews; arrange for pay, uniform fittings, and all medical and dental work; obtain ID cards; mark uniform equipment; and arrange to pick up records, orders, and transportation when you complete training.

CLASSIFICATION

This process helps the Navy select and train the right person for the right job. Classification identifies you in two ways— through your Armed Services Vocational Aptitude Battery

(ASVAB) scores, and through Navy Enlisted Classification (NEC) codes. Classification tests measure your basic aptitudes and are designed to find out how much you can *learn*, rather than how much you already *know*. The ASVAB testing and classification interviews have already been given to you at the Armed Forces Examining and Entrance Station (AFEES) in or near your home town. Besides these tests, a trained Navy classifier has already asked about your hobbies, interests, previous job experience, education, and what you think you would like to do in the Navy.

While you're in recruit training you'll be given your final classification.

SCHOOLS

The chief objective of Navy enlisted training—which costs millions of dollars a year—is to develop recruits into petty officers who can handle the technical requirements of their ratings. Some men may put in two or three tours of sea duty and go through several schools to become tops in their ratings. Recruit training at the Class R school is the first step. Next comes either apprentice training, or a Class A school; then assignment to the fleet. The Navy maintains about 60 Class A schools, which train more than 50,000 persons a year. About 60 percent of all recruits are selected for an "A" school, at Great Lakes, San Diego, or Orlando.

All training in the Navy is under the control of the Chief of Naval Education and Training (CNET), whose headquarters are in Pensacola, Florida. CNET plans and directs training programs for several hundred activities—everything from basic recruit training to postgraduate instruction for officers. CNET also handles dependents' educational programs.

APPRENTICESHIP TRAINING

When your unit completes basic military training, some members of the unit will go on to Class A schools, while others will enter apprenticeship programs. Those selected for such training will receive intensive instruction as seamen, firemen, or airmen. Apprenticeship courses last four weeks.

COMPETITION

The Navy is based on competition. Sailors compete with one another for advancement in rating, and ships compete with each other in gunnery, engineering, and communications. In recruit training, your unit will compete for a series of weekly awards for athletic skill, scholastic achievement, military drill, inspections, and overall excellence.

Flags awarded to winning training units are carried in dress parades and reviews. The training unit guidon, bearing the unit number, may also carry athletic streamers for awards won in competition on the obstacle course, in swimming, tug-of-war, volleyball, and various track-and-field events. At the weekly graduation review, one person is selected from all graduating honor men or women and recruit chief petty officers (RCPOs) to receive the American Spirit Honor Medal. Honor men and women also receive special recognition certificates.

Personal Affairs

When you report for training, your parents or next of kin will receive notice of your correct address. Your civilian clothing may be donated to charity or sent home at government expense. Because of the great number of recruits in training, and the tight schedule, you cannot receive telephone calls; but usually, during evenings and weekends, you may make long-distance collect calls.

Visitors are not permitted during the first few weeks of training. Later, a visiting time will be scheduled and you may send this information to your family. You will also be given information to send home about graduation review. You will probably be allowed to invite your parents to dine in the mess hall with you on graduation day.

PAY

All hands in the Navy are paid twice a month, usually by check if ashore and in cash if at sea. While at RTC you will not receive pay until you are granted your first liberty—permission to leave the base. On transfer from the RTC, you will be paid up to date, minus deductions for allotments, and for the chit book and ditty bag you were issued.

LIBERTY AND LEAVE

You may expect liberty once during recruit training and again at the end of that training. After completion of all entry training, including your apprenticeship program and "A" school, you will normally be allowed to take leave en route to your first duty station.

RECREATION

In your spare time, you will be allowed to use the center's recreational facilities, which include a library, movie theater, swimming pool, bowling alleys, pool room, TV lounge, gym, snack bars, and cafeteria.

RELIGION

You will be given full opportunity to attend the church of your choice. All training centers have chapels in which Catholic, Jewish, and Protestant services are conducted by chaplains, who are also available for pastoral counseling and religious education. Recruit choirs are organized and trained to sing at the services.

ORDERS

Before you know it, recruit training will be over. And it won't be long before you will be an apprentice instead of a recruit—you'll have another stripe and be getting higher pay. Some of your "shipmates," those who went through training with you, may go with you to your next assignment. Some you will never see again. Others you may meet years later when you are a petty officer.

Being handed a set of orders means going on to new experiences, meeting new people, and moving one step along in your Navy career. Better yet, orders mean a new start in a new job—perhaps even aboard a new ship. No matter how things went before, you have an opportunity to do better. There's even the possibility that, years later, with two or three hashmarks on your sleeve, you may be right back at the RTC, training recruits.

15

2. Classification, Rates, and Ratings

The recruit training curriculum is a concentrated course in basic naval skills and knowledge. In just a few weeks, this "cram" course starts everyone off on an equal footing. During basic training you will take a series of tests and interviews that will determine which way you go in the Navy.

Early in recruit training you will be scheduled for a classification interview. This kind of vocational counseling enables the Navy to train and select the right person for the right job. The classification process will identify you in two ways—by the results of the Armed Services Vocational Aptitude Battery (ASVAB) and by your Navy Enlisted Classification (NEC) code.

Navy Classification Tests

The ASVAB test—formerly called the BTB (basic test battery)—which you took before entering the Navy, is used to measure your basic aptitudes. In other words, this test finds out what you learned in school or on civilian jobs, and how you compare with other recruits. It is mainly concerned with how much you can *learn*, rather than how much you *know*.

In addition to the ASVAB, two other types of tests are administered: the Nuclear Field Qualification Test (NFQT) and the Defense Language Aptitude Battery (DLAB). These tests are used to screen candidates for advanced specialized training. Your eligibility to take these tests is based on your ASVAB scores.

Test scores are important in your Navy career. They determine whether you go to a service school or to the fleet; and they help determine your eligibility for advanced training. Be sure you know your scores in the ASVAB. They show your strong and weak points, they will save you time and effort by eliminating ratings or duties that would be very difficult for you, and they will give you a good idea of the ratings and duties for which you are best suited.

Ratings and Rates

Ratings and Rates

A rating is a Navy job—a duty calling for certain skills and aptitudes. The rating of engineman, for example, calls for persons who are good with their hands and are mechanically inclined. A paygrade (such as E-4, E-5, E-6) within a rating is called a rate. Thus an engineman third class (EN3) would have a rating of engineman, and rate of third class petty officer.

The term *petty officer* (PO) applies to anyone in paygrades E-4 through E-9. E-1s through E-3s are called non-rated personnel. Personnel in general apprenticeships are identified as recruit (E-1), apprentice (E-2), or, at the E-3 level, by their apprenticeship field—such as seaman, fireman, airman, constructionman, dentalman, or hospitalman. A person training for a specific job in paygrades E-1 through E-3 is called a *striker*—one who has been authorized to "strike" or train for a particular job.

Enlisted seniority is determined by time in rate and time in the Navy. If two petty officers are in the same paygrade, the one in that grade the longest is considered senior. In the case of two POs in the same paygrade with the same amount of time, the one having the most time in the next lower paygrade is senior.

RATINGS

These are divided into three categories—general, service, and emergency.

General ratings are broad occupational fields for paygrades E-4 through E-9. Each general rating has a distinctive badge. General ratings are sometimes combined at the E-8 or E-9 level, when the work is similar, to form even broader occupational fields. For example, senior chief instrumentman (IMCS) and senior chief opticalman (OMCS) can be combined to form the rating of master chief precision instrumentman (PICM). Some general ratings include service ratings; others do not.

Service ratings are subdivisions of a general rating, which require specialized training. There are service ratings at any petty officer level; however, they are most common with E-4s and E-5s. In the higher paygrades, service ratings merge into a general rating, usually at the E-8 level. For example, a chief fire control technician G (gun fire control) is an FTGC until the E-8 level and then becomes an FTCS. As an FTCS, he must be knowledgeable about both guns and missiles.

Emergency ratings are used to identify civilian occupational fields that are only used in time of war; e.g., stevedore, transportationman, and welfare and recreation leader. There are no emergency ratings in use today.

RATES

A *rate* identifies the level of your rating. For example, the yeoman rating is broken down into rates E-1 through E-9. *General rates* (not to be confused with general ratings) are the general apprenticeships that identify enlisted personnel in grades E-1, E-2, and E-3. Within these apprenticeships, enlisted personnel receive their recruit training and initial technical training, as preparation for advancement to petty officer or a service rating. E-1 is generally where recruits start. E-2s (apprentices) perform the routine duties of their occupational groups, but they also perform duties with more responsibility. General rates are identified by various colored stripes.

Title	Color of Stripe
Seaman (SN)	White
Hospitalman (HN)	White
Dentalman (DN)	White
Fireman (FN)	Red
Constructionman (CN)	Blue
Airman (AN)	Green

Stripes are navy blue on white uniform except for FN, CN, and AN which are the same color as described above on all uniforms.

18

The following is a basic description of the duties of E-3s:

Seaman (SN): Keep compartments, lines, rigging, decks, and deck machinery shipshape. Act as lookouts, members of gun crews, helmsmen, and security and fire sentries.

Hospitalman (HN): Arrange dressing carriages with sterile instruments, dressings, bandages, and medicines. Apply dressings. Give morning and evening care to patients. Keep medical records.

Dentalman (DN): Assist dental officers in the treatment of patients. Render first aid. Clean and service dental equipment. Keep dental records.

Fireman (FN): Care for and operate boilers. Operate pumps, motors, and turbines. Record readings of gauges, and maintain and clean engineering machinery and compartments. Stand security and fireroom watches.

Constructionman (CN): Operate, service, and check construction equipment. Perform semiskilled duties in construction battalion. Stand guard watches.

Airman (AN): Perform various duties for naval air activities ashore and afloat. Assist in moving aircraft. Load and stow equipment and supplies. Maintain compartments and buildings. Act as members of plane-handling crews.

Petty officer rating groups include paygrades E-4 through E-9, as follows: *E-4*, petty officer third class (PO3); *E-5*, petty officer second class (PO2); *E-6*, petty officer first class (PO1); *E-7*, chief petty officer (CPO); *E-8*, senior chief petty officer (SCPO); and *E-9*, master chief petty officer (MCPO).

Figure 2–1 Enlisted seniority is determined by time in rate and time in the Navy.

Navy Enlisted Classification (NEC) Codes

While the ASVAB measures your basic aptitudes when you enter the Navy, Navy Enlisted Classification (NEC) codes show the aptitudes, special skills, and qualifications that you have *now*. The rating system is a form of classification; for instance, you probably have a pretty good idea what a quartermaster third class (QM3), a fireman (FN), or a chief yeoman (YNC) do. But,

there are certain things a rate doesn't show, and this is where the
NECs come in.

An NEC is a four-digit number that indicates your skills, qualifications, and aptitudes. Every enlisted person has both a primary
and a secondary code number. Some sailors are identified only
by a primary code, but will have an all-zero secondary code,
such as a 3221/0000. A 3221 is a Navy Broadcast Journalist; the
secondary code (0000) indicates that the individual holds no
other qualification beyond the primary code.

NECs determine where you will work and what you will do.
They are invaluable to detailers—the administrative people at
the Naval Military Personnel Command (NMPC) in Washington,
D.C.—who are responsible for filling the Navy's job requirements. The codes are of three types: entry series, rating series,
and special series.

ENTRY SERIES

These codes are assigned to personnel who are not yet designated as strikers but have received training, are in training, or
have the aptitude to be trained for the appropriate rating. There
are two types of codes: defense grouping (DG) codes and rating
conversion codes. All DG codes end in 0 and are assigned to
personnel in paygrades E-1 through E-3, except for designated
strikers, and men and women in the ratings of hospital corpsman
(HM) and dental technician (DT). The code DG-9700, for example, is assigned to sailors who will become either boatswain's
mates (BMs) or quartermasters (QMs). Rating conversion codes,
which end either in 99 or a letter plus 9, are assigned to persons
in training for conversion to another rating. For example: a PN-
2699 is a person converting to the personnelman (PN) rating; a
YN-2599 is a convertee to the Yeoman (YN) rating. Entry NECs
are always primary codes.

RATING SERIES

These NECs supplement the general and service ratings. Most
are prefixed by two-letter abbreviations (but there are exceptions). Rating series NECs may appear as either primary or secondary codes. For example, an HM1—hospital corpsman first
class—who has experience in the preparation and maintenance
of eye glasses would have an NEC of HM-8463, which identifies
that person as an Optician Technician.

SPECIAL SERIES

These NECs are assigned only as secondary codes. They
usually are not directly related to a particular rating. Examples of
special series NECs are: Drug Detector Dog Handler, 9542; Petroleum Specialist, 9561; and Locksmith, 9583.

With a few exceptions, all NECs are assigned at NMPC. Changes in your NECs are made only when a training command reports that you have completed a course (earning you a specialty code), when a command shows that your specialty code should be canceled, or when a command reports that you have earned a code through on-the-job training (OJT).

Because NECs identify billets and the personnel qualified to fill them, make sure your NECs actually reflect your qualifications. Not keeping your codes up to date may keep you from getting the duty you want. You may have up to five NECs, although the two most important ones will appear as your primary and secondary codes. All of them are kept in your permanent record at NMPC and are available to the detailers there when you become eligible for reassignment.

Navy Enlisted Occupational Fields

There are 24 major occupational career fields for enlisted personnel. By combining all the foregoing information, the Navy can place each person into one of the 24 fields, which are made up of general ratings. The purpose of all this is to simplify the identification process, enabling the Navy to match the most qualified person to the job.

A complete analysis of each field may be found in Section I of the Manual of Navy Enlisted Manpower and Personnel Classifications and Occupational Standards (NAVPERS 18068). Section II contains a listing of all NECs.

All ratings in which Navy men and women work are described on the following pages. You will notice that these jobs are not all mechanical or technical; in fact, many would be known in civilian life as "white-collar" jobs. The specialty mark of each rating is included with the rating description. Specialty marks were added to enlisted uniforms in 1866. They originally represented the instrument used to perform the particular task. For example, the quartermaster (QM) has a ship's helm while a gunner's mate (GM) has two crossed cannons. The custom of representing the type of work with a specialty mark for each rating continues, but often the design has been stylized. For instance, the journalist (JO) is represented by crossed quill and scroll, and the cryptologic technician (CT) is crossed quill and spark.

OCCUPATIONAL FIELDS
1. General Seamanship—BM, SM
2. Ship Operations—OS, QM
3. Marine Engineering—BT, EM, EN, GS, IC, MM
4. Ship Maintenance—HT, IM, MR, ML, OM, PM

5. Aviation Maintenance/Weapons—PR, AX, AE, AT, AQ, AD, AZ, AO, AM
6. Aviation Ground Support—AB, AS
7. Air Traffic Control—AC
8. Weapons Control—ET, FT
9. Ordnance Systems—GM, MN, MT, TM
10. Sensor Operations—EW, OT, ST
11. Weapons System Support—TD
12. Data Systems—DP, DS
13. Construction—BU, CE, CM, EA, EO, SW, UT
14. Health Care—DT, HM
15. Administration—LN, NC, PN, PC, YN, RP
16. Logistics—AK, DK, MS, SH, SK
17. Media—DM, JO, LI, PH
18. Musician—MU
19. Master-at-Arms—MA
20. Cryptology—CT
21. Communications—RM
22. Intelligence—IS
23. Meteorology—AG
24. Aviation Sensor Operations—AW

Here's how the general rates of E-2, and E-3 fit into the occupational fields:

SA, SN—1, 2, 4, 8, 9, 10, 12, 15, 16, 17, 18, 20, 21, 22
FA, FN—3, 4
CA, CN—13
AA, AN—5, 6, 7, 11, 16, 17, 23, 24
HA, HN—14
DA, DN—14

AB

Cross anchors, winged

Aviation Boatswain's Mate: ABs operate, maintain, and repair aircraft catapults, arresting gear, and barricades. They operate and maintain fuel and lube oil transfer systems. ABs direct aircraft on the flight deck and in hangar bays before launch and after recovery. They use tow tractors to position planes and operate support equipment used to start aircraft.

AC

Microphone, winged

Air Traffic Controller: ACs assist in the essential safe, orderly, and speedy flow of air traffic by directing and controlling aircraft. They operate field lighting systems, communicate with aircraft, furnish pilots with information regarding traffic, navigation, and weather conditions. They operate and adjust GCA (ground-controlled approach) systems. They interpret targets on radar screens and plot aircraft positions.

AD

Two-bladed propeller, winged

Aviation Machinist's Mate: ADs usually are assigned to billets concerned with maintaining turbojet aircraft engines and associated equipment, or to any one of the several types of aircraft maintenance activities. ADs maintain, service, adjust, and replace aircraft engines and accessories, as well as perform the duties of flight engineers.

23

AE

Globe, winged

Aviation Electrician's Mates: AEs maintain, adjust, and repair aircraft electrical power generating and converting systems, lighting, control and indicating systems, as well as install and maintain wiring and flight and engine instrument systems.

AG

Circle on vertical arrow, winged

Aerographer's Mate: The Navy has its own weather forecasters—AGs, who are trained in meteorology and the use of aerological instruments that monitor such weather characteristics as air pressure, temperature, humidity, wind speed, and wind direction. They prepare weather maps and forecasts, analyze atmospheric conditions to determine the best flight levels for aircraft, and measure wind and air density to aid the accuracy of antiaircraft firing, shore bombardment, and delivery of weapons by aircraft.

AK

Crossed keys, winged

Aviation Storekeeper: AKs ensure that the materials and equipment needed by naval aviation activities are available and in good order. They take inventory, estimate future needs, and make purchases. AKs store and issue flight clothing, aeronautical materials and spare parts, as well as ordnance, electronic, structural and engineering equipment.

AM

Crossed mauls,
winged

Aviation Structural Mechanic: The maintenance and repair of aircraft parts (wings, fuselage, tail, control surfaces, landing gear and attending mechanisms) are performed by AMs working with metals, alloys, and plastics. AMs maintain and repair safety equipment and hydraulic systems.

AO

Flaming spherical
shell, winged

Aviation Ordnanceman: Navy planes carry guns, bombs, torpedoes, rockets, and missiles to attack the enemy on the sea, under the sea, in the air, and on land. AOs are responsible for maintaining, repairing, installing, operating, and handling aviation ordnance equipment; their duties also include the handling, stowing, issuing and loading of munitions and small arms.

AQ

Range finder,
winged

24

Aviation Fire Control Technician: AQs test, maintain and repair aviation fire-control equipment, as well as inspect, clean, lubricate, test, and adjust bomb directors, armament control systems, computers, gyros, optical components, and fire-control radars. They also maintain air-launched guided-missile test equipment.

AS

Crossed maul and
spark, winged

Aviation Support Equipment Technician: ASs perform intermediate maintenance on "yellow"— aviation accessory—equipment at naval air stations and aboard carriers. They maintain gasoline and diesel engines; hydraulic and pneumatic systems; liquid, gaseous oxygen, and nitrogen systems; gas turbine compressor units; and electrical systems.

AT

Helium atom,
winged

Aviation Electronics Technician: Modern aircraft depend on radio, radar, and other electronic devices for rapid communications, efficient navigation, controlled landing approaches, detection of (and guidance to) objectives, and neutralizing enemy equipment and tactics. ATs are responsible for the test, maintenance, and repair of this equipment.

AW

Spark-pierced
electron orbits over
wave, winged

Aviation Antisubmarine Warfare Operator: AWs operate airborne radar and electronic equipment used in detecting, locating, and tracking submarines. AWs also operate radars to provide information for aircraft and surface navigation. They act as helicopter-rescue crewmen and serve as part of the flight crew on long-range and intermediate-range aircraft.

AX

Sparked arrow piercing water, winged

Aviation Antisubmarine Warfare Technician: AXs inspect and maintain ASW systems and equipment, including those related to magnetic anomaly detection, long- and short-range underwater detection, nuclei detection, integrated displays, and associated ASW equipment. AXs install and remove equipment in aircraft, test for short circuits, grounds, broken cables, and pressure leaks.

AZ

Two-bladed propeller on open book, winged

Aviation Maintenance Administrationman: The many clerical, administrative, and managerial duties necessary to keep aircraft maintenance activities running smoothly are handled by the AZs. They plan, schedule, and coordinate the maintenance workload, including inspections and modifications to aircraft and equipment.

BM

Crossed anchors

Boatswain's Mate: BMs are expert seamen who maintain the ship, serve as steersmen, take command of tugs and other small craft, serve as gun captains, look after rigging, paint, handle and care for deck equipment, and serve on working parties and damage-control teams. BMs in upper grades train and supervise others in caring for and handling deck equipment and small boats.

25

BT

Hero's boiler

Boiler Technician: Because the propelling agent of our large naval ships is steam, the Navy relies on BTs to keep its ships moving. BTs operate and repair marine boilers and fireroom machinery, and they transfer, test, and inventory fuels and water.

BU

Carpenter's square on plumb bob

Builder: Navy BUs are like civilian construction workers. They may be skilled carpenters, plasterers, roofers, cement finishers, asphalt workers, masons, painters, bricklayers, sawmill operators, or cabinetmakers. BUs build and repair all types of structures, including piers, bridges, towers, underwater installations, schools, offices, houses, and other buildings.

CE

Spark on telephone pole

Construction Electrician: CEs are responsible for the power production and electrical work required to build and operate airfields, roads, barracks, hospitals, shops, and warehouses. The work of Navy CEs is like that of civilian construction electricians, powerhouse electricians, telephone and electrical repairmen, substation operators, linemen, and others.

CM

Double-headed
wrench on nut

Construction Mechanic: CMs are specialists in maintaining heavy construction and automotive equipment—buses, dump trucks, bulldozers, rollers, cranes, backhoes, pile drivers, and other construction equipment and service vehicles. They keep gasoline and diesel engines running, work on ignition and fuel systems, transmissions, electrical systems, and on hydraulic, pneumatic, and steering systems.

CT

Crossed quill and
spark

Cryptologic Technician: CTs control the flow of messages and information. The kind of work they do depends on the career area in which they specialize. The six areas are: *administration,* which includes administrative and clerical duties involved in controlling access to classified material; *interpretive,* which includes radiotelephone communications and foreign language translation; *maintenance,* which includes the installation, servicing, and repair of electronic and electromechanical equipment; *communications,* which includes operation of naval security group communications systems; *collection,* which includes Morse code communications and operation of radio direction-finding equipment; and *technical,* which includes communications by means other than Morse code and electronic countermeasures.

26

DK

Key on check

Disbursing Clerk: DKs maintain the financial records of Navy personnel. They prepare payrolls, determine transportation entitlements, compute travel allowances, and process claims for reimbursement of travel expenses. DKs also process vouchers for receiving and spending public money, and they make sure accounting data are accurate. They maintain fiscal records and prepare financial reports and returns.

DM

Draftsman's
compass on triangle

Illustrator-Draftsman: DMs prepare mechanical drawings, blueprints, charts, and illustrations needed for construction projects and other naval activities. They specialize in a number of areas, among them graphics, structural drafting, electrical drafting, graphic arts mechanics, and illustrating.

DP

Quill on gear

Data Processing Technician: The Navy needs an extensive accounting system to maintain personnel records, to keep tabs on the receipt and transfer of supplies and disbursement of money, and to keep track of all equipment the Navy owns. DPs operate and maintain transceivers, sorters, collaters, reproducers, interpreters, alphabetic accounting machines, and digital electronic data processing (EDP) machines for accounting and statistical purposes.

DS

Helium atom with
input/output arrows

Data Systems Technician: DSs are electronics technicians who specialize in computer systems, including digital computers, video processors, tape units, buffers, key sets, digital-display equipment, data-link terminal sets and related equipment. They clean, maintain, lubricate, calibrate, and adjust equipment. They run operational tests, diagnose problems, make routine repairs, and evaluate newly installed parts and systems units.

DT

"D" on caduceus

Dental Technician: Navy dentists, like many civilian ones, are assisted by dental technicians. DTs have a variety of "chairside," laboratory, and administrative duties. Some are qualified in dental prosthetics (making and fitting artificial teeth), in dental X-ray techniques, in clinical laboratory procedures, in pharmacy and chemistry or in maintenance and repair of dental equipment.

EA

Measuring scale
fronting level rod

Engineering Aide: EAs provide construction engineers with the information needed to develop final construction plans. EAs conduct surveys for roads, airfields, buildings, waterfront structures, pipelines, ditches, and drainage systems. They perform soil tests, prepare topographic and hydrographic maps, and survey for sewers, water lines, drainage systems, and underwater excavations.

27

EM

Globe with
longitude, latitude
lines

Electrician's Mate: The operation and repair of a ship's or station's electrical powerplant and electrical equipment is the responsibility of EMs. They also maintain and repair power and lighting circuits, distribution switchboards, generators, motors, and other electrical equipment.

EN

Gear

Engineman: Internal combustion engines, either diesel or gasoline, must be kept in good order; this is the responsibility of ENs. They are also responsible for the maintenance of refrigeration, air-conditioning, and distilling-plant engines and compressors.

EO

Bulldozer

Equipment Operator: EOs work with heavy machinery such as bulldozers, power shovels, pile drivers, rollers and graders, etc. EOs use this machinery to dig ditches and excavate for building foundations, to break up old concrete or asphalt paving and pour new paving, to loosen soil and grade it, to dig out tree trunks and rocks, to remove debris from construction sites, to raise girders, and to move and set in place other pieces of equipment or materials needed for the job.

ET

Helium atom

Electronics Technician: ETs are responsible for all electronic equipment used to send and receive messages, detect enemy planes and ships, and determine the distance of targets. This responsibility includes maintaining, repairing, calibrating, tuning, and adjusting all electronic equipment used for communications, detection and tracking, recognition and identification, navigation, and electronic countermeasures.

EW

Spark through
helium atom

Electronics Warfare Technician: EWs operate and maintain electronic equipment used in navigation, target detection and location, and for preventing electronic spying by enemies. They interpret incoming electronic signals to determine their source. EWs are advanced electronic technicians who do wiring, circuit testing, and repair. They determine performance levels of electronic equipment, install new components, modify existing equipment, and test, adjust, and repair equipment cooling systems.

28

FT

Range finder

Fire Control Technician: Complicated electronic, electrical, hydraulic, and mechanical equipment is required to ensure the accuracy of guided missiles, gunfire, and underwater weapons. FTs maintain and repair fire control systems, including radars, weapons direction systems, target designation systems, and electro-hydraulic fire-control servo-mechanisms.

GM

Crossed cannons

Gunner's Mate: Navy GMs operate, maintain, and repair all gunnery equipment, guided-missile launching systems, rocket launchers, guns, gunmounts, turrets, projectors, and associated equipment. They also make detailed casualty analyses and repairs of electrical, electronic, hydraulic, and mechanical systems. They test and inspect ammunition and missiles and their ordnance components, and train and supervise personnel in the handling and stowage of ammunition, missiles, and assigned ordnance equipment.

GS

Turbine with ducting

Gas Turbine System Technician: GSs operate, repair, and maintain gas turbine engines, main propulsion machinery (including gears, shafting and controllable pitch propellers), assigned auxiliary equipment, propulsion control systems, electrical and electronic circuitry up to the printed circuit modules, and alarm and warning circuitry. They perform administrative tasks related to gas turbine propulsion system operation and maintenance.

HM

Caduceus

Hospital Corpsman: HMs assist medical professionals in providing health care to service people and their families. They act as pharmacists, medical technicians, food service personnel, nurses' aids, physicians' or dentists' assistants, battlefield medics, X-ray technicians and more. HMs' work falls into several categories: first aid and minor surgery, patient transportation, patient care, prescriptions and laboratory work, food service inspections, and clerical duties.

HT

Crossed fire ax and maul with carpenter's square

Hull Maintenance Technician: HTs are responsible for maintaining ships' hulls, fittings, piping systems, and machinery. They install and maintain shipboard and shorebase plumbing and piping systems. They also look after a vessel's safety and survival equipment, and perform many tasks related to damage control.

IC

French phone over globe

Interior Communications Electrician: ICs operate and repair the electronic devices used in the ship's interior communications systems—SITE TV systems, public address systems, electronic megaphones, and other announcing equipment, as well as the gyrocompass systems.

29

IM

Calipers

Instrumentman: The Navy uses many meters, gauges, watches and clocks, typewriters, adding machines, and other office machines. Repairing, adjusting, and reconditioning them is the IM's job. An IM also repairs mechanical parts of electronic instruments, and is often called upon to manufacture parts, such as bushings, stems, jewel settings, mainsprings, and spring hooks.

IS

INTELLIGENCE TECH.

Intelligence Specialist: Military information, especially secret information about enemies or potential enemies, is called "intelligence." The IS is one of the people involved in collecting and interpreting intelligence data. An IS analyzes photographs and prepares charts, maps, and reports that describe in detail the strategic situation all over the world.

JO

Crossed quill and scroll

Journalist: JOs are the Navy's information specialists. They write press releases, news stories, features, and articles for Navy newspapers, bulletins, and magazines. They perform a variety of public relations jobs. Some write scripts and announcements for radio and TV; others are photographers or radio and television broadcasters and producers. The photo work of JOs ranges from administrative and clerical tasks to film processing.

LI

Crossed lith crayon
holder and scraper

Lithographer: LIs run the Navy print shops and are responsible for producing the printed material used in naval activities. LIs print service magazines, newspapers and bulletins, training materials, official policy manuals, etc. They operate printing presses, do layout and design, and collate and bind printed pages. The usual specialties are cameraman, pressman, and binderyman.

LN

Vertical millrind
crossing quill

Legalman: Navy LNs are trained aides who assist professionals in the field of law. They work in Navy legal offices, performing administrative and clerical tasks necessary to process claims, to conduct court and administrative hearings, and to maintain records, documents, and legal reference libraries. They give advice on tax returns, voter registration procedures, immigration and customs regulations, regulations governing social security and veterans' benefits, and perform many duties related to courts-martial and nonjudicial hearings.

30

MA

Star embossed in
circle within shield

Master-at-Arms: Members of this rating help keep law and order aboard ships and shore stations. They report to the executive officer, help maintain discipline, and assist in security matters. They make sure regulations are enforced, conduct investigations, take part in correctional and rehabilitative programs, and organize and train sailors assigned to police duty. In civilian life, they'd be detectives and policemen.

ML

Crossed bench
rammer and stove
tool

Molder: MLs make molds, cores, and rig flasks. They make castings of ferrous and nonferrous metals, alloys, and plastics for the repair of ships, guns, and other machined equipment. MLs identify metals and alloys, heat-treat them, and test them for hardness. They operate the furnaces used to melt metals for castings, and they use a variety of special hand and power tools.

MM

Three-bladed
propeller

Machinist's Mate: Continuous operation of the many engines, compressors and gears, refrigeration, air-conditioning, gas-operated equipment, and other types of machinery afloat and ashore is the job of the MM. In particular, MMs are responsible for the ship's steam propulsion and auxiliary equipment and the outside (deck) machinery. MMs also may perform duties in the manufacture, storage, and transfer of some industrial gases.

MN

Floating mine

Mineman: MNs test, maintain, repair, and over-haul mines and their components. They are respon-sible for assembly, testing, handling, issuing, and delivering mines to the planting agent and for main-taining and repairing minehandling and minelaying equipment.

MR

Micrometer and gear

Machinery Repairman: MRs are skilled machine tool operators. They make replacement parts and re-pair or overhaul a ship's engine auxiliary equip-ment, such as evaporators, air compressors, and pumps. They repair deck equipment, including winches and hoists, condensers, and heat exchange devices. Shipboard MRs frequently operate main-propulsion machinery, besides performing ma-chine-shop and repair duties.

MS

Crossed keys with
quill on open ledger

Mess Management Specialist: MSs operate and manage Navy dining facilities and bachelor enlisted quarters. They are cooks and bakers in Navy dining facilities ashore and afloat, and order, inspect, and stow food. They maintain food service and prepara-tion spaces and equipment, and keep records of transactions and budgets for the food service in liv-ing quarters ashore.

31

MT

Guided missile and
electronic wave

Missile Technician: MTs assemble, maintain, and repair missiles carried by submarines. They main-tain the specialized equipment used in these func-tions. Although missile components and related test-ing and handling equipment are primarily electrical and electronic, MTs also must work with the me-chanical, hydraulic, and pneumatic units in the launcher systems, fire control systems, and missile flight control systems.

MU

Lyre

Musician: MUs play in official Navy bands and in special groups such as jazz bands, dance bands, and small ensembles (such as trios, quartets, and quintets). They give concerts and provide music for military ceremonies, religious services, parades, and such social occasions as receptions and dances. Of-ficial unit bands usually do not include stringed in-struments, but each MU must be able to play at least one brass, woodwind, or percussion instrument. Performing is only part of the job. Musicians prac-tice individually and in group sessions.

NC

Anchor crossed with
quill

Navy Counselor: NCs offer vocational guidance on an individual and group basis to Navy personnel aboard ships and at shore facilities, and to civilian personnel who are considering enlistment in the Navy. They assess the interests, aptitudes, abilities, and personalities of individuals.

OM

Lens crossed by lines
of light

Opticalman: OMs perform organizational and intermediate level maintenance on small navigational instruments, binoculars, night-vision sights, range finders, turret and submarine periscopes, and other optical instruments. OMs must be able to perform close, exact, and painstaking work and possess high mechanical aptitude.

OS

Arrow through
oscilloscope

Operations Specialist: OSs operate radar, navigation, and communications equipment in shipboard combat information centers or bridges. They detect and track ships, planes, and missiles. They operate and maintain IFF (identification friend or foe) systems, ECM (electronic countermeasures) equipment, and radiotelephones. OSs also work with search-and-rescue teams.

OT

Neptune's trident
crossed by waves

Ocean Systems Technician: OTs operate special electronic equipment used to interpret and document oceanographic data, such as the depth and composition of the ocean floor and how sound travels through water. They operate tape recorders and related equipment, prepare reports and visual displays, and convert analyzed data to be used in statistical studies.

PC

Postal cancellation
mark

Postal Clerk: The Navy operates a large postal system manned by Navy PCs, who have much the same duties as their civilian counterparts in the Postal Service. PCs collect postage-due mail, prepare customs declarations, collect outgoing mail, cancel stamps, and send the mail on its way. They also perform a variety of record-keeping and reporting duties, which include maintaining an up-to-date directory service and locator file.

PH

Lens pierced by light
lines

Photographer's Mate: PHs photograph actual and simulated battle operations, and make photo records of historic and newsworthy events for the Navy. They expose and process light-sensitive negatives and positives, maintain cameras, related equipment, photo files and records, and perform other photographic services for the Navy.

PM

Wooden jack plane

Patternmaker: The PM is the important link between the draftsmen (DMs), who make the drawings, and the molders (MLs) in a Navy foundry, who produce the castings. PMs make patterns in wood, plaster, or metal, from which castings are made. PMs use drafting, carpentry, metalworking skills, and shop mathematics to create their patterns.

32

PN

Crossed manual and quill

Personnelman: PNs provide enlisted personnel with information and counseling about Navy jobs, opportunities for general education and training, promotion requirements, and rights and benefits. They also assist enlisted persons' families with legal aid or reassignments in hardship situations. PNs keep records up to date, prepare reports, type letters, and maintain files.

PR

Parachute, winged

Aircrew Survival Equipmentman: Parachutes are the lifesaving equipment of aircrewmen when they have to bail out. In time of disaster, a parachute may also be the only means of delivering badly needed medicines, goods, and other supplies to isolated victims. PRs must pack and care for parachutes as well as service, maintain, and repair flight clothing, rubber life rafts, life jackets, oxygen-breathing apparatuses, protective clothing and air-sea rescue equipment.

QM

Ship's helm

Quartermaster: Ship safety, skillful navigation, constant vigilance for ships and natural obstacles, and reliable communications with other vessels and shore stations are the responsibilities of quartermasters. In addition, they maintain charts, navigational aids, and records for the ship's log. They steer the ship, take radar bearings and ranges, make depth soundings and celestial observations, plot courses, and command small craft. QMs stand watches and assist the navigator and officer of the deck (OOD).

33

RM

Four sparks

Radioman: Naval activities often involve people working at many different locations on land and at sea, and RMs operate the radio communications systems that make such complex teamwork possible. RMs operate radiotelephones and radioteletypes, prepare messages for international and domestic commercial telegraph, in addition to sending and receiving messages via the Navy system.

RP

Globe on anchor within circle

Religious Program Specialist: RPs assist Navy chaplains with administrative and budgetary tasks. They serve as custodians of chapel funds, keep religious documents and keep in contact with religious and community agencies. They also prepare devotional and religious educational materials, set up volunteer programs, operate shipboard libraries, supervise chaplains' offices and perform administrative, clerical and secretarial duties. They train personnel in religious programs and publicize religious activities.

SH

Crossed key and quill

Ship's Serviceman: Both ashore and afloat, SHs manage barber shops, tailor shops, ships' uniform stores, laundries, dry-cleaning plants, and cobbler shops. They serve as clerks in exchanges, soda fountains, gas stations, warehouses, and commissary stores. Some SHs function as Navy club managers.

SK

Crossed keys

Storekeeper: SKs are the Navy's supply clerks. They see that needed supplies are available—everything from clothing and machine parts to forms and food. SKs have duties as civilian warehousemen, purchasing agents, stock clerks and supervisors, retail sales clerks, store managers, inventory clerks, buyers, parts clerks, bookkeepers, and even fork lift operators.

SM

Crossed semaphore flags

Signalman: SMs serve as lookouts and, using visual signals and voice radios, alert the ship of possible dangers. They send and receive messages by flag signals or flashing lights. They stand watches on the signal bridge, encode and decode messages, honor passing vessels, and maintain signaling equipment. Signalmen must have good vision and hearing.

34

ST

Earphones pierced by arrow

Sonar Technician: STs are responsibile for underwater surveillance, assistance in safe navigation, and aiding in search, rescue, and attack operations. They operate and repair sonar equipment and jam enemy sonars. They track underwater objects and repair antisubmarine warfare fire control equipment and underwater radiotelephones.

SW

I-beam suspended from hook

Steelworker: SWs rig and operate all special equipment used to move or hoist structural steel, structural shapes, and similar material. They erect or dismantle steel bridges, piers, buildings, tanks, towers, and other structures. They place, fit, weld, cut, bolt, and rivet steel shapes, plates and built-up sections used in the construction of overseas facilities.

TD

Spark passing through gear

Tradevman: TDs install, repair, modify, and maintain audio/visual training aids. They perform organizational and intermediate level maintenance on training devices and related auxiliary equipment.

TM

Torpedo

Torpedoman's Mate: TMs maintain underwater explosive missiles, such as torpedoes and rockets, that are launched from surface ships, submarines, and aircraft. TMs also maintain launching systems used to fire underwater explosives. They are responsible for the safe shipping and storage of torpedoes and rockets.

UT

Valve

Utilitiesman: UTs plan, supervise, and perform tasks involved in the installation, operation, maintenance and repair of plumbing, heating, steam, compressed air and fuel storage and distribution systems, water treatment and distribution systems, air conditioning and refrigeration equipment, and sewage collecting and disposal facilities.

YN

Crossed quills

Yeoman: YNs perform secretarial and clerical work. They deal with visitors, telephone calls, and incoming mail. YNs organize files and operate duplicating equipment, and they order and distribute supplies. They write and type business and social letters, notices, directives, forms, and reports. They maintain files and service records.

Enlisted Service Record

Your service record contains all the papers and records concerning your Navy career. It is the Navy's official file on you.

Actually, you have two service records—one in the personnel office of your ship or station, which goes with you when you are transferred, and another in the Naval Military Personnel Command. At the end of your naval service, the two records are combined and sent to a records storage center. You should check your record at least once a year to make sure that it is correct and up to date.

When looking it over, remember that it is government property. Do not take anything out, put anything in, or make any changes. If you have comments or questions, the yeoman (YN) or personnelman (PN) on duty will help you.

A look at your service record can be arranged through your division officer or division chief. Some ships and stations have regular hours for sailors to check their service records.

Your record is important during your Navy career and after. When you leave the Navy, you may need information from your record for collecting veterans' benefits, for federal or civilian employment, or for school credits.

Your service record contains copies of such vital documents as birth certificate, school certificates, letters of commendation, etc. But its main contents are the NAVPERS forms that make up the right side of your record and are filed, beginning with the first page listed, from bottom to top. In the early days of your enlistment you will have less than half of these pages; more are added as needed.

Enlistment Contract: This is the contract you signed when you joined the Navy.

Agreement to Extend Enlistment.

Assignment to and Extension of Active Duty.

Dependency Application/Record of Emergency Data: This page is probably the most important part of your record and should be constantly updated. It contains names and addresses of persons to be notified in case of emergency or death, persons to receive the death gratuity if you have no spouse or child, persons to receive earned pay and allowances, dependents to receive allotment of pay if you are missing or unable to transmit funds, commercial insurance companies to be notified in case of death, and information about government life insurance.

You should make out a new form in the event of any of the following: reenlistment, recall to active duty, promotion from enlisted to commissioned status, change of permanent address of those to be notified in case of emergency, changes in names of those to be notified, and any major changes in status—such as marriage, an additional child, divorce.

Enlisted Classification Record: It contains information about aptitude test scores, civilian education and training, personal interests, civilian experience, and recommendations and remarks from your initial classification interview.

Navy Occupation/Training and Awards History: This page provides a complete chronological record of your classification codes and designations; service schools attended, personnel advancement requirements (PARs), performance test scores, personnel qualification standards (PQS), advancement exam results, reductions, changes in rate and rating, and decorations.

History of Assignments: This is a record of your duty assignments, ashore and at sea. It also reflects your record of enlistments, extensions of enlistments, discharges, etc., and the amount of any reenlistment bonuses you've been paid.

Record of Unauthorized Absence: This is used to record unauthorized absences of more than 24 hours, and lost time due to confinement by civil authorities.

Court Memorandum: This is a record of courtmartial action when a guilty finding is made by the court and approved by the convening authority (CA). It's also used to report nonjudicial punishment (NJP) that affects pay.

Enlisted Performance Record: This chronologically records your performance of duty. Far more than any other part of your service record, this page shows how you are doing in the Navy. It shows how those you serve under judge your performance—the petty officer who acts as your immediate supervisor, the division CPO, the division officer, the executive officer, and the commanding officer.

Your evaluations—also called "marks"—are used in determining performance factors (multiples) for advancement in rate, for selection to training which can lead to a commission, for selection to special programs and advanced schooling, for the awarding of the Good Conduct Medal, for your type of discharge (honorable or otherwise), and to determine whether you'll be recommended for reenlistment.

In general, there are four types of marks: a required evaluation, assigned annually; an entry for transfer or permanent change of station (PCS) orders; an entry when performance indicates special cognizance should be taken of particularly meritorious or derogatory performance; or a memorandum entry for a significant event, such as a note on meritorious mast, recommendation for advancement, or special performance of duty. The evaluation form is also used to report changes in ratings (in the same grade only), and for advancement or reduction in rate.

Regularly scheduled marks are completed on the following schedule: E-1 through E-3, 31 January; E-4, 30 June; E-5, 31 December; E-6, 30 November; E-7, 30 September; and E-8 and E-9, 31 October.

Record of Personnel Actions: This is a record of changes of rate, proficiency pay, citizenship, and other administrative information.

Record of Naval Reserve Service: This page is used to record reservist retirement points.

Transfers and Receipts: This gives details about your transfers from past duty stations and your reporting aboard new duty stations.

Administrative Remarks: This is a place for significant entries not provided for elsewhere; it is also used when more detailed information may be required to clarify entries on other pages.

Record of Discharge, Release from Active Duty, or Death: This is prepared when active duty is terminated because of discharge, release from active duty, change of status, or death.

Record of Discharge from the U.S. Naval Reserve: This records an honorable discharge of an enlisted person on inactive duty because of expiration of enlistment or expiration of obligated service.

Report of Separation from Active Duty.

3. Uniforms

Your Navy uniform marks you as a professional, a member of a military service over 200 years old, and a person currently in the service of your country. Over the decades there have been many uniform changes; the oldest part of the enlisted person's uniform is the petty officer rating badge, which has been used since 1886. A major uniform change came in 1973, when enlisted men began wearing CPO-type double-breasted coats, shirts, ties, and caps.

This decision, however, was changed in 1977, after an overwhelming majority of enlisted sailors had expressed the desire to return to the traditional jumper, bell-bottom-style uniforms. The first phase of the return to the bells began on 1 January 1978, when a year-long test by 20,000 fleet unit personnel was begun. The new bells are worn by those men who entered the Navy after 1 May 1980 and will remain an optional uniform for other E-1 through E-6 through 1 May 1983. The traditional white hat, known affectionately as the "dixie cup," is part of the new uniform and authorized as optional wear by all E-1 through E-6 with all uniforms except the utility/dungaree and service dress blue coat-style uniforms.

There has been considerable modernization of Navy uniforms for both men and women recently. Some changes are effective immediately; others will be phased in over a period of months. Consult U.S. Navy Uniform Regulations (NAVPERS 15665) for up-to-date information concerning uniforms and how to wear them.

The uniform is the first big change in your appearance after you join the Navy. A man may still wear sideburns and a woman may still wear eye shadow, but once you're in Navy blue you represent the United States government; and when overseas, you're an unofficial American ambassador. Not only must you wear the proper uniforms correctly, but you must set a good example by your conduct.

The matter of ranks, rates, and insignia will seem confusing at first, but once you learn the system you'll find it fairly simple. Become familiar with all the officers' rank, line and corps insignia, and special identification marks. Also learn all enlisted rates, rating badges, and special qualification devices.

There are many special uniforms worn by submariners, aviators, sailors on cold-weather operations and others, but you won't see these everywhere in the Navy. There also are various uniforms for women, including a variety of maternity uniforms.

Service
Record

Figure 3-1 Enlisted men wear, clockwise from top, bell bottom uniform with white hat, winter blue, summer blue without tie, and service dress blue.

Identification

The first thing to look for in identifying a person in the Navy is the hat—usually called the "cover"—which differs for flag officers, commissioned or warrant officers, chief petty officers, and enlisted personnel. They also differ for men and women. Sleeve markings, shoulder boards, and collar insignia for officers show rank, corps, and specialty. Rating badges for enlisted personnel

40

Figure 3–2 A lieutenant models the service dress blue uniform, left, and a lieutenant (junior grade) wears service dress whites. A lieutenant commander wears the women's new khaki uniform for officers and CPOs.

Figure 3–3 Women's uniforms shown are, from left, lieutenant (junior grade) service dress blues, Nurse Corps white working uniform, a lieutenant commander in summer blue and summer white.

Figure 3–4 Enlisted men wear service dress blues, left, summer blues, tropical white longs, and lightweight blue coverall uniform.

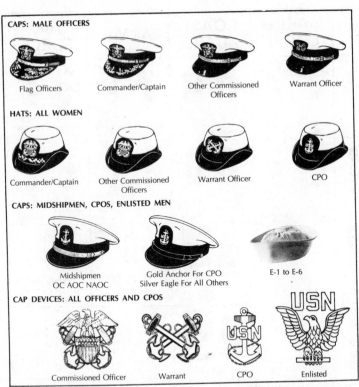

CAPS: MALE OFFICERS

Flag Officers   Commander/Captain   Other Commissioned Officers   Warrant Officer

HATS: ALL WOMEN

Commander/Captain   Other Commissioned Officers   Warrant Officer   CPO

CAPS: MIDSHIPMEN, CPOS, ENLISTED MEN

Midshipmen OC AOC NAOC   Gold Anchor For CPO Silver Eagle For All Others   E-1 to E-6

CAP DEVICES: ALL OFFICERS AND CPOS

Commissioned Officer   Warrant   CPO   Enlisted

Figure 3–5 Cap devices are the same for men and women in the same rank. The CPO device is a gold anchor with USN superimposed. Enlisted persons wear a silver eagle with USN above the wings. The midshipman's cap is also worn by all officer candidates.

show both their rate and rating. The various breast insignia and ribbons indicate the special qualifications, awards, and service of officers and enlisted personnel.

HEADGEAR

Male officers, warrant officers, CPOs, and enlisted men wear hats with bills on them. The white hat is worn by sailors entering the Navy after 1 May 1980 and optionally by all E-1 through E-6. Women, both officers and enlisted, wear hats with the sides turned up. At sea, and when specified ashore, all hands wear baseball-type working caps. Other types of headgear are authorized for optional wear: the beret and garrison cap for women; the garrison cap for male officers and CPOs.

Cap or hat devices for commissioned officers consist of a shield, eagle, and crossed anchors. Chief petty officers wear one anchor mounted vertically, with the letters USN. The device for senior chief petty officers has one star above the anchor; there

Identification

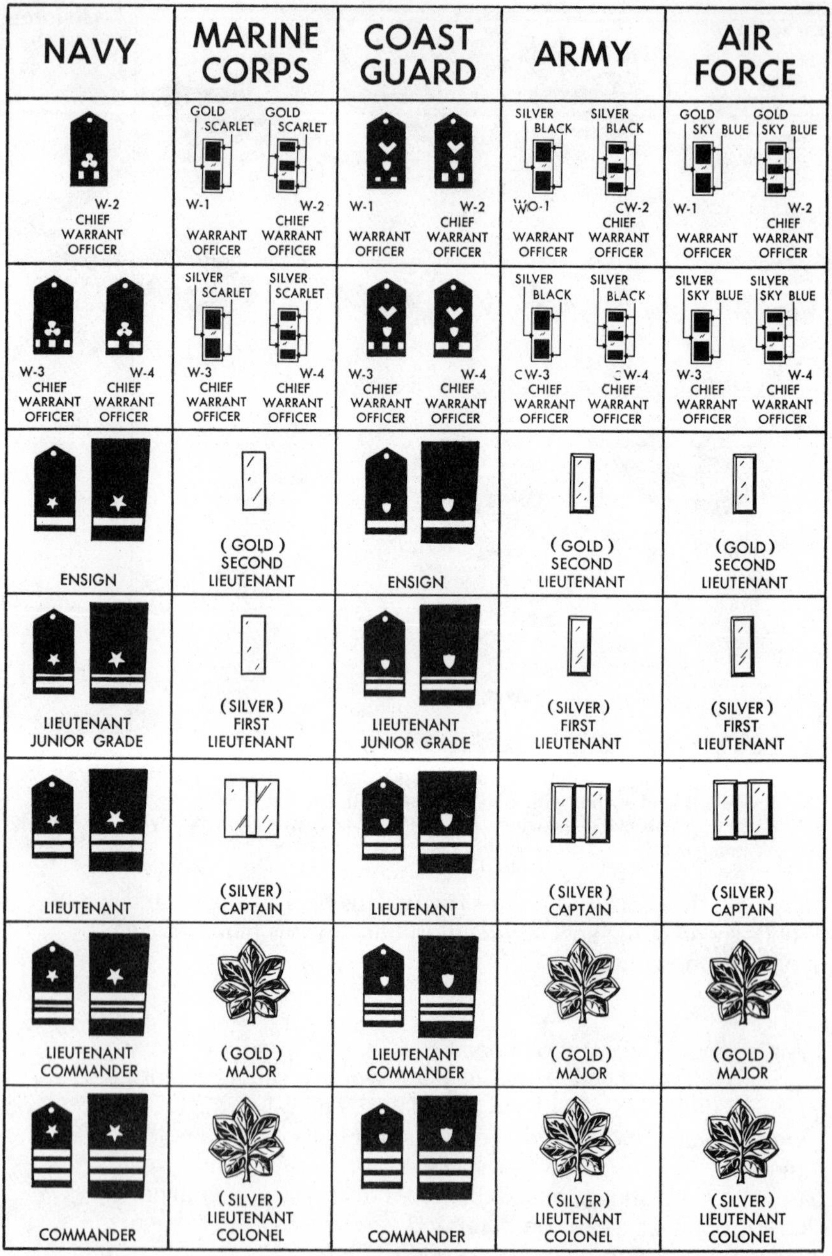

NAVY	MARINE CORPS	COAST GUARD	ARMY	AIR FORCE
W-2 CHIEF WARRANT OFFICER	GOLD SCARLET / GOLD SCARLET — W-1 WARRANT OFFICER / W-2 CHIEF WARRANT OFFICER	W-1 WARRANT OFFICER / W-2 CHIEF WARRANT OFFICER	SILVER BLACK / SILVER BLACK — WO-1 WARRANT OFFICER / CW-2 CHIEF WARRANT OFFICER	GOLD SKY BLUE / GOLD SKY BLUE — W-1 WARRANT OFFICER / W-2 CHIEF WARRANT OFFICER
W-3 CHIEF WARRANT OFFICER / W-4 CHIEF WARRANT OFFICER	SILVER SCARLET / SILVER SCARLET — W-3 CHIEF WARRANT OFFICER / W-4 CHIEF WARRANT OFFICER	W-3 CHIEF WARRANT OFFICER / W-4 CHIEF WARRANT OFFICER	SILVER BLACK / SILVER BLACK — CW-3 CHIEF WARRANT OFFICER / CW-4 CHIEF WARRANT OFFICER	SILVER SKY BLUE / SILVER SKY BLUE — W-3 CHIEF WARRANT OFFICER / W-4 CHIEF WARRANT OFFICER
ENSIGN	(GOLD) SECOND LIEUTENANT	ENSIGN	(GOLD) SECOND LIEUTENANT	(GOLD) SECOND LIEUTENANT
LIEUTENANT JUNIOR GRADE	(SILVER) FIRST LIEUTENANT	LIEUTENANT JUNIOR GRADE	(SILVER) FIRST LIEUTENANT	(SILVER) FIRST LIEUTENANT
LIEUTENANT	(SILVER) CAPTAIN	LIEUTENANT	(SILVER) CAPTAIN	(SILVER) CAPTAIN
LIEUTENANT COMMANDER	(GOLD) MAJOR	LIEUTENANT COMMANDER	(GOLD) MAJOR	(GOLD) MAJOR
COMMANDER	(SILVER) LIEUTENANT COLONEL	COMMANDER	(SILVER) LIEUTENANT COLONEL	(SILVER) LIEUTENANT COLONEL

Figure 3–6 Rank insignia are worn as shoulder and sleeve markings in the Navy and Coast Guard, and correspond to Marine Corps, Army, and Air Force collar devices.

NAVY	MARINE CORPS	COAST GUARD	ARMY	AIR FORCE
CAPTAIN	COLONEL	CAPTAIN	COLONEL	COLONEL
COMMODORE ADMIRAL	BRIGADIER GENERAL	COMMODORE	BRIGADIER GENERAL	BRIGADIER GENERAL
REAR ADMIRAL	MAJOR GENERAL	REAR ADMIRAL	MAJOR GENERAL	MAJOR GENERAL
VICE ADMIRAL	LIEUTENANT GENERAL	VICE ADMIRAL	LIEUTENANT GENERAL	LIEUTENANT GENERAL
ADMIRAL	GENERAL	ADMIRAL	GENERAL	GENERAL
FLEET ADMIRAL	NONE	NONE	GENERAL OF THE ARMY	GENERAL OF THE AIR FORCE
NONE	NONE	NONE	AS PRESCRIBED BY INCUMBENT GENERAL OF THE ARMIES	NONE

are two stars for the master chief petty officers, and three stars for the master chief petty officer of the Navy (MCPON). The cap or hat device for enlisted personnel is a silver eagle with wings spread and the letters USN mounted above the wings.

INSIGNIA

Naval officers who are eligible to assume command of ships (and stations) are designated unrestricted line officers; other officers are members of a staff corps or are specialists in various fields.

Staff corps includes: Medical, Supply, Chaplain, Civil Engineer, Judge Advocate General's, Dental, Medical Service, and Nurse. (The Medical Corps consists entirely of physicians and surgeons; the Medical Service Corps is made up of pharmacists, medical administrative officers, medical technologists, etc.)

An officer's grade is indicated in the following ways: by gold sleeve stripes on blue coats; by black sleeve stripes on aviation green coats; by shoulder boards on white coats and white shirts, blue overcoats and reefers; and by metal grade insignia on the shoulder straps of blue raincoats or aviation overcoats, and on collars of khaki and blue shirts. Above the stripes, line officers wear a five-pointed star; staff corps officers wear the appropriate corps device as shown in Figure 3–7.

Corps devices for commissioned warrant officers appear in Figure 3–8. Sleeve stripes and shoulder boards indicating grades are shown in Figure 3–6.

Officers also wear pin-on grade insignia on the collars of shirts. Line officers wear the device on both collar tips; staff corps officers wear the pin-on grade device on the right collar tip, and the corps device on the left.

Enlisted Personnel

The rate, rating and special qualifications of enlisted men and women are indicated by their sleeve and breast insignia. These include group-rate marks, striker's identification, rating badges, service stripes, specialty marks, and various breast insignia denoting special qualifications or designations.

GROUP-RATE MARKS

These marks consist of short diagonal stripes indicating the paygrade, and the color indicating the apprenticeship of persons rated E-2 and E-3. They are worn on the left sleeve. These are not worn on the peacoat or dungaree (utility blue shirt).

Seaman Apprenticeship: Seamen and seaman apprentices wear white stripes on blue uniforms, blue stripes on white uniforms.

Fireman Apprenticeship: Firemen and fireman apprentices wear red stripes on blue and white uniforms.

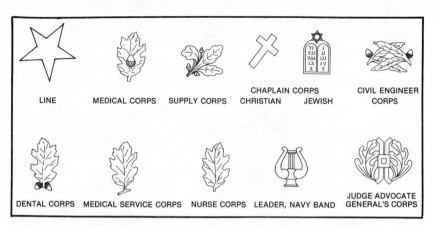

Figure 3–7 Line and staff corps insignia are worn on both sleeves, above the stripes, and on shoulder boards. Officers other than line officers also wear them on collar tips.

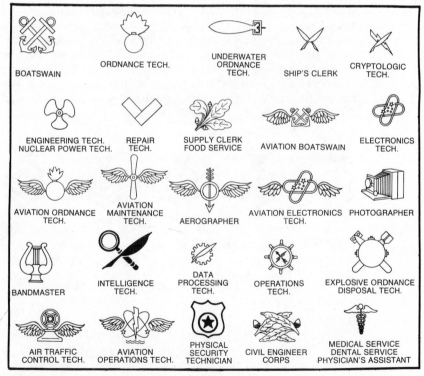

Figure 3–8 Warrant officer insignia are worn on sleeves, above the stripes, on shoulder boards, and as pin-on collar devices.

Construction Apprenticeship: Constructionmen and construction apprentices wear light blue stripes on blue and white uniforms.

Airman Apprenticeship: Airmen and airman apprentices wear emerald green stripes on blue and white uniforms.

Hospital Apprenticeship and Dental Apprenticeship: Hospitalmen and hospital apprentices, dentalmen and dental apprentices, all wear white stripes on blue uniforms and Navy blue stripes on white uniforms. They also wear specialty marks which indicate their particular apprenticeship and distinguish them from seaman apprentices.

RATING BADGES

Rating badges, worn on the left sleeve, consist of an eagle (called a "crow"), chevrons indicating the wearer's rate, and a specialty mark indicating rating.

Once you reach paygrade E-7 (chief petty officer), a rocker, or arch, is added to the rating badge. The specialty mark is centered in the space between the eagle and upper chevron. Senior chief petty officers (E-8) also have a single silver star, centered above the eagle's head, while master chief petty officers (E-9) have two silver stars arranged horizontally above the eagle's wing tips. The rating badge for command master chiefs is the same as that for master chief petty officers except an inverted five-point silver star takes the place of the specialty mark. The badge for the fleet/force master chiefs is the same as that for master chief petty officers of the command except that all the stars are gold. The master chief petty officer of the Navy has three gold stars instead of two appearing in a horizontal line above the eagle's head.

| MCPON | FM/C CM/C | MCPO | SCPO | CPO |

Enlisted people in all services wear chevrons which indicate their paygrade. These are shown, along with the Navy paygrades, in Figure 3–9. Coast Guardsmen, for the most part, wear badges identical to those of the Navy.

SERVICE STRIPES

Service stripes, or "hashmarks," are worn on the left sleeve below the rating badge and indicate length of service. Each stripe signifies completion of four full years of active or reserve duty (or any combination thereof) in any of the armed forces. Scarlet

NAVY	MARINES	ARMY	AIR FORCE	
MASTER CHIEF P.O.	SGT. MAJOR / MASTER GUNNERY SGT.	STAFF SGT. MAJOR / COMMAND SGT. MAJOR / SPEC. 9	CHIEF MASTER SGT. / CHIEF MASTER SGT. OF THE AF	E-9
SENIOR CHIEF P.O.	1ST SGT. / MASTER SGT.	1ST SGT. / MASTER SGT. / SPEC. 8	SENIOR MASTER SGT.	E-8
CHIEF P.O.	GUNNERY SGT.	SGT. 1ST CLASS / SPEC. 7	MASTER SGT.	E-7
P.O. 1ST CLASS	STAFF SGT.	STAFF SGT. / SPEC. 6	TECHNICAL SGT.	E-6
P.O. 2ND CLASS	SGT.	SGT. / SPEC. 5	STAFF SGT.	E-5
P.O. 3RD CLASS	CORPORAL	CORPORAL / SPEC. 4	SGT.	E-4
SEAMAN	LANCE CORPORAL	PRIVATE 1ST CLASS	AIRMAN 1ST CLASS	E-3
SEAMAN APPRENTICE	PRIVATE 1ST CLASS	PRIVATE	AIRMAN	E-2
SEAMAN RECRUIT	PRIVATE	PRIVATE	BASIC AIRMAN	E-1

Figure 3–9 Navy enlisted rates and paygrades compared with those of the other services. The Coast Guard's badges are the same as the Navy's. Chevrons are red on blues with a white eagle, blue on whites with a blue eagle. CPO's are red or gold as appropriate. Specialty marks are the same color as the eagle. Badges worn on dungaree shirts have dark blue chevrons but no specialty marks.

Figure 3–10 Breast insignia.

stripes are worn on blue uniforms, Navy-blue stripes on forest green uniforms (worn by aviation personnel).

GOLD BADGES AND STRIPES

Petty officers with a total of 12 years' active duty (broken or unbroken service) in the Navy or Naval Reserve, who have fulfilled the requirements for successive awards of the Navy Good Conduct Medal, are required to wear the gold rating badge and gold service stripes on their service dress blue uniforms.

STRIKER'S MARKS

Striker's marks are worn by enlisted men and women in paygrades E-2 and E-3 who have been designated as strikers by the Naval Military Personnel Command. The specialty mark of the rating for which the sailor is qualified is centered immediately above the rectangular background of the group-rate marks on the left sleeve of blue and white uniforms.

Breast Insignia

Metal or embroidered insignia are worn on the breast to indicate a special qualification or designation. Certain officers may wear insignia for aviation, submarine service, surface warfare, command, special warfare, parachuting, and underwater or explosive ordnance disposal. Insignia for enlisted personnel are awarded in aviation, submarine, surface warfare, command, special warfare, parachuting, and underwater and explosive ordnance disposal. Only one warfare specialty may be worn at a time.

All insignia are worn on the left breast, except those for command at sea or ashore, small craft, and craftmaster; these are worn on the right breast. Approved insignia are:

OFFICER INSIGNIA

Aviation: naval astronaut, naval aviator, naval aviation observers and flight meteorologists, naval flight surgeons, naval flight nurse, naval flight officers, aviation experimental psychologist and aviation physiologists.

Submarine: submarine (dolphins), submarine medical, submarine engineer duty, submarine supply, submarine combat patrol, and SSBN deterrent patrol.

Surface warfare: surface warfare insignia.

Command: command at sea, command ashore/project manager.

Special warfare: special warfare insignia.

Parachutists: naval parachutist and basic parachutist.

Underwater: diving and diving (medical).

Explosive ordnance disposal: EOD insignia.

ENLISTED INSIGNIA

Aviation: aircrew, aviation warfare specialist.

Submarine: submarine (dolphins), submarine combat patrol, and SSBN deterrent patrol.

Surface warfare: surface warfare insignia.

Command: small craft and craftmaster.

Special warfare: special warfare insignia.

Parachutists: naval parachutist and basic parachutist.

Underwater: master diver; diver, first class; diver, second class; diver, scuba and diving medical technician.

Explosive ordnance disposal: EOD insignia; senior, master.

Usually only one insignia may be worn at a time, but when ribbons or medals are worn, two insignia may be worn. When two are worn they must be of different categories, except for the submarine combat patrol, and the SSBN deterrent patrol insignia. When two insignia are worn with ribbons or medals, one is centered above and the other below the ribbons or medals. The insignia of the current specialty should be the one worn above.

Command at sea, small craft, and craftmaster insignia may be worn by officers and enlisted even though they are not currently assigned to such duties. In such cases the insignia are worn on the left breast. Details for wearing all insignia are contained in U.S. Navy Uniform Regulations.

Identification Badges

These badges publicly identify personnel on special assignments. The first four (Figure 3–11) are worn by members of *all* military services.

Presidential Service: Worn by those on duty at the White House who have been awarded a Presidential Service Certificate. The badge is worn on the upper right pocket during and after the period of detail.

Vice Presidential Service: Worn by personnel assigned to the Office of the Vice President who have been awarded a Vice Presidential Service Certificate. The badge is also worn on the right pocket both during and after the period of detail.

Office of Secretary of Defense: Worn only during the period of detail by those who have received a certificate of eligibility from the Office of the Secretary of Defense authorizing them to wear the insignia. It's worn on the upper left pocket.

Joint Chiefs of Staff: Worn during, and the miniature may be worn after, the period of detail by those assigned to the JCS organization. It goes on the upper left pocket.

Recruiting Command: Worn by all personnel assigned to duty with the Navy Recruiting Command. It's worn on the upper left

Figure 3–11 Identification badges, from upper left, are worn by persons performing Presidential, Vice Presidential service, those assigned to the Office of the Secretary of Defense, Joint Chiefs of Staff (second row, left), those in the recruiting service, Navy/Fleet/Force/Command master chief petty officers, and career counselors.

pocket. Excellence of performance is acknowledged with the addition of a gold-colored metal wreath and gold or silver stars.

Navy/Fleet/Force/Command Master Chief Petty Officers: Worn by personnel serving in these billets, who must be designated to the positions in writing. The badge is worn on the upper left pocket during the period of detail, and a miniature one may be worn afterwards. A raised block in the center indicates the position held, i.e., "Navy," "Fleet," "Force," or "Command."

Career Counselor: Worn by a designated person who is assigned to duty as a career counselor or a career information and counseling school instructor. It's worn on the upper left pocket.

Recruit Company Commander: Worn by personnel assigned as recruit company commanders. It's worn on the upper breast pocket only during the period of service.

Ceremonial Guard Patch: Enlisted persons below the paygrade E-7 are authorized to wear an identifying sleeve patch while assigned to the U.S. Ceremonial Guard, Washington, D.C. The insignia is prescribed and worn at the discretion of the Commandant, Naval District Washington (NDW).

Uniform of the Day

This uniform is prescribed for all naval personnel within a command or geographical area. Usually the plan of the day (POD) for every ship or station lists the uniform for officers and enlisted personnel. A working uniform will be prescribed for "turn to" hours and a uniform of the day will be prescribed for after working hours. The uniform for liberty, leave, special occasions, or ceremonies also will be prescribed in the plan of the day. Changes in uniform appear in ship or station notices.

The area coordinator is responsible for establishing and controlling uniform policies within his jurisdiction. He designates uniforms for the season, day, or special occasion. Uniform policies afloat and ashore outside his jurisdiction are the responsibility of the senior officer present.

Uniforms in General

Since the abolishment in 1975 of the traditional uniform for sailors—white hat, rolled neckerchief, jumper, and bell-bottom trousers—all enlisted men, petty officers and non-rated alike, have been issued the same type of uniform worn by officers and CPOs. However, as previously mentioned, the decision was reached in 1977 to return to the traditional uniform. This is the uniform now being issued to all recruits entering the Navy. It remains optional for all E-1 through E-5 who entered the Navy prior to 1 May 1980 and will become mandatory for all sailors through paygrade E-5 on 1 May 1983.

Uniforms for women, officers and enlisted, are very much alike. The main difference is in the wearing of formal attire, which is generally authorized only for senior officers.

UNIFORMS FOR ENLISTED MEN

Service dress blue (jumper): blue jumper, blue broadfall trousers, neckerchief, white hat, ribbons, black shoes and socks. Service dress white (jumper): substitute white jumper and trousers.

Summer blue: blue belted trousers with tropical white shirt.

Summer white: white belted trousers with tropical white shirt.

Dinner dress uniform: same as service dress.

Full dress uniform: same as service dress, but with large medals.

Tropical uniforms: tropical white shirt, white shorts and knee-length socks. Tropical white long: with long trousers. Tropical khaki: black socks, dungaree or working blue trousers, undershirt (no outside shirt), blue working cap.

Working uniforms: enlisted working blue trousers and shirt, blue working cap. Dungaree: blue working cap, blue chambray shirt, black socks, dungaree trousers. Winter working blue: white hat, black tie, winter working blue shirt, blue belted trousers.

UNIFORMS FOR ENLISTED WOMEN

Service dress blue: blue coat and skirt with white shirt and gloves, black handbag and black necktie, combination hat, with ribbons. Bravo is slacks in lieu of skirt. Summer blue: short sleeve open-collar white shirt, blue skirt, black shoes, and combination hat. Bravo: same with slacks. Winter blue: same as summer but with long-sleeve blue shirt and tie. Winter working blue is the same without tie and with either skirt or slacks. The summer white is the same as the summer blue but with a white skirt.

Dinner dress blue: same as service dress blue, with miniature medals.

Full dress blue: same as service dress blue, with large medals.

Working uniform: indoor duty white cap and uniform, white hose, white shoes. Dungaree: blue chambray shirt, blue polyester/cotton slacks, blue garrison cap.

Sports uniform: exercise shorts, gym shoes, blue chambray shirt.

Today's enlisted woman also has several optional uniform items. For instance, she can wear a white scarf with an overcoat or raincoat; she can wear a blue sweater (at command discretion) with any uniform while in working spaces; she may wear a white sweater with ward uniform and pantsuit; and overcoat, overshoes, raincoats, and an umbrella (plain black) may be used with any uniform. Women's uniforms are also undergoing modernization. Check Navy Uniform Regulations for changes.

Decorations and Awards

Awards include any decoration, medal, badge, ribbon, or an attachment thereof bestowed upon an individual or a unit. A decoration is awarded to an individual for an act of gallantry or meritorious service. A unit award is presented to an operating unit and can be worn only by members who participated in the action cited. A service award is made to those who have participated in designated wars, campaigns, and expeditions, or who have fulfilled a specified service requirement. The Navy Cross, Bronze Star Medal, and Purple Heart are examples of decorations; the Presidential Unit Citation (PUC) and Meritorious Unit

Commendation (MUC) are examples of unit awards. Service awards, often called "campaign or theater" awards, include the Good Conduct Medal and the Vietnam Service Medal.

The Navy recognizes 17 military decorations, 4 unit awards, 18 nonmilitary decorations, 32 campaign and service awards and a number of others by foreign governments. Many foreign awards may be accepted, but cannot be worn. There are over 150 awards, including those bestowed by military societies.

Military decorations and unit awards may be given at any time. They are listed below in order of precedence, with the four unit awards last. All other decorations are worn following these.

Medal of Honor
Navy Cross
Defense Distinguished Service
  Medal*
Distinguished Service Medal
Silver Star Medal
Legion of Merit
Distinguished Flying Cross
Navy and Marine Corps Medal
Bronze Star Medal
Defense Meritorious Service Medal
Meritorious Service Medal

Air Medal
Joint Service Commendation
  Medal*
Navy Commendation Medal
Navy Achievement Medal
Purple Heart
Combat Action Ribbon
Presidential Unit Citation Ribbon
Navy Unit Commendation Ribbon
Meritorious Unit Commendation
  Ribbon
Navy "E"

Ribbons for decorations and awards are worn on the left breast. One, two, or three ribbons are worn in a single row, centered above the pocket. When more than three ribbons are authorized, they are worn in horizontal rows of three each. If not in multiples of three, the uppermost row contains the lesser number, with the ribbon(s) centered over the row beneath. Women wear one or two rows of ribbons centered above the left pocket flap, with additional rows continuing upward.

Order of precedence for all decorations and unit awards are listed in U.S. Navy Uniform Regulations, Chapter 5, Section 2.

Ownership Markings

Articles of clothing shall be legibly marked with the owner's name and social security number in black marking fluid for white clothes and chambray shirts and utility blue shirts. White marking fluid is used for blue clothes and dungaree trousers; or indelible ink when labels are provided for the purpose. All markings other than those on labels should be made with a half-inch stencil or stamp.

Recruits are furnished detailed instructions on marking when they're issued clothing. These instructions must be followed explicitly. As a general rule, instructions for marking clothes, as laid down in Uniform Regulations, should be followed when additional uniform articles are obtained.

* Not Navy decoration—listed for precedence only.

The word "right" or "left" means the owner's right or left when it's worn. On towels, it means the owner's right or left when standing behind the article laid out for inspection. Markings on all articles, when properly rolled or laid out for bag inspection, will appear right-side-up to the inspecting officer and upside-down to the person standing behind them.

ENLISTED MEN

Belts: Inside.

Blue chambray shirt: Inside of collar, centered, last name only on left, one inch above pocket.

Blue working cap: Initials only on sweatband.

Blue working jacket: Inside of hem at back, right of centerline.

Drawers: On the inside of the right half of the waistband, or immediately beneath the waistband on drawers with elastic waistbands.

Duffel bag: Along carrying strap on outer side; and opposite side from carrying strap, around the bag about one foot from top.

Dungaree trousers: On waistband inside front, right of centerline; last name only on outside, one inch above right hip pocket.

Enlisted working blue trousers: On waistband inside front, right of centerline; last name only on outside, one inch above right hip pocket.

Gloves: Initials only, on inside, near top.

Knit watch cap: On label, inside, one-half inch from bottom.

Jumper (blue and white): turn inside out, front down, stencil initial left of center and $1/4$-inch below collar seam; last 4 digits of SSN same on right of seam.

Neckerchief: diagonally across center.

Peacoat (reefer coat): On label, inside breast pocket.

Raincoat: Inside on lining, 3 inches below collar seam.

Shoes: Initials only, inside, near top.

Socks: Initials only on the foot.

Sweater: On inside label, below back of collarette.

Swim trunks: Inside on hem, right center of back.

Towel: Right corner on hem, parallel to end.

Tropical white shirt: Inside of collar.

Trousers (blue and white): turn inside out; on left rear pocket stencil initials and last 4 digits of SSN in between the two horizontal seams.

Undershirt: On outside, front, one inch from bottom of shirt, right of center.

White dress shirt: Inside of collar.

White hat: on inside brim close to crown so as not to show when turned up.

White trousers: On waistband, inside front, right of centerline.

Winter working blue shirt: Inside of collar.

ENLISTED WOMEN

Anklets: On the foot.

Black service shoes: On inside, initials only, inside of tongue.

Black shoes: Inside, initials only, to right of heel.

Blue coat: On nameplate.

Blue skirt: On nameplate.

Blue polyester/cotton slacks: Center back inside; on waist-band.

Chambray shirt: Center back, inside; on lower part of collar and on nameplate.

Combination hat: On nameplate.

Garrison cap: On nameplate.

Gloves: Initials only, inside cuff.

Gym shoes: On inside, initials only, on tongue.

Handbags: On nameplate.

Hatcovers: Center back, inside band.

Havelock: On nameplate.

Hosiery: Initials only, inside top.

Necktie: Center back, inside.

Overcoat (raincoat type): On nameplate, and inside left front panel.

Raincoat: On nameplate, and inside left front panel.

Scarf: Inside, along seam, near end.

Sweater: On nameplate.

Towel: Right corner on hem, parallel to end.

White dress shoes: Inside, initials only, to right of heel.

White shirt: Center back, inside, on lower part of collar, and on nameplate.

Optional articles of clothing are marked similarly to comparable items of required clothing.

No transfer or exchange of uniform clothing may be made without the authority of the commanding officer. When a transfer or exchange is authorized, or when clothing belonging to another is disposed of, the name of the former owner is stamped over with the mark "D.C."—for discarded clothing—and the purchaser's name is placed above, below, or next to it.

Take care of your uniforms. They cost money to replace. Your money.

Miscellaneous Uniform Items

Aiguillettes are usually worn by officers while performing specialized staff duty. They're worn by aides to the President, the Vice President, the White House, the Secretary of Defense, the Secretary and other officials of the Navy Department, the Deputy

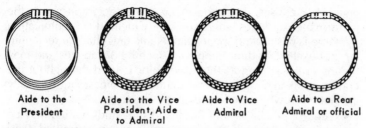

Aide to the President

Aide to the Vice President, Aide to Admiral

Aide to Vice Admiral

Aide to a Rear Admiral or official

Figure 3–12 Aiguillettes are worn by various aides to officials. Service aiguillettes are shown here. Dress aiguillettes are much more ornate and are fastened across the chest to the coat collar.

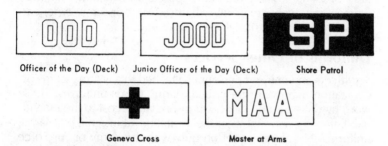

Officer of the Day (Deck)   Junior Officer of the Day (Deck)   Shore Patrol

Geneva Cross   Master at Arms

57

Figure 3–13 Brassards are worn on the right arm, midway between the shoulder and elbow. The officer of the day (or deck) wears the OOD brassard, the junior officer of the day (or deck) wears JOOD, shore patrol the SP, corpsmen the Geneva Cross, and masters-at-arms the MAA.

or Assistant Secretaries of Defense, and aides to flag officers. You probably already know of two enlisted people who wear them—your company commander, who has one red loop, and your assistant recruit company commander, who has one light-blue loop.

Brassards are bands of cloth, suitably marked with symbols, letters, or words, indicating a temporary duty to which the wearer is assigned. They are worn on the right arm, midway between the shoulder and elbow, on outer garments. They are usually worn by officers of the day (OOD), junior officers of the day (JOOD), shore patrol (SP), masters-at-arms, armed forces police, and by personnel who are members of ambulance and first-aid parties (Geneva Cross) and by damage-control personnel of shore stations during drills and tests within a naval activity (Damage Control). The mourning badge, made of black crepe, is worn on the left sleeve of the outer garment, halfway between shoulder and elbow, for officers; in the same position, on the right sleeve, for enlisted personnel.

A commanding officer may direct that officers and enlisted personnel wear name tags for easy identification during confer-

Uniform Items

ences, VIP cruises, open houses, or similar occasions, or in the performance of duties where some easy method of identification by name is desirable or beneficial. Name tags shall be rectangular, not exceeding dimensions of 1 inch by 3½ inches and may be any color as long as the same color is used throughout the command. Name tags are worn on the right breast, but generally are not worn when medals are prescribed.

Except for tie clasps, cuff links, and shirt studs, which may be worn as prescribed, no other personal items are permitted. Pencils, pens, watch chains, pins, combs, smoking material, or jewelry (except for rings, wrist watches, and identification bracelets) are not to be worn or carried exposed on a uniform. Enlisted women may wear small silver ball (¼″ post or screw type) earrings while in uniform. Officers wear gold.

Uniforms of Other Services

Officers and enlisted personnel attached to a Marine Corps organization may wear prescribed Marine Corps uniforms. Those worn by enlisted men will be furnished at no cost to the individual. Enlisted personnel wear their usual naval insignia on Marine uniforms. Naval personnel on duty with the Army or Air Force normally wear their own uniforms. In some instances, they are authorized to wear Army or Air Force uniforms, provided these uniforms are furnished at no cost.

Wearing of Uniforms

Along with the rules and regulations involved in proper wearing of the uniform, some things are a matter of common sense. The hat or cap is part of the uniform, but if a particular duty or operation interferes, it may be removed. Persons riding in motor vehicles with insufficient headroom may remove their headgear. Those riding two- or three-wheeled motor vehicles should remove uniform headgear and wear safety helmets; they may also wear protective clothing over their uniform. A cap no longer has to be worn at sea, except on specific watches and specific occasions. It is always worn squarely on the head, bottom edge horizontal.

Shoes are kept in good repair; those worn on watch, liberty, and for inspections should be shined. White shoes should always be freshly cleaned.

Grooming Standards

Good grooming standards of neatness, cleanliness, and safety are essential to your military image. They're not intended to be restrictive nor to isolate Navy men and women from society;

they are meant to promote a favorable image for the Navy. They're not unreasonable, and they permit a degree of individuality.

MEN

Your grooming should be neat, clean, and presentable at all times.

The hair should be tapered around the neck, three-quarters of an inch up from the lower hairline. Don't let it hang over your ears. And don't let the hair on the back of the neck touch your collar. The "block cut" is permitted as long as it looks tapered. Don't let your hair grow longer than four inches. The hair on the top of your head, after you've groomed it, should not extend more than two inches from the scalp.

There's a reason for men having their hair shorter than shoulder length—safety. For instance, the headgear you wear—the helmet that could save your life—will not fit properly if you have long hair.

The three-quarter-inch rule is not ironclad. In the cases of curly, kinked, and wavy hair, a slightly greater length is acceptable, providing it doesn't interfere with the proper wearing of your headgear. Plaited or braided hair may not be worn while in uniform or on duty.

Keep your sideburns neat and trimmed, no lower than the ear lobe. Flares, muttonchops, and other exaggerations are not permitted.

If you wear a beard or mustache, keep it trimmed and neat. The beard must be short—no longer than three-quarters of an inch—so that the oxygen mask you may need one day will fit you. Medical personnel who like beards have to wear face masks —or shave—if they're working in areas where they have direct contact with patients or with food. If you're going to wear a mustache and beard, they must blend smoothly. Don't grow your mustache below the top line of your upper lip. If you're wearing a mustache without a beard, don't let it grow beyond the corners of your mouth, nor more than a quarter-inch up from the corners.

If you're assigned to a Marine Corps unit, abide by its standards for grooming.

You may wear a hairpiece or wig on active duty and in uniform only if it is used to cover up baldness or a deformity. Make sure the wig fits, presents a natural appearance and doesn't interfere with your safety.

WOMEN

Keep your hair clean, neatly arranged, and no longer than the lower edge of your collar. Your hair must not show under the front brim of the combination hat or garrison cap. Various hair-

Figure 3–14 Enlisted women wearing summer blue, blue coverall, service dress blue, and winter working blue.

styles are permitted, including Afros, as long as they are not exaggerated, and do not interfere with wearing headgear.

Plaited or braided hair is out.

You may wear pins, combs, and barrettes if they match your hair color, but not gaudy ornaments and ribbons. Hairnets are O.K. when authorized. The rule for wigs is the same as it is for men: it must have a natural appearance, good fit, and must not interfere with your safety.

Grooming   Keep cosmetics in good taste.

4. Leadership, Discipline, and the UCMJ

Navy training comes in two general areas: professional and military. You get professional training by attending service schools, qualifying for advancement, studying, and working at your job. You get military training by learning and understanding the qualities of leadership, discipline, standards of conduct, watchstanding, drills, and first aid. You learn most aspects of military training by following the example of the petty officers and officers who are senior to you.

Leadership

Before you can lead, you must have followers. Before you can be a *good* leader, you must have *willing* followers. Navy recruits are expected to be good followers, and they should learn the qualities of good leadership so they can assume important responsibilities in the future.

But what makes a good leader? First, he must know his job, his men, and how to set a good example. He never orders someone to do something unless he knows how to do it himself. The idea is to *inspire* those under you to follow you, not to *order* them to.

Your first chance to demonstrate some leadership will probably come when you're a leading seaman. You'll be part of the chain of command, with men and women you outrank and others who outrank you.

The chain of command exists to ensure that:

1. The Navy and its sailors do their jobs without confusion and without wasting time and effort.
2. Those in charge know what their responsibilities are.
3. Everyone accounts to someone for his job and actions.
4. There is a sense of direction, so that everyone knows what he's supposed to do.
5. There is clear communication, so there will be no doubt where you or anyone else stands in the chain of command.

The Meaning of Leadership

Different leaders define the term in different ways. Eight chief petty officers who have served from 14 to 23 years each have described what leadership means to them. Ask yourself the ques-

Figure 4–1 The chain of command is essential in establishing clear communication between experienced leaders and new sailors.

tion. Do you see leadership as the ability to inspire others, or is it the ability to keep them in line? Here's what the eight CPOs said.

The first chief pointed out that, in the past, leaders were more educated than their followers. Since they knew more, they took charge. But today, the chief says, those expected to follow are educated, and in many cases may be smarter than the people who outrank them. The educated follower needs motivation. He wants to know the reason for his work. If his boss can't give him the reason and fails to motivate him, the job will suffer.

Another CPO sees honesty as a key to leadership—honesty with yourself and those you work with. A leader earns respect by being willing to listen to others' ideas before forming his own opinions on what to do—more respect than one who decides immediately to do everything "his way." This chief says a leader should be flexible and willing to compromise when it's the best thing to do. He wants his leaders to be friendly, willing to help, and knowledgeable about the Navy and their professional fields.

A third chief, who because of his rating has always led small, closely knit groups, likes the personal touch. By personal example, close direction, and a soft approach, chief No. 3 can get his men to do their jobs well. And this makes his job easier. "We don't have to yell and scream at our people," he said. "We treat them as intelligent people, which they are."

Chief No. 4 stresses the ability to get along with her people. A leader doesn't have to be exceptionally smart, she feels, as long as she knows the capabilities of her people.

A fifth CPO feels the word "leadership" is worn out. "It's better to talk about management or directed effort," he says. But he adds: "I've always looked at my job as a morale-type petty officer. Treat subordinates as human beings rather than coolies or slaves." Chief No. 5 denounces the old adage, "Do as I say, not as I do." He urges leaders to stand up for their men, back them up. The chain of command involves respect down as well as up.

Chief No. 6 feels a person's leadership is determined by his ability to get a job done promptly and efficiently, by making the

Figure 4–2 Leadership calls for experienced personnel who know "there is a fine line between being one of the guys and being their leader."

best use of the workers available. A good leader will get the job done and still keep the respect of the men and women working for him. To accomplish this the people should work willingly, not out of fear.

The seventh CPO feels that the followers must believe that the leader knows how to get the job done. "I don't ask anyone to do anything that I can't do myself. In other words, personal example." This chief points out the need to be paternalistic occasionally—father-and-son treatment. When you have to lay down your convictions, be firm, and be sure of them, he urges. "Praise in public, reprimand in private," he believes. "Sarcasm and ridicule have no place in leadership."

The last chief says leadership is based on common sense: "Treat a young man under your command as you'd want to be treated." Respect his problems. They may seem trivial, but they're important to him. Offer him the guidance he needs. But, he warns, "avoid the trap of becoming one of the guys. If a discipline situation arises, your men can't be sure what your position is." He adds: "There is a fine line between being one of the guys and being their leader." Stay on the right side of that line.

64

The Quality of Leadership

When you look at a group, you can almost always tell who the leader is. It's the person who takes charge and directs the others in getting the job done.

To some people, leadership is simply getting the job done. To others, it's *how* the job gets done. The "how" is important, for what good is a leader who gets a job done but loses the respect of his men in the process? What good is a leader whose efforts result in dissension, disorganization, and ineffectiveness, not to mention poor morale? A leader who alienates his men is hurting himself, because he'll have to count on those men the next time he's in charge of a job. And that job could be in combat.

Good leadership can be defined as the art of influencing people to win their obedience, confidence, respect, and willingness to cooperate. As a petty officer, you are given formal authority to lead. But to be a true leader, you must earn a different kind of authority—the kind that comes from those you're leading. Without it, you lose.

Personal Relations

Getting along in the Navy means more than just learning new duties, obeying regulations, standing watches, and showing up for drills. It means working and living with all kinds of people— enough to populate a small town—crowded into a space no larger than a big hotel. Going to sea involves not only crowded living conditions, but extreme operating conditions and long working hours, in intense heat or bitter cold, for perhaps weeks at a time. There are certain qualities and characteristics a person must possess, or acquire, to endure these conditions.

ATTITUDE TOWARD OTHERS

Attitude involves respect, tolerance, and consideration. Perhaps for the first time you will be living with people from different social backgrounds and various levels of education. They will be of different races and have different religions. In fact, they will be just as different from you as you are from them. There is only one thing each of the half-million people in the Navy have in common—they're all in the Navy.

Because of all the differences in race, creed, religion, or national origin, discrimination may crop up, but it is the goal of the Navy to eliminate every vestige of prejudice. The Navy has, in recent years, been successful in fostering racial harmony. The Navy's Affirmative Action Plan (NAAP) has done much toward establishing and maintaining equal opportunity in the Navy, countering racism, fostering equal opportunity for Navy women, and recognizing the dignity and worth of every individual.

While many individuals are available in the naval establishment and in individual commands for counseling and assistance in dealing with discriminatory practices, the ultimate responsibility for extending equal opportunity to all rests with each commanding officer. Assistance to commanding officers is provided by equal opportunity program specialists and human resource management specialists (who operate under the control of the commanders-in-chief, type commanders or other appropriate second echelon commanders) and by the human resource management centers/detachments (HRMC/Ds). Their job is to help make the Navy a place where all persons have equal opportunities, where minority groups are represented in enlisted and commissioned ranks, where bias is eliminated, and where racial and interracial understanding and cooperation is promoted and practiced.

RELATIONS WITH THE PUBLIC

When you put on the Navy uniform, you represent the United States Navy. When you go ashore, civilians will base some of their ideas about the Navy on the way you look and act. So be careful to make a good impression. Remember that at all times, no matter where you may be or what position you hold in the Navy, you are performing a public-relations duty. In a foreign country, you represent the United States, and the people you meet will take your appearance and behavior as representative of all Americans.

OVERSEAS DIPLOMACY

You, as a modern American sailor, will serve overseas and in foreign nations more than any of your predecessors. Overseas service has, of course, always been part of the sailor's expectations. In the past, there were small forces permanently stationed in places like China or the Caribbean; but most of our fleet remained close to home, save for occasional trips to "show a flag." Despite the slogan "Join the Navy and see the world," the average American sailor of the past was apt to be much more familiar with San Diego, Long Beach, Brooklyn, or Norfolk, than he was with Hong Kong, Bangkok, Naples or Marseilles.

But the international situation since the end of World War II has demanded a new policy, often called "foreign strategy."

Figure 4–3 Attitude toward others, respect, tolerance, and consideration underscore the one thing all sailors have in common—they're all in the Navy.

Put simply, it means the U.S. Navy must have ready combat units in places where combat may occur. For the individual sailor, this means more time overseas.

There are three basic kinds of overseas duty:

Regular deployment: This is the most common type, involving service aboard a ship, with an aircraft squadron, or in a construction battalion. Deployed ships and aircraft engage in operational and training missions, and regularly call on foreign ports for maintenance and for crew R&R (rest and recreation). Some of these are regular ports of call for Navy ships: Subic Bay in the Philippines, Hong Kong, Kaohsiung, Yokosuka, Naples, and Rota. Others are visited only occasionally, such as Mombassa (in Kenya), Bangkok, Inchon, and Abadan.

Depending on the needs of the Navy, each command is rotated to duty in a forward area for six to nine months and then returns to CONUS (the continental United States) for repair, reassignment of personnel, and training.

Overseas homeporting: Some ships are permanently assigned to foreign ports for periods of two years or longer. This type of duty permits crewmembers to have their dependents in the country and thus reduces long periods of family separation. Homeported units operate at sea and visit other foreign ports in the area.

Overseas shore: To support fleet operations and carry out its other missions, the Navy needs foreign naval stations and other facilities. Overseas shore duty may be on a large naval base not too different from those in CONUS; or it can be as part of a small unit in such remote locations as Afghanistan, Iceland, and Kuwait.

For the Navy man and woman all of these types of duty present an unparalleled opportunity to learn about the world, to see strange and famous places, and to become acquainted with people of other cultures and points of view. But, with all privileges, overseas service also carries with it a responsibility—to act as a positive representative of the Navy and the nation.

This duty is one which is best fulfilled by enjoying things to the fullest and taking advantage of opportunities offered. The sailor who spends all his overseas liberty in the "sailor trap" waterfront bars will soon grow bored and dissatisfied with overseas duty. Similarly, a Navy family which does not learn about the country and the people but only longs for the familiar sights and sounds of home is not going to look forward to another overseas assignment. And in neither case is the Navy's mission being fully accomplished.

The Navy's Overseas Diplomacy Program (ODP) is designed to help Navy members and their families enjoy their tours overseas and at the same time foster good relations between ourselves and host-country nationals. That is an important term—host country—because we are guests and should act like it. Often people do not enjoy foreign service because of fear of the unknown and unfamiliar, and fear of not knowing the language. To help overcome these fears, ODP provides—through local command overseas diplomacy coordinators (ODCs)—accurate up-to-date information about host countries. Also, every effort is made to explain local transportation systems, point out recreational opportunities, and to teach local customs. Above all, the program points out the benefits of learning and appreciating different ways of solving common human problems. Orientation lectures, publications and other materials are provided.

As a U.S. citizen, you regard people from other countries as foreigners. But bear in mind that when you visit another country, *you* are the foreigner. The customs of other people may seem strange to you, but that's their way of doing things, and they like it. Don't make fun of anyone or anything in another country. At best it's impolite, and at the worst such thoughtlessness can result in serious trouble. (The United States came close to war with Mexico once because some sailors at a bullfight cheered for the bull instead of the bullfighter.)

Discipline

Discipline is sometimes understood to mean *punishment,* but its real goal is the best possible attitude, efficiency, and morale. A well-disciplined crew or team has the right attitude, does its work efficiently, and shows high morale. And its members do the right thing because they *want* to, not because they *have* to. Such men and women willingly perform with enthusiasm and zest, individually or in groups, in order to carry out the mission of their organization. They will do their work without specific instructions.

When discipline fails, punishment may be necessary. In the Navy, as in civilian life, there is a system of punishment for those who fail to observe rules and regulations. (See pp. 73–76.) Punishment is governed by the U.S. Navy Regulations, the Articles for the Government of the Navy, and the Uniform Code of Military Justice (UCMJ). You must be familiar with certain parts of all of them. A brief outline of the UCMJ is contained in Appendix C, pages 544–46.

THE U.S. FIGHTING MAN'S CODE

Any member of the military who may be captured by enemy or unfriendly forces, in war or peace, must be guided in his actions by the six articles of this code. Each article is followed here by a brief discussion of its meaning. You must be familiar with the code and understand what you must do, or not do, if captured.

"I am an American fighting man. I serve in the forces which guard my country and our way of life. I am prepared to give my life in their defense."

A member of the armed forces is always a fighting man. As such, it is his duty to oppose the enemies of the United States, regardless of the circumstances in which he may find himself, whether in active combat, or as a prisoner of war.

II

"I will never surrender of my own free will. If in command, I will never surrender my men while they still have the means to resist."

As an individual, a member of the armed forces may never voluntarily surrender himself. When he is isolated and can no longer harm the enemy, it is his duty to evade capture and rejoin the nearest friendly forces.

The responsibility and authority of a commander never extends to the surrender of his command while it still has power to resist or evade. When isolated, cut off, or surrounded, a unit must continue to fight, until it is relieved or able to rejoin friendly forces.

69

III

"If I am captured I will continue to resist, by all means available. I will make every effort to escape and aid others to escape. I will accept neither parole nor special favors from the enemy."

The duty of a member of the armed forces to continue resistance by all means at his disposal is not lessened by the misfortune of capture. He will escape, if he can, and will help others escape. Parole agreements are promises given the captor by a prisoner of war, on his faith and honor, to fulfill stated conditions (such as not to bear arms or not to escape) in consideration of special privileges—usually release from captivity or lessened restraint. He will never sign or enter into any parole agreement.

IV

"If I become a prisoner of war, I will keep faith with my fellow prisoners. I will give no information nor take part in any actions which might be harmful to my comrades. If I am senior, I will take command. If not, I will obey the lawful orders of those appointed over me and will back them up in every way."

Informing, or any other action which harms a fellow prisoner, is shameful. Prisoners of war must avoid helping the enemy identify fellow prisoners who may have knowledge of value to the enemy, and may therefore be tortured.

Strong leadership is essential to discipline. Without discipline, camp organization, resistance, and even survival may be impossible. Personal hygiene, camp sanitation, and care of sick and wounded are imperative. Officers and noncommissioned officers of the United States will continue to carry out their responsibilities and exercise their authority after capture. The senior line officer or noncommissioned officer within the POW camp or group will assume command according to rank (or precedence), without regard to branch of service. This responsibility and accountability may not be evaded. If the senior officer or noncommissioned officer is incapacitated or unable to act for any reason, the next senior takes over.

V

"When questioned, should I become a prisoner of war, I am required to give only name, rank, service number, and date of birth. I will evade answering further questions to the utmost of my ability. I will make no oral or written statements disloyal to my country and its allies or harmful to their cause."

When questioned, a prisoner of war is permitted to disclose his name, rank, service number, and date of birth. A prisoner of war may tell the enemy about his individual health or welfare as a prisoner of war, and, when appropriate, on routine matters of camp administration. Forbidden are: oral or written confessions (whether true or false), questionnaires, personal history statements, propaganda recordings and broadcasts, appeals to other prisoners of war, signatures of peace or surrender appeals, criticisms, or any other oral or written communication on behalf of the enemy or critical or harmful to the United States, its allies, its armed forces, or other prisoners.

It is a violation of the Geneva Convention to subject a prisoner of war to physical or mental torture or any other form of coercion to secure information of any kind. If, however, a prisoner is subjected to such treatment, he will endeavor to avoid by every means the disclosure of any information, or the making of any statement or the performance of any action harmful to the interests of the United States or its allies, or which will provide aid or comfort to the enemy.

VI

"I will never forget that I am an American fighting man, responsible for my actions, and dedicated to the principles which made my country free. I will trust in my God and in the United States of America."

The provisions of the UCMJ continue to apply to members of the armed forces while prisoners of war. On release, the conduct of prisoners will be examined based on the circumstances of
capture and the time of detention, with due regard for the rights

of the individual and consideration for the conditions of captivity.

A member of the armed forces who becomes a prisoner of war has a continuing obligation to remain loyal to his country, his service and his unit.

The life of a prisoner of war is hard, but he must never give up hope. He must resist enemy indoctrination. Prisoners of war who stand firm and united against the enemy will help one another survive this ordeal.

PRISONERS OF WAR—GENEVA CONVENTION

Article 1123 of U.S. Navy Regulations defines the duties of an individual when captured by the enemy. A person in the Navy who is captured by the enemy shall not disclose any information other than his name, grade or rank, social security number, and date of birth. He should try to communicate this same information, along with his prison address and state of health, to the Central Prisoners of War Agency, normally the International Committee of the Red Cross in Geneva, Switzerland.

In turn, Article 0741 makes the commanding officer responsible for all enemy prisoners of war to assure they are treated with humanity, that their personal property is preserved and protected, that they are allowed to use what they need to take care of their health, that they are supplied with proper rations, that they are guarded properly and deprived of all means of escape and revolt, as provided by the Geneva Convention, 12 August 1949.

UNAUTHORIZED ABSENCE (UA)

This includes absence from duty station (quarters for muster, cleaning station, battle station), leaving your duty station, and overstaying leave.

Overstaying leave is a serious offense. No matter what the reason for your absence, make every effort to return to duty and to notify your commanding officer of your whereabouts. If you can't contact your ship, report to the nearest naval activity.

When going on leave, allow plenty of time to get back. If, for reasons beyond your control, you are going to be late, notify your ship. There may be an excuse for lateness because of sickness, accident, or other emergency. But there is never any excuse for not notifying your commanding officer, the American Red Cross, or the nearest naval activity if you are going to be late. If you are sick or in jail, a family member, a friend, or the shore patrol can send a message for you.

Furnish enough information so that the commanding officer can understand the situation and can send instructions. Don't use the mail, use the telephone. You can always reach the duty

Figure 4–4 Strong leadership ensures good discipline.

officer of any station, or a shore patrol headquarters on any Navy base if your ship has gone to sea.

In most cities some naval activity is listed in the telephone directory under "U.S. Government"; or "Information" can give you the number. Remember, we have recruiting offices in nearly every major U.S. city. The officer or petty officer will advise you of the best course to follow.

MASTERS-AT-ARMS AND POLICE PETTY OFFICERS

The masters-at-arms (MAA) and the police petty officers have the task of maintaining order on a ship or station. They are assistants of the executive officer. Large ships will have a chief master-at-arms (CMAA) with several assistants. Men are assigned to the MAA force for several months or longer. While acting as MAAs, they are relieved of most of their normal watches and duties. Police petty officers usually remain with their divisions for work and watches. Their duties also include maintaining order, making reveille and taps, directing traffic, and turning lights on and off.

SHORE PATROL AND ARMED FORCES POLICE

The shore patrol (SP) is the military police unit in the Navy. It consists of officers and petty officers assigned to maintain order among naval personnel off ship or station. They are identified by brassards (armbands) with the letters SP.

The Army and Marines have their military police (MP) and the Air Force has its air police (AP). You must obey the MPs and APs as well as the SPs. In some areas a combined or unified armed forces police detachment (AFPD) is organized, with military po- lice from all the services under one command.

These military patrols assist military personnel, protect them from harmful practices of civilian establishments and investigate accidents and offenses involving military personnel.

The shore patrol and the military police have authority to stop, question, apprehend, or take into custody any member of the armed forces. If stopped by the SP or AFPD, you must show your ID card, leave or other orders, and obey any directions.

If you need advice, directions, or help, you should call or visit the nearest SP petty officer or headquarters. It's their job to help and protect naval personnel.

Uniform Code of Military Justice

As a civilian you were subject to the criminal laws of your local, state, and federal governments.

To a large extent you still are. But by enlisting, you have submitted yourself to the jurisdiction of the Uniform Code of Military Justice (UCMJ) as well. The basic criminal laws of the Navy are stated in the UCMJ. It is a "uniform" law because Congress made it apply equally to the Army, Navy, Air Force, Marine Corps and Coast Guard—and it is under this law that the various services bring criminal charges against their personnel who violate military law.

Under the UCMJ, all service personnel are required to obey all laws established by Congress for the regulation of the military, and all lawful orders and regulations of the service and of their superior officers.

In the event of violations of the code—refusal to obey lawful orders, insubordination, or disrespect of superior authority—a sailor receives punishment from his commanding officer by captain's mast, or if the offense is more serious, through Navy court-martial. UCMJ articles dealing with punishment for various crimes (Articles 77 through 134) are to be explained to all Navy personnel when they enter active duty, six months thereafter, and on reenlistment. Additionally, military law requires that the UCMJ be made available to all personnel. It is therefore posted in a conspicuous place on all ships and stations.

The Navy has three types of mast: meritorious, request, and captain's mast. *Meritorious mast* is held for award presentations or commendations to personnel who have earned them. *Request masts* are simply audiences with the commanding officer requested by personnel who have matters to discuss with him. A *captain's mast* is a hearing at which minor charges against personnel are resolved. At this hearing, which is non-judicial, an accused sailor is given a chance to rebut or explain charges

brought against him. The accused may call witnesses or even be
represented by an attorney if he so elects.

On hearing the evidence, both for and against, the commanding officer (CO) determines whether the person has committed the infraction he is charged with. If the CO concerned (usually a lieutenant commander or above in rank) finds that the accused is guilty, he may order punishments to the offender, such as: restriction of not more than 60 days, extra duties not more than 45 days, reduction in grade, correctional custody not more than 30 days, confinement on bread and water not more than three days if the parties concerned are aboard ship at sea, forfeiture of not more than half a month's pay per month for two months, or detention of half a month's pay for three months. All punishments imposed are non-judicial; this means there is no criminal "record" for the offender. It also means that a sailor punished under this provision may appeal to a higher commander who will review the matter for strict compliance with Navy law and procedure.

Commanding officers below the rank of lieutenant commander also may impose punishments at captain's masts, but the power of stiff punishment is reserved for officers of higher rank. A person may refuse to submit to captain's mast (unless he is attached to or embarked on a vessel at sea) by submitting a demand for trial by court-martial instead of captain's mast.

If an alleged offense, in the opinion of the CO, is too severe to dispose of by captain's mast, he may recommend court-martial. The commander may recommend trial by three different levels of military court. The lowest level is summary court-martial, the next is special court-martial, and the highest or most serious level of military court is general court-martial.

If the offense is minor, and if the CO has ruled out non-judicial action, he may refer the charges to trial by *summary court-martial.* This involves "summary" or shortened procedure, but a summary court-martial is still a properly recognized United States court, and its actions are judicial in nature. One officer serves as the judge, jury, prosecution, and defense counsel. He takes evidence on the charges and makes judgment according to judicial standards. The accused may be represented by an attorney if he or she desires, but this is not mandatory. The accused may also refuse trial by summary court-martial by demanding trial by special court-martial.

If an accused is convicted by summary court-martial, the court may impose confinement of up to one month in the stockade, or hard labor without confinement for 45 days. The court may also restrict him to specified limits for a total of 60 days, or it may deny him two-thirds of his monthly pay. An E-5 and above may be reduced only one grade in pay, and may not be confined or ordered to perform hard labor. An E-4 and below may be confined for one month or assigned hard labor for 45 days, and may be reduced to the lowest enlisted paygrade.

If a CO feels that a charged offense against a service person is moderate-to-severe he may refer the charges to trial by *special court-martial*. The special court-martial consists of three or more members. A legally trained judge may also be added at the discretion of the convening authority. An accused might, if he or she wishes, waive the right to trial before the court-martial jury, and face the military judge alone. An accused standing trial before a special court-martial can also request that up to one-third the total membership of the jury be comprised of enlisted personnel. A special court-martial may order a bad conduct discharge and up to six months' imprisonment, with loss of all pay and allowances for that time. Every accused person who stands trial by special court-martial is entitled to an attorney; usually an attorney from the Navy is appointed for him.

The *general court-martial* is reserved for the more serious charges, such as the common-law felonies (murder, rape, robbery, and arson) and the more serious military charges (lengthy AWOL, desertion, refusal to fight). It is comprised of a military judge, five or more members who serve as the jury, and military defense and prosecution attorneys. An accused may request trial before military judge alone, or may be tried by the full court-martial. If he so elects, one-third of the court members must be enlisted persons.

This is by far the most serious of all military courts. Its sentencing power extends to the death penalty and life imprisonment. This does not mean that a general court may sentence *anyone* convicted of an offense before that court to such extreme sentences. The court is limited by the sentences in the table of maximum punishments (which is found in the Manual for Courts-Martial). In other words, the table lists maximum sentences that may be imposed by all military courts for each offense punishable under the UCMJ. Nor does this mean that military courts routinely impose maximum sentences under law. The court may sentence an accused to any sentence less than the maximum— but in no case may it impose a greater sentence.

As was mentioned before, service personnel are also subject to civil trial and punishment; this must be understood with certain reservations, however. Service personnel are not answerable to civil authorities for violations of a strictly military nature, such as absence without leave, desertion, or misbehavior before the enemy. These offenses are subject to trial by military authorities only. Service personnel, however, are subjected to joint jurisdiction (both civil and military) for certain types of offenses—such as murder, robbery, or rape committed on a military post. In

75

many situations involving crimes of this nature, both civil and military authorities can try an offender. Normally, he would be subjected to trial before only one jurisdiction in such circumstances, but there are situations where he is tried in succession, by both civil and military jurisdictions, for the same offense.

Finally, there are certain offenses committed by a service person that can only be tried by a civil jurisdiction. These would include, for example, an off-post rape committed against a civilian without connections to the military. In other words, the Navy cannot try a sailor for an offense, even though the act is prohibited by the UCMJ, unless it is, in some fashion, "service-connected."

On the other hand, the civil courts allow military tribunals to try military personnel arrested for selling narcotics off-post to civilians without military ties. This offense is considered "service-connected" because a service person who pushes drugs, even to off-post civilians, poses a threat to the military community, since he may at any time start pushing drugs to service personnel, on or off-post. Hence, the question of what is a "service-connected" offense and can be tried by court-martial is resolved on a case-by-case basis.

Military law relating to trial by court-martial is a complex subject, covered by thousands of books. The finer points of military law and court-martial procedure may, therefore, never be completely understood by non-legal personnel. But Navy lawyers are at your disposal, should the need arise, and will represent you, at no cost, on all military justice matters.

5. Courtesies, Customs, and Ceremonies

The Salute

The hand salute is the military custom you will learn first and use most. It is centuries old, and probably originated when men in armor raised their helmet visors so they could be identified. Salutes are customarily given with the right hand, but there are exceptions. A sailor with his right arm or hand encumbered may salute left-handed, while people in the Army or Air Force never salute left-handed. On the other hand, a soldier or airman may salute sitting down or uncovered (without cap on); in the Navy, a sailor does not salute when uncovered (unless failure to do so would mean embarrassment or misunderstanding), but may salute when seated in a vehicle.

Women in the Navy follow the same customs and rules as men in saluting, with one exception. A woman in uniform indoors, where men customarily remove their hats, does not remove her hat, nor does she salute. She does, of course, use the proper spoken greeting, just as she would outdoors.

HOW TO SALUTE

Salute from a position of attention. If you're walking, salute from an erect position. Your upper arm should be parallel to the deck or ground, forearm inclined at a 45-degree angle, hand and wrist straight, palm slightly inward, thumb and fingers extended and joined, with the tip of the forefinger touching your cap beak, slightly to the right of the right eye. Face the person saluted, or if you're walking, turn your head and eyes toward the person. Hold the salute until the officer has returned or acknowledged it, then bring your hand smartly to your side.

WHOM TO SALUTE

Salute all officers, men and women, of all U.S. services and all allied foreign services. Officers in the U.S. Merchant Marine and Public Health Service wear uniforms that closely resemble Navy uniforms, and they too rate a salute.

When chief or senior petty officers perform duties normally assigned to an officer—such as standing JOOD watches or taking a division muster—they rate the same salute as an officer.

There is one simple rule of saluting: When in doubt, salute.

The Address

ADDRESSING OFFICERS

Officers are always addressed and referred to by their title or rank, such as "Admiral," "Captain," or "Commander." If several officers of the same rank are together, it is proper to use both title and name, such as "Admiral Taylor" or "Captain Smith," to avoid confusion. Warrant officers are addressed in the same manner as officers. Midshipmen and aviation cadets are addressed as "Mister" or "Miss."

By tradition, the commanding officer of any ship or station, no matter what his rank, is addressed and referred to as "Captain." The executive officer, likewise, is "Commander." Other captains or commanders in the same command should be addressed by rank and name.

An officer in the Medical Corps and Dental Corps is addressed and referred to by title, or as "Doctor." A chaplain may be called "Chaplain" no matter what the rank. An officer below the rank of admiral who is in command of a squadron, task unit, or convoy of ships is customarily addressed and referred to as "Commodore." The rank of commodore, between the ranks of captain and admiral, is not used in peacetime.

Army, Air Force, and Marine Corps officers are addressed and referred to by their ranks.

ADDRESSING ENLISTED PERSONNEL

A chief petty officer is addressed as "Chief Petty Officer Smith," or more informally as "Chief Smith," or as "Chief" if you do not know his name. But in recruit training all chiefs acting as company commanders rate "Mister" and "Sir." Master and senior chief petty officers are customarily addressed and referred to as "Master Chief Smith," or "Senior Chief Smith," or as "Master Chief" or "Senior Chief" if you do not know their names.

Other petty officers are addressed and referred to by their specific rates. "Non-rated" personnel—in paygrades E-1 through E-3—are addressed and referred to as "Seaman Wells," or "Fireman Clifton," regardless of their specific paygrade.

In civilian life, it is customary to introduce men to women, and young people to older ones. The same general rules are followed in military life, except that in most cases, rank establishes the order of introduction: introduce the junior to the senior, regardless of either one's sex. Navy personnel, regardless of rank or sex, are introduced to a chaplain.

Flags and Flag Etiquette

Salutes to the American flag are prescribed in U.S. Navy Regulations, Article 1007, as follows:

Each person in the naval service, upon coming on board a ship of the Navy, shall salute the national ensign if it is flying. He shall stop on reaching the upper platforms of the accommodation ladder, or the shipboard end of the brow, face the national ensign, and render the salute, after which he shall salute the officer of the deck. On leaving the ship, he shall render the salutes in inverse order. The officer of the deck shall return both salutes in each case.

When passed by or passing the national ensign being carried, uncased, in a military formation, all persons in the naval service shall salute. Persons in vehicles or boats shall follow the procedure prescribed for such persons during colors.

The salutes prescribed in this article shall also be rendered to foreign national ensigns and aboard foreign men-of-war.

COLORS

The ceremony of hoisting the national ensign and union jack at 0800 and lowering them at sunset on ships in port is referred to as morning colors and evening colors. Shore stations make colors but do not fly the jack. All ships follow the motions of the senior officer present afloat (SOPA) in making colors. At 0755 "first call" is sounded on the bugle. (Ships without a bugle may play a recording, or the boatswain's mate of the watch may pipe and pass the word, "first call to colors.")

At 0800, the bugle sounds "attention," then "to the colors," and the ensign and jack, respectively, are hoisted smartly to the top of the flagstaff. If the ship has a band, the national anthem is played. Aboard ships with no bands or bugle, a whistle signal and the word "attention to colors" is passed. At the end of the music "carry on" is passed or whistle signals are made.

The procedure for evening colors is the same, with "first call" sounded at five minutes to sunset. This can vary from about 1700 to 2100, according to time of year and latitude.

During colors everyone within sight or hearing renders honors. Personnel in ranks cease work, face the colors, and salute until the last note of the anthem. Passengers in a boat, seated or standing, remain at attention. The boat officer or coxswain salutes. Persons wearing civilian clothes or athletic gear stop and face the colors at attention. If a hat is worn, it should be held in the right hand, over the heart. If no hat is worn, salute by holding the right hand over the heart. A woman in civilian clothes, with or without a hat, stands at attention and places her right hand over her heart. Drivers of motor vehicles pull over and stop if traffic safety permits.

SHIFTING COLORS

On unmooring, at the instant the last mooring line leaves the pier or the anchor is aweigh, the Boatswain's Mate of the Watch

(BMOW) will blow a long whistle blast and pass the word "shift colors." The jack and ensign, if flying, will be hauled down smartly. At the same instant the "steaming" ensign will be hoisted on the gaff and the ship's call sign and other signal flags will be hoisted or broken. On mooring, the moment the anchor is let go or the first mooring line is made fast on the pier, the BMOW passes the word "shift colors," the ship's call sign and the "steaming" ensign are hauled down smartly, and the jack and ensign are raised.

Ships underway do not make morning or evening colors, but do fly a "steaming" ensign at the gaff from sunrise to sunset. The jack is not flown at sea.

The ensign is sometimes flown at half-mast as a tribute to the dead. Whenever the ensign is to be half-masted, it is first closed up and then lowered to the half-mast position. The same procedure is used when lowering the ensign; it first must be closed up and then lowered.

On Memorial Day, the ensign is half-masted from 0800 until completion of the 21-gun salute fired at 1200, or until 1220 if no salute is fired.

During burial at sea, the ensign is at half-mast from the beginning of the funeral service until the body is committed to the deep.

DIPPING

Merchant ships "salute" Navy ships by dipping their ensigns. When a merchant ship of any nation formally recognized by the United States salutes a ship of the U.S. Navy, it lowers its national colors to half-mast. The Navy ship, at its closest point of approach, lowers the ensign to half-mast for a few seconds, then closes it up, after which the merchant ship raises its own flag. If the salute is made when the ensign is not displayed, the Navy ship will hoist her colors, dip for the salute, close them up again, and then haul them down after a suitable interval. Naval vessels dip the ensign only to answer a salute; they never salute first.

UNION JACK

The jack is a replica of the blue, star-studded field of the national ensign; it is flown by ships at anchor from 0800 to sunset. A union jack is hoisted at a yardarm when a general court-martial or a court of inquiry is in session. The jack is half-masted if the ensign is half-masted, but it is not dipped when the ensign is dipped.

COMMISSION PENNANT

The commission pennant is long and narrow with seven white stars on a blue field covering one-fifth of it nearest the hoist. The

rest of the pennant is divided lengthwise, red on top and white below. The commission pennant flies from the time a ship is commissioned until she is decommissioned (except as noted below); it is hoisted at the after truck or, aboard a mastless ship, at the highest and most conspicuous point of hoist. A commission pennant is also flown from the bow of the boat in which the commanding officer makes an official visit. The commission pennant is not flown when a ship flies a personal flag or command pennant.

The commission pennant is not a personal flag, but sometimes it is regarded as the personal symbol of the commanding officer. Along with the ensign and the union jack, it is half-masted on the death of the ship's commanding officer. When a ship is decommissioned, the commanding officer keeps the commission pennant.

The ship carrying an officer who commands a fleet or unit of a fleet flies his personal flag from the main truck at all times, unless he is absent for more than 72 hours. This is a blue flag with five white stars for a fleet admiral, four for admiral, three for vice admiral, two for rear admiral, and one for commodore admiral.

COMMAND PENNANTS

An officer below flag rank, when in command of a force, flotilla, squadron, carrier or cruiser-destroyer group, aircraft wing or carrier air wing, flies a broad command pennant, white with blue stripes top and bottom. An officer in command of any other unit, such as an aircraft squadron, flies a burgeé command pennant, which is white with red stripes top and bottom.

ABSENCE INDICATORS

When a commanding officer or any flag officer is absent, an "absentee pennant" is flown. The absence of the admiral or unit commander, whose personal flag or pennant is flying, is indicated by the "first substitute indicator," flown from the starboard yardarm. The "second substitute," flown from the port yardarm, indicates that the chief of staff is absent. "Third substitute," also flown from the port yardarm, indicates the absence of the commanding officer. (If he is to be gone more than 72 hours, then the pennant shows the absence of the executive officer.) The "fourth substitute" means that the civil or military official whose flag is flying (such as the Secretary of Defense) is absent. It is flown from the starboard yardarm.

CHURCH PENNANT

The church pennant is the only flag ever flown over the national ensign at the same point of hoist. It is displayed only during church services conducted by a chaplain, both ashore and afloat.

OTHER FLAGS AND PENNANTS

Both in port and at sea, ships fly many single flags or pennants with special meanings. The Senior Officer Present Afloat (SOPA) may prescribe certain flag hoists for local use, such as request for garbage or trash lighter, or water barge. At anchor, ships awarded the Presidential Unit Citation (PUC), Navy Unit Commendation (NUC), or Meritorious Unit Commendation (MUC) fly the pennant at the foretruck from sunrise to sunset.

Honors

GUN SALUTE

In olden days it took as much as 20 minutes to load and fire a gun, so that a ship that fired her guns in salute did so as a friendly gesture, making herself powerless for the duration of the salute.

The gun salutes prescribed by Navy Regs are fired only by ships and stations designated by the Secretary of the Navy. A national salute of 21 guns is fired on Washington's Birthday, Memorial Day, and Independence Day, and to honor the President of the United States and heads of foreign states. Salutes for naval officers are: admiral, 17 guns; vice admiral, 15 guns; rear admiral, 13 guns; commodore admiral, 11 guns. Salutes are fired at intervals of 5 seconds, and always in odd numbers.

MANNING THE RAIL

This custom evolved from "manning the yards" hundreds of years ago. Men aboard sailing ships stood evenly spaced on all

Figure 5–1 Crew members man the rails before their ship renders honors.

the yards and gave three cheers to honor a distinguished person. Now men are stationed along the rails and superstructure of a ship when honors are rendered to the President, a head of a foreign state, or a member of a reigning royal family. Men so stationed do not salute.

DRESSING AND FULL-DRESSING SHIP

Commissioned ships are *full-dressed* on Washington's Birthday and Independence Day, and *dressed* on other national holidays.

When a ship is dressed, the national ensign is flown from the flagstaff and, usually, from each masthead. When a ship is full-dressed, in addition to the ensigns a "rainbow" of signal flags is displayed from bow to stern over the mastheads, or as nearly so as the construction of the ship permits. Ships not underway are dressed from 0800 to sunset; ships underway do not dress until they come to anchor during that period.

PASSING HONORS

Passing honors are ordered by ships and boats when vessels, embarked officials, or officers pass (or are passed) close aboard —600 yards for ships, 400 yards for boats.

Such honors are exchanged between ships of the U.S. Navy, between ships of the Navy and the Coast Guard, and between U.S. and most foreign navy ships passing close aboard. "Attention" is sounded and the hand salute is rendered by all persons, in view on deck and not in ranks.

Smaller ships use whistle signals when rendering honors. Attention to starboard is indicated by one blast; two blasts indicate attention to port. Subsequent commands are one blast for "hand salute," two blasts for ending the salute, and three blasts for signaling "carry on."

THE NATIONAL ANTHEM

When the national anthem is played, sailors stand at attention and face the direction of the music. If the anthem is played at colors, those present face in the direction of the ensign. When covered, they salute from the sounding of the first note to the last. Those in ranks salute together, on command. Persons in vehicles or in boats remain seated or standing; only the boat officer or the coxswain stands and salutes.

The same marks of respect prescribed during the playing of our national anthem are shown during the playing of a foreign national anthem. When uncovered, in uniform, it is customary to stand at attention during the playing of U.S. or foreign anthems.

If in civilian clothes and covered, remove the hat with your right hand and place it over your heart. Women in civilian dress also salute in this manner.

There are many occasions besides colors when honors are rendered to the ensign or national anthem. The usual rule is if the flag is displayed, face it. If the flag is not displayed, face the music. Hold the salute until the music has stopped or the flag has been hoisted, lowered, or has passed.

THE QUARTERDECK

The quarterdeck is that part of the ship designated by the commanding officer for official and ceremonial functions. It is normally on the main deck, but may vary according to the type of ship. It is marked off by appropriate lines, deck markings, decorative cartridge cases, or fancy work, and is always kept particularly clean and shipshape. Observe these rules concerning the quarterdeck:

Men on watch on the quarterdeck must be in the proper uniform of the day and present a smart and military appearance at all times.

Men not in the uniform of the day may appear on or cross the quarterdeck only as their work requires.

Aboard large ships with well-defined quarterdeck limits, salute every time you enter it.

Do not smoke or engage in any recreational athletics on the quarterdeck except with permission of the captain, and then only after working hours.

Never walk on the starboard side of the quarterdeck except in the performance of duty as a quarterdeck watch.

The starboard gangway to the quarterdeck is used by all commissioned officers, warrant officers, and their visitors; the port gangway is used by enlisted men, their visitors, workmen, and other civilians. Changes in the rule are made at the discretion of the commanding officer. In heavy weather, the lee gangway is used by everyone. Flagships are sometimes equipped with an additional starboard gangway which is used by the embarked flag officer (admiral) and senior officers of his staff. Aboard small ships with only one gangway, it may be rigged to either side and is used by all hands.

SIDE BOYS

Side boys are a part of the quarterdeck ceremonies when an important person or officer comes on board or leaves a ship. Large ships will have side boys detailed to the quarterdeck from 0800 to sunset. When the side is piped by the boatswain's mate of the watch (BMOW), from two to eight side boys, depending on the rank of the officer, will form a passageway at the gangway. They salute on the first note of the pipe and finish together on the last note.

Figure 5–2 With a huge Spanish sombrero applied to her sail, the USS *Mariano G. Vallejo* (SSBN 658) goes down the ways at Mare Island, California.

Side boys must be particularly smart in appearance and grooming, with polished shoes and immaculate uniforms. There is nothing in Navy Regulations stating that side boys must be male. In ceremonies ashore when side boys are required, enlisted women may be, and have been, detailed. (Yes, they're still called "side boys!")

Shipboard Customs

The quarterdeck is the most important place on a ship in port, but when the ship gets underway, the bridge becomes the center of operations. Like the quarterdeck, the bridge is a place where only those on watch are permitted.

Many ships require all non-watch personnel to request permission from the OOD to come on the bridge, accompanying their request with a salute. If the captain is on the bridge, officers and civilians—and on some ships, senior enlisted personnel—will make a point of greeting him at this time.

BOARDING OR LEAVING SHIP

The OOD or the JOOD, who may be either an officer or senior petty officer, will meet all persons leaving or boarding the ship. Usually the OOD will attend the starboard side, the JOOD the port side. There are definite procedures to be used at all times on boarding or leaving a ship; learn them.

Boarding your own ship: At the gangway, if the ensign is flying, salute in its direction, then turn to the OOD or his representative, salute and say, "I report my return aboard, sir." The OOD will return both salutes and say, "Very well."

Leaving your own ship: Salute the OOD and say, "I request permission to leave the ship, sir," or if you are going to the pier to work and do not need the permission of your division officer and the executive officer, you salute and say, "I request permission to go on the pier to (check the after mooring lines), sir." When the OOD says "Permission granted," and returns your salute, drop your salute and step to the gangway. If the ensign is flying, salute in its direction and leave.

Boarding ship other than your own: Stop at the top of the gangway, salute the ensign if it is flying, then turn to the OOD or his representative, salute and say, "I request permission to come aboard, sir." You may be asked to identify yourself, or state your business, then the OOD will salute and say, "Permission granted (denied)."

Leaving ship other than your own: Salute the OOD or his representative, and say, "With your permission, sir, I shall leave the ship." After he has said, "Permission granted," and has returned your salute, step to the gangway and, if the ensign is flying, salute in its direction before leaving.

86

In a party of men: Only the person in charge makes the request to the OOD to board and leave the ship. All salute the ensign, if it is flying, and the OOD, both coming and going.

Crossing nests: Destroyers and smaller ships sometimes tie up in nests (clusters) alongside a tender or pier and a man may have to cross several ships to get to his own. The usual quarterdeck procedure described for boarding and leaving a ship does not apply when crossing a ship, but there is still a procedure to be followed. On boarding the inboard ship, salute the colors and the quarterdeck, request "Permission to cross" of the quarterdeck watch. Do not salute the quarterdeck or colors on leaving. Repeat this procedure on each ship until you reach your own. Going from your ship in a nest to the pier or tender, the procedure is reversed; after leaving your own ship, request permission to cross from the quarterdeck watch on each inboard ship.

DIVINE SERVICES

When divine services are held on board ship, the church pennant is flown and the word is passed, "Divine services are being held in (name of space). Maintain quiet about the decks." A person entering the area where services are held will uncover, even if he is on watch and wearing duty belt and sidearm. There is one exception: remain covered for a Jewish ceremony.

SICKBAY

In sailing-ship days it became customary to uncover when entering the sickbay, out of respect to the dying and dead. Due to modern medicine, the sickbay is instead a place where men are usually healed and cured; but the custom remains. As in any hospital, silence is maintained. Smoking is usually not permitted in the sickbay, partly because the oxygen used for medical purposes is a fire hazard.

OFFICERS' AND CPO COUNTRY

Officers' country includes all staterooms and the wardroom. CPO country includes CPOs' living spaces and mess. Do not enter these areas except on business, and do not use their passageways as thoroughfares or short cuts. When entering the wardroom, or any compartment or office in officer or CPO country, uncover. Men on watch and wearing the duty belt or sidearm remain covered, unless a meal is in progress. Always knock before entering any officer's or chief petty officer's room.

MESS HALL

The mess hall for enlisted men is treated with the same courtesy as the wardroom. If you enter while a meal is in progress, uncover, even if you are on watch and wearing the duty belt.

Boat Etiquette

BOAT, VEHICLE, AND PASSAGEWAY MANNERS

The basic rule in Navy manners, as in civilian life, is to make way for a senior quickly, quietly, and without confusion.

The procedure for entering boats and vehicles is: seniors in last and out first. The idea is that the captain should not have to wait in a boat for anyone. The senior gets out first because normally his business is more important and pressing than that of the men under him.

A ship is judged by her boats and their crews. Whether in dungarees or dress blues, crews should observe the courtesies and procedures that build and maintain their ship's reputation. Boats play an important part in naval ceremonies, and each crew member ought to know what is expected of the boat and him. In general, boats exchange salutes when passing, in much the same way that men and officers do when walking on land.

It is not the size or type of boat that determines seniority, but who is embarked; a whaleboat carrying a commander is senior to a large boat with only an ensign aboard.

When one boat passes another carrying an officer, the coxswain and the boat officer, if embarked, render the hand salute. Others in the boat stand or sit at attention. If standing, they face the boat being saluted; if seated, they sit at attention but do not turn toward the passing boat. It is usually possible to tell by the uniform of the passenger officer or the flag flown which boat is senior. But if in doubt, salute.

The senior officer in the boat salutes if he is visible outboard. Officers do not rise when saluting.

Boats passing U.S. or foreign men-of-war during colors on board must lay to.

Only the boat officer—or, in his absence, the coxswain—stands at attention and salutes if safety permits. All others remain seated at attention.

If the boat is carrying an officer or official for whom a salute is being fired, the engine is slowed and clutch disengaged after the first gun is fired, and the person honored rises.

SALUTES WHILE NOT UNDERWAY

A boat is not underway when it is anchored, moored, or lying at a boom, gangway, or landing. It is considered underway if it is merely stopped dead in the water, as when standing off from a ship or dock, waiting to be called.

The rules of saluting while not underway are as follows:

Only the person in charge of the boat salutes.

Coxswains in charge of boats salute when officers enter or leave their boats, unless there is an emergency. The coxswain also salutes when the officer in his boat salutes or returns a salute. The coxswain salutes at the same time with his officer, and not before.

Men working aboard a boat do not salute unless "attention" is sounded.

Men seated in boats in which there is no officer, petty officer, or acting petty officer in charge, rise and salute the officers passing near. When an officer, PO, or acting PO is in charge of a boat, he alone renders the salute.

Enlisted men seated well forward in a large boat do not rise and salute when officers enter or leave the stern sheets. Men in the after section of a boat always rise and salute when a commissioned officer enters or leaves.

OTHER COURTESIES

The command "gangway" should be given by anyone who observes an officer approaching where passage is blocked. The courtesy is also extended to important civilians. The senior petty officer present must be responsible for clearing the gangway properly and promptly. Enlisted men do not clear a passage for themselves or other enlisted men in this way, but should say "coming through."

The command "attention" should be given, if possible, when officers are escorting visitors through their own ship. The requirements of "attention" and "gangway" must be strictly obeyed, whether the visitors are officers or civilians. If the party does not intend to move on promptly, the passing dignitary should order "carry on."

Do not overtake and pass an officer without permission. When it is necessary to walk past him, overtake him on his left side, salute when you are abreast, and ask, "By your leave, sir?" When the officer returns the salute and says "Very well," or "Permission granted," you drop your salute and continue past.

When walking with a senior, always walk on his left; that is, with him on your right. When walking with a woman, it is customary to have her on your right side, which is the position of honor. When a man and woman, both in uniform, are walking together, the man may insist that the woman walk on the right side even though she is junior. If so, she should defer to his preference and accept the honor.

6. Sentry Duties and Recruit Drills

One of the first military duties a recruit will perform is a sentry or security watch. Security means protecting a ship or station against damage by storm or fire, and to guard against theft, sabotage, and other subversive activities. Chapter 7 discusses security in greater detail.

Security involves sentry duty, guard duty, fire watches, and barracks watches. *Sentry duty* is formal military duty, governed by specific orders. *Guard duty* may be the same as sentry duty; at other times a guard may be permitted to relax military bearing, so long as he is on the job and ready to act. A *fire watch* may mean covering an assigned area on foot or in a vehicle, or it may mean assignment to a certain place for a specified period. A *barracks watch* may sometimes mean standing sentry duty, or merely being available to answer a phone, check people in and out, turn lights off and on, and preserve order and cleanliness.

Requirements for standing sentry duty are the same as those for all watches: keep alert, attend to duty, report all violations, preserve order, and remain on watch until properly relieved. The rules or orders for sentries are basic for all security watches.

Detail to a sentry watch involves two sets of orders: special orders and general orders. *Special orders* apply to a specific type of watch. They will be passed on and explained to you by the petty officer of the watch or the petty officer of the guard. *General orders* never change. You will—on any watch or duty, now and in the future—be responsible for carrying them out, whether or not anyone explains them to you or reminds you of them. The 11 general orders, with a brief explanation of each, follow. Memorize them and be ready to recite them whenever called on to do so.

The General Orders

1. To take charge of this post and all government property in view.

2. To walk my post in a military manner, keeping always on the alert, and observing everything that takes place within sight or hearing.

3. To report all violations of orders I am instructed to enforce.

4. To repeat all calls from posts more distant from the guard house than my own.

5. To quit my post only when properly relieved.

6. To receive, obey, and pass on to the sentry who relieves me all orders from the commanding officer, command duty officer, officer of the deck, and officers and petty officers of the watch only.

7. To talk to no one except in line of duty.

8. To give the alarm in case of fire or disorder.

9. To call the officer of the deck in any case not covered by instructions.

10. To salute all officers, and all colors and standards not cased.

11. To be especially watchful at night, and, during the time for challenging, to challenge all persons on or near my post and to allow no one to pass without proper authority.

Orders 1, 2, and 3 mean that all persons in the service, whatever their ranks, are required to respect you in the performance of your duties as a sentinel and a member of the guard.

You report immediately, by telephone or other means, every unusual or suspicious event.

You apprehend and turn over to proper authority all suspicious persons involved in a disorder on or near your post, and anyone who tries to enter your post without authority.

Report violations of orders when you are inspected or relieved. If it is urgent and necessary, apprehend the offender and call the petty officer of the guard.

Order 4 means that you "pass the word" by calling "petty officer of the guard, number __," giving the number of your post, when you need him for any purpose other than relief, fire, or disorder.

Order 5 means that if you become sick or for any reason must leave your post, you call "petty officer of the guard, number __, relief." Do not leave your post for meals or other reasons unless properly relieved. If your relief is late, telephone or call the petty officer but do not leave your post.

Order 6 names the officers whose orders you must obey. However, any officer can investigate apparent violations of regulations when he observes them.

You give up possession of your rifle only on receiving a direct order to do so from the person who can lawfully give you orders while on your post. No other person may require a sentinel to hand over his rifle or even require it to be inspected.

Order 7 is self-explanatory, but when challenging or holding conversations with any person, you take the position of "port arms" if you are armed with a rifle, and take the position of "raise pistol" if you are armed with a pistol.

Order 8 means that if fire is discovered, you must immediately call, "Fire, Number __," then turn in the alarm, or make sure it has been turned in. If possible, put out the fire.

Order 10 covers saluting. (More details on saluting are on page 77.) A sentry salutes as follows: If walking post, he halts. If armed with a rifle, he salutes by presenting arms; if otherwise armed, he renders the hand salute. If on patrol duty, he does not halt, unless spoken to, but renders the hand salute. If in a sentry box, he stands at attention in the doorway upon the approach of the person or party involved, and renders the hand salute (or, if armed with a rifle, he presents arms).

When a sentry is required to challenge, he salutes an officer as soon as he is recognized.

The sentry salutes an officer as he comes on the post. If the officer stops to hold conversation, the sentry assumes the position of "port arms" if armed with a rifle, or the position of "attention" throughout the conversation, and salutes again when the officer leaves.

When talking to an officer, the sentry does not interrupt to salute another officer unless the officer being addressed salutes. Then the sentry follows his example.

When the flag is raised at morning colors or lowered at evening colors, the sentry stands at attention at the first note of the National Anthem or "To the Colors" and salutes. A man engaged in duty that would be hampered doesn't have to salute. He should face the flag while saluting, but if duty requires he may face in another direction.

Order 11 means when a person or party approaches a post during challenging hours, the sentry should advance rapidly toward them, and at 30 paces, challenge sharply: "Halt! Who is there?" Unless circumstances prevent it, the sentry should continue to advance while challenging. He then assumes the best position to pass or apprehend the person and requires him to advance, remain halted, or face toward the light to determine whether he should be passed or turned over to the guard.

If a person is in a vehicle, the same procedure is followed. If necessary, the sentry may require the person to get out of the vehicle.

A sentry permits only one member of a group to approach to be recognized. If he is not satisfied with the identification, he detains that person and calls the petty officer of the guard.

When two or more individuals approach from different directions at the same time, the sentry challenges each in turn and requires each to halt and remain halted until told to proceed.

A sentry must never let himself be surprised nor should he permit two persons to advance at the same time.

A sentry should always say, "Advance one to be recognized." If the party has replied properly, he says, "Advance, friend (or officer of the day, etc.)." As soon as recognition is certain, he salutes and permits the person to pass.

Guard duties aboard ship will differ somewhat from those ashore. Some of the variations follow:

Where there are no Marines, guard duty, if required, is performed by details from the ship's divisions and is known as the security watch.

The guard of the day is mustered only at morning and evening colors and in the daylight hours between the times honors are to be rendered.

Sentries do not challenge.

The guard does not raise nor lower the colors.

The guard, except the sentry on the brig post, is not responsible for any prisoners aboard ship.

The chief master-at-arms (CMAA) or his assistants always have access to prisoners.

The relief does not make the rounds of all posts as a unit when going on watch.

The petty officer of the guard visits sentinels when required by the commanding officer and as directed by the OOD.

Use of Weapons

Besides sentry and guard duties, others who may be armed are the guard mail officer, brig or prisoner guards, pay line guards, gangway watches and in some cases, shore patrols. Armed men are authorized to fire their weapons only under the following conditions:

To protect their own lives or the life of another person where no other means of defense will work.

To prevent the escape of someone known to have committed a serious crime, when there is no other effective means available to prevent it.

To prevent sabotage, arson, or other crimes against the government after all other means have failed.

No one is to be assigned to any duty requiring the use of a weapon until he has been properly trained and instructed in it, including all safety precautions.

Drill Commands

Preparatory commands are indicated in this chapter by *small italic letters* and those of execution by *CAPITAL ITALIC LETTERS.*

There are two parts to a military drill command:

1. The preparatory command, such as *hand,* indicates the movement that is to be executed.

2. The command of execution, such as *SALUTE,* brings about the desired movement.

When appropriate, the preparatory command includes the name or title of the group concerned, as *"First Division, hand SALUTE."*

In certain commands, the preparatory command and the command of execution are combined, as in: *FALL IN, AT EASE,* and *REST.*

To call back or revoke a command or to begin again a movement that was not intended, give the command *AS YOU WERE.* The movement is supposed to stop and the former position is taken.

THE POSITIONS

Position of Attention: Command: *a-ten-HUT* or *FALL IN.* Heels close together, feet turned out to form an angle of 45 degrees, knees straight, hips level, body erect, with the weight resting equally on the heels and balls of the feet. Shoulders squared, chest arched, arms hanging down without stiffness so that the thumbs are along the seams of the trousers, palms and fingers relaxed. Head erect, chin drawn in, and eyes front. In coming to "attention," the heels are brought together smartly and audibly.

The Rests: Commands: *FALL OUT, REST, AT EASE,* and (1) parade, (2) *REST.*

FALL OUT. Men break rank but remain nearby. Men return to places and come to attention at the command *FALL IN.*

REST. Right foot is kept in place. Sailors are silent, but may move about.

(1) *Parade,* (2) *REST.* Move the left foot smartly 12 inches to the left from the right foot. At the same time, clasp the hands behind the back, palms to the rear, the right hand clasping the left thumb, arms hanging naturally. Be silent and be still.

To resume attention from any rest other than *FALL OUT* the command is, for example, (1) detail, (2) *a-ten-HUT.*

Eyes Right or Left: The commands are: (1) eyes, (2) *RIGHT* (or *LEFT*), (3) ready, (4) *FRONT.* At the command *RIGHT,* each man turns his head and eyes smartly to the right. Those on the extreme right file keep head and eyes to the front. At the command *FRONT,* head and eyes turn smartly to the front. The opposite is carried out for eyes *LEFT.*

Hand Salute: Command: (1) hand, (2) *SALUTE,* (3) *TWO.* The command *TWO* is used only when saluting by command. At the command *SALUTE,* raise the right hand smartly in the hand salute, then turn the head and eyes toward the person saluted. At the command *TWO,* drop the arm to its normal position by the side in one movement and turn the head and eyes to the front. While passing in review, execute the hand salute in the same way. Hold the salute until you are six paces beyond the person saluted.

Right or Left Face: Command: (1) *right (left)*, (2) *FACE*. At the command *FACE*, slightly raise the left heel and right toe. Face right, turning on the right heel, putting pressure on the ball of the left foot and holding the left leg straight. Then place the left foot smartly beside the right one.

Half Right or Left: Command: (1) *right* (or *left*) *half*, (2) *FACE*. Execute half face as prescribed above, turning only 45 degrees.

About Face: Command: (1) *about*, (2) *FACE*. At the command, place the toe of the right foot about a half-foot to the rear and slightly to the left of the left heel without moving the left foot. Put the weight of the body mainly on the heel of the left foot, right leg straight. Then turn to the rear, moving to the right on the left heel and on the ball of the right foot. Place the right heel beside the left to complete the movement.

STEPS AND MARCH COMMANDS

All movements executed from the halt, except right step, begin with the left foot. Forward, half step, halt and mark time may be executed one from the other in quick or double time.

The following table prescribes the length in inches and the cadence in steps per minute of steps in marching.

STEP	TIME	LENGTH	CADENCE
Full	Quick	30	120
Full	Double	36	180
Full	Slow	30	–
Half	Quick	15	120
Half	Double	18	180
Side	Quick	12	120
Back	Quick	15	120

The Full/Slow step is executed only as a funeral escort approaches the place of internment. The cadence, in accordance with that set by the band, varies with different airs that may be played.

All commands of execution are given on the foot, right or left, in the direction of the movement. For example, if the march is to be to the right—as (1) *by the right flank*, (2) *MARCH*—the command *MARCH* is given on the right foot.

Quick Time: All steps and movements are executed in quick time, which is what most people understand as normal marching pace, unless the unit is marching double time, or unless double time is added to the command. Example: (1) *squad right, double time*, (2) *March*.

Marching: At halt, to march forward in quick time, the commands are: (1) *forward*, (2) *MARCH*. At the command *forward*, shift the weight of your body to the right leg. At the command

MARCH, step off smartly with the left foot and continue marching with 30-inch steps taken straight forward without stiffness or exaggeration. Swing the arms easily in their natural arcs about six inches straight to the front and three inches to the rear of the body.

Double Time: To march in double time, the commands are: (1) *double time,* (2) *MARCH.*

1. If at halt, at the command *double time,* shift the weight of the body to the right leg. At the command *MARCH,* raise the forearms, fingers closed, knuckles out, to a horizontal position along the waistline, and take up an easy run with the step and cadence of double time, allowing the arms to take a natural swinging motion across the front of the body. Be sure to keep the forearms horizontal.

2. If marching in quick time, at the command: (1) *double time,* (2) *MARCH,* given as either foot strikes the ground, take one more step in quick time and then step off in double time.

3. To resume the quick time from double time, the commands are: (1) *quick time,* (2) *MARCH.* At the command *MARCH,* given as either foot strikes the ground, advance and plant the other foot in double time, then resume the quick time, dropping the hands by the sides.

Halt: The commands are: (1) *squad* (*platoon, company*), (2) *HALT.*

1. When marching in quick time, at the command *HALT,* given as either foot strikes the ground, execute the halt in two counts by advancing and planting the other foot and then bringing up the rear foot.

2. When marching in double time, at the command *HALT,* given as either foot strikes the ground, advance and plant the other foot as in double time, then halt in two counts as in quick time.

3. When executing right step or left step, at the command *HALT,* given as the heels are together, plant the foot next in cadence and come to the halt when the heels are next brought together.

Mark Time: The commands are: (1) *mark time,* (2) *MARCH.*

1. Being in march, at the command *MARCH,* given as either foot strikes the ground, advance and plant the other foot. Then bring up the rear foot, placing it so that both heels are in line, and continue the cadence by alternately raising and planting each foot.

2. Being at a halt, at the command *MARCH,* raise and plant first the left foot, then the right as described before.

3. Mark time may be executed in either quick-time cadence or double-time cadence. While marking time, any errors in alignment should be corrected.

4. The halt is executed from mark time, as from quick time or double time. Forward march, halt, and mark time may be executed one from the other in quick time or double time.

Half Step: The commands are: (1) *half step*, (2) *MARCH*.

1. Being in march at the command *MARCH*, take steps of 15 inches in quick time instead of the normal 30 inches. The half step is executed in quick time only.

2. To resume the full step from half step, the commands are: (1) *forward* (2) *MARCH*.

Right Step: The commands are: (1) *right step*, (2) *MARCH*. At the command *MARCH*, carry the right foot 12 inches to the right. Then place the left foot beside the right, left knee straight. Continue in the cadence of quick time. The right step is executed in quick time from a halt for short distances only.

Left Step: The commands are: (1) *left step*, (2) *MARCH*. At the command *MARCH*, carry the left foot 12 inches to the left. Then place the right foot beside the left, right knee straight. Continue in the cadence of quick time. The left step is executed in quick time from a halt for short distances only.

Back Step: The commands are: (1) *backward*, (2) *MARCH*. At the command *MARCH*, take steps of 15 inches straight to the rear. The back step is executed in quick time for short distances only.

To Face to the Right (or Left) in Marching: The commands are: (1) *by the right* (or *left*) *flank*, (2) *MARCH*.

1. To face to the right in marching and advance from a halt, at the command *MARCH*, turn to the right on the ball of the right foot. At the same time, step off with the left foot in the new direction with a half or full step in quick time or double time as the case may be.

2. To face to the right in marching and advance, being in march, at the command *MARCH*, which is given as the right foot strikes the ground, advance and plant the left foot. Then face to the right in marching and step off with the right foot in the new direction with a half or full step in quick or double time as the case may be.

To face to the left, reverse directions for the above instructions.

To Face to the Rear in Marching: The commands are: (1) *to the rear*, (2) *MARCH*.

1. Being in march at quick time, at the command *MARCH*, given as the right foot strikes the ground, advance and plant the left foot. Then turn to the right all the way about on the balls of both feet and immediately step off with the left foot.

2. Being in march at double time, at the command *MARCH*, given as the right foot strikes the ground, advance two steps in the original direction. Then turn to the right all the way about while taking four steps in place, keeping cadence; then step off.

To Change Step: The commands are: (1) *change step,* (2) *MARCH*.

1. Being in march in quick time, at the command *MARCH,* given as the right foot strikes the ground, advance and plant the left foot. Then plant the toe of the right foot near the heel of the left and step off with the left foot.

2. The same movement may be executed on the right foot by giving the command of execution as the left foot strikes the ground and planting the right foot. Then plant the toe of the left foot near the heel of the right and step off with the right foot.

Figure 6–1 Members of the first all "bell bottom" recruit division to graduate from basic training since reintroduction of the "old" enlisted uniforms to the fleet march to the graduation ceremony.

To March at Ease: The commands are: (1) *at ease*, (2) *MARCH*. At the command *MARCH*, men adopt an easy natural stride, without any requirement to keep in step or a regular cadence. But they are still required to maintain silence.

To March at Route Step: The commands are: (1) *route step*, (2) *MARCH*. At the command *MARCH*, men adopt an easy natural stride, without requirement to keep step or a regular cadence, or to maintain silence.

7. Security of Information

The word security, as it is used in the Navy, can mean many things, but its most common usage refers to the safeguarding of classified information. Security can also mean the protection of ships and stations or property, which will be discussed later under "external security" (pages 106–108).

Because the safety of the United States in general, and of naval operations in particular, depends greatly on the protection of classified information, it is important that you understand what classified information is, who may have access to it, some rules for safeguarding it, and the penalties for security violations.

Security Classification

Information is classified when it requires protection in the interests of national security. It is assigned a classification designation, which tells you that it needs protection and how much protection it requires. There are three classification designations —Top Secret, Secret, and Confidential—keyed to the anticipated degree of damage to national security that could result from unauthorized disclosure. The expected impact for each designation is: Top Secret—exceptionally grave damage; Secret—serious damage; and Confidential—identifiable damage. Regardless of the level, all classified information must be protected against unauthorized disclosure. Unauthorized disclosure, or "compromise," means that the classified information becomes available to a person who is not authorized to have it.

There is another category of information: *For Offical Use Only* (FOUO). This is not classified information because it does not involve the national security, but it is of such a nature that it cannot be divulged to everyone. Results of investigations, examination questions, bids on contracts, etc., are "privileged information," kept from becoming general knowledge as *For Official Use Only*.

MARKING OF MATERIAL

All classified material—publications, equipment, films, etc.— is plainly marked or stamped with its classification designation. Some material may have additional markings following the classification that signal extra precautions in handling. For example,

Classifi-
cations

"RESTRICTED DATA" means that the material pertains to nuclear weapons or power and cannot be released to anyone who is not a United States citizen.

Security Clearance

Before a person is allowed to have access to classified information, he or she must have a security clearance. A security clearance is a determination that you are eligible for access to classified information up to the specified level—Top Secret, Secret, or Confidential. The standards for clearance are listed in the Information Security Program Regulation (OPNAVINST 5510.1) or "Security Manual," as it is commonly called. In general you must be trustworthy, of excellent character, and able to show discretion and good judgment. A man loyal to his country may not be eligible for clearance because he cannot meet the standards for a position of trust and confidence. Bad conduct, such as excessive drinking, gambling, promiscuity, and poor credit can lead to denial of clearance. This could cost a promotion. A clearance may be denied or revoked because of emotional disturbance, homosexuality, general ineptitude, drug abuse, general disciplinary causes, AWOL, or larceny.

An investigation is conducted to acquire information on which to base the security determination. A final Top Secret clearance requires a satisfactory Background Investigation (BI). As a BI may take several months to complete, an interim clearance may be issued on the basis of a satisfactory National Agency Check (NAC), or the Entrance NAC (ENTNAC) which is conducted on all first-term enlistees.

A final Secret clearance is based on an NAC or ENTNAC. An interim clearance may be granted based on a check of the Defense Central Index of Investigations (DCII) by the Naval Investigative Service and a favorable review of the records available to the issuing command.

The investigative basis for a final Confidential clearance is also an NAC or ENTNAC, so a final Confidential clearance is usually not issued. If you have a favorable NAC or ENTNAC, the clearance will be issued at the Secret level. An interim Confidential clearance may be issued, however, after a favorable local records review, while awaiting the results of the NAC or ENTNAC.

Your clearance is recorded and becomes a permanent part of your service record. It remains valid as long as you are in the Navy unless it is revoked because you can no longer be considered trustworthy.

ACCESS AND NEED TO KNOW

A clearance means that you are *eligible* for access to information up to the level shown. The commanding officer at each duty station then decides what *access* you actually need at his command to perform the duties assigned. Though you may have a Top Secret clearance, you may only require access to Secret at your command, so that is the level of access the commanding officer will authorize. Even then, you are not entitled to all information classified at the Secret level in other locations or departments not related to your billet.

You are responsible for protecting any classified information you know. Before allowing another person to have access to that information, it is *your* responsibility to determine that the person has the proper clearance and need to know, not the responsibility of the one asking for it. For example: You have Secret information on "The Flight of the Humming Bird." Two sailors, with Secret clearances, ask you for the information. You find that proper authority has established that the first sailor needs the information to carry out his duties. The second sailor is only curious. You may disclose the information only to the first sailor because he has a "need to know."

SAFEGUARDING INFORMATION

Classified information or material may only be discussed, used, or stored where adequate security measures are in effect. When removed from storage for use, it must be kept under the continuous observation of a cleared person. It is never left unattended.

Classified information may only be communicated over secure circuits, so you must never discuss classified information on the telephone.

Classified material may not be removed from the command without permission. Authorized protective measures must be used when classified material is being sent or carried from one place to another and when it is being destroyed.

If you accidently come across some classified material—a letter, booklet, or device—that has been left unguarded, misplaced, or not secured, do not read or examine it or try to decide what to do with it. Notify your security manager or your commanding officer, then stand by to keep unauthorized personnel away until a responsible person arrives to take charge.

Aboard ship, depending on the type of equipment installed, there will be various types of security areas, such as:

An Exclusion Area is where access to the area means access to classified information because the equipment cannot be covered.

A Limited Area is the one with classified information a visitor could gain access to, such as uncovered gauges, etc.

A Controlled Area is next to, or surrounds, an exclusion or limited area. All of these areas are clearly marked by signs reading, "Security Area—Keep Out."

A proper topside (quarterdeck or gangway) watch, where everyone coming aboard is required to identify himself, is in itself a controlled area. A man on watch in such an area must not be afraid to ask for identification. No responsible person in the Navy will object to being stopped politely but firmly until identified.

Don't talk about classified information to unauthorized persons, including family, friends, shipmates, and especially strangers. Classified information can be revealed unintentionally to unauthorized persons in many ways.

Bragging can snowball into a dangerous situation. A person brags about how much he knows to impress friends or family. They in turn brag about how much they know, and the next step is for the sailor to reveal classified information. Don't talk too freely. It is natural to talk with shipmates, but classified subjects should be avoided. The fact that you may be entrusted with certain classified information gives you no right to divulge it to anyone else.

Interest in your own job is natural and desirable, but it must not lead to revealing classified information to unauthorized persons. In an argument, enthusiasm may cause a man to blurt out classified facts and figures to prove his point. Such a situation may develop from a discussion of a news item. Never add to a news story that appears to be incomplete, no matter how much you may know. By doing so, you may make public exactly what the Navy has tried to keep secret.

THREATS TO SECURITY

Unfriendly foreign nations are always interested in classified information on new developments, weapons, techniques, and materials, as well as ship and aircraft movements and their operating capabilities.

The people who collect such information cannot be stereotyped or categorized. That's why they succeed in their work. A person who has access to classified material should never talk to any stranger about any classified subjects. A foreign intelligence agent collects many odd little bits of information, some of which might not even make sense to him; but when they are all put together in his own country, they may tell experts much more than we want them to know. Don't make their work easier for them.

When security breaks down, the Navy becomes vulnerable to sabotage and espionage. Especially vulnerable are factories, large hard-to-protect shipyards, piers, ships, planes, and stations.

The FBI and other agencies say that thousands of people, many of them American citizens, are associated with espionage. Thus, someone attending such events as the replenishing of ships, could sabotage the operation—even if only in a small way. Worse yet, they'd do it without being detected.

So who's vulnerable to espionage tactics? You are if you talk about security matters at a booze-fest while someone not on your side is eavesdropping. Servicemen with relatives in communist countries aren't immune. Members of minorities can be tempted to go along with an enemy system if they feel the one they're in isn't fair to them. And people with personal problems and no guts can be intimidated into doing favors for the enemy. The problems can be financial, alcoholic, sexual, or a need for attention. If an enemy offers to solve those problems, you could be placed in the awkward position of accepting—without even knowing that your new "friend" is indeed the enemy. All this may sound like a scene from a James Bond movie, but it happens in real life—and during wars.

Here's how not to be exploited:

1. Don't talk about your sensitive job to people who don't "need to know"—not even your family or friends.

2. Know how to handle classified material.

3. Don't be careless with carbons and typewriter ribbons used in connection with classified material. They're as classified as the original material.

4. Secure your working area before leaving if it has classified material.

5. If you have personal problems you feel might be exploited, use the chain of command to solve them. No one in the Navy is going to hit you over the head because you have a problem that might be solved by a senior petty officer or officer. And if one of them can't help, go to the chaplain. Chaplains are in the service for more than promoting religion; they're there to help, whatever your problem is.

Any contact with a citizen of a communist-controlled country must be reported immediately. That includes contacts between ham radio operators, "pen pals," neighbors, or any other kind of contact. The contact will be reported to the Naval Investigative Service who will then advise you of any further action. Such contacts are not, in themselves, wrong or illegal. It is just that NAV-INVSERV agents are the experts who will be able to evaluate the contact and tell whether it is an attempt to "target" you for espionage purposes.

If you suspect someone of gathering intelligence for an enemy, or if you suspect someone of violating security, report it. If someone is compromising the security of the Navy or of the United States, that person is compromising you. Who would you be without the security of the United States and the military? You're either on our side or theirs. Reporting a security problem is not like "telling" on someone. It's protecting yourself and the country you're serving.

What if you're confronted by a spy? Don't try to catch him. Just report him. If a citizen of an unfriendly nation tries to turn you against the United States, report him.

Make your reports by way of your chain of command. Every member of the chain has a superior. If you suspect someone in the chain of not being trustworthy enough to receive what you have to report, request permission to see the next higher-up. And the next, if necessary.

If you feel you can't approach the people in your chain of command, go to the Naval Investigative Service office. If you can't find one, look in the white pages of the phone book under "U.S. Government, Naval Activities."

If you're going to make a report, make a note of the date, time, place, and nature of the encounter. Take names. Describe how you were approached and mention who else in the Navy was also approached. State your own name, grade, social security number, and anything else you feel is pertinent.

Operational Security (OPSEC)

OPSEC's purpose is to keep the enemy from finding out about military operations before, while, and after they occur. Operations are military actions, missions, and maneuvers. They are destinations of ships and planes and their cargoes. They are your assignments and those of your shipmates.

The word "information" in connection with OPSEC means any detail that helps the enemy. With enough "information," an enemy can determine what the operation is for and sabotage it.

Cargo loaded aboard a ship or plane may seem unimportant, but it can be vital information for an enemy who's wondering whether it's destined for the tropics or the arctic regions. The kind of ship carrying the cargo does not escape the enemy's attention. Is it a troop carrier or an icebreaker? Are the planes bombers or supply transports? What you take for granted as being unimportant, the enemy takes seriously. By piecing together bits of information from here and there, a spy can easily determine the general purpose of an operation before it even starts.

The OPSEC program has four parts:

Communications security: This covers communications by telephone, telegraph, radio, teletype, documents, mail, and any other means of communication.

Electronic security: This includes radar, sonar, or any non-communication signal. For example, if you're tracking one of our planes by radar, the echo of radio waves can tip off an enemy to that plane's whereabouts.

Operational information security: This means the protection of plans, maps, photographs, equipment (such as tanks, guns and ships), attack and defense tactics, and unit movements and locations.

Physical security: This means guarding classified areas, documents, equipment, buildings, or people from unauthorized access, sabotage, and other dangers.

ENEMY ACTIONS

During the war in Vietnam, the communists were able to find out about many U.S. operations before they took place. They found out not because there were security leaks, but because much of what they learned came from sources who didn't realize they were contributing information that would be valuable to the enemy. The slightest change in daily routine was noted and reported to an expert, who knew that any change, no matter how innocent or trivial, could be a piece in the puzzle of U.S. operations.

An example: Medical supplies are being loaded aboard a supply ship at the same time Marines board an LPH. Then an air squadron makes an urgent request for maps of an area that would be ideal for an amphibious assault. Spies paying attention in those three areas could quickly determine that something is up. Once they figure out what is likely to happen, they can take the steps necessary to ruin the operation—and kill a lot of American servicemen.

Unclassified news releases about our casualties and those of our allies can be a big help to the enemy who is trying to determine the strength of our forces. Enemies collect any and all publications that are released before an operation takes place. They read what they collect, and try to figure out what will happen. If they guess right, we lose.

Enemies like to infiltrate social gatherings where U.S. servicemen dance, drink, and talk. The enemy is there for one reason only—to listen. Then he passes on what he hears to the super spies. Some enemies even move into communities with servicemen so they can pump their neighbors for information.

So watch your mouth in the bars. Loose talk and a skilled listener can mean trouble.

External Security

Everyone aboard ship, whether on watch or not, must always be security-minded and on the alert for any sign of danger to the ship. A ship in port should be relatively safe, but it can be threatened in many ways—by hurricanes, tidal waves, flooding, fire, explosions, sabotage from within the ship, foreign saboteurs, sneak attacks, civil disorders, or riots.

Threats to security may originate outside the ship. Strangers approaching the ship should be regarded with suspicion, even though they appear to be ordinary visitors, salesmen, newsboys,

Figure 7–1 A Marine guard maintains shipyard security.

or delivery men. All individuals coming aboard must be identified by the officer of the deck or his representative; and all items like packages, parcels, briefcases, and tool boxes should be inspected. Men standing gangway or quarterdeck watches assist the OOD in identifying approaching boats, screening visitors, and checking packages.

Sentries and guards posted for security purposes are guided by written instructions and must know how to challenge boats in order to identify occupants before they come alongside. All sentries may be armed when the situation demands. Armed guards should be reasonably proficient in the use of their weapons. An armed man who does not know his weapon is useless at his post and a danger to his ship and shipmates.

Moored or anchored ships are vulnerable to sneak attacks and sabotage, particularly at night. The ship can be approached by swimmers, small boats, or a submarine. Boarders may pose as gunboat crews. Saboteurs may mingle with a returning liberty party, pose as visitors, or sneak aboard when ships are moored to a pier. When such dangers of attack exist, the operations officer will organize special watches and issue instructions to them.

The signal bridge watches report to the OOD any boats approaching the ship or operating in the vicinity of the ship in a suspicious or aimless manner, as well as any unusual disturbances or signs of distress in the harbor, aboard other ships, or ashore.

108   Internal Security

The safety of a ship also may be threatened from within. Sabotage is possible, especially during times of great international tension. Abrasives in oil, nails driven into multiple conductor cables, or foreign objects placed in turbines or reduction gears can cause great damage. Fire and flooding, accidental or otherwise, are always a danger.

All ships maintain these two watches for internal security:

The sounding and security watch: This is stood underway and in port by men from the "R" division, who make routine checks for watertight closures and security. The team also checks for fire hazards, takes soundings in shaft alleys and voids not in use, and makes draft readings.

The cold iron watch: Besides routine security and sounding patrols, a ship whose main machinery is inactive, or which does not have an auxiliary watch on duty below, stations a "cold iron watch." This watch consists of men from the "B" and "M" divisions who are required to check all machinery spaces for violations of watertight integrity.

During war, because modern science enables an enemy to detect almost any electronic emission, a condition known as EMCON—emission control—is set. When EMCON is set, even personal radios aboard ship cannot be played if they have signal-emitting characteristics.

Internal security is also maintained by setting two other conditions: Darken ship and quiet ship. *Darken ship* must be observed by everyone going topside. The glow of a cigarette can be seen for miles on a dark night. The light from an improperly shielded hatchway will let a submarine make a successful periscope attack. A *quiet ship* condition is just that, maintaining quiet about the ship. Banging or hammering can give away the position of an otherwise perfectly silent submarine, for instance.

Orders covering trash disposal and pumping bilges must be strictly obeyed. A ship littering the ocean with debris can be tracked down by an alert enemy.

Shipyard Security

When a ship is in a shipyard, all workmen coming aboard must be identified. Compartments containing classified matter must be secured, either by locking or by sentries. Fire watches are normally assigned to each welder and burner who comes on board. Also, special precautions must be taken after each shift to inspect spaces for fire hazards.

The commanding officer has custody of all keys to the magazines, but the CO may designate others to have duplicate keys. Heads of departments are responsible for keys to locked spaces under their cognizance. Keys to other spaces are in the custody of designated officers and petty officers. Each department head maintains a locker containing all keys to spaces in his department. Keys to these lockers are always available to the OOD in case of emergencies.

Every sailor must provide a lock for his own locker and should carry his keys always. Any other keys with which he may be entrusted should never be carried off the ship.

Censorship

In war or during certain peacetime emergency conditions, censorship of personal mail may be imposed. The main intent of censorship is to avoid security violations that might occur through carelessness or lack of judgment in writing letters. Under such emergency conditions, all letters written aboard a ship, or in a forward area, must be passed by a censor. When censorship is imposed, instructions will be issued detailing subjects not to be discussed in letters. These will include ships' movements, mention of combat actions, details of weapons, etc. Photographs may be censored too. Cameras may be barred and all pictures taken aboard ship may require clearance for release.

8. Hygiene, Health, and First Aid

The Navy will train you to perform your military and professional duties, but your ability to perform them quickly and efficiently will depend on your physical and mental condition. Good health and a cheerful attitude will make your job easier and improve your relations with others. However, no one can order you to stay healthy and keep cheerful. That's up to you.

In the days of "iron men and wooden ships," disease killed more men than cannonballs did. Sailors lived for months aboard damp and cold ships, ate salted or rancid meat and moldy or wormy bread, drank foul-smelling water, and bathed—if at all—in cold salt water. A man with a smashed leg received quick "kill or cure" treatment—the surgeon sawed it off. Good surgeons heated the saw so it wouldn't hurt so much, and sometimes the man got a shot of rum to take his mind off his troubles.

Sailors in the Navy today live better and are safer and healthier than most of the people in many nations of the world. Even the smallest ship has facilities to provide nourishing meals, well-ventilated and heated berthing spaces, medical and dental attention, laundry service, hot and cold running fresh water, and sanitary living conditions.

It's almost impossible not to be healthy, but a few people will always manage. They will be the ones with athlete's foot, ringworm, jungle rot, or "crabs," who make things difficult for their shipmates.

Good Health Habits

Good health is no accident. You can achieve it through careful attention to personal and oral hygiene, a balanced diet, moderation in using alcohol and tobacco, plenty of fresh air and exercise, good posture, and proper rest. Exercise invigorates and stimulates the whole body.

Mild exercise for a few minutes everyday is important for your efficiency. If an exercise area is not available, or an exercise period is not provided in the daily routine, work out your own system of conditioning exercises and follow it every day. These should include warming-up exercises in various positions: standing, kneeling, sitting, and lying prone. Follow with limbering exercises: body stretching, twisting, bending, knee bending, and running in place. Include deep breathing exercises.

Remember that cleanliness and health are very nearly the same. The person with athlete's foot or ringworm is generally not just unlucky; he's just not smart enough to keep clean. Sometimes it's not easy to keep clean where washrooms are crowded, but the effort is worthwhile. Shower daily in warm weather or when you are sweating heavily. In cool weather, once every other day should be enough—but wash your face and hands well with hot water and soap before every meal. Wash your hair at least once a week.

CARE OF TEETH

The three most common dental diseases are: tooth decay (carries); inflammation of the gums (gingivitis); and an affliction of the gums and bone surrounding the teeth (pyorrhea). They all can lead to the loss of teeth—which is needless, since they can be prevented or controlled.

There is no positive way to prevent all tooth decay, but it can be cut down by brushing the teeth correctly and by cutting down on sweets. At the first sign of tooth decay, see a dentist.

Normal and healthy gums are pale pink and firm in texture. If they are swollen or puffy, hang loosely about the teeth, and bleed easily, then you have *gingivitis*.

If gingivitis goes untreated you may notice pockets or crevices between the tooth and gum, an indication of *pyorrhea* (or periodontitis). Surprisingly, more teeth are lost from these two diseases

Figure 8–1 Sailors now live better and are healthier than ever. They receive regularly scheduled medical and dental checkups.

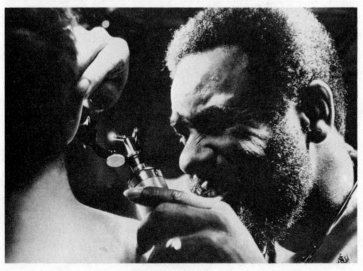

than from tooth decay. Most dental diseases result from poor mouth hygiene combined with inadequate brushing.

The Navy is doing what it can to prevent dental disease by requiring all sailors to have their teeth checked at least once a year. Every commanding officer must see that the checks are indeed made, and individuals are notified when their checks are due. Navy regulations also require all personnel to have stannous flouride treatments before deployment to an area without adequate dental facilities.

DRUG AND ALCOHOL ABUSE

Most drug abuse involves substances—like marijuana, LSD, and heroin—which have no legitimate medical use. However, some of the drugs which are abused—principally morphine, amphetamine, and the barbiturates—are invaluable tools for the physician in his effort to cure and alleviate disease.

The important factor in drug abuse is the abuser, not the drug. Drug abuse has a particularly important consequence for the armed forces. Unlike civilians, those in military service have a special dependency on each other. The lives of all hands on a Navy ship may depend on the alertness of one man assigned to close a certain watertight door. No commander can trust the fate of his unit, ship, or plane to a man who may be under the influence of drugs.

Since 1971 the Navy has had a drug abuse control program. Objectives of the program are: to identify all naval personnel involved in drug abuse, to restore to full duty all Navy members involved in drug abuse who have potential for further useful service, and to ensure that every sailor has the facts necessary to make an intelligent decision concerning drug abuse. These objectives are pursued by three basic elements of the program: identification, rehabilitation, and education.

Drug abusers are identified through the exemption program, the urinalysis testing program, or through normal investigative and law enforcement procedures.

The exemption program encourages drug abusers sincerely concerned about their problem to voluntarily come forward to seek assistance. By doing so, these sailors are provided rehabilitative help without fear of disciplinary actions under the UCMJ. Further, should separation from the Navy for drug abuse be necessary, their discharge will be an honorable one. Exemption does not necessarily mean that you will lose your security clearance, be reassigned, or lose special status (for instance, as an aircrewman). If you are apprehended for a drug offense you lose the right for exemption. Exemption, however, once granted cannot be revoked. (SECNAV instruction 5355.1 series outlines the drug exemption program.)

The urinalysis screening is normally given to sailors 25 years of

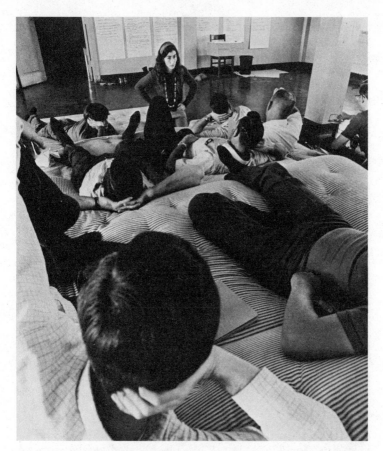

Figure 8–2 Sailors undergo treatment at a Navy alcohol rehabilitation center.

age and younger. Commanding officers, however, may have all personnel tested when they feel it is in the best interests of the command.

Investigative and law-enforcement assistance is provided to commanding officers by the Naval Investigative Service (NIS), base police, masters-at-arms, and various civilian law-enforcement authorities. The Navy also has 53 drug detector dog teams, located at 34 places which have a heavy concentration of Navy personnel.

When drug abusers are identified, they must be detoxified, if required. After any pending disciplinary action is concluded, the abusers are rehabilitated, if necessary. Rehabilitation is available at three levels: (1) locally, within the command (2) at a counseling and assistance center (CAAC) (3) at a Navy drug rehabilitation center (NRDC). After the abuser has been identified, the parent command is required to evaluate the extent of his drug

involvement, and his potential for further useful service. There
are 52 CAACs ashore; 14 others are located aboard various
ships.

In military law, wrongful acts concerning narcotics and marijuana are charged as "conduct prejudicial to good order and military discipline." There is no article of the Uniform Code of Military Justice (UCMJ) specifically dealing with drug offenses, so
such offenses are prosecuted as violations of the "general article"—Article 134. Drug abuse offenses may also be prosecuted
under Article 112, entitled "drunk on duty." It's immaterial
whether drunkenness was caused by liquor or drugs; any intoxication which is sufficient to impair "the rational and full exercise
of the mental and physical facilities" is drunkenness for purposes
of a military court. Violations of specific service regulations dealing with drugs may be prosecuted as violations of Article 92 of
the UCMJ.

The Manual of Courts-Martial (MCM) provides for a maximum
punishment of a dishonorable discharge (DD) and a confinement
of 10 years for narcotic offenses, and a DD and five years for
marijuana offenses—whether the offenses involve use, possession, or sale.

The Navy, recognizing that alcoholism is a disease which can
be treated, is determined to aid every sailor suffering from alcoholism. Alcoholism is usually preceded by several years of drinking, although increasing incidence is being observed among
Navy personnel in their teens and early 20s. Since 1971 the
Navy has undertaken an intense program to educate, assist, and
rehabilitate Navy men and women who are afflicted with the disease. Today, experts in alcohol education, alcohol abuse, and alcoholism—including over 1,500 rehabilitated alcoholics—are
offering their experience and assistance to other Navy men and
women.

Treatment of the identified alcoholic can be done locally at a
"drydock"—an alcohol rehabilitation unit drydock (ARD) or a
counseling and assistance center (CAAC) for habitual abusers
and early-stage alcoholics. More serious cases are treated at the
alcohol rehabilitation center (ARC) of a naval hospital unit.

Serious drinking problems afflict 17 percent of all active duty
sailors, impairing performance of duty and personal life. It is estimated that 10 percent of the total Navy force are chronic problem drinkers, in need of help. Post-treatment studies show that
about 70 percent of patients treated at Navy rehab facilities are
effectively restored to duty and complete their enlistments. In
purely financial terms—measured by the cost necessary to replace highly trained personnel who would otherwise have been
lost to the Navy through alcoholism—the Navy saves many millions of dollars annually through its rehabilitation programs.

Dysentery is common in the tropics, but it's not unknown in the United States. The major symptom is loose bowels, although nausea, stomach cramps, and vomiting also occur. Bad water and flies definitely are causes, but dysentery is more likely to be spread by food handlers or through vegetables fertilized with human waste. Ashore, wherever dysentery is known to be a problem, avoid any uncooked food—particularly lettuce, celery, cabbage, and radishes. If you must eat ashore, eat in reputable restaurants, and avoid "dives." In areas where dysentery is easily contracted, water should be boiled for at least five minutes and then put into sterile containers. It's safer, though, to drink bottled water. Never buy food from small stands or pushcarts in a foreign country. Don't eat raw seafood (oysters, clams, shrimp) in a foreign country, particularly in hot climates.

HOMOSEXUALITY

There are a lot of mistaken ideas about homosexuality. Some examples: a homosexual can be detected by speech characteristics, manner, or dress. (This is not true in most cases.) VD cannot be contracted through homosexual acts. (It can, and frequently is.) The Navy will "cure" homosexuals. (The Navy does not have facilities or personnel for this; and even if it did, treatment is not always successful.)

The Navy is concerned about homosexuals. They can be poor security risks, and can be susceptible to blackmail. Persons who commit or attempt to commit homosexual acts can be separated from the service through court-martial or administrative discharge. However, there may be circumstances in which a sailor recommended for discharge may have his case reviewed by the Secretary of the Navy. According to SECNAVINST 1900.9C, issued in early 1978, anyone who attempts or engages in a homosexual act on a single occasion and who does not profess or demonstrate a strong leaning to repeat the act may be considered for retention. But a person will be allowed to stay in the service only if his or her conduct is not likely to have an adverse impact on his or her continued performance of duty, or on the readiness, efficiency, or morale of that sailor's unit. Each person processed for homosexuality will be evaluated on a case-by-case basis.

VENEREAL DISEASES (VD)

Venereal diseases, like alcoholism, were for many years "swept under the rug" and not mentioned in polite society. "Nice people" didn't even know what to call the various types of infection, although that didn't prevent both royalty and riff-raff from getting them. Now VD is no longer a hush-hush subject. It is discussed in newspapers and magazines, and it should be a matter of concern for everyone because, despite "wonder drugs" such as penicillin, it is on the increase.

Many contagious diseases can be transmitted from one person to another without the two people coming near each other—by mosquitoes, fleas, flies, sneezing, dirty dishes, improper food handling, contaminated water, or clothing. But VD is an infectious disease that can be transmitted only by sexual contact between one person and another. The "contact" is not always from what are considered the usual sources, such as prostitutes or "bar flies." More and more, VD is infecting young people. It is one disease whose prevention depends almost completely on the individual—no contact, no VD.

The five general types of VD are: syphilis (syph, pox, old Joe), gonorrhea (clap, dose, the drip, GC), chancroid (bubo, hair cut), granulema inguinale, and lymphogranuloma venereum. All can be transmitted from an infected person to an uninfected person through sexual intercourse. Syphilis can also be transmitted by a kiss if an infected person has an open sore on the lips or in the mouth. A woman can transmit syphilis to her unborn child or gonorrhea to her newly born child.

The incubation period—time from contact until first symptoms appear—varies. It's 10 to 90 days for syphilis, 2 to 14 days for gonorrhea and chancroid, and longer for the others. However, a person who has become infected can transmit the disease to another before signs of infection appear. There's no way to tell that a person is not infected.

The results of VD infection may appear years later. Latent syphilis, the state in which clinical signs and symptoms of infec-

Figure 8–3 First aid is the immediate, temporary treatment of a sick or injured person before a doctor can take over.

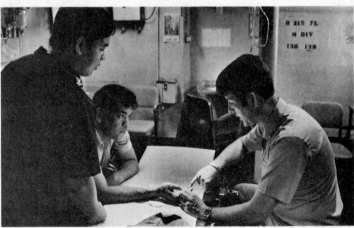

tion are absent, may appear "early"—four years after infection— or "late" as much as 20 years afterward. Among the infinite variety of results to be expected then are destructive ulcers, loss of position sense, disease of the heart or blood vessels, blindness, and insanity. Other kinds of VD have other effects, none of them pleasant.

First Aid

First aid is emergency treatment for sick or injured people. It consists *only* of immediate, temporary assistance necessary to save life, prevent further injury, and preserve the victim's vitality and resistance to infection. In administering first aid, first *stop severe bleeding,* then begin artificial respiration, and finally treat for shock.

Don't move a patient unless it's absolutely necessary to save him from fire, gas, drowning, or gunfire. A fractured bone may cut an artery or nerve. A broken neck or back may result in a spinal cord injury, paralysis, or death. Make an injured person comfortable. Cover him to keep him warm. If a victim must be moved, make sure you know how to do it (see "Transportation of the Injured," p. 138).

Know what to do, then do it. Serious bleeding must be stopped. If someone is bleeding from the mouth (or vomiting), roll him on his belly with his head turned to one side and lower than his feet. Clear his mouth or throat, start artificial respiration if needed, then treat for shock.

CONTROL THE SITUATION

Ask for medical assistance by telephone, radio, or messenger. Have someone keep bystanders clear. Loosen clothing around the patient's neck, chest, and abdomen.

Determine the extent of injuries. Look for bleeding, wounds, fractures, or burns. Notice the color of his face. To determine if he is conscious, ask him questions. Bleeding from the nose and ears is often a symptom of a fractured skull. Bloody froth coming from the mouth often indicates damaged lungs. Check the pulse rate and strength. Check dogtags for blood type. See if the victim carries anything (bracelet, tag, or card) about drugs or medicines he must or cannot take.

ARTIFICIAL RESPIRATION

The standard methods of artificial respiration are mouth-to-mouth and manual (back-pressure, armlift). Mouth-to-mouth (or mouth-to-nose) is considered best (Figure 8–4). Follow these procedures:

Mouth-to-mouth method: Place the victim on his back imme-

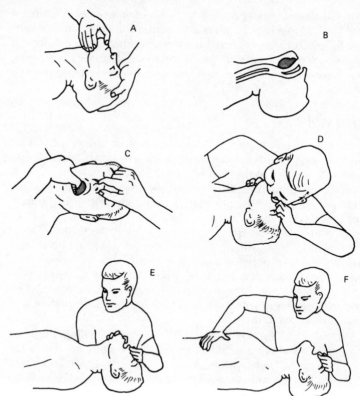

Figure 8–4 The above steps illustrate the proper method of administering mouth-to-mouth artificial respiration.

diately. Don't waste time moving him to a better place, loosening his clothing, or draining water from his lungs.

Quickly clear his mouth and throat. Remove any dentures, mucus, food, and other obstructions.

Tilt the victim's head as far back as possible (step A) so it's in a "chin-up" position, with neck stretched to ensure an open airway (step B).

Lift his lower jaw forward. Grasp the jaw by placing your thumb into the corner of his mouth (step C). Do not hold or depress his tongue.

Pinch his nose shut (or seal his mouth). Prevent any air leakage. Open your mouth wide and blow in. Take a deep breath and blow forcefully (except with babies) into his mouth or nose until you see his chest rise (step D).

Quickly remove your mouth when his chest rises. Listen for exhalation. If the victim makes snoring or gurgling sounds, his jaw is not high enough (step E).

Repeat these two steps 15 to 20 times per minute. Continue until the victim begins to breathe normally.

Remove air blown into the victim's stomach. Periodically, between breaths, if the stomach is distended, place your hand on his upper abdomen and gently but firmly press the air out of his stomach (step F).

For an infant seal both the mouth and nose with your mouth. Blow with small puffs of air from your cheeks.

Sometimes the mouth-to-mouth method cannot be used, such as when there are injuries to the face with bleeding around the mouth, or when gas masks must be worn in contaminated areas. Then a manual method must be used. Manual methods are not always effective because they fail to maintain a free and unobstructed airway. In all manual methods the first consideration must be proper positioning of the head to avoid airway obstruction. Two manual methods—the chest pressure, armlift method (Figure 8–5) and back pressure, armlift method (Figure 8–6)—are discussed below.

Chest pressure, armlift method: Place the victim in a face-up position and put something under his shoulders to raise them and to allow the head to drop backward (step A).

Kneel at his head. Grasp his arms at the wrists. Cross them, then press them over the lower chest (step B). This should cause air to flow out.

Immediately release this pressure and pull the arms outward and upward over his head, and backward as far as possible (step C). This should cause the air to rush in.

Repeat this cycle about 20 times a minute, checking the mouth frequently for obstruction. A victim in a face-up position may take vomit or blood into his lungs. So keep his head extended and turned to one side. If possible, the head should be a little lower than the trunk. If a second rescuer is on hand, have him continuously check the victim's head so that the jaw juts out and the mouth is kept as clean as possible.

Back pressure, armlift method: Place the victim face down. Bend his elbows and place his hands one upon the other, under his chin. Turn his head slightly and extend it as far as possible, making sure that the chin juts out (step A).

Kneel at the head of the victim. Place your hands on the flat of his back so that the palms lie just below an imaginary line running between the armpits (step B).

Rock forward until your arms are approximately vertical, and allow the weight on the upper part of your body to exert steady, even pressure downward on your hands (step C).

Immediately draw his arms upward and toward you, applying enough lift to feel resistance and tension at his shoulders (step D). Then lower his arms to the ground. Repeat this cycle about 20

Figure 8–5 Artificial respiration can also be administered manually by the chest pressure, armlift method.

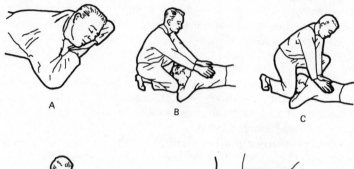

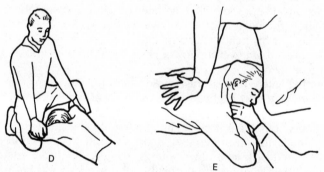

Figure 8–6 The back pressure, armlift method is another manual artificial-respiration technique.

times a minute. If a second rescuer is available, have him hold the victim's head so the jaw juts out (step E). Check the mouth for any stomach contents and keep it as clean as possible.

Time your application of pressure to coincide with the victim's first attempt to breath for himself. If he vomits, turn him on his side, wipe out his mouth, then re-position him.

Normally, recovery should be rapid except in cases of electrical shock, drug poisoning, or carbon-monoxide poisoning, when the nerves and muscles that control the breathing system may be paralyzed or deeply depressed, or carbon monoxide may have displaced oxygen in the bloodstream. Artificial respiration must continue for long periods in such cases.

When the victim is revived, keep him quiet until he can breathe regularly. Keep him covered and otherwise treated for shock until suitable transportation is available. Since respiratory and other disturbances may develop, a doctor's care is necessary during the recovery period.

ASPHYXIATION

This is loss of consciousness due to lack of oxygen. Drowning, electric shock, and gas poisoning are the most common causes, but suffocation, strangulation, and choking will produce the same results. Breathing stops, but the heart may continue to pump blood for some time. Even when the victim's heartbeat cannot be felt, artificial respiration should be administered.

BANDAGES

Bandages may consist of gauze, a gauze square, an adhesive compress, a bandage compress, or a plain strip of cloth. The compress, which directly covers the wound, should be sterile if possible. Bandages need not be sterile because they do not touch the wound. They should not be made of anything adhesive that will stick to the skin. The bandage may be applied in turns—circular, spiral, figure-eight, or recurrent turns. Triangular bandages may be tied on the head or face, shoulder or hip, chest or back, foot or hand. Cravat bandages are used on head, neck, eye, temple, cheek, ear, elbow, knee, arm, forearm, or palm wounds. Roller bandages are wrapped on the hand and wrist, forearm or leg. The Standard First Aid Training Course (NAVPERS 10081) and First Aid Textbook prepared by the American Red Cross are invaluable for learning about the application of bandages, or any other first-aid problem.

BLEEDING

An average human body contains five quarts of blood. One pint can be lost without harmful effect. A loss of two pints will

Figure 8–7 Control bleeding by applying direct pressure to the wound.

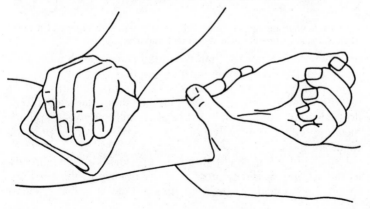

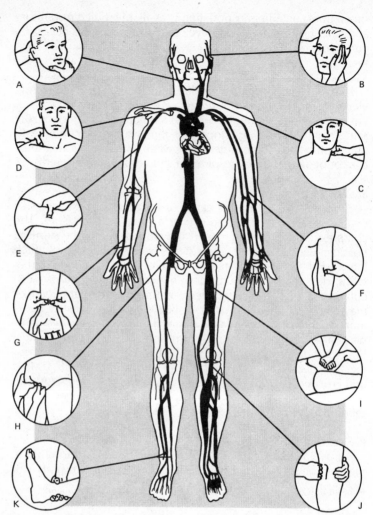

Figure 8–8 Bleeding can be controlled when pressure is applied at a point where the main artery lies near the surface and over a bone.

usually produce shock. If half the blood is lost, death almost always results; thus bleeding must be stopped quickly.

In arterial bleeding, bright red blood spurts out; this sort of bleeding is very serious. In venous bleeding, dark red blood flows steadily; this type of bleeding also can be serious. Capillary bleeding, which is usually not serious, comes from a prick or small abrasion.

Usually, bleeding can be stopped if pressure is applied directly to the wound. If direct pressure does not work, the pressure should be applied at the right pressure point. Where severe bleeding cannot be controlled by these methods, pressure by means of a tourniquet should be applied. (This, however, can be very dangerous, because if circulation is cut off entirely, gangrene can set in.)

Direct pressure: Use a sterile dressing or the cleanest cloth available—a freshly laundered handkerchief, a towel, or an article of clothing. Fold it to form a pad, place it directly over the wound, and fasten it in position with a bandage (Figure 8–7).

If the bleeding does not stop, try applying direct pressure by hand steadily, for five or six minutes, over the pad of cloth.

In cases of severe bleeding, don't worry about infection—stop the blood. If nothing else is available, jam a shirt into the wound. Remember, direct pressure is the *first* method to use in controlling bleeding.

Pressure points: Bleeding from a cut artery or vein often can be controlled by applying pressure to the right pressure point (Figure 8–8). A pressure point is a place where a main artery lies near the skin surface and over the bone. Pressure there compresses the artery against the bone and shuts off the flow of blood to the wound.

A. Face, below the eyes: Pressure point is the lower jawbone, at a notch you can feel with your finger.

B. Temple or scalp: Pressure point is just in front of the ear. You can feel the pulse in the artery there with your finger.

C. Neck: Apply pressure below the wound, just in front of the neck muscle. Press inward and slightly backward. Apply pressure here only if absolutely necessary, since you may accidentally press on the windpipe and choke the victim.

D. Shoulder or upper part of the arm: The pressure point is back of the collar bone. Press forward against the collar bone or down against the first rib.

E. Middle of the upper arm and elbow: Pressure point is on the inner side of the arm, about halfway between shoulder and elbow.

F. Lower arm: Pressure point is at the elbow.

G. Hand: Pressure point is at the wrist. If the arm can also be held up, the bleeding will stop sooner.

H, I, J. Upper part of thigh: Pressure point is in the middle of the groin (H). Sometimes it is better to apply pressure on the upper thigh (I). Heavy pressure is needed here, however. Use a closed fist and press at the side of the knee, or else push one fist against the back of the knee and hold one hand in front of the knee (J). As a last resort, fold a bandage behind the knee and bend the leg against it.

K. Foot: Pressure point is at the ankle. Elevating the leg will help control bleeding.

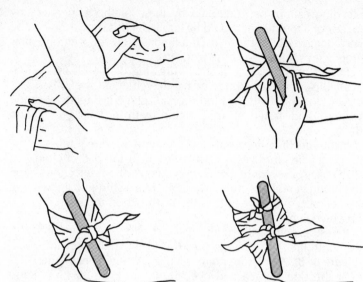

Figure 8–9 When applying a tourniquet, tie the bandage with an overhand knot, tie a square knot over the stick, and twist the stick to tighten the tourniquet.

Remember to apply pressure at the point nearest the wound, between the wound and the heart.

It is very tiring to apply finger pressure, and it can seldom be maintained for more than 15 minutes. As soon as possible, use a compress held securely over the wound by a bandage.

If the bleeding is still severe, you may have to apply a tourniquet. Remember—tourniquets are dangerous and may result in gangrene when left on too long.

A tourniquet (Figure 8–9) consists of a pad (pressure object), a band, and a device for tightening the band as the blood vessels are compressed. The type found in many Navy first-aid kits consists of a web band, two inches wide and five feet long, with a buckle for fastening. The tourniquet is applied above the wound —that is, between the wound and the heart.

Wrap it once about the limb, then run the free end through the buckle. Draw the band tightly enough to stop the flow of blood. In an emergency, any round, smooth pressure object may be used—a compress, roller bandage, stone, rifle shell—and any long piece of cloth may be used as the band. At least a quarter of an inch from the top edge of the wound, place a thick compress of folded cloth that is four to six inches square. Do not use a rope, wire, string or narrow pieces of cloth. They will cut into the flesh. A short stick may be used to twist the band and tighten the tourniquet.

A tourniquet is *never* used unless bleeding cannot be controlled in any other way.

By the time a tourniquet is put on, the victim has already lost a considerable amount of blood; the additional loss resulting from loosening the tourniquet may easily cause death. Thus, once a tourniquet is used, it should be released only by qualified medical personnel. Mark the patient's forehead with a "T" and the time, using a felt-tip pen, lipstick, or iodine, so that there is no doubt about how long the tourniquet has been in place. To avoid the necessity of amputating part of the limb on which a tourniquet has been placed, seek assistance from qualified medical personnel as soon as the tourniquet is applied.

Internal bleeding: If the patient is bleeding internally, he may be thirsty, restless, fearful, and in shock. Don't give the victim anything to eat or drink, even if he is thirsty, for if anesthesia has to be administered he might vomit and take material into his lungs. Bleeding in the stomach may be determined from the location of the wound and bloody vomiting. The treatment for internal bleeding is the same as that for shock, except that stimulants must not be given. Seek medical care immediately, since internal bleeding can lead to death.

BLISTERS

The skin covering a blister is better protection than any bandage. If the blister is in a place where it can easily be broken, open it with a sharp knife or needle that has been heated in flame. Press out the fluid with a bit of sterile gauze and apply a sterile bandage.

BURNS AND SCALDS

Burns and scalds are caused by exposure to intense heat (fire, bomb flash, sunlight, hot metal solids, hot gases, or hot liquids). Electrical current also can cause severe burns. The chief dangers from burns are shock and infection. Thus, first aid should be directed towards relieving pain, combating shock, and preventing infection.

Burns are usually classified according to the depth of tissue injury. A burn that reddens the skin is a *first-degree burn*. One that raises a blister is a *second-degree burn*. One in which the skin is destroyed and the tissues are actually charred is a *third-degree burn*. Severe third-degree burns extend to the muscles and bones. Third-degree burns, for many hours after the injury, frequently appear as white areas, surrounded by the reddened or blistered skin.

The size of the burn may be far more important than its depth. A first-degree burn that covers a large area of the body is almost always more serious than a small third-degree burn.

Rule of nines: The "rule of nines" is used to establish the extent and percentage of burn for determining the amount of fluid the body would need during the first 24 hours after the injury. The front and back of the trunk and the lower legs are each rated as 18 percent for a total of 72 percent. The arms and head are individually rated at 9 percent and the genital area at 1 percent for a total of 28 percent. A first-degree burn over 72 percent of the body is more serious than a third-degree burn of the arm.

Minor burns: Dress the burns immediately. Do not apply ointments or other medicines to the burn. Cover the burn with a sterile bandage to prevent infection. The pain will be lessened greatly if the bandage is airtight and fairly firm.

Cold-water treatment is comforting and effective. Use compresses wrung out of ice water, or submerge the burned part in water containing enough ice to chill (but not freeze). Continue until no pain is felt when the burned part is withdrawn from the water. An ounce or so of germicidal detergent in the chilled water will help control infection.

Serious burns: Extreme pain increases the severity of the shock. Relieve pain with morphine. (See page 134.) Treat for shock immediately, before trying to treat the burns.

Keep the patient's head slightly lower than his feet, and see that he is warm. Do not remove clothing immediately. Cover him with a blanket if he appears to be cold, but do not overheat him. Remember, too, that exposure to cold also will increase shock.

A seriously burned person badly needs fluids. Give him water, sweet tea, fruit juices, or sugar water—if he is conscious, able to swallow, and has no internal injuries.

Burns of the eyes: See "Eye Injuries," pages 127–28.

Chemical burns: Chemicals in contact with the skin or other body membranes may cause burns by direct destruction of the body tissues. This kind of injury can be caused by acids—such as nitric acid, sulfuric acid, and hydrochloric acid—or caustic alkalis—such as potassium hydroxide (lye), sodium hydroxide (caustic soda, soda lye), and calcium oxide (quicklime). Phenol (carbolic acid) also causes chemical burns. Strong concentrations of various bleaches and disinfectants cause chemical injuries to the skin. Chlorine, ammonia, and other industrial chemicals—whether in liquid or vapor form—may cause serious chemical burns of the skin or eyes. Phosphorus burns are a combination of heat burns and chemical injury.

These are some guidelines for treating chemical burns:

Wash off the chemical immediately with large amounts of clean, fresh, cool water. If it is not possible to put the victim under running water, immerse the affected areas, or pour plenty of water over the burns.

Neutralize any chemical that remains on the skin. For acid

burns, apply a solution of sodium bicarbonate (baking soda) or another mild alkali. For alkali burns, apply vinegar, lemon juice, or a mild acid. For phenol (carbolic acid) burns, apply alcohol. Don't try to neutralize any chemical unless you know *for sure* what the chemical is and what substance will effectively neutralize it!

Flooding the area with lots of cool water will suffice when in doubt. Wash the affected areas again with fresh water, then dry gently with sterile gauze. Do not break the skin or open any blisters.

Do what you can to relieve pain and treat for shock. See also "Eye Injuries," below.

CHOKING

When a person has something lodged in his throat, he'll start choking and coughing. If the obstruction goes deep enough to block the victim's air passage, he'll die. Don't try to dislodge the object with your finger. Here's a quick and effective lifesaving treatment:

Stand behind the victim and wrap both arms around his waist, clasping one hand around your other wrist.

Place your interlocked hands against the victim's abdomen just below the breast bone. Press into the victim's abdomen with quick upward thrusts until the object is forced out of the throat.

Your thrusts force air out of the victim's lungs. As the air moves up, its pressure will be enough to cause the object to fly out of the victim's mouth.

If the victim is lying down, turn him on his side and strike him with your hand on his back between the shoulders. But the first method is better, if you can get him to stand.

If breathing has stopped, you can try artificial respiration. But it won't do much good if the air passage is completely blocked.

EYE INJURIES

For eye wounds, apply thick, dry, sterile bandages. If the eyeball is injured, do not let the bandage press against it. If soft tissue around the eye is injured, apply a pressure bandage. Keep the patient lying down while he is being transported and until he receives medical aid.

To remove something from the eye, have the patient look up. Use the corner of a clean handkerchief or a cotton swab moistened in clean water, and gently pull the lower lid down with your finger, or turn the upper lid back over a match stick or cotton swab applicator by grasping the lashes of the upper lid between the fingers and the stick. If these methods fail, use a sterile syringe or medicine dropper to irrigate the eye with sterile water at body temperature, holding the lids apart with the fingers. If the object still cannot be removed, cover the eye by bandaging and obtain medical help. Never try to remove a foreign body from the eye with your fingers.

Heat burns: Drop clean mineral oil or olive oil into the eye, and cover it with a thick gauze compress. Do not let the patient rub his eye. Get medical help.

Chemical burns: Flush the eye immediately with large quantities of clean water. Hold the victim's head over a drinking fountain so that the water flows from the inside corner of his eye toward the outside corner, or have the victim lie down with his head turned slightly to one side. Then pour water into the inside corner of his eye and let it flow·gently across the eyeball to the outside corner. If he is unable to open his eyes, hold the eyelids apart so that the water can flow across the eyeball. Do not use anything except water.

Another way to wash out chemical substances is to have the victim open and close his eyes several times while his face is immersed in a pan of fresh water.

Cover the eye with a small, thick compress. Fasten the compress in place with a bandage or an eyeshield, and get medical care as soon as possible.

FAINTING

This is a reaction of the nervous system, slowing the flow of blood to the brain. A worried or tired person suffering a mental setback may faint. To prevent fainting a person should lie flat for 10 minutes, with the head lower than the rest of the body. If a person who appears to have fainted does not recover consciousness almost immediately, he has not simply fainted. Unconsciousness may also be caused by asphyxia, deep shock, poisoning, head injury, heat stroke, heart attack, apoplexy, or epilepsy. Get medical help at once.

FISH HOOKS

If the barb is buried in the flesh, clean the area, paint it with antiseptic, then push the hook entirely through so the barb comes out on the other side. Then cut off the barb. The rest of the hook can be backed out. Watch out for infection. Check your medical record to see if you need a tetanus shot.

FISH STINGS

Many sea creatures (Portuguese men-of-war, jellyfish, stingrays, scorpion fish) have a poisonous sting. The symptoms can be burning, stinging, reddening of the skin, hives, pus sores, abdomenal cramps, numbness, dizziness, pain in the groin and armpits, nausea, muscular pain, difficulty in breathing, constriction of the chest, prostration, and shock.

For Portuguese man-of-war stings, remove the tentacles immediately and wash the skin with alcohol. Apply calamine lotion or ammonia water. The treatment for jellyfish is about the same. Apply ammonia water, vinegar, or a soothing lotion; then treat for shock.

A stingray wound should be washed immediately with cold salt water. Much of the toxin will wash out. The cold water causes blood vessels to constrict, slowing circulation and acting as a mild pain-killing agent. The wound should be immersed in hot water for 30 to 60 minutes, with the temperature as high as the victim can stand without injury. (Hot compresses can be applied for wounds in areas that cannot be immersed.) A sterile dressing should be applied after the soak.

FRACTURES

Simple fracture means a bone is broken, but there is no break in the skin. In a compound fracture, the broken bone protrudes through the skin. All fractures require careful handling—send for medical aid as soon as possible. Don't move a victim until the fracture has been splinted, unless it's necessary to save his life or prevent further injury. Do not try to set a broken bone.

Treat for shock if the victim shows signs of suffering from it. But don't give morphine if there is a head injury. Stop the bleeding in a compound fracture by using direct pressure or the pressure point system.

Apply splints over clothing if the patient is to be moved a short distance or if a doctor will see him soon. Otherwise, apply well-

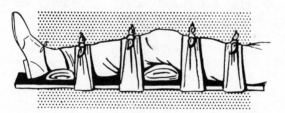

Figure 8–10 Make sure splints are tied securely to prevent any movement of the limb.

padded splints after the clothing has been cut away. Be careful when you handle any fracture to avoid additional shock or injury. Splints vary according to the area and nature of the fracture. Follow these rules:

Forearm: Two well-padded splints, top and bottom, from elbow to wrist. Bandage in place. Hold the forearm across the chest with a sling.

Upper arm: For a fracture near the shoulder, put a towel or pad in the armpit, and bandage the arm to the body. Support the forearm in a sling. For a fracture of the middle upper arm, use one splint on the outside of the arm, shoulder to elbow. Fasten the arm to the body and support the forearm in a sling. For a fracture near the elbow, don't move the arm at all—splint it the way you find it.

Thigh: Use two splints—the outside one from the armpit to foot, the inside one from the crotch to foot. Fasten the splints around the ankle, over the knee, below the hip, around the pelvis, and below the armpit. Tie both legs together. Don't move the patient until all this has been done.

Lower leg: Use three splints, one on each side and one underneath. They must be well padded, especially under the knee and at the ankle bones. Or use a pillow under the leg, with edges brought around in front and pinned, along with two side splints.

Kneecap: Carefully straighten the leg, place a four-inch-wide padded board under it, reaching from buttock to heel. Fasten it in place just below the knee, just above the knee, at the ankle, and at the thigh. Do not cover the knee.

Collarbone: On the injured side, place the forearm across the chest, palm turned in, thumb up, with the hand four inches above the elbow. Support the arm in this position with a sling. Fasten the arm to the body with several turns of bandage around the body and down over the hand.

Rib: A broken rib can puncture a lung. If this happens, the patient may cough up frothy bright blood. If there is no pain, no action is required. To relieve pain, put a wide bandage around the upper part of the chest and tie in a loose knot on the uninjured side. Place two more bandages a little lower down, and tie loosely. Put a compress or pad under each knot on the injured side. Then tighten each bandage after the patient has breathed out, one at a time, starting at the top.

Jaw: If the injury interferes with breathing, pull the lower jaw and tongue forward and keep them there. Apply a four-tailed bandage under the jaw, with two ends tied on top of the front of the head and the other two on top at the back, so the bandage pulls the jaw forward. It must support and immobilize the jaw but not press on the throat.

Skull: It is not necessary to determine if the skull is fractured when a person has a head injury. The primary aim is to prevent brain damage. Do not let the patient move. Try not to move him any more than necessary. Do not let him get cold, do not give him anything to drink and do not give him morphine. Stop any bleeding and get immediate medical assistance.

Spine: Pain, shock, and partial paralysis result from damage to the spine. Severe pain in the back or neck after injury should be treated as a fractured spine. Treat for shock, and give morphine for severe pain. Keep the patient flat, and do not move his head.

If the patient cannot move his legs or toes, the fracture is probably in his back. If he cannot move his fingers, it is probably in his neck. If the patient must be transported, carry him face up on a rigid stretcher, a door, or a wide frame. Never try to lift such a patient with fewer than four men. Pick him up by his clothing and slide him onto the stretcher.

Pelvis: Treat a patient with a pelvis injury for shock, but do not move him unless absolutely necessary. If a patient must be moved, handle him just as you would a victim of a fractured spine. Bandage legs together at ankles and knees. Place a pillow at each hip and fasten them in place. Fasten the patient securely to the stretcher.

FROSTBITE

Exposure to dry cold causes frostbite, especially in the cheeks, nose, chin, ears, forehead, wrists, hands, and feet. The skin turns white or gray, then bright pink.

Frostbite also may be caused by contact with certain chemicals that cause rapid freezing, such as liquid oxygen, carbon dioxide, Freon, and other industrial gases. Such injuries are often called chemical "burns," but the body tissue is actually frozen.

When the frostbitten area is warmed up, it immediately becomes red and swollen. Large blisters develop. Severe frostbite causes gangrene, which destroys soft body tissues—and sometimes even bone. If deep tissue is destroyed, the injured part may have to be amputated.

First aid for frostbite is rapid thawing of the frozen tissues.

Get the victim into the warmest available place as soon as possible and get him undressed. If his feet or legs are frostbitten, do not let him walk. Do not handle the frostbitten area unnecessarily, and do not exert pressure against it. Do not thaw a frozen extremity until you can transport the patient to a place where the following steps can be taken:

Immerse the injured part in water kept at a temperature of 107 to 109 degrees F. If you have no thermometer, make sure that the water is just comfortably warm. Warming should not continue after thawing. Stir the water.

Dry the victim carefully. Place him in bed and keep him covered. Don't let anything touch the frostbitten parts. Keep a sterile gauze or cloth pads between toes and fingers, and keep frostbitten parts elevated. Get medical assistance as soon as possible.

Caution: Never rub or massage frostbite with ice or snow. Do not apply cold water. And do not expose a frostbitten area to cold air.

GENERAL LOSS OF BODY HEAT

Abnormally low body temperature usually results from total immersion in cold water and loss of consciousness. The victim will appear pale and unconscious, and may even be taken for dead. Breathing is slow and shallow, his pulse faint or undetectable. Body tissues feel semi-rigid, and the arms and legs may be stiff.

First aid consists mainly of bringing the body temperature to normal. The patient should be wrapped in warm blankets in a warm room. Do not give him hot drinks or other stimulants until he has regained consciousness. Get medical attention as soon as possible.

HEAT EXHAUSTION AND HEAT CRAMPS

In heat exhaustion, there is no failure of the heat-regulating mechanism, but there is a serious disturbance of the blood flow, similar to the circulatory disturbance of shock. Through prolonged sweating, the body loses large quantities of salt and water.

Heat exhaustion may begin with a headache, dizziness, nausea, weakness, and profuse sweating. The victim may collapse and lose consciousness, but can usually be aroused rather easily. His temperature is usually normal or even below normal. Sometimes it may drop to as low as 97 degrees. The pupils of his eyes are usually dilated. The pulse is weak and rapid. And the skin is pale, cool, and sweaty. Sometimes there may be severe cramps in the abdomen, legs, and arms.

Follow these first-aid measures:

Move the victim to a cool place, but not one where he will be exposed to strong drafts or become chilled.

Loosen his clothing and make him as comfortable as possible. Keep him quiet. Keep him lying down, with feet and legs somewhat elevated. Be sure that he is neither too hot nor too cold. You may have to cover him with blankets, even if the air around him is warm. If the victim is conscious and able to swallow, give him plenty of warm water to drink with one-fourth to one-half teaspoonful of salt in each glass. This is probably the most important part of the treatment; replacement of the salt and water that has been lost by sweating often brings rapid recovery.

Give hot coffee or hot tea when the patient is able to drink it. If recovery is not prompt, get medical attention quickly.

HEATSTROKE (SUNSTROKE)

Heatstroke and heat exhaustion both are caused by excessive exposure to desert or jungle heat, the direct rays of the sun, or heat in machinery spaces, foundries, or bakeries. Under similar circumstances, one person may develop heatstroke and another heat exhaustion. There are important differences, however, between the two conditions.

Each represents a different bodily reaction to excessive heat. Thus the symptoms and treatment are also different.

Heatstroke results from failure of the heat-regulating mechanism of the body. The body becomes overheated, the temperature rises to 105 to 110 degrees F., but there is no sweating or cooling of the body—the victim's skin is hot, dry, and red. He may have preliminary symptoms such as headache, nausea, dizziness, or weakness. But often the first signs are sudden collapse and loss of consciousness. Breathing is likely to be deep and rapid, and the pulse is strong and fast. Convulsions also may occur. Heatstroke may cause death or permanent disability; at best, recovery is slow and complicated by relapses.

The longer the victim remains overheated, the more likely he is to die. These first-aid measures are designed to immediately lower the body temperature:

Move the victim to a cool place, remove his clothing, and place him on his back with head and shoulders slightly raised.

Sponge or spray his body with cold water, then fan him so the water will evaporate rapidly.

When he regains consciousness, give him cool (not cold) water to drink.

Don't give stimulants or hot drinks.

Get him to a medical facility as soon as possible. Keep him cool while he is being transported.

IMMERSION FOOT (OR TRENCH FOOT)

This is caused by prolonged exposure to a combination of moisture and cold. Men on life rafts or in unprotected lifeboats are most likely to suffer immersion foot from exposure to near-freezing sea waters. Such cases have also occurred as a result of lengthy immersion in warmer waters. This condition can affect other parts of the body, such as knees, hands, or buttocks.

A person remaining for a long time in a cold, wet place, standing or crouching in one position, is likely to develop this condition.

Immersion foot brings with it a feeling of heaviness or numbness. All sensitivity may be lost, and the affected areas become swollen. The skin is first red, then waxy white, then a yellowish color, and finally a mottled blue or black. The injured parts remain cold, swollen, discolored, and numb. Or if they thaw, the swelling increases and the skin becomes hot, dry, red, and blistered. In severe cases gangrene may set in. Get the victim off his feet quickly, keep him as warm as possible, and expose the injured part to warm, dry air.

If the skin is not broken or loose, the injured part may be left exposed. However, if it is necessary to move the victim, cover the injured part with loosely wrapped fluff bandages of sterile gauze. Do not apply salves or ointments. Be careful not to rupture blisters.

If there is pain, give the victim no more than one-fourth grain of morphine.

INSECT BITES

Wash insect bites with soap and water and apply a paste of baking soda and water. Ice or ammonia applied to bee stings will prevent pain and swelling. Ticks can be dislodged by holding a lighted cigarette close to their behinds. Be careful not to crush the insect or leave its jaws embedded in flesh. Certain types of ticks can transmit Rocky Mountain spotted fever, which can be fatal. Inflamed bites require medical assistance.

MORPHINE

Morphine relieves severe pain and helps prevent shock. It should *not* be given if there is a head injury, chest injury, any injuries or burns that impair breathing, if there is evidence of severe or deepening shock, or if there is massive bleeding. Morphine should never be given to an unconscious man. Morphine should not be given if a doctor can be summoned in less than four hours. If morphine is given, the dosage must not be repeated for four hours.

Ordinarily, there is no need for anyone giving first aid to administer morphine. If it must be used, follow these steps:

Inject morphine on the outer surface of the upper arm or into the thigh if the arms are injured. In very cold climates, morphine is sometimes injected into the back of the neck to avoid undressing the victim. If a tourniquet has been applied, the morphine must be injected above it (that is, between the tourniquet and the heart).

Sterilize the skin with antiseptic, alcohol, soap and water, or plain tap water. Pick up the tube with the syrette at its shoulder, using your fingertips. Remove the shield, grasp the wire loop and push the wire into the tube to break the seal. Pull out the wire and discard. Push the needle through the skin to its full length, then slowly squeeze out the contents of the syrette.

Withdraw the syrette. Remove and discard the needle. Pin the empty syrette tube to the man's shirt collar to show that morphine has been given. Also, with a skin pencil, colored antiseptic, ballpoint pen, etc., write the letter M and the time of the injection on his forehead.

POISONING

First-aid treatment here depends partly on how the poison enters the body—whether by swallowing, inhalation, skin contact or injection. Here is a brief discussion of the symptoms and proper first aid for common types of poisoning.

Symptoms: Intense pain frequently follows poisoning. Nausea and vomiting may occur. The victim may become delirious, or collapse and fall unconscious. He is almost always likely to have trouble breathing. Some poisons cause paralysis; others produce convulsions. Shock always follows acute poisoning.

Ingested poisons: Many substances are poisonous, if swallowed. *Corrosives* (substances that rapidly destroy or decompose body tissues on contact) may be *acids* (hydrochloric, nitric, sulfuric), *phenols* (carbolic acid, creosol [Lysol], creosote), or *alkalies* (lye, lime, ammonia). Iodine is also a corrosive.

Corrosives cause a burning pain in the mouth, severe burning pain in the esophagus and stomach, retching, and vomiting. The inside of the mouth is eaten away. Swallowing and breathing become difficult. The abdomen is tender and distended with gas, and body temperature soars.

Irritants (substances that do not directly destroy body tissues but inflame in the area they touch) are potassium nitrate, zinc chloride, zinc sulfate, arsenic, iodine, and phosphorus. Irritants cause faintness, nausea, vomiting, diarrhea, and cramps in the abdomen.

Depressants (substances that depress the nervous system) include atropine, morphine and its derivatives, bromides, barbiturates, alcohol, and most local anesthetics. They usually have a stimulating effect at first, and then cause drowsiness, slow breathing, snoring, cold moist skin (with the face and fingers a bluish color), relaxed muscles, and dilated or contracted pupils.

Excitants (substances that stimulate the nervous system) are strychnine, camphor, and the fluorides. They cause delirium (mental disturbances, physical restlessness, and incoherence), a feeling of suffocation, hot dry skin, rapid and weak pulse, convulsions or jerking muscles, and dilated or contracted pupils.

Antidotes: *Emetics* cause vomiting. Effective ones are: one to three teaspoons of powdered mustard in a glass of warm water; two teaspoons of salt in a glass of warm water; warm water with soapsuds (not detergents); or large quantities of warm water. Emetics are not very effective in depressant poisoning, because depressants inhibit vomiting. In such cases, vomiting may be brought on by tickling the throat.

Demulcents will soothe the stomach and delay the absorption of poison. Periodically, after the victim has vomited, he should be given raw egg whites, milk, or a thin paste of cooked starch or flour.

A universal antidote, especially effective against irritants, excitants, and depressants, consists of two parts of activated charcoal, and one part each of magnesium oxide and tannic acid. The dose is half an ounce of this compound, dissolved in half a glass of water. It should be followed by an emetic, except when the poison is corrosive. You can substitute burned toast or charred wood for activated charcoal, milk of magnesia for magnesium oxide, and strong tea for tannic acid.

Antidotes for acids are milk of magnesia, magnesium oxide, lime water, or soap in large amounts of water. Follow this with a demulcent. Do not give emetics.

Antidotes for alkalies are diluted vinegar, lemon juice, or grapefruit juice. Follow this by a demulcent. Do not give emetics.

In treating of poisoning by mouth, identify the poison if possible. Give an emetic (except for corrosives), then give an antidote. Repeat both procedures every 10 minutes. Give a demulcent after the patient has vomited. Get medical assistance as soon as possible.

Inhaled poisons: These can come from refrigeration machinery, fire fighting equipment, paints and solvents, photographic materials, and other types of shipboard equipment that contain volatile and sometimes poisonous chemicals. Fuel oil and gasoline vapors are special hazards. Other poisonous gases are found in voids, double bottoms, empty fuel tanks, and similar places.

Carbon monoxide, the most frequent cause of gas poisoning, is colorless, odorless, and tasteless. It gives no warning. Carbon monoxide is present in exhaust gases of internal-combustion engines.

First aid for carbon monoxide, and other gases, is:

1. Get the victim out of the toxic atmosphere into a well-ventilated space.

2. Remove his contaminated clothing.

3. Watch his breathing. Give artificial respiration if necessary.

4. Give oxygen, or an oxygen–carbon dioxide mixture, if either is available and you know how to use it. (Carbon dioxide, which we breathe out, counteracts carbon monoxide. In mouth-to-mouth artificial respiration, you're breathing carbon dioxide into the victim of the carbon monoxide poisoning.)

5. Keep the victim lying down. Keep him quiet. Treat him for shock.

6. Call a medical officer as soon as possible.

Gasoline, benzene, naphtha, and other petroleum products are poisonous if they are ingested, inhaled, or come into prolonged contact with the skin. The inhalation of gasoline fumes causes a kind of intoxication similar to drunkenness. The victim may become violent and self-destructive, or may injure others unless he is very carefully guarded. Caution: do not give morphine.

Carbon tetrachloride and other chlorinated hydrocarbons, such as methylene chloride, chloroform, dichloromethane and tetrachlorethane, are used for dry cleaning, for degreasing metal articles, for cleaning electrical and electronic equipment in various manufacturing processes, and in some fire extinguishers. They are extremely dangerous as fire-extinguishing agents because heat causes them to decompose, forming phosgene gas.

Someone exposed to these vapors may not realize his condition until he becomes dangerously ill with nausea, mental confusion, and in some instances, a kind of drunken behavior. Those required to work with chlorinated solvents must not drink liquor. Alcohol greatly increases their susceptibility to this poisoning.

No antidote is known for poisoning by carbon tetrachloride and the other chlorinated hydrocarbons. Standard first-aid instructions should be followed.

Freon, a colorless, odorless gas used as a refrigerant, is toxic in high concentrations. First aid is the same as for other gases. Because even a very small amount of Freon can freeze the delicate tissue of the eye, medical attention must be obtained as soon as possible in order to avoid permanent damage. Meanwhile, put drops of clean olive oil, mineral oil, or other non-irritating oil in the eyes and make sure that the victim does not rub his eyes.

Hydrogen sulfide smells like rotten eggs. Its presence cannot always be detected because the gas paralyzes the sense of smell. It is flammable and poisonous.

The general signs of hydrogen sulfide poisoning are eye, nose, and throat irritation, and an abundant flow of tears. Breathing is first deep, noisy, and grasping. Later it becomes feeble and irregular. Death is caused by paralysis of the brain.

Ammonia, an industrial gas used in many ways, is pungent, biting, and extremely irritating. No one can breathe a concentration of one-tenth of 1 percent ammonia; the irritation causes coughing and a spasm of the air passages. Death may occur from asphyxiation.

Administer standard first aid. In addition, hold vinegar or a weak solution of acetic acid close enough to the victim's face so that he can inhale the fumes. But stop if this does not give him relief.

Poisoning by skin contact: Poisoning by skin contact is not usually a first-aid problem. Such poisoning frequently is fatal, but it builds over a long period of time. There is no real cure, except to know the substances that can poison by contact and be careful in handling them. These include gasoline, benzene, naphtha, lead compounds, mercury, arsenic, carbon tetrachloride, and TNT.

SHOCK

When the nervous system is subjected to excessive shock, the nerves lose control of the blood vessels, allowing them to relax and thus reducing the supply of blood to the brain. Unconsciousness or "fuzzy-headedness" may result. The heart quickens its pace but the pulse is weak. All injury is attended by shock, which may be slight, lasting only a few seconds, or serious enough to kill. Shock may begin immediately, or it may be delayed as long as several hours.

How to recognize shock: The pulse is weak and rapid. Breathing may be shallow, rapid, and irregular. The skin feels cold to the touch and may be covered with sweat. The skin will be pale. In dark-complexioned people, the gums and beds of fingernails will be ash gray. The pupils of the eyes are usually dilated. A shock victim may complain of thirst. He may feel weak, faint or dizzy, and nauseated. He may be restless, frightened, and anxious. As shock deepens, these signs gradually disappear and he becomes less and less responsive, even to pain. A man in shock may insist that he feels fine, and then pass out.

Treatment: It is important to keep the patient flat on his back, feet higher than his body. Keep him warm with blankets, not artificial heat. Do all you can to relieve pain, but do not try to give any drugs. A person in shock is often thirsty. Moisten his mouth with cool water, but don't give him anything to drink unless medical personnel will not be available for a long time.

Never give alcohol to a person who is in shock or may go into shock. Alcohol increases the blood supply to surface vessels, cutting the blood supply to the brain and other vital organs.

TRANSPORTATION OF THE INJURED

Take these precautions before transporting an injured person: Locate all injuries to the best of your ability. Treat serious bleeding, breathing trouble, shock, fractures, sprains, and dislocations. Relieve the victim's pain and make him as comfortable as possible.

Use a regular stretcher. If you must improvise, be sure that the stretcher is strong enough to hold the victim. Have several men carry the stretcher. Don't drop the victim; fasten him in the stretcher so that he cannot slip, slide, or fall off. Tie his feet together unless injuries make this impracticable. Use blankets, garments, or other materials to pad the stretcher and to protect the victim from exposure.

An injured person usually should lie on his back while being moved, but one having difficulty breathing because of a chest wound may be more comfortable if his head and shoulders are slightly raised. Fracture cases should be moved very carefully, so the injury will not be made worse. A man with a severe injury to the back of his head should be kept on his side. A patient should always be carried feet first, unless there is some special reason for carrying him head first.

The three-man lift (Figure 8–11) and the fireman's lift (Figure

Figure 8–11 The three-man lift is a recommended method of transporting an injured person.

8–12) are recommended for carrying an injured person, and the tied-hands crawl (Figure 8–13) is used to transport a patient under special circumstances.

Three-man lift: No. 1 man takes head and shoulders of victim; No. 2, back and buttocks; No. 3, legs and feet. No. 1 says, "Ready, lift," and all lift together and keep the body straight. If the man has a chest wound, he is placed on his stomach. If he has a stomach wound, keep him on his back with knees bent.

Fireman's lift: Turn the patient face down. Kneel over his head, facing his shoulders (A). Pass both your hands under his armpits and lift him to his knees. Then slide your hands down lower and clasp them around his back (B). Raise him to a standing position, stick your right leg between his legs (C), take his right wrist in your left hand and swing his arm around the back of your neck, holding him close to you. Put your right arm between his thighs (D), stoop quickly, pull his trunk across your shoulders, and straighten up (E).

To lower the patient, kneel on your left knee. Grasp his left knee with your right hand. Slide him around in front of you and down your right thigh into a sitting position. Shift your hands to his head and place him gently on his back.

Tied-hands crawl: Use this method when you must remain close to the deck, or when you must have both hands free for climbing a ladder.

Lay the patient on his back. Lie on your back alongside him and to his left. Grasp his right arm above the elbow with your right hand. With your left hand, grasp the same arm below the elbow. Entwine your legs with his and roll over on your chest, pulling him over onto your back. Now pull his free hand (the left one) under your armpit. Tie his wrists together with a handkerchief or any other available material, then crawl forward.

Strokes stretcher: This is a wire basket adaptable to a variety of uses. It will hold a person securely in place even when tipped. The Strokes stretcher is generally used for transferring the injured to and from boats or ships. It can be used to rescue men from the water. The stretcher should be padded with two blankets placed lengthwise so that one will be under each of the victim's legs, and a third folded in half and placed in the upper part of the stretcher to protect his head and shoulders. He should be lowered gently into the stretcher and made as comfortable as possible. His feet must be fastened to the end of the stretcher so

Figure 8–12 One person can transport an injury victim by using the fireman's lift.

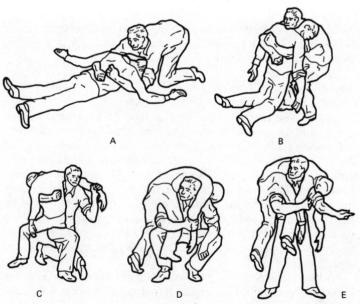

A

B

C

D

E

Figure 8–13 Transport an injured person with a tied-hands crawl when you must remain close to the deck or when you must have both hands free for climbing a ladder.

that he will not slide up and down, and he must be fastened into the stretcher by straps over his chest, hips, and knees. The straps go over the blanket or over the covering.

Neill–Robertson stretcher: The stretcher is specifically designed for vertically removing victims in close spaces. It is all wood and canvas construction, and completely encloses the victim.

Army litter: This consists of two wooden poles, six and one-half to seven feet long, with canvas stretched across the poles. It is used for evacuation of the injured at land-based facilities. Check it for deterioration before using it.

II. The Navy Career

9. Duty Assignments and Advancements

While you are in training or at school, everything will be organized for you, and after you report to your new ship or station, everything there will be organized too. But between the time you pick up your orders at your old station and turn them in at your new station, you may feel like a lost person. If you don't keep yourself organized, you might end up being just that.

Some transfers are simple; others are extremely complicated. You may be lucky and receive orders to a ship which is in port near where you are. Or you may end up flying halfway around the world, check in at a base for a few days, ride a cargo ship somewhere else which is to be unloaded on a dock, and find out that your ship has just sailed back to where you came from. Suddenly you belong to no one. What do you do?

Remember, it's all one Navy, and no matter where you are, you can find someone to help. Always keep your orders in hand and not in your baggage, which may be lost. If you are given your records and pay accounts, keep them with your orders. You can obtain further transportation with your orders, and with your pay accounts you can draw pay—even from an Army or Air Force activity—if needed.

Make certain when you're checking out from your old duty station that you understand your orders. If they authorize DELREP—delay in reporting to count as leave—check the date on which you must report in at the new station. If commercial transportation is authorized at government expense, pick up the tickets or travel vouchers. If you have any questions at all, ask the transfer yeoman or personnelman before you leave; this may save you a lot of trouble later.

If you are ordered to a service school or other shore activity, any taxi driver at the airport, bus, or railroad terminal will know how to take you there. But finding a particular ship in a port city such as Norfolk or San Diego can be difficult—the ship could be anywhere within thirty or so miles. First check in with the Navy Shore Patrol. If you can't find the SP, look in the telephone directory under "U.S. Government," to find some naval activity where you can obtain help. The Navy Recruiting Command, with recruiters in most major cities across the country, can be contacted if you're unable to contact a naval installation.

No matter what you wore on leave, be in a complete and proper uniform when you report in for duty. Be sure you have all your gear with you—the ship may sail the same day and what you checked at the airport or station will do you no good at sea. Hand your orders to the watch, either at the main gate or the quarterdeck, so that they can be endorsed with the time and date of reporting in, and you can be logged in.

Centralized Detailing

At any one time, about two-thirds of the enlisted personnel in the Navy are in seagoing billets and the other third in shore billets. To make certain that everyone gets a fair share of each kind of duty assignment, a system of centralized detailing has been set up by the Naval Military Personnel Command (NMPC). Because it is a complicated system, full details are contained in the Enlisted Transfer Manual (TRANSMAN, NAVPERS 15909). Always check with the personnel office before making any requests under this system.

All personnel, except nondesignated seamen (SN), firemen (FN), and airmen (AN) who are under the control of the Enlisted Personnel Management Center (EPMAC) in New Orleans, are assigned by NMPC.

DUTY TYPE CODES

Six duty type designations are used to establish an equitable rotation of sea and shore assignments. Each of these duty types is credited as sea, shore, or neutral duty for rotational purposes. These codes are assigned (and, when necessary, changed) exclusively by NMPC.

The six types are:

Type 1 Shore Duty: Duty performed in CONUS (the continental United States) at land-based activities and other CONUS activities designated as "long-term" schooling programs. (Long-term is defined as 18 or more months; school assignments of less than 18 months are considered neutral duty.)

Type 2 Sea Duty: Also known as "arduous sea duty." This duty is performed in commissioned active-status vessels, homeported or homebased in CONUS, which operate away from their permanent homes for extended periods.

Type 3 Overseas Shore Duty: Duty performed in overseas land-based activities, including Alaska and Hawaii, at locations where the prescribed tour length is less than 36 months.

Type 4 Nonrotated Sea Duty: Duty performed in commissioned active-status vessels homeported overseas (outside CONUS); or performed in activities which operate away from overseas homeports or bases for extensive periods.

Type 5 Neutral Duty: Duty in activities which would normally be designated as shore duty for rotational purposes, but where the personnel assigned are absent, for a significant length of time, from the corporate limits of their duty station while accomplishing their assigned tasks. It also includes school assignments of less than 18 months.

Type 6 Preferred Overseas Shore Duty: Duty performed in specified overseas land-based activities, including Alaska and Hawaii, at locations having suitable dependent accommodations and support facilities. The tours normally last at least 36 months.

For rotational purposes, Types 1 and 6 count as shore duty credit; Types 2, 3, and 4 for sea duty credit; and Type 5 for neutral duty credit.

The length of tours at sea and ashore for each rating depends primarily on the ratio of shore billets to sea billets. In order to provide both personal and command stability, every effort is made to achieve a goal of a three-year sea/shore rotation pattern. Tour lengths for all rates and certain NEC (Navy Enlisted Classification) codes are contained in the TRANSMAN.

ENLISTED DUTY PREFERENCES

For planning purposes, each person in the Navy is provided with a projected rotation date (PRD) which estimates the tentative month and year of next assignment. Although the Navy will try to transfer you at a PRD, this date is established for planning purposes and will not always be the precise time of your reassignment. PRDs are established and modified by NMPC.

There are two important forms used in the enlisted duty preference system: the enlisted duty preferences (NAVPERS 1306/63), and the enlisted transfer and special duty request (NAVPERS 1306/7).

Duty Preferences Form: In order for a sailor to be considered for the type of duty he prefers, he should complete a 1306/63. This allows individuals to state their preferences as to type of ship; homeport for sea duty, overseas duty, and shore duty; and localities preferred for overseas or shore duty. Concisely stated, detailing is the process whereby available personnel assets are matched up with existing Navy-wide requirements in such a manner as best to satisfy the individual's duty preferences. If an individual has no duty preferences on file, his assignment will be to any valid requirement.

Submission of the duty preferences form is an individual responsibility. The initial 1306/63 is submitted upon arrival at your first permanent duty station. Subsequent forms may be submitted anytime the member's duty preferences change, and must be submitted when significant personal changes occur; for instance, a change in dependency status, or a change in the physical location of household goods.

Although the 1306/63 was designed to reflect the information most pertinent to an individual's assignability, it is recognized that no form of this type can be all-encompassing. Accordingly, a "remarks" section has been incorporated to allow for the indication of additional useful information. Examples of such information are: any skill possessed by the member not identified by NEC; community-supportive skills possessed by a dependent (e.g., as a teacher, nurse, dental technician, secretary, or hairdresser); handicapped dependents and areas where the appropriate treatment facilities are; and expected delivery date if wife is pregnant.

Enlisted Transfer and Special Duty Request: This request form, NAVPERS 1306/7, is designed to give you an opportunity to request participation in programs of a more immediate nature. In general, the form is to be used only to request a program, school, reassignment, or special duty for which a particular requesting format has not been specified. These unspecified formats could include humanitarian assignments, reenlistment incentive, and the SCORE program. There is one important consideration for all such requests: You must be eligible for the type of duty requested.

ROTATION FOR ENLISTED WOMEN

The rotation for enlisted women is identified as OUTUS—outside the continental limits of the United States—or CONUS, instead of sea or shore. Women who fall into the OUTUS (Type 3 and 6 duty) rating category may expect no more than two back-to-back overseas tours, and no less than one tour in CONUS. Women who fall into the CONUS (Type 1 duty) rating category may expect shore tours paralleling those of their male counterparts. Assignments to Type 3 and 6 duty is for prescribed DOD area tour length. When assignments to Type 3 or 6 duty are not practical, a voluntary (or involuntary) extension on a CONUS tour is used, to aid in minimizing permanent change of station (PCS) transfers.

Assignment to Programs

In order to provide for the increasing complexity of the Navy's mission, it is often necessary to establish special programs for tasks requiring skills not identified by existing ratings. Once a long-term requirement for a particular skill is known to exist, such a program is integrated into the regular naval organization and, if necessary, a new rating is established for the specific skill required.

One of the most recent illustrations of this is the establishment of the NC (Navy counselor) rating. It has been evident for some time that the existing Navy rating structure didn't provide a rating

Figure 9–1 Rotation for enlisted women is categorized as either in the United States or out of the United States, instead of for sea or shore duty.

for personnel skilled in the fields of recruiting and retention. While the majority of the billets in career counseling and field recruiting are still filled by persons from a variety of ratings, NCs are now beginning to take over more and more of these specialized responsibilities. (The Navy Counselor rating is more fully discussed on page 31.)

Some of the programs discussed below have specific rating requirements, others do not. Since all of them are subject to change, you'll do well to check with your personnel office for the exact details.

NAVY FOOD MANAGEMENT TEAMS

Navy Food Management Teams provide technical and management assistance to mess management specialists (MS) in the operation of enlisted dining facilities and afloat wardrooms. They get on-the-job instruction in areas of food preparation and service, mess management, and sanitation. They assist both fleet units and shore activities. Teams are located at Norfolk, Charleston, San Diego, and Pearl Harbor.

MOBILE TECHNICAL UNIT PROGRAM

The mobile technical units (MOTUs) provide specialized electronic and weapons technical and training service to the fleets and systems commands for special projects. They also play an important part in maintaining readiness of fleet electronic and weapons equipment. MOTU headquarters are in Washington, D.C., at the Naval Sea Systems Command (NAVSEASYSCOM). There are presently ten MOTUs located at Pearl Harbor, Norfolk, New London, San Diego, San Francisco, Charleston, and Mayport. Three of these are at overseas locations: Naples, Italy; Subic Bay, R.P.; and Yokosuka, Japan.

ARMED FORCES POLICE DETACHMENTS (AFPDs)

Armed Forces Police Detachments are located in Washington, D.C., New Orleans, Brooklyn, Boston, San Francisco, Seattle, Honolulu, and Fort Gordon (Ga.). AFPDs function as do most community police forces.

CORRECTIONAL CENTER STAFF

Correctional centers are located in nearly all naval districts and at a few overseas locations. They provide an exceptional opportunity for personnel to enhance their leadership qualities, regardless of their military speciality.

CAREER COUNSELING PROGRAM

The NMPC-controlled counseling program provides for the assignment of full-time career counselors, in ratings other than NC, to billets under assignment control of NMPC. Personnel so assigned assist commanding officers and unit commanders in maintaining an effective career-motivation program.

NAVAL INTELLIGENCE SUPPORT CENTER

The requirements exists for a small, but growing number of submarine-qualified sonar technicians (STs) at the Naval Intelligence Support Center, Washington, D.C.

SPECIAL STAFF ASSIGNMENTS

These assignments include duty in Military Assistance Advisory Groups (MAAGs), Naval Missions, Military Groups (and similar activities), NATO commands, and joint staff and Navy staffs. While the largest percentage of these billets is for yeoman (YN), radioman (RM), and storekeeper (SK) ratings—in paygrades E-3 through E-9—some requirements also exist for a variety of other ratings and NECs. Those interested should contact the MAAGs/mission desk in NMPC to see if a requirement exists for a particular rating and paygrade.

HUMAN RESOURCE MANAGEMENT SUPPORT
SYSTEM (HRMSS) PROGRAM

The HRMSS program provides for the assignment of full-time

human resource management specialists, instructors, and consultants, in billets under the distributional control of NMPC. Persons so assigned assist commands in establishing and maintaining an effective human resource management plan. There are currently five different specialists assigned to the program: human resource management specialist, collateral duty alcoholism counselor (CODAC), race relations education specialist (RRES), drug and alcohol education specialist (DAES), and alcoholism treatment specialist (ATS).

ASSIGNMENT OF SEABEES TO STATE DEPARTMENT UNITS

The Navy has established the Naval Support Unit of the State Department to provide continuing Seabee support to the State Department security program. This duty involves the security surveillance of foreign contract construction, and the accomplishment of minor construction repairs and maintenance within the Foreign Service establishment. Personnel are desired on a volunteer basis. Non-volunteers are also sometimes used. Tours are normally three years in duration, and consist of a one-year unaccompanied tour followed by a two-year accompanied tour in the same general area.

OPERATION DEEP FREEZE

Each year the Naval Support Force, Antarctica and Air Development Squadron Six (VXE 6) participates in the Antarctic expedition. Personnel requirements for the summer support group are open to most rates and ratings on a continuing basis. An NMPC notice, published annually, outlines the specific qualifications desired of participants in the wintering-over party, known as "Detachment Alfa."

BLUE ANGELS

The U.S. Navy Flight Demonstration Team—known as the Blue Angels, or "The Blues"—is based at NAS Pensacola. A number of enlisted support billets are available with the team. Due to the extensive time away from their permanent duty station, this duty is neutral duty for rotation and is for a period of three years. Requests may be made to NMPC through your chain of command and via the officer-in-charge of the team.

USS *CONSTITUTION*

The USS *Constitution,* affectionately known as "Old Ironsides," is an important part of the U.S. Navy's history. The *Constitution,* berthed in Boston, represents the Navy as it was in the 1800s. Because the *Constitution's* crew are in constant contact with the public, they must have an excellent personal appearance and exemplary military bearing. Enlisted crew members are assigned directly from recruit training. Petty officers are selected from those eligible for shore duty.

OTHER PROGRAMS

Special programs are also provided so that personnel can qualify for assignment to the Aircrew Program, for the UDT, SEAL, and EOD Program (underwater demolition teams, sea-air-land teams and the explosive ordnance disposal teams), for the Deep Sea Diver Program, and for the Service Craft Program. The latter includes persons designated as tugmasters (NEC 0161) and yard craft boat captains (NEC 0162).

Figure 9–2 Sailors in a special unit undergo underwater demolition and sea-air-land training at a Navy amphibious base.

Instructor Duty

Due to the level of expertise required in these highly responsible assignments, applicants for instructor duty must be petty officers. Requests should be indicated on the DPC. Personnel selected as instructors are first ordered to instructor school on a temporary-duty basis, enroute to their final duty station. Instructor schools are located in Great Lakes, San Diego, Norfolk, and Millington, Tennessee. The four-week course covers the methods and techniques of training.

Those received for instructor duty are initially in a probationary status for a period of at least 90 days, under the direct supervision of a seasoned instructor. After this period the probation is usually terminated and a recommendation is made for the assignment of an appropriate NEC instructor designation.

In addition to the many sailors needed to teach throughout the Navy's large schooling system, there are also a number of other specialized instructor assignments. These include recruit company commanders and instructors at activities concerned with survival training, Naval Reserve, aviation, and nuclear propulsion.

Recruiting Duty

While the highest standards of personal conduct and characteristics are required of all members of the naval service, it is

Figure 9–3 Personnel in all ratings may apply for recruiting duty.

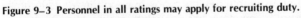

especially important that personnel assigned to the Navy Recruiting Command exemplify these high standards. A recruiter is constantly under the scrutiny of civilians in the surrounding community. Enlisted personnel in paygrades E-5 and above (E-4 and above for women) are assigned mainly to recruiting districts located within CONUS. There are also a limited number of assignments available in Alaska, Hawaii, Guam, Puerto Rico, the Philippines, and Europe.

Personnel in all ratings may apply for assignment to recruiting duty. If selected, male personnel in YN, SK, PN, DK, and JO ratings are normally assigned to recruiter support billets only. Female personnel of all ratings can apply for recruiter/canvasser duty.

On your way to recruiting duty you'll stop off at ENRO (Enlisted Navy Recruiting Orientation) in Orlando for five weeks of intensive training and instruction. The orientation course covers approximately 200 hours of instruction. At the completion of this course, prospective field recruiters should be thoroughly familiar with the many career programs available for volunteers, the proper method of explaining and presenting this information, and the necessary paper work involved.

154

Exchange of Duty

There are occasions when the assignment of an individual to a specific area would be highly beneficial to the individual's morale, but not justifiable in view of the expenditure of government funds required. The Navy has provisions for effecting such transfers on a no-cost-to-the-government basis, provided the individual agrees to bear all expenses involved. There are two types of exchange of duty—usually called "swaps." One is negotiated by NMPC and is based upon a letter request from you. The other is self-negotiated, and is requested on the NAVPERS 1306/7—the enlisted transfer and special duty request. The specific requirements are contained in the TRANSMAN.

Humanitarian Reassignments

Detailing authorities are aware of the hardships which confront Navy families and of the additional aggravation imposed by long absences of service members from their families. Emergency leave frequently provides sufficient time to alleviate such hardships; however, when an individual requires more time than leave can provide and has a reasonable chance of resolving the hardship within a specified time-frame, reassignment for human-itarian reasons (HUMS) may be requested.

Your personnel office can give you additional information regarding HUMS assignments and help you determine your eligibility for such assignment.

The Navy also will make provision for the assignment or reassignment of members of the same family. According to the rules governing these assignments, family members include: spouse, father, mother, sons, daughters, brothers, sisters, step-brothers, step-sisters, and adopted brothers and sisters. The specific requirements are also contained in the TRANSMAN.

Enlisted Advancement System

Many of the above special duty assignments require that applicants be senior petty officers. The following is a detailed examination of the system you go through to get there—the enlisted advancement system.

All advancements in the Navy (except for a few meritorious advancements under the Sailor of the Year program) are made through a centralized competitive system. Because the requirements sometimes change, it is always best to consult with your personnel office or educational services office for the latest information.

GENERAL REQUIREMENTS

In general, there are certain qualifications each person must meet to be eligible to compete in the semi-annual or annual Navy-wide examinations for advancement in rate. These include:

Have the required time in rate (TIR). The specific TIR requirement for advacement to E-2 is 6 months as E-1; for E-3, 6 months; E-4, 9 months; E-5, 12 months; E-6, 36 months; E-7, E-8, and E-9 are 36 months each. Time in service (TIS) is no longer a factor in establishing requirements for advancement. The elimination of TIS enables superior performers to advance commensurate with their ability and performance. It is possible, with hard work and diligent study, to become a chief petty officer within nine years.

Completion of established personnel advancement requirements (PARs) for the projected paygrade. Each PAR contains descriptive information, instructions for administration, special rating requirements (such as physical, citizenship, or security clearance), and advancement requirements of the following types: administrative requirements; formal school and training requirements; and occupational and military ability requirements.

Figure 9–4 Sailors who have met certain criteria for advancement take part in a formal ceremony marking their promotions.

Successfully pass the military leadership examination. This is a prerequisite for competing for advancement to paygrades E-4 and E-5. There is an examination for each grade. Personnel in paygrades E-2 and E-3, who are not eligible to take the professional exam (the semi-annual or annual Navy-wide tests), may take the military leadership examination. You need only pass once in each grade to establish eligibility.

If required, pass a performance test. For example, a typing test for YNs, PNs, RMs and JOs; a semaphore test for SMs; and a flashing-light test for QMs.

Complete required Navy training courses or correspondence courses and service schools, as required.

Meet requirements for proficiency marks.

And the most important requirement to be met in the advancement system—be recommended by your commanding officer.

FINAL MULTIPLE SCORE (FMS)

The competitive system uses a combination of factors to determine the final multiple for each person. For E-4s and E-5s, the maximum percentage you can earn is 35 percent from the examination, 30 percent for performance, 13 percent for length of service, 13 percent for service in paygrade, 4.5 percent for awards, and 4.5 percent for high quality or passed but not advanced points. The percentages for E-6s are identical, except they receive 30 percent from the examination and 35 percent for performance.

Because of selection board screening for E-7s, the FMS system for advancement is somewhat different. Weight factors for computing the E-7 FMS are based on 60 percent for the examination and 40 percent from the leadership evaluation (directing/counseling).

These are the only factors used in determining E-7 FMS. The system is designed to give more advancement consideration to members who, through their outstanding performance and demonstrated leadership ability, have exhibited the potential to assume increased levels of responsibility. Based on the final multiple score, each candidate's examination results fall within one of three categories: (1) SBE (selection board eligible), (2) SBI (selection board ineligible), or (3) fail. SBE candidates comprise 50 percent of the test-takers for E-7.

Promotion examinations for the top two enlisted grades, E-8 and E-9, are no longer given. Those who have three years in rate, have satisfactorily completed Military Requirements for senior and master chief petty officer (NAVTRA 91209), and are recommended will automatically be eligible for selection board consideration.

Figure 9–5 Formal classroom study is an important part of the Navy's system for advancement and ensures a more proficient sailor for the fleet.

Senior Enlisted Grades

Until 1958, a person who had advanced to chief petty officer (E-7) had gone as high as possible in the enlisted rating structure. Then the grades of senior chief petty officer (E-8 or SCPO) and master chief petty officer (E-9 or MCPO) were established to give additional recognition to people with outstanding technical, leadership, and supervisory abilities.

While advancement to E-7 is considered normal for a 20-year career, the E-8 and E-9 paygrades are regarded as 30-year career plans. Candidates for E-8 and E-9, having met all the requirements, have their service records closely screened by a selection board at NMPC. This is where a good record becomes extremely important—those with the best records are selected over those with records that may be good, but not good enough.

MASTER CHIEF PETTY OFFICER OF THE NAVY

The Master Chief Petty Officer of the Navy (MCPON) is the Navy's senior enlisted member. Assigned to the office of the Chief of Naval Personnel for a four-year tour of duty, the MCPON serves as senior enlisted representative of the Navy and acts as the senior enlisted adviser to the Chief of Naval Operations and the Chief of Naval Personnel in all matters pertaining to enlisted personnel.

The MCPON also serves as an adviser to many boards dealing with enlisted personnel; accompanies the CNO or Inspector General on some trips; serves as the enlisted representative of the Department of the Navy at special events, celebrations, and ceremonies; and maintains a liaison with the Navy Wives' Club of America.

FLEET, FORCE, AND COMMAND MASTER CHIEF PETTY OFFICERS

The Fleet and Force Master Chief Petty Officers (F M/Cs) and the Command Master Chief Petty Officers (C M/Cs) function as principal enlisted advisers to unit commanders and commanding officers. They have made better communications possible at all levels of command throughout the Navy and have fostered a keener sensitivity to the needs and viewpoints of enlisted men and women, as well as their dependents.

They have the responsibility of keeping their commanders or commanding officers up to date on situations, procedures, and practices that affect the welfare, morale, and well-being of the enlisted crew. F M/Cs and C M/Cs have direct access to their commanders or commanding officers.

At present, there are 5 fleet and 16 force F M/C billets in the

Navy, as well as 67 major command "billeted" C M/C jobs which are staffed directly by NMPC. Every Navy command with more than 250 personnel has a designated C M/C. When an MCPO is not available, a senior chief is designated as the Command Senior Chief Petty Officer (C S/C); if neither an MCPO or SCPO is available, the senior CPO is designated as the Command Chief Petty Officer (C Ch). Their function is identical to that of a C M/C.

The MCPON and F M/C are in continual liaison, and C M/Cs are constantly in touch with the appropriate F M/Cs. This liaison ensures that proper communications channels are established.

CHIEF OF THE BOAT

The Navy's submarine service also has assignments simular to those of the C M/Cs; they are called Chiefs of the Boat (COBs). But there are subtle differences. COBs are a little bit like the C Chs, a little like the CMAAs (chief masters-at-arms) and a little like the LCPOs (leading chief petty officers) of the surface and shore Navy. While their duties include many of the administrative duties associated with C Chs, many of the law-and-order functions associated with CMAAs, and much of the extensive hands-on experience that LCPOs have, there are still a number of differences.

Detailed to his assignment by NMPC, the COB must first make himself available for the assignment by volunteering. COBs are E-8s or E-9s. A special NEC is awarded to a man selected for COB duty. As you'll see, his responsibilities are varied.

He assigns bunks and lockers; supervises men detailed to compartment cleaning, mess cooking and special details; and assists the executive officer (XO) in maintaining the watch, quarter and station (WQ&S) bill. He also ensures proper stowage and upkeep of lifejackets, escape hoods, oxygen breathing equipment, lines, and cables. In addition, he instructs men in marlinespike seamanship, riggings, mooring, and anchoring.

Under direction of the first lieutenant, he supervises the care and preservation of the hull, superstructure, and all topside equipment not assigned to other departments.

One of his most important functions is assisting the XO in the administration of the on-board enlisted submarine qualification program. He also coordinates and supervises—through division leading petty officers—the conduct, performance, and administration of all enlisted personnel. The COB also monitors leave and special liberty.

The COB is considered an executive petty officer in all matters affecting enlisted personnel. He is charged with departmental coordination on the leading petty officer level. As such, he reports directly to the XO. By virtue of his position, he works with and for all department heads.

LEADING CHIEF PETTY OFFICER

The enlisted man or woman selected for the assignment of leading chief petty officer plays a key role in every command. By tradition, the position of top leadership over the enlisted personnel of a command usually goes to the most senior petty officer; but the job involves more than seniority.

No matter what his or her rating, an LCPO must be highly skilled in leadership and personnel management.

Normally the LCPO is directly responsible to the executive officer and assists him in carrying out his responsibilities in assigning and administering enlisted records, preparing watchbills, material inspections, personnel inspections, leave, and liberty. The LCPO advises the captain, through the XO, on matters of crew morale, personal problems of enlisteds or their dependents, and problems affecting living conditions. The LCPO encourages enlisted personnel to bring personal problems to him, and takes the initiative in solving them.

160

A deciding factor in selecting an LCPO is his ability as a leader. An LCPO must know how to guide and handle enlisted people, and must present an outstanding example of proper military dress, grooming, and moral traits.

10. Educational and Commission Opportunities

Education in the Navy begins with recruit training and continues throughout your naval career—whether it lasts for 4 years or 30. Navy vocational/technical schools are only one phase of Navy education. Those not attending school can take Navy training courses (self-study texts). And every sailor at one time or another is involved in a formal or informal on-the-job training (OJT) program.

Every enlisted person must complete a training course or attend the equivalent school in order to become eligible for promotion. He also must demonstrate a mastery of the requirements for the next higher paygrade—measured by the personnel advancement requirement (PAR) system—before becoming eligible to compete for advancement.

Promotion in the Navy is determined by time in rate (TIR), quality of work, examination marks, and demonstrated ability. The Navy's promotion system is unique; no one fails to advance simply because he is assigned to a unit that doesn't need another person in the next higher paygrade. Competition for advancement is Navy-wide. Anyone who is qualified and recommended may take the exam. Typically, it takes 12 years or more to become a chief petty officer; it is possible, however, to advance from recruit to CPO in 9 years.

While no specific amount of education is required for joining the Navy, it is obvious that a good education will contribute to the effectiveness of those who work in a vast technical organization. The greater majority of those joining the Navy today are at least high-school graduates.

Young men and women who want to learn and improve themselves have unlimited opportunities in the Navy today. They can take simple correspondence courses and attend a wide range of schools, both within the Navy and at civilian educational institutions. Those who have not completed high school can earn an equivalency certificate, and those who qualify can take a full four-year college course for a bachelor's degree or, through selection for officer training programs, earn a commission in the Navy.

162

Figure 10–1 To advance your Navy career, you've got to study, and you've got to keep up.

Personnel Qualification Standards (PQS)

From the moment a person begins training for advancement to E-2, until the paygrade of E-9 is attained, every step of the way is governed by the personnel qualification standards (PQS) manual—often called the "quals book" or the "PQS manual."

The manual sets up standards for the training courses and publications you will use, curricula for the schools you will attend, and the specific programs for on-the-job training (OJT) you will enter. The PQS manual also sets the standards for the Navy-wide advancement exams and, in general, governs all preparations for advancement in the Navy. Your career counselor, master chief petty officer of the command, or someone in the personnel or educational services office, is best qualified to explain the fine points to you.

Minimum requirements for advancement to specific paygrades, including professional knowledge and practical work,

PQS

are part of the military standards listed in the PQS. Occupational standards—specific practical skills and knowledge you'll need for advancement in a general rate or rating—are also listed. The career pattern section of the manual outlines the path of advancement you will normally take. It also determines some of the schools you must attend.

Service Schools

Navy service schools are located at the three training centers, and at Memphis, Tennessee; Gulfport and Meridian, Mississippi; Norfolk, Virginia; Port Hueneme (pronounced Y-neemee), California; and other places. For some rates, graduation from a particular service school is necessary for advancement—the PQS manual will tell you which rates. Selection for a service school depends on the rate held, time in service, current duty assignment, school quotas, and the operational schedule of your unit. Although you can attend a service school, on a temporary additional duty (TAD) basis, from your current duty station, most school assignments are made with a permanent change of station (PCS).

Figure 10–2 Basic and advanced schools provide the technical knowledge sailors need to perform their jobs.

The five types of enlisted service schools are:

Class A: Provides the basic technical knowledge required for job performance and later specialized training. A Navy Enlisted Classification (NEC) code may be awarded to identify the skill achieved.

Class C: Advanced knowledge, skills, and techniques needed to perform a particular job are taught. This category includes schools and courses previously identified as Class B. An NEC code may also be awarded to identify the level of skill acquired.

Class E: Designed for professional education, leading to an academic degree.

Class F: Trains fleet personnel who are enroute to, or are members of, ships' companies. Also provides individual training such as refresher, operator, maintenance, or technical training of less than 13 calendar days. An NEC code is not awarded.

Class R: This is the basic school and provides your initial training after enlistment. It prepares the recruit for early adjustment to military life by providing skill and knowledge in basic military subjects. Class R schooling does not include the apprenticeships. However, apprenticeship schools are conducted at the three RTCs. Everyone attends one of three Class R schools—in San Diego, Great Lakes, or Orlando.

The two remaining types of schools, Class P and Class V, are designed for officers. Class P is for officer-acquisition programs and is designed to provide undergraduate education and training for midshipmen, officer candidates, and all other newly commissioned officers, except those acquired through Class V programs. Class V schools provide the training that leads to designation as a naval aviator or naval flight officer.

Since the eligibility requirements for schools vary, and are changed frequently, you should check the Catalog of Navy Training Courses (CANTRAC), NAVEDTRA 10500. CANTRAC has information on schools and courses under the direction of the Chief of Naval Education and Training (CNET). Besides CANTRAC, you have three other sources of information on schools—your educational services office, your career counselor, and your personnel office. They can provide you with full information on how to apply for any of the following programs.

Selective Training and Reenlistment (STAR) Program

This program can guarantee early reenlistment, career designation, a variety of school programs, automatic advancement, and payment of a selective reenlistment bonus (SRB). Applicants must be E-5s, E-4s, or qualified E-3s. They also must have at least 21 months, but not more than five years, of continuous naval service (and not more than eight years of total military service). Applicants also should be recommended by their commanding officers, be serving in their first enlistments, meet the minimum test-score requirements for entrance into the appropriate Class A school, and agree to reenlist or extend for a period of six years.

Nuclear-power-trained personnel normally will serve a tour of three years in an operational nuclear billet before attending the guaranteed school.

Although all ratings are eligible, the emphasis is on those serving in critical ratings or those with critical NECs.

Selective Conversion and Retention (SCORE) Program

SCORE is for people in ratings that are overmanned or have limited advancement opportunities. It helps them make the shift into a critical rating. The program offers a variety of schooling guarantees, automatic advancement, early reenlistment, and payment of the selective reenlistment bonus (SRB)—although SRB is not considered a SCORE guarantee. Applicants in pay-grades E-6, E-5, E-4, and identified E-3 strikers who have more than 21 months of continuous active naval service (but not more than 15 years of total active military service) are eligible.

Applicants must be recommended by their commanding officers, be within four months of the minimum activity tour, and must meet the obligatory service and test-score requirements to enter the appropriate Class A school. One of SCORE's chief benefits is that candidates have an opportunity to work in the rating to which they are converting before being assigned to school. SCORE requires a six-year obligation. A candidate failing in formal schooling will be dropped from the program but is required to fulfill his service obligation.

Guaranteed Assignment Retention Detailing (GUARD III) Program

The purpose of the GUARD III program is to guarantee assignment as a reenlistment incentive to all career petty officers and eligible E-3s with less than 25 years of service. GUARD III is also designed to encourage direct contact between reenlistment-eligible persons who are approaching the expiration of active obligated service (EAOS) and their detailers in NMPC. This should be done after counseling by the command career counselor, informally (by telephone or personal letter) at any time within the six months prior to EAOS.

GUARD III provides for two guaranteed assignments: one must be used at first reenlistment, and the second may be used anytime before beginning the 25th year of service.

To be eligible for GUARD III, you must: not possess PCS orders; be within six months of your EAOS; be qualified under current NMPC instructions; be eligible for the duty requested in accordance with the sea/shore or OUTCONUS/CONUS rotation pattern. Candidates must also be recommended by their commanding officer, be willing to reenlist for four or more years, and have a consistent record of above-average or steadily improving performance.

Assignments are normally made for the appropriate sea, shore, or area tour.

The above GUARD III program does not apply to nuclear-trained personnel. A separate program, known as the Nuclear GUARD, provides for the guaranteed assignment of top-quality nuclear-trained personnel who are qualified for operational reactor plant duty.

The Nuclear GUARD program also encourages direct contact between those qualified for the program and their NMPC detailers. The program applies only to persons in the ET, EM, IC, MM, EN, and BT ratings, who have specific NECs. Specific options are detailed in a Nuclear GUARD letter sent to qualified individuals. Here are the general options:

(1) Persons serving in an operational nuclear billet at sea may request a guaranteed assignment to shore duty; they may also request sea or neutral duty, in a nuclear ship or at the homeport of their choice.

(2) Persons serving in a non-operational nuclear billet, or non-nuclear billet classified as sea or neutral duty, may request guaranteed assignment to a nuclear ship or to the coast of their choice.

(3) Persons serving on shore duty may request a guaranteed assignment to a nuclear ship or the coast of their choice.

Assignment to School Incentive

The Navy also has provisions to guarantee reenlistees a specific school. Generally, a sailor must meet the obligated service and entrance requirements for the appropriate school. Consideration of requests is based on: composite training, sea/shore rotation, paygrade versus skill requirement, and Fleet Reserve eligibility. Assignments to schools normally occur at the member's projected rotation date (PRD).

Changes in Rate or Rating

Since the Navy wants each sailor to serve in the rate or rating for which he has the greatest aptitude and interest, regulations provide for lateral changes in rate and rating. "Lateral change" means that you can change your apprenticeship field or occupa-

Figure 10–3 Among the Navy's modern schools is a computerized instruction center.

tional specialty without changing your paygrade. The program is rather complex, so that if you're contemplating a change in rate or rating, you would do well to check current directives or to consult with your career counselor, personnel office, or educational services office.

Change of apprenticeship field can be done by your commanding officer, and normally will be approved if a greater need exists in the apprenticeship you want to switch to. Changes in rate or rating may also be accomplished via formal school training or "in-service training," through direct conversion, through successful competition in a Navy rating exam, and, in rare cases, through forced conversion.

167

Nuclear Field Program (NFP)

The supervision, operation, and maintenance of naval nuclear power plants require a high level of competence. Consequently, all personnel assigned to operate the engineering plants of nuclear-powered ships are carefully screened, and rigorously trained in nuclear-power-plant theory and operation. Although it is expected that the majority of nuclear field personnel will volunteer for submarine duty, the nuclear surface-ship requirement must also be met. Therefore, not all persons in the nuclear field who volunteer for submarine duty will be assigned to it.

NFP training leads to qualification as a mechanical operator, electrical operator, or reactor operator. Mechanical operators are drawn from the MM rating, electrical operators from the EM and IC ratings, and reactor operators from the ET rating. All nuclear operators, regardless of rating, should expect to qualify as engineering watch supervisors.

Training, which requires more than a year of study, normally begins in boot camp, where the nuclear field candidate is screened and classified into one of the program ratings (MM, EM, IC, or ET), according to his capabilities and the needs of the service. According to his prospective rating, the NF trainee attends Class A rating training, which is from 2 to 5 months in length. On completion of Class A school, trainees are ordered directly to Nuclear Power School in Orlando for a 6-week fundamentals course. It is designed to provide instruction in general mathematics, physics, problem-solving techniques, and a simple introduction to power plants.

The basic nuclear-power course follows the fundamentals course. The basic course is 24 weeks long and covers all academic subjects required for an understanding of the theory and operation of a nuclear propulsion plant. Subjects include mathematics, physics, reactor principles, thermodynamics, radiological fundamentals, water chemistry, and the study of typical reactor-plant systems.

From Nuclear Power School, an NF trainee proceeds to one of the nuclear-power training units located near Idaho Falls, Idaho; Ballston Spa, New York; or Windsor, Connecticut. There the trainee is enrolled in a 24-week course of instruction qualifying him as a nuclear-propulsion-plant operator on one of several land-based nuclear reactor plants located at these places.

Two additional courses are available for graduates from the above training: the 13-week engineering laboratory technician (ELT) course, at the nuclear-power training sites; or the 13-week nuclear-propulsion-plant operator welding course (for MMs only), at the Naval Submarine School, Groton, Connecticut, or at the Naval Training Center, San Diego.

Basic requirements for entering the NF program: Meet the listed ASVAB or BTB (basic test battery) requirements; meet the minimum test score on the nuclear field qualification test (NFQT); be at least 17 but less than 24 years old; be a U.S. citizen and meet the eligibility requirements for a security check (you should at least pass an entrance National Agency Check [ENTNAC]); be a high school graduate; meet certain physical qualifications; and accept a commitment of six years' active service.

Submarine Training

Only volunteers are assigned submarine duty. More than 14 ratings (E-4 and E-5) and identified strikers are eligible for submarine training. All must be under 30 years of age before beginning training. They must meet certain test-score minimums and eligibility requirements for a secret clearance (although all applicants must first obtain a security clearance through an entrance National Agency Check [ENTNAC]).

Enlisted Basic Submarine School lasts eight weeks and is located at Groton, Connecticut. On completion of the basic course, 60 percent of the students are assigned additional training at Groton. Graduates will be assigned at least 12 months of duty aboard a submarine in commission or under construction.

Other Educational Opportunities

NAVY CAMPUS FOR ACHIEVEMENT (NCFA)

NCFA maintains a worldwide network of professional education specialists who assist Navy personnel in formulating their educational plans. NCFA also helps eligible persons take advantage of the in-service educational benefits of the GI Bill of 1966 and the Veteran's Educational Assistance Program (VEAP).

Key educational programs under NCFA are:

College Degree and Certificate Program: Under this program, Navy students may obtain academic degrees or vocational/technical certificates by combining education, training, and work experience received both in civilian life and the military. About 20 institutions of higher learning are part of this program. Some schools grant up to 75 percent of the degree requirements for prior education, training, and work experience. Navy students enrolled in this program are encouraged to seek financial assistance through other programs, like the Tuition Assistance Program or PACE.

Tuition Assistance Program: This program provides financial assistance to eligible personnel who attend higher-education institutions on a voluntary, off-duty basis. Tuition assistance may be provided to regular Navy personnel, Naval Reserves on continuous active duty and Naval Reserves ordered to active duty for 120 days or more. Tuition assistance cannot, by law, exceed more than 75 percent of the cost of tuition (up to 90 percent for E-5 and above with less than 14 years service); other expenses—including books, fees, and the individual's share of tuition—must be paid by the student.

Program for Afloat College Education (PACE): Under this program, even the sailor at sea has an opportunity to take college courses and, in some instances, vocational/technical courses. A number of fully accredited colleges and universities conduct tuition-free courses for seagoing students. These courses are taught by college teachers living aboard ship. When teachers are not on board, students can use study guides. Credits are assigned and transcripted just as if the courses had been offered on the campus of one of the participating institutions.

Instructor Hire Program: The purpose of this program is to enable commanding officers to hire qualified instructors to teach off-duty courses on a wide variety of subjects. The objective of

169

Figure 10–4 A sailor at sea must know which technical manual to go to and how to look up the critical information required to perform his daily tasks. Being at sea doesn't mean the end of personal study. He even has an opportunity to take college courses offered through PACE—the Program for Afloat College Education.

such instruction is to raise individual educational levels and to increase effectiveness on the job. Classes may be organized in academic, professional, technical, and vocational subjects at all educational levels. Instructors may be either military or civilian, but must be qualified in the subject or skill taught. Courses such as remedial mathematics, English, small engine repair, American history, and speedreading have been taught under this program. The student pays no tuition.

High School Studies Program: The Navy would like all personnel to complete high school before enlisting so they can be more effective in today's technical Navy. For those unable to do so, NCFA provides the opportunity to earn a diploma from your local high school, earn a certificate of high school completion, or qualify for a high school equivalency certificate. Books and tuition are provided by NCFA.

Servicemen's Opportunity College (SOC): Although SOC is neither managed nor funded by NCFA, it is available to sailors and is well-known to NCFA education specialists. SOC is a two- and four-year college program available to all members of the armed services. SOC, like the College Degree and Certificate Program, is based on partnerships with civilian educational institutions.

Enlisted Education Advancement Program: EEAP allows career enlisted personnel to obtain an associates degree in 24 months or less. Selectees receive full pay and allowances but must finance their own education. Applicants must have at least 4 years, or be an E-5 with a minimum of 3 years, but no more than 14 years active duty, and be willing to obligate for six years.

VA EDUCATIONAL BENEFITS

The Veterans Administration (VA) has two programs for veterans seeking financial assistance for education. For those with service between 1 February 1955 and 31 December 1976, assistance is available under the GI Bill of 1966. For those who entered the Navy on or after 1 January 1977, assistance is available under the Veterans Educational Assistance Program (VEAP).

GI Bill: Under the GI Bill of 1966, as amended, the VA provides financial assistance to veterans enrolled in approved educational institutions, such as high schools, junior colleges, or universities. Benefits are also available to veterans enrolled in approved correspondence schools, farm cooperative programs and OJT programs.

An eligible veteran is entitled to financial assistance for a period of 1½ months (or the equivalent in part-time training) for each month of active duty service, up to a maximum of 45 months. If an eligible veteran served on active duty for 18 *continuous* months or more, he or she is entitled to the full 45 months. The amount of financial assistance varies, depending on the number of courses taken and the number of dependents of the recipient. Active duty personnel eligible under this program are also eligible for certain in-service benefits.

Veterans Educational Assistance Program (VEAP): Like its predecessor above, VEAP is designed to provide sailors with financial aid to further their education. Unlike the GI Bill, VEAP requires voluntary rather than automatic participation by active duty sailors. You must elect to make monthly contributions from your paycheck, with the government adding two dollars for each dollar you contribute.

You may contribute between $25 and $100 per month in $5 increments. Once you decide to contribute to the fund, you must continue your contributions for at least 12 months. The maximum you can contribute is $2,700 (based on $75 for 36 months or $50 for 54 months). If you elect maximum participation, the government will have contributed $150 for each of these months (based on your $75 per month contribution) or $5,400. You may also make a lump sum contribution of $2,700 to the fund. The total accumulation will then be $8,100.

If you decide not to go to school after release from active duty, your deposits are refunded in full, but you forfeit the government contributions. Benefits from VEAP are also available to eligible persons who remain on active duty. The monthly payback is $225 per month for 36 months if you contributed $75 per month for 36 months. This will give you enough time to acquire a bachelor's degree in most colleges and universities. You have up to 10 years after separation from active duty to pursue your education and take advantage of the government contribution.

Commission Opportunities

If a commission is your goal, a number of programs can help you get one. The following officer programs lead to an appointment in the Naval Reserve for enlisted persons with bachelor's degree or higher:

Officer Candidate School (Men) Program
Officer Candidate School (Women) Program
Aviation Officer Candidate School Program
Navy JAG Corps Direct Appointment Program
Chaplain Corps Direct Appointment Program
Civil Engineer Corps Direct Appointment Program
Nuclear Power Instructor and Naval Reactor Engineer Direct Appointment Program

172

The requirements are generally the same for all programs: You must be a U.S. citizen, have a bachelor's degree from an accredited college or university, meet the age requirements for the desired program, be physically qualified, be serving on active duty in an enlisted status (in any rate and paygrade), and be entitled to an honorable discharge. Women applicants must meet the dependency requirements as outlined in the BUPERS manual. Applicants for OCS, AOC, NFOC, NAOC-AI, AEDO-AM, and OC(W) must have at least six months of obligated service remaining on their current enlistment upon assignment to the program. (Enlistments may be extended for one year to meet this last requirement.)

ENLISTED COMMISSIONING PROGRAM

The Enlisted Commissioning Program is an undergraduate education program for enlisted personnel on active duty who have previous college credit. Selectees will be ordered to ECP on a permanent change of station basis and enrolled as full-time students in a participating NROTC host college or university to complete their degrees in not more than 24 months. They will maintain their enlisted status during training with all pay and allowances but must pay all expenses incurred in the education program themselves. Upon completion of the program, ECP can-

Figure 10–5 If a commission is your goal, a number of programs can help you get one.

didates will be ordered to OCS at Newport. Upon graduation they will be commissioned ensign, USN, in the URL. Enlisted applicants must be between 22 and 31 years of age at time of enrollment and have completed 4 years but not more than 11 years of active service and be willing to obligate for 6 years upon enrollment.

NAVAL ACADEMY

Most midshipmen are appointed from among high school or prep school graduates, but about 85 enlisted men and women who have passed the entrance exams are appointed by the Secretary of the Navy. Enlisted candidates for Naval Academy appointments must be U.S. citizens, at least 17 but not more than 22 years of age in the entering year, unmarried with no children, with at least one full year of enlisted naval service and a minimum of 24 months' active obligated service. They must also meet certain physical requirements and be recommended by their commanding officer.

Midshipmen receive one-half of an ensign's base monthly pay, plus tuition, room, and board. On graduation, they receive a bachelor of science degree in one of 18 majors, and a commission in the regular Navy or Marine Corps.

BROADENED OPPORTUNITY FOR OFFICER
SELECTION AND TRAINING (BOOST)

This educational opportunity is designed for men and women who have leadership potential, but haven't had enough education to compete successfully for commissioning programs. Participants spend six months to two years at the Service School

Command in San Diego, where they study algebra, geometry, physical science, chemistry and communications skills. Through a program of individually tailored academic and military instruction, participants can acquire the knowledge they need to compete for admission to one of the other officer programs.

A BOOST applicant must meet certain requirements for admission to the program: Be an enlisted member on active duty in the Navy or Naval Reserve, have two years of active service as of 1 January of the year in which BOOST training begins, agree to accept the minimum service requirements if selected for a specific program, meet certain physical requirements, and be recommended by the commanding officer.

WARRANT OFFICER (WO) PROGRAM

Chief petty officers (paygrades E-7 to E-9) may apply under the WO program. There is no age requirement. Applicants must have completed at least 12 but not more than 24 years of naval service as of 16 January of the year in which they apply. Appointments are made to the grade of chief warrant officer (W-2). E-9s with two years in grade may apply for appointment to chief warrant officer (W-3).

Other specific requirements are that a candidate must be a U.S. citizen, physically qualified, a high school graduate or equivalent, have a "clean" record for at least two years, and be recommended by the commanding officer. Applications must be submitted before 1 April. They are considered by a board that is convened by the Secretary of the Navy in August or September. Names of selectees are released by an NMPC notice or an ALNAV (all-Navy commands) message. Nonselectees are not notified.

LIMITED DUTY OFFICER (LDO) PROGRAM

The LDO program is open to warrant officers with more than 2 years of service as warrants, and to enlisted personnel in paygrades E-6 through E-8. Enlisted applicants must have completed at least 8 but not more than 16 years of active naval service. E-6s must compete in the E-7 examination and be designated as "LDO selection board eligible".

The LDO program has the same basic requirements as the WO program. Deadline for application by WOs, E-7s, and E-8s is 1 April; the E-6 deadline is 16 May. Warrant applicants are appointed to the temporary grade of lieutenant (junior grade); all enlisted applicants are appointed temporary ensigns. If you accept the appointment, you must agree to remain on active duty for three years.

Enlisted persons may also enter the NROTC Scholarship Program, which can lead to a commission in the regular Navy or Marine Corps. You must be a U.S. citizen, under 27$\frac{1}{2}$ years of age on 30 June of the year you become eligible for commissioned status, be a high school graduate or equivalent, be physically qualified, and have a "clean" record. Tuition, fees, books, uniforms, and a monthly subsistence allowance are paid for by the NROTC Scholarship Program. The program is available at more than 50 civilian colleges and universities. An NROTC student can get a bachelor's degree in various academic fields, although at least 80 percent of the program's participants must be majoring in engineering, mathematics, physics, or chemistry.

MEDICAL AND DENTAL PROGRAMS

MSC of the Naval Reserve: The Medical Service Corps of the Naval Reserve program is open to qualified enlisted members on active or inactive duty. The program leads to a reserve commission. Applicants must be U.S. citizens, physically qualified, and must meet the requirements for an appointment (outlined in the BUPERS manual). Maximum age requirements are 39 years old for lieutenant, 38 for lieutenant (junior grade) and 35 for ensign.

Health Care Administration: The Medical Service Corps In-Service Procurement Program is a continuing program that allows senior regular Navy HM and DT personnel, in paygrades E-6 through E-9, to obtain a commission.

Armed Forces Health Professions Scholarship Programs: The Navy, along with the Army and Air Force, offers scholarships to qualified students in the health professions. To be eligible, students must be enrolled in or accepted for admission to study: medicine/osteopathy, dentistry, clinical psychology, or optometry. This scholarship provides up to four years' full tuition including books, fees, and necessary equipment, plus monthly pay. Selectees are commissioned as ensigns in the Naval Reserve. In return for the scholarship, students serve one year on active duty for each year in the program, with a three-year minimum, exclusive of periods of postgraduate professional education.

General Military Training (GMT)

This service-wide program provides the nontechnical orientation and follow-up training needed by everyone in the Navy. The training is designed to help Navy personnel fulfill their oath of service, and to inform them on matters affecting their morale, both as citizens and as members of the Navy.

Presentation methods include the use of closed-circuit television, lectures, plan-of-the-day notes, spots on internal radio programs, and general-interest films. There has been nearly an 80 percent reduction in the number of formal GMT sessions. The American Forces Radio and Television Service (AFRTS) outlets, which provide information and entertainment to forces overseas, are also used as GMT forums.

The following subjects are covered: blood donorship program, career counseling, character education, code of conduct, democracy and communism, dependents assistance, educational advisement, financial responsibility, health and fitness, human resource management, information security, legal assistance, naval safety, savings-bond program, sea power, Uniformed Services Health Benefits Program (USHBP) and voting.

An education and training program (ETP) is also administered by the Defense Department. This program deals chiefly with informational materials, such as pamphlets, movies, and booklets. It also produces various overseas "pocket guides."

LEADERSHIP TRAINING

It is a well-known fact that leaders are made, not born. Although leadership comes easier to some than to others, the process of becoming an effective leader is a difficult one, requiring years of training and a lot of practice. To assist you in understanding and accepting your responsibilities as a leader, the Navy will provide extensive leadership training at various times throughout your career. These courses are taught at all major training centers throughout the fleet and vary in length from 5 to 12 days.

From E-4 through E-6, Petty Officer Leadership will supply essential information concerning leadership principles and the practical application of these principles. The Petty Officer Leadership courses also provide information concerning methods of interpersonal communication, psychological factors affecting behavior, evaluation techniques, counseling skills, and Navy programs.

As you advance in rate, you will have more opportunities to exercise your authority as a leader; therefore, additional leadership training will be required. When you are selected for chief petty officer, you will have the opportunity to attend the Leadership Management Education and Training (LMET) course for leading chief petty officers. This course provides advanced training in efficiency and effectiveness, advising and counseling, skillful influence, problem solving, and process management. The course is geared to help you resolve the special problems you will face as a chief petty officer.

These courses, together with the leadership training you receive aboard ship and through other Navy training courses, will help you attain the level of skill required to become a professional Navy leader.

11. Navy Pay, Benefits, and Retirement

All Navy pay accounts are handled by the Navy Finance Center in Cleveland, Ohio, through a computerized pay and leave accounting system called JUMPS (Joint Uniform Military Pay System).

JUMPS sends you a monthly leave and earning statement (LES) showing the pay you've earned for that month, the amount you can expect to receive on your next two paydays, the allotments you have in effect, the deductions taken from your pay, and the status of your leave account. This information is also sent—in the LES form—to your disbursing office. The LES helps you check the accuracy of your entitlements and manage your own earnings more effectively.

JUMPS: The Personalized System

Since your monthly JUMPS leave and earning statement contains a great deal of information on you and your progress in the Navy, you should know how to read the form. Because the system is personalized, no two forms are exactly the same; but the following paragraphs give a block-by-block description of the sample LES in Figure 11–1.

Blocks 1, 2 and 4 should contain no surprises, but *block 5* may be something new to you—the unit identification code (UIC) of your present activity. This five-digit number is more important than it looks. The Navy uses this number to distribute all LESs. Your monthly LES is prepared at the Cleveland center; a copy is also forwarded to your disbursing office.

Blocks 6 through 8 won't be new to you either. PAY GRADE is your current paygrade, YRS is your total years of service (rounded "down" to the nearest whole year), and PEBD is your pay entry base date—the day you contracted for your military service.

Block 9 shows a clothing allowance, if applicable.

Block 10 is the date your enlistment expires. EAOS means "expiration of active obligated service"

Block 11 is not used.

Block 12 is the symbol number assigned to your disbursing office.

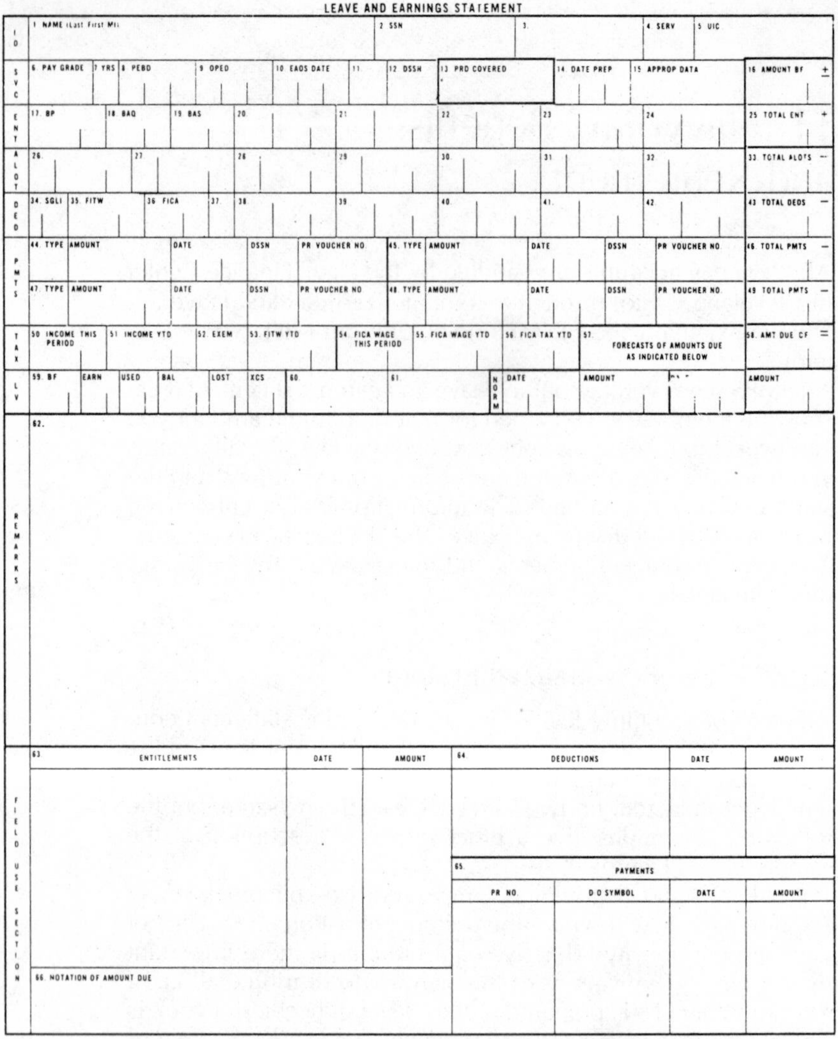
LEAVE AND EARNINGS STATEMENT

I D: 1 NAME (Last First MI) | 2 SSN | 3. | 4 SERV | 5 UIC

S V C: 6 PAY GRADE | 7 YRS | 8 PEBD | 9 OPED | 10 EAOS DATE | 11 | 12 DSSN | 13 PRD COVERED | 14 DATE PREP | 15 APPROP DATA | 16 AMOUNT BF +

E N T: 17 BP | 18 BAQ | 19 BAS | 20 | 21 | 22 | 23 | 24 | 25 TOTAL ENT +

A L O T: 26 | 27 | 28 | 29 | 30 | 31 | 32 | 33 TOTAL ALOTS −

D E D: 34 SGLI | 35 FITW | 36 FICA | 37 | 38 | 39 | 40 | 41 | 42 | 43 TOTAL DEDS −

P M T S: 44 TYPE | AMOUNT | DATE | DSSN | PR VOUCHER NO | 45 TYPE | AMOUNT | DATE | DSSN | PR VOUCHER NO | 46 TOTAL PMTS −

47 TYPE | AMOUNT | DATE | DSSN | PR VOUCHER NO | 48 TYPE | AMOUNT | DATE | DSSN | PR VOUCHER NO | 49 TOTAL PMTS −

T A X: 50 INCOME THIS PERIOD | 51 INCOME YTD | 52 EXEM | 53 FITW YTD | 54 FICA WAGE THIS PERIOD | 55 FICA WAGE YTD | 56 FICA TAX YTD | 57 FORECASTS OF AMOUNTS DUE AS INDICATED BELOW | 58 AMT DUE CF =

L V: 59 BF | EARN | USED | BAL | LOST | XCS | 60 | 61 | NORM | DATE | AMOUNT | AMOUNT

REMARKS: 62.

FIELD USE SECTION: 63 ENTITLEMENTS | DATE | AMOUNT | 64 DEDUCTIONS | DATE | AMOUNT

65 PAYMENTS: PR NO. | D O SYMBOL | DATE | AMOUNT

66 NOTATION OF AMOUNT DUE

Figure 11–1 Your leave and earning statement is a vital record of your pay, allowances, allotments, and deductions.

Block 13 indicates the pay period for which your LES was prepared.

Block 14 is the specific day your LES was prepared.

Block 15 includes the abbreviated pay appropriation account. MPN 71130 would be shown for regular Navy enlisted personnel.

JUMPS *Block 16* is brought forward from Block 58 of your last LES.

Blocks 17 through 25 make up the next important aspect of the LES—your entitlements. These blocks contain the amounts accrued in each item of pay entitlement during the period covered by the LES. (If an entitlement started, stopped, or changed during the period, an explanatory remark will appear in block 62.) *Block 17* (BP) is your basic pay . *Block 18* (BAQ—basic allowance for quarters) will be filled in if you are entitled to this allowance. If you are entitled to compensation for subsistence (BAS—basic allowance for subsistence) the amount will appear in *block 19.* (The specific kind of BAS will be stated in block 62.) Entitlements besides those already mentioned appear in *blocks 20 through 24* and are identified by a three-digit code; the reverse side of your LES explains these codes and others used on the statement. The items are totaled in *block 25.*

Blocks 26 through 32 show which of your allotments were in effect on the last day of the pay period. (A remark will be printed in block 62 when an allotment starts or stops. If an allotment is registered for a definite number of months, the expiration date will precede the monthly amount.) The most common classes of allotments are: D for dependency, S for savings, and I for insurance. The total of your allotments appears in *block 33.*

Blocks 34 through 43 contain deductions other than allotments. *Block 34* (SGLI) shows the amount being deducted for your servicemen's group life insurance policy—0.00 appears if you've decided not to be insured. The federal income tax withholding (FITW) for the period is printed in *block 35.* FICA (your social security tax), appears in *block 36. Block 37* is your current state of record. In *blocks 38 through 42* are miscellaneous deductions—such as forfeitures, state taxes, fines, recoupment of reenlistment bonuses, liquidation of advanced pay, charges for excess household goods shipments, etc. *Block 43* is the total of blocks 34–42.

Blocks 44, 45, 47 and 48 each represent a payment. There are five items within each payment block containing details of the payments. TYPE will be blank unless the payment was made to a third party, such as TXL (tax levy); or DEP (dependents' emergency evacuation). AMOUNT and DATE of payment are indicated. The DSSN (disbursing station symbol number) stands for the disbursing office making the payment. PR VOUCHER NO is the five-character payroll number. *Blocks 46 and 49* show totals of the payments.

Blocks 50 through 56 contain information on your personal taxes, both income tax and social security. *Block 53* is the total federal income tax paid to date, and *block 56* is the total social security paid to date (cumulative for the year).

Blocks 57 and 58 are important to you. *Block 58,* AMT DUE/CF is obtained by adding blocks 16 and 25, and subtracting blocks 33, 43, 46 and 49. This amount is the pay due on the last regular payday of the period covered. *Block 57* contains forecasts of your pay for the next month following the current period.

Blocks 59 through 61 show the status of your leave. Each month, your LES itemizes your leave brought forward (BF— *block 59*), the cumulative leave you have earned (EARN), and the leave you have used (USED) since the previous balance (BF) was established. The fourth item, BAL, shows the leave balance at the end of the LES reporting period. An adjustment for lost leave (LOST) is made only at the end of the fiscal year. Excess leave (XCS) is used only when your pay is checked for excess leave, which is done only at the end of your tour of active duty. *Block 60* shows the same information as block 53. *Block 61* shows your state taxes, if applicable, for year-to-date.

Last but not least is *block 62*—REMARKS. Within this sacred area will be those notations mentioned above, and many more. It's very important that you read this. Each remark pertains to you alone, and thus deserves your immediate attention.

180

Pay

BASIC PAY

Basic pay depends on your paygrade and years of service. It's the largest single item in your pay.

You will be paid twice a month, usually on the 15th and 30th. Payment is by check, whether you're aboard ship or on shore or overseas stations. Aboard ship, you may cash your paycheck when you present it, with the proper identification, to a representative of the disbursing office.

You may be paid while on leave if you make prior arrangements with your disbursing office. While on leave from an overseas station or enroute between duty stations, you can be paid at any military disbursing office—Navy, Marine Corps, Army, or Air Force. But you must have your last LES with you. Without it, you won't be paid. See page 181 for the 1980 11.7% pay raise.

BASIC ALLOWANCES

Allowances are extra payments designed to help you meet certain expenses of Navy life. Some are paid automatically; others you must apply for. Amounts and conditions under which they are paid are subject to change, so always check with your disbursing office for the latest information.

Basic Allowance for Quarters (BAQ): There are two kinds of BAQ. If you have dependents—wife, husband, children or stepchildren (under 21 years old), parent or stepparent—who rely on you for more than half of their support, you can draw married

Years of Service	E-1	E-2	E-3	E-4	E-5	E-6	E-7	E-8	E-9
Under 2	501.30	558.60	580.50	603.60	627.90	715.20	828.00	—	—
2	501.30	558.60	612.30	637.50	683.40	779.70	893.70	—	—
3	501.30	558.60	636.90	674.70	716.40	812.40	927.00	—	—
4	501.30	558.60	662.10	727.20	747.60	846.60	959.10	—	—
6	501.30	558.60	662.10	756.00	796.50	878.10	992.10	—	—
8	501.30	558.60	662.10	756.00	828.90	910.20	1023.30	1185.90	—
10	501.30	558.60	662.10	756.00	862.20	943.50	1056.30	1219.20	1413.60
12	501.30	558.60	662.10	756.00	893.70	992.10	1089.00	1251.60	1445.70
14	501.30	558.60	662.10	756.00	910.20	1023.30	1138.20	1284.30	1478.40
16	501.30	558.60	662.10	756.00	910.20	1056.30	1170.60	1317.90	1512.60
18	501.30	558.60	662.10	756.00	910.20	1072.20	1203.60	1348.50	1546.20
20	501.30	558.60	662.10	756.00	910.20	1072.20	1219.20	1381.50	1576.20
22	501.30	558.60	662.10	756.00	910.20	1072.20	1301.10	1462.80	1659.30
26	501.30	558.60	662.10	756.00	910.20	1072.20	1462.80	1626.00	1820.40

BAQ. (It is not payable, however, when you are occupying public [government] quarters.) Single BAQ is also available to a member without dependents. Persons entitled to BAQ (at the married rate) may also draw a Family Separation Allowance (FSA) if (1) their ship is away from homeport for more than 30 days; (2) if their dependents are not transported to their new duty station; or (3) if they are on temporary additional duty (TAD) for a period of 30 days or more. High-cost CONUS areas now qualify you for increased BAQ in the form of a Variable Housing Allowance (VHA). The rates vary by area and paygrade.

Basic Allowance for Subsistence (BAS): This allowance is paid if you are not provided meals at government expense. The rates vary, depending on (1) whether "rations in kind" (a government mess or government-provided mess) are not available; (2) whether permission has been granted to mess separately (commuted rations or leave rations); or (3) whether you are assigned to duty under emergency conditions where no government messing facilities are available. Separate rations (SEPRATS) are usually limited to people living off-base who have permission to eat away from their duty station. They are required to pay for each meal they eat in the mess hall.

SPECIAL PAY

This includes sea pay, foreign-duty pay, proficiency pay, reenlistment bonuses, and numerous types of hazardous-duty pay.

Sea and Foreign Duty: The rates vary for each paygrade. In general, sea pay begins the day you report aboard ship for duty. Increased rates are received after three years of accumulative sea duty. Foreign duty pay begins the day you report aboard a designated foreign duty station.

Selective Reenlistment Bonus (SRB): As the name implies, this retention incentive is paid to members serving in certain selected ratings or with certain NECs. These members can reenlist or extend their enlistments for a period of at least three years. SRB is computed by using applicable award levels, ranging from one to six. The actual amount received depends on your award level, multiplied by your monthly basic pay and the term of your enlistment. The maximum SRB is $16,000. The SRB program is extremely complicated. You'll do well to check with your career counselor or personnel office for additional facts.

INCENTIVE PAY FOR HAZARDOUS DUTY

Several types of incentive payments are made, the most common of which are aviation pay and submarine-duty pay. Rates for those two types are based upon your paygrade and years in service. Additional monthly incentive payments are made for flight-deck hazardous duty (FDHD), parachute duty, demolition duty, and experimental stress duty (such as high/low pressure tests).

Diving pay, for members serving in an authorized diving billet, varies according to the skills involved. A scuba diver gets less per month than a master saturation diver. Nuclear pay is available to certain qualified enlisted members. Payment is in the form of selected reenlistment bonus and goes up to a maximum of $20,000. Hostile-fire pay is paid to members subject to hostile fire. The only form of proficiency pay today is the special duty assignment (SDA) pay.

MISCELLANEOUS ALLOWANCES

Clothing: The first clothing allowance is the initial clothing monetary allowance (ICMA), which differs for men and women. Second is the special initial clothing monetary allowance (SICMA), for those who must wear a uniform not worn by the majority of Navy personnel. It goes to those assigned to certain Navy bands, for example, and is also paid upon promotion to CPO. The rates vary. Third is the clothing maintenance allowance (CMA), a monthly payment. This allowance is of two types: basic maintenance allowance (BMA) and standard maintenance allowance (SMA). For the recruit who draws ICMA, the BMA starts six months later; then, after 36 months of active service, the SMA begins.

Travel and Transportation (T&T): The T&T allowances are paid to you when you receive orders to travel. You might be authorized to travel by automobile (called POV—privately-owned vehicle) or by government or commercial transportation. In addition, you may be paid a per diem (daily) allowance to cover the cost of lodging, meals, and other incidentals not included in the cost of transportation. An allowance for transportation of dependents at government expense is also provided for a permanent change of station (PCS) if you're in paygrade E-4 with over two years' service. (If you're authorized transportation of dependents and own a mobile home that you're taking on a PCS move, you'll be reimbursed up to the actual amount of the mobile home move costs. Be sure to see your disbursing office for all of the details before making the move.

You can get an allowance for transportation of household goods (HHGs) or personal effects when you make a PCS move. A reduced weight allowance is sometimes allowed for temporary additional duty (TAD) orders. Partial reimbursement for incidental expenses incurred in a PCS move of HHGs is paid as a dislocation allowance (DLA). If you're an E-4 with dependents and have at least two years' service, you're eligible to receive DLA at the "with dependents" rate. Single personnel and married E-1s through E-3s, and E-4s with less than two years' service, may also qualify for this entitlement.

There are several other allowances specifically designed to help you with excessive costs while you're on permanent duty outside the U.S. Overseas stations will give you a housing allowance (HA), a cost-of-living allowance (COLA), and a temporary lodging allowance (TLA). The HA is based on the average cost of local housing in the overseas area, compared with your BAQ. Items considered include rent, utilities, minor maintenance expenses, and initial occupancy expenses. COLA is derived by comparing the cost-of-living in your overseas area with the average cost-of-living in the U.S. for a similar area. TLA provides partial reimbursement for the expenses incurred when you're moving to or from overseas areas. The amount is a graduated percentage, depending on the number of your dependents and the per diem allowances for travel to that specific area.

Other Pay Benefits

ALLOTMENTS

Through allotments, you may assign a part of your pay regularly to a spouse, parents, bank, or insurance company. (Through an allotment, you can take part in the Navy's Savings Bond Program, too.) Disbursing officers make out the allotment forms. Checks are mailed out monthly from the finance center at Cleveland.

INCOME TAX

Generally, all pay (except uniform, quarters, and subsistence allowances) is taxable as income. For this reason a part of your pay is withheld, just as it would be in most civilian jobs. The amount depends on the amount of pay and the number of dependents you have. When filling out your annual income-tax form, you will be able to credit the amount that's been withheld against the tax. Most ships and stations have an expert to assist you with tax matters.

FICA SOCIAL SECURITY

While on active duty, you build up social security and Medicare coverage. You work toward social security benefits in addition to Navy retirement benefits.

Other Benefits

There's no doubt that the pay in today's Navy is one of the real benefits. There are others, such as commissary and exchange privileges, medical care in uniformed services facilities or through CHAMPUS, and an extensive educational program. And other somewhat less tangible benefits also go to you (and in some cases to your family) because you're in the Navy.

Figure 11–2 A retiree takes advantage of his exchange privileges, one of the Navy's many benefits.

LEGAL ASSISTANCE

The legal assistance officer (LAO) can draw up wills, powers of attorney, deeds, affidavits, contracts, and many other documents. The LAO also can advise on transfer of property, marriage and divorce, adoption of children, taxation, personal injury, and other legal problems. The advice is free, and may help you avoid a lot of trouble. The Navy's legal assistance program is specifically designed to interview, advise, and assist sailors and their dependents who have legal problems. All matters are treated confidentially.

All sailors are given the opportunity to review their personal legal affairs and obtain necessary advice and counseling from qualified legal assistance officers. A handy legal assistance questionnaire (NAVJAG form 5801/10) can, when filled out completely, tell you if you need legal counseling or assistance.

FAMILY HOUSING PROGRAM

The family housing program includes: public quarters (government rental units), mobile-home parks, government-insured privately owned projects, and leasing of privately owned units. The Navy tries to make sure adequate housing facilities are available for sailors and their dependents, at a reasonable cost and within reasonable commuting distance. Where Navy housing is not available, housing referral offices are provided to assist in locating private housing in the community.

MORTGAGE HOUSING PLAN

Military personnel who purchase housing with FHA-insured mortgages may do so without paying the 0.5 percent insurance premium; this is paid for by the Department of Defense (DOD). As long as the serviceman remains on active duty, DOD pays the premium; on his release from active duty, he must pay this fee himself.

INSURANCE PROGRAMS

Dependency and indemnity compensation (DIC) and dependents indemnity compensation (DICOMP) provide protection for your family if you die. Eligible survivors—including unmarried widows, unmarried children under 23 (with restrictions), and certain parents—are provided basic benefits for members who die on active duty, or after separation as a result of a service-connected disability. Social security survivor's benefits are added to this income.

You can also have a $20,000 life insurance policy while on active duty, through servicemen's group life insurance (SGLI). The cost is $3.00 per month. You may request that the amount be reduced to $15,000, $10,000 or $5,000 with a reduction in your premium of 75 cents per $5,000 of coverage. (You may also decline this policy.) On separation, SGLI can be converted to a five-year non-renewable term policy.

UNIFORMED SERVICES HEALTH BENEFIT
PROGRAM (USHBP)

Free medical and dental care are provided to all active duty and retired personnel, and to dependent wives and children (with some exceptions). USHBP provides for diagnosis and treatment of acute medical and surgical conditions, immunization, maternity and infant care, and medication. Dependents admitted to a uniformed hospital pay a small daily rate. There is no charge for outpatient or dental care when authorized. Dependent dental care is limited.

CIVILIAN HEALTH AND MEDICAL PROGRAM
OF THE UNIFORMED SERVICES (CHAMPUS)

Dependents of active duty personnel, retired Navy personnel and their dependents, and dependents of members who died on active duty or after retirement may receive health care benefits as civilian outpatient and inpatient care under the CHAMPUS program.

Dependents with a serious physical handicap may also receive special education, training, rehabilitation and instructional care in civilian facilities.

A plan entitled "Interpretive Guidelines for Cooperative Care," permits military hospital commanders to send their patients to civilian medical facilities for diagnostic tests, physical therapy, and other services not available at some military hospitals. The cooperative-care plan was developed chiefly for hospital patients, though some CHAMPUS beneficiaries receiving psychiatric or psychological care as outpatients can also benefit.

COUNSELING ASSISTANCE

If a sailor is faced with a situation that is too involved for him to handle, the Navy has experts in human relations who are ready to advise and help with personal and family affairs. A Navy chaplain, like a minister or priest at home, can perform marriage ceremonies or baptisms, conduct funerals, and offer family counseling.

A large staff of professionally trained specialists is also available through the human resources management system (HRMS) for counseling of problems relating to alcoholism, drug abuse, family and personal affairs, and the effects of discriminatory practices, in and out of the Navy. Chapter 8 contains additional information on how to cope with alcohol and drug abuse (pages 112–14).

DEPENDENTS' OVERSEAS SCHOOLS

The Department of Defense (DOD) operates many educational facilities for minor dependents of all U.S. active-duty military and DOD civilian personnel stationed overseas. Of the more than 170 schools worldwide, 21 are Navy-sponsored. Navy schools extend from Spain to Japan, and from Iceland to the West Indies. Army and Air Force schools in many countries are open to Navy dependents. From first grade through high school, Navy juniors can receive an education overseas—at the Navy's expense.

FEDERAL CREDIT UNIONS

Most major Navy installations provide credit union facilities for Navy personnel. In addition, the Navy Federal Credit Union (NFCU) in Washington, D.C. serves enlisted men and women stationed in the D.C. area, in foreign countries, or aboard ships homeported in foreign countries. NFCU has worldwide wire facilities plus an 800-number which allows members to call toll-free, anywhere in the continental United States (CONUS). It offers signature loans, loans based on equal collateral, automobile loans, and personal loans for mobile homes and furniture. NFCU also has a policy of free life insurance that ensures loan protection for members. It pays interest on all savings accounts.

Leave

All personnel on active duty earn leave at the rate of 2½ days each month, except for brig time or unauthorized absences of 24 hours or more. *Earned leave* is the amount credited to you "on the books" at any given date. If you take more leave than you are entitled to, then you are taking *advance leave*. This means you have a minus leave balance on the books. *Excess leave* is the amount you exceed what you've earned, along with any advance leave you've been granted. Advance leave is taken out of the amount you would normally earn during the remainder of your enlistment.

Recruits are usually granted 14 days' leave on completion of training. Part of this is advance leave.

As leave accumulates, it is carried over from one fiscal year to the next. No more than 60 days can be carried over; thus, if you have 67 days' leave on the books on 30 September (the end of the fiscal year), you lose seven days.

Persons discharged with leave still on the books are paid a lump sum equal to their daily pay for each day. The most leave you can "sell back" in a 20-year career is 60 days. Those discharged with minus leave will pay approximately a day's pay for each day's leave owed.

Your commanding officer has the authority to grant (on a yearly basis) all earned leave, plus up to 30 days' advance leave. You cannot take more than 60 days' leave at any one time—except for reenlistment leave, which can go up to 90 days. Personnel lacking enough earned leave during an emergency can be granted advance and excess leave up to 60 days.

Convalescent leave is an authorized absence while you're under medical care and treatment. It must be authorized by your commanding officer on orders of a medical officer, or by the commanding officer of a military hospital. It is usually granted following a period of hospitalization, and is not charged as leave.

In a personal emergency, such as a death in the family or a serious illness, you will normally be granted emergency leave to take care of personal matters that no one else can handle. Such emergencies must be verified by the Red Cross.

Off-Duty Hours

Hobby shops, entertainment programs, and recreational facilities provide sailors on shore stations and many ships with plenty of leisure activities. More than 30 sports are offered in the Navy Sports Program, part of the special services organization of the Navy. There is also a program for high-caliber athletes in the Navy to be considered for selection to national and international-level sports.

The Navy Sports Program provides formal and informal organized sports. Formal programs include intramural, intercommand, area, and All-Navy competitions. Informal sports for self-directed activities use multi-purpose courts, gymnasiums, tennis courts, football, and softball fields.

Other offerings include marina facilities, golf, swimming, and so on. A variety of arts and crafts facilities, including woodworking, photography, ceramics, leatherworking, boatbuilding, and electric shops, are also available.

Service Organizations

Many organizations provide assistance and services to sailors and their dependents. Three of the most important are:

NAVY RELIEF SOCIETY (NRS)

Supported entirely by private funds, NRS assists sailors and their families in time of need. Though not an official part of the Navy, NRS is the Navy's own organization for taking care of its people. It is staffed and supported largely by naval personnel. Navy Relief can give you financial aid, in the form of an interest-free loan, a grant, or a combination of both.

Figure 11–3 Golf courses at naval installations offer the off-duty sailor a chance to improve his game.

AMERICAN RED CROSS (ARC)

The ARC supplies financial aid to naval personnel, does medical and psychiatric casework, and provides recreational services for the hospitalized. It also performs services in connection with dependency discharge, humanitarian transfer, emergency leave, leave extensions, and family welfare reports.

NAVY WIVES CLUB OF AMERICA (NWCA)

This group is composed chiefly of wives of enlisted men serving at sea in the Navy, Coast Guard, and Marine Corps. Besides its many social activities, NWCA sponsors a special scholarship

Figure 11–4 A family welcomes their sailor home from the sea.

fund for children of sailors. The club assists chaplains, and participates in the blood donor program and Navy Relief Society projects. Local chapters hold dances, picnics, and similar affairs, and participate in community projects.

Reenlistment

A sailor who completes an enlistment or cruise in the Navy and enters on another enlistment is said to reenlist, or "ship over." If you reenlist on the expiration date of your current term of service, it's called a "continuous service reenlistment." Those who reenlist after having been released from active duty make a "broken service reenlistment." The first type is better; on the broken service reenlistment, you may have to come back in a lower rate, and may not receive a bonus.

Reenlistment is not a right, it's a privilege. To earn that privilege, you must be recommended by your commanding officer, be physically qualified, and meet certain standards of performance. If you reenlist with no break in service, you reenlist "on board." Those with a break in service may reenlist only at recruiting stations.

Reenlistment

Because of large reenlistment bonuses offered in many specialties, many sailors choose to ship over for 6 years. But reenlistments for 2, 3, 4, 5, or 6 years are also available.

EXTENSIONS OF ENLISTMENT

There are two types of enlistment extensions. *Conditional extensions* may be made at any time during an enlistment, if you wish to qualify for advancement, for a cruise or deployment, for entrance into a service school, for any special program, for any other duty requiring additional obligated service, or to obtain maternity benefits for a dependent wife. Extensions are executed in increments of one or more months, not to exceed an aggregate of 48 months on any single enlistment. *Unconditional extensions* also may be made at any time for a period of not less than 24 nor more than 48 months.

SEPARATION

This term includes discharge, release from active duty, transfer to the Fleet Reserve, or transfer to the Retired List—including the temporary disability retired list (TDRL). Separations from active duty because of death or desertion are not included.

Types of Discharges

The type of discharge you receive will affect you after you leave the Navy. Certain discharges eliminate some veterans rights and benefits. And many employers will reject an ex-serviceperson who cannot produce an honorable-discharge certificate.

Honorable discharge: An honorable discharge means separation with honor. It is for one of the following reasons: expiration of enlistment, convenience of the government, dependency, minority, or disability. To receive an honorable discharge, the final average of your performance marks must be at least 2.7, with an average of not less than 3.0 in military behavior. You can't have been convicted by a general court-martial, or more than once by a special court-martial. This rule won't apply if you held an average of at least 3.0 during the last 24 months of active duty.

Regardless of a sailor's record, if he or she has received certain decorations or awards—ranging from the Medal of Honor through the Silver Life Saving Medal—then that sailor will be entitled to an honorable discharge, as long as subsequent service is good.

General discharge: A general discharge is given "under honorable conditions" for any reason that applies to honorable discharges, plus such other reasons as ineptitude and unsuitability. In most cases, a general discharge goes to those whose conduct and performance, though technically satisfactory, has not been good enough to deserve an honorable discharge.

Other discharges: These are the *undesirable discharge* (UD), *bad conduct discharge* (BCD), and *dishonorable discharge* (DD). The UD is given by administrative action for misconduct or breach of security; the BCD only by approved sentence of a general or special court-martial, and the DD only by approved sentence of a general court-martial (GCM).

FORMAL REASONS FOR DISCHARGE

There are 12 formal reasons for discharge:

A. Expiration of enlistment: The date an enlistment ends is normally the day before the fourth or sixth anniversary date of the enlistment, or the day before the 21st birthday in the case of a minority enlistee. Depending on circumstances, it may be later. If you have "lost" days—because of injury, sickness, or disease caused by misconduct—you can be kept on active duty until the lost days are made up. Also, your expiration date can be postponed if you are undergoing medical care, or awaiting trial or necessary official papers. All enlistments can be extended by the government during war or national emergency.

B. Fulfillment of service obligation: This discharge is given to regular Navy enlisteds on completion of their service obligation; or to reservists who are released to inactive duty after completing their active obligated service.

C. Disability: Given to sailors unable to carry out their duties because of a mental or physical disability.

D. Convenience of the government: This term includes general demobilization after a war, acceptance of a permanent commission, and for women, parenthood or pregnancy.

E. Dependency: Discharges for reasons of dependency or hardship are authorized when it is shown that undue and general hardship exists at home. The hardship must be permanent and must have arisen or worsened since the person joined the Navy. Dependency discharges, commonly called "hardship discharges," are not authorized merely for financial or business reasons, or for personal convenience.

F. Minority: Everyone under 18 years of age, must have the written consent of their parents or guardians to enlist. If they lie about their age in order to enlist, and this is later discovered, they may be (and in some cases must be) given a minority discharge.

G. Misconduct: A misconduct discharge is given to deserters who have not returned to military jurisdiction, to persons convicted by civil authorities, and to those who have made fraudulent enlistments.

H. In Absentia: Deserters absent longer than 18 months can be discharged *in absentia*. In absentia permits discharges for those who flee to foreign countries, where the United States has no jurisdiction, or for whom the statute of limitations has run out. This applies only during peacetime. Deserters who have committed more serious offenses would not be given *in-absentia* discharges. Authorities would continue searching for them until they're apprehended and brought back for court-martial.

I. Security: Given to personnel who are considered "security risks."

J. Sentence of court-martial: As the title implies.

K. Unsuitability: Given for such reasons as ineptitude, apathy, alcoholism, financial irresponsibility, as well as character and behavior disorders.

L. Personal abuse of drugs: This discharge is given to a drug abuser—identified either by a urinalysis test or the abuser's own admission.

M. Good of the Service: This type of discharge can be issued for the good of the service, instead of taking action under the Uniform Code of Military Justice (UCMJ). Although a sailor may request an administrative discharge under other-than-honorable conditions (OTH), he is still subject to the results of any disciplinary proceedings in his case.

Planning a Second Career

Planning for a second career or retirement is an important step that requires you to weigh many considerations. It can be a new life, offering fun, zest or relaxation—or it can be a headache with stress, strain, and boredom thrown in.

The first step is getting to know yourself, especially if your second career includes finding a job. Often a sailor undersells his talents—or worse yet, his potential. If you've climbed the promotion ladder to senior petty officer or officer, you've showed not only talent but potential and leadership. In examining your career, look for areas that will support your job aims in civilian life. Don't think that because you've spent 20 years as a signalman, the only job you're qualified for on the outside is that of a construction flagman. In general, don't limit yourself to work that's directly related to your Navy occupation. Your experience as a supervisor or manager is probably even more important in the eyes of an employer.

You should also brace yourself for the social and psychological shock that comes from leaving military society—where the rules and the paths ahead are well defined—and entering the civilian world. Don't expect this transition to happen overnight. It may take weeks, months, or even longer to make the adjustment.

A good way to begin is by listing potential occupations, and then checking the list with people who know you, to see if they agree with your choices. If you find that your list is not broad enough, prepare another based on major categories such as:

Federal, state, and local government
Big business
Small businesses, including the field of franchising
Agriculture
Public service institutions, such as hospitals
Education and educational services

Retirement

When enlisteds complete more than 20 years of active service, they are eligible for release to inactive duty and for transfer to the Fleet Reserve. After 30 years of combined active service and inactive duty in the Fleet Reserve, they are transferred to the Navy's Retired List. Those with 30 or more years of active service may be transferred directly to the Retired List.

Legislation effective 31 December 1977 prohibits the accumulation of "constructive service credit" and the option to transfer to the Fleet Reserve with less than 20 years service. Certain sailors are permitted to retire with less than 20 years of service if they have accumulated constructive service credit. In other words, sailors who have already accumulated constructive time can keep it; but, as of 31 December 1977, no one can accumulate any "new" constructive time.

Technically, the pay received by a Fleet Reserve member is a retainer, while that received by those on the Retired List is retired pay. Since both types are received by those who have "retired from active service," both are popularly called retired pay.

In either case, an estimate of your retired pay can be figured on this basis: 2½ percent of basic (active duty) pay times the number of years on active service. (This is an estimate, because other factors are used in computing the precise amount.) Thus, the longer the active service and the higher the paygrade, the greater the amount of retired pay.

A family protection plan called Survivor Benefit Plan (SBP) is available to provide for the continuation of up to 55 percent of retired pay to a deceased retiree's beneficaries. Enrollment in SBP at the maximum coverage level is automatic unless the retiree requests a lessor level or not to participate in the program. There are four types of coverages: spouse only; spouse and children; children only; and insurable interest coverage. The monthly amount deducted from retired pay varies with the program elected and the upward change over the years for Consumer Price Index adjustments. Your career counselor should be consulted for up-to-date SBP information.

Appendix J of this manual (page 559) has a separate listing of references that can assist you in planning your retirement and preparing for a second career. The following additional list may also prove helpful:

Navy Guide for Retired Personnel and their Families (NAVPERS 15891 series). Naval Military Personnel Command. Washington, GPO.

Provides comprehensive information on the rights, benefits, privileges, and responsibilities of members of the U.S. Navy and Naval Reserve entitled to retired or retainer pay.

Disability Separation (NAVEDTRA 46601 series). Armed Forces Information Service, Department of Defense.

Contains information about procedures leading to disability retirement or discharge and describes benefits accruing when physical disability ends an active military career.

Federal Benefits for Veterans and Dependents (VA Fact Sheet IS-1). Washington: GPO.

Contains general information concerning most federal benefits enacted by the Congress for veterans, their dependents, and beneficiaries.

195

Once a Veteran (NAVEDTRA 46602 series). Armed Forces Information Sheet, DOD.

Contains information on benefits available from the Veterans Administration and other federal agencies for service members who are to be released from active duty.

Reference Guide to Employment Activities of Retired Naval Personnel (NAVSO P-1778). Office of the Judge Advocate General, Department of the Navy, Washington, D.C. 20370.

Explains the Dual Compensation Act, conflict and interest, and other restrictions on civilian employment.

Your Social Security. Social Security Administration, U.S. Department of Health, Education and Welfare.

Contains information concerning social security benefits as a result of military service.

Your Personal Affairs (NAVEDTRA 46600 series). Office of Information for the Armed Forces, DOD.

Contains general information about matters affecting the personal affairs, including insurance and benefits, of service members and their families.

Opportunities in the Federal Service for Veterans (BRE 48). U.S. Civil Service Commission, Washington, GPO (25¢).

Explains the preference given to veterans in federal employment.

Retired Military Personnel in Federal Jobs (PMS 21). U.S. Civil Service Commission, Washington, GPO (25¢).

Explains the restrictions imposed upon retired military personnel in federal employment.

Federal Job Information Centers Directory (BRE 9). U.S. Civil Service Commission, Washington, D.C. 20415.

A listing of Federal Job Information Centers throughout the U.S. where answers can be provided to questions about federal employment.

Your Retirement System (Pamphlet 18). U.S. Civil Service Commission, Washington, GPO (85¢).

Contains questions and answers concerning the Federal Civil Service Retirement Law.

Survivor Benefit Plan for Retired Members of the Uniformed Services (NAVEDTRA 0503-LP-003-0280). American Forces Information Service, DOD.

Contains information about the Survivor Benefit Plan under which members of the armed forces can provide incomes for their widows and eligible surviving children after their death in retirement.

III. Ships, Planes, and Weapons

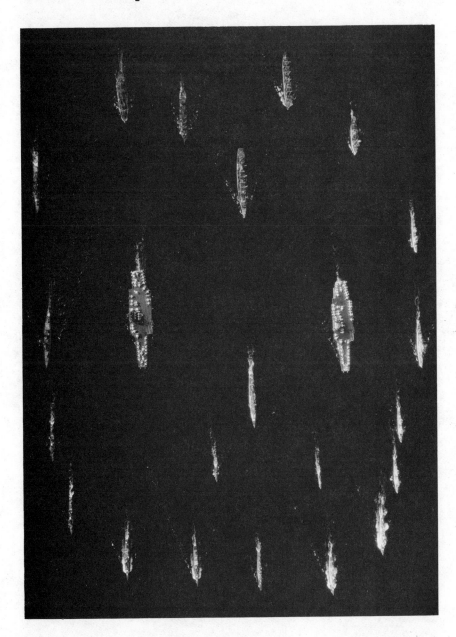

12. Ship Construction

Navy ships are highly complicated machines with their own propulsion plants, weapons, repair shops, and facilities to provide for the crew's living, sleeping, and eating needs. Although there are great differences in types and missions of ships (see Chapter 14) all ships have certain essential qualities.

Armament consists of all the weapons used to give battle to an enemy: missiles, guns, rockets, torpedoes, mines, depth charges, and aircraft.

Protection means the features that help a ship survive the effects of combat. Aside from weapons, a ship's sturdy steel construction is her best protection. Compartmentation, double bottoms, and other structural components all help provide protection.

Seaworthiness means those features that enable a ship to operate in high winds and heavy seas. A ship's stability, the way she recovers from a roll, is an essential part of her seaworthiness.

Maneuverability means the way a ship handles—in turns, in backing down, in going alongside another ship, or in evading enemy weapons.

Speed gets a ship to the scene of action quickly, helps her overtake an enemy, or avoid being overtaken by a superior force. Key factors are the power of her engines in relation to her size, and the shape of her underwater hull.

Endurance is the maximum time a ship can steam at a given speed. Most oil-powered ships can do so for one to two weeks without needing to be refueled. The Navy's nuclear-powered ships can cruise for years.

Habitability refers to whatever makes the ship comfortable for the crew. Adequate heads and washrooms, laundries, air conditioning, and well-lighted and roomy berthing and messing spaces are some habitability features.

Terminology

Part of your first cruise will be spent aboard ship. No matter how specialized your professional training may be, you still must be thoroughly familiar with basic nautical terminology and ship construction. You need this knowledge to carry out routine orders and commands, and to act quickly during combat or emergency situations.

Figure 12–1 Submarine maneuvering controls are more like those of an aircraft than those of a surface ship, since a sub moves up and down.

In some respects a ship is like a building. It has outer walls (forming the *hull*), floors (called *decks*), inner walls (called *partitions* and *bulkheads*), corridors (called *passageways*), ceilings (called *overheads*) and stairs (called *ladders*). But, unlike a building, a ship moves around—so you'll also have to learn new terms for directions and for getting around. When you go up the stairs from the dock to a ship, you're using the *accommodation ladder* to *go onboard;* and what might be an entrance hall or foyer in a building is the *quarterdeck* on a ship.

The forward part of a ship is the *bow;* to go in that direction is to *go forward.* The after part is the *stern;* to go in that direction is to *go aft.* The uppermost deck that runs the entire length of the ship from bow to stern is the *main deck.* Anything below that is *below decks* and anything above is *superstructure.* The forward part of the main deck is the *forecastle* (pronounced fōc'sle) the after part is the *fantail.* To proceed from the main deck to a lower deck you *go below.* Going back up again is *going topside.* As you face forward on a ship, the right side is *starboard,* the left side is *port.* An imaginary line running full length down the middle of the ship is the *centerline.* The direction from the centerline toward either side is *outboard,* and from either side toward the centerline is *inboard.* A line from one side of the ship to the other runs *athwartship.*

Basic Ship Structure

The hull is the main body of the ship. Structurally it is a big box girder, similar to a bridge. *Shell plating* forms the sides and bottom, and the *weather deck* or *main deck* forms the top. The intersection of the weather deck with the shell or side plating is called the *deck-edge* or *gunwale*. The intersection of the side plating with the bottom plating is called the *bilge*.

The shape and construction of the hull depends on the type of ship. Ships designed for high-speed operations—destroyers and cruisers—have long, narrow hulls with fine lines and rounded bilges. Aircraft carriers and auxiliary ships have hulls with square center sections, vertical sides and flat bottoms for greater carrying capacity. Submarines, designed to operate underwater, have hulls that are generally rounded in sections, like an egg, because that shape withstands great pressure.

Most ships have unarmored hulls. The hull consists only of the basic shell plating. Ships with armored hulls have a waterline armor belt of very thick steel running fore and aft to protect enginerooms and magazines from torpedoes or shellfire, and thinner armor steel plates on one or more decks to protect against bombs and shells.

The keel is the backbone of the hull. (Figure 12–2 shows the hull and other structural members discussed in this section). It usually looks like an I-beam running the full length of the ship with heavy castings fore and aft called *stem* and *stern posts*. *Frames,* fastened to the keel, run athwartships and support the watertight skin or shell plating. Most ships built for the Navy also have *longitudinal* frames running fore and aft. The longitudinal and athwartships frames form an egg-crate structure in the bottom of the ship called the *double bottom*. *Deck beams, transverse bulkheads,* and *stanchions* support the decks and help

Figure 12–2 A ship's deck is strengthened by transverse beams and longitudinal girders.

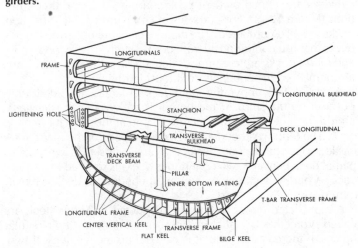

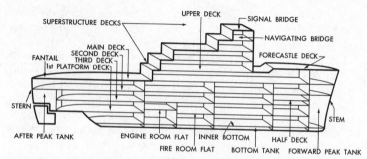

SUPERSTRUCTURE DECKS

UPPER DECK

SIGNAL BRIDGE

NAVIGATING BRIDGE

MAIN DECK
SECOND DECK
THIRD DECK
1st PLATFORM DECK

FANTAIL

FORECASTLE DECK

STERN

STEM

AFTER PEAK TANK

ENGINE ROOM FLAT
FIRE ROOM FLAT

INNER BOTTOM
BOTTOM TANK

HALF DECK
FORWARD PEAK TANK

Figure 12–3 Decks are named and numbered by their position and function on a ship.

strengthen the sides against water pressure. The framework is assembled by electric-arc welding, which is lighter than riveting.

Compartments are the rooms of a ship. Some compartments are called rooms, such as *wardroom, stateroom, engineroom,* but generally speaking, you don't use the word "room." You don't refer to the space where you sleep as the bedroom, nor the place where you eat as the dining room. They are called the *berthing compartment* and the *messdeck,* respectively.

The decks of a ship divide it into tiers or layers of compartments, in the same way the floors of a building divide it into stories. The deck normally consists of steel plates, strengthened by transverse (athwartships) deck beams and longitudinal (fore and aft) girders. On some ships the weather deck is covered by wood, to provide better footing in wet weather and to insulate below-deck space from heat and cold. Decks above the waterline are usually cambered, or arched, to provide greater strength and to drain off water.

Decks are named by their position in the ship and their functions (Figure 12–3). For purposes of compartment identification, decks are also numbered. The *main deck* is the uppermost of the decks that run continuously from bow to stern. The *second, third,* and *fourth decks* are continuous decks below the main deck and are numbered in sequence from topside down.

A partial deck above the main deck is named according to its position on the ship. At the bow it is called a *forecastle deck,* amidships it becomes an *upper deck,* and at the stern it is a *poop deck.* The term *weather deck* includes all parts of the main, forecastle, upper, and poop decks that are exposed to weather. A partial deck between two continuous decks is referred to as a *half deck.* A partial deck below the lowest continuous deck is a *platform deck.*

Armor-plated decks, or those constructed of armor steel, are called *protective* or *splinter decks,* in addition to their regular names. If there is only one, it is called a protective deck. If two, the heavier is the protective deck and the lighter the splinter deck.

Flats are platings or gratings installed only to provide working or walking surfaces above bilges.

Any deck above the main deck, forecastle deck or poop deck is called a *superstructure deck*. The top deck of an aircraft carrier is the *flight deck*. The deck below it, where aircraft are stored and serviced, is the *hangar deck*.

The *quarterdeck* is not a true deck or structural part of the ship, but merely a location designated by the commanding officer as a place for ceremonies.

Figure 12–4   Aboard an aircraft carrier, the main deck is the flight deck, and the superstructure is called the island.

Compartmentation and Watertight Integrity

If a ship were built like a rowboat, one hole below the waterline could sink it. To prevent this from happening, naval ships are built with watertight bulkheads, which divide the hull into a series of watertight compartments. Cargo ships have widely spaced bulkheads in order to provide large hold areas. Ships designed to carry troops or passengers have smaller holds, and much of the interior is divided into smaller living compartments. Navy vessels are divided into many compartments, so that in case of damage flooding can be limited to as few compartments as possible.

Watertight doors and *watertight hatches* allow access through all bulkheads and decks. Any ship could be made virtually unsinkable if it were divided into enough watertight compartments; but too much compartmentation may interfere with the arrangement of mechanical equipment and with the ship's operation. Today's ships are designed so that a given number of compartments must be flooded before the ship will sink.

Large ships have outer and inner *double bottoms*. These are divided athwartships and longitudinally into tanks, which are used for fuel oil, boiler-feed water, fresh water, or sea-water ballast. In armored hulls the double-bottom compartmentation may extend past the turn of the bilge (where the bottom meets the side of the hull) and all or part way up the side, as protection against torpedoes and other weapons.

Tanks at the extreme bow and stern, called the *forward peak* (or *forepeak*) tank and the *after peak* (or *aftpeak*) tank, are used for trimming the ship. Sometimes they may carry potable (drinking) water.

A strong watertight bulkhead at the after side of the forepeak tank is called the *collision bulkhead*. If one ship rams another head on, the bow structure would collapse to a point, hopefully, somewhere forward of the collision bulkhead, thus preventing flooding of compartments aft of it.

All tanks are connected to a pumping and drainage system so

Figure 12–5 Compartment and deck numbers are assigned starting with the main deck.

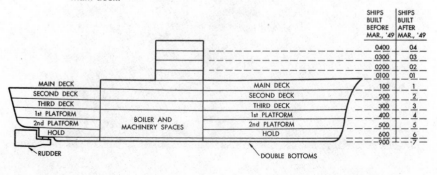

that fuel, water, and ballast may be transferred from one part of the ship to another or pumped overboard.

Maintenance of *watertight integrity* is a function of damage control (Chapter 18). All doors and hatches through watertight bulkheads or decks must also be watertight. Wherever water, steam, oil, air piping, electric cables or ventilation ducts go through a watertight bulkhead or deck, the hole is plugged by a stuffing tube, pipe, spool or other device to prevent leakage. All watertight doors and hatches carry markings that determine when they may not be opened (See pages 315–317.)

Compartment and Deck Numbering

Trying to find your way around a ship that is several hundred feet long, with many decks, is like trying to get around in a strange town where the street signs have been torn down. This is why the compartment numbering system was devised. It gives each compartment an "address," so that you can go directly to any designated compartment—once you understand the system.

Every space aboard ship (except for minor spaces, like peacoat, linen, and cleaning-gear lockers) is assigned an identifying letter-number symbol, which is marked on a label plate secured to the door, hatch, or bulkhead of the compartment. There are two numbering systems, one for ships built before March 1949, the other for ships built since then.

SHIPS BUILT BEFORE MARCH 1949

The compartment designation first has a letter that tells in which of three divisions the compartment is located. The letter is followed by three digits. The first digit indicates the deck, and the last two indicate the number of the compartment within the division. Even numbers indicate port side and odd numbers starboard side on that deck. A letter following the digits indicates the primary use of the compartment.

Divisions of the ship are: A (from the bow to the forward bulkhead of the engineering spaces), B (all engineering spaces), and C (everything aft of the engineering spaces). Decks are numbered from the main deck down, 100, 200, etc., and from the deck above the main deck up, 0100, 0200, etc. Double bottoms are always numbered in the 900 series, no matter how many or how few decks the ship has.

The primary use of a compartment is indicated by the following letters:

A—Supply and storage	M—Ammunition
C—Control	T—Trunks and passages
E—Machinery	V—Voids
F—Fuel	W—Water
L—Living quarters	

For example, C-217-A identifies a compartment in the C, or after part of the ship, on the second deck below the main deck, starboard side, which is used for supply and storage.

SHIPS BUILT AFTER MARCH 1949

The compartment numbers contain the following information: deck number, frame number, relation to the centerline of the ship and use of the compartment.

The *deck number* is the first part of the compartment number. Where a compartment extends to the bottom of the ship, the number assigned to the bottom compartment is used.

The *frame number,* the second part of the compartment number, is found at the forward end of the bulkhead of a compartment. If the bulkhead is between frames, the frame number is forward of the bulkhead.

The third part of the compartment number refers to the compartment's relation to the centerline. Compartments located on the centerline carry the number 0. Those to starboard have odd numbers, while those to port have even numbers. Where two or more compartments with the same deck and frame number are entirely to starboard or port of the centerline, they are numbered consecutively odd or even, from the centerline moving outboard. Thus, the first compartment outboard of the centerline to starboard is 1, the second is 3, and so on. The first compartment outboard of the centerline to port is 2, the second is 4, and so on.

When the centerline of the ship passes through more than one compartment, the compartment having that portion of the forward bulkhead through which the centerline of the ship passes, carries the number 0, and the others carry the numbers 01, 02, 03, etc.

The fourth and last part of the compartment number is the letter that identifies the compartment's primary use. On dry- and liquid-cargo ships, a double-letter identification designates cargo-carrying compartments as follows:

A Dry stowage—storerooms, issue rooms, refrigerated compartments.

AA Cargo—cargo holds, cargo refrigerated compartments.

C Ship and fire control operations—CIC, plotting rooms, communication centers, radio, radar, sonar operating spaces, pilothouse.

E Engineering control centers (manned)—main propulsion spaces, boiler rooms, evaporator rooms, steering gear rooms, auxiliary machinery spaces, pumprooms, generator rooms, switchboard rooms, windlass rooms.

F Oil Stowage (ship's use)—fuel oil, diesel oil, lubricating oil, and fog oil compartments.

FF Oil stowage (cargo)—all types of oil in cargo.

G Gasoline stowage (ship's use)—tanks, cofferdams, trunks, and pumprooms.

GG Gasoline stowage (cargo)—all gasoline in cargo.

K Chemicals and dangerous materials (other than oil and gasoline)—stowage, either for ship's use or as cargo.

L Living spaces—berthing and messing spaces, staterooms, washrooms, heads, brigs, sickbays, hospital spaces, passageways.

M Ammunition—magazines, handling rooms, turrets, gun mounts, shell rooms, ready service rooms, clipping rooms.

Q Spaces not otherwise designated—shops, offices, laundry, galley, pantries, unmanned engineering or electrical spaces.

T Vertical access trunks—escape trunks or tubes.

V Voids—cofferdam compartments (other than gasoline), void wing compartments, wiring trunks.

W Water—drainage tanks, fresh water tanks, peak tanks, reserve feed water tanks.

Hull Reference Terms

Ballast: Weight added in a ship's inner bottom to balance her topside weight, or to keep her down in the water under light loads. Some ships carry permanent concrete ballast. Others pump salt water into tanks for the same purpose.

Bilge Keels: Long, narrow fins fitted to both sides of the hull at the turn of the bilge to prevent the ship from rolling.

Bulwarks: Vertical extensions above the deck edge of the shell plating. Bulwarks are built high enough to keep men and equipment from going overboard.

Draft: The vertical distance from the waterline to the keel. Draft is measured in feet and inches, by scales marked on the hull at the stem and stern post. Draft numbers are six inches high and spaced six inches apart. The bottom of each number indicates foot marks, the top indicates half-foot marks.

Freeboard: Vertical distance from the waterline to the weather deck.

Lifelines: Light wire ropes supported on stanchions. They serve the same purpose as bulwarks.

Propeller Guards: Steel braces at the stern, directly above the propellers. They prevent them from striking a dock, pier or another ship.

Stem: The point of the hull at the bow, where port and starboard sides meet.

Stern: The point of the hull at the after end, where both sides of the ship meet.

Trim and List: *Trim* refers to the relation between the fore and

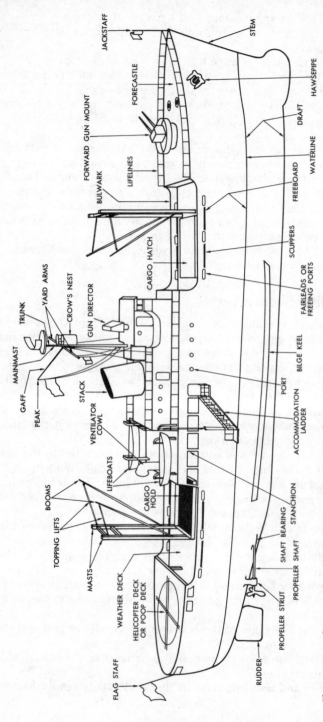

Figure 12–6 These are the principal parts of a typical auxiliary ship.

aft draft. A ship properly balanced fore and aft is "in trim," otherwise she is "down by the head" or "down by the stern." *List* refers to athwartships balance. A ship with one side higher than the other has a "starboard list" or "port list." List is measured in degrees by an inclinometer, mounted on the bridge, exactly on the centerline of the ship.

Waterline: The line where the hull meets the surface of the water.

Superstructure

The superstructure includes all structures above the main deck. The superstructure will vary according to the type of ship, but all ships have a wheelhouse, bridge, signal bridge, chart room, combat information center, radio room, and probably a sea cabin or emergency cabin for the captain. (These are discussed later in this chapter.)

The superstructure is topped off by the mast. In its simplest form, a mast is a single pole, fitted with a yardarm (spar) that extends above the ship and carries flag halyards, and navigational and signal lights. Generally a mast consists of several structural members in tripod form. In addition to the usual yardarm, the mast may support various electronic devices, radar antennas, and radio aerials.

On older ships, and particularly on small escort and patrol craft, the mast is a distinct feature. If the ship has two masts, the one forward is called the *foremast,* the one after the *mainmast.* On single-masted ships, the mast, whether forward or amidships, is usually part of the superstructure and is simply called "the mast."

The top of a mast is called the *trunk.* The top of the forward mast is the *foretrunk,* while the top portion of the main mast is the *maintrunk.* The *pigstick* is a slender vertical extension above the mast from which is flown the ship's commission pennant or an admiral's personal flag. The *gaff* extends abaft the mainmast. It is from the gaff that the national ensign is flown when the ship is underway.

The small vertical spar at the bow and the slightly raked one at the stern are called the *jackstaff* and *flagstaff,* respectively. When a Navy ship is at anchor or moored, it flies the union jack on the jackstaff and the national ensign on the flagstaff from 0800 to sunset.

The *stack* of a ship serves the same purpose as the smokestack on a power plant ashore. It carries off smoke and hot gases from the boilers, and exhaust from the diesel engines. (Nuclear-powered ships do not need stacks, since their reactors produce no smoke or gas.) Some diesel-powered ships have their exhaust in the sides. On some new ships the masts and stacks have been combined to form large towers called *macks*.

Propulsion Plant

A typical steam propulsion plant consists of *boilers, main engines, reduction gears, propeller shafts* and *propellers*. There are many variations, involving turbo-electric drive, direct diesel drive, diesel-electric drive and gasoline engines. Nuclear-powered ships have steam propulsion, but the steam is produced in a reactor instead of in oil-fired boilers.

A *boiler* consists of a box-like casing containing hundreds of water-filled steel tubes. These tubes are arranged so that heat from the fireboxes passes over them. Fuel oil, heated and sprayed into the fireboxes under high pressure, burns intensely, turning the water into steam. The steam then flows through pipes to the turbines. *Forced-draft blowers* increase the air pressure—either in the fire rooms where the boilers are mounted, or in the boilers themselves—for better combustion. Fresh water used in the boilers is made from salt water by *evaporators* and *condensers*.

A *turbine* consists of a revolving rotor, with several rows of blades mounted in a steam-tight casing with several rows of stationary blades. Rotor and casing blades are set in alternate rows. Thus, as the steam passes through the turbine, each row deflects the steam to the next row. Most turbines have both high pressure (HP) and low pressure (LP) stages. After steam has passed through both stages, it is cooled, condensed into water, and then returned to the boilers.

Turbines cannot be reversed, so to reverse the shaft, a *backing turbine* has to be installed, or else one section of the main turbine called an *astern element* is fitted inside a separate casing. Because backing turbines or astern elements have fewer rows of blades than the main turbine, they produce less power. A ship never has as much power for backing down as she has for going ahead.

Reduction gears connect turbines and shafts. They are required because turbines operate most efficiently at several thousand rpm, but propellers are not very effective above 400 rpm. With reduction gears, two turbines frequently drive one shaft.

In ships where the main drive is by electric motors, the current is generated either by steam turbines (turbo-electric) or diesel engines (diesel-electric). Submarines powered by diesel engines use electric drive when submerged, but their motors draw current from storage batteries that are charged by diesels when running on the surface.

Propeller shafts carry the power to the propellers. They run

from the reduction gears through long watertight spaces, called
shaft alleys, in the very bottom of the ship. They enter the water
through *stern glands* and *stern bearings* and may be supported
outside the hull by *struts.*

Propellers drive the ship. All aircraft carriers and most cruisers
have four propellers. Most older destroyers have two, as do older
submarines. Newer destroyer types and most nuclear submarines
have one propeller. Ships are classed as four-screw, two-screw
or single-screw types. Newer single-screw-type ships have ad-
justable-pitch propellers. With this type of propeller, instead of
reversing the direction of rotation to back down, the curvature of
the blades is reversed.

For relatively small ships which need no more than 5,000–
6,000 horsepower, diesel engines are frequently used. Diesels
are lighter, take up less space and are more efficient than steam
turbines. The diesel can be coupled directly to the shaft through
reduction gears and perhaps a clutch; or it can drive a generator
which produces current for the main drive.

Gasoline engines are very dangerous for marine use because
the highly volatile gas fumes are heavier than air and tend to collect in such places as the bilge, where the slightest spark can
cause an explosion. Diesel fuel is much safer because it does not
vaporize as readily.

NUCLEAR POWER PLANT

A nuclear power plant uses a reactor (instead of oil-fired
boilers) to provide heat for the generation of steam. The primary
system is a circulating water cycle, consisting of the reactor,
loops of piping, primary coolant pumps, and steam generators.
Heat produced in the reactor by nuclear fission is transferred to
the circulating primary coolant water, which is pressurized to
prevent it from boiling. This water is then pumped through the
steam generator and back into the reactor by the primary coolant
pumps. It can then be reheated for the next cycle.

In the steam generator, the heat of the pressurized water is
transferred to a secondary system, where water is turned into
steam. This secondary system is isolated from the primary system.

From the steam generator, steam flows to the engineroom
where it drives the turbo-generators which supply the ship with
electricity, and the main propulsion turbines which turn the propeller. After passing through the turbines, the steam is condensed
and the water is fed back to the steam generators by feed pumps.

The generation of nuclear power does not require oxygen.
Thus, submarines can operate completely submerged for extended periods of time.

During the operation, because there are high levels of radiation around the reactor, men are not permitted to enter the reactor compartment. Heavy shielding protects the crew so that they receive less radiation than they would from natural sources ashore.

Nuclear power plants give a ship the advantage of unlimited endurance at high speed. Instead of refueling every few thousand miles, as oil-burning ships do, a nuclear-powered ship can operate for years on one reactor core. This means they require far less logistical support or maintenance. Such ships can be better sealed against NBC attack, and they emit no corrosive stack gas. As of 1 March 1981, the Navy had a total of 126 nuclear-powered ships in service; of this number 114 are submarines and the remaining 12 are surface ships—3 carriers and 9 cruisers.

Figure 12–7 The combat information center (CIC) is the nerve center of a ship.

Steering

Any ship or boat is steered by a rudder. The rudder is controlled by a tiller in an open boat (such as a motor whaleboat or motor launch), and by a wheel in the cockpit of a larger boat or on the bridge of a ship. In a boat, the motion of the wheel is transmitted to the rudder by a cable or shaft. On a ship the rudder is turned by an electric or steam steering engine in the steering-engine room. This electrical or hydraulic engine is controlled by the wheel on the bridge.

A rudder acts by the force of water pushing against one side of it. There is no rudder action when the ship is motionless. The greater the speed, the greater the effect the rudders have. That's why they are usually mounted just astern of the screws, where the wash pushes directly against them. When a ship is backing down, the propeller wash goes forward and the rudder has very little effect, especially at slow speeds.

To prevent loss of control in case of damage to the bridge (sometimes called the main conn), there is usually a second steering wheel mounted elsewhere (called the secondary conn). If that wheel is disabled, the ship can be hand-steered by several men using special gear in the steering-engine room.

When a single-engine ship or boat moves at low speed, there is a tendency for the stern to swing to one side or the other. This is due to a *side effect* set up by the propeller. The blades below the shaft get a better bite in the denser water and push the stern sideways. This effect is even more noticeable when the ship is backing down, because the propeller wash is moving forward and exerts no force on the rudder.

Ships or boats with two screws can be steered fairly well without a rudder by using the engines. If one screw turns faster than the other, the bow will swing toward the slower screw. If one screw goes ahead while the other goes astern, the bow of the ship will swing toward the backing screw. Boats, and even very large ships, can turn within their own lengths using this method.

Ground Tackle

This term covers all the gear used to anchor a ship or moor it to a buoy. A ship is *anchored* when it is held in position by an anchor on the bottom, and *moored* when it is made fast either to a buoy or a pier. A ship is moored to a buoy by anchor chain, but moored to a pier by mooring lines. Details on the ground tackle (pronounced *tay-kle*) are contained on pages 413–22.

All ground tackle is located on the forecastle. Some ships, particularly amphibious craft, may also carry a stern anchor used in retracting, or in hauling off from the beach.

Ladders and Booms

Although not permanent parts of the hull, they are rigged out for use when necessary.

Boat Boom: A spar swung out from the ship's side from which boats can be hauled out or made fast. This permits boats to ride safely alongside when the ship is anchored.

Accommodation Ladder: A "stairway" suspended over the side of the ship, with a platform at the bottom that serves as a landing for boats. A *boat rope* or *sea painter* is provided to secure boats alongside while they load and unload.

Brow: A form of gangway used when the ship is moored alongside a pier or "nested" alongside other ships. Its size and construction depend on the size of the ships and the distance from the ship to the pier.

Chains: A small platform rigged out over the side for use by the leadsman in taking soundings.

Ship's Equipment and Operations

Much of the hull space in most ships is taken up by the engines, engineering equipment, and related piping and electrical systems.

Fire rooms contain the boilers which provide steam for the main engines. The enginerooms contain the main engine and reduction gears, which drive the ship. Auxiliary enginerooms contain generators that produce electricity for the ship, as well as evaporators and condensers to make fresh water out of salt water. The steering engineroom contains the machine which powers the rudder. Fuel-oil tanks carry the oil burned in the boilers.

ELECTRICAL SYSTEM

A large ship has hundreds of electric motors driving everything from fans and tape decks to 50-ton elevators. Every other system in the ship depends on electric motors. The main power supply is produced in the engineering spaces by steam-driven generators. Emergency diesel-electric generators in other parts of the ship automatically cut in to supply power if the main generators are disabled for any reason.

DRAINAGE SYSTEM

This system includes the piping, valves, and pumps that discharge water from the ship. Its functions include the supply of water for flushing systems and firefighting, and the removal of sea water that enters the hull because of damage, collision, or heavy weather. The main eductor is a large pipe in the bottom of the ship, to which other drain pipes are connected. The secondary eductor is a smaller pipe running the length of the ship. This system connects all watertight compartments. Boiler rooms have independent drainage systems and sea valves. Motors and valve controls for boiler-room centrifugal pumps are located on higher decks so that they can be operated even if the boiler room is submerged. Parts of the system can be used to flood compartments when counter-flooding is required for damage control.

VENTILATION SYSTEM

This system includes air supply, exhaust, and air-conditioning equipment. There are many separate systems so that ducts do not have to run through watertight bulkheads.

FRESH-WATER SYSTEM

Water for the crew—for drinking, showers, and cooking—and for boilers is provided by this system. Fresh-water tanks may be filled in port from shore supplies. At sea, fresh water is made from salt water by condensers and evaporators.

SALT-WATER SYSTEM

This system provides water for fire protection, including turret sprinkling, magazine flooding, NBC washdown, and flushing. Flushing water may come directly from the fire main or from separate lines. The fire main is a large pipe running the length of the ship, with risers and branch mains connected to it.

FUEL-OIL SYSTEM

This system includes fuel-storage tanks, filling lines, and feed lines to the boilers. It also includes lines and connections for pumping oil from one tank to another to control trim or list when the ship is damaged.

COMPRESSED AIR SYSTEM

Compressors, storage tanks, and high-pressure lines to eject gases from guns after firing are part of this system. Compressed air is also used for testing and blowing out compartments; for charging torpedoes; and for operating pneumatic tools, dispatch tubes, and other equipment.

MAGAZINES

Ammunition for all guns is stored in magazines, which are placed well below the waterline whenever possible. Projectiles and powder may be stored in separate compartments. In case of fire, all magazines can be flooded by remote control (or automatically, with heat-sensitive sprinkler systems). Ammunition is passed to handling rooms, where hoists take it up to the gun mounts or turrets.

CARGO HOLDS

Cargo holds are large spaces, with hatches opening on the main deck, where auxiliaries carry material for other ships.

STOREROOMS

Storerooms are spaces where ships carry their own supplies. These may be clothing, dry or refrigerated provisions, and various types of spare parts and supplies.

CREW ACCOMMODATIONS

The many compartments throughout the ship include the wardroom, officer's cabins (or staterooms), berthing compartments, pantrys, messes, heads, washrooms, and sickbay. Other spaces provided for the health and comfort of the crew include barber and tailor shop, cobbler shop, laundry, galleys, bake shops, butcher shops, library, chapel, ship's store, soda fountain, reception room and hobby shops. Some larger ships, such as aircraft carriers, have several of each of these "services"-type compartments.

SHOPS AND OFFICES

Besides offices for the captain and executive officer, a ship has office space, or a separate office, for every department and activity on board. Even a small ship will have a carpenter's shop and electrical shop. Larger ships, such as tenders and repair ships, will have print shops, photographic laboratories and many special repair shops handling everything from typewriters to torpedoes.

BRIDGE

This is the primary control position for the ship when she is underway, and the place where all orders and commands affecting the ship's movements and routine originate. The OOD is always on the bridge when the ship is underway. The captain is on the bridge during general quarters, during most special sea evolutions, and when the ship is entering and leaving port. The ship can also be handled from the *secondary conn* (secondary control station), the GQ station for the executive officer. Thus if the bridge is knocked out or the captain disabled in battle, the executive officer can take over.

BRIDGE AND PILOTHOUSE EQUIPMENT

Sometimes called the wheelhouse, the pilothouse contains equipment and instruments used to control the movements of the ship. Usually the bridge extends out on both sides of the pilothouse. Some pilothouse equipment is duplicated on the bridge.

Ship Control Console: This consists of the engine and propeller order sections, which control the speed and direction (ahead or astern) of the ship. The *engine order section* has a dial for each engine, divided into sectors marked flank, full, standard, $2/3$, and $1/3$ speed ahead; stop; and $1/3$, $2/3$, and full speed astern. When a hand lever is moved to the speed sector ordered by the OOD, the engineroom watch sets the engine throttle for the same speed and notifies the bridge by moving an answering pointer to the same sector. The ship control console is manned by the lee helmsman, who is sometimes also a telephone talker. The *propeller order section* enables the OOD to make minor changes in speed by ordering the enginerooms to increase or decrease the rpm of the propellers.

Steering Control Console: This contains the controls and indicators required to maintain the course of the ship. The steering wheel (helm) is operated by the helmsman. On the panel in front of him are various indicators and switches. The ship's course indicator is a gyro compass repeater that shows the ship's true course. Another indicator shows the course to be steered. Two more important indicators show the rudder angle (number of degrees) left or right of amidships, and the helm angle (number of degrees) left or right of amidships.

Tachometer: This is the same type of instrument used on a sports car; it shows shaft rpms. There's a tach for each propeller.

Lighting Panels: The two primary lighting panels in the pilothouse are the signal and anchor light supply and control panel and the running lights supply control panel.

Lights installed on combatant ships usually include aircraft warning lights; blinker lights; breakdown, man overboard, and underway replenishment lights; steering lights; stern lights (blue); wake lights; and speed lights. Switches are located on the signal and anchor light supply and control panel.

The location of bridge equipment varies among ship types, and may be different on ships of the same type. A bridge watchstander not only has to know where everything is located, but must be able to find it in the dark.

CHARTHOUSE

The charthouse is normally just aft of the pilothouse and on the same deck; but it can also be on another deck and some distance away. On some ships the dead reckoning tracer (DRT) is in the charthouse. The charthouse also contains navigational instruments, such as sextants, stadimeter, bearing circles and stopwatches, parallel rulers, protractors, position plotters and navigational books and tables.

SECONDARY CONN

This area contains steering equipment, engine order telegraph, phone circuits, and other equipment that would be necessary for ship control, in the event primary control is unable to perform because of battle damage. The ship's magnetic compass may also be located here.

SIGNAL BRIDGE

This is an open platform located near the navigational bridge and equipped with yardarm blinker controls, signal searchlights and flag bags. From here signalmen communicate with other ships.

MESSAGE CENTER

This is the station of the communication watch officer. Here, outgoing traffic is prepared for transmission and incoming messages are readied for local delivery. All messages, except tactical signals received and sent direct from shipboard control stations, go through the message center.

CRYPTOGRAPHIC CENTER

The cryptographic center is the exclusive working area of the crypto board, which is responsible for encoding and decoding all cryptographic information. Access to the center is strictly controlled. It has a single entrance and an authorized entry list posted nearby.

COMBAT INFORMATION CENTER

The combat information center (CIC) is the nerve center of the ship. It has a five-fold function: to collect, process, display, evaluate, and disseminate information from sources both inside and outside the ship. A wide range of electronic equipment is installed in CIC: radar, sonar, electronic warfare intercept receivers, IFF (Identification Friend or Foe), radio and visual communications, PPI (plan position indicator) repeaters, display screens, and computers. Radar installations include both air and surface search, plus fire control.

DAMAGE CONTROL CENTRAL

Damage control central (DCC) maintains damage control charts, machinery charts and liquid loading diagrams. DCC sees that the proper conditions of readiness are set and maintained. The conditions of stability and damage throughout the ship are known in DCC at all times, and reported directly to the bridge. All repair parties report to DCC. (More details on actual DCC operation are contained in Chapter 18, pages 311–339.)

Submarines

Because they are designed to operate underwater, submarines have very few topside features and practically no superstructure as such. About all that projects above the hull is the *sail*, a streamlined tower on which diving planes are mounted, and where a few people can stand a topside watch when the submarine operates on the surface.

Submarine hulls are nearly circular in cross section and built to withstand tremendous pressure. The hull consists of the bow compartment, containing living accommodations; the operations compartment, containing control room, sonar and radar rooms, torpedo room, and some staterooms; the reactor compartment; the missile rooms; and the engineroom. A feature of submarines not found on surface ships is the sub's ballast tanks; these can be quickly flooded when the boat is to submerge, or pumped out when she is to surface.

The controls by which a submarine is maneuvered are more like those of an aircraft than a surface ship (which merely steers left or right) because a sub also moves up and down. In fact, when operating submerged, it banks in its turns exactly as an aircraft does.

Aside from these basic differences, a submarine contains all the systems and features found in a surface vessel.

13. Ships and Aircraft

Ships

The Navy operates approximately 542 ships. There are 460 active, "full-time" ships, oceangoing vessels operating under a commanding officer. Some 34 more fleet support ships are manned by civilian crews; there are 49 ships in the Naval Reserve Force. In addition to these, there are over 1,000 service craft. Some have part-time crews, but most are without crews. Most service craft have no self-propulsion.

Most Navy ships have both a name and number. The number —called a designation—tells you two things about a ship: its type (general use) and its hull number. The USS *Texas,* for instance, is CGN 39. CGN is its classification symbol and 39 its hull number. The C means cruiser, the G means that it carries guided missiles, and the N means nuclear propulsion. Hull numbers also indicate the sequence in which ships of a type were ordered for construction. For example, the USS *Barry,* (DD 2) was commissioned in 1902; another *Barry* (DD 248), was commissioned in 1920; and a third *Barry* (DD 933) went into commission in 1956 and is still active.

Designations are used in correspondence, records, and plans, and appear on ships' boats, ships' bows, and in other places. Refering to a ship by her designation can help avoid confusion. For instance, the Navy operates a USS *George Washington* and a USS *George Washington Carver.* The former is designated SSBN 598 and the latter is SSBN 656. Also, as you can see, designations are often shorter than ships' names.

No matter what a ship's formal name is, sailors have traditionally given nicknames to their seagoing homes. Among aircraft carriers, for instance the *John F. Kennedy* is the *JFK;* the *Enterprise* is the *Big E;* the *Constellation* is the *Connie;* and the *Eisenhower* is the *Ike.*

AIRCRAFT CARRIERS

We currently have 13 active aircraft carriers. Our carrier force has 3 nuclear-powered ships and 10 oil-powered ones. The former are the *Enterprise* (CVN 65), commissioned in 1963, the *Nimitz* (CVN 68) of 1975, and the *Dwight D. Eisenhower* (CVN 69) of 1977. These are the world's largest warships. A fourth, the *Carl Vinson* (CVN 70) is under construction; another, CVN 71, has been authorized.

Our non-nuclear carrier force has four ships of the *Kitty Hawk,* (CV 63) class—the *Kitty Hawk, Constellation, America,* and *John F. Kennedy* (sometimes referred to as a single-ship class); four of the *Forrestal* (CV 59) class of the late 1950s and early 1960s—the

Forrestal, Saratoga, Ranger and *Independence;* and two of the
1945 *Midway* (CV 41) class: the *Midway* and *Coral Sea.* Older
carriers are progressively modernized over the years to enable
them to accommodate newer types of aircraft and advanced ship
technologies.

The *Nimitz* is a good example of what, in many respects, is
one of the world's most powerful warships. She is 1,092 feet in
overall length, 252 feet in extreme beam, has a full-load displacement of 91,400 tons, and rides 38 feet deep in the water. At
the heart of her engineering plant are two nuclear reactors (compared to eight for the *Enterprise*) whose energy takes form as a
280,000-horsepower drive turning four propellers. A nuclear-
powered ship's reactors take the place of the oil furnaces in the
boilers of an oil-fueled ship. The reactors generate heat to turn
water into steam and power the turbines that drive the ship's propellers. Unlike oil-burners, nuclear ships can operate at high
speeds for long periods of time without refueling. Weight and
space taken by fuel tanks in conventional ships can be used for
other purposes. As with all Navy warships, her precise top speed
is classified, but is listed as being "in excess of 30 knots."

When the *Nimitz* has an air group embarked, she accommo-
dates about 570 officers and 5,720 enlisted men. From her decks
operate nearly 100 aircraft—fighter, attack, ECM, AEW, reconnaissance planes, and helicopters. For defense she has, in addition to her own aircraft, three basic point defense missile systems
(BPDMS). (See Chapter 15, pages 256–71, for details on weapons.)

The four *Forrestal*-class carriers exemplify the oil-powered
types. They are 1,040 feet long, 252 feet in beam, displace
78,000 tons, have a crew of 5,000, and carry up to 90 aircraft.
Eight oil-burning boilers give these ships a steam-turbine drive
rated at 260,000 horsepower.

The oldest and smallest active CVs are two of the *Midway*
class. Sizeable in comparison with cruisers or destroyers, but
small by comparison with later carriers, they displace 64,000
tons, are 979 feet long and 238 feet in beam.

One modernized *Essex*-class carrier, the *Lexington,* originally
built during World War II, serves as a training carrier (AVT 16).
Five of her sister ships remain in the "mothball fleet." Reactivation of one or more of these is currently proposed.

CRUISERS

In a sense, cruisers may be regarded as large destroyers, since
the two types have many similarities. But where the DD is primarily intended to operate with a task force, cruisers can operate
independently as well. Larger than destroyers, active cruisers
also have more weapons and more elaborate electronics suits,
larger crews, and greater steaming endurance.

Figure 13–1 The carrier USS *Enterprise* and the combat support ship USS *Sacramento* demonstrate the Navy's increased at-sea capability, made possible by improved methods of underway replenishment.

The Navy has 27 active cruisers; all of these are missile ships. The last of the part-gun, part-missile cruisers is inactive, with two all-missile conversions of World War II gun-cruiser hulls. Like carriers, some cruisers are oil-burning (CGs) and some have nuclear power plants (CGNs). There are two CGNs of the *California* class: the *California* (CGN 36) and the *South Carolina* (CGN 37) of 1975 and 1976. These ships can travel around the world 28 times before having their nuclear cores replaced. One of their principal roles is the screening and protection of fast carrier task forces. They are 596 feet long, 63 feet in extreme beam, displacing 11,000 tons. They have crews of about 540.

Closely following the *California* class is the *Virginia* (CGN 38) class of the mid- and late 1970s: the *Virginia, Texas,* and *Mississippi* are active, with the *Arkansas* just commissioned. Though slightly smaller than their predecessors, they are equally well armed. Vital to their firepower is the Mark 86 weapon system, which can track up to 120 targets at a time, and which aims and controls the ship's guns and missiles. Each *Virginia* class CGN has two multi-purpose missile launchers, firing such missiles as Standard or Harpoon against air or surface targets, and ASROC against submarines. Antisubmarine torpedo tubes and two quick-firing 5-in./54-cal. lightweight guns are also fitted.

The *Bainbridge* (CGN 25) and *Truxtun* (CGN 35), completed in 1962 and 1967 respectively, were originally classed as missile frigates. They are the forerunners of the later *California*s and *Virginia*s and the larger *Long Beach* (CGN 9) is our first nuclear-propelled surface warship.

The name *Ticonderoga* has been given to CG 47, the first of a projected new class of missile ships to be armed with the Aegis fleet air defense system (see Chapter 15). Their basic design was derived from the *Spruance* (DD 963) class, which they will generally resemble. A second ship of this class is projected, with others expected to follow.

The nine CGs of the *Belknap* (CG 26) class (1964–1967) form a large part of the Navy's cruiser force. Their displacement is 7,840 tons. They are 547 feet long and carry a 430-man crew. Weapon features are a Terrier/ASROC launcher, a 5-in./54-cal. gun and torpedoes.

Nine *Leahy* (CG 16)-class cruisers are slightly smaller than the *Belknap*s and lack their 5-inch gun. Commissioned in 1962–64, they employ missiles, torpedoes, and ASROC.

Three *Des Moines* (CA 134)-class cruisers, completed in 1948–49, are in the inactive fleet. These ships are armed with rapid-firing 8-inch turret guns developed as a result of World War II battle experience. With four *Iowa* (BB 61)-class battleships, mounting 16-inch guns, also in the inactive fleet, these cruisers are the last ships in the Navy's inventory to have guns larger than 5-inch in caliber. Conversion programs now projected call for the reactivation of two Iowa-class ships and the replacement of some of their guns by missiles.

DESTROYERS

In today's Navy, destroyers perform a wide range of duties. For example, as part of a screen unit in a carrier task group, they can detect and engage enemy submarines, enemy aircraft and missiles, and enemy surface ships. In an amphibious assault a destroyer's weapons can help protect against enemy forces at sea and ashore.

The *Spruance* (DD 963) destroyers form the Navy's newest class. They are 563 feet long, 55 feet in beam, displace 7,800 tons and have a crew of 250. Their 80,000-horsepower, gas-turbine-drive engineering plants can go from "cold iron" to full speed in 12 minutes. The *Spruance*s were the Navy's first major ship class to be powered by gas turbines. Their weaponry consists of antisubmarine torpedoes, two rapid-fire 5-in./54-caliber guns, antisubmarine rockets (ASROC), and Sea Sparrow antiair missiles. The class will have 30 ships; about 25 of these are now in service.

The first *Spruance*s were commissioned in 1975–76. Before these there were fourteen ships of the *Forrest Sherman* (DD 931) class of the mid-1950s. Armed with guns and antisubmarine weapons, they are 418 feet long, 45 feet in beam and displace 4,050 tons. Preceding these DDs were a number of *Gearing* (DD 710)-class ships, built around the end of World War II and modernized early in the 1960s. About 9 of them are with the Naval Reserve.

In contrast to the conventionally armed destroyers just dis-

Figure 13-2 Current Navy ship types

USS Dwight D. Eisenhower (CVN 69)

USS South Carolina (CGN 37)

USS Truxtun (CGN 35)

USS Claude V. Ricketts (DDG 5)

USS Paul F. Foster (DD 964)
and USS Kinkaid (DD 965)

USS Brooke (FFG 1)

USS Garcia (FF 1040)

USS Mariano G. Vallejo (SSBN 658)

USS Dixon (AS 37)

USS Guadalcanal (LPH 7)

USS Alamo (LSD 33)

USS Tarawa (LHA 1)

Figure 13–3 Current Navy ship types

Figure 13–4 Current Navy ship types

USS *Mount Whitney* (LCC 20)

USS *Juneau* (LPD 10)

USS *Fairfax County* (LST 1193)

USS *St. Louis* (LKA 116)

USS *Los Angeles* (SSN 688)

USS *Beaufort* (ATS 2)

cussed are the DDGs—guided missile destroyers—such as the 23 ships of the *Charles F. Adams* (DDG 2) class of 1960–1964. In size, engineering plant, and general appearance they are fairly close to the *Forrest Sherman* destroyers. Weaponry differs, however. Besides two 5-in./54-cal. gun mounts, the DDGs have launchers for firing Tartar or Standard surface-to-air missiles. Four more *Forrest Sherman*s, with two former *Mitscher*-class frigates of the early 1950s, have been converted to DDGs similar to the *Charles F. Adams* class in function.

FRIGATES

The frigate first appeared during World War II (when 500 were built) as the "destroyer escort" (DE). It was later called an escort vessel, and in 1975 it received the name "frigate" (FF).

The largest class is the *Knox* (FF 1052) with 46 units. That class started with the *Knox* in 1969 and ended with the *Moinester* (FF 1097) in 1974. These ships carry crews of 230, and may be viewed as scaled-down destroyers specializing in antisubmarine work. With 10 ships of the earlier *Garcia* (FF 1040) class, they protect amphibious forces, underway replenishment groups, and merchant ship convoys.

Six *Brooke* (FFG 1)-class frigates have Tartar or Standard air-defense missiles. The *Oliver Hazard Perry* (FFG 7) was commissioned in 1977 as the first of a large new class of missile frigates, slightly larger than the *Knox* class, with gas turbines like those of the *Spruance* (DD 963) class. Presently in the building program are 39 FFG-7-class ships.

SUBMARINES

The Navy's submarines include attack and ballistic missile types. Submarines are also assigned secondary missions, which may include surveillance and reconnaissance, direct task-force support, landing-force support, minelaying, and rescue.

Five diesel-electric submarines are designated SS. These were built in the 1950s. All other submarines are nuclear-powered.

The Navy's 75 nuclear attack submarines (SSN) may be compared to the "fleet boats" of World War II, since their main job is to attack enemy ships and submarines. The SSN's principal weapon is the high-speed, wire-guided Mark 48 torpedo, which permits the launching SSN to correct for changes of target motion up to the torpedoes' point of impact. SSNs also carry SUBROC, a rocket-assisted depth charge launched from a torpedo tube. Some carry Harpoon missiles for use against surface targets. Latest of the SSNs is the 6,900-ton *Los Angeles* (SSN 688) class. This class will continue building well into the 1980s, for a total of 28 subs. They are the largest and most powerful of the SSNs, and are capable of operating faster, deeper, and more quietly than any of their predecessors.

The fleet ballistic missile submarines (SSBN) have a strategic mission. They are on constant patrol in the world's oceans. Each is armed with 16 long-range Polaris/Poseidon missiles (except for the new *Ohio*-class boats just launched, which will carry 24 Trident I missiles). They also carry torpedoes, mainly as defense weapons. (Any weapon carried by attack submarines may also be used by the SSBNs.)

The earliest of the pre-Trident SSBNs is the three-unit *George Washington* (SSBN 598) class of 1959–1961. This class is now carrying 16 Polaris A3 missiles. Next is the *Ethan Allen* (SSBN 608) class of 1963–1964, also three units, carrying the Polaris A2. Then the 19-boat *Lafayette* (SSBN 616) class was built, in 1963–1964. Finally, there's the 12-boat *Benjamin Franklin* (SSBN 640) class; it was commissioned in 1965–1967. The *Lafayette* and *Franklin* classes can launch Poseidon missiles. Largest of these four classes are the *Lafayette*s: 8,200 tons submerged displacement, 33-foot beam, 425-foot length, 16 vertical missile tubes and a crew of 168.

SSBNs are operated during alternate periods by separate crews. One is called the Blue Crew and the other the Gold Crew. On return from an extended patrol, one crew relieves the other and the ship returns to patrol following a brief period alongside her tender. The relieved crew, now enroute to the United States, enters a month-long period of rest, recreation, and leave, followed by two months of training. This system allows each crew to enjoy an extended period ashore, while keeping the entire force of SSBNs cruising on deep patrol except for very brief periods.

All successful ship types have a follow-on. The follow-on to the Navy's Polaris/Poseidon units is the Trident SSBN. It will be the mainstay of our strategic submarine force for the 1980s and beyond. Trident is the name of the sub's long-range missile system. The Trident SSBN weighs 18,000 tons—twice as much as current SSBNs. It is 560 feet long—135 feet longer than the *Lafayette*s; its greater size permits it to carry 24 missiles rather than the regular 16. Like our newer guided missile cruisers, the Trident units are given state names. The lead ship of this new class, still under construction, is the *Ohio* (SSBN 726).

PATROL COMBATANTS

The principal vessels in this group are the two *Asheville*-class patrol combatants (PG). Though displacing less than 250 tons, these gas-turbine-powered craft carry a good punch in their Standard missiles. The Navy is also doing experimental work with hydrofoils and surface effect systems.

MINE WARFARE SHIPS

This category includes the ocean minesweepers of the *Aggressive* (MSO 422) class. They are 172 feet long, displace 775 tons, and carry out a variety of mine warfare tasks. While three are assigned to the Atlantic Fleet, 22 more serve with the Naval Reserve.

AMPHIBIOUS WARFARE SHIPS

Often referred to as the "amphibs" or "gators," these ships work mainly where the sea and land meet, and where assault landings are carried out by the Navy–Marine Corps team. Such operations call for many different types of ships. The 64 active fleet amphibs are divided into seven types. Most are transports designed to sealift Marines and their equipment from bases to landing beaches. The differences lie in the ship's designs and in the way troops and their gear are moved from the ship to the shore, which can be done by means of landing craft, helicopters, or tracked amphibious vehicles.

Tank Landing Ships (LST): LSTs merely run up to the beach, lower their extended bow ramp, and offload tanks, artillery, and logistic vehicles. All 20 active "T"'s are in the *Newport* (LST 1179) class. They displace 8,400 tons and carry up to 430 troops.

Dock Landing Ships (LSD): These ships have a well deck that can be flooded so that waterborne landing craft can be floated out of the ship's after section. The 13 active units are divided into two classes: the *Thomaston* (LSD 28) and *Anchorage* (LSD 36) classes. Ships of the latter, newer class are 555 feet long, displace 13,700 tons, have crews of 400 and can embark 340 Marines. A new class, LSD 41, is projected.

Amphibious Transports Dock (LPD): These ships land troops and equipment by landing craft carried in a well deck and floated out through a stern gate, and by helicopters operating from a flight deck. The *Raleigh* (LPD 1) class displace 14,651 tons, are 521-feet long with a 104-foot beam, and carry a crew of 462 and 1,069 troops. *Austin* class (LPD 4 through 15) displace 16,900 tons, are 569-feet long with a 105-foot beam, and carry a crew of 474 and 904 troops. They are similar in appearance and function to the LSD, but have more extensive helicopter facilities.

Amphibious Cargo Ships (LKA): There are three of these ships, all in the *Charleston* (LKA 113) class of 1969–1970. They usually land combat cargo rather than troops. Large ships of over 20,500 tons, they have an elaborate array of masts and booms. This allows them to offload cargo over the side into landing craft.

Amphibious Assault Ships (LPH): These are among the most advanced of the amphibs. The seven ships of the 18,000-ton *Iwo Jima* (LPH 2) class were the world's first helicopter carriers designed for that purpose. Twenty large Sea Knights are on board to do the job. LPHs are designed to carry and land the 2,000 men and equipment of a Marine battalion landing team (BLT).

Amphibious Command Ships (LCC): LCCs serve as floating command centers, providing control facilities for embarked sea, air, and land commanders and their staffs. Two are active: *Blue Ridge* (LCC 19) and *Mount Whitney* (LCC 20). These measure 620 feet in length, displace over 18,000 tons, and have a crew of 1,514.

General Purpose Assault Ships (LHA): Of all the ship types discussed so far, only aircraft carriers are larger than these. The five ships of the *Tarawa* (LHA 1) class are, at over 39,000 tons displacement, nearly twice the displacement of the LPHs. They are capable of simultaneous helicopter and landing-craft operations, for they have both a flight deck and a well deck.

Auxiliary Ships

UNDERWAY REPLENISHMENT SHIPS

Our warships must be able to remain at sea for weeks at a time. To do so, they must have fuel, provisions, and ammunition. The Navy has several types of underway replenishment (UNREP) techniques that use ships fitted with special cargo-handling gear to make transfers from one ship to another while the two are steaming abreast or, in some cases, astern. Vertical replenishment (VERTREP) is another form of UNREP, in which cargo-carrying helicopters are used. The Navy has 34 active UNREP ships.

Fleet Oilers (AO): Currently there are four AOs in fleet service. The *Ponchatoula* (AO 148) is of the *Neosho* class. There are three jumboized AOs—51, 98 and 99—of the *Ashtabula* class. AOs carry a variety of petroleum products needed by other ships and their embarked aircraft. Several shipboard stations are available from which fuel can be supplied to replenish ships. Twelve more AOs are operated by the Military Sealift Command (MSC) with civilian crews.

Fast Combat Support Ships (AOE): At 52,480 tons these are the largest and most powerful of the Navy's non-combatant seagoing units. All four AOEs are of the *Sacramento* (AOE 1) class. They are 793 feet long, 107 feet wide, and have a

100,000-horsepower drive. They can operate with the fast task forces. AOEs combine features of fleet oilers, ammunition ships, and store ships.

Replenishment Oilers (AOR): These ships came on the scene in the early 1970s. All are of the seven-ship *Wichita* class and are similar in size to the *Neosho* class AOs, which are 655 feet long and displace 38,000 tons. Like the AOE, the AOR is a multipurpose replenishment ship. They transfer fuel, spare parts, provisions, freight, and ammunition.

Combat Store Ships (AFS): AFSs provide general stores, dry stores, and refrigerated food. They have a constant-tension wire highline system and a built-in helicopter deck aft with capability to maintain and store H-46 helicopters. There are seven ships in this class, headed by the *Mars* (AFS 1).

Ammunition Ships (AE): Of the 12 AEs, eight are in the *Kilauea* (AE 26) class. They are 564 feet long and displace more than 19,000 tons. Providing ammunition and missiles is their principal task. Besides having equipment for transferring materials to ships close by or alongside, many UNREP ships have their own VERTREP helicopters.

FLEET SUPPORT SHIPS

So far the ship categories have had a degree of similarity. This does not hold true for the Navy's more than 70 active auxiliaries. It is difficult, for instance, to find similarities between a 21,000-ton *Simon Lake*-class submarine tender and a 1,640-ton *Cherokee*-class fleet ocean tug. They don't look alike and have far different jobs.

"Auxiliaries" is not a "catch all" category. Rather, the wide variety of auxiliary ships demonstrates the great variety of functions needed to keep the fleet's other ships in operating condition. Of the 14 types of auxiliary ships, nine are represented by only a single ship.

Destroyer Tenders (AD) and Submarine Tenders (AS): These ships are the largest of the active auxiliaries. The newer ones displace from 16,000 to 22,000 tons. Their crews are formed mainly of technicians and repairmen. Some submarine tenders specialize in supporting SSN types, while others support SSBNs, and are often based overseas for this purpose. Those of the *L.Y. Spear* (AS 36) class can take four submarines alongside and can support another dozen.

Despite their title, destroyer tenders service a variety of ships. Among these, the *Samuel Gompers* (AD 37) class ADs can accommodate ships up to and including the highly complex *Virginia*-class nuclear-powered missile cruisers.

Repair Ships (AR): Four *Vulcan* (AR 5)-class repair ships are 530 feet long and displace 17,000 tons. These versatile floating

Figure 13–6 "Yard" tugs, usually skippered by chief petty officers, are among the few vessels in the Navy with all-enlisted crews. They aid large ships in docking and undocking.

machine shops, like ADs and ASs, have the ability to accomplish a wide range of repair and service jobs for the fleet.

Salvage Ships (ARS) and Salvage and Rescue Tugs (ATS): Six ships of the *Bolster* (ARS 6) class, built during World War II, and three *Edenton* (ATS 1)-class ships, built in England and completed in 1971–72, are designed to salvage ships and support diving operations.

Submarine Rescue Ships (ASR): Seven World War II built ships of the *Chanticleer* class generally resemble the *Bolster* class ARSs. Two ships of the *Pigeon* (ASR 21) class, completed in 1973, have a twin-hull catamaran design, with a 34-foot-wide well between their two hulls. They have a new system that can support divers at a depth of up to 1,000 feet, and can operate Deep Submergence Rescue Vehicles (DSRV) for the rescue of submarine crews.

So far, only active Navy ships have collectively been discussed. Another group of ships, 59 in all, are in an inactive status or other degrees of standby, including four battleships (BBs), six aircraft carriers, and six cruisers. Others include transports and cargo ships. These warships, and support ships alike, could be placed in service in an international crisis, as many already have been since World War II.

Whether large or small, the ships discussed earlier in this chapter are commissioned vessels with full-time crews under commanding officers.

SERVICE CRAFT

Also among the Navy's waterborne resources is a large and varied group of 900 active and 180 standby service craft. There are 56 different types. Some are huge vessels like the large auxiliary floating dry docks that can take aboard, and raise out of the water for repairs, vessels as large as aircraft carriers.

Barracks craft (non-self-propelled) accommodate ships' crews when their ships are in overhaul or under major repair. Open lighters and covered lighters—there are 340 of them—are barges used to store materials and to house pierside repair shops. Under tow, other lighters haul freight or cargo.

Some gasoline barges, fuel-oil barges and water barges are self-propelled while others are not, and thus depend on tugs. These service ships moor at Navy bases, or anchor out in harbors or roadsteads, as do garbage lighters.

Diving tenders support diving operations and are essential in diver training. Aircraft transportation lighters carry complete or dismantled aircraft and parts. Ferryboats or launches, which carry people, automobiles, and equipment, are usually located at Navy bases where facilities are spread out over large distances.

Best known of the service craft are the 170 harbor tugs: large, medium and small. Under a chief petty officer or bluejacket skipper, and with an all-enlisted crew, these highly essential craft can be found at Navy bases the world over. They aid ships in docking and undocking. Harbor-side and at sea, they tow non-self-propelled craft, act as people carriers, fight fires, and perform rescue duties when needed.

MILITARY SEALIFT COMMAND SHIPS

Any summary of the Navy's ships must include those in the Navy's Military Sealift Command (MSC), the Defense Department's water transport service. These are designated USNS (United States Naval Ship) rather than USS (United States Ship). They are "in service" rather than "in commission." About six cargo ships and 20 oilers serve the Army and Air Force as well as the Navy.

Another two dozen perform "special duty" projects. Some of these are missile range instrumentation ships. Others do ocean-bottom laying and repairing of cables used for detecting enemy submarines. Much of their work is done for other government agencies.

Of special interest are 20 to 30 MSC fleet-support ships. As with other MSC ships, they have civilian officers and crews. They operate under Navy orders, have a military department of 10–15 Navymen aboard, performing visual and radio communications, and otherwise assisting the ship's master and crew in operations with naval units.

These fleet-support vessels include storeships, oilers, fleet ocean tugs and cargo ships supporting our fleet ballistic missile (FBM) submarines. Often referred to as "AK-FBMs," these latter units carry supplies of all sorts from stateside ports to the overseas-based tenders that support our SSBNs. * Asterisk denotes "full-time" active ships, which collectively number over 460.

AALC	Amphibious Assault Landing Craft
*AD	Destroyer Tender
*AE	Ammunition Ship
AF	Store Ship
AFDB	Large Auxiliary Floating Dry Dock (non-self-propelled)
AFDL	Small Auxiliary Floating Dry Dock (non-self-propelled)
AFDM	Medium Auxiliary Floating Dry Dock (non-self-propelled)
*AFS	Combat Store Ship
*AG	Miscellaneous
*AGDS	Deep Submergence Support Ship
AGEH	Hydrofoil Research Ship
AGER	Environmental Research Ship
*AGF	Miscellaneous Command Ship
*AGFF	Frigate Research Ship
AGM	Missile Range Instrumentation Ship
AGMR	Major Communications Relay Ship
AGOR	Oceanographic Research Ship
AGP	Patrol Craft Tender
AGS	Surveying Ship
*AGSS	Auxiliary Research Submarine
AH	Hospital Ship
AK	Cargo Ship
AKR	Vehicle Cargo Ship
*AO	Oiler
*AOE	Fast Combat Support Ship
AOG	Gasoline Tanker
*AOR	Replenishment Oiler
*AOT	Transport Oiler
AP	Transport
APB	Self-Propelled Barracks Ship
APL	Barracks Craft (non-self-propelled)
*AR	Repair Ship
ARB	Battle Damage Repair Ship
ARC	Cable Repair Ship
ARD	Auxiliary Repair Dry Dock (non-self-propelled)
ARDM	Medium Auxiliary Repair Dry Dock (non-self-propelled)
ARL	Repair Ship, Small
*ARS	Salvage Ship
*AS	Submarine Tender
ASPB	Assault Support Patrol Boat
*ASR	Submarine Rescue Ship
ATA	Auxiliary Ocean Tug
ATC	Mini-Armored Troop Carrier

234

Ships

*ATS	Salvage and Rescue Ship
*AVM	Guided Missile Ship
*AVT	Training Aircraft Carrier
BB	Battleship
CA	Heavy Cruiser (8-inch guns)
CC	Command Ship
CCB	Command and Control Boat
*CG	Guided Missile Cruiser
*CGN	Guided Missile Cruiser (nuclear propulsion)
CPC	Coastal Patrol Boat
CPIC	Coastal Patrol and Interdiction Craft
*CV	Multi-Purpose Aircraft Carrier
*CVN	Multi-Purpose Aircraft Carrier (nuclear propulsion)
CVS	ASW Aircraft Carrier
*DD	Destroyer
*DDG	Guided Missile Destroyer
DSRV	Deep Submergence Rescue Vehicle
DSV	Deep Submergence Vehicle
*FF	Frigate
*FFG	Guided Missile Frigate
IX	Unclassified Miscellaneous
LCA	Landing Craft, Assault
LCAC	Landing Craft, Air Cushion
*LCC	Amphibious Command Ship
LCM	Landing Craft, Mechanized
LCPL	Landing Craft, Personnel, Large
LCPR	Landing Craft, Personnel, Ramped
LCSR	Landing Craft, Swimmer Reconnaissance
LCU	Landing Craft, Utility
LCVP	Landing Craft, Vehicle, Personnel
*LHA	Amphibious Assault Ship (general purpose)
*LKA	Amphibious Cargo Ship
LPA	Amphibious Transport
*LPD	Amphibious Transport Dock
*LPH	Amphibious Assault Ship (Helicopter)
*LSD	Dock Landing Ship
LSSC	Light SEAL Support Craft
*LST	Tank Landing Ship
LWT	Amphibious Warping Tug
MIUW	Mobile Inshore Underseas Warfare Craft
MON	Monitor (small armored river gunboat)
MSB	Minesweeping Boat
MSC	Minesweeper, Coastal (non-magnetic)
MSD	Minesweeper, Drone
MSI	Minesweeper, Inshore
MSL	Minesweeping Launch
MSM	Minesweeper, River (converted LCM-6)
*MSO	Minesweeper, Ocean (non-magnetic)

235

Aircraft

MSR	Minesweeper, Patrol
MSS	Minesweeper, Special (device)
MSSC	Medium SEAL Support Craft
NR	Submersible Research Vehicle (nuclear propulsion)
PB	Patrol Boat
PBR	River Patrol Boat
PCF	Patrol Craft (fast)
PCH	Patrol Craft (hydrofoil)
*PG	Patrol Combatant (ex-Patrol Gunboat)
PGH	Patrol Gunboat (hydrofoil)
*PHM	Guided Missile Patrol Combatant (hydrofoil)
PTF	Fast Patrol Craft
SDV	Swimmer Delivery Vehicle
SES	Surface Effect Ship
*SS	Submarine (conventional)
*SSBN	Ballistic Missile Submarine (nuclear propulsion)
SSG	Guided Missile Submarine
*SSN	Submarine (nuclear propulsion)
SWAL	Shallow Water Attack Craft, Light
SWAM	Shallow Water Attack Craft, Medium
SWCL	Special Warfare Craft, Light
SWCM	Special Warfare Craft, Medium
SWOB	Ship Waste Off-loading Barge

Aircraft

As 1981 began, the Navy had an inventory of 5,393 aircraft—4,364 active plus 1,029 in the assembly "pipeline." These include approximately 829 fighters, 148 antisubmarine, 404 patrol, 189 transport, 1,285 rotary wing, 1,211 attack, 120 early warning, 54 in-flight refuelers, 86 observation, 58 utility, and 1,004 trainers, which include jet and propeller aircraft, and 235 drones. Aircraft operate in squadrons and airwings. There are about 150 squadrons in service.

Many types, designs, and modifications of aircraft—far more than Navy ships—form "naval air." A system of letters and numbers (aircraft designations) is used to distinguish them.

AIRCRAFT DESIGNATIONS

Navy aircraft may be considered as fixed-wing or rotary-wing (helicopter). The purpose of a designation in letters and numbers is simply to tell what the airplane is. At the root of it all is a simple letter/number combination. F-14, for example, indicates a Tomcat fighter plane. The F stands for fighter and the 14 for the design number.

Basic Mission and Type Symbols:

A Attack
C Cargo/transport
E Special electronics
F Fighter
H Helicopter
O Observation
P Patrol

R Reconnaissance
S Antisubmarine
T Trainer
U Utility
V V/STOL
X Research

Series Symbol: Follow-on changes to the F-14 would call for a series symbol, indicating an improvement on, or change to, the same design. F-14A or F-14C, for example.

Modified Mission Symbol: When the basic mission of an airplane has been considerably modified for other than the original or intended purpose, a modified mission symbol is added. For example, an F-14C modified to be principally a reconnaissance plane would become RF-14C.

Modified mission symbols are:

A Attack
C Transport
D Director
E Special electronics
H Search/rescue
K Tanker
L Cold weather
M Mine countermeasures

Q Drone
R Reconnaissance
S Antisubmarine
T Trainer
U Utility
V Staff
W Weather

237

Status Symbol: Finally, there is the status symbol, a letter prefix that tells that the aircraft is being used for special work and experimentation; or that it is in planning, or a prototype.

Consider our imaginary RF-14C. If it were to be used for a permanent special test, it would have an N added to the designation and become an NRF-14C. Despite this, the basic airplane is still the F-14, and most Navymen would recognize it as such despite its several changes.

Status prefix symbols are:

G Permanently grounded
J Special test, temporary
N Special test, permanent

X Experimental
Y Prototype
Z Planning

PARTS OF A FIXED-WING AIRCRAFT

All fixed-wing aircraft have the same basic parts: fuselage, wings, tail assembly, landing gear, and powerplant. These are defined as follows:

Fuselage: The main body of the plane.

Figure 13–7 Operational Naval Aircraft

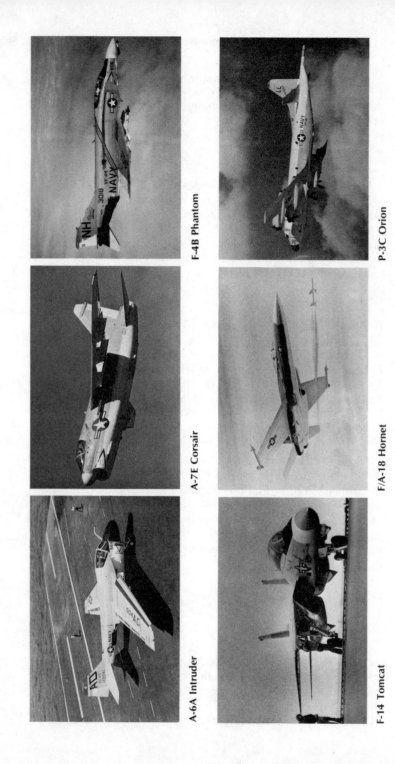

A-6A Intruder

A-7E Corsair

F-4B Phantom

F-14 Tomcat

F/A-18 Hornet

P-3C Orion

C-9B Skytrain

S-3A Viking

SH-60B Seahawk

E-2C Hawkeye

H-3A Sea King

UH-46A Sea Knight

Figure 13–8 Operational Naval Aircraft

Wings: Strong structural members attached to the fuselage. Their airfoil shape provides the lift which supports the plane in flight. Wings are fitted with control surfaces—ailerons and flaps—and may carry fuel tanks, guns, rockets, missiles and other weapons, engines, and landing gear.

Tail assembly: Carries vertical and horizontal stabilizers, rudder and elevators.

Landing gear: Usually means the wheels, but in certain aircraft these may be replaced by skis or floats.

Powerplant: Develops the thrust or force that provides forward motion in flight. May consist of reciprocating (piston) engines that drive propellers, jet engines that develop thrust (turbojet and turbofan), or jet engines and propellers or rotors in combination (turboprop or turboshaft).

The most common naval aircraft are listed below, categorized by mission. Each mission name is followed by a two-letter abbreviation which indicates the type of squadron in which the units usually serve. The V indicates fixed-wing aircraft.

(A note on aircraft speed listings. For higher-speed aircraft, figures are listed not as miles per hour (mph) but as a Mach factor. Mach 1 is the speed of sound in the air through which the airplane is moving. It varies with altitude and temperature. At sea level at 32 degrees Fahrenheit, a plane traveling at Mach 1 is going about 760 mph. Mach 2 is approximately twice that speed.)

ATTACK (VA)

The attack aircraft's main job is to destroy enemy targets, at sea and ashore, with rockets, guided missiles, torpedoes, mines, and conventional or nuclear bombs.

A-6 Intruder: All-weather, day and night bomber. Has twin jet engines and carries nearly eight tons of weapons. Weight, 60,600 lbs.; Length, 54 ft. 7 in.; Span, 53 ft.; Speed, 600 mph; Range, over 3,000 miles.

A-7 Corsair II: Single-seater and subsonic light attack plane. Can carry 10 tons of ordnance. Weight, 38,000 lbs.; Length, 46 ft.; Span, 38 ft. 8 in.; Speed, 595 mph; Range, 3,800 miles.

FIGHTER (VF)

Like attack planes, fighters are both carrier-based and land-based. They are faster and more maneuverable than attack planes. They intercept and engage enemy aircraft, defend surface forces, escort attack and reconnaissance aircraft, and support ground troops. They can be equipped to carry nuclear weapons, guided missiles, and a mix of other weapons.

F-4 Phantom: An all-weather fighter carrying a pilot and radar intercept officer (RIO). Weight, 54,600 lbs.; Length, 53 ft. 3 in.; Span, 38 ft. 5 in.; Speed, Mach 2; Range, over 2,000 miles.

F-14 Tomcat: Two-seater, twin jet, variable sweep wing, all-weather fighter-interceptor. Fires air-to-air missiles to destroy enemy aircraft. Weight, 55,000 lbs.; Length, 61 ft. 10 in.; Span, 64 ft.; Speed, Mach 2; Range, 1,500 miles.

F/A-18 Hornet: Under development and currently under service acceptance trials as a replacement for the F-4 and A-7 and a complement to the F-14. Expected to be the key Navy fighter/attack of the early 1980s.

PATROL (VP)

These large airplanes, with low speeds but very long flying range, have the primary mission of antisubmarine patrol. They also mine and bomb. They have infrared, acoustic, and magnetic detection devices for finding and tracking submarines.

P-3 Orion: Land-based, long-range, over-water patrol plane. It carries a crew of 12. Weight, $63\frac{1}{2}$ tons; Length, 117 ft.; Span, 99 ft.; Speed, 380 mph; Range, 4,800 miles.

TRANSPORT (VR)

Transport planes carry cargo and personnel. They are mostly land-based, long-range types.

C-131 Convair Liner: Primarily a cargo transport, but can carry 47 passengers. Weight, 53,200 lbs.; Length, 79 ft. 2 in.; Span, 105 ft. 4 in.; Speed, 274 mph; Range, 2,000 miles.

C-9B Skytrain: This Navy version of the commercial DC-9 can carry cargo or 90 passengers. It replaces three earlier transport types. Gross weight is 54 tons.

ANTISUBMARINE (VS)

Searching out submarines visually or by radar and magnetic detection, or by signals sent from floating sonobuoys, these airplanes attack with rockets, depth charges, or homing torpedoes.

S-3 Viking: This carrier-based plane is powered with two turbofan engines. It can loiter near sea level at relatively low speeds while sub-hunting. Length, 49 ft.; Span, 68 ft. 8 in.; Speed, 440 mph.

RECONNAISSANCE (VQ) (VAQ) (VW)

Many aircraft have been modified for these complex missions.

RF-8 Crusader: Originally a fighter. Has four forward and side-mounted motion-picture cameras for rapid terrain photo-reconnaissance work.

EA-3B/KB-3B Skywarrior: A heavy attack aircraft modified as a special electronics or refueling tanker. Carries a crew of three.

WP-3A Orion: This is the basic P-3 modified to monitor weather conditions and do hurricane tracking.

TRAINER (VT)

Trainers are two-seat airplanes (instructor and student). Most are jets, designed with an emphasis on safety and versatility.

T-2 Buckeye: Trainer used in primary and basic training, instrument flying, combat maneuvers, and pre-carrier work. Weight, 13,180 lbs.; Length, 38 ft. 3 in.; Span 38 ft.; Speed, 465 mph.

TA-4F Skyhawk: This trainer model of the A-4 is used primarily in advanced jet training. It has a speed of 590 mph. Other prominent trainers are the propeller-driven, twin-engine T-34C, the single-engine T-44A, and the basic trainer, the T-28B.

AIRBORNE EARLY WARNING (VAW)

Electronic search and radar countermeasures equipment is used by these airplanes to provide early warning of hostile aircraft, missiles, ships, submarines, and even bad weather.

E-2 Hawkeye: Easily recognized by the large revolving radar saucer above its fuselage, this carrier-based plane has two turboprop engines and a five-man crew. One version, the E-2C, provides a long-range, early warning and command-data link to the F-14.

EA-6B Prowler: Has a role of electronic warfare and radar countermeasures, and is the most advanced airborne electronic warfare aircraft in existence.

HELICOPTER (ROTARY WING)

The other main type of aircraft, the helicopter—identified by an H designation—joined the fleet in the mid-1940s, 35 years after the Navy bought its first fixed-wing airplane. A score of different designs are in service, and they are as likely to be ship-based as they are shore-based.

Helicopters—also called choppers, helos and copters—get their lift from rotating airfoils (or blades) called rotors. The helo's flight characteristics are determined by the speed and pitch of the rotor blades. Helicopters have relatively low speeds and short ranges.

Helicopter missions include antisubmarine activity, minesweeping, general utility, vertical envelopment, and vertical replenishment (VERTREP).

Antisubmarine: For these duties the helo is equipped to detect the submarine and destroy it. When using sonar, the helo lowers a sonar "ball" into the water, and attacks the target with torpedoes or depth charges.

Minesweeping: With minesweeping gear in tow, mostly submerged, the helo flies a few feet above the water along the route being swept. When a mine pops to the surface, surface ships destroy it by gunfire.

General utility: These tasks may include transporting mail, light cargo, and men from one ship to another; searching for

leads in the ice; searching for, and rescuing downed flyers or
shipwreck survivors: and helping ships check radar accuracy.

Vertical envelopment: Assault landings of this nature are possible with helicopters. The copter pilots and the troops, usually Marines, operate from amphibious assault ships.

Vertical replenishment (VERTREP): Helos help speed up alongside cargo transfer between ships. Underway replenishment ships have one or two copters assigned for such duties.

LAMPS: The light airborne multipurpose system, LAMPS, built around the Seasprite helicopter, was installed in about a dozen destroyers in 1972. By 1982 about 200 ships will have this system. The Navy recently introduced a prototype of the SH-60B *Seahawk*, the airborne platform segment of the LAMPS MK III integrated ship/air weapon system, which is slated to go aboard frigates and destroyers in the mid-1980s. The current LAMPS helicopter carries surface search radar, MAD (magnetic anomaly detector), sonobuoys, ESM (electronic support measures) equipment, TACAN and a UHF direction finder. A ship using LAMPS can station its helicopter 30 to 40 miles away in the direction of any expected enemy action. The helicopter can give the ship instant information on any radar contact within 15 miles.

243

AIRCRAFT CLASSIFICATIONS

Fighters		**Antisubmarine**		**Patrol**	
F-4	Phantom	EA-4F		P-2	Neptune
QF-4B		TA-4F		DP-2E	
RF-4B		TA-4J		SP-2H	
F-4J		A-4L		P-3	Orion
YF-4J		A-4M		P-3A	
F-4N		OA-4M		EP-3A	
F-4S		A-6	Intruder	RP-3A	
F-8	Crusader	A-6A		WP-3A	
RF-8G		EA-6A		P-3B	
F-86	Sabre	A-6C		EP-3B	
QF-86F		KA-6D		P-3C	
QF-86H		A-6E		RP-3D	
F-14	Tomcat	EA-6B	Prowler	EP-3E	
F-14A		A-7	Corsair II		
F/A-18	Hornet	A-7A		**Early Warning**	
F-18A		A-7B		E-2	Hawkeye
A-18A		YA-7B		TE-2A	
F-18B		TA-7C		E-2B	
		A-7E		E-2C	
Attack		**Antisubmarine**		TE-2C	
A-3	Skywarrior	S-2	Tracker	YE-2C	
A-3B		TS-2A			
EA-3B		US-2A		**V/STOL**	
KA-3B		US-2B		OV-10	Bronco
RA-3B		US-2C		OV-10A	
TA-3B		ES-2D		YOV-10D	
ERA-3B		S-2G		OV-10D	
A-4	Skyhawk	S-3	Viking	AV-8	Harrier
A-4E		S-3A		AV-8A	
A-4F		US-3A		YAV-8B	

Ships,
Planes,
and
Weapons

244

Aircraft

Research
X-22
X-22A
X-26A

Helicopters

H-1	Iroquois
UH-1B	
UH-1E	
AH-1G	
UH-1H	
AH-1J	
HH-1K	
TH-1L	
UH-1L	
UH-1N	
AH-1T	
H-2	Seasprite
UH-2C	
HH-2D	
SH-2D	
YSH-2E	
SH-2F	
H-3	Sea King
HH-3A	
SH-3A	
UH-3A	
VH-3A	
SH-3D	
SH-3G	
SH-3H	Aircraft
H-46	Sea Knight
CH-46A	
HH-46A	
UH-46A	
CH-46D	
CH-46E	
CH-46F	
H-53	Sea Stallion
CH-53A	
CH-53D	
RH-53D	
MH-53D	
CH-53E	Super Stallion
TH-57A	SeaRanger
SH-60B	Seahawk

Utility

U-11	Aztec
U-11A	

Cargo/Transport

C-1A	Trader
C-118	Liftmaster
C-118B	
VC-118B	
C-130	Hercules
DC-130A	
C-130F	
KC-130F	
LC-130F	
EC-130G	
EC-130Q	
LC-130R	
C-131	Convair Liner
C-131F	
C-131G	
VC-131H	
C-2	Greyhound
C-2A	
C-4	Gulfstream
TC-4C	
C-9B	Skytrain

Trainers

T-2	Buckeye
T-2B	
T-2C	
T-28	Trojan
T-28B	
T-28C	
T-33	Shooting Star
QT-33A	
T-33B	
T-34	Mentor
T-34B	
T-34C	
T-39	Sabreliner
T-39D	
CT-39E	
CT-39G	
T-44	unnamed
T-44A	

14. Ship and Squadron Organization

Every Navy ship operates under the authority of an officer ordered to command that ship by the Naval Military Personnel Command. No matter what his rank, he is called "captain." The commanding officer (CO) is the line officer in actual command of a ship. In case of absence or death his duties are assumed by the line officer next in command—usually the executive officer.

Though the absolute responsibility for the safety, well-being, and efficiency of his command rests with the captain, in practice he delegates the duties of the ship to the executive officer, department heads, and the officer of the deck (OOD)—and through them, to the crew.

The executive officer, often called "the exec" or "XO," is the line officer next in rank to the captain. He is responsible for all matters relating to the personnel, routine, and discipline of the ship. All orders issued by him have the same force and effect as though issued by the CO. In case of the captain's disability, the XO takes charge. He is, by virtue of his position, senior to all staff officers on board.

Executive's Assistants

Depending on the size of the ship, certain officers and enlisted men are detailed as executive assistants. Among them are the following:

The *administrative assistant* relieves the XO of as many administrative details as possible.

The *chaplain* has primarily religious duties, although he is involved in all matters pertaining to the mental, moral, and physical welfare of the ship's company.

The *chief master-at-arms* (CMAA) is responsible for the maintenance of good order and discipline. The CMAA enforces Navy regulations, ship's regulations and pertinent directives and assists the officer-of-the-deck (OOD) in the execution of the ship's routine.

The *career counselor* runs the ship's career counseling program, and makes sure that current programs and opportunities are available to all crew members.

The *drug abuse program adviser* advises the CO/XO on drug and alcohol abuse aboard ship and the approaches necessary to

Figure 14–1 A high degree of organization and coordination is called for when ships steam in formation for underway replenishment of supplies and fuel. Here the *Sample* (FF 1048) and *Kitty Hawk* (CV 63) take on fuel from the *Sacramento* (AOE 1), while the *Goldsborough* (DDG 20), *Bainbridge* (CGN 25), and *Badger* (FF 1071) cruise behind.

cope effectively with the problem. He also coordinates Navy policies and procedures on drug and alcohol education, rehabilitation, identification, and enforcement.

The educational services officer handles coordination and planning for officer and enlisted education programs.

Lay leaders may be appointed when a chaplain is not available to meet the need. For instance, a unit might have a Protestant chaplain, but no priest or rabbi. Hence, the command may appoint Roman Catholic and Jewish lay leaders. The lay leader must be a volunteer, either officer or enlisted.

The legal officer is an adviser and staff assistant to the CO/XO on the interpretation and application of the Uniform Code of Military Justice (UCMJ), the Manual for Courts-Martial (MCM) and other laws and regulations concerning discipline and the administration of justice within the command.

The personnel officer is responsible for the placement of enlisted personnel and for the administration and custody of enlisted personnel records.

The postal assistant looks after the administration of mail services to the command.

The public affairs assistant prepares briefing material and information pamphlets, assists with press interviews, generates newsworthy material about the unit's operation, and publishes the command's newspaper.

The safety officer promotes maximum cooperation in safety matters at all levels.

The master chief petty officer of the command (C M/C)—who in some instances may be a designated senior chief petty officer of the command (C S/C), or chief petty officer of the command (C Ch)—assists the commanding officer in matters of morale and crew welfare. (Details of the C M/C's job are contained in Chapter 9.)

The senior watch officer, under the direction of the executive officer, is responsible to the CO for assigning and supervising all deck watchstanders, underway and in port.

The ship's secretary is responsible for administering and accounting for ship's correspondence and directives, for administering officers' personnel records, and for establishing and maintaining a forms control point. He also acts as the captain's writer and supervises the preparation of his personal correspondence.

The special services assistant administers the command's special services program, which comprises all organized welfare, recreational, and athletic activities not assigned to other departments or officers.

The training officer handles the formulation and administration of the unit training program.

The 3-M coordinator directly supervises the unit's 3-M (maintenance and material management) program.

The security manager is responsible for proper classification management, personal security, information systems security, physical measures for protecting classified material, and security education and training material.

Departments

All ships have these basic departments: operations, navigation, weapons (or deck), engineering, and supply. Aircraft carriers, LPHs, ships with VERTREP capabilities, and some tenders will have an air department. Most ships have a medical department.

Certain other departments are established on ships, according to the type of vessel and its operational mission. These include repair departments on repair ships and communications relay ships. Besides an air department, carriers have aircraft intermediate maintenance (AIMD) and safety departments. Ships assigned for special purposes may have other departments authorized by the Chief of Naval Operations (CNO).

Departments, in turn, consist of divisions which are further subdivided into watches, sections, or both.

Figure 14–2 Members of the deck division haul in a line.

Each ship's department has a department head, an officer who is responsible for its organization, training, and performance. All departments fall into one of three categories: command, support, or special.

COMMAND DEPARTMENTS

Command departments include air, aircraft intermediate maintenance, aviation, communications, deck, engineering, navigation, operations, reactor, and safety. When embarked, there also may be air-wing or air-group departments.

Air: On ships that have air departments, the air officer (called *air boss*) supervises and directs launchings, landings, and the handling of aircraft and aviation fuels.

The department consists of the V division. If additional divisions are assigned, they'll include V-1, plane handling on the flight deck; V-2, catapults and arresting gear; V-3, plane handling on the hangar deck, and V-4, aviation fuels.

The following, where assigned, report to the air officer: flight deck officer, catapult officer, arresting gear officer, hangar deck officer, aviation fuels officer, aircraft handling officer, and training assistant (air).

Aircraft intermediate maintenance: Head of AIMD is the aircraft intermediate maintenance officer. He supervises and directs the intermediate maintenance effort of the embarked air wing or other aircraft, and maintenance for assigned ship aircraft. He also keeps up ground support equipment. When there's only one division aboard ship, it's called the IM division. Ships having more than one division include the IM-1 division, responsible for administration, quality assurance, production and maintenance/material control, and aviation 3-M analysis; IM-2 division, for general aircraft and organizational maintenance of ship's as-

Depart-
ments

signed aircraft; and IM-3 division, for maintenance of aviation and armament systems, as well as the precision measuring equipment.

Communications: In units with a communications department, the head of the department is the communications officer. He is responsible for visual and electronic exterior communications and for administering internal communications systems. In units without a communications department, the communications officer reports to the operations officer. Assistants may include a radio officer, a signal officer, a communications security material system (CMS) custodian, a cryptosecurity officer and a message center (traffic) officer.

Deck: On ships having a deck department, the first lieutenant is the head of that department. He is responsible for the supervision, direction, and use of the equipment associated with deck seamanship and, aboard ships without a weapons department, of the ordnance equipment. The following report to the first lieutenant: the gunnery officer (on ships whose chief jobs don't involve ordnance or aircraft), cargo officer, ship's boatswain, and boat group commander. On ships with a deck department but without one for weapons, the weapons officer is an assistant.

Engineering: This department, headed by the engineering officer, is responsible for operating and maintaining the ship's machinery, damage and casualty control, repair of hull and machinery, power lighting, water maintenance, and underwater fittings. All repairs beyond the capability of other departments are handled by engineering. When the department consists of a single division, it's called the E division. Multiple-division ships have a B division, boilers; M division, main engines; A division, auxiliaries; E division, electrical; and R division, repair.

The engineer may have assistants for main propulsion, reactor control, damage control, and administration; an electrical officer; and specialists such as a technical assistant for nuclear, biological, and chemical (NBC) defense, and a fire marshal.

Executive: This department is headed by the executive officer and normally contains a single X division, which includes personnel assigned to work in the captain's office, executive officer's office, chaplain's office, print shop, security office, training office, legal office, and hospital corps (when no medical officer is assigned). It may also include an I division for indoctrination of recruits and newly reported personnel. Embarked staff enlisted personnel are a part of C division—normally called the "flag division"—in one-division ships. Ships with multiple divisions may have C-1 division, administrative, operations, logistics, and other clerical personnel; C-2 division, communications (radio and visual); C-3 division, barge and boat crews, drivers, and orderlies; and C-4 division, mess personnel.

Navigation: This department, headed by the navigator, is responsible for the safe navigation and piloting of a ship and the care and maintenance of navigational equipment. It consists of the N division.

Operations: Ops is headed by the operations officer, who is responsible for collecting, evaluating, and disseminating tactical and operational information. If the department consists of a single division, it is called the O division. For ships with more than one division, the department could include OA, OI, OL, OR, OS, OE, OC, and OP divisions. OA includes intelligence, photography, drafting, printing and reproduction, and meteorology. OI includes the combat information center (CIC) and sometimes lookouts. OL is the lookouts division. OR (radio communications) and OS (visual communications) are normally combined into the OC division. (On carriers, OC is the carrier air traffic control center [CATCC] division.) OP is the photographic intelligence division.

The following officers, when assigned, report to the ops officer: air intelligence, carrier air traffic control center (CATCC) officer, combat information center (CIC) officer, communications (COMM) officer, electronics material officer (EMO), electronic warfare (EW) officer, intelligence officer, meteorological officer, photographic officer, strike operations officer, and computer programmer (or computer maintenance officer).

Reactor: The reactor officer heads this department. He is responsible for the operation and maintenance of the installed reactor plants and their associated auxiliaries aboard nuclear-powered ships. Assistants to the reactor officer may include a reactor control assistant and a reactor mechanical assistant.

The special responsibilities of running a reactor plant require the reactor and engineering officers to closely coordinate their activities in the operation and maintenance of the propulsion plant.

Weapons: The weapons officer supervises and directs the use of ordnance and seamanship equipment, except for what is specifically assigned to other departments. Weapons, of all the shipboard departments, is the most complicated and often the largest. Some intricacies include the assignment of assistants to the weapons officer:

On ships with a weapons department but without a deck department, the first lieutenant is an assistant. On small ships, the duties of the weapons officer and the first lieutenant may be assigned to one officer.

On ships with antisubmarine warfare (ASW) arms and a weapons department, the ASW officer is an assistant.

On ships with missile arms and a weapons department, the missile officer is an assistant.

On ships with guns and a weapons department, the gunnery officer is an assistant.

On ships with nuclear weapons, the nuclear weapons officer is an assistant.

On ships requiring additional groups in the weapons department, the ordnance officer and the commanding officer of the Marine detachment may be assistants.

A fire control officer may also be assigned to the weapons department.

The weapons department has a complicated division organization. A single division would be designated as the first division. Ships with more than one division may have up to nine divisions responsible for gunnery and deck seamanship. Other divisions and divisional responsibilities include: W division, nuclear weapons assembly and aviation ordnance; F division, fire control; F-1 division, missile fire control; F-2 division, antisubmarine warfare (ASW); V division, aviation (for ships without an air department but with an aviation detachment embarked); G division, ordnance handling; and GM division, guided missiles.

SUPPORT DEPARTMENTS

Support (also called staff) departments include dental, medical, and supply.

Dental: The dental officer is responsible for preventing and controlling dental diseases and supervising dental hygiene. As-

Figure 14–3 Assault transports have a department not found on most other ships—the boat group.

sistant dental officers are sometimes assigned to larger ships. The D division is the only dental division.

Medical: The head of this department must be an officer of the medical corps (MC). He is designated as the medical officer. He is responsible for maintaining the health of personnel, making medical inspections, and advising the CO on hygiene and sanitation conditions. Assistant medical officers may be assigned. The H division is the only medical division. When no medical officer is assigned, hospital corps personnel run the department, but are assigned to the operations department for military and administrative functions.

Supply: Headed by the supply officer, this department handles the procurement, stowage, and issue of all stores and equipment of the command. The supply officer pays the bills—and pays the crew. He is also responsible for supervising and operating the general and wardroom messes, the ship's laundry and store, and the sale and issuing of clothing and small stores. A single-division ship has the S division only. Others have an S-1 division, general supply support; S-2 division, general mess; S-3 division, clothing, small stores, ship's stores, and services; S-4 division, disbursing; S-5 division, officers' messes; S-6 division, aviation stores; and S-7 division, data processing.

On larger ships, the supply officer may have assistants for disbursing, food service, ship's store, or wardroom mess.

SPECIAL DEPARTMENTS

The eight special departments are aviation, boat group, deep submergence, ordnance repair, repair, research operations, safety, and transportation.

Aviation: On a non-aviation-facility ship with a helicopter detachment embarked, an aviation department is organized and headed by the aviation officer. He is responsible for the specific missions of the embarked aircraft. His principal assistant is the helicopter control officer, but often one officer performs both functions. The single divisional unit is known as the V division.

Boat group: Assault transports (LPDs and LSDs) have a boat group department. The division is the BG division.

Deep submergence: Headed up by the deep submergence officer, this department launches, recovers, and services deep submergence vehicles (DSVs) or deep submergence rescue vehicles (DSRVs).

Ordnance repair: The ordnance repair officer is in charge. This department, found only on submarine tenders, usually has a single division, designated SR. A large department may be subdivided into the SR-1 division, repair and service; and the SR-2 division, maintenance of repair machinery.

Repair: On ships with a repair department, the repair officer is in charge. On single-division ships, there is only the R division. Multiple-division ships have an R-1 division, hull repair; R-2 division, machinery repair; R-3 division, electrical repair; R-4 division, electronic repair; and R-5 division, ordnance repair.

Research operations: Units with this department are headed by the research officer, who is responsible for the operation, maintenance, and security of research, special-purpose communications, and associated equipment.

Safety: The safety officer heads this department, which is found only aboard aircraft carriers. He is responsible for ship and aviation safety. The AS division is the only designated safety department division.

Transportation: Only Military Sealift Command (MSC) transports have this department, headed by the transportation officer. This department is responsible for loading and unloading, berthing and messing, and general direction of passengers. On ships without a combat cargo officer, the transportation officer is also the liaison with loading activities ashore. The single T division is used on small ships. Larger ones may have a T-1 division, which has the physical transportation responsibilities, and T-2 division, which handles the administrative end of transportation.

MARINE DEPARTMENT

The commanding officer of the Marine detachment, though not a department head, is in charge of matters pertaining strictly to the Marine Corps. He is generally assigned as a division officer of the weapons department. On a cruiser the detachment could be made up of 25 to 40 men with larger detachments aboard carriers. Responsibilities include comprising the ship's landing party; security of ship; providing gun crews; operating the ship's brig; serving as orderlys for the ranking officers; and other duties.

Division Organization

The division is the basic working unit of the Navy. It may consist of 20 specialists on small ships or as many as several hundred persons in a division on an aircraft carrier. The boss is the division officer, who reports to the department head. Division officers are assigned by the commanding officer.

The division officer is the one officer with whom division personnel come into contact every day. The junior division officer (who also functions as the division's training officer) and the leading chief petty officer (LCPO) are his principal assistants. (Some divisions have a technical and material assistant, usually a warrant officer or limited duty officer, to supervise the maintenance and repair of material or equipment.) Each division is organized into sections—the number depends on how many watch sections there are. A petty officer, who is a section leader, heads up each section.

You'll note that the person to whom you're immediately responsible, your section leader, is enlisted. So is the next in the chain of command, the LCPO. Any requests you make, whether to the division officer, the commanding officer, or the Navy Department in Washington, must first go through them. This is what is meant by going through the proper chain of command.

QUARTERS FOR MUSTER AND INSPECTION

Depending upon the type of ship and the ship's operating schedule, quarters for muster and inspection are held every work day before 0800. At this time, a muster of the entire crew is taken, every person on board is accounted for—including those on watch, on the sick (binnacle) list, late sleepers, prisoners, and those authorized to be absent. Unauthorized absentees are reported to the executive officer. Leading petty officers muster their divisions and report to the division officer, who inspects the division and gives the department head an accounting. Department heads report to the executive officer at "officer's call."

Each division is also assigned a parade—a space on deck for its formations. Fair-weather parades are on uncovered decks. Foul-weather parades are on covered decks and in designated living spaces.

Aircraft Squadron Organization

Operating squadrons, like ships, have a commanding officer, executive officer, department heads, and division officers.

COMMANDING OFFICER

The commanding officer, also known as the squadron commander, has the usual duties and responsibilities of any captain, insofar as they are applicable to an aircraft squadron. These include looking after morale, discipline, readiness, efficiency, and the issuing of operational orders to the entire squadron.

EXECUTIVE OFFICER

The executive officer, the second senior naval aviator in the squadron, is the direct representative of the commanding officer. He sees that the squadron is administered properly, and that the squadron commander's orders are carried out.

SQUADRON DEPARTMENTS

The XO is assisted by various department heads who are responsible for the organizing and training of their departments, the assignment of personnel within the department, the effective-

Figure 14–4 A jet is catapulted after the pilot receives the launch signal from the catapult officer.

ness of operation and planning, the security, safety, and cleanliness of assigned areas, and the maintenance of records and reports.

Administrative: This department is headed by the administrative officer, whose duties include handling classified and unclassified correspondence and required reports.

Operations: The operations officer heads the operations department. He is responsible for the operation of all squadron aircraft; the enforcement of all ground, water, and air rules concerning the movement of aircraft; and the supervision and instruction of all pilots and flight crews.

Maintenance: This department is headed by the maintenance officer, who is responsible for planning, coordinating, and executing all maintenance work on aircraft; for inspection, adjustment, and replacement of aircraft engines and equipment; and for the keeping of logs, records, and reports of the maintenance department.

Safety: The safety officer is designated a department head and has direct access to the commanding officer. He is a member of the accident board which investigates all accidents. As safety officer, he ensures compliance with all safety orders.

Ordnance: The head of this department, the ordnance officer, prepares the squadron rearming bill, issues safety precautions on aviation armament, supervises the training and execution of gunnery exercises, and advises pilots and crewmen of the tactics best suited to derive maximum effect from the available armament.

Supply: This department is headed by the supply officer, who is responsible for all squadron supplies, including procurement of materials, the supervision and control of all property and material for squadron use, maintenance of required records, and submission of supply and fiscal reports.

15. Weapons and Weapon Systems

To understand the weapons used by the Navy, one should first be familiar with these terms:

Ordnance: An overall term including everything that makes up a ship's firepower: guns, gun mounts, turrets, ammunition, guided missiles, rockets, and units that control and support these weapons.

Gun: Basically a tube closed at one end from which a projectile is propelled by the burning of gunpowder.

Rocket: A weapon containing an explosive section and a propulsion section. A rocket is unable to change its direction of movement after it has been fired.

Missile: A vehicle containing an explosive section, propulsion section, and a guidance section. A missile is able to change its direction of movement, after it is fired (launched), to hit the target.

Torpedo: Self-propelled underwater missile used against surface and underwater targets.

Mine: An underwater explosive weapon put into position by surface ships, submarines, or aircraft. A mine explodes only when a target comes near or into contact with it.

Depth Charge: Antisubmarine weapons fired or dropped by a surface vessel or aircraft, and set to either explode at a certain depth or in proximity to a submarine—no longer used by surface ships.

Bomb: Any weapon other than a torpedo, mine, rocket, or missile, dropped from an aircraft.

Weapons are the mainstay of the military. Without them, the Navy could not carry out its combat missions or defend its ships, planes, bases, and personnel. This chapter deals with two kinds of weapons: small ones for individual use, and big ones—like missiles and rockets—which help the Navy's combatant ships fulfill their missions. The Navy's overall mission is to maintain sufficient military capability to deter the use of military power against this nation and its allies, or against other countries important to our security and well-being. To this end the Navy must be prepared to conduct prompt and sustained combat operations at sea.

Missiles and Rockets

Missiles are self-propelled, unmanned vehicles that carry conventional explosives or nuclear warheads. Each missile has a

Missiles

guidance system that controls its direction in flight. A rocket is a small missile—2.5 to 12.75 inches in diameter—and has no self-contained guidance system.

MISSILE COMPONENTS

Each missile has four basic parts: the airframe, powerplant, warhead, and guidance system. Compared to an airplane, a missile's basic parts represent—in the same order—the aircraft, its engines, its bomb load, and its pilot.

A missile's airframe is a streamlined package that houses the powerplant, guidance system and warhead. It must be light, because the other parts are heavy. Airframes are made of aluminum alloys, magnesium, and high-tensile (which means high-stress) steel. The metals can withstand extreme heat and pressure.

The powerplant must propel the missile at supersonic speeds to minimize its vulnerability and increase its chance of intercepting a target. The missile must be able to operate at altitudes where there is no atmosphere. Therefore, when liquid or solid propellants are used, the missile must carry both the fuel and an oxidizer. Air-breathing plants carry only the fuel—gasoline, kerosene or other petroleum products—but they cannot operate above about 70,000 feet.

Air-breathers are cheaper to use than rocket engines. The three types of air-breathing plants are:

Pulse jet: This type of jet engine uses a flapper valve which alternately compresses and ejects air. Also called aerojet.

Turbojet: This plant is complex, expensive, and capable of producing higher combustion temperatures than most metals can withstand.

Ramjet: A supersonic lightweight that is easy to build. It uses a lot of fuel, however, and develops no thrust until it reaches a supersonic speed. It has to be carried aloft by another vehicle, or its takeoff must be rocket-assisted.

The warhead is the part that does the damage. Its explosive may be conventional—TNT or another chemical—or nuclear.

MISSILE GUIDANCE SYSTEMS

Missiles are either ballistic or guided. *Ballistic missiles* have a two-stage flight path. During the first stage, the guidance system corrects the flight path to the target. In the second stage, the missile flies a free or unsteered trajectory.

Guided missiles have a guidance system that constantly corrects the flight path until it intercepts the target. These missiles have one of five guidance systems: preset gyro, inertial, homing, command, or beam rider.

Preset gyro guidance was used in missiles built during World War II. Gyros kept the missile on a set course, and an onboard computer checked the angle of climb and acceleration. When the missile reached proper velocity and direction, power was shut off and the missile continued toward the target as a free projectile.

Inertial guidance uses a predetermined path programmed into the onboard missile computer. Missile speed and direction are checked constantly, and the computer makes corrections to keep it on course.

Homing guidance means the missile picks up and tracks a target by radar, optical devices, or heat-seeking methods. The homing system will follow a target's evasive movements, and the missile is fast enough to overtake a target trying to escape.

Command guidance means a missile is controlled by signals from a ground equipment system. After a missile is launched on an intercept course, a computer tracks both missile and target and transmits to the missile orders to change its track so it can hit the target, even though the target takes evasive action.

Beam-rider guidance requires the missile to follow a radar beam to the target. A computer in the missile keeps it centered within the radar beam. Several missiles may ride the beam simultaneously. If the missile wanders, it will automatically destroy itself.

MISSILE AND ROCKET DESIGNATIONS

All rockets and missiles carry three-letter designations, describing their launch environment, mission, types, and status:

Launch Environment	*Mission*	*Type Vehicle*	*Status*
A Air	D Decoy	M Guided Missile	J Special Test, Temporary
B Multiple	E Special	N Probe	
C Coffin	Electronic	R Rocket	N Special Test, Permanent
F Individual	G Surface Attack		
M Mobile	I Intercept, Aerial		X Experimental
P Soft Pad	Q Drone		Y Prototype
R Ship	T Training		Z Planning
U Underwater	U Underwater Attack		
	W Weather		

MISSILE CATEGORIES

Missiles may be air-to-air, air-to-surface, surface-to-air, or surface-to-surface. Some surface-launched missiles can be used against air or surface targets. Missiles can be fired from surface ships, submarines, or aircraft; the Marines use ground-launched weapons.

The chief air-to-air missiles are the Sidewinder (AIM-9) and the newer Phoenix (AIM-54). The Sidewinder is a supersonic homing weapon that uses passive infrared target detection, proportional navigation guidance, and torque balance control. The newest Sidewinder (AIM-92), with infrared seekers, is flown on the Tomcat (F-14) and Phantom (F-4) fighters and will be used by the new F/A-18. The Phoenix (AIM-54) was originally intended for the ill-fated F-111B aircraft. It, too, is flown on the Tomcat. The long-range Phoenix has a high-explosive warhead and proximity fuze, active-radar terminal homing, and an AWG-9 airborne missile-control system (AMCS). The Sparrow I became operational in 1956 and was replaced by Sparrow III (AIM-7F). An improved version, AIM-7M, of this all-weather radar-intercept missile is under development.

The principal air-to-surface missiles are the Shrike and the Harpoon. The Shrike (AGM-45) comes in four sections and consists of a guidance-control system, warhead, and solid rocket motor. The Shrike senses and homes in on radiation targets. The widely used Harpoon (AGM-84) is an anti-ship missile with active-radar terminal guidance. The wave-skimming Harpoon climbs rapidly in the last few seconds before hitting its target to avoid the ship's point defense.

Other air-to-surface missiles include the Bullpup (AGM-12), a short-range missile used against small targets; the Condor (AGM-53), a rocket-powered, TV-guided, conventional warhead weapon; the Walleye (AGM-62), a TV-guided glide bomb (a larger version, the Walleye II, is nicknamed "Fat Albert"); the Standard ARM (AGM-78), a tactical anti-radiation missile; the Bulldog (AGM-83), a modified Bullpup with laser guidance used for more effective close air support; the Focus I (AGM-87), a modified Sidewinder that is under test and evaluation; and the HARM (AGM-88), a high-speed anti-radiation tactical missile evolved from the Strike and Standard ARM for suppressing and destroying enemy radar air defense systems.

Surface-to-air/surface missiles include: Tartar (RIM-24), developed as a medium-range air-defense missile for use in destroyers.

Terrier (RIM-2) is a supersonic, solid-fuel, radar-guided missile used for task force defense against surface and air attack. It can be armed with nuclear or conventional warheads.

Sea Sparrow (RIM-7E), a surface-to-air version of the AIM-7E, has folded wings for use in a shipboard launcher. It can be used against ships. The improved NATO Sea Sparrow (RIM-7H) is an allied development. Both versions of the Sea Sparrow are designed for close-in protection of individual ships against attack by planes or missiles.

Talos (RIM-8), a long-range, two-stage supersonic missile that uses a mid-course beam-riding continuous wave interferometer (CWI) homing. It can be used against single or massed groups of high-speed aircraft or against surface targets. The Talos is presently being phased out. The *Long Beach* (CGN 9) is the only active ship still armed with it.

Standard MR (RIM-66) is a medium-range surface-to-air

weapon with surface-to-surface capability for shipboard use. It's roll-stabilized and replaces the Tartar (RIM-24B).

Standard ER (RIM-67) is an extended-range version of the RIM-66. It replaces the Terrier (RIM-2E). The difference between ER and MR is the propulsion system. ER has a separable booster and a sustainer rocket motor. MR has an integral dual-thrust-level rocket motor.

An improved Standard MR is being developed for use with the new Aegis fleet air-defense system; a new version of the ER will have increased range and may use a nuclear warhead.

Harpoon is an anti-ship cruise missile, fired from ships (RGM-84), submarines (VGM-84), or planes (AGM-84). It can operate in any weather, with active target acquisition and terminal guidance.

Figure 15–1 The Polaris submarine USS *Sam Rayburn* (SSBN 635) nears completion of its yard period.

The most recent addition to the Navy's missile arsenal is the Tomahawk (BGM-109) cruise missile. It is nuclear-armed and can make a highly accurate, long-range attack against land targets. A conventionally armed version can be used against enemy surface ships. The Tomahawk is an all-weather missile that can be launched from submarines, surface ships, land vehicles, and aircraft. It can fit into a submarine torpedo tube. The guidance system of the land-attack version is updated from time to time to match the contour of the terrain. A digital map is stored inside the missile. The anti-ship cruise missile has a modified Harpoon guidance system.

The principal ground-launched missile is the Redeye (MIM-43), a shoulder-fired air defense weapon used by the Marines. Two other ground-launchers are the Hawk (MIM-23), a low-altitude air defense weapon with an anti-missile capability, also used by the Marines, and the Stinger (XFIM-92), an improved Redeye. The Stinger has passive infrared homing and proportional navigation with a head-on launch capability. TOW (MGM-71) is an anti-tank weapon launched from helicopters or light vehicles. It is optically sighted and wire-guided.

Submarine-launched missiles include strategic and tactical types. The Polaris A-1 and A-2 strategic ballistic missiles were introduced during the 1960s in fleet ballistic-missile submarines (SSBN). Both have been replaced by the Polaris A-3 (UGM-27), which arms eight early SSBNs, and the Poseidon C-3 (UGM-73), used in 31 *Lafayette*-class submarines. The *Ohio* (SSBN 726) class, now under construction, will use the longer-range Trident C-4 (UGM-96). This missile has been designed to fit Poseidon launching tubes, and will eventually replace it in the *Lafayette* class. Each Trident strategic-deterrent missile is a three-stage solid-fuel weapon with improved guidance. Like Poseidon, it carries multiple independently targeted (MIRV) warheads.

Tactical submarine weapons include SUBROC (UUM-44), launched from a conventional torpedo tube. This is the submarine version of ASROC (RUR-5) and consists of a rocket carrying either a nuclear depth charge or a Mark 46 antisubmarine homing torpedo. When fired, SUBROC surfaces, ignites its rocket motor, and flies to the vicinity of the detected target before landing and activating its payload. The submarine version of Harpoon (UGM-84) is contained in a capsule for torpedo-tube launching. Like SUBROC, it comes to the surface before taking off.

Antisubmarine weapons include SUBROC, mentioned above, and its surface-ship equivalent, ASROC. The 12.75-inch Mark 46 homing torpedo is launched from ships, planes, and helicopters. The 21-inch Mark 48 torpedo is a long-range, wire-guided, homing weapon fired from submarine tubes against other submarines. It can also be used against surface ships.

The principal target missile (drone) is Firebee 1 (BQM-34A), a jet-powered, swept-wing, subsonic aircraft target system. It can be launched from the air or the ground and is recoverable. The Firebee II (BQM-34E) is a high-altitude supersonic version, capable of simulating enemy aircraft. The BQM-34T is a modified BQM-34E with a transponder and auto pilot. The Navy and Air Force have many versions of the Firebee.

Another target missile/drone is the Chukar (MQM-74), a recoverable gunnery aircraft weapon. It's a high-midwing monoplane that can be launched from shore or ships. It can be used as a decoy aircraft.

Still other target missiles/drones include the Bomarc, HAST (high-altitude supersonic target drone), LAST (low altitude), the rocket-propelled Gunrunner, and several decoys and unnamed missiles.

Fleet Operational Missiles

Name	Designation	Length	Weight	Speed	Range
Tartar	RIM	14 ft. 10 in.	1,425 lbs.	Mach 2.5	10 miles
Terrier	RIM	26 ft. 6 in.	3,070 lbs.	Mach 2.5	20 miles
Talos	RIM	33 ft.	7,800 lbs.	Mach 2.5	70 miles
Sea Sparrow	RIM	12 ft.	450 lbs.	Mach 2.5	12 miles
ASROC	RUR	15 ft.	1,000 lbs.		
SUBROC	UUM	20 ft. 6 in.	4,000 lbs.		
Polaris A3	UGM	32 ft.	35,000 lbs.	Mach 5/10	2880 miles
Poseidon	UGM	34 ft.	65,000 lbs.	n/a	2900 miles
Sparrow III	AIM	12 ft.	350 lbs.	Mach 3	5 miles
Sidewinder	AIM	9 ft. 6 in.	185 lbs.	Mach 2	5 miles
Phoenix	AIM	13 ft.	838 lbs.	Mach 2	30 miles
Harpoon	AGM/RGM	12 ft. 7 in.	1,160 lbs.		60 miles
	VGM	15 ft.	1,450 lbs.		
Standard MR	RIM	14 ft. 8 in.	1,350 lbs.		25 miles
Standard ER	RIM	26 ft. 2 in.	2,962 lbs.		40 miles

Bombs

Bombs have four chief parts. The case or body is normally made of steel and contains the explosive. The fuze or fuzes explode the bomb on contact or after a predetermined time interval. A surface blast is produced by instantaneous fuzing, an explosion delayed after contact is produced by a delayed-action fuze, and an underwater explosion is produced by a delayed-action fuze triggered by water pressure. The fin or tail assembly stabilizes the bomb during flight. The arming wire assembly keeps the fuze or fuzes from being armed until after the bomb is dropped. Bombs are classed as explosive, chemical, or practice.

Figure 15–2 An ordnanceman fuzes a 500-pound bomb on an A-6A Intruder aircraft.

EXPLOSIVE BOMBS

General purpose (*GP*), weighing 100 to 2,000 pounds, are generally used against unarmored ships or ground targets, for blast or fragmentation effect.

Semi-armor piercing (*SAP*), weighing 1,000 pounds, are used against carriers, cruisers, and "hardened" ground targets. They are designed to blow up after penetrating the ship.

Fragmentation bombs are very small explosives dropped in clusters against troops and ground targets.

CHEMICAL BOMBS

Gas bombs, containing mustard gas, phosgene, tear gas or vomiting gas, are used to harass or kill troops.

Smoke bombs, containing white phosphorus that ignites when the bomb explodes, spread over an area of 30 to 50 yards. It produces intense smoke for about five minutes and is used to conceal movements of ships or troops.

Incendiary bombs containing a mixture of gasoline or jet fuel and an agent that produces intense fire when ignited, are used against troops and ground targets. (These are also called napalm bombs.)

Practice and drill bombs used in training may be loaded with sand or water, but are inert and will not explode.

Torpedoes

The torpedo is a self-propelled explosive-carrying underwater weapon with its own automatic guidance system.

A torpedo consists of tail, afterbody, midsection, and head. The tail section includes the screws, fins, and control surfaces. The propulsion system is contained in the afterbody. The midsection houses batteries, compressed air, or liquid fuel. The head contains the explosive charge, fuze, and any acoustic or magnetic sensing devices.

Guidance systems are either preset, wire-guided, or homing. Preset torpedoes follow a set course and depth after they are launched. Wire-guided torpedoes have a thin wire connecting the torpedo and the firing ship. Through this wire, guidance signals can be transmitted to the torpedo to intercept the target. Homing torpedoes are either active or passive types. Active types depend on the sensing signals generated and returned to the torpedo through a sonar device inside the torpedo. Passive types listen for the noise generated by the target and thus home in on it.

Destroyer-type ships launch torpedoes from tubes mounted topside, or propel them to the target area with an antisubmarine rocket (ASROC). Submarines launch torpedoes from bow or stern tubes. Torpedoes from helicopters and fixed-wing aircraft are parachuted from the craft. They activate once they're in the water.

Weapon-Control Systems

A weapon, however powerful, is only as good as its accuracy. The process by which a projectile, missile, bomb, or torpedo is guided to its target is called weapon control. A potential target is first *detected* by a sensor (radar, sonar, lookout). It is then *evaluated;* if it proves to be hostile, a *decision* is made, according to prescribed weapons doctrine, whether or not to *engage*. If the target is to be engaged, the appropriate weapon is selected. All available information is assimilated by a computer to produce a weapon-control solution that will guide the weapon to produce a hit.

Ships, aircraft, and submarines all incorporate various types of weapon-control systems. Surface- and air-search radars have been continuously improved since World War II to detect high-performance targets at long ranges in any weather. The newer surface-ship control systems work with guns and missiles, and include radars and digital computers that can quickly acquire and track targets while directing shipboard weapons. The Mark 92 Fire Control System is being installed in destroyers and larger ships, while the lightweight Mark 86 system is going into missile frigates and smaller combatants. Perhaps the ultimate weapon-control system so far is the Aegis Weapon System Mark 7, a rapid-reaction long-range fleet air-defense system developed for use against aircraft and missiles. It includes the greatly improved AN/SPY-1 radar, a quick-reaction tactical computer for overall command control, a digital weapon-control system, and guided-missile launchers that will use the Standard-1 missile until the improved Standard-2 is ready for deployment. The Aegis system can also assist a force commander in controlling the surface and aerial weapons of a battle group, particularly in a modern tactical environment in which electronic warfare (detection and jamming) is heavily used. The first operational Aegis system will join the fleet with the commissioning of the missile cruiser *Ticonderoga* (CG-47), now under construction.

Many older electromechanical analog director systems are still in use in the surface fleet. Submarines and aircraft have their own control systems, similar in general principle to those used in surface ships; submarines, of course, detect and track their targets by sonar rather than by radar. Fleet ballistic missiles are controlled by a missile fire-control system, which is connected to the submarine's inertial navigation system. The navigation system keeps accurate track of the ship's position. When missiles are to be fired, the fire control system takes current position data and quickly computes firing information to direct the missiles on the proper ballistic course to hit their targets. While in flight, the missile keeps itself on course with the aid of an inertial navigation system; the new Trident missile can supplement this with stellar navigation.

Mines

Most information on mines is classified, so there can be only a very general discussion here. The several types of mines can be described according to the method of actuation (firing), method of planting, and position in the water.

METHOD OF ACTUATION

A contact mine fires when a ship strikes it. Usually it has lead horns containing glass tubes filled with an electrolyte. When the horn is struck, the glass breaks and the electrolyte generates enough current to fire the mine. Influence mines may be actuated by the underwater sound generated in a passing ship's current, by the ship's magnetic field, or by the mine's sensitivity to reduced water pressure caused by a passing ship.

METHOD OF PLANTING

Mines may be planted by surface craft, submarines, and aircraft. Surface planting mines are subject to enemy interception. Submarines can plant mines secretly, but cannot return to plant more mines until those planted have been destroyed or become inactive. Aircraft can plant mines in shallow waters where submarines and surface craft cannot operate.

POSITION IN THE WATER

Moored mines are anchored in place and float near the surface of the water, where a ship can strike them. They are usually contact types. Bottom mines lie on the ocean floor so they can only be used in relatively shallow water. They are influence mines, set off by sound, magnetism, or pressure.

Guns

Caliber, as applied to naval guns, has two meanings. In its first sense, it refers to bore diameter, expressed in inches (in.) or millimeters (mm). In its second sense, it expresses the ratio of the gun's length (in inches) divided by the bore diameter. Thus you can find the nominal barrel length of a gun if you multiply the bore diameter by the caliber of the gun. For example, a 5-inch/54-caliber gun has a barrel 270 inches long. The higher a gun's caliber, the longer it is; for example, the 5-inch/54 caliber gun is longer than a 5-inch/38 caliber gun, though both have the same bore diameter.

Guns are categorized as *major* (eight inches and larger), *intermediate* (less than eight inches but larger than four inches), and *minor* caliber (less than four inches). Guns may be described as:

Case guns: All modern Navy guns are case types. The propelling charge of powder is contained in a metal cartridge or case. Ammunition for case guns is either fixed or semi-fixed. Fixed ammunition has a propellant powder case and projectile attached as one unit. Small arms and minor-caliber guns use fixed ammu-

Figure 15–3 Gunnery crewmen keep their hands away from the moving parts of a 3-inch SODP gun mount during exercises at sea.

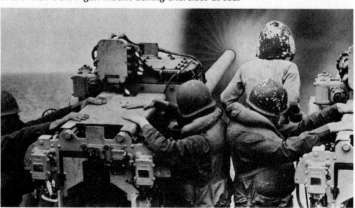

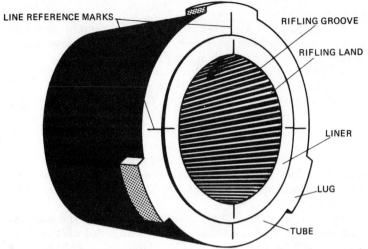

LINE REFERENCE MARKS

RIFLING GROOVE

RIFLING LAND

LINER

LUG

TUBE

Figure 15–4 A view through the barrel of a rifled gun shows the lands, grooves, and right-hand twist.

nition. Semi-fixed ammunition has two parts—powder case and projectile. All Navy guns 5 inches and larger use semi-fixed ammunition.

Bag guns: Heavy-caliber guns using silk bags, rather than cases, to contain their powder charges. The only bag guns remaining in the fleet are the 16-inch guns in four inactive *Iowa*-class battleships.

Automatic guns: These use the recoil of the gun to eject the fired case and reload the gun; 5-inch/54-caliber and 3-inch/50-caliber guns are automatic.

Semiautomatic guns: These guns eject the fixed case and leave the breech open in a proper position for hand loading, as in the 5-inch/38-caliber gun.

Dual Purpose (DP) guns: These can be used against both surface and air targets. The 5-inch/54-caliber and 5-inch/38-caliber guns are dual purpose.

Saluting gun: This gun fires salutes, normally black-powder blanks.

Line-throwing guns: These resemble single-barrel shotguns. They are used to shoot a light line across a space too great for a heaving line to be thrown.

A *battery* is a group of guns of the same size, normally controlled from the same point. The main battery of a ship consists of the largest guns aboard. The secondary battery consists of dual purpose guns or guns of the next size aboard. An antiaircraft (AA) battery consists of small caliber guns. It's usually called the machine-gun battery.

PARTS OF A GUN

The function and size of a gun mount will determine its major parts, but all guns have these components: stand, carriage, slide, housing, barrel, and breech assembly.

The *stand* is firmly attached to a ship's superstructure and contains the roller bearings on which the mount rotates.

The *carriage* usually has two parts, the base and gun carriage. The base is a platform that supports the gun carriage and rotates on the stand. The gun carriage supports the gun assembly in the vertical pivot points, called trunnion bearings.

The *slide* does not move, but it contains the bearing surfaces that support and guide the moving (recoiling) barrel and housing. The slide also contains the trunnions, which enable the gun to be elevated.

The *housing* moves within the slide during firing. The housing contains the breech assembly, barrel (which is locked to the housing by a bayonet joint), and a locking key.

The *barrel* is a rifled tube closed at one end to contain the pressure of the rapidly burning powder. The rear end of the barrel is attached to the breech housing, which contains the breech-block, sometimes called a plug. Forward of the breech end is an enlarged chamber that holds the propelling charge. The forward

268

Figure 15–5 These are the main assemblies of a 5-inch dual-purpose gun, and a cross-section of the barrel and housing.

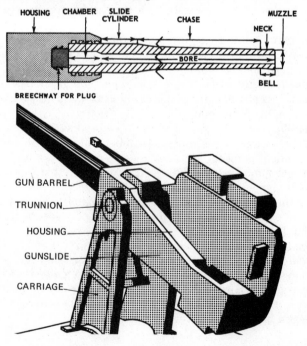

end of the chamber is tapered down to guide the projectile into the rifling, where it is seated prior to firing. The bore of the barrel is rifled in a right-hand twist of a uniform diameter, end to end. Rifling in a barrel causes a projectile to spin. This spinning motion keeps the projectile from tumbling once it leaves the barrel, and ensures greater accuracy. The slide cylinder area is a bearing surface for the slide during recoil and counter-recoil. The chase area is the tapered part of the barrel. Some guns have an enlarged area at the muzzle called the bell, which prevents any tendency of the barrel to split.

The *breech assembly* is the plug or block, which closes off the chamber end of the barrel. The breech assembly contains the firing mechanism that ignites the powder primer in the propellant case, and the extractors that remove the fired case from the gun chamber.

Guns now in use in the fleet include the following:

Size	Range	Type	Projectile Weight
8"/55 cal.*	30,400 yds.	Case—Semi-Fixed	335 lbs.
5"/54 cal. (MK 45)	25,900 yds.	Case—Semi-Fixed	75 lbs.
(MK 42)	25,900 yds.	Case—Semi-Fixed	75 lbs.
5"/38 cal.	17,300 yds.	Case—Semi-Fixed	55 lbs.
3"/50 cal.	14,000 yds.	Case—Fixed	13 lbs.

Recent experience has shown a need for new gun systems to meet contemporary requirements. The Mark 45 lightweight 5-inch/54-caliber gun system was developed for general use in surface ships. It is an automatic weapon designed with reliability and ease of maintenance in mind. The 76-mm Mark 75 is a remote-controlled, water-cooled, automatic gun of Italian design, being procured for use in smaller warships. Phalanx, the Mark 15 close-in weapon system (CIWS), is an all-weather weapon for ship defense against planes and anti-ship missiles. It includes its own automatic radar system and an electrically controlled, hydraulically operated 20-mm multi-barrel "Gatling" gun.

AMMUNITION

Ammunition is either fixed or semi-fixed and consists of a propellant charge (powder), the primer that sets off the propellant charge, and the projectile.

All naval guns use smokeless powder shaped into cylindrical grains. This shape, with holes through the powder grain, ensures that the powder will burn completely and predictably.

AMMUNITION HANDLING

Ammunition is perfectly safe to handle, as long as it is handled cautiously. Ammunition safety precautions (see Chapter 20) are

---

* In inactive fleet cruisers.

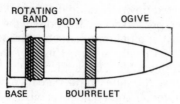

Figure 15–6 External features of a gun projectile.

Figure 15–7 Right front view of a 7.62 mm M14 rifle.

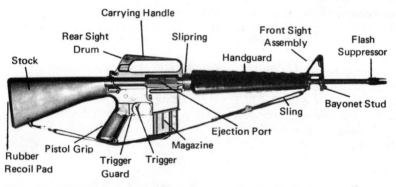

Figure 15–8 The 5.56 mm M16 rifle.

Figure 15–9 The 7.62 mm M60 machine gun.

posted in handling areas; learn them and follow them strictly. They're based on past experiences and disasters that cost lives, ships, and port facilities. Strict adherence to proper procedures can avert such accidents.

PROJECTILES

A projectile consists of five distinct parts. The *ogive* (pronounced o-jive) is the nose, the streamlined forward part. The *bourrelet* is the forward bearing surface of the body, which steadies the projectile in the gun barrel. The *body* is the main part of the projectile, and it carries the explosive charge. The *rotating band,* normally of brass, seals the projectile in the bore of the gun so that the full force of the propellant gases is exerted on the projectile. The *base* houses the base fuze tracer, or solid base plate. General types of projectiles include:

Thin-walled projectiles designed to damage by blast effect and fragmentation. The two subdivisions of this projectile type are high capacity (HC) for use against troops or surface targets, and antiaircraft (AA) for use against aircraft.

Thick-walled projectiles are armor-piercing (AP). They are designed to penetrate armor plating or thick concrete before exploding.

Common (COM) projectiles have a wall thickness midway between that of thin-walled projectiles and AP projectiles.

Special-purpose projectiles are not intended to inflict damage by explosion or fragmentation.

Illumination projectiles, called starshells, drop a flare attached to a parachute.

Smoke projectiles use white phosphorus to provide a smoke screen.

Window projectiles scatter metal foil strips to confuse radar.

Target projectiles do not contain explosives and are used for target practice.

Projectiles may be fitted with any of these types of fuzes or any combination of them:

The point-detonating fuze (PDF) explodes on impact.

The mechanical time fuze (MTF) contains a clock mechanism to explode the projectile at a preset time.

The proximity fuze (VT) contains a miniature radio transmitter that explodes the projectile when it senses a nearby target.

The auxiliary detonating fuze (ADF) acts as a booster in conjunction with a nose fuze.

The base-detonating fuze (BDF) is set to explode a fraction of a second after impact so that the projectile can penetrate its target before it explodes.

All fuzes in naval guns begin to function, or arm themselves, after the projectile leaves the gun barrel and has traveled a safe distance.

SMALL ARMS

Any weapon with a bore diameter of .60 inches or less is called a small arm. The military also classifies any hand-held or carried weapon as a small arm. The largest Navy small arm is the .50-cal. machine gun and the smallest is the .22-caliber pistol. The bore size of small arms is designated by caliber (cal.) or gauge (ga.) in the case of shotguns. Small arms have one of the following firing systems:

A semiautomatic weapon unlocks the bolt, extracts the fixed case from the chamber, ejects the fired case from the mechanism, cocks the hammer, and reloads automatically. The trigger must be released and pulled again to fire the weapon.

An automatic weapon follows the same chain of events as a semiautomatic weapon, except that as long as the trigger is held in the fire position, the weapon will continue to fire.

A double-action weapon, such as a revolver, operates off the trigger pull. When the trigger is pulled back, the cylinder rotates to align a chamber with the barrel, and the hammer is cocked and then released to fire the weapon. To fire again, the trigger must be released and pulled again.

272

The .45-caliber M1911A1 automatic pistol, in use for more than 60 years, is one of the most dependable small arms ever made. It is a recoil-operated, air-cooled, magazine-fed, semi-automatic hand weapon, and the only American service arm in use with a left-hand rifling. It contains five safety devices; two automatic safeties (disconnector and grip safety) and two manual safeties (thumb safety, and a half-cock notch). Anyone using a hand firearm must always remember that the only really effective safety system is responsible handling by the user. Mechanical safeties are never fool-proof and were never intended as a substitute for proper handling.

The .38-caliber revolver is a cylinder-loaded, exposed-hammer, single or double action, air-cooled, hand weapon. For single-action firing, the hammer is pulled back to the full cock position and then the trigger is pulled to fire the weapon. In double-action firing, the pull back on the trigger both cocks the hammer and then releases it to fire the weapon. Double-action firing requires two or three times the trigger-pull pressure of single-action firing. The revolver has two built-in safety mechanisms, the rebound slide and the hammer block.

The M14 rifle is an air-cooled, gas-operated, 20-round, magazine-fed, semiautomatic or automatic weapon. The rifle is normally issued with a selector shaft lock preventing full automatic fire. The M14 is the standard issue rifle to all ships and shore stations. It has a manual safety located in front of the trigger guard; to place the weapon on safe, press the lever back into the trigger guard.

Guns

The M16 Rifle is a gas-operated, magazine-fed, air-cooled, lightweight shoulder weapon, capable of either semiautomatic or automatic fire through the use of a selector lever on the left side of the receiver. Once the last round is fired from the magazine, the bolt is held open by the bolt catch. The weapon is equipped with a manual safety, a three-position fire selector lever on the left side of receiver (safe, semiautomatic, and fully automatic). It is considered safe only when the magazine is out, the chamber is empty, the bolt carrier is to the rear, and the selector is on safe. This is the standard issue rifle for all deployed and combatant forces.

The M60 machine gun is an air-cooled, belt-fed, gas-operated weapon firing the 7.62 mm (NATO) cartridge. The M60 machine gun may have either a bipod or tripod mount.

The .45-caliber line throwing gun is not used as a weapon, although the projectile it fires can be extremely dangerous. It resembles a small shotgun and is used for putting a light line across to another ship or to the beach when the distance is too great for a heaving line. It fires a .45-70 blank cartridge.

Shotguns issued to the Navy are civilian models procured for training, skeet shooting, and certain guard duty. All shotguns are 12 gauge.

IV. The Sailor at Sea

16. Living Aboard Ship

All ships have standard routines for in port and at sea. The routine varies on different ships; a submarine on extended patrol will run on a schedule different from that of an aircraft carrier on around-the-clock flight operations. Below is a sample standard routine. Departures from the normal routine are published in the plan of the day.

Plan of the Day (POD)

This is "the word"—the daily schedule of events, prepared and issued by the executive officer. It will name duty officers, assign various watches, and include any changes or additions to the normal routine and orders of the day—drills, training schedule, duty section, liberty section and hours, working parties, movies, examinations, or inspections.

The plan of the day—distributed to the OOD, all offices, officers, and division bulletin boards—is carried out by the OOD and all division officers.

Daily Routine at Sea

Note: When time is left blank, it is specified in the POD. Standard reports are in quotation marks.

Weekdays	Sundays and Holidays	Routine
0030	0030	JOOW (Junior Officer of the Watch) inspects the lower decks; hourly thereafter until sunrise.
0330	0330	Call the morning watch. Call galley force.
0400	0400	Reveille for duty cooks (cooks may specify time to be called by signing up in the wake-up log kept by the Boatswain's Mate of the Watch).
Sunrise	Sunrise	Turn off running lights. If the ship is darkened, light ship. Hoist pennants and flags as necessary.
0530	0600	Call masters-at-arms, division police

Weekdays	Holidays	Routine
		petty officers and mess cooks; early mess for designated men.
0600	0630	"Up all idlers." (Non-watchstanders).
0605	0635	Announce weather.
0615	0645	"Turn to. Scrub down weather decks. Sweep down all compartments. Empty all trash cans."
		"Lay below to the master-at-arms office for muster, all restricted men." Pipe sweepers, MAA report to OOD, "Idlers turned out." Clean boats and fuel boats as necessary.
0655	0655	"Clear mess decks." Mess call.
0700	0700	Pipe to breakfast. "Testing general alarm." On completion: "Test of general alarm completed." "Uniform of the day is _____," or "Uniform for captain's inspection is _____."
0720	0720	"Relieve the watch, on deck the _____ section. Lifeboat crew of the watch to muster."
0755	0755	OOD reports "8 o'clock" to the admiral if embarked, and "8 o'clock; request permission to strike eight bells" to the captain.
0800		Officers' call.
0805		Assembly.
0815	0815	Sick call.
	0815	Rig for church. "Knock off ship's work; shift into uniform for inspection." "The uniform for inspection is _____."
	0915	Officers' call. "All hands to quarters for inspection."
	0930	"Knock off work. Shift into clean uniform of the day." Church call. "Maintain quiet about the decks during divine service." Hoist the church pennant. At the end of service, pennant is hauled down. Commence holiday routine.
1115	1115	Pipe sweepers. "Sweepers, man your brooms. Make a clean sweep down fore and aft. Empty all trash cans." Early mess for cooks, mess cooks, and MAA.
1145		"Knock off all ship's work."
1150	1150	Quartermaster reports "Chronometers wound and compared" to OOD. OOD

		reports "12 o'clock" to the admiral if embarked, and "12 o'clock, chronometers wound and compared; request permission to strike eight bells" to the captain.
1200	1200	Pipe to dinner.
1220	1220	"Relieve the watch, on deck the _____ section. Lifeboat crew of the watch to muster."
1300		"Turn to." At this time, extra duty men muster at MAA office.
1300	1300	Pipe sweepers. "Sweepers, man your brooms. Make a clean sweep down fore and aft. Empty all trash cans."
1300		Friday, or when ordered, inspections call; "Stand by for inspection on lower decks."
1545		"Relieve the watch, on deck the _____ section. Lifeboat crew of the watch to muster."
1600	1600	Pipe sweepers. "Sweepers man your brooms. Make a clean sweep down fore and aft."
1600		"Knock off all ship's work."
1600 (or at least one hour before sunset)	1600	Test running lights and emergency identification signals, report their readiness to the OOD.
1630	1630	Early mess for mess deck MAA and mess cooks.
1645		"Observe sunset." Set the prescribed material condition. Division damage control petty officers report closures to Damage Control Central or sign the closure log maintained by the OOD on the bridge.
1655	1655	Mess call. "Clear the mess decks."
Sunset	Sunset	If the ship is to be darkened: "Darken ship. The smoking lamp is out on all weather decks." If ship is not to be darkened, turn on running lights, and haul down colors following motion of senior officer present afloat (SOPA). Lookouts report running lights bright; lifebuoy watch on fantail reports stern light and lifebuoy light bright (and on the half hour thereafter until sunrise). Boatswain in-

	Weekdays	Holidays	Routine
			spect weather decks and boats; when secured, report to the OOD.
	1700	1700	Pipe to supper. Close watertight doors, etc.: "Set material condition _____ throughout the ship."
	1720	1720	"Relieve the watch. On deck, the _____ section. Lifeboat crew of the watch to muster."
	1730	l730	Security patrols make reports to the OOD, and hourly thereafter. Coxswain of lifeboat reports lifeboat crew mustered and boat ready for lowering (every half hour) and engine tested (once each watch). Corporal of the guard reports police conditions (and half-hourly thereafter).
	1745	1745	Sick call.
	1800	1800	Pipe sweepers. "Sweepers, man your brooms. Make a clean sweep down on lower decks and ladders. Empty all trash cans." "Lay below to the MAA office for muster, all restricted men."
			Rig for movies. Movie call. Time and place as designated in plan of the day.
	1930	1930	"Now lay before the mast all 8 o'clock reports."
	1945	1945	"Relieve the watch. On deck, the _____ section. Lifeboat crew of the watch to muster."
	1955	1955	OOD reports "8 o'clock" to the admiral if embarked, and "8 o'clock, lights out and galley ranges secured; prisoners and lower decks secure; request permission to strike eight bells," to the captain.
	Dark	Dark	Dump trash and garbage. Pump bilges (Oil Pollution Act permitting). Blow tubes if wind favorable and plant requires it.
	2000	2000	Hammocks. "Out lights, and silence in all berthing spaces."
	2100	2100	MAA reports to the OOD "9 o'clock, lights out."
	2155	2155	Tattoo
	2200	2200	MAA reports to the OOD "10 o'clock, lights out."
	2330	2330	Call the watch.

278

Routine at Sea

Weekdays	Holidays	Routine
2345	2345	Relieve the watch, on deck, the _____ section. Lifeboat crew of the watch to muster.

Daily Routine in Port

Weekdays	Sundays and Holidays	Routine
0030	0030	JOOW inspects lower deck and boats in water (and hourly thereafter until reveille).
0330	0330	Call the watch.
0350	0350	Relieve the watch.
Daylight		Call galley force. Turn off all unnecessary lights.
Sunrise		Turn off anchor, boom, and gangway lights. Hoist guard flags, absentee pennants as necessary. If darkened, light ship; the smoking lamp is lighted on the top side.
0540	0600	Call MAA, division police petty officer, mess cooks, and boat crews. Early mess for designated personnel.
0600		Reveille. "Reveille, all hands, heave out and trice up."
0605		Announce weather to the crew.
0615		"Turn to. Scrub down weather decks, sweep down compartments, empty all trash cans." Pipe sweepers. Division police petty officers report to the duty MAA that men of their division are turned out. MAA reports to OOD "Crew turned out." Fuel all boats and test engines.
0655	0715	Mess call. "Clear all mess decks."
0700	0720	Pipe for breakfast, "Uniform of the day is _____," or "Uniform for inspection is _____," Meal pennant is hoisted.
0705		Announce weather over officer's circuit.
0720	0740	"Relieve the watch."
0750	0750	Guard of the day.
0755	0755	First call. Hoist PREP signifying prepare for colors. OOD reports "8 o'clock" to the admiral if embarked, and "8 o'clock, request permission to strike eight bells" to the captain.

	Weekdays	Holidays	Routine
	0800	0800	Morning colors. Meal pennant hauled down.
	0800		All hands to quarters for muster. Officers' call.
	0805		Assembly.
	0815		Pipe retreat. "Turn to, commence ship's work."
		0800	"Turn to, sweep and clamp down weather decks and living spaces.
	0815	0815	Sick call.
		0815	Rig for church. "Knock off work. Shift into uniform for inspection. The uniform for inspection is _____," Officers' call. "All hands to quarters for inspection."
		0915	"Knock off work. Shift into clean uniform of the day."
		0930	Church call. "Maintain quiet about the decks during divine service." Hoist the church pennant. At the end of divine service, haul down the church pennant. Commence holiday routine. Inspection of mess cooks.
	1115	1115	Early mess for mess deck MAA and cooks.
	1115	1115	Pipe sweepers. "Sweepers, man your brooms. Make a clean sweep down fore and aft. Empty all trash cans."
	1145		"Knock off all ship's work."
	1150	1150	Quartermaster reports "Chronometers wound and compared" to the OOD.
	1155	1155	Mess call. "Clear the mess decks." OOD reports "12 o'clock," to the admiral if embarked, and "12 o'clock, chronometers wound and compared; request permission to strike eight bells" to captain.
	1200	1200	Pipe to dinner. Hoist meal pennant.
	1220	1220	"Relieve the watch." "Commence holiday routine." Extra duty men muster at MAA office.
	1300		"Turn to."
	1300	1300	Pipe sweepers. "Sweepers, man your brooms. Make a clean sweep down fore and aft. Empty all trash cans."
	1300		Haul down meal pennant. Friday, or when ordered, inspection call. "Stand by for inspection of lower decks."

Routine
in Port

Weekdays	Holidays	Routine
1545	1545	"Relieve the watch."
1600	1600	Pipe sweepers. "Sweepers man your brooms. Make a clean sweep fore and aft."
1600		"Knock off all ship's work. All hands shift into the uniform of the day. Extra duty men muster at MAA office.
1600 (or at least one hour before sunset)	1600	Test anchor and boom lights. Rig and test gangway and flood lights. Report their readiness to OOD. Liberty call.
Half hour before sunset		Guard of the day.
5 minutes before sunset		First call. Hoist PREP.
Sunset		Evening colors. Turn on anchor, boom, accommodation ladder (brow), and flood lights. If ship is to be darkened, "Darken ship. The smoking lamp is out on the topside."
1645	1645	Early mess for mess deck MAA and mess cooks.
1700	1700	Closure of watertight doors, etc.; "Set material condition _____ throughout the ship."
1730	1730	Pipe to supper. Hoist meal pennant, if before sunset.
1750	1750	"Relieve the watch."
1800	1800	Haul down meal pennant at sunset or completion of supper. Rig for movies.
1815	1815	Pipe sweepers. "Sweepers man your brooms. Make a clean sweep down all lower decks and ladders. Empty all trash cans." Lay below to the MAA office for muster, all restricted men." Movie call. Time and place as designated in plan of the day.
1930	1930	"On deck, all the 8 o'clock reports."
1950	1950	"Relieve the watch."
1955	1955	OOD reports "8 o'clock" to the admiral if embarked, and "8 o'clock, lights out and galley ranges secured. Request permission to strike eight bells" to the captain. Executive officer (or command duty officer) reports to captain (if on board) "All departments secure for the night (or as appropriate)."

	Weekdays	Holidays	Routine
	2000	2000	Hammocks, "Out all lights and silence in all berthing spaces."
	2100	2100	MAA reports to OOD "9 o'clock, lights out." Tattoo. "Turn in, keep silence about the decks." Taps (5 minutes after Tattoo).
	2200	2200	MAA reports to OOD "10 o'clock, lights out."
	2350	2350	"Relieve the watch."

Standard Organization and Regulations of the U.S. Navy

If a sailor had to learn a new set of regulations and an entirely different organization every time he moved from one division, department, or ship to another, he would waste time. The Navy has standardized everything—routine, regulations, and organization—as much as possible on all ships.

This information is contained in the current edition of the Standard Organization and Regulations of the U.S. Navy (OPNAV-INST 3120.32). You will be loaned a copy. Your daily and weekly routine aboard ship will be governed by this instruction, as will the organization of your division and your department. You must first know and become familiar with the general regulations, a list of which follows. You must read all of the regulations and sign a statement to the effect that you have done so, and that you understand them. Whether you are aboard a minesweeper or an aircraft carrier, the titles and numbers of the general regulations will be the same.

Figure 16–1 Part of life aboard ship is swabbing decks—and getting your feet wet.

The Battle Bill

This bill assigns sailors to specific jobs at general quarters (GQ) stations, and for all other conditions of readiness. Battle station and duty assignments are made by billet number—a combination of number and letter indicating a man's division, section within the division, and his seniority within that section.

Once you've reported aboard your ship and are assigned to a division, you will receive a billet slip which contains your billet

Figure 16–2 Watches are maintained for communication, security, and safety of a ship and crew.

number and the duties for the various bills. It's your responsibility to know your station and the duties required of you for each bill.

A new system of manning some classes of ships, called the *ship manning document* (SMD), is now in effect. Rather than basing crew assignments on billets in the battle bill, it relates tasks to man-hours as already implemented in the Navy's 3-M maintenance system. Each ship included in this system receives an SMD outline from which assignments are made. All new ships joining the fleet are organized under the SMD system.

Watch, Quarter, and Station Bill

This bill displays in one place the duties of each man in each emergency and watch condition. It also shows your duty requirements in the administrative and the operational bills.

WATCH ORGANIZATION

A ship in commission always has sailors on watch. Even when the ship is tied up in port and is receiving steam and electricity from the pier or another ship, it is necessary to maintain a watch for communications, security, and safety. Those assigned to watches are called watchstanders. "Watch" may refer to the location of the person on watch, such as the forecastle watch or bridge watch; or it may refer to the section of the ship's crew on duty, as in "Relieve the watch, on deck the third section."

Traditionally, the 24-hour day is divided into seven watches:

0000–0400	Mid-watch	1600–1800	First dog watch
0400–0800	Morning watch	1800–2000	Second dog
0800–1200	Forenoon watch		watch
1200–1600	Afternoon watch	2000–2400	Evening watch

The "dog watches"—from 1600 to 1800, and 1800 to 2000—serve to alternate the daily watch routine so sailors with the mid-watch one night will not have it again the next time. It also affords each watchstander an opportunity to eat the evening meal.

CONDITIONS OF READINESS

Officers and men assigned to watch-keeping duties are trusted with the safety of the ship, its machinery and equipment, and all the people on board. Watch officers are in charge of the various watches. The commanding officer may assign as a watch officer any commissioned or warrant officer he considers qualified. When conditions require, the CO may assign petty officers to such duty. The watch organization varies according to a ship's condition of readiness:

Condition I: General quarters, all hands at battle stations.

Condition II: Modified general quarters, used on large ships to let the crew relax.

Condition III: Wartime cruising. Usually only one of three sections on watch and only certain stations manned or partially manned.

Condition IV: Peacetime cruising. Only necessary men on watch, rest of crew engages in work or training.

Condition V: Peacetime watch in port. Enough of the crew is on board to get the ship underway or handle emergencies.

Variations of these conditions include:

Condition IA: All hands on station to conduct amphibious operations and limited defense of the ship.

Condition IAA: All hands at battle stations to counter an air or surface threat.

Condition IAS: All hands at battle stations to counter a submarine threat.

Condition IE: Temporary relaxation from GQ for brief periods of rest and distribution of food at battle stations.

Condition IM: All hands at battle stations to take mine countermeasures.

Depending on the condition of readiness, which affects disposition of the crew and condition of armament, the ship establishes certain material conditions, concerned with watertight doors and hatches and the damage control systems. (For details on markings of fittings and the various material conditions, see Chapter 18, pages 315–17.)

The watch organization for Condition IV, the normal peacetime cruising condition, is shown in Figure 16–3. It includes an adequate number of qualified personnel for the safe and effective operation of the ship, yet allows for the most economical use of personnel in watch assignments. In Condition IV, no weapon batteries are manned, the engineering plant is ready for speeds as ordered, Material Condition YOKE is modified for access in daylight, and aircraft are in the condition of readiness required by the flight schedule. The combat information center (CIC) and the exterior and interior communication systems are manned for routine purposes. Complete surface lookout coverage is provided, and when flight operations are in progress, air lookouts are posted.

WATCH SECTION

Each sailor is assigned to a numbered section of the watch. When the word is passed that a specific section has the watch, everyone in that section immediately reports to his watch station. A ship may have as many as five watch sections.

On some ships, especially for in-port watches, a division may
consist of a port watch and starboard watch. Each is divided into

two sections. Odd-numbered sections, 1 and 3, are in the starboard watch. Even-numbered sections, 2 and 4, are in the port
watch.

**Living
Aboard
Ship**

RELIEVING THE WATCH

The oncoming watch should be on station 15 minutes before
the hour so the relief can receive information and instructions
from the off-going watch. Some ships muster the oncoming
watch to make sure each man is ready ahead of time. Relieving
the watch must be a controlled and precise function. Experience
has shown that a ship's ability to handle casualties and tactical
decisions is significantly reduced during the transition period between watches.

When reporting for watch, say "ready to relieve." The man on
watch then passes on pertinent instructions or information.
When you understand all conditions and instructions say, "I relieve you." Thereafter you assume complete responsibility for
the watch.

UNDERWAY WATCH

There are seven key watch assignments for the underway
watch. All other members of the watch section have important
responsibilities to one or more of them.

Command Duty Officer (CDO): Although an official watchstander, the CDO may be on duty for a period of several
watches. The CDO is eligible for command at sea. He is designated and empowered by the captain to advise, supervise, and
direct the OOD in matters concerning the general operation and
safety of the ship.

Officer of the Deck (OOD): The OOD is in charge of the ship
and is responsible to the CO for the safe and proper operation of
the ship. This includes navigation, ship handling, communications, routine tests and inspections, reports, supervision of the
watch, and carrying out the plan of the day (POD).

Junior Officer of the Deck (JOOD): The JOOD is the principal
assistant to the OOD. Anyone making routine reports to the
OOD normally makes them through the JOOD or the JOOW.

Junior Officer of the Watch (JOOW): The JOOW, when assigned, is a line officer on watch, in training for qualification as
the OOD. He normally stands his watch in the pilot house but
may be stationed on the open bridge during complex tactical operations or when directed by the OOD for indoctrination.

CIC Watch Officer: He supervises the operation of the combat
information center (CIC), which reports, tracks, and evaluates air,
surface, and submarine contacts during the watch.

Engineering Officer of the Watch (EOOW): The EOOW is the
officer or petty officer on watch, who has been designated by the

Figure 16–3 Watch organization underway.

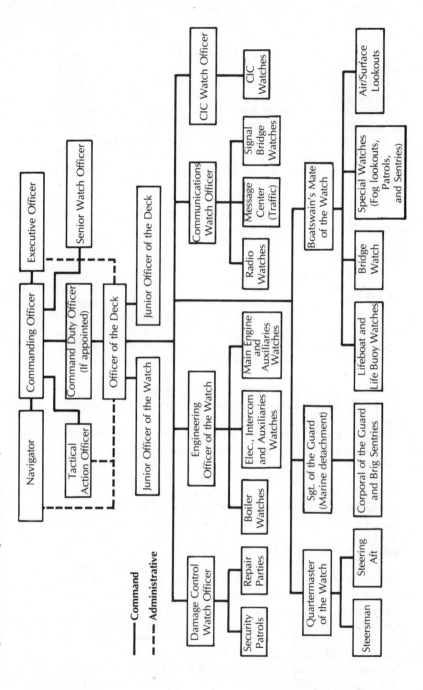

—— Command
--- Administrative

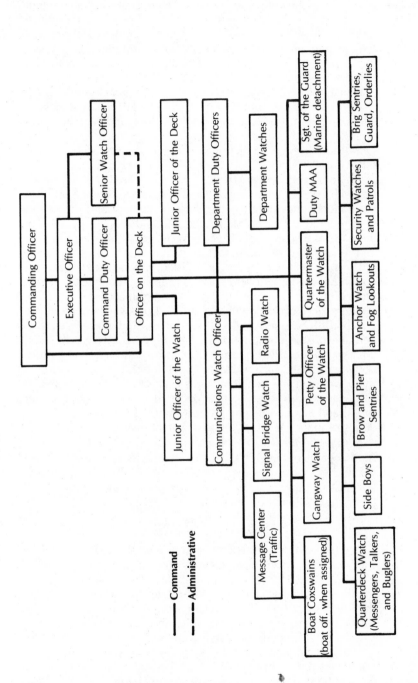

Figure 16–4 Watch organization in port.

engineering officer to take charge of the engineering department watches. He is responsible for the safe and proper performance of all engineering watches except damage control. He sees that the engineering log, the engineer's book, and other records are kept properly and that all orders from the OOD are promptly and properly executed.

Damage Control Watch Officer: The DC watch officer is responsible for maintaining any material condition of readiness in effect on the ship and for checking, repairing and keeping in full operation the various hull systems. He reports directly to the OOD on all matters affecting watertight integrity, stability, and other conditions that affect the safety of the ship.

On certain occasions a *tactical action officer* (TAO) may be assigned by the commanding officer. He is the CO's representative in all matters concerning the tactical employment and defense of the unit, and is responsible for the safe and proper operation of the combat systems. The TAO normally stands his watch in CIC, and reports directly to the CO.

The numbers and duties of enlisted watchstanders vary according to the type of ship and the operation being carried out.

On the bridge, the minimum will be: helmsman, lee helmsman, quartermaster of the watch (QMOW), boatswain's mate of the watch (BMOW), lookouts, phone talker, and messenger. Depending on the construction of the ship, signalmen will stand their watches on the bridge deck or the signal bridge. Other underway watches—again depending on the ship and operation—include lifebuoy watches, lifeboat watches, various watches in CIC, main radio, brig, hangar deck, main engineroom, boiler room, and auxiliary engineroom (Chapter 17 discusses specific duties of these and other enlisted watches.)

A "bare-bones watch" is sometimes used in Condition III and IV. It consists of the OOD, helmsman, one lookout, one quartermaster, and one signalman. Ships using the bare-bones watch system are equipped with automatic bell loggers, fog signal timers, and steering devices.

IN-PORT WATCH

The basic in-port peacetime watch (see Figure 16–4) is based on Condition V. In an emergency or war, additional watches may be required for security, antisabotage, and weapons-systems manning. As in the underway watch, the principal officers are the CDO and OOD. The OOD reports directly to the CO for the safety and general duties of the ship, and to the CDO (XO when CDO is not assigned) for carrying out the ship's routine. He also carries out the plan of the day, handles honors and ceremonies, conducts routine inspections, observes safety precautions, inspects liberty parties, and prepares the deck log. A JOOD is also assigned in port. Assignment of a JOOW is optional; if assigned, he is an additional officer or petty officer on watch for qualification as an in-port OOD.

Other important people in the in-port watch organization include:

Boat Officer: When assigned, he is responsible to the OOD for the safe and proper operation of his boat, and the proper conduct of all personnel embarked.

Department Duty Officer: He is the officer or petty officer responsible for the proper functioning of a department. He reports to the CDO.

Communications Watch Officer (CWO): The CWO, as a representative of the communications officer, is responsible to the OOD for the reliable, rapid, and secure conduct of external, visual, and radio communications (other than tactical and air control voice radio); and for the efficient administration of internal routing and related communications system.

Some of the enlisted bridge watchstanders—BMOW and messenger—move to the quarterdeck when in port. The signal watch continues on the signal bridge and most of the engineering watches continue if the ship is providing her own steam, heat, and power. If a quarterdeck petty officer of the watch (POW) is assigned, neither a BMOW nor QMOW is assigned. Other important watches include side boys, duty master-at-arms, gangway watch (when required), sergeant of the guard (when Marines are embarked), and various security watches and patrols. (Chapter 17 describes details of these other watch assignments.)

Special Evolutions

The movement of ships—in and out of restricted waters, getting underway or returning to port—is complex and tedious. The job requires a concentrated effort by most of the ship's crew. When a special detail is needed, the captain does what a professional football coach does—he calls on the specialty team. In most cases, the special unit supplements the regular watch; in other instances the special unit relieves the regular watch until the evolution is completed.

SPECIAL SEA DETAIL

Whenever a ship is leaving or returning to a pier or anchorage, the special sea detail is set. Getting a small ship underway, or bringing her to anchor, can be a fairly simple and quiet operation when everyone concerned is on his toes. But the checklist for getting a big ship underway is like the count down on a space shot. Each ship has its own list and preparations may start up to eight hours in advance of the actual event. There may be literally hundreds of things to do, and responsible sailors see that they are all done properly and promptly.

Those assigned to the special sea detail must be well trained and experienced, for moving a ship into or out of a crowded harbor can be difficult and dangerous. No mistakes are allowed.

GETTING UNDERWAY

This is the typical routine for getting underway. The times listed are the hours prior to the occurrence of the actual event:

8 hours: Start gyros; energize and calibrate all radar repeaters.

6 hours: Verify schedule for lighting off boilers.

3 hours: Verify arrangements for discontinuing services from the pier, such as shore power and crane service.

2 hours: Ascertain from the XO:

(1) Whether there is any variation in standard sequence of setting special sea and anchor detail, (2) the time of heaving short or "singling up" lines, (3) the disposition of boats, (4) his instructions concerning U.S. and guard mail, and (5) the number of passengers and expected time of arrival.

After obtaining permission from the XO, start hoisting boats and vehicles as soon as they are no longer required and rig in booms and accommodation ladders not in use; secure for sea. Have the word passed as to the time the ship will get underway. Energize all radars except those prohibited by local electromagnetic emission restrictions.

1½ hours: Muster the crew.

1 hour: Set Condition YOKE; MAA inspects for stowaways; tune and peak radars; conduct radio checks on all required circuits; and ensure that pit sword is in a raised position.

45 minutes: Underway OOD, JOOD and JOOW take stations on bridge. N, A and E divisions man the after steering and pilothouse, and test steering engine, controls, communications, and emergency steering alarm. Ship is cleared of all visitors.

30 minutes: Set the special sea and anchor detail; prepare both anchors for letting-go; OOD shifts watch to the bridge. Sound-powered phone circuits are tested. Departmental reports of readiness to get underway are received, as is the MAA report of inspection for stowaways. Draft of the ship, fore and aft, is recorded, and, if required, the deck-edge antennas are raised.

15 minutes: CO's permission is obtained to test main engines; after screws are checked for clearance, engineering control is directed to test engines. Report ready for getting underway to the XO. Test whistle; "heave short" or "single up" lines when so ordered; standby to receive tugs and pilots; and if alongside a pier, ensure that all shore connections are broken and that the brows are ready to be removed. When required, sound "quarters for leaving port."

10 minutes: The command "maneuvering bells" is ordered by setting the engine revolution indicator system on a certain repetitive number combination beyond the range of the engines— such as 999, if applicable. Warn engineering control to stand by to answer all bells. If a flag officer is embarked, request permission to get underway as scheduled.

Zero time: Underway.

ENTERING PORT

The schedule for entering port or restricted waters is:

(When directed): Deballast as far in advance as possible and for as long as regulations permit. Pass the word "go to your stations, all the special sea and anchor detail." Have both anchors ready for letting-go prior to arrival at channel entrance. Determine and record fore and aft draft of the ship; blow tubes; dump all trash and garbage overboard; pump bilges when conditions permit; and, subject to the concurrence of the navigator, raise the pit sword. Ensure smart appearance of the ship.

1 hour: Ascertain expected time of anchoring or mooring from the navigator and notify the engineering officer, weapons officer, first lieutenant, and engineering control. Pass the word "make all preparations for entering port. Ship will anchor (moor _____ side to) at about _____. All hands shift into the uniform of the day." Man depth-determining devices. Weather permitting, remove the canvas covers that are normally off when in port. Obtain information concerning boating from XO and inform first lieutenant. Lay out mooring lines, if required, and set up and check all harbor and tug radio frequencies.

30 minutes: Sound "man all boats" as signal of execution for boat crews, winch crews, boat handlers, and boom and gangway rigging details to take their stations. Obtain information from navigator on depth of water at anchorage, and on the anchor and scope of chain to be used from the XO (and so inform the first lieutenant). When mooring to a pier, inform first lieutenant on the tide and time of high water.

20 minutes: When required, designated personnel fall in at quarters for entering port. Direct CMAA to inspect upper decks to see that crew is in proper uniform.

15 minutes: Station in-port deck watches. Instruct to stand by on the quarterdeck the guard mail PO, mail clerk, movie operator, shore patrol, and any other details leaving the ship in the first boat. If mooring to a buoy, lower a motor whaleboat with buoy detail as directed. Stand by to receive tugs and pilots.

On anchoring or mooring: Set the in-port watch. Secure main engines, gyros, and navigational radars as directed. Record draft of ship fore and aft.

When the special sea detail is set, the CO (with an experienced telephone talker), the navigator (with quartermasters), and others will be on the bridge. The first lieutenant and anchor detail will be on the forecastle, the line handlers will be at stations on the main deck and fantail. Other stations manned will include CIC, main engine control, signal bridge, and sonar control.

LOGS AND REPORTS

A log is a permanent, written record. The ship's deck log, the engineering log, magnetic compass record, and engineer's bell book are the official records of a ship. No erasures may be made in any of these logs. When a correction is necessary, a line can be drawn through the original entry so it remains legible, and the correct entry inserted. Corrections, additions, or changes in any log shall be made only by the person required to sign it, and shall be initialed by him on the margin of the page.

Ship's Deck Log: This is the official, chronological record of events occurring during a watch, which may concern the crew, operation, and safety of the ship, or may be of historical value.

The OOD supervises the keeping of the log, and the quartermaster of the watch (or other designated watchstander) writes the log, with each event recorded as directed by the OOD, or in accordance with standing instructions. All log entries are made with a ballpoint pen, using black or blue-black ink.

The navigator examines the log daily, and the commanding officer approves it at the end of each month. The original ship's deck log goes to the Chief of Naval Operations every month. A duplicate copy is kept on board for six months, after which it may be destroyed.

Magnetic Compass Record Book: This is a complete record of all magnetic compasses on board. It also records gyro compass errors. When the ship is underway, comparisons between the gyro and magnetic compasses are made on every course change and entered in the book.

Engineer's Bell Book: This is kept in the engineroom. It is the official record of the engine orders received from the bridge.

Logs may be consulted many years after they were written—even after the ship has been sunk or scrapped—in connection with claims for pensions by men who served in the Navy, or as evidence before courts and other legal bodies. For such reasons, log entries should be complete, accurate, and in standard naval language. Names should be printed, and figures must be recorded carefully. Sample ship's deck log entries are contained in the *Watch Officer's Guide,* which should always be available in the quarterdeck or bridge desk.

Daily routine reports are made to the commanding officer at 0800, 1200 and 2000. About 0750 the crew is mustered, the day's orders read, and a report of absentees made to the XO by department heads. The results are reported to the CO by the exec.

At 1200, the 12 o'clock reports, which consist of the fuel and water report, magazine temperature report, and the 1200 position report, are made to the OOD by the engineer officer, the weapons officer, and navigator, respectively. The OOD messenger makes the 12 o'clock report to the commanding officer in somewhat this form.

"Good morning, Captain. The officer of the deck sends his respects and reports the hour of 12 o'clock. All chronometers have been wound and compared. Request permission to strike eight bells on time, sir." (This procedure will vary from ship to ship depending on the skipper's instructions.)

Underway, the 8 o'clock reports are made by all department heads at 1930 to the executive officer, who then takes them to the CO. These usually consist of equipment status reports and 2000 position reports. In port, the 8 o'clock reports are made to the CDO by the departmental duty officers.

Ship's Bell: Before timepieces were common, time aboard ship was marked by a so-called hour-glass, which ran out every 30 minutes. Then the glass would be turned over, to start measuring another 30 minutes, and the bell would be struck so all hands knew a half-hour had passed. At the end of each half-hour, the bell would be struck one more time. Thus it was struck once at the end of the first half-hour and eight times at the end of the fourth hour. This practice still continues despite the use of clocks and watches. After eight bells are struck, the sequence starts all over again. An odd number of bells marks a half-hour, and an even number marks an hour. For the relation between Navy time, bells, and watches, see the table below.

Midwatch		Morning Watch		Forenoon Watch		Afternoon Watch		Evening Watch		Night Watch	
time	bells	time	bells	time	bells	time	bells	time	bells	time	bells
0030	1	0430	1	0830	1	1230	1	1630	1	2030	1
0100	2	0500	2	0900	2	1300	2	1700	2	2100	2
0130	3	0530	3	0930	3	1330	3	1730	3	2130	3
0200	4	0600	4	1000	4	1400	4	1800	4	2200	4
0230	5	0630	5	1030	5	1430	5	1830	5	2230	5
0300	6	0700	6	1100	6	1500	6	1900	6	2300	6
0330	7	0730	7	1130	7	1530	7	1930	7	2330	7
0400	8	0800	8	1200	8	1600	8	2000	8	2400	8

Bells are struck from reveille to taps, but not during divine services or when fog requires that the bell be used as a fog signal. When the church call is sounded, the bell is struck once at the end of each phase of the call. When the bell is used as a fog signal at anchor, it is rung rapidly for five seconds at the end of each minute. On some ships it is customary for the youngest member of the crew to strike eight bells on New Year's Eve.

17. Shipboard Duties and Watchstanding

There are literally hundreds of different jobs aboard a large ship, each important to the mission of the ship. Because organization and routine are standardized as much as possible throughout the Navy, the jobs—what you do—are pretty much standardized, and the employment of your ship—what she does—is standardized to a degree. (Shipboard organization is covered in Chapter 14; shipboard routine in Chapter 16.)

Shipboard Operations

What your ship does depends on what type of ship she is. Most versatile are the warships—aircraft carriers, surface combatants, command ships and submarines—all of which have many-faceted missions.

Carriers perform a variety of tasks, all centered around their most unique feature—the ability to deliver aircraft within striking range of designated targets. Destroyers also perform a wide range of duties; they screen carrier task groups, carry out antisubmarine warfare, and provide fire support for amphibious assault operations. The principal function of cruisers is anti-air and anti-missile defense of fast carrier task forces. Submarines are grouped in two general categories based on their primary mission: attack and ballistic missile. Submarines are also assigned secondary missions, which may include surveillance and reconnaissance, direct task-force support, landing-force support, minelaying, and rescue.

In most other cases, the name of the category suggests the ships' primary missions: amphibious warfare ships, mine warfare ships, combatant craft (which include patrol, landing, mine countermeasures, and riverine warfare craft), auxiliaries, and service craft.

FLIGHT OPERATIONS

Flight ops are interesting and exciting—and very often dangerous. They require the combined efforts of many men who prepare the planes, brief the pilots, plot the weather, fuel and arm the aircraft, evaluate the results of missions, and interpret photo-

Figure 17–1 Crewmen in the flight deck control and launch operations room move the pieces that represent the flight deck activity aboard the carrier USS *Kitty Hawk* (CV 63).

graphic findings. Flight quarters stations for air department and air wing squadron personnel are the general-quarters (GQ) stations prescribed in the battle bill.

For a morning launch, aircraft are usually spotted (positioned) on the flight deck the night before. Jet aircraft, which must be catapulted, are spotted forward in position to taxi onto the catapults. The rescue helicopter is usually the first aircraft in the air and the last recovered (brought aboard).

At "flight quarters" men swarm on the flight deck. When the order is given, pilots man their aircraft and start engines. The carrier turns into the wind to increase relative wind speed down the flight deck and the air officer (also called the "air boss") gives the catapult officer (the "cat officer") a green light—meaning aircraft may be launched. An entire deckload of carrier aircraft can be launched within a few minutes.

Landing aboard a carrier is the most dangerous part of flight ops. All hands not directly involved must clear the flight deck and catwalks. Arresting-gear crews raise the arresting-deck pendants slightly above the deck, to engage the aircraft's tailhook. As the ship steams into the wind, the air boss orders the optical landing system (made up of mirrors) to be turned on, and gives the arresting gear officer the okay to commence landing operations. Aircraft fly a rectangular pattern on the port side of the carrier and use the optical landing system in their approach in order to maintain a constant angle of descent and correct air speed.

The landing signal officer (LSO), located aft on the port side of the flight deck, monitors all approaches. If the plane is not on the glidepath or the deck is not prepared to receive aircraft, the LSO flashes the pilot a waveoff—and the pilot applies full power, goes around the traffic pattern, and makes another approach. On a good approach with a clear deck, the pilot stays on the glidepath at full power until the aircraft touches the deck and the arresting gear brings the plane to a stop. If he misses the arresting gear, the pilot can fly off the angled deck and go around again. (A plane that misses the arresting gear and goes around again is known as a "bolter.")

After all aircraft have landed, they are respotted for the next launch. Tractors tow the aircraft to their final position. When the refueling and rearming are complete, the carrier is again ready to launch aircraft.

Flight-deck and hangar crews wear helmets and jerseys in the following combinations for quick identification:

Blue and blue	Plane-handling crews, chockmen.
Yellow and yellow	Plane-handling officers, directors.
White and blue	Elevator operators.
Green and green	Arresting-gear crews, catapult crews, hook runners, maintenance crews, photographers.
Green and yellow	Arresting-gear and catapult officers.
Red and red	Ordnance, crash and salvage, explosive ordnance disposal (EOD) crews.
Purple and purple	Fueling crews.
Brown and brown	Plane captains.
Red and brown	Helicopter captains.
White and white	Medical and transfer officer.
Green and white	Plane inspector.
White and blue	Messengers and telephone talkers.

You will hear various flight-deck personnel referred to as "a yellow shirt," or "a red shirt"—this is a reference to their jobs.

AMPHIBIOUS OPERATIONS

The goal of amphibious warfare operations is the establishment of a military force on an enemy shore. Marines are normally included in landing operations and, very often, units from all the armed forces take part.

A modern amphibious landing is a complicated operation that may involve hundreds of ships and small craft, and thousands of men. Planning for such an operation may take months. After planning is completed an operation order (OPORD) is issued—this covers organization, ships and units assigned, communications, minesweeping, naval gunfire and bombardment, air strikes, actual assault operations, and logistics. There will be training operations, perhaps even a full-scale rehearsal, before the actual amphibious operation takes place.

ASW OPERATIONS

The basic mission of antisubmarine warfare is to deny the enemy the effective use of his submarines. Our destroyers and many of our helicopter and fixed-wing aircraft are specifically designed for ASW. In addition, most of our major warships have an ASW capability. ASW operations include protective and offensive phases. Protective ASW includes escorting merchant convoys and carrier task force operations; offensive ASW include strike operations, missions designed to search out and destroy the submarine. The principal ASW weapons are torpedoes, antisubmarine rockets (ASROCs), submarine rockets (SUBROCs), and the light airborne multi-purpose system (LAMPS).

Sonar is the principal instrument used to detect submarines. In "active" sonar, signals sent out by a transmitter unit, are reflected off the submarine, and return to their source. This method is called "pinging," from the noise the transmitter makes. Another form, called "passive" sonar, keys into the signals or noises emitted by underwater vessels. Sonar is used by surface ships, submarines, and aircraft to detect and pinpoint enemy submarines. Helicopters hunt submarines by hovering in one spot and lowering a cable holding a transducer (transmitter and re-

Figure 17–2 The Marine Corps experimental vehicle LACH (lightweight amphibious container handler) removes an Army MilVan from an assault craft. In the background, a crane on the Navy's new elevated causeway removes a MilVan from another assault craft.

ceiving unit) into the water. Fixed-wing aircraft drop expendable sonobuoys equipped with radio hydrophones that pick up the broadcast underwater sounds. Patrol planes use the magnetic airborne detection device (MAD) to sweep a wide path.

Shipboard Duties

A compartment cleaner's job on a destroyer is the same as it is on a nuclear-powered aircraft carrier. The hundreds of ships in the Navy all go through the same cycles—repairs, post-repair trials, underway training, deployment, upkeep, and material and

Figure 17–3 A USS *Coronado* crewman prepares to flood the ballast tanks to allow amphibious craft to enter the ship's well deck.

military inspections. Details of the job and employment will differ, but it's the same Navy, no matter where you are.

A day's work aboard ship involves professional and military duties. "Turn to on ship's work" means that you carry out the professional duties of your rating. During general drills and when on watch, you may perform both general military assignments and professional duties. Duties of the various ratings are described in Chapter 2. General bills and drills are detailed in Chapter 19. The daily routine, at sea and in port, also requires men on duty at all times as watchstanders—see details in Chapter 16.

Enlisted Watchstanders

A Navy ship in commission can never be left unattended. The boilers must be kept fired, water and electricity must be maintained, and the magazines and other vital equipment must be guarded. While at sea, the lookout stations, the helm, and other stations must be adequately manned. All these functions are maintained 24 hours a day—not just 9 A.M. to 5 P.M., as with most office jobs ashore.

The watch system, divided into two parts—underway and in-port—is detailed in Chapter 16. Some key assignments for officers in the watch organization include the CDO, OOD, JOOD, and JOOW. There are also a number of important assignments for enlisted watchstanders within the top echelon. (In fact, many senior petty officers can qualify for some of the officers' assignments.) While there are scores of other enlisted watch assignments, those described below are the most important and most responsible jobs. The majority of other enlisted watchstanders report to, or through, these sailors.

UNDERWAY WATCH SECTION

The two basic types of enlisted watches in the underway section are: deck watches and navigational watches. The boatswain's mate of the watch (BMOW) is the petty officer in charge of the watch. His principal assistants include sky and surface lookouts, the messenger, the bridge sound-powered telephone talkers, lifeboat watch, lifebuoy and after lookouts, and fog lookouts. The navigational portion of the watch includes the quartermaster of the watch (QMOW), the helmsman, the lee helmsman, and the aft steering watch.

Boatswain's Mate of the Watch (BMOW): The BMOW is the most important enlisted assistant to the OOD. His status in these respects is the same—regardless of the readiness condition in effect, or the watch (sea or in-port) that has been set. It is his responsibility that all deck watch stations are manned, and that all men in previous watch sections are relieved. Although it is the duty of the section leader and the division petty officer to instruct the men they send on watch, the BMOW must verify that every man in his watch has been properly instructed and trained. A BMOW must be a qualified helmsman.

Sky and Surface Lookouts: Lookouts, who are trained in their duties by the CIC officer, perform their duties in accordance with the ship's lookout doctrine. Navy regulations require that night lookouts report on the navigational lights every half-hour: By tradition, the starboard lookout reports, "Starboard side light, masthead light, bright lights, sir"; the port lookout reports, "Port side light, range light, bright lights, sir." (Details of specific lookout duties and techniques are covered in Chapter 23.)

Messenger: The messenger stands his watch on the bridge. He delivers messages, answers telephones, and carries out other duties assigned by the OOD. The messenger normally comes from the weapons or deck department.

Bridge Sound-Powered Telephone Talkers: The JV talker mans the JV circuit on the bridge and must be familiar with other stations on the circuit. He relays all messages between the OOD and these stations; this includes forwarding all orders to the engine-order telegraph. The JV talker is normally a helmsman under instruction and is assigned from the weapons or deck department. The JL/JS talker mans the JL/JS bridge phones. He has the same responsibilities for receiving and relaying information as the JV talker. The JL/JS talker is normally assigned from the operations department. The use of sound-powered phones is described in Chapter 24.)

Lifeboat Watches: Each ship must be capable of rapidly recovering personnel from the sea. Lifeboat watches are set as necessary to ensure this capability. The maneuvering characteristics of the ship, sea conditions, the availability of rescue helicopters, and the nature of the ship's operations are some of the factors that are considered when establishing the readiness required for lifeboat watches. Although lifeboat watches are not necessarily required to be on station at the lifeboat, crews are always designated when at sea and are mustered as required.

Lifebuoy and After Lookout: This watch is stationed at a designated after station. The watch has a life ring and must be alert for men overboard. In addition, he mans sound-powered phones and checks communications with the bridge every half-hour. During periods of low visibility this watch is augmented by the phone talker.

Fog Lookouts: Stationed during periods of low visibility, the watch is stood where approaching ships can best be seen or heard. The fog lookout must also be in communication with the OOD and is normally assisted by a phone talker.

Figure 17–4 Sound-powered phones are an essential part of shipboard communications and control. Telephone talkers must speak clearly, be specific, and act businesslike.

Quartermaster of the Watch (QMOW): Assigned from the navigation department, the QMOW maintains the ship's log, assists the OOD in navigational matters, including changes of weather and the movement of shipping. He is a qualified helmsman.

Helmsman: The helmsman, also called the steersman, is normally assigned from the weapons or deck department. His qualifications must be recorded in his service record. He steers courses prescribed by the conning officer.

Lee Helmsman: Stands watch at the engine-order telegraph on the bridge and rings up the conning officer's orders to the engines, ensuring that all bells are correctly answered. He must also be a qualified steersman. The lee helmsman is normally assigned from the weapons or deck department.

Aft Steering: This watch is stationed in after steering to line up and operate the steering engines as directed by the OOD and to take over steering control in the event of a steering casualty. This watch, normally stood by a machinist's mate (MM) or electrician's mate (EM) must be qualified to shift steering units and handle emergencies in connection with this equipment.

IN-PORT WATCH SECTION

Although the in-port watch section is similar to that of the underway watch, there are some significant differences. Most importantly, the location of the primary watch station is shifted from the bridge to the quarterdeck. When the need arises, en-

Enlisted
Watch

listed personnel may be designated as quarterdeck watch officers. The section is generally headed by the petty officer of the watch (POOW), although his duties are sometimes carried out by the boatswain's mate of the watch (BMOW). The remainder of the watch section consists of messenger, side boys, duty masters-at-arms (duty MAAs), the gangway watch, and various security watches and patrols.

Quarterdeck Watch Officer: This is one of the most responsible jobs an enlisted man can have. It is provided for by Article 1003, U.S. Navy Regulations, as follows:

> When the number of commissioned or warrant officers qualified for watchstanding is reduced to an extent which may interfere with the proper operation of the command or may cause undue hardship, the commanding officer may assign to duty in charge of a watch, or to stand a day's duty, subject to such restrictions as may be imposed by a senior in the chain of command, or by these regulations, any petty officer or noncommissioned officer who is subject to his authority and who is, in the opinion of the commanding officer, qualified for such duty.

There should be no confusion as to the official status of these petty officers. They are officers of the deck, subject only to the orders of the commanding officer, executive officer, and command duty officer. The assignment of petty officers as OODs is made in writing either in the ship's organization book, the senior watch officer's watch list, or in the plan of the day (POD).

Petty Officer of the Watch (POOW): The POOW is the OOD's primary enlisted assistant in port. He supervises and instructs sentries and messengers, and carries out the daily routine and orders as the OOD directs. When neither the OOD nor the JOOW is at the gangway, he returns salutes. He calls away boats in sufficient time to ensure they are ready to leave the ship at the time prescribed in the boat schedule; keeps a list of men who may be expected to be absent on duty from the ship (and notifies the duty ship's cook of the approximate time they will return for meals), and assembles liberty parties for inspection by the OOD. If a QMOW is not assigned he also notifies the OOD and JOOW of any changes in weather or barometric pressure (readings are taken by the messenger), and requires the messenger to make calls listed in the call book kept on the quarterdeck.

Messenger: The OOD messengers stand a four-hour watch with the OOD and JOOD. They should be familiar with various departments of the ship and key ship's-company personnel.

Side Boys: The side boys are stationed for rendering formal honors. They are mustered, inspected, and instructed in their duties by the BMOW (or POOW). (Their duties are described on pages 84–85.)

Gangway Watch: When required, the gangway watch will be posted at the foot of the brow or gangway. He performs such duties as directed by the OOD; these duties normally include security of the brow and ceremonial duties.

Security Watches and Patrols: Besides those watches described elsewhere in this chapter, other security watches and patrols may be prescribed by the commanding officer. They are established to increase the physical security of the ship. Personnel assigned to these watches are trained and qualified by the appropriate department heads. Duties include making hourly reports to the OOD; checking classified stowage, including spaces containing classified equipment; being alert for evidence of sabotage, theft, and fire hazards; checking security of weapons magazines; obtaining periodic soundings of tanks and spaces; and periodically inspecting damage control closures.

Quartermaster of the Watch (QMOW): When assigned, the QMOW performs duties assigned by the OOD. These include: maintaining the deck log, handling absentee pennants, checking anchor and riding lights, hailing boats, and assisting in the rendering of honors. He takes bearings (when at anchor) and temperature and barometer readings, and keeps the OOD appropriately informed. He also maintains a call book. (When a QMOW is not assigned, the duties of this watch are carried out by the duty QM, the POOW, or a messenger of the watch.)

Anchor Watch: When the ship is at anchor, this watch is stationed according to instructions from the captain. The watch is posted in the immediate vicinity of the ground tackle and maintains a continuous watch on the anchor chain to observe the strain and how the chain is tending. Conditions are reported to the OOD every half-hour (or more often if directed by the OOD). The anchor watch must have rapid and continuous communication with the OOD.

DECK AND ENGINEERING LOGS

Although numerous records are kept by watch sections, four sets of logs have significant official and historical purposes. They are the deck log, the magnetic compass record, the engineering log, and the engineer's bell book.

The deck log is a daily record, by watches, describing every circumstance of interest concerning the crew and ship. Information contained includes: ship's operating orders, changes in sea state or weather, courses and speeds, position of the ship, bearing and distance of objects and other ships, tactical formation of ships in company, draft, soundings, zone description, and particulars of anchoring and mooring. The deck log also records changes in status of ship's personnel or passengers (except for transfers and receipts); damage or accident to ship, cargo, or equipment; death or injuries to personnel, passengers, visitors, longshoremen, harborworkers, or repairmen; arrests, suspensions, and restorations to duty.

The log, which is written by the quartermaster of the watch (QMOW), is supervised by the officer of the deck (OOD), who signs the log after the last entry made during his watch. The ship's navigator examines the log daily to see that it is properly kept, and he certifies it on a monthly basis. Then at the end of each month the commanding officer approves the log with his signature.

The log is prepared according to a form prescribed by the CNO. Under two specific circumstances the log may not be filled out: (1) when designated ships are conducting special operations directed by the CNO, and (2) when a ship is undergoing a scheduled period of regular overhaul, conversion, or inactivation. In these cases, "noteworthy events" are recorded as they occur; daily entries are not made.

The magnetic compass record contains all readings of the magnetic compass. It also records errors of the ship's gyro compass. While the ship is underway, compass comparisons are made and entered every half-hour (or whenever a new course is set). One magnetic compass is compared with the master gyro compass or the ship's course indicator used for steering. Compass comparisons are not required at half-hour intervals when the ship is involved in emergency operations or when frequent changes occur, as in harbor maneuvering.

Signed and submitted to the commanding officer on the last day of every quarter, the magnetic compass record is the responsibility of the navigator.

The engineering log is a daily watch record of important events or data pertaining to the engineering department and to the operation of the ship's propulsion plant. It includes: average hourly speed in revolutions and knots, and total number of miles steamed for the day; draft and displacement; amounts of fuel, water, and lubricating oil on hand, received, or expended; disposition and changes of engines, boilers, and principal auxiliaries; and injuries to personnel and material casualties in the department.

Prepared according to the COMNAVSHIPSYSCOM—Commander, Naval Ship Systems Command—the engineering log is signed by the engineering officer.

The engineer's bell book is a chronological record of orders of engine speed. It shows, for each shaft, when each order for directing a propeller speed is received, the meaning of the order, and the corresponding revolutions per minute. Ships and craft equipped with controllable-pitch propellers also record propeller pitch for each signaled change in speed. Shaft counter readings are recorded on getting underway, then hourly thereafter, and finally when the engine is shut down. All other entries are made at the time of receipt. The throttleman makes the entries in this book.

DEPARTMENTAL WATCHES

Many other watches may be introduced on your ship. The actual decision to do so rests with the type commander and commanding officer. The following list contains some of the more common ones and, where necessary, a brief description of the duties is also included:

Air Department: The air department watch petty officer, air department integrity watch messenger, aviation-fuel security watch, conflagration-station watch, flight-deck security watch, and hangar-deck security watch are all carrier watches. They are stood by personnel from embarked squadrons or detachments, and from ship's company in the V division. In addition, the department may have a person from each of the rating specialty groups assigned; for example, duty AM (aviation structural mechanic), duty AD—sometimes called the "duty mech"—(aviation machinist's mate), etc.

Engineering Department: Watches include auxiliary engineering watch, damage-control watch, electrical-equipment watch, engineroom watches, fireroom watches, and the sounding and security patrol.

Engineroom watches generally consist of the lower-level watch, upper-level watch, evaporator watch, shaft-alley watch and throttle watch. The pumpman is in charge of the lower-level watch and is responsible for maintaining a considerable number of pumps—main lube oil, lube-oil coolers, main condenser, main feed, main-feed booster and fire pipes—as well as other auxiliary machinery. Duties on the upper-level watch include responsibility for recording periodic temperature and pressure readings, for making required valve adjustments to correct slight variations, and for reporting unusual conditions. The shaft-alley watch inspects all equipment for proper lubrication and temperature and sees that the shaft-alley bilge is pumped. The evaporator watch must constantly check pressures, temperatures, vacuum, and salt content of sea water being distilled by the ship's evaporators. The throttleman must have knowledge of all gauges, instruments, and indicators on the throttle board. The throttleman also logs speed changes in the engineer's bell book.

Fireroom watches usually include a burnerman, blowerman, and checkman. The burnerman maintains steam pressure by cutting burners in or out, or by regulating the fuel-oil pressure of the burners. The blowerman is responsible for operating the forced-draft blowers that supply combustion air to the boiler. It is important that the burnerman and blowerman cooperate with each other because both are concerned with the combustion of the fuel oil. The checkman is responsible for operating the feed stop and feed-check valves. This is his only job, since it requires his full attention. (In some ships equipped with automatic feedwater controls, a checkman is not normally needed.)

The sounding and security patrol—a continuous patrol of unmanned spaces below decks—is stood on most ships from the end of the working day until 0800 the next morning. On larger ships the watch is stood around the clock. This watch also is responsible for maintaining the proper condition of material readiness by checking all watertight air ports, doors, hatches, scuttles, and other damage-control fittings. Besides making his own hourly report to the POOW or BMOW, he frequently relays the report of the cold-iron watch (discussed on p. 108).

The engineering department also provides boat engineers, although this is not necessarily considered a watch. The department will also have various rating specialities available, such as duty HT (hull technician), duty IC (interior communications electrician), duty MM (machinist's mate), duty EN (engineman), etc.

Two other watches are unique to engineering: the oil king and the fresh-water king. The oil king is a petty officer assigned to keep records of fuel oil, make tank soundings and assist when taking on fuel. The fresh-water king is another name for the evaporator watch.

Executive Department: The duty master-at-arms (MAA) is one of the principal watches of this department. The duty MAA is a regular member of the master-at-arms force who stands his watch under the direction of the executive officer. On ships without Marines, he also performs the duties of the sergeant of the guard. In this capacity, he is responsible for posting and supervising the performance of brig sentries and orderlies.

In port the executive department normally provides several duty drivers. Other common departmental watches include a duty YN (yeoman) or duty PN (personnelman). On aircraft carriers there may also be a duty JO (journalist).

Navigation Department: Besides providing personnel for signalman of the watch, quartermaster of the watch (QMOW), and bridge and signal watches, navigation also has many responsibilities in special evolutions—for example, the special sea and anchor detail. The department also provides a fog-signal watch and a gyrocompass watch. Other times the department has available a duty QM (quartermaster) and duty SM (signalman).

Operations/Communications Department: Besides supplying

a variety of watchstanders serving under the combat information center watch officer, this department has a guard-mail petty officer, a radio watch, a signal watch and a telephone switchboard watch. Operations/communications also has personnel on duty representing their specialties—such as a duty RM (radioman), a duty PH (photographer's mate), or a duty AG (aerographer's mate).

Weapons/Deck Department: Besides providing deck, forecastle, and fantail sentries, and duty-boat crews, the weapons/deck department is also responsible for providing and training the ship's helmsmen and lee helmsmen. This department also provides an ordnance security patrol.

The ordnance security patrol watch is composed of the magazine security patrol and battery security patrol. Operating under the gunnery officer, the patrol inspects and reports every half-hour to the OOD on the security of magazines, ready rooms, hoists, ordnance shops, radar-control rooms, guns, and directors.

Other Departments: The ship's medical/dental department has a duty HM (hospital corpsman) and a duty DT (dental technician) available; the supply department has a duty SK (storekeeper), duty MS (mess management specialist), duty SH (ship's serviceman), and on occasion, a duty DK (disbursing clerk). In the supply department the man in charge of the provision issue room is traditionally known as the jack o' the dust.

Each division within a department has a division police petty officer (DPPO) who is an assistant to the ship's MAA. He performs his duties in the part of the ship which his division is responsible for. The DPPO makes taps and reveille in his own division spaces, turns standing lights on at sunset and off at reveille, and during drills he directs traffic and clears the compartments. When the commanding officer designates the posting of the anti-sneak/anti-swimmer attack watch, a number of departments may be called upon to contribute personnel. This watch normally consists of topside sentries, a picket-boat crew, sonar operator and main engine personnel.

Sometimes departments may be called on to furnish orderlies and sentries. On ships with Marines, the Marines stand orderly watches. Otherwise, the executive officer assigns sailors to this duty. Orderlies may be assigned to flag officers or commanding officers of large ships. Their duties are much the same as those of messengers.

Men posted as sentries must know the general orders (see Chapter 6, pages 90–93). All sentries posted for security reasons are guided by written instructions that specify the limits of the post, steps to be taken in case of an alarm or breach of security, specific instructions on how and when to use assigned arms (rifle, nightstick, etc.), and the requirements for periodic inspections and reports to the OOD. Some of the most common sentry assignments are fantail, forecastle, and pier sentry.

Another common assignment is brig sentry. When Marines are embarked, they stand the watch. Otherwise, the watch is maintained by personnel of the MAA force, or by personnel assigned from the departments having men in the brig.

When a ship moves alongside a repair ship or tender, or into a naval shipyard, and is receiving power from these activities, a security and fire watch is usually set by each department. The watch is commonly called the cold-iron watch. Each cold-iron watch makes frequent inspections to see that there are no fire hazards, that there are no unauthorized persons in the area, that all spaces are cleaned, and that no tools, rags, gear, and the like are left adrift. The watch reports hourly to the OOD.

ENLISTED DETAIL

Although not a watch in the strictest sense, the "man overboard" emergency should be considered a permanent watch, to be stood by all hands at all times. It is everyone's responsibility to be constantly on the lookout for a man overboard. If it happens, you should sound the alarm immediately.

Many jobs involve work and responsibilities not covered by a particular rating. Men may be assigned to these jobs by a division officer, department head, or the executive officer.

Perhaps best known are the assignments of duty as a messman (or, more commonly, messcook) and as a compartment cleaner. Generally, personnel assigned these duties do not stand watches but take part in all drills. Also in this category are assignments to the beach guard and shore patrol (SP). The beach guard is responsible for the in-port control of boat traffic and helps maintain good order at a fleet landing during liberty hours. The shore patrol assists naval personnel ashore on leave or liberty and maintains good order and discipline.

Other non-specific enlisted rating assignments are: master chief petty officer of the Navy (MCPON), master chief petty officer of the fleet or force (F M/C), and master chief petty officer of the command (C M/C)—or, on submarines, chief of the boat (COB). Others may be, when qualified, assigned as career counselors, Navy recruiter/canvassers, recruit company commanders, or to counseling and assistance jobs within the human resource management support system (HRMSS). These are discussed in Chapter 9.

18. Damage Control and Firefighting

A ship's ability to do her job may someday depend on her crew's damage control response. Damage control covers firefighting, collision, grounding, and explosions. Its objectives are:

Preventing damage by making the ship watertight and gas tight, maintaining reserve buoyancy and stability, removing fire hazards, and making emergency equipment ready.

Keeping the damage from spreading, while helping those who are hurt.

Repairing and restoring damaged equipment; this includes supplying emergency power.

Damage Control Organization

The damage control assistant (DCA) works under the engineering officer and is responsible for preventing and repairing damage, training the crew in damage control, and caring for machinery, drainage and piping assigned to the organization.

There are two types of damage control organizations. One is a vital part of the engineering department. The other is the damage control battle organization, which varies from ship to ship, depending on size, type and mission. The latter organization includes Damage Control Central (DCC) and repair parties.

On large ships the department damage control petty officer (DDCPO), a qualified senior petty officer, coordinates the relieving, qualifying, training, and duties of departmental personnel as directed by the DCA and fire marshal. Section leaders are designated as duty DDCPOs outside normal working hours in port. DDCPOs and duty DDCPOs normally serve three months. They check in and out with the fire marshal and DCA on being assigned duties or released from them.

DDCPOs and their duty counterparts do the following:

Supervise all phases of the ship's damage control firefighting and defense procedures.

Teach division sailors damage control, firefighting, and nuclear-biological-chemical (NBC) warfare defense procedures.

Keep checkoff lists and set specified damage control conditions within their division spaces.

DC Organization

Weigh portable carbon dioxide (CO_2) bottles, inspect and test damage control and firefighting equipment and ensure that battle lanterns, dog wrenches, spanners, etc. are in place.

Inspect division spaces daily for fire hazards and cleanliness.

BATTLE ORGANIZATION

Battle organization includes: Damage Control Central (DCC); repair parties for hull, propulsion, electronics, weapons, and air; and battle dressing stations. DCC is the place where the reports from damage control units come. DCC assesses the damage and decides which area is most in need of repairs. It also reports to and receives orders from command concerning matters affecting buoyancy, list, trim, stability, watertight integrity, and NBC defensive measures. DCC is normally the battle station for the DCA.

DCC uses a variety of administrative tools to keep track of a casualty. These include:

Charts and diagrams that show the subdivisions of the ship and its systems.

A casualty board to visualize the damage sustained and the corrective action in progress (based on repair-party reports).

A stability board to show liquid loading, the location of flooding boundaries, the effect of list and trim, and the corrective action taken.

A list of access routes for ready shelter, deep shelter, electronic casualty control, and battle dressing.

Graphic displays to record corrective damage control and electrical systems.

Deck plans to indicate areas contaminated by NBC agents, the location of battle dressing stations and decontamination stations, and safe routes to them.

REPAIR PARTIES

Repair parties are the DCA's representatives at the scene of the casualty or damage. They are the primary units in the damage control organization. Parties may be subdivided to let personnel cover a greater area more rapidly, and to prevent loss of the entire party from a single hit.

The number and ratings of men assigned to a repair party, as specified in the battle bill, are determined by: the location of the station, the size of the area assigned to that station, and the total number of men available for all stations.

Each repair party will usually have an officer or chief petty officer in charge, a scene leader to supervise all on-scene activities (he also functions as the assistant repair-party leader), a phone talker, and OBA men and messengers. Additional men assigned will include petty officers and non-rated men from various departments, such as electrician's mates (EMs), hull technicians (HTs), storekeepers (SKs) and hospital corpsmen (HMs).

Repair parties and teams are designated as follows:

Repair 1: Main deck repair. Comprised of deck petty officers and non-rated men, storekeepers, radiomen (RMs), electrician's mates, hospital corpsmen, and aviation details (except on aircraft carriers). Engineering petty officers may also be required.

Repair 2: Forward repair. Comprised of petty officers of the deck and engineering branches, electrician's mates, storekeepers, hospital corpsmen, and non-rated men.

Repair 3: After repair. Similar to Repair 2.

Repair 4: Amidship repair. Similar to Repair 2.

Repair 5: Propulsion repair. Comprised of an electrical officer or senior electrician's mate and a broad cross-section of engineering ratings. Assignment to this unit is based more on fireroom/engineroom takeover qualifications than on damage control qualifications.

Repair 6: Ordnance repair. Comprised of gunner's mates, fire control technicians, and electrician's mates. This party is sometimes divided into forward and after groups.

Repair 7: Gallery deck and island structure repair. This unit is used primarily on aircraft carriers and other ship types where it is needed. It consists of personnel from air, engineering, damage control, and other areas.

Repair 8: Electronics repair. Comprised of electronics, sonar, and fire control technicians—ETs, STs and FTs—as well as electrician's mates. This party works under electronics casualty control.

Aviation fuel repair teams and *crash and salvage teams* are peculiar to aircraft carriers and ships equipped for manned helicopter operations. On carriers the teams consist of air department personnel. On ships equipped for helo operations the appropriate deck, engineering and damage control personnel are assigned.

The ordnance disposal team is made up of specially trained personnel, deployed aboard ships as required. The team is administered as a unit of the weapons department.

All ships except submarines, patrol and yard craft, minecraft, and small auxiliaries maintain at least one *at-sea firefighting team*. A smaller ship whose complement is not large enough to warrant formation of such a team may organize a fire party as appropriate.

Functional teams within each repair party include: hose teams; dewatering, plugging, and patching teams; investigation teams; shoring, pipe repair, structural repair, casualty power, IC communications repair, and electrical repair teams; radiological monitoring, biological sampling, chemical detection, and NBC decontamination teams; and stretcher bearers.

Every man in the repair party should be able to perform effectively on any team.

FUNCTIONS OF REPAIR PARTIES

In general, repair parties must be:

Capable of controlling and extinguishing all types of fires.

Capable of giving first aid and transporting the injured to battle dressing stations without seriously reducing the damage control capabilities of the party.

Capable of detecting, identifying, measuring dosage and intensity of radiation, and carrying out decontamination procedures.

Organized to evaluate and report correctly on the extent of damage in its area.

Besides the general functions required, certain repair parties are also responsible for:

Maintaining watertight integrity (Repair 1, 2, 3, 4, and 5).

Maintaining the ship's structural integrity and maneuverability (Repair 1, 2, 3, and 4).

Maintaining the ship's propulsion (Repair 5).

Protecting ordnance and magazines (Repair 6), and maintaining deck and hangar bays in aircraft carriers (Repair 7, plus the crash and salvage team and the EOD team).

Maintaining electronics equipment on certain ships (Repair 8).

Protecting exposed ordnance (EOD team).

Each repair party has an officer or senior petty officer in charge. The second in charge of a repair party is also a petty officer, qualified in damage control and capable of supervising the party. Damage Control Central holds continuing drills in fire-fighting, flooding, plane attack, collision, communications, and general quarters.

EQUIPMENT AND FACILITIES

Damage control equipment is stowed in repair lockers. It includes patches for ruptured water lines, steam lines, broken seams, and for ship's hull; plugs made of soft wood for stopping the flow of liquids in a damaged hull or in broken lines; soft wood wedges for shoring; radiological defense equipment; an electrical repair kit for isolating damaged circuits and restoring power; and such tools for forcible entry as axes, crowbars, wrecking bars, claw tools, hacksaws, bolt-cutters, and acetylene cutting torches. This equipment is reserved for damage-control use only and should never be removed for any other purpose.

Most ships have at least two *battle dressing stations* equipped to handle personnel casualties. They're manned by medical personnel and are so located that stretcher cases may be brought directly to them by the repair party. Emergency supplies of medical equipment are also placed in first aid boxes throughout the ship.

At least two *decontamination stations* are provided in widely separated parts of the ship, preferably near battle dressing stations. These stations differ from ship to ship, but the basic requirements are the same. To prevent recontamination of personnel and ship locations, each station is divided into two areas: a contaminated or unclean section with a washing area, and a clean section. Stations are manned by medical and repair-party personnel to ensure that proper decontamination procedures are followed.

Communication is vital to the damage control organization. Without it the entire organization could fail in its primary functions. Normal communications include the battle telephone circuit (sound-powered 2JZ), interstation two-way systems (the 4MC circuit), ship's service telephones, the ship's general announcing system (the 1MC circuit), and messengers. (More on sound-powered telephones in Chapter 24, pages 485–90).

Compartmentation

The success of damage control depends partly on the proper use of watertight-integrity equipment. Each ship is divided into compartments to control flooding, to withstand NBC attacks, to segregate activities, to provide underwater protection with tanks and voids, to strengthen the structure of the ship, and to control buoyancy and stability.

Every Navy ship is divided by decks and bulkheads, both above and below the waterline, into as many watertight compartments as possible. In general, the more extensive a ship's compartmentation, the greater her resistance to sinking will be. The original watertight integrity, which is established when the ship is built, may be reduced or destroyed by enemy action, storms, collisions, or negligence.

MATERIAL CONDITIONS OF READINESS

These refer to the degree of access into an area and the system of closing hatches and other openings to limit the damage. Maximum closure is not always maintained because it would interfere with the normal operation of the ship. For damage-control purposes, Navy ships have three material conditions of readiness, each representing a different degree of tightness and protection. They are X-RAY, YOKE, and ZEBRA. These titles are used in all spoken and written communications concerning material conditions.

Condition X-RAY provides the least protection. It is set when the ship is in no danger of attack, such as when she is at anchor in a well-protected harbor, or secured at home base during regular working hours. During this condition all closures marked with

Markings	Purpose
W (William)	Classification W is applied to sea suction valves that supply water to the condensers and fire pumps, and to other fittings and equipment necessary for fire protection and mobility. These fittings are normally open or running.
Circle W	Ventilation fittings and certain access openings are marked Ⓦ (circles are black). Normally open, these fittings are closed only to prevent NBC contamination or smoke from entering a vent system.
Red Circle Z (Zebra)	Special fittings marked Ⓩ (circles are red) may be opened during long periods of general quarters to allow for preparation and distribution of food or for cooling vital spaces such as magazines. When open, these fittings are guarded so that they can be closed immediately if necessary.
Black circle X and Y	Fittings marked with Ⓧ or Ⓨ permit access to battle stations, are used for transfer of ammunition, or are part of vital systems. They may be opened without special permission, but must be kept closed when not actually in use.
Dog Zebra	Ⓩ is applied to accesses to weather decks that are not equipped with light traps or door switches that will turn lights off when the access is opened during darkened ship conditions.

Condition	Circumstances	Close fittings marked
X-Ray	In well-protected harbors; at home base during regular working hours.	X, Ⓧ. These fittings are kept closed at all times except when actually in use.
Yoke	At sea; in port outside of regular working hours.	X, Ⓧ, Y, Ⓨ. Ⓧ and Ⓨ fittings may be opened for access, to pass ammunition, for inspection, etc.
Zebra	General quarters; fire or flooding; when entering or leaving port in war-time.	X, Ⓧ, Y, Ⓨ, Z, Ⓩ. Ⓩ fittings may be opened to permit distribution of food, use of sanitary facilities, and ventilation of vital spaces. Must be guarded when open.

Figure 18–1 Types of watertight fittings.

a black X are secured; they are also closed when setting Conditions YOKE and ZEBRA.

Condition YOKE provides somewhat more protection than Condition X-RAY; YOKE is set and maintained at sea. In port, it is maintained at all times during war, and at times outside of regular working hours during peacetime. YOKE closures, marked with a black Y, are secured during Conditions YOKE and ZEBRA.

Condition ZEBRA is set before going to sea or when entering port during war. It is set immediately, without further orders, when general quarters stations are manned. Condition ZEBRA is also set to localize and control fire and flooding when not at GQ

Compart-
mentation

stations. When Condition ZEBRA is warranted, all closures marked with a red Z are secured.

Once the material condition is set, no fitting marked with a black X, black Y or red Z may be opened without permission of the commanding officer (through the DCA or OOD).

Additional fitting markings for specific purposes are modifications of the three basic conditions, as follows:

Circle X-RAY fittings, marked with a black X in a black circle, are secured during Conditions X-RAY, YOKE, and ZEBRA. *Circle YOKE* fittings, marked with a black Y in a black circle, are secured during Conditions YOKE and ZEBRA. Circle X-RAY and Circle YOKE fittings may be opened without special authority when going to or from general quarters, when transferring ammunition, or when operating vital systems during GQ. The fittings must be secured when not in use.

Circle ZEBRA fittings, marked with a red Z in a red circle, are secured during Condition ZEBRA. These fittings may be opened during prolonged periods of general quarters, when the condition is modified. Opening these fittings enables personnel to prepare and distribute battle rations, open limited sanitary facilities, ventilate battle stations, and provide access from ready rooms to the flight deck. When open, these fittings must be guarded for immediate closure if necessary.

Dog ZEBRA fittings, marked with a red Z in a black D, are secured during Condition ZEBRA and during dark ship condition. The Dog ZEBRA classification applies to weather accesses not equipped with light switches or light traps.

WILLIAM fittings, marked with a black W, are kept open during all material conditions. This classification applies to vital sea suction valves supplying main and auxiliary condensers, fire pumps, and spaces that are manned during Conditions X-RAY, YOKE, and ZEBRA. It also applies to vital ship valves that, if secured, would impair the mobility and fire protection of the ship.

Circle WILLIAM fittings, marked with a black W in a black circle, are normally kept open (as WILLIAM fittings are) but must be secured against NBC attack.

Remember: It is the responsibility of all hands to maintain the material condition in effect. If it is necessary to break the condition, permission must be obtained (from the OOD or Damage Control Central). A log is maintained in DCC at all times to show where the existing condition has been broken; the number, type and classification of fittings involved; the name, rate, and division of the man requesting permission to open or close the fitting; and the date the fitting was opened or closed.

The number of times and circumstances in which DCC may give permission to break watertight integrity is determined by the commanding officer.

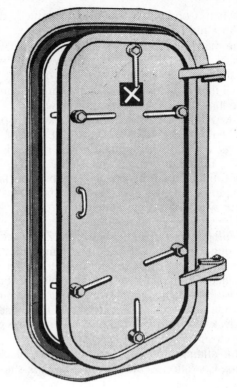

Figure 18–2 The individually operated dogs on this watertight door are in the closed position, but would have to be opened before the door can be closed.

WATERTIGHT INTEGRITY

The purpose of damage control is to keep the ship watertight. She may sustain a great deal of damage, but with proper watertight integrity, the ship will remain afloat.

Doors, hatches, and manholes giving access to all compartments must be securely dogged (closed down). Manhole covers to double bottoms should always be bolted except for inspection, cleaning, or painting. They must never be left open overnight or when men are not actually working.

Watertight (WT) doors and hatches will work longer and require less maintenance if they are properly closed and opened. When closing a door, first set up on a dog opposite the hinges, with just enough pressure to keep the door shut. Then set the other dogs evenly to obtain uniform pressure all around. When opening a door, start with the dogs nearest the hinges. This procedure will keep the door from springing and make it easier to operate remaining dogs.

Compartmentation

When the ship sustains damage, watertight doors, hatches, manholes, and scuttles should be opened only after making sure

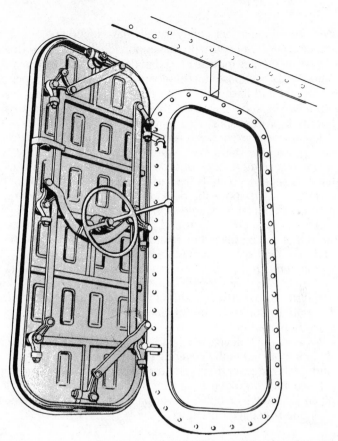

Figure 18–3 The control wheel operates all dogs at once on the quick-acting WT door.

that the compartment is dry or has little flooding, so that there won't be more flooding when the closures are opened. They should never be opened without DCC permission. Extreme caution is always necessary in opening compartments below the waterline, near any damage.

TYPES OF CLOSURES

The strongest doors are classified as *watertight (WT) doors*. They are used in watertight bulkheads or lower-deck compartments and are designed to resist the same amount of pressure as the bulkheads. Some doors have dogs that must be individually closed and opened. Others, known as *quick-acting watertight doors* have handwheels that operate all dogs simultaneously.

Non-watertight doors (NWT), used in non-watertight bulkheads, usually do not have dogs.

Airtight doors (AT) are also flame-tight and fire-retarding.

Compartmentation

When used in air locks, they usually have lever-type, quick-acting closures. Others usually have individually operated dogs.

Passing scuttles may be placed in doors through which ammunition must be passed. These are small, tube-like openings, watertight and flashproof.

Spraytight doors are used topside in vessels with low freeboard, to prevent spray and seawater from getting in.

Joiner doors are ordinary shore-type metal doors used to provide privacy for staterooms, wardrooms, etc.

Hatches are horizontal doors used for access through decks. A hatch is either set with its top surface flush with the deck, or on a coaming raised above the deck. Hatches usually are not quick-acting, but must be secured with individually operated dogs.

An *escape scuttle* is a round opening with quick-acting closures that can be placed in a hatch, bulkhead, or deck to permit rapid escape from a compartment.

Bolted manholes normally provide access to water, fuel tanks, and voids. They are sections of steel plate which are gasketed and fastened over deck openings where access may be required. They are seldom used by ship's personnel. Manholes are occasionally placed in bulkheads.

Most closure devices depend on a rubber gasket, which is usually mounted in the covering part to close against a fixed position knife edge for their tightness. Gaskets of this type are either pressed into a groove or secured with retaining strips held in place by screws or bolts. Never paint or "doctor" gaskets. If a new one is needed, install it.

Investigating and Reporting Damage

In order to investigate damage properly, you must know your ship and be familiar with the basic principles of investigating and reporting damage.

Be cautious. Each investigating team should consist of two or more men, using safety equipment (oxygen breathing apparatus [OBA], explosimeter, flame safety lamp) in case toxic or combustible gases are present.

Be thorough and determined. Find out what type of damage exists, its location and extent, and how it can be best repaired or controlled.

Report the damage. A prompt, accurate report should be made to DCC by the best method available, telephone or messenger.

DAMAGE REPAIRS

Battle-damage repair is strictly emergency action, taken to keep the ship afloat. Damage control drills will teach everyone how to use damage control equipment. Do your best with what you have in an emergency. If you are calm, alert, and work fast

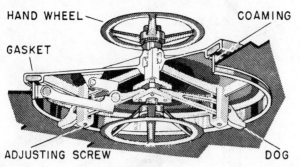

HAND WHEEL

GASKET

COAMING

ADJUSTING SCREW

DOG

Figure 18–4 This cutaway section of an escape scuttle shows quick-acting hand wheels above and below.

with the tools you have at hand, you can do much to keep the ship afloat and make her ready for action again.

Any rupture, break, or hole in the ship's outer hull plating, particularly below the waterline, can let in sea water. If flooding is not controlled, the ship will sink. When the underwater hull is pierced, there are only two possible courses of action. The first, obviously, is to plug the holes. The second is to establish and maintain flood boundaries within the ship, and thus prevent more extensive flooding.

Plugging and patching materials include wooden plugs and wedges, wooden shoring, prefabricated wooden box patches, rags, pillows, mattresses, blankets, kapok life jackets, metal plate, folding metal plate patches, flexible sheet metal patches, prefabricated steel box patches, bucket patches, and welded steel patches.

Securing materials include assorted hook bolts, manila line, wire rope, chain, machine bolts, and angle clips for welding and shoring.

Backup materials include mess tables, panel doors, buckets, plywood or lumber, and sheet metal.

Gasket materials include sheet and strip rubber, leather, canvas, rags, oakum, white lead, and paint.

There are two general methods of making temporary repair to a hole in the hull: put something in it, or over it. In either case, the effect is to reduce the area through which water can enter the ship, or through which water can pass from one compartment to another.

A riveted joint is not inherently watertight or oil-tight, because the surfaces or edges that are held together are not machined or ground. Therefore riveted joints or boundaries tend to loosen from shock of gunfire, collision, vibration, explosion, and racking of the ship from high-speed maneuvering. Repairs to this type of damage are usually made by calking the loosened joint. These repairs must be made as soon as defects are discovered.

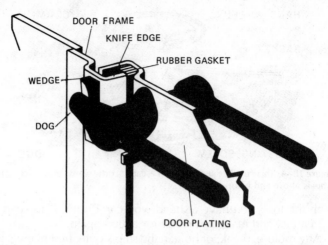

Figure 18–5 This cutaway section of a WT door shows how the knife edge sets up against the rubber gasket for a tight seal.

Shoring is often used aboard ship to support ruptured decks, to strengthen weakened bulkheads and decks, to build up temporary decks and bulkheads against the sea, to support hatches and doors, and to provide support for equipment that has broken loose.

Knowing the proper time to shore is a problem that cannot be solved by any one set of rules. Sometimes the need for shoring is obvious, as in the case of loose machinery or damaged hatches. But sometimes dangerously weakened supports under guns or machinery may not be so noticeable. Although shoring is sometimes done when it is really not necessary, the best general rule is: in case of doubt, it is always better to shore.

The basic materials required are shores, wedges, sholes, and strongbacks. A shore is a portable beam. A wedge is a block, triangular on the sides and rectangular on the butt end. A shole is a flat block that may be placed under the end of a shore for the purpose of distributing pressure. A strongback is a bar or beam of wood or metal, often shorter than a shore, which is used to distribute pressure or to serve as an anchor for a patch. Many other pieces of equipment can also be used in connection with shoring.

Fire Protection

Fire aboard ship is a constant threat. All measures must be taken to prevent fires. Fires may start from spontaneous combustion, carelessness, hits by enemy shells, or collision. If a fire is not controlled quickly, it may cause more damage than the initial casualty and could mean loss of the ship.

Although firefighting is chiefly the responsibility of repair parties, you must learn all you can about it, so you can help if called upon.

For there to be a fire, three conditions must be met. There must be a burnable material, the substance must be heated enough to start burning, and there must be sufficient oxygen to sustain combustion. These requirements form what is called the *fire triangle,* whose sides consist of fuel, heat, and oxygen. Removing any side of the triangle will result in extinguishing the fire. But that's not always easy to do.

Removing the fuel, for instance, is not always possible, nor even practical. But one case where this method might work is a flammable liquid fire being fed by a pipeline. The flow of fuel can be stopped by closing valves in the pipe, and the fire can then be left to burn itself out. Or one or both of the other sides of the triangle can be eliminated.

Removing the heat side of the triangle, the most often used method, is another way of saying the fire must be cooled. The usual cooling method is to use lots of water, both solid stream and fog (spray).

Oxygen can be removed in two ways. In a closed space, carbon dioxide (CO_2) can be used to dilute the oxygen content of the air, thus starving the fire. The other method is to smother the fire with a blanket of foam or sand.

CLASSES OF FIRES

Fires have four classifications, indicating the type of material burning and the agents and methods required to extinguish them.

Class A fires involve solid substances—wood, cloth, paper—that usually leave an ash. Explosives are in this category. Water is the usual means of extinguishing Class A fires. Carbon dioxide may be used on small fires but not on explosives. A large fire usually requires knocking down (cooling) the flames with fog, then usually a solid stream to break up the material for further cooling.

Class B fires involve flammable liquids—oil, gasoline, paint, etc. For small fires or in confined spaces, CO_2 is a good extinguisher. For large fires, other agents such as water and fog foam must be used. Never use a solid stream on Class B fires. The steam only penetrates the fuel's surface, scatters the fuel, and spreads the fire.

Class C fires are those in electrical/electronic equipment. The primary extinguishing agent is CO_2. Fog is used only as a last resort. Foam should not be used because it will damage the equipment and may be a shock hazard. A solid stream should *never* be used. If possible, the equipment should first be de-energized.

Class D fires involve combustible metals such as magnesium,

Combustible	Class	Extinguishing agent
Woodwork, bedding, clothes, combustible stores	A	Fixed water sprinkling, high-velocity fog, solid water stream, foam, dry chemical, CO_2.
Explosives, propellants	A	Magazine sprinkling, solid water stream or high velocity fog, foam.
Paints, spirits, flammable liquid stores	B	CO_2 (fixed system), foam, installed sprinkling system, high-velocity fog, PKP, CO_2.
Gasoline	B	Foam, CO_2 (fixed), water sprinkling system, PKP.
Fuel oil, JP-5, diesel oil, kerosene	B	Foam, PKP, water sprinkling system, high-velocity fog, CO_2 (fixed system).
Electrical and radio apparatus	C	CO_2 (portable or hose reel), high-velocity fog, fog foam or dry chemical (only if CO_2 not available).
Magnesium alloys	D	Jettison overboard, low-velocity fog.

Figure 18–6 The classes of fires and recommended extinguishing agents are listed in order of priority.

sodium, and titanium. These metals are used for building certain parts of aircraft, missiles, electronic components, and other equipment. An example is the magnesium aircraft parachute flare, which can burn at a temperature above 4,000 degrees F., with a brilliancy of 2 million candlepower. Water coming in contact with burning magnesium produces highly explosive hydrogen gas, so use only low-velocity fog on this type of fire. One important safety precaution: wear welder's goggles with very dark (No. 6) lenses to protect your eyes from the intense light of the fire.

FIRE PREVENTION RULES

You can't win against a fire. You can fight it and hold down its damage. But some property will be destroyed, productive work is interrupted, and additional effort and materials are required to clean up the mess. The objective, therefore, is to prevent fires from starting.

Keep things squared away—clean, shipshape, and in their proper places. Keep flammable products (gasoline, oily rags, paint, etc.) away from fire-starting articles (such as torches, cigarettes, and sparking equipment). Don't take open flames near gasoline tanks and don't bring flammable liquid near a welder's torch.

Make sure the correct firefighting equipment is in the right places and in good condition. If a fire does start, you'll want to have the right equipment on hand, ready to go into operation. You may not be able to prevent a fire from starting, but you can prevent a little one from getting bigger.

Some fire prevention rules for each class of fire:

Class A fires: Don't throw lighted cigarettes or matches in trash cans. Don't smoke in bunks. Be careful of where and how you

Figure 18–7 A team of students practices using foam during firefighting school.

stow rags, and oily paint-smeared cloth and paper. When welding or burning, protect Class A materials against flame and hot droppings. Inspect opposite bulkheads and maintain a fire watch.

Class B fires: Expect all low places, bilges, tanks, and bottoms to have an accumulation of extremely flammable gasoline or oil vapors. Remember the danger of flashback where gasoline is concerned. Use only non-sparking tools in areas where Class B substances have been or are stored. Don't carry matches, lighters, or keys, and don't wear metal buttons or nylon clothing near gasoline or oil vapors. Don't turn on lamps, flashlights, or electrical equipment which are not certified as sparkproof in an area where gasoline or oil fumes can accumulate.

Class C fires: Do not paint or splash paint, oil, grease, or solvents on electrical insulation or wires. Report all frayed or worn wires and all sparking contacts, switches, and motors. Report any electrical equipment that is hot, smokes, or makes unusual noises. In case of fire, secure all electrical equipment in the space. Don't try to use unauthorized equipment, such as hot-plates, shavers, extension lights, or radios, except in authorized spaces.

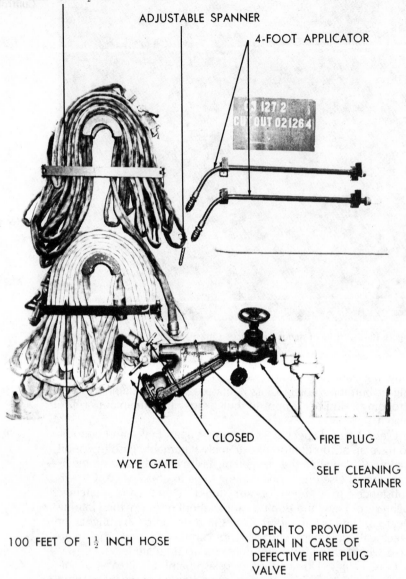

100 FEET OF 1½ INCH HOSE

ADJUSTABLE SPANNER

4-FOOT APPLICATOR

CLOSED

FIRE PLUG

WYE GATE

SELF CLEANING STRAINER

100 FEET OF 1½ INCH HOSE

OPEN TO PROVIDE DRAIN IN CASE OF DEFECTIVE FIRE PLUG VALVE

Figure 18–8 In a standard shipboard installation of the fire plug, strainer, and hose sections, note that the lower valve on the wye gate is open to provide drain in case of a defective fire plug valve.

Class D fires: Protect Class D fuels from welding and burning operations. Do not store Class D fuels in areas that are susceptible to intense heat. Some of these fuels do not require flame for ignition.

SHIPBOARD FIREFIGHTERS

Despite the most careful precautions, fires still occur. When one is discovered, report it immediately so firefighting operations can begin. The efforts of one person may be enough to contain the fire until the fire party arrives. If you discover a fire, report it immediately to the OOD. State the type of fire and its location (compartment name and designation); then do what you can to fight it. Always report the fire before taking any action. A delay of even half a minute might result in a minor fire becoming a major one.

To some extent, the procedures for fighting a shipboard fire depend on the condition under which the fire occurs. Fires during action, normal steaming, or when a full crew is aboard are handled as battle casualties and the ship goes to GQ. These fires, which may occur in port or at sea, are normally fought by the firefighting party from the repair station in that section of the ship. Aboard larger ships it may not always be feasible to go to GQ. Then a nucleus fire party is organized.

When a fire occurs in port and there is only a partial crew on board, the duty repair party handles it. The regular firefighting party is shown in Figure 18–9, page 329.

FIREFIGHTING PARTY ORGANIZATION

Every firefighting party consists of two *hose teams* (known as the attack party). The No. 1 hose team is the attacking unit, and the No. 2 team is the back-up.

The *scene leader* is in charge of the firefighting party. His first duty is to get to the fire quickly, to investigate and evaluate the situation and to determine the nature of the fire. Then he must decide what type of equipment should be used and inform DCC. Later developments may require different or additional equipment, but the scene leader must decide the equipment needed first.

Nozzlemen have their oxygen-breathing apparatus (OBA) on and ready for immediate use. They assist the scene leader with investigating the fire when OBAs are needed to enter a compartment. Nozzlemen man an all-purpose nozzle and applicator (Figure 18–10) and wear complete battle dress, with gloves and miner's headlamp.

Hosemen lead out the hose from the fireplug, remove kinks and sharp bends and tend it. When fighting the fire they too wear OBAs.

Fire boundaries, established by DCC, are set by *investigators.* They accomplish this by removing burnable materials from bulkheads and cooling down bulkheads if necessary. They also investigate the area for further damage, take soundings, and lead personnel trapped in smoke-filled compartments to safety.

OBA tenders are in charge of tending lines (when used) and keeping spare OBA canisters readily available.

Plugmen stand by to operate fireplug valves when ordered. They rig and stand by jumper lines, and clear fireplug strainers when necessary.

Access men open doors, hatches, scuttles, and other closures. They clear routes to gain access to the fire. They carry equipment necessary to open jammed fittings and locked doors.

Foam supply men prepare foam equipment and obtain foam can spares from racks.

CO_2 *supply men* bring CO_2 extinguishers.

The closure detail secures all doors, hatches, and openings around the area to isolate the fire. All ventilation closures and fans in the smoke and heat area are secured by this detail. They also establish secondary fire boundaries by cooling down nearby areas.

The electrical kit man de-energizes and re-energizes electrical circuits in the fire area. He also rigs power cables for portable lights, tools, and blowers.

The hospital corpsman provides on-scene first aid. He is also responsible for supervising the movement of seriously injured men back to sickbay for more extensive treatment.

The sound-powered telephone talker plugs into the nearest JZ circuit to establish and maintain communication with DCC, either directly or through the local repair party.

The messenger carries written communications from the scene leader to the repair party leader.

Additional personnel and equipment assigned to a firefighting party may include foam equipment operators, additional hosemen, firefighting suit men, oxyacetylene cutting outfit, pumping equipment, dewatering equipment, de-smoking equipment, the flame safety lamp, and a combustible gas indicator.

FIREFIGHTING EQUIPMENT

All firefighting equipment is located in readily accessible positions and is inspected frequently to ensure its reliability and readiness for instant operation. At any time you may be called upon to serve on a repair/fire party or you may be the only person present to combat a fire. If you don't know how to use the equipment available, or what equipment to use, the result could be disaster.

The firemain system is designed to deliver seawater to fireplugs and sprinkler systems. It has a secondary function of sup-

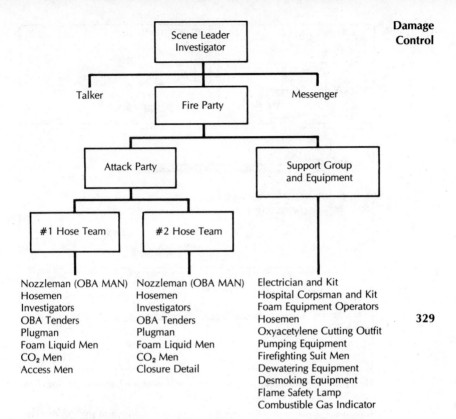

Figure 18–9 Organization of a firefighting party.

plying water to flushing systems and auxiliary machinery as a coolant.

The piping usually is four inches in diameter and is either a single line running fore and aft near the centerline (on small ships), or in a loop system (on larger ships) running along each side of the ship inside protective bulkheads or armor. In both systems the main is located on or below the damage control deck. There are many cross-connection points and shutoff valves throughout the system to allow any damaged sections of piping to be isolated or "jumped." Risers lead from the main to fireplugs throughout the ship.

Aboard larger ships most fireplug outlets are 2½ inches in diameter. A wye gate provides two 1½-inch outlets, or a reducing fitting can be used to provide a single 1½-inch outlet. On destroyers and smaller ships, fireplug outlets are 1½ inches throughout the ship.

The standard Navy firehose has an interior lining of rubber, covered with cotton jackets. It comes in 50-foot lengths with a

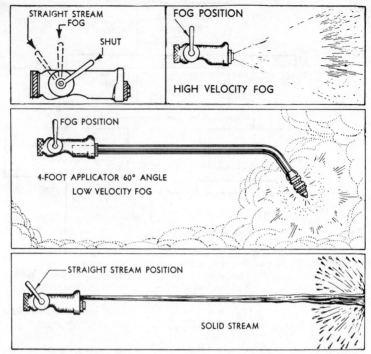

Figure 18–10 The all-purpose hose nozzle is used for high-velocity fog, low-velocity fog, and a straight stream.

female coupling at one end and a male coupling at the other. The female coupling is connected to the fireplug. The male coupling is connected to another length of hose or receives a nozzle.

Destroyers and smaller ships use 1½-inch hose. Larger ships use 2½-inch hose on the weather decks and 1½-inch below deck and in the superstructure.

One or more racks are provided at each fireplug for stowing the firehose. The hose must be faked on the rack so that it is free-running, with the ends hanging down so that couplings are ready for instant use. On large ships, each weather deck fire station has 100 feet of 2½-inch hose faked on a rack and connected to the plug. Below deck, 200 feet (two lines) of 1½-inch hose is stowed by each plug, but only one line is connected to the plug. On smaller ships, 100 feet of 1½-inch hose is faked on the racks, with 50 feet connected to the plug. A spanner wrench for tightening connections, and one or two applicators, are also stowed at each fire station. Spare lengths of hose are rolled and stowed in repair lockers.

The all-purpose nozzle can produce a solid stream of water, high-velocity fog, or low-velocity fog. It is available for both 1½-inch and 2½-inch hose. The nozzle can be adjusted easily and

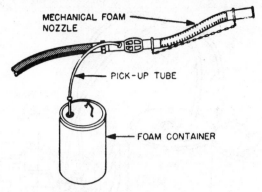

MECHANICAL FOAM
NOZZLE

PICK-UP TUBE

FOAM CONTAINER

Figure 18–11 The straight-type pickup proportioner.

quickly by a handle. Never pick up a charged hose by the handle
of the all-purpose nozzle. The handle could easily move to the
fog or open position and the high water pressure (about 100 psi)
could make the hose whiplash dangerously.

Sprinkler systems are installed in magazines, turrets, ammuni-
tion-handling rooms, spaces where flammable materials are
stowed, and in hanger bays aboard aircraft carriers. Water for
these systems is piped from the firemain. Some systems are automatically triggered when the protected compartment reaches a
certain temperature, but most are operated manually by control
valves.

Foam, a frothy mixture of air, water and chemicals, is used to
fight Class B fires. The foam provides a blanket that floats on top
of the burning liquid and smothers the fire. Mechanical or pro-
tein foam is non-toxic, and once the fire is out, can prevent a reflash for up to 24 hours. Foam will not damage surfaces, but it
should not be used on Class C fires because of the obvious
cleanup problems. It is not used, unless absolutely necessary, on
either Class A or C fires.

Mechanical foam is produced by mixing a foam concentrate
with water under pressure. A proportioner puts in the correct
mixture (6 percent concentrate, 94 percent water). Two types of
proportioners may be used.

Easiest to use is the straight-type proportioner. The mechanical
nozzle is a 21-inch length of two-inch diameter flexible metal or
asbestos hose, with a suction chamber (the proportioner) and an
air port at the pump end. The pickup tube siphons the correct
amount of foam concentrate into the water stream. As the stream
crosses the air port, air is mixed with the solution to produce the
foam. Foam concentrate comes in five-gallon cans; each can
lasts 90 seconds and produce 660 gallons of foam.

The FP-180 water motor proportioner consists of a foam liquid
pump driven by a water motor. It has 2½-inch connections at

331

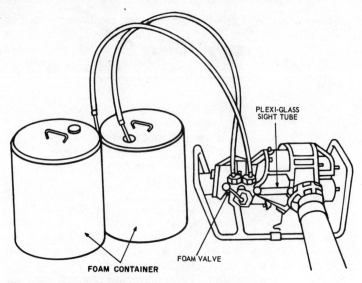

PLEXI-GLASS
SIGHT TUBE

FOAM VALVE

FOAM CONTAINER

Figure 18–12 The portable water motor proportioner.

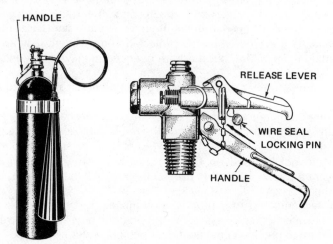

HANDLE

RELEASE LEVER

WIRE SEAL

LOCKING PIN

HANDLE

Figure 18–13 The portable CO₂ extinguisher, with detail of handle, release lever, and locking pin.

both the inlet and outlet sides, and use two half-inch pickup tubes. When the foam valve is in either of the two foam positions, the pump injects foam liquid into the water stream. With the valve in the "off" position, no foam is delivered, and the fire line can be used for conventional firefighting.

Two types of portable extinguishers are used. Both are effective in fighting Class B and Class C fires.

Carbon dioxide (CO_2) extinguishers are used mainly for putting out electrical fires, but they are effective on any small fire, including burning oil, gasoline, paint, and trash cans. Because CO_2 is heavier than air, it forms a smothering blanket over the fire. Maximum range of the extinguisher is five feet from the horn.

To use the extinguisher, remove the locking pin from the valve, grasp the insulated handle of the horn with one hand, and squeeze the grip with the other. If you are in the open, approach the fire from the windward side. This type extinguisher is quick to use and leaves no mess, but carbon-dioxide "snow" produced can be blown away by wind or draft. While not poisonous, it will not support life, and can smother men as well as fires in confined spaces. When CO_2 is released from the container, it expands rapidly to 450 times its stored volume. This expansion causes the gas's temperature to drop to -110 degrees F. Contact with the carbon-dioxide snow can cause painful skin blisters.

Dry chemical extinguishers are provided primarily for Class B fires. The chemical used is potassium bicarbonate (similar to baking soda); it is called purple-K powder, or simply PKP.

PKP is non-toxic and four times as powerful as CO_2 for extinguishing fires. It is also effective on Class C fires, but should not be used if CO_2 is available. Neither substance should be used on internal fires in gas turbines or jet engines, since both leave residues that cannot be completely removed without disassembling the engine.

The dry chemical extinguisher weighs 18 pounds and uses CO_2 as a propellant. The extinguisher shell is not pressurized until it is to be used.

Its use is simple. Pull the locking pin from the seal-cutter assembly and strike the puncture lever to cut the gas cartridge seal. The extinguisher is then charged and ready for use. Discharge the chemical in short bursts by squeezing the grip on the nozzle. When you're finished, invert the cylinder, squeeze the discharge lever and tap the nozzle on the deck. This releases all pressure and clears the hose and nozzle of powder.

Dry chemical is an excellent firefighting agent, but its effects are temporary. It has no cooling effect and provides no protection against reflash. Therefore, it should always be backed up by foam. In confined spaces, PKP should be used sparingly. Prolonged discharge of the chemical reduces visibility, and makes breathing difficult.

Two types of fixed fire-extinguisher installations are often provided, in areas like machinery spaces and hangar decks.

Fixed carbon dioxide extinguishers provide a dependable, ready means of flooding spaces that are more-than-ordinary fire hazards. Cylinders of the system each have a 50-pound capacity and are mounted either singly or in banks of two or more. Installed CO_2 extinguishers are either hose-and-heel type for machinery spaces, or flooding systems for spaces not continually occupied by personnel (such as paint lockers).

As mentioned before, PKP cannot prevent reflash. Nor can it be used with mechanical foam, because it causes a chemical breakdown in the foam. It is fully compatible, however, with an agent called "light water." Light water is a 6 percent concentration that, when mixed with water, produces foam. As the water drains from the foam, a vapor-tight film is formed on top of the fuel.

A light water/PKP combination will extinguish a fire up to three times faster than mechanical foams. The dry chemical beats down the fire and the light water prevents a reflash.

Aircraft carriers have a portable light water/PKP system mounted on a truck, known as a *twinned agent unit* (TAU). The unit can be operated by one man. Mechanical foam is being phased out in favor of the combination light water/PKP system.

PUMPS

There are three types of portable gasoline-powered pumps, but this discussion will be confined to the P-250 model, since this pump is now replacing the P-60 (called the "handy billy") and the P-500.

The P-250 is a self-priming centrifugal pump designed to pump 250 gpm, with a suction lift of 16 to 20 feet. The pump has a three-inch outlet, to which may be attached a 2½-inch hose, or a trigate having either three 2½-inch outlets, or two 1½-inch and one 2½-inch outlets for dewatering with an eductor.

Like any other gasoline engine, the P-250 produces carbon monoxide. When it is used below deck, its exhaust must be led outside the ship. The engine should never run in a space with explosive vapors.

When fighting a fire, a vast amount of water is used on the ship. For example, 2½-inch hose with a pressure of 100 psi pumps nearly a ton of water per minute. Obviously this water must be removed or the ship's stability will become greatly impaired.

The P-250 pump can be used for dewatering by straight pumping, at the rate of 300 gallons per minute. (The rate is higher than that for firefighting because of lower discharge pressure requirements.)

While the foregoing pumping rate may be sufficient in some instances, it's usually better to pump at a faster rate. The dewatering rate of a single pump can be doubled by using a pump called an *eductor*.

Eductors are also used when the liquid to be pumped (gasoline

Figure 18–14 Crash crewmen at a firefighting school test light water, which makes water actually float on gasoline or JP-5 fuel.

or other flammables) cannot be handled by the pump itself. This practice eliminates the chance of damaging the pump or of igniting the flammable liquid. Eductors can be used when the required suction lift is greater than the pump's capability. When the two are rigged together, lifts of more than 20 feet may be accomplished. This arrangement can be used both for dewatering and for firefighting.

PROTECTIVE CLOTHING AND EQUIPMENT

Any clothing that covers your skin will protect it from flash burns and other short-duration flames. In situations where there is a likelihood of fire or explosion, keep covered as much as possible, and protect your eyes with anti-flash goggles.

If your clothes catch fire, don't run. This fans the flames. Lie down and roll up in a blanket, coat, or anything that will smother the flames. If nothing is available, roll over slowly, beating out the flames with your hands. If another person's clothes catch fire, throw him down and cover him (except his head) with a blanket or coat.

Asbestos suits do not burn, but they conduct heat. Such suits offer only short-term protection against flames. The wearer should be heavily clothed before putting one on.

Anyone wearing an asbestos suit should not be sprayed with water while working on a fire because the suit becomes soaked and heavy. If it becomes necessary to do this, do not stop the stream of water until the man is clear of the fire and the suit has cooled. If the water is stopped after the suit is wet and while still hot, the water will turn to steam and scald the wearer.

The proximity firefighting suit, which consists of a one-piece coverall, gloves, hood, and boots, is made of glass fiber and asbestos. It is an aluminized surface and is designed to replace the asbestos suit. Its hood provides a protective cover for the OBA (see below) which is normally worn with it. It is lightweight and resists penetration of liquids. The suit allows men to enter overheated or steam-filled compartments and to make crash fire rescues.

The Navy uses Type A-4 *oxygen breathing apparatus (OBA).* The self-contained unit is designed to protect the wearer in an atmosphere lacking oxygen or containing harmful gases, vapors, smoke, or dust. The wearer breathes in a closed system in which oxygen is supplied by chemicals in a canister that purifies exhaled air.

The wearer's breath is circulated through the canister of chemicals, which react with the carbon dioxide and the moisture in his breath to produce oxygen. The process continues until the oxygen-producing capacity of the chemicals is used up—in

Figure 18–15 Navy Type A-4 Oxygen Breathing Apparatus.

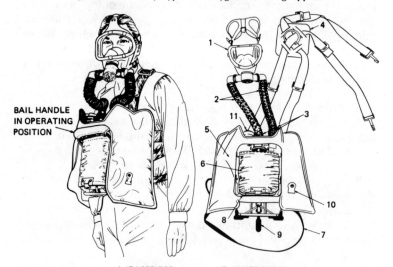

BAIL HANDLE
IN OPERATING
POSITION

1. FACEPIECE
2. BREATHING TUBES
3. BREATHING TUBE COUPLINGS
4. BODY HARNESS AND PAD
5. BREATHING BAG
6. BREASTPLATE

7. WAIST STRAP
8. BAIL ASSEMBLY HANDLE (STANDBY POSITION)
9. CANISTER RELEASE STRAP
10. PRESSURE RELIEF VALVE AND PULL TAB
11. TIMER

about 45 minutes, depending on the amount of physical labor involved.

All OBA equipment requires special instruction and practice. Don't try to use one until you have been properly instructed. Always observe these precautions:

Never enter a danger area until you are sure the apparatus is working correctly. Start the timer every time you start a new canister; when the timer goes off, or when it becomes difficult to exhale (meaning the canister needs to be changed), return to fresh air.

A used canister is very hot. Wear asbestos mittens, leather-palmed work gloves, or equivalent protection for your hands.

The chemical in canisters is very caustic to skin. Open canisters with care. If the chemical is accidently spilled on deck, clean it up immediately and dump it overboard, using a metal, nonflammable material for a scoop.

Oil, gasoline, or similar substances coming in contact with the chemicals will cause an explosion. When you drop the used canister, be sure it is on dry deck. Also be sure there is no chance for it to drop through or off a grating, and into the bilges.

When the facepiece needs cleaning, use only soap and water —never alcohol. Never grease or oil any part of the OBA.

Do not throw a canister overboard if there is an oil slick on the water, or if the ship is in port. Always punch several holes in the bottom with a clean tool, so it will sink immediately. Never hold your face or any part of your body over a canister opening.

The air-line mask (Figure 18–16) may be used for entering smoke-filled compartments or to rescue crew members. Since it produces no oxygen of its own, it should never be used when actually fighting a fire. The mask is a demand flow air-line respirator with a speaking diaphragm, monocular lens with adjustable head harness, breathing tube, and a belt-mounted demand regulator with quick-disconnect fittings. A 25-foot hose, also with quick-disconnect fittings, is provided.

If compressed air cylinders are not available, low-pressure ship's service air may be used, if it is reduced to the proper operating pressure. Never use an oxygen bottle with this equipment. Oil, grease, or oily water in the apparatus might combine with the oxygen and explode.

Before entering a space filled with toxic gases or smoke, check the mask to be sure it is working properly. Take a breath to determine whether there is sufficient airflow.

Life lines are 50-foot nylon-covered steel-wire tending lines used with the OBA or the air-line mask. Snap hooks are at each end of the line.

Tending lines are used as a precautionary measure for rescuing an overcome fire investigator or firefighter. Rescue should be accomplished by having men equipped with OBAs follow the tending lines to the person being rescued, rather than by dragging him out by the tending line. Never attach a line to the rescuee's waist. If pulled, it might interfere with his breathing or cause him internal injuries. A man should only be dragged out of a space when no other method of rescue is possible. OBAs are equipped with a hook on the harness to facilitate fastening of the life-line snap hook.

Life-line signals are:

	Pulls on life line	Meaning
Tender to wearer	1	Are you OK?
	2	Advance
	3	Back out
	4	Come out now
Wearer to tender	1	I am OK
	2	I am going on in
	3	Keep slack out of line
	4	Send help

A new *fire escape mask* consists of a transparent plastic head covering that can be donned in 20 seconds. Each mask carries a cartridge of compressed air—enough for eight minutes—which should enable the wearer to escape from any part of a ship to topside. It is especially designed to protect against smoke inhalation.

Two types of atmosphere-testing indicators are used. All closed or poorly ventilated compartments (and particularly those in which a fire has just occurred) are dangerous because the air in them may lack oxygen, may contain poisonous gases, or may present fire and explosion hazards.

Combustible gas indicators are used to detect various flammable gases and vapors. Several different types of indicators are available, but all operate on the same principles. A condensed operating routine is attached to the inside of the case cover. This type of indicator can quickly, safely, and accurately detect all combustible gases or vapors associated with fuel oils, gasoline, alcohol, acetone vapors, illuminating gas, fuel gas, hydrogen, and acetylene in mixtures with air or oxygen.

The indicator is sensitive to small quantities. Although it does not identify the combustibles present, it indicates that they are present in a certain proportion. The instrument is equipped with a flame arrester to prevent flashbacks.

Intended solely for the detection of oxygen deficiency in the atmosphere in which men must work, the *flame safety lamp* will detect the presence of flammable vapors. Its intentional use in areas where there are suspected flammable or explosive gases or vapors is dangerous and expressly forbidden.

When atmospheric conditions are normal, the flame of the safety lamp appears normal. When the atmosphere undergoes certain changes, the appearance of the flame is altered. If the oxygen in the atmosphere becomes lower than normal, the flame grows dim. If the oxygen is less than 16 percent by volume, the flame is extinguished. Before using the flame safety lamp, as with the combustible gas indicator, you should become very familiar with the instructions on its operation.

Fires that seem to be out may start again from a smoldering fragment or through vapor ignition. The final step in firefighting is the establishment of a *reflash watch*. After a fire has been extinguished, it is usually necessary to desmoke the compartments. This is done by using natural or forced ventilation.

Several cautions should be noted:

Be sure the fire is really out.

Investigate the ventilation systems in the affected areas to make sure they are free of burning or smoldering materials.

Have fire parties and equipment standing by the blower and controller of the ventilation systems.

Obtain permission from DCC (or the engineer) to open ventilation-system closures to start the blowers.

It is best to use exhaust systems, rather than supply systems, for desmoking. Portable ventilating blowers—often called red devils —can be used for desmoking, although they are not as efficient or convenient as permanent ventilating systems. When explosive vapors or fumes are present, it may be dangerous to use the installed systems. Under these circumstances, use only portable blowers.

Figure 18–16 Air-Line Mask with Buddy Fitting.

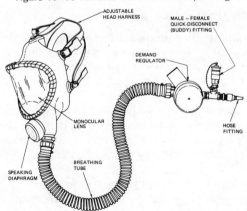

19. General Bills and Drills

Since the days of John Paul Jones, ships of the Navy have existed for one specific purpose—to fight. Everything a ship does in the way of training and maintenance is aimed at making her better able to fight when the time comes. As Navy Regulations says, "The requirements for battle shall be the basis for the organization of the ship."

If a ship is to perform her primary function well, she has to be organized in such a way that her crew can be effectively directed and controlled at all times. This means that every sailor aboard ship must know his station and duty—where he is to be and what he must do—for every drill or emergency. It is the responsibility of the commanding officer to see that this is done.

Since no one officer could handle all the details of assigning hundreds of men to their various duties, every ship has been organized under a standard system, so that the various departments and divisions handle much of this detail.

This system involves the use of "bills," which are established by three official documents: Standard Organization and Regulations of the U.S. Navy; the battle bill; and the watch, quarter, and station (WQ&S) bill. A bill is written to cover a certain emergency or job. It describes the duties involved, the stations to be manned, and lists the rates required to perform the duties and man the stations. The Standard Organization and Regulations of the U.S. Navy describes administrative bills, operational bills, emergency bills, and special bills.

Administrative Bills

These bills set procedures for the everyday administration of the ship's company, determine where a specific assignment of each member of the crew is required, and include the bills list.

BERTHING AND LOCKER

The personnel officer is responsible for establishing and maintaining uniform policies for assignment of berthing and locker facilities to personnel, both officers and enlisted. Division officers assign bunks and lockers for men within their divisions.

CLEANING, PRESERVATION, AND MAINTENANCE

General procedures for cleaning and preservation are contained in the bill. Duties involve maintaining, preserving, and cleaning the exterior and interior of the hull, hull fittings, machinery, and equipment. Cleaning stations are assigned by division officers—except for side cleaners, who are assigned by the first lieutenant to care for the ship's exterior.

FORMATION AND PARADE

Quarters and formations which may be required are held in accordance with the bill. Included are regular divisional quarters —fair- and foul-weather parades, personnel inspections, and mustering on station; officers' quarters; quarters for entering and leaving port; manning the rail; and general assembly. The XO is responsible for this bill.

GENERAL VISITING

Also the responsibility of the executive officer, this bill specifies procedures and restrictions necessary for the control of visitors to naval units, ensures physical security, integrity of classified information, and reasonable privacy of the unit's company.

OFFICIAL CORRESPONDENCE AND
CLASSIFIED MATERIAL CONTROL

Designed to coordinate the receiving, sending, marking, accounting, inventorying, controlling, and destroying of official correspondence and classified material. The executive officer, assisted by the security manager (SM), is responsible.

ORIENTATION

Provides procedures for the indoctrination of newly reported enlisted personnel with the unit, its departmental functions, and its routine. The I-division officer, under the XO, is responsible. The bill applies to personnel in paygrades E-1 through E-4.

PERSONNEL ASSIGNMENT

Provides for the assignment and reassignment of officers and enlisted personnel to billets within the unit's organization, including collateral and special duties. This bill, also the responsibility of the XO, covers temporary assignment of a chief master-at-arms (CMAA), mess deck master-at-arms, and personnel as food servicemen and compartment cleaners.

SECURITY

Assigns responsibilities for the handling and safeguarding of classified material (except nuclear weapons) and information. The security manager (SM) is responsible for this bill.

SECURITY FROM UNAUTHORIZED VISITORS

The XO is responsible for this bill, which ensures the maintenance of security of the unit when "repel boarders" action is not appropriate. Situations can occur wherein an unauthorized person (commercial agent, occupant of a pleasure boat, member of a non-military organization, etc.) would attempt to board the unit for various reasons, including sheer mischief, revelry, or even for political reasons. This bill includes the handling of these and similar situations.

SECURITY WATCH

To provide the maximum security of the unit consistent with the performance of assigned missions and routine functions, certain security watches are established by this bill. The bill is the responsibility of the security officer.

UNIT SECURITY

The purpose of this bill is to provide for the particular security measures required by nuclear-capable ships. The procedures and responsibilities in this bill are in addition to the general shipboard security measures provided elsewhere—such as sounding and security patrols, bow and stern sentries, and the gangway watch. The security officer (or weapons officer, if none is assigned) is responsible.

ZONE INSPECTION

Frequent zone inspections are necessary to see that proper measures are being taken to maintain machinery, spaces, and equipment in a satisfactory state of operation, preservation, and cleanliness. The XO is responsible for this bill.

Operational Bills

As the name implies, operational bills deal with specific evolutions by the ship's company. Most spell out specific duties and responsibilities for special operations.

BOAT

The boat bill defines policies and methods for employing the ship's boats. The first lieutenant, under the XO, is responsible for the bill, which also assigns specific responsibilities to the navigator, the engineer, the OOD, the boat officers, and the coxswains.

CIVIL DISASTER

Through this bill the XO provides for an effective, organized force, capable of participating in civil disaster relief work. In providing disaster relief, units expect to deal with demoralized, hysterical, or apathetic survivors who are incapable, at least temporarily, of intelligent cohesive action in their own behalf. Planning takes all of these factors into account.

COLD WEATHER

This bill is placed into effect prior to deployment in areas of extremely cold weather. It involves among many other things, seeing that a full allowance of cold-weather clothing is available; that a sufficient quantity of additional life and safety lines and de-icing equipment is on board; and establishing a shipboard "heating patrol" to monitor temperatures in all living spaces. The XO is the coordinator.

DARKEN SHIP

Ships may steam at night with all lights out to avoid detection by enemy forces; this is called "darken ship." When darken ship is set, all topside doors and hatches are closed, ports are blacked out and smoking is prohibited on all weather decks. To perform efficiently during darken ship, you must be able to find your way around topside in complete darkness, and know how to open and close doors, plug in telephones, locate switches, and handle all other equipment at the underway or general quarters station. During darken ship, only flashlights or hand lanterns with red lens covers can be used topside, and only when absolutely necessary. The DCA is responsible for maintaining this bill.

DIVING

This bill is intended primarily for scuba diving and is designed to establish procedures and precautions for diving operations. The guidelines may also be applied to dives made with light-

Figure 19–1 Divers prepare for a swim under the ice in the arctic during cold-weather operations.

Figure 19–2 An aquanaut trainee emerges during diving operations in California.

weight diving equipment. The diving officer is responsible for the bill.

DRYDOCKING

This bill, the responsibility of the engineer officer (under the supervision of the XO), includes responsibilities and duties necessary to prepare the ship for entering drydock and to provide required services for the ship while in dock. The provisions of Navy Regulations govern this bill. Since docking and undocking are normally all-hands evolutions and require coordination with the docking facility, adequate preparations, smart seamanship and adherence to sound procedures are necessary. Provisions must also be made on nuclear ships to shut down the reactor before the water level in the dock is permitted to fall below the ship's minimum draft.

EMCON

The necessary procedures for setting EMCON (emission control) conditions, ensuring the maintenance of EMCON conditions when set, and designating an emission control center (EMC or EMCON center) are contained in this bill. EMCON is the management of electromagnetic transmissions to provide a command with essential information, while presenting an enemy with a controlled probability of detecting, identifying, position, and homing. The operations officer is responsible for this bill.

EMERGENCY TOWING

Whenever towing or being towed, a towing watch is maintained for the purpose of observing towing conditions, keeping the OOD informed and being prepared to cast off if so ordered. This bill defines all of the procedures to be used, including establishment of policies for assignment of personnel to duties and stations. The weapons (or deck) officer is responsible for the bill.

EQUIPMENT TAG-OUT

This bill outlines procedures to be used to prevent improper operation when a component, equipment, a system, or portion of a system is isolated or is functioning in an abnormal condition. The bill is designed to standardize all tag-out procedures used by ships and repair activities. The commanding officer is responsible for this bill; it is administered through his department heads, who see that assigned personnel understand and comply with the procedures of this bill.

FLIGHT OPERATIONS

All of the necessary assignments to flight quarters stations for air department and air wing or detachment personnel are covered in this bill. Departmental responsibilities are also defined for engineering, communications, and medical. Responsibility for the bill rests with the air officer.

HEAVY WEATHER

This bill is designed to provide for heavy weather conditions both at sea or in port. The first lieutenant, under the XO, is responsible. In addition to the two officers already mentioned, the navigator, operations officer, engineer officer, gunnery officer, supply officer, medical department, and the OOD all have specific responsibilities and duties.

HELICOPTER OPERATIONS

Since the role of the helicopter has been extensively expanded in recent years, this bill is designed to ensure safe helicopter operations by establishing standard operating procedures. Helo

Figure 19–3 Helo operations offer a wide-range view of Norfolk harbor.

missions now include search and rescue, vertical replenishment (VERTREP), antisubmarine warfare (ASW), amphibious assault, and minesweeping. Helicopters operate with virtually all fleet units. The XO assigns an officer to maintain this bill.

HELICOPTER INFLIGHT REFUELING

This bill ensures safe helicopter inflight refueling operations. Standard operating procedures are specified for each ship. The operations (or weapons) officer, as directed by the CO, is responsible.

INTELLIGENCE COLLECTION

Although collection of intelligence information is a secondary mission (following after operations and training), this bill provides for the collection and reporting of that information, as long as it doesn't interfere with the ship's principal mission. The intelligence officer, under the supervision of the operations officer, is responsible for maintaining the bill; the OOD is responsible for its execution.

LANDING PARTY

When required, units form a landing party capable of quelling riots or disorders in the vicinity of the ship, able to assist in disaster relief ashore, and available for parades and ceremonies as required. The landing party is organized on the basis of the size of the ship's crew: one 10-man squad per 100 crewmembers, with a minimum of one squad. The size cannot exceed one company. Squads are commanded by petty officers; platoons and companies by junior officers. The weapons officer (or CO of the Marine detachment, if assigned) is responsible for the bill.

NAVIGATION

This bill, the responsibility of the navigator, prescribes uniform responsibilities and procedures for the safe navigation of the ship, including navigation in restricted water under conditions of low visibility. It should be noted that the safe navigation of the ship ultimately rests with the commanding officer.

REPLENISHMENT

Assignment of personnel to duties and stations, as well as the establishment of certain procedures for replenishing the ship at sea, transferring passengers and light freight, fueling, defueling the internal transfer of fuel—all these are spelled out in this bill. The first lieutenant, under the supervision of the XO, is responsible for this bill. (Replenishment operations are also covered in Chapter 21, pages 427–35.)

RESCUE AND ASSISTANCE

It is through this bill that the engineer officer, under the XO, provides for a special organization of qualified personnel within each duty section to render emergency assistance to persons or activities outside the unit, without lowering the unit's own security standards. It is this bill that also prescribes the procedures for recovering one or more persons from the water.

RESCUE OF SURVIVORS

This bill, similar to the one above, is designed to provide an organization capable of rescuing large numbers of survivors from the water. The weapons officer, under the supervision of the XO, is responsible. The organization created by this bill is supplemented, as necessary, by personnel from all repair parties in order to meet the needs of a particular rescue operation.

SHIP'S SILENCING

The engineer, working with and through the ship silencing board, is responsible for reducing his ship's noise in order to enhance the performance of installed sonars, and decrease the acoustic detectability of his own ship. Although shipboard noise may have an adverse physical or psychological effect on the crew, this bill is primarily connected with "tactical" noise.

SHORE FIRE CONTROL PARTY

This bill provides for the organization and command responsibilities of the shore fire control party, provides lists of equipment to be used, and outlines the conditions under which the party may be called into service. The operations officer, under the XO, is responsible for the bill. The primary mission of the ship's shore fire control party is to provide shore fire control for the ship's guns (or other naval guns) in support of limited operations ashore. The party also has a secondary mission of providing tactical control of available aircraft support. The shore fire control party is sent ashore under varying combat conditions.

SPECIAL SEA AND ANCHOR DETAIL

Personnel assignments, and specific duties for periods when the ship is being handled in restricted waters and preparing to get underway or return to port, are covered in this bill. The special sea and anchor detail supplements the regular steaming watch; in some instances, the detail personnel relieve the regular watch. The operations officer has responsibility for the bill. (The specific procedures for getting underway or returning to port are discussed in Chapter 16.)

VISIT AND SEARCH, BOARDING AND
SALVAGE, AND PRIZE CREW

Such operations were much more liable to take place in the old days of square riggers and muzzle loaders, but they can still happen. The operations officer is responsible for maintaining the bill and for bringing to the XO's attention any matters that may have an effect on the bill. The purpose of visit and search is to determine the nationality of ships, character of their cargo, nature of their employment, and other pertinent factors. The boarding and salvage party is dispatched, when necessary, by the commanding officer to board and take command of the ship, restrain the crew, and conduct necessary salvage operations. A prize master, although still responsible to his commanding officer, has the full range of responsibilities of any commanding officer over the prize crew.

Emergency Bills

Emergency bills are probably the most important of all shipboard bills because they affect all hands. It is extremely important that you know what your responsibilities are for each situation, and that when the alarm is sounded, you go to your station on the double. You go forward and up the starboard side, aft and down the port side. Maintain silence; only men in charge should speak.

The organization, procedures, and responsibilities for controlling the effects of a major emergency or disaster suffered by the ship are contained in this bill. Such situations as collision, grounding, internal and external explosion, NBC (nuclear-biological-chemical) contamination, earthquake, storm, or battle damage are included. This bill, the responsibility of the engineer officer, also provides for the orderly and controlled egress of personnel if abandon ship is required, and for salvage of the ship if feasible.

The training program to prepare for emergencies is a long-range one, encompassing the following factors:

Formal shore-based schools for training in firefighting, basic damage control procedures, and NBC defense.

All officers and leading petty officers have the responsibility to indoctrinate and train their personnel in the fundamentals of controlling the effects of any emergency.

In major catastrophies, the availability of personnel trained in first aid will drastically reduce the number of serious casualties and fatalities. Therefore, the medical officer (or senior HM when no medical officer is assigned) is charged with conducting an ac-

Figure 19–4 A damage control repair party drills for emergency situations until their response to an alarm is second nature.

tive training program for all hands in first-aid procedures, including measures necessary in NBC defense.

Division officers have the responsibility for training their personnel in the use of individual protective equipment and the performance of their duties while wearing the gas mask and other protective clothing.

General emergency drills are held as ordered by the XO; there is generally at least one each month. During drills the actions and duties prescribed in this (and other supplemental bills) must be fully carried out.

The general provisions of this bill are effective whether the ship is underway or in port. The bill is placed in effect in the event of fire or other emergency which may present a danger to the ship. The bill also provides details for specific situations: for example, emergency with full crew on board; in-port general emergency with partial crew; NBC attack; or abandon ship.

AIRCRAFT CRASH AND RESCUE

Each ship must be prepared to rapidly implement this bill. Since the wide variances in ship characteristics, organization, and capabilities preclude the establishment of a general bill applicable to all units, each must establish its own guidelines. Type commanders distribute bills which are generally applicable to ships of their forces. Each ship, within the guidelines set by the type commander, prepares a bill to meet its specific requirements. The XO is responsible for appointing an officer to maintain this bill.

EMERGENCY STEERING

Since many of the detailed measures used to control a steering casualty are peculiar to the installed equipment, supplemental instructions to this bill are necessary. It does, however, provide the general guidelines and defines the responsibilities of the OOD, the steersman in the pilothouse, the quartermaster of the watch (QMOW), the boatswain's mate of the watch (BMOW), the duty electrician's mate (EM), and the auxiliary machinist's mate (MM). The navigator, with the technical assistance of the engineer officer, is responsible for this bill.

MAN OVERBOARD

Each sailor should be instructed in the action he should take if he falls overboard and he should understand what action he can expect from a rescuing ship. The watch sections get frequent drill and instruction, and rescue details are conducted to ensure the successful execution of this bill, which is designed to recover one man or a small number of men from the water. The first lieu-

Figure 19–5 A dummy called Oscar—named after the flag—is used in man-overboard drills.

tenant is responsible for the adequacy and currency of this bill and makes all necessary changes to it, subject to the approval of the executive officer.

NUCLEAR REACTOR PLAN CASUALTY

The engineer/reactor officer, under the supervision of the XO, is responsible for this bill and for conducting drills to test the adequacy of the bill and evaluate the state of training. Although it is unlikely that reactor conditions will degrade in such a way as to produce a power-plant casualty, resulting in a nuclear accident, the ship must be prepared to meet such an emergency. The bill also outlines the procedures for control, monitor, and decontamination of affected areas and personnel.

NUCLEAR WEAPONS ACCIDENT/INCIDENT

A nuclear weapons accident/incident is a potential or actual casualty to a nuclear weapon or related system which endangers personnel, the ship, or its vital equipment. This bill, which defines the specific hazards and basic considerations involved, is the responsibility of the weapons officer, under the supervision of the XO. A nuclear safety officer, if this duty is assigned to an officer other than the weapons officer, is the weapons officer's assistant in maintaining the currency and effectiveness of the bill.

TOXIC GAS

Procedures, duties, and responsibilities are outlined in this bill which deals with controlling and minimizing the effects of toxic gases within the ship. The bill provides for gases whose presence indicates an emergency condition (chlorine, smoke, or tear gas) and for those which are generated by the ship (such as carbon monoxide, ammonia, or carbon dioxide). The damage control assistant (DCA) maintains this bill. A complete listing of toxic and hazardous gases and vapors that may be encountered aboard ship is contained in the bill, including information as to how the gases are usually produced, how they are detected, and the effects of overexposure.

Special Bills

The four bills in this category are employed in special situations. All but the first one are the responsibility of the executive officer. (The operations officer maintains the anti-sneak/anti-swimmer attack bill.)

ANTI-SNEAK/ANTI-SWIMMER ATTACK

When moored in foreign ports or anchored in foreign or hostile waters, ships are very vulnerable to attack by swimmers and small boats. This bill ensures that the ship is capable of detecting and defeating sneak attack. The anti-sneak/anti-swimmer watch is set at the discretion of the commanding officer.

EVACUATING CIVILIANS

The plans and procedures outlined in this bill are intended to serve as a guide for the execution of an evacuation mission involving civilian personnel. Each situation will differ in regard to

the number and sex of passengers embarked, and the length of
time they would be on board; therefore, detailed plans must be
formulated after assignment to a specific evacuation mission.

PRISONERS OF WAR

This bill applies to combat forces of the enemy, as well as to
individuals traveling with an armed force (such as newspaper
correspondents, contractors, technicians), and the officers and
crews of enemy merchant ships. This bill also provides for the
particulars of custody, berthing, messing and otherwise meeting
the needs of prisoners of war.

TROOP LIFT

Although the conditions under which troops are transported
will vary, the basic procedures and responsibilities prescribed in
this bill are considered the standards for the transportation of
troops. In addition to the executive officer, who is responsible for
the organization, supervision and coordination of all phases of
the troop lift, the weapons officer, first lieutenant, supply officer,
operations officer, and personnel officer also have assigned responsibilities.

Drilling for Emergencies

During a major emergency, you will hear the continuous
sounding of the general quarters (GQ) alarm or (on smaller ships)
a siren, horn, or bell, plus the words "General Quarters! General
Quarters! All hands man your battle stations" over the 1MC system. Don't try to find out what's happened, move . . . you'll
know soon enough.

MAN OVERBOARD

The first necessity when a man goes overboard is prompt action. Anyone who sees a man go overboard immediately sounds
the alarm "Man overboard, port (starboard) side," and drops a
life ring or lifejacket. If possible, keep the man in sight. If a smoke
float and dye marker are available, drop them too.

Every underway watch is organized to handle this situation.
The OOD will maneuver the ship to reach a recovery position.
At the same time the word will be passed twice and you'll hear
six or more short blasts on the ship's whistle. The lifeboat crew
will stand by to lower away when directed. If available, a helo
may be launched. The helo can quickly spot a man in the water
and can pick him up even if he is unable to help himself. If the
identity of the man is not known, a muster of the crew may be
held in order to find out who is missing.

There is always the possibility that the man overboard may be you. If this should happen, keep your head. Don't panic or despair. Hold your breath when you hit the water; the buoyancy of your lungs will bring you to the surface. Don't swim frantically away from the ship—the screws won't suck you under because they are too deep in the water. Just keep afloat and try to stay right where you went in. The ship will maneuver so as to come right back down her track to you.

Even if no one saw you go over, keep afloat. When a man is missed, ships and aircraft begin an intensive search.

If a man goes overboard in port, the alarm is sounded as usual, and the OOD uses the best available method of rescue. Boats in the water will assist in any emergency.

NBC DEFENSE

In the event of nuclear, biological, or chemical (NBC) attack, the crew can do a great deal to minimize casualties and damage. For those ships located at or near ground zero in a nuclear attack, or in an area of high concentrations of biological or chemical agents, casualties and damage will, of course, be very great. However, tests have shown that ships not receiving the direct effects of such attacks would have a very good chance of survival with relatively few casualties, and with weapons systems intact. Since formations are generally widely dispersed, it is probable that nearly all of the fleet units would escape the direct effects of the NBC attack.

Before the attack: The preparatory measures taken when attack is declared imminent are as follows:

Go to general quarters to "button up" the ship. Conduct a preattack washdown of all topside areas using the water washdown system. The entire outer surface of the ship is kept wet so that NBC contaminants will tend to wash overboard and not adhere to the external surfaces of the ship.

All nonvital openings of the ship are closed in order to maintain as complete a gas-tight envelope as possible. Personnel who are manning stations below decks, and must breathe air conducted directly into the ship during an attack, should have gas masks. These areas are generally in firerooms, diesel-generator rooms and other main propulsion spaces that require large volumes of air to support combustion.

All topside personnel in exposed positions don protective clothing and masks. Personnel are also issued detectors which will indicate what kind of NBC agent the wearer might be exposed to, and the degree of exposure.

The extreme effectiveness of some bacteriological agents, the toxicity of chemical agents, and the danger of radioactive fallout dictate that protective clothing and gas masks be carefully used.

It is mandatory that all personnel be periodically retrained in the use of protective clothing and masks.

Protective clothing worn in NBC defense is of four types:

Ordinary work clothing is initially effective in preventing droplets of chemicals or bacteriological agents from making easy contact with the skin; however, they quickly become contaminated and must then be discarded.

Foul-weather clothing, including parka, trousers, rubber boots, and gloves, protects the skin against penetration by liquid chemical agents and low-energy radioactive particles. It, too, retains contamination and must be discarded when the garments can no longer be decontaminated by being hosed down.

Permeable protective clothing has been treated with chemicals that neutralize blister-agent vapors and aerosols. It loses its ability to neutralize these agents once soaked down. It is thus not effective for long-term protection.

Impermeable protective clothing has a rubberized outer covering and hence will not permit air or water to pass through. Needless to say, this clothing is hot and uncomfortable in warm climates. It will provide, however, the best overall protection against BW and CW agents and alpha particles. Gamma and high-energy beta radiation will penetrate it, however.

There are several protective masks available for general use in the Navy, and some can be used in NBC defense. Masks are generally of two types. The first type includes all masks that do not provide oxygen to the user. This type of mask employs a system of mechanical and chemical filters that remove solid or liquid particles and absorb or neutralize toxic and irritating vapors.

The MK V gas mask is a good example of this type. This mask will protect against the inhalation of some nerve, blister, choking, vomiting, and tear agents. It will not protect against carbon monoxide, carbon dioxide, ammonia, and many fuel gases or vapors. This mask is not used in connection with firefighting or smoke, or in an atmosphere containing less than 16 percent oxygen, the amount necessary to support life.

The oxygen breathing apparatus (OBA) is an example of the second type of mask. (It is described on page 336.) The chemicals in the OBA canister can provide for about 60 minutes of use —less than that, if the user engages in heavy work. Various other masks will provide some protection against NBC agents—but only for short periods of time, and only if air supplies to them are kept uncontaminated.

After the attack: The detection of NBC agents—which generally are invisible, odorless, tasteless, and give no hint to the senses of their presence—requires special equipment and training.

Radioactive particles betray their presence by giving off several kinds of radiation. Some types of radiation contain no detectable mass or charge and are classed as high-energy electromagnetic radiation, called gamma rays. Other types have charge or mass and are further classed into neutrons, electrons, alpha particles, neutrinos, and other subatomic particles too numerous to mention. The ionizing radiations—alpha particles, beta electrons, and gamma waves—are the easiest to detect. The three primary types of radiation can be detected by instruments known as radiacs (radiation, detection, indication, and computation).

The use of radiacs depends on their specific internal configuration. They are used as intensity meters for measuring the highly penetrating gamma radiation or the less penetrating beta and alpha radiation. They are also used as survey meters detecting alpha particles, or as dosimeters for measuring the total amount of radiation an individual has received during an attack. The present individual dosimeter is the DT-60/PD; it is worn around the neck on a chain. It records accumulated whole-body gamma radiation from 10–660 roentgens and is read by a computer. Film badges are also issued to measure whole-body beta and gamma radiation.

If early detection of the radiation is made, with prompt decontamination and removal of radiation hot spots from the ship, many lives can be saved and much radiation sickness avoided.

In biological warfare detection, samples must be taken, cultured, and subjected to thorough laboratory testing before the agent used can be identified. This is slow, exacting work; and if viruses are involved, they can greatly increase the difficulty of identification. Since identification is difficult, by the time the BW agent has been identified, many people could already be casualties.

Chemical agents are somewhat easier to detect, but no one procedure will detect all known chemical agents. Some of these are lethal in extremely small concentrations and hence could be deployed upwind over a very great area with devastating results.

Monitoring and surveying of ships and stations is a vital part of NBC defense. The location of the hazard, isolation of the contaminated areas, recording of the results of the survey, and the reporting of the findings up the chain of command are the functions of every military unit encountering contamination.

On board ship, two more types of survey are required after an NBC attack. A gross survey, including weather decks, interior spaces, and machinery, is taken to locate any obvious contamination. Personnel decontamination starts as soon as the decontamination area itself is ready.

Specific instructions for making monitoring surveys cannot be specified for all situations, but generally after a gross survey has been made, gross decontamination begins. This entails flushing the contaminated surfaces with large amounts of water. The water washdown system would be used for external surfaces. For internal contamination, firehoses and manual scrubbing is necessary. Steam is a useful agent for decontamination, especially if BW agents are suspected or if the contamination is lodged in greasy or oily films.

Detailed decontamination would be the next step, its purpose being to reduce the contamination to such a low level that no significant hazard would remain. These are three general procedures: surface decontamination to reduce the agent without destroying the use of the equipment; aging and sealing to allow the contaminant to decay or lose its potency through evaporation or dissolution; and disposal or removal of contaminated materials to a place where they can do little harm.

EMERGENCY DESTRUCTION

This action, ordered by the commanding officer, requires the destruction of classified documents and equipment to prevent their falling into enemy hands. Persons assigned duties under this bill are given specific and detailed instructions when the need arises.

ABANDON SHIP

This is one emergency in which many senior officers and petty officers may be lost as battle casualties, and full responsibility may fall on the shoulders of very junior men.

Abandon-ship stations and duties are noted on the watch, quarter, and station (WQ&S) bill. Careful planning takes care of who goes in which boat or raft, what emergency equipment is to be supplied, and who supplies it. Know your abandon-ship station and duties. Know all escape routes to topside from berthing spaces or working spaces below decks. Know how to inflate a lifejacket. Know how to lower a boat or let go of a life raft. Know how to handle survival gear. And, if necessary, know how to do it all in the dark.

Only the commanding officer can order abandon ship. He will do so only after all efforts to save the ship prove futile. When the abandon-ship alarm sounds, act fast. It's your last chance. Survival at sea depends on knowledge, equipment, training, and self-control.

Disaster can strike suddenly at sea. A ship can go down within three minutes after a collision or explosion. If you don't know what to do before it happens, there won't be time to find out after it does.

Going over the side: Make certain your lifejacket is secured properly and that your knife, whistle, and flashlight are fastened to it. Go down a cargo net, boat falls, fire hose or line if you can, but don't slide down and burn your hands. If you have to jump, look out for wreckage or swimmers in the water. Don't try a fancy dive; go feet first, with legs crossed and arms over your face. If you have a pneumatic lifejacket, don't inflate it until you are in the water—otherwise you will pop right out of it.

If possible, go over the windward side and swim upwind. If you go over the leeward side, the wind may blow the ship, or burning oil, down on you. Swim underwater to avoid burning oil; when you come up for air, splash the oil away as you break the surface. To protect yourself from underwater explosions, swim away for at least 150 yards, then climb aboard a raft, boat, or piece of wreckage, or float on your back. Stay calm. If you panic, you are more than halfway to being lost.

In the water: Rafts, boats, nets, and floating wreckage should be tied together; this makes it easier for searchers to find you. Wounded men should be put in boats or rafts first, others should hang on the sides. In cold water, everyone must get into a raft or boat as soon as possible. If you must remain in the water, stay as still as possible to prevent heat loss which escapes most rapidly from the head, hands, and feet. Use whatever clothing is available to protect these areas. Numbness occurs in waters below 35 degrees. Breathe slowly and remain still.

Frostbite and immersion foot can occur quickly in cold water. Don't rub; this will damage frozen tissues. Warm affected parts against your own body, or a shipmate's.

In a hot climate, keep your shirt, trousers, and shoes on— you'll need them for protection against sun and salt water.

Boat handling: In a power boat, the slowest possible speed will give the best mileage. If the boat is fitted for sails, use them and save the motor for an emergency. Otherwise, rig a jury mast and sails out of oars, boathooks, clothing, and tarpaulins. If wind and sea are driving you away from the nearest land or rescue area, rig a sea anchor to slow the drift.

Organization: The abandon-ship bill assigns an officer or senior enlisted man to each boat or raft, but serious casualties may make you the senior man in a boat. If so, take charge.

Make wounded as comfortable as possible. Make a list of all survivors, and try to list all known casualties. Inventory all water and provisions and set up a ration system based on the expected number of days to land. No one should eat or drink for the first 24 hours.

Organize a watch. Lookouts must be alert and know how to use available signal gear. Get underway for the nearest known land or well-travelled shipping route.

Secure all gear so nothing will be lost. If fishing gear is aboard, use it; otherwise, make some. Rig a tarp for protection against the sun and to catch rain water.

Try to keep all hands alert and cheerful. Save their energy; unnecessary exertion uses up food and water.

Equipment: *Vest-type life preserver:* This is the most important item of abandon-ship equipment. Learn how to use it. The vest preserver goes on over other clothes. Tie the upper tape at the waist fairly tight to keep it from sliding up in the water; adjust the chest strap and fasten the snap hook into the ring; tie collar tapes to keep them down under your chin; and pull straps between the legs from behind, as tightly as possible without becoming uncomfortable. Adjust the straps on an unconscious man before he is put overboard; the design of this preserver will keep his head upright and prevent him from drowning.

Inflatable life preserver: This one is carried in a pouch at your back and fastens around your waist on a web belt. It can be inflated by CO_2 cartridge or by mouth. To inflate the preserver, pull the pouch around in front, remove the preserver, slip it over your head, and jerk the lanyard down as far as possible to release the CO_2 gas into the chamber. For more buoyancy you can add more air through the mouthpiece. To deflate, open the valve.

Inflatable lifeboat: The 15-man Mark 5, the type carried aboard most ships, is a compact, relatively light, easily stowed, and easily launched boat. The boat is constructed of separate tubes: the upper, lower, and canopy support tubes are inflated by CO_2 cylinders; the thwart tubes are inflated with hand pumps. A fabric bottom is attached to the lower tube to support manually inflatable floors. The floors are equipped with hand lines and are removable for emergency use.

The boat is contained in a carrying case, with a release cable extending outside the case; pulling the cables will open and inflate the boat in about 30 seconds. Normally the boat should be inflated after it's in the water. As soon as the boat is inflated, use the boarding net and grab ladders to board it. The first person to enter stays at the entrance to help others; the second in goes forward to open the other entrance, check the sea anchor, and help others board at that end.

Each boat is equipped with three waterproof containers of survival equipment. These containers are packed in the carrying case, not in the boat, so don't let the case get away—it is secured to the boat by a length of line. Two of the containers each hold two cartons of rations and one carton of water. The third container holds one carton of rations and the following items: sea marker dye, flashlight, two "C" batteries, jackknife, signal mirror, two sponges, whistle, first-aid kit, and distress signal kit. The rations are sufficient to sustain 15 men for five days.

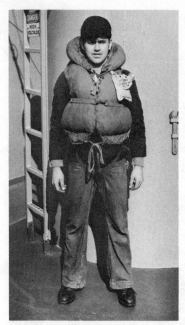

360

Figure 19–6 Front and back views of the kapok-type vest life preserver.

Figure 19–7 Front and back views of the CO_2-type jacket life preserver.

Signaling equipment is extremely important because of the difficulty of spotting life rafts from the air, and from the surface in heavy weather. The signal mirror can be seen at a distance of 10 miles or more, if used properly. Hold the mirror to reflect sunlight onto a nearby object, then look through the hole in the center. You will see a bright spot which shows the direction of the reflected beam of sunlight. Keep your eye on the dot and move the mirror slowly until the dot is on the target.

The signal kit contains a dozen Mark 13 distress signals for day and night use, and for providing wind-drift information to helicopters picking up personnel. One end of the signal tube produces an orange smoke for day use; the other end produces a red flare for night use. The night-flare end can be identified in the dark by a series of small beadlike projections embossed around the edge. Each signal will burn for about 18 seconds.

Dye markers consist of a powder which produces a brilliant yellowish-green fluorescence when sprinkled on water. Under good conditions the dye will be a good target for only about an hour, but it will retain some of its color for up to four hours. From an altitude of 3,000 feet the detection range of the dye marker may be as great as 10 miles. The range decreases as the dye deteriorates. Unless the moonlight is very bright, the dye is not effective at night.

Never discard any article that will hold water. When it rains, every container that can possibly hold water will be invaluable. To assist you in filling the containers, a raincatcher tube is attached to the lifeboat canopy. The 15-man lifeboat carries no equipment for turning sea water into fresh water. Other types of rafts, however, such as those carried in aircraft, have solar stills.

In polar areas, fresh water can be obtained from old sea ice— this type of ice is bluish, splinters easily, and is nearly free from salt. Fresh water may also be obtained from icebergs—but be careful. As the berg's underwater portion melts, it gets top-heavy and can capsize without warning.

FIRE

Alarm for a real fire may be given at any time. For drill purposes, a fire may be assumed to be in a specific place—for example, in an ammunition space or berthing compartment.

The word for fire is passed twice over the general announcing system, giving the fire's compartment location; this is followed by rapid ringing of the ship's bell, followed by one stroke if forward, two if amidships, three if aft. Ships with nuclear weapons have a special FZ alarm, a rapid ringing bell which is triggered automatically if temperature in a weapons space exceeds authorized temperatures, or if security there is violated.

The man who discovers an actual fire must give the alarm. The most important thing he can do is notify at least one other person who can go for help. Too often a fire has gotten out of control because a man tried to put it out by himself, without calling help.

Once the alarm has sounded, men nearby should act promptly messenger, or word of mouth to notify the OOD, or Damage Control Central (DCC).

Once the alarm has sounded, men nearby should act promptly to check or extinguish the fire, using the means nearest at hand. All others respond to the alarm in accordance with the watch, quarter and station (WQ&S) bill. If you and several other men have begun to fight the fire, do not leave the scene until the fire or repair party arrives. Chapter 18, pages 323–39, gives a comprehensive picture of shipboard firefighting operations and associated equipment.

20. Safety and Maintenance

Safety

Safety is a job for all hands, 24 hours a day. Some danger exists in every single operation aboard a naval vessel. Going to sea involves working with powerful machinery, high-speed equipment, steam which has intensely high temperature and pressure, volatile and exotic fuels and propellants, heavy lifts, high explosives, stepped-up electrical voltages, and the unpredictable forces of weather. It is the responsibility of everyone aboard ship to observe all safety precautions.

Safety precautions for each piece of equipment used in the Navy are available and should be read and understood. The Navy Ships Technical Manual (NAVSHIPSTECHMAN), Standard Organization and Regulations of the U.S. Navy, and numerous bureau and systems manuals all contain written safety regulations.

Another important part of safety is the regular maintenance of equipment and systems. Maintenance involves much more than just cleaning and painting. For safety and efficiency, every item aboard ship—from the simplest valve to the most complicated electronic gear—must be clean and operable.

The following general instructions, listed alphabetically, serve as an introduction to the most important principles regarding shipboard safety.

AIRCRAFT OPERATIONS

During aircraft operations, only those actually involved are allowed in the flight-deck area. All other personnel remain clear or below decks. Personnel engaged in flight ops must wear appropriate safety equipment.

Passengers must be led to and from a helicopter or aircraft by a member of the transfer crew, handling crew, or flight crew. All loose gear in the flight-deck area must be stowed elsewhere or secured to the deck. Personnel must be instructed on the shrapnel effect caused when rotor blades or propellers strike a solid object. Be careful around props and helo rotors. When turning they are nearly invisible. A helicopter's rotor tips cover a wide area and they often will dip close to the deck when the helo lands.

Engine noise of the plane you are watching will drown out the noise of ones you are not watching. Don't move without looking in all directions and don't direct all your attention to a single aircraft.

Also beware of jet blast. Any place within 100 feet of a jet engine is dangerous. A jet blast can burn a man, knock him to the ground, or blow him over the side.

AMMUNITION HANDLING

Everyone required to handle ammunition must be instructed in safety regulations, methods of handling, and storage and uses of all ammunition and explosives. Only careful, reliable, mentally sound and physically fit sailors are permitted to work with explosives or ammunition.

Anyone knowing of defective ammo or other explosive ordnance, defective containers or handling devices, rough or improper handling, or willful or accidental violation of safety regs must report the facts to his immediate superior.

All persons supervising the inspection, care, preparation, handling, use, or disposal of ammunition or explosives must see that all regulations and instructions are observed, remain vigilant throughout the operation, and warn subordinates of the need for care and constant vigilance. Supervisors must also ensure that subordinates are familiar with the characteristics of the explosive materials involved, the equipment to be used, safety precautions to be observed, and the hazards of fire, explosion, and other catastrophies which the safety regs are designed to prevent. Supervisors must be alert to hazardous procedures, or symptoms of a deteriorating mental attitude, and take immediate corrective action when these are found.

Smoking is not permitted in magazines or near the handling or loading operations. Matches, lighters, and spark- or flame-producing devices are permitted in certain designated spaces, such as torpedo rooms, but only when specific written permission is received from command authority.

Crews working with explosives or ammunition are limited to the minimum number required to perform the operation properly and safely. Unauthorized personnel are not permitted in magazines or in the immediate vicinity of loading operations, except for authorized inspections. All authorized visitors must be escorted.

Productivity of persons or units using explosive ordnance is never evaluated on a competitive basis, except in servicing weapons in training, or under prescribed conditions.

When fuzed or assembled with firing mechanisms, mines, depth charges, rockets, projector charges, missiles, and bombs
are treated as if armed.

Live ammo, rockets, or missiles are loaded into guns or on
launchers only for firing, except where otherwise approved by
NAVSEASYSCOM, or as permitted below.

No ammo other than inert types are used for drill purposes. But
the following may be used aboard aircraft carriers for loading
drills, when specifically authorized by the CO, and when applicable radio-frequency hazard restrictions and other safety regulations are adhered to: (1) aircraft gun ammunition, (2) conventional, high-explosive bombs, (3) rockets and rocket launchers
with installed rockets, and (4) guided missiles and torpedoes with
exercise heads only.

Supervisors must require good housekeeping in explosive
spaces. Nothing is to be stored except explosives, containers,
and authorized handling equipment.

No warhead detonator should be assembled in or near a magazine containing explosives. Fuzing is performed at a designated fuzing area.

BOATS

In motor launches only the coxswain and the boat officer or
senior line officer may ride on the coxswain's flat, although not
more than two persons may be on deck at once.

No boat may be loaded beyond the capacities established by
the CO and published in the boat bill, without specific permission of the CDO, and then only in emergencies.

No person may smoke in a boat under any circumstances.

No person is assigned to a boat crew unless he can swim.

Additionally, boat crewmen must demonstrate a practical
knowledge of boat seamanship, rules of the road, and boat safety
regulations. Qualification is by the ship's first lieutenant.

No one who is not specifically designated by the engineer officer is to operate or attempt to operate a boat engine; to test, remove, or charge a boat's battery or tamper in any way with the
boat's electrical system; or to fuel a ship's boat.

No person may board a boat from a boat boom unless someone is standing by on deck or in a boat at the same boom.

All members of a boat's crew wear rubber-soled canvas shoes
in the boat.

All boats leaving the ship must have local charts with courses
to and from their destinations indicated. They must have a properly adjusted lighted compass installed. Boats also must have
enough life preservers to accommodate each person embarked.
These should be readily available when rough seas, reduced visibility, or other hazards threaten.

No boat is dispatched or permitted to proceed unless released
by the OOD. Releases will not be granted until it has been determined that the crew and passengers are wearing life preservers

and, when advisable, that weather and sea conditions are suitable for small-boat operations.

CHEMICALS

Adequate precautions should be taken in the stowage, handling, and disposal of hazardous chemicals and materials. A review of the potential hazards is not possible here, but substantial chemical safety information is available in the following references:

The NAVSHIPSTECHMAN has requirements and safety guidelines on a wide variety of hazardous chemicals, including cleaning agents, solvents, paints and associated chemicals, chlorinated hydrocarbons, mercury, oxidizing materials, corrosive liquids, and materials in aerosol containers.

NAVMAT P-5100, titled Safety Precautions for Shore Activities, includes information on hazards and precautions in using laboratory, photographic, and painting chemicals, alkalies, acids, various solvents, cleaning agents, cyanides, organic phosphates, toxic metals/dusts, halogenated hydrocarbons, etc.

NAVSUP P-4500, titled Consolidated Hazardous Item List (CHIL), lists hazardous federal stock items, classifies the material according to type of hazard, and recommends proper stowage. NAVSUP P-485—Afloat Supply Procedures—also contains information on receipt, custody, and proper stowage of hazardous materials.

Guidelines for use and procedures to follow when seeking information on the nature, hazards, and precautions of unknown chemicals and materials are outlined in the Hazardous Material Safety Program (NAVMAT instruction 5100.3).

COMPRESSED GAS

Precautions must be taken when working on high-pressure air systems to keep from opening lines which are not completely isolated and bled down.

No person should attempt repairs of any nature on an air flask or receiver under pressure. Bottles containing compressed gases must be kept capped and well secured when not in use.

Oxygen bottles and fittings must be kept away from oil and grease. Never substitute oxygen for compressed air.

DIVERS

Diving precautions and safety regulations are in the U.S. Navy Diving Manual.

ELECTRICAL AND ELECTRONIC EQUIPMENT

Electrical equipment includes generators, electrically powered machinery and mechanisms, power cables, controllers, trans-

Figure 20–1 Extreme caution must be used when working with electrical power machines.

formers, and associated equipment. Electronic equipment includes radars, sonars, power amplifiers, antennas, electronic warfare equipment, computers, and associated controls. The most important precaution with all such equipment is to never work alone.

No one shall operate, repair, or adjust any electrical or electronic equipment unless he has been assigned that duty, except

in definite emergencies, and then only when no qualified operator is present. (Electric light and bulkhead electric fan switches
are exempted.)

No one shall operate, repair, or adjust electrical and electronic
equipment unless he has demonstrated a practical knowledge of
its operation and repair and applicable safety regulations, and
then only when duly qualified by the head of the department.

No one shall remove, paint over, destroy, or mutilate any
markings, nameplates, cable tags or other identification on electrical or electronic equipment.

No one shall hang anything on, or secure a line to, any power
cable, antenna, wave guide, or other electrical or electronic
equipment.

Only authorized portable electric equipment that has been
tested and certified by the electric shop may be used. Portable
electric equipment is tested weekly.

Electric equipment should be de-energized and checked with
a voltage tester or voltmeter to ensure that it's de-energized before servicing or repairing it. Circuit breakers and switches of de-
energized circuits must be locked or placed in the "off" position

while work is in progress, and a suitable warning tag attached.

If work on live circuits or equipment is required, it is done only
when specific permission has been received from the commanding officer. The person performing the work must be insulated
from the ground and must follow all safety measures. Rubber
gloves will be worn. Another man will stand by to cut the circuit
and render first aid. Medical personnel are also to be alerted before work begins.

Personal electrical or electronic equipment used aboard ship
must be inspected by the electrical or electronic workshop for
conformance to NAVSHIPSTECHMAN regulations.

Never intentionally take a shock of any voltage. Even 115 volts
can kill.

Bare lamps or fixtures with exposed lamps should not be installed in machinery spaces. Only authorized fixtures are installed in such spaces to minimize fire hazards from flammable
fuels.

No one is permitted aloft near energized antennas unless it is
determined no danger exists. If there is any danger from rotating
antennas, induced voltages in rigging and superstructure, or from
high-power radiation causing direct biological injury, the equipment must be secured and a suitable warning tag attached to the
main supply switches. These precautions are also observed if any
other antenna is in the vicinity, as on an adjacent ship.

Electrical and electronic safety precautions must be conspic-
uously posted. Personnel must be instructed and drilled in their

observance. All electrical and electronics personnel must be qualified to administer first aid for electrical shock. Procedures for emergency resuscitation and use of airway breathing tubes must be posted in spaces containing electronic equipment.

Rubber matting (except where vinyl sheet is specified) must be installed in front and in back of propulsion control cubicles, power and lighting switchboards, IC switchboards, test switchboards, fire control switchboards, ship announcing-system amplifiers and control panels; areas in and around radio, radar, sonar, and countermeasures equipment spaces that may be entered while servicing or tuning energized equipment; and around work benches in electrical and electronic shops where equipment is tested or repaired. A "shorting stick" should be available in every working space for electronic equipment.

Protective electrical enclosures must be closed and permanent electrical grounds maintained. Fuse boxes, lever-type boxes, and wiring accessories should be closed except when necessary to perform maintenance. Ground straps should not be painted and care should be taken to maintain a positive ground to the ship's hull from all metal enclosures for electrical and electronic equipment.

FIRE AND EXPLOSION PREVENTION

Cutting fire and explosion hazards is every sailor's responsibility. All potential hazards should be eliminated, including nonessential combustibles. Whenever possible, replace combustible materials with less flammable ones. Limit the amount of combustibles. Stow and protect essential combustibles to reduce the chance of fire.

Avoid accumulating oil and other flammables in bilges and inaccessible areas. Any accumulations should be flushed out or removed immediately. Oily rags should be stowed in air-tight metal containers. After use, stow paint, brushes, rags, thinners, and solvents only in authorized locations.

Do not use compressed air to accelerate the flow of liquid from containers of any type.

Keep damage control equipment ready for any emergency.

FORKLIFTS

Only authorized persons should operate forklifts. Before operating, check condition of equipment. Keep feet and hands inside the running line of the forklift. No one other than the operator should ride, unless an additional permanent seat is provided.

Slow down on wet or slippery decks and corners.

No one should stand under loads being hoisted or lowered.

All cargo should be transported with the load lifting rails tipped back. When moving, keep forks four to six inches above the deck, whether loaded or not. Do not exceed the specified load capacity. Lower and rest forks on deck when not in use.

Never bump or push stacks of cargo to straighten them. Forks should be all the way under the load. Inspect each load before lifting. An unstable load should be repiled or banded. Once the load is lifted and moving, it's too late.

Come to a full stop before reversing directions of travel.

Set the parking brake when completing work, park the forklift in a fore and aft position near the centerline of the ship, and secure with chains or cables. Use only special personnel pallets for lifting personnel.

HAND TOOLS

Cold chisels should be held between the thumb and other four fingers. On horizontal cuts, the palm should be up. Do not use a burred chisel, one with a mushroomed head or one that is not properly tempered or sharpened. Wear goggles and allow no one close enough to be hit by flying chips.

Wood chisels should be free of cracks. Don't use one with a mushroomed head. Cup the chisel handle in the palm of your hand and exert pressure away from the body. Be sure no one is close enough to be hurt if the chisel slips.

Select the right hammer for the job. The head should be wedged securely and squarely on the handle and neither the head nor handle should be chipped, cracked or broken. Keep the hammer clean and free of oil or grease; otherwise it might slip from your hands or the face of the hammer might glance off the object being struck. Grasp the handle firmly near the end, and keep your eye on the part to be struck. Strike so the hammer face hits the object squarely.

HYDRAULIC MACHINERY AND FLUIDS

Hydraulically operated equipment must not be used until it is certain that all personnel are clear of moving parts. This is particularly important in the operation of masts, periscopes, rudders, and planes in port when they are operated only with the permission of the duty officer.

Because of the greater danger of auto-ignition explosions in systems where high pressure, air, and petroleum fluids are in proximity, make sure:

All hydraulic system operating instructions are followed.

When operating any manual valve in hydraulic systems, especially those isolating dead-ended piping, the valve is opened slowly until the pressure on both sides is equalized.

Machinery is secured and all equipment thoroughly checked when a hydraulic leak is detected.

Figure 20–2 Two Navy women work on an aircraft engine. Before any hydraulic equipment is turned on, hands must be clear of moving parts.

INTEGRITY OF SEAWATER SYSTEMS

To minimize the chance of flooding a ship, in case seawater systems fail, observe the following principles:

Systems not in use must be fully secured and proper log and status board entries made.

Supervisory and watch personnel must be aware of sea valves that are open.

No seawater system will be broken into for repairs, except as authorized by the appropriate department head. The duty officer or OOD will be kept fully informed and adequate provisions will be made to preclude the possibility of flooding the ship. A hydrostatic test is made on reassembly. Before restoring the system to normal operation a test must be conducted as specified in the system technical manual or NAVSHIPSTECHMAN.

Reach rods on all sea valves in the bilge must be kept in proper mechanical condition to permit operation from the platform deck.

LIFEJACKETS, LIFE RINGS, AND SAFETY HARNESSES

Lifejackets and approved topside shoes are worn on weather decks when required.

A life ring with attached distress light marker is available topside near the quarterdeck, at each man-overboard station and at each replenishment station. Submarines provide a life ring topside when on the surface for prolonged periods. Aircraft float lights, two at each man-overboard station, must be available

Figure 20–3 Sailors working over the side wear lifejackets and make use of life rings and safety harnesses.

when the ship is underway. Ships with an ASW capability have three available floats on both the port and starboard sides.

Submarines, when moored or anchored, have a Jacob's ladder rigged from the safety track to the waterline near the torpedo-loading hatch.

Whenever someone is required to wear a lifejacket in open-sea operations, the jacket must be buoyant.

Lifejackets are also worn when working over the side in port and at sea, on stages, on boatswain's chairs, or in boats and punts. They are worn during heavy weather, when handling lines or other deck equipment during transfers between ships, when fueling underway, during towing operations, when in boats being raised or lowered, when entering boats from a boom or Jacob's ladder, and when in boats underway and in rough water or low-visibility conditions.

LIFELINES, LADDERS, AND SAFETY NETS

No one shall lean, sit, stand, or climb on any lifeline in port or underway. Men working over the side in port may climb over lifelines when necessary, but only if they are wearing lifejackets and safety lines that are tended.

No lifeline shall be dismantled or removed without specific permission of the first lieutenant, and then only if temporary lifelines are promptly rigged.

No person shall hang or secure any weight or line to any lifeline unless authorized by the CO.

Ladders must not be removed without permission from the department head in charge. All accesses must be carefully and adequately roped off, or suitable railings installed. Work on ladders must, when possible, be performed when there is the least traffic.

No one may enter a flight-deck safety net or cargo net, except as authorized. The parachute-type safety harness is worn by all working aloft or over the side. The following components are used: safety line with dynabrake shock absorbers, nylon working line (wire when doing hot work), and nylon tending line.

In heavy weather additional inboard life and safety lines are rigged when personnel are required to be on weather decks.

LIGHTS

When in port at night, weather decks, accommodation ladders, gangways, and brows must be well lighted.

LINE HANDLING

Under no circumstances stand in the bight of a line or on a taut fall.

Don't try to check a line that is running out rapidly by stepping on it.

When handling lines, the standing part is coiled or faked down to prevent fouling in case the line runs out rapidly.

Nylon, dacron, and other synthetic-fiber lines are widely used for mooring and rigging. These lines are characterized by high elasticity and a low friction. The following rules apply:

An extra turn is required when securing to bitts, cleats, capstans and other holding devices.

When easing out from holding devices, use extreme caution because of the high elasticity, rapid recovery and low friction.

Nylon line, on parting, is stretched 1½ times its original length and snaps back. Do not stand in the direct line of pull of nylon line when heavy loads are applied.

Put a strain gauge on all synthetic mooring lines.

LINE-THROWING GUN

Bolo heavers and line-throwing-gun crew members must wear red helmets and highly visible red jackets for easy identification. Bolos and gun lines must be properly prepared for running. For the gun line, a loose coil in a bucket is better than a spindle.

When the receiving ship reaches the proper position, both ships pass the word: "Stand by for shot line. All hands take cover." The officer in charge at each replenishment station in the firing ship sounds a one-blast signal on a mouth whistle or passes the word "stand by" on the electric megaphone. The officer in charge of the corresponding station on the receiving ship replies with a two-blast signal on a mouth whistle or passes the word

Figure 20–4 Before a line-throwing gun is fired, all personnel not involved in the operation must stay clear.

the shot line and all of his crew has taken cover. After ascertain-
ing that all hands in the target area are clear, the officer in charge
on the firing ship gives the order to fire.

Only those designated by the officer in charge may leave cover to retrieve the bolo or shot line. All others must keep clear until all bolos or shot lines are on board and the word "shot (bolo) lines secure" is passed.

The receiving ship (except in the case of an aircraft carrier) does not fire her line-throwing guns unless ordered or asked to do so by the delivering ship.

LUMINOUS DIAL DEVICES

No luminous dial devices using radioactive paints are permit-ted on board any time. Personal luminous dial devices, such as wrist watches, are subject to the control of the engineer officer when atmosphere control is in effect.

MATERIALS HANDLING

Safety shoes or toe guards must be worn when handling heavy stores or equipment.

Gloves must be worn when carrying, lifting or moving objects that have sharp edges or projecting points. Always remove rings when wearing gloves.

Material must not be thrown from platforms or trucks to the floor or ground. Use suitable lowering equipment.

Lifting or lowering operations performed by several persons should be done only on the signal from one man, and only after everyone is in the clear.

Don't overload hand trucks. On a ramp or incline, keep the load below you—pull the load up, and push it down.

To lift objects, stand close to the load, with your feet solidly placed and slightly apart. Bend your knees, grasp the object firmly, and lift by straightening your legs, keeping your back as straight as possible.

MEN WORKING ALOFT

No person may climb the masts or stacks without first obtain-ing permission from the OOD, and then only to perform neces-sary work or duty. Before authorizing men aloft, the OOD must ensure that all power on radar and radio antennas in the vicinity is secure when they are aloft. Controls and related equipment are tagged "SECURED! MEN ALOFT." Main engine control is noti-fied to refrain from lifting safety valves and, if men are to work nearby, to secure steam to the whistle. The OOD ensures that men assigned to work near the stack gases wear protective breathing masks and remain there for only a short time. The

OOD determines that wind and sea conditions will not endanger men aloft, and he ensures that men wear parachute-type safety harnesses with safety lines attached to the ship's superstructure at the same level.

All tools, buckets, paint pots, and brushes must be secured by a lanyard when used in work on masts, stacks, upper catwalks, weather decks or sponsons that overhang areas where other personnel may be.

OPERATION OF MACHINERY

Machinery includes engines, motors, generators, hydraulic systems, and other equipment supplying power or moving force.

Except in emergencies, and then only when no qualified operator is present, no one should operate, repair, adjust or otherwise tamper with any machinery and controls unless assigned by a department head to perform a specific function on such machinery.

No one should operate, repair, or adjust machinery unless he has demonstrated a practical knowledge of its operation and repair and of all applicable safety regulations, and then only when qualified by the head of the department responsible for the machinery.

Machinery undergoing repair will have its power or activation sources tagged out to prevent accidental use of power.

PERSONNEL PROTECTION

Avoid wearing clothing with loose ends or loops when working on or near rotating machinery. Suitable leather, asbestos, or other heavy-type gloves must be worn when working on steam valves or other hot units. Keep the body well covered to reduce the danger of burns when working near steam equipment.

Goggles or helmet and leather welding jacket must be worn when brazing, welding, or cutting. Fire watches *must* wear protective goggles. Protective goggles should also be worn whenever working with substances corrosive to the eyes, such as acid, alkali, monoethemolamine, and vinyl paint. Water in plastic squeeze bottles or other containers should be readily and quickly available.

When using an oxygen-breathing apparatus (OBA), two men normally work together. An insulated line may be attached to the men using the OBA, but the line is used only to signal, not to pull. The OBA is not authorized aboard submarines.

Plastic face shields must be worn when handling primary coolant under pressure, and suitable eye protection—a shield, goggles or safety glasses—must be worn when buffing, grinding, or doing similar eye hazard operations.

Fumes from burning teflon are very dangerous. There should be no smoking where work can produce teflon chips or dust. Precautions should be taken when working in asbestos dust, such as when lagging is being removed.

PETROLEUM, OIL, AND LUBRICANTS

Because of hazards in the widespread use of NSFO (Navy standard fuel oil), Navy distillate (ND) fuel, aviation fuel, and other petroleum products, and the varying circumstances under which they are used and handled, everyone must be indoctrinated in their dangers and the procedures for preventing fires and explosions. Portions of the NAVSHIPSTECHMAN and the Navy Precautions for Forces Afloat contain details.

PORTABLE ELECTRIC AND PNEUMATIC TOOLS

The rated speed of a grinding wheel cannot be less than that of the machine or tool on which it is mounted. Grinders are not operated without wheel guards. Face shields or safety goggles are required for all types of grinding, chipping, or scaling. Automatic securing devices, such as dead-man switches, must be tested for satisfactory operation before they're used.

RADIATION

Radioactive material is present in nuclear reactors and warheads, in the sources used for calibration of radiation monitoring equipment, and in certain electronic tubes.

Radiation sources must remain installed in the radiation detection equipment, or be stowed in their shipping containers in a locked storage.

Spare radioactive electronic tubes and fission chambers must be stored in clearly marked containers and locked stowage.

All hands must scrupulously obey radiation warning signs and remain clear of radiation barriers.

RADIATION HAZARDS (RADHAZ)

The power generated by electronic equipment can result in biological injuries. Where such danger is possible, an r-f (radio frequency) radiation hazard exists, and warnings must be posted.

No visual inspection of any opening, such as a wave guide, that emits r-f energy is allowed unless the equipment is secured for inspection.

All r-f hazard signs posted in the operating area must be inspected to ensure that the equipment is operating so that anyone near it is not subjected to hazardous radiation. Observe r-f warning signs.

When there may be exposure while the antenna is radiating, someone must be stationed topside, within view of the antenna (but well out of the beam), and in communication with the operator.

Radiation warning signs must be permanently posted and used to temporarily restrict access to certain parts of the ship where equipment is radiating.

REPLENISHMENT AT SEA

Safety regulations are reviewed immediately before each replenishment operation. Only essential personnel are allowed near any transfer station. Lifelines should not be lowered unless absolutely necessary. If lowered, temporary lines are rigged. When line-throwing guns or bolos are used, all hands on the receiving ship take cover.

Topside personnel engaged in handling stores and lines must wear safety helmets and orange-colored, buoyant, vest-type life preservers. If helmets are not equipped with a quick-acting,

Figure 20–5 When replenishing at sea, sailors must observe a number of safety regulations. Note the helmets, life vests, and tucked-in pants legs.

378

breakaway device, the chin strap is fastened behind the head or worn unbuckled. VERTREP (vertical replenishment) personnel may wear flight-deck-type vests and cranial impact helmets instead.

Cargo handlers must wear safety shoes. Those handling wirebound or banded cases must wear work gloves.

Personnel must keep clear of bights, handle lines from the inboard side, and be at least six feet from any block through which the lines pass. They must keep clear of suspended loads and rig attachment points until loads have been landed on deck.

Care should be taken to prevent shifting of cargo, and no one should get between any load and the rail.

Deck space near transfer stations should be covered with something slip-resistant.

A lifebuoy watch must be stationed well aft on the engaged side. If a lifeguard ship is not available, a boat or rescue helicopter should be kept ready for anyone who falls overboard.

Measures must be taken to avoid hazards associated with radio frequencies. This is important when handling ammunition and petroleum products.

Dangerous materials, such as acids, compressed gases, and hypochlorites, are transferred separately from one another and from other cargo.

When transferring personnel by highline, only manila line (hand-tended by at least 25 people) must be used. Persons being transferred wear orange-colored life preservers (except patients in litters equipped with flotation gear). When the water temperature is 59 degrees or below or when outside air/water temperature is a total of 120 degrees or below, immersion suits should be worn, if possible.

When aviation fuel and fuel oil is received or transferred, no naked light or electrical or mechanical apparatus likely to spark is permitted within 50 feet of an oil hose, an open fuel tank, the vent terminal from a fuel tank, or an area where fuel-oil vapors may be present. The term "naked light" includes all forms of oil lanterns, lighted candles, matches, cigars, cigarettes, cigarette lighters, and flame or arc welding and cutting apparatus. Portable electric lights used during fueling must have explosion-proof protected globes and must be inspected for proper insulation and tested prior to use. Portholes in the ship's structure on the side from which fuel is being received must be closed and secured during operations.

A ground wire must connect the two ships when they are transferring gasoline. This must be accomplished before the hose is brought aboard, and the wire is disconnected only after the hose is clear. Gas hoses are blown down by an inert gas when transfer is completed.

SAFETY CLOTHING

Personnel who may be exposed to mechanical, physical, or chemical dangers must have adequate protective clothing and devices. Specifics are covered in the Safety Equipment Manual (NAVMAT P-10470), Safety Precautions for Shore Activities (NAVMAT P-5100), Illustrated Shipboard Shopping Guide (NAVSUP P-4400), and applicable sections of the NAVSHIPSTECHMAN, Aircrew Systems Manual, and the Federal Supply Catalog.

SAFETY DEVICES

Mechanical, electrical, and electronic safety devices are inspected at intervals specified by the preventive maintenance system (PMS), by type-commander instructions, or as usual circumstances or conditions warrant. When practical, these inspections include operation of the device while the equipment or unit is in actual operation. Machinery or equipment is not operated unless safety devices are working.

No one should tamper with or render ineffective any safety device, interlock, ground strap, or similar device without the commanding officer's approval.

SAFETY TAGS

DANGER, CAUTION, OUT-OF-COMMISSION and OUT-OF-CALIBRATION tags and labels must be posted to ensure the safety of personnel and to prevent improper operation of equipment. Posted safety tags will not be removed without proper authorization.

SHORE POWER

All onboard shore-power equipment must be checked out for safety. Shore-power cables should be thoroughly inspected and merged. Spliced portable cables are dangerous and should not be used except in an emergency.

Cables should be long enough to allow for the rise and fall of the tide, but not so long as to allow the cable to dip in the water or become wedged between the ship and the pier. Cables should not rest on sharp or ragged edges such as ship gunwales. Personnel should not step or walk on shore power cables.

SMOKING

There is no smoking in holds, storerooms, gasoline-tank compartments; gasoline pump rooms, voids, or trunks; in any shop or space where flammable liquids are being used or handled; in the ship's boat; in bunks or berths; in magazines, handling rooms, ready service rooms, gun mounts or turrets; in gasoline control stations, oil relay tank rooms, and battery and charging rooms; in the field projection room or in the vicinity of motion picture stowage; in the photo lab; anywhere that there is bleeding oxygen; in any area where vinyl or saran paint is being applied; on the flight deck, flight-deck catwalks, and gun platforms; or in hangar and gallery spaces open to the hangar.

No smoking is permitted in any area of the ship or alongside when ammunition is being handled; in any part of the ship when receiving or transferring fuel oil, diesel oil, aviation gasoline, or other volatile fuel, except in spaces designated as smoking areas by the commanding officer.

There is no smoking during general quarters, general drills, or during emergencies except as authorized by the CO. And there is no smoking when the word "the smoking lamp is out" is passed.

TANKS AND VOIDS

No one is permitted to enter any closed compartment, tank, void, or poorly ventilated space aboard a naval or Navy-operated ship until the space has been ventilated and determined to be gas-free. In an emergency, if a space must be entered without gas freeing, a breathing apparatus, such as airline mask, must be worn. In all cases at least two persons must be present when such a space is occupied. One acts as tender or safety observer.

Additional precautions: the space entered should be continuously ventilated; a reliable person must be stationed at the entrance to keep count of the number of persons inside as well as to maintain communications; suitable fire-extinguishing equipment must be at the scene; non-sparking tools will be used; and persons entering will not carry matches or lighters, or wear articles of clothing that could cause a spark.

TOXIC MATERIALS

The use of all materials that are potential health hazards is controlled by the medical officer or other designated person.

Methyl alcohol—commonly used as duplicator fluid, "canned heat," paint thinner, cleaner, and antifreeze—is hazardous if inhaled, absorbed through the skin, or swallowed. Even small amounts can cause permanent blindness or death. Therefore, only the amount required to do a specific job is released. It may be used only in well-ventilated spaces, and contact with the skin should be avoided.

Solvents, refrigerants, fumigants, insecticides, paint removers, dry-cleaning fluids, and propellants for pressurized containers are hazardous if inhaled, swallowed, or absorbed by the skin. They too are used only with adequate ventilation, by authorized personnel under supervision, and in such a way that contact with the eyes and skin is prevented. Use of carbon tetrachloride is prohibited aboard ship, except in laboratory and pharmacological work.

WELDING AND BURNING

Welding or burning is not permitted without permission of the CO or the OOD. The area of "hot work" must be cleared of flammable matter before work begins. Fire watches must be posted to prevent fire and stand by until materials cool.

Various synthetic materials yield toxic gases when burned or heated. Use caution when burning or welding vinyl resin-coated surfaces. Vinyl coating must be chipped or scraped clear of work area whenever possible; welders, fire watch, and others required to be in the immediate area will be equipped with line respirators; and a local exhaust ventilation will be provided in the work area and must have a minimum capacity of 200 cubic feet per minute for each three-inch suction hose.

Although the ship's force normally doesn't weld on the hull, if such work is required, proper precautions must be taken. An X ray of the hull must be accomplished at the first opportunity.

When they are cutting galvanized material, ship's personnel in the area wear air-line respirators. The area must be adequately ventilated to avoid illness caused by toxic fumes.

FIRE WATCH

A shipboard fire watch is assigned for the purpose of detecting and immediately extinguishing fires caused by welding or burning operations. Usually at least two persons are assigned—one with the operator, the other in the space behind, below, or above the site of the cutting, grinding, or welding. Remember, heat generated by welding or burning passes through a bulkhead or deck and can ignite material on the other side. A fire watch must remain alert at all times even though the assignment may become boring and dreary. When the ship is undergoing a shipyard overhaul, for example, the ship's firemains may be inoperative. If the watch is "goofing off" or is absent from the watch station, a fire could gain considerable headway before the arrival of the fire-fighting crew—resulting in extensive, and unnecessary, damage to the ship and possibly in casualties to the crew.

The fire watch should obtain safe and workable equipment and know how to operate it before going on watch. The watch inspects the work site with the hot-work operator and indicates a thorough understanding of the requirements of the assignment. The watch should be familiar with the location of all installed fire-fighting equipment in the work space and adjoining spaces and know how to use it. The watch must know where and how to sound the fire alarm and know all the assigned escape routes from the space.

When the hot-work operation is completed, the fire watch inspects both sides of the work area and remains on station for at least 30 minutes to be sure that there are no smoldering fires or sparks left and that the hot metal has cooled to the touch. The watch returns all fire-watch equipment at the conclusion of the watch.

WORKING OVER THE SIDE

No work is done over the side without the permission of the OOD, who must first notify the engineering officer to determine whether the screw will be turned over. If the screw is to be turned for any reason, men working over the side will be cleared. Men working over the side on stages, boatswain's chairs and on work floats or boats along the side of the ship must wear buoyant life preservers and shall be equipped with parachute-type safety harnesses with safety lines tended from the deck above. When another ship comes alongside, all men working over the side should be cleared.

Division officers have the responsibility for instructing personnel in all safety regulations and ensuring that they are qualified before allowing them to work over the side. Responsibility for ensuring that a competent petty officer is available for constant supervision also rests with the division officer.

All tools, buckets, paint pots, and brushes used over the side must be secured by lanyards to prevent loss overboard and injury to personnel below.

No person may work over the side while the ship is underway without permission of the commanding officer.

Maintenance

Because of the Navy's size and complexity, and the variety of equipment that must be maintained ready for use, a carefully planned program is required. The program must be the same for all equipment of the same type, regardless of the type of ship or location, so that a person transferred from one location to another can take on a new task without confusion. This procedure is called the 3-M (maintenance and material management) system.

Some of your shipboard duties include aiding in the maintenance of equipment associated with your rating. At first your responsibilities will be of a minor nature, but as you gain knowledge through training and experience you will be given more difficult tasks.

Broadly speaking, maintenance is preventive and corrective. Preventive maintenance forestalls equipment failure. It includes inspection, cleaning, testing, and lubrication of equipment. Corrective maintenance is another name for repair and is required only after the equipment has failed.

Preventive maintenance is accomplished according to procedures and schedules established by the 3-M system. Objectives of the system are: (1) to maintain equipment at maximum operating efficiency, reducing the cost of maintenance in both money and man-hours, and (2) to provide data on the costs of spare parts, failure rates, man-hours expended, and other information directly related to maintenance. More simply, the objective of 3-M is to improve the material readiness of the fleet.

The two main features of the system with which you will be concerned are the planned maintenance subsystem (PMS) and the maintenance data collection subsystem (MDSC).

PLANNED MAINTENANCE SUBSYSTEM (PMS)

PMS is designed to simplify maintenance by defining the maintenance required, scheduling its performance, describing the tools and methods used, and providing for the detection and prevention of impending casualties. PMS also provides a good foundation for training in equipment operation and maintenance.

This portion of 3-M also gives shipboard department heads the means to manage, schedule, and control the maintenance of their equipment. There are three components in the PMS: the PMS manual, maintenance schedules (cycle, quarterly and weekly), and maintenance required cards (MRCs).

The MRC is the feature of PMS that you will use almost daily. The work center will have a complete MRC group for all work handled by the center. When the weekly schedule names you for a job, pull the required MRC from the holder and take it with you for step-by-step guidance while doing the task. The MRC has a code that tells when or how often a job is done: D, daily; W, weekly; M, monthly; Q, quarterly; S, semi-annually; A, annually; C, overhaul cycle; and R, situation requirement (such as before getting underway or as a pre-firing measure).

If the MRC shows a "related maintenance," both jobs are done together. When a piece of equipment must be opened up, it saves time to do more than one job, if possible.

Safety precautions are listed for each job. Be careful to read, understand, and observe all precautions. "Caution" means that a worker can damage the equipment and "warning" means that the equipment could damage the worker. Be careful both ways. The section on "tools, parts, materials, and test equipment" tells you exactly what to use. Don't substitute. If a particular grease is called for but not available, don't use just any grease. Check with the leading petty officer to see if there is an approved substitute.

MAINTENANCE DATA COLLECTION SUBSYSTEM (MDCS)

The MDCS is a management tool used by systems commands and fleet and type commanders to identify and correct maintenance and logistics support problems. This system has resulted in improvements in maintenance procedures, equipment design, allocation of resources and long-range cost accounting. The

MDCS provides a means of recording planned and corrective maintenance actions. All planned maintenance actions, except daily and weekly preventive maintenance and routine preservation, are recorded in substantial detail. Recorded information concerns the number of man-hours required to make a repair, the repair parts and materials used, delays encountered, reasons for delays, and the technical specialty or repair activity that performed the work.

In recording maintenance actions, codes are used to convert information to a language that can be handled by automatic data processing (ADP) machines. These codes are contained in the equipment identification code (EIC) manual.

3-M INSTRUCTION

Many sailors are sent to a basic 3-M school for instruction on the entire system, but all the necessary manuals and instructions are on every ship, and expert work supervisors can show you what is to be done and how to do it. The best source of information is the 3-M manual; read it and ask questions of the work center supervisor or the 3-M coordinator and you'll become a reliable part of the Navy's 3-M system. There are also several self-training courses available on the system.

CONSERVATION

Every job you do in the Navy, whether it has to do with maintenance, cleanliness, preservation, or almost anything else, requires you to practice conservation. Conservation doesn't mean that you should pack-rat away extra stores because you think you might need them sometime. Nor does it mean that you should try to save a bit by using one coat of paint where two are required.

It *does* mean that you must make effective use of material—and time—in order to do the most work at the least possible cost. The Navy is a business, just like a major corporation, and everything used must be paid for. Just because you merely have to sign a chit for what you draw from supply doesn't mean it's free. Someone has to pay for it—you, as an American taxpayer, help pay.

General Preservation and Cleaning

You might think that a ship at sea would not get very dirty, but it does—and quickly. In the interest of sanitation and appearance, daily cleanups are required.

SWEEPERS

"Sweepers" is always piped by the boatswain's mate of the watch shortly after reveille, at the end of the regular working day, and at other times as necessary. At these times, all men assigned as sweepers draw their gear and sweep and swab down their assigned areas, and empty all trash receptacles. All trash and dirt should be picked up in a dustpan. If you try to sweep the dirt over the side, the wind may blow it back aboard, necessitating another sweepdown. Or the dirt may stick to the side, giving the ship an unsightly appearance and eventually requiring the side to be scrubbed or chipped and painted sooner than normally expected.

COMPARTMENT CLEANERS

If you are assigned duty as a berthing compartment cleaner, you won't have to sweep down topside decks. Unless your division is short-handed, you may not have any watches. But you will be expected to keep the compartment scrupulously clean. Neither you nor your shipmates want to live in a dirty compartment.

Periodically, a field day is held. Field day is cleaning day, when all hands turn to and thoroughly clean the ship inside and out, usually in preparation for an inspection by the captain. Fixtures and areas (overhead cables, piping, corners, spaces behind and under equipment, etc.) that sometimes are neglected during regular sweepdown are cleaned; bulkheads, decks, ladders and all other accessible areas are scrubbed; knife edges and door gaskets are checked, and any paint, oil, or other substances are removed; all brightwork is shined; and clean linen is placed on each bunk. Field days improve the appearance and sanitary condition of the ship, aid in the preservation of the ship by extending paint life, and reduce the dirt intake of operating equipment. Dirt intake must be held to a minimum to prevent overheating of electronic equipment, and to prevent abrasive action in rotating machinery.

If you are in charge of a compartment, you present the space to the inspecting officer by saluting and greeting him in the following manner: "Good afternoon (morning), sir; Seaman Jones, compartment (name and number), _____ division, standing by for inspection."

TOPSIDE AREAS AND DECK COVERINGS

Because of weather conditions, there will be many days at sea when personnel cannot clean topside areas. At the first opportunity, these surfaces should be cleaned with fresh water and an inspection made for signs of rust and corrosion. If such signs are discovered, tend to the area immediately. A little work at that time will save a lot of work later.

Deck coverings aboard ship receive more wear than any other material. Early and costly replacement of deck covering is necessary unless proper care is given. Several types of material are used for deck coverings, the most common are resilient and non-slip.

These deck coverings do not require painting. Upkeep is by observance of the general rules of sweeping up loose dirt daily and wiping away spills as soon as possible. This type of deck covering is clamped down (cleaned with a wet swab) frequently, allowed to dry, then buffed with an electric buffing machine. For more thorough cleaning, when the deck is unusually dirty, apply a solution of warm water and detergent with a stiff bristle brush or circular scrubbing machine. Use water sparingly. Wet the deck with the cleaning solution, but do not flood it. Remove the soiled solution with a swab and rinse with clean water to remove residual detergent. Stubborn dirt and black marks left by shoes can be removed by rubbing lightly with a scouring pad, or fine steel wool, or a rag moistened with mineral spirits.

No waxing should be done when the ship is going out to sea or when heavy weather is anticipated. This is an added precaution against slipping, even though the approved emulsion floor waxes are designed to be slip-resistant.

When rubber switchboard matting, ceramic tile, or painted decks need cleaning, they should be washed with a detergent solution, rinsed with a minimum amount of water, and dried.

Static conductive linoleum ordinarily is used as the deck covering for the medical operating room. Cleaning procedure for it is the same as for resilient deck covering, except no wax, oil, or polish should be used on it. Waxes, oils, and polishes act as electrical insulators, and reduce the inherent conductivity of this type of deck covering. Gloss may be increased by buffing the deck covering lightly with a fine steel wool pad on the floor-polishing machine.

The cleaning procedure for non-skid paint is to use a solution consisting of one pint of detergent cleanser and five tablespoons of dishwashing compound or 10 tablespoons of metasilicate. This preparation is diluted with fresh water to make 20 gallons of solution. Apply with a handscrubber, let it soak for five minutes, then rinse with fresh water. Non-skid deck coverings should not be waxed or painted because to do so will tend to reduce their non-skid properties.

Aluminum surfaces aboard ship present a special problem because, if not treated properly, considerable corrosion can result. Corrosion is greatest when dissimilar metals (such as aluminum and steel) are in contact with each other and are exposed to sea water.

The corrosive condition is first indicated by white, powdery residue in the area of contact, later by pitting and scarring of the aluminum surface, and finally by complete deterioration of the aluminum. Holes in aluminum plate enlarge, and the screws, bolts, or rivets pull out, or they may even disintegrate.

The best way to prevent aluminum corrosion is to insulate the aluminum from other materials. Insulation is especially important when the joint is exposed to moisture.

Where aluminum is to be joined to other metals, each surface is given one coat of pretreatment formula and two coats of zinc primer. Never use red lead as a primer on aluminum. If the joint is exposed to the weather, insulation tape must be placed between the two surfaces and the joint filled with calking compound. When aluminum is joined to wood, the wood is given one coat of phenolic varnish.

When preparing aluminum surfaces for painting, power sanders must be used with great care. It is best to use handscrapers, hand and power wire brushes, or sandpaper of a very fine grit. Do not use scaling hammers.

Painting

In the Navy, paint is used primarily for the preservation of surfaces. It seals the pores of wood and steel, arrests decay, and helps prevent rust. Paint serves several other purposes. It is valuable in cleanliness and sanitation because of its antiseptic properties and because it provides a smooth, washable surface. Paint is also used to reflect, absorb, or redistribute light.

Knowledge required for painting includes selecting suitable paints for the surfaces to be covered, the proper preparation of the surfaces before painting, and the correct methods of applying paint.

TYPES OF PAINT

Most Navy paints are named according to color and use, such as exterior gray deck and pretreatment coating. The most common types and uses for them are:

Primers: Primers are base coats of paint that adhere firmly to bare woods and metals, providing a smooth surface for finishing coats. They also serve to seal the pores, and those applied on steel are rust inhibitors as well. Two principal primers are used by the Navy: zinc chromate and red lead. Use only zinc chromate primers on galvanized and aluminum surfaces.

At least two coats of primer should always be used after the surface is cleaned down to bright metal. A third coat should be added at all outside corners and edges. At least eight hours' drying time should be allowed between primer coats.

Exterior paints: Vertical surfaces above the upper limit of the boot topping (water line area, which is painted black) are given two coats of haze gray. Horizontal surfaces are painted with ex-

Figure 20–7 Paint helps preserve the surfaces of a ship that are exposed to weather.

terior deck gray (darker than haze gray), except the undersides of deck overhangs, which are painted white.

A non-skid deck paint is used on main walkways. It contains a small amount of pumice, which helps to give a better footing.

The tops of stacks and tophamper, which are subject to discoloration from smoke and stack gases, are painted black.

Interior paints: Depending on the use to which individual compartments are put, several color schemes are authorized or prescribed for interior bulkheads, decks, and overheads.

The choice of colors for berthing, messing, and recreation spaces usually is left to the individual ship. All other spaces are painted the color prescribed by the Naval Ship Systems Command (NAVSHIPSYSCOM). Deck paint colors, for example, are dark green in the wardroom and in officers' quarters, dark red in the machinery spaces, and light gray in enlisted men's living spaces.

Some common bulkhead colors are: green for offices, radio rooms, pilot house, and medical spaces; gray for flag plot, CIC, and sonar control; and white for the storerooms and sanitary and commissary spaces.

Overhead colors are either the same as the bulkhead or white.

Painting

For paint to adhere to a surface, all salt, dirt, oil, grease, rust, and loose paint must be removed completely, and the surface must be thoroughly dry.

Salt and most dirt can be removed with soap or detergent and fresh water. Firmly imbedded dirt may require scouring with powder or with sand and canvas. Do not use lye or other strong solutions because they may burn or soften the paint. When oil and grease fail to yield to scrubbing, they must be removed with diesel oil or paint thinner. If diesel oil is used, scrub the surface afterward to remove the oil. After scrubbing or scouring, the surface should be rinsed with fresh water.

Removing rust, mill scale, and loose paint requires the use of handtools or powertools, paint and varnish removers, or blowtorches. Handtools usually are used for cleaning small areas; powertools are for larger areas and for completely cleaning decks, bulkheads, and overheads covered with too many coats of paint. (Normally, paint in interior spaces is not removed if in good condition, unless its thickness exceeds 0.005 inch or a total of four coats. Thickness on exterior surfaces may be determined by general appearance, and sometimes is indicated by cracks.) Paint and varnish removers and torches are used to remove paint from wood.

Handtools: The most commonly used handtools are sandpaper, a steel wire brush, and a handscraper.

Sandpaper is used to clean corners and to feather paint—that is, taper the edges of chipped areas down to the cleaned surface so that no rough edges remain.

A hand wire brush is useful for light work on rust or light coats of paint. Such a brush also is used for brushing weld spots and cleaning pitted surfaces.

Scrapers are made of tool steel. The most common type is L-shaped, with each end tapered to a cutting edge like a wood chisel. They are most useful for removing rust and paint from small areas and from plating less than ¼-inch thick, when it is impractical or impossible to use powertools.

Occasionally it is necessary to use a chipping or scaling hammer, but care must be taken to exert only enough force to remove the paint. Too much force dents the metal, resulting in the formation of high and low areas. In subsequent painting, the paint naturally is thinner on the high areas. Consequently, thin paint wears off quickly, leaving spots where rust will form and, in time, spread under the good paint.

Powertools: The most useful powertool is the portable grinder. It usually is equipped with a grinding wheel that may be replaced by either the rotary wire brush or the rotary cup wire brush. Light-duty brushes, made of crimped wire, will remove light rust. Heavy-duty brushes, which are fashioned by twisting several wires into tufts, are needed to remove deeply imbedded rust.

Scaling may be done with a chisel and pneumatic hammer, and with the hand scaling hammer. Using the pneumatic hammer and chisel you must take care that the chisel strikes the surface at approximately a 45-degree angle. You must use the same caution when using the hand scaling hammer to avoid denting the surface.

The rotary scaling and chipping tool—called a "deck crawler"—has a bundle of cutters or chippers mounted on either side. As it is pushed along the surface to be scaled, the rotary cutters do the work. This piece of equipment is particularly helpful on large deck areas.

The electric disc sander is another handy tool for preparing surfaces. However, great care must be exercised in its use. If too much pressure is applied, or if it is allowed to rest in one place too long, it will quickly cut into the surface, particularly that of wood and aluminum.

Paint and varnish removers: Paint and varnish removers are used mostly on wood surfaces but may be used on metal surfaces that are too thin to be chipped or wire brushed.

Three types of removers are in general use. They are the flammable, nonflammable, and water-base alkali types. All are hazardous, and all safety precautions must be observed; they should be used only in well-ventilated spaces. The alkali type is not to be used on aluminum or zinc because of the caustic properties of alkalis.

Procedures for using paint and varnish removers are the same, regardless of type. Wet the surface with a smooth coat of the remover. Permit it to soak in thoroughly until the paint or varnish is loosened, then lift the paint off with a handscraper. After the surface is cleaned, wet it again with the remover, and wipe it off with a rag. Finally, wash the surface thoroughly with paint thinner or soap and water. This final rinse gets rid of any wax left by the remover and any acids that may have worked into the grain of the wood.

Fillers: Holes, dents, and cracks in all surfaces and open-grained woods should be filled before finishing. Putty, wood fillers, and even sawdust mixed with glue can be used on wood. Deep cracks and checks in wooden booms, spars, and the like should first be calked with oakum or cotton calking and then covered with putty. Epoxy cements are available for use on steel and aluminum surfaces. Methods of use vary with the type of cement, so carefully follow the included instructions. All fillers should be allowed to dry and then should be sanded smooth before you apply the first finishing coat.

Flat	Fitch	Sash Tool	Flat Varnish	Lettering	Painter's Dusting

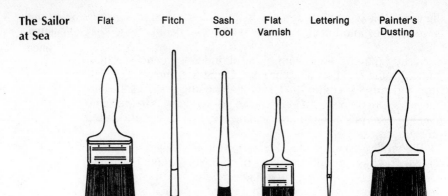

Figure 20–8 Types of brushes.

USE OF BRUSHES AND ROLLERS

Smooth and even painting depends as much on good brush-work as on good paint. There is a brush for almost every purpose, so use the proper brush and keep it in the best condition.

The two most useful brushes are the flat brush and the sash tool brush. These and some others commonly used aboard ship are shown in Figure 20–8.

With a flat brush a skillful painter can paint almost anything aboard ship. Flat brushes are wide and thick, carry a large quantity of paint, and provide a maximum of brushing action. Sash brushes are handy for painting small items, for cutting in at corners, and for hard-to-get-at places. The fitch brush also is useful for small surfaces. The painter's dusting brush is used for cleaning surfaces.

Using a brush: Following are some general hints to help you use a paint brush properly.

Grip the brush firmly but lightly. Do not put your fingers on the bristles below the metal band. This grip permits easy wrist and arm motion. To hold it otherwise restricts your movements and causes undue fatigue.

When using a flat brush, don't paint with the narrow edge. This practice wears down the corners and spoils the shape and efficiency of the brush. When using an oval brush, don't let it turn in your hands. An oval brush, if revolved too much, soon wears to a pointed shape and becomes useless. Don't poke over-sized brushes into corners and around moldings. Such a practice bends the bristles, eventually ruining a good brush. Use a smaller brush that fits into such odd spots.

Dip the brush into the paint but not over halfway up the bristles. Remove excess paint by patting the brush on the inside of the pot. (Avoid overfilling the brush; otherwise paint will drip on the deck or other surfaces and run down the handle.)

Hold the brush at right angles to the surface being painted, with the ends of the bristles just touching the surface. Lift the brush clear of the surface when starting the return stroke. If the brush is held obliquely and is not lifted, the painted surface will be uneven, showing overlaps and spots and a daubed appearance. Also, a brush held at any angle other than a right angle will soon wear away at the sides.

Paint applications: For complete and even coverage, follow the Navy method and first lay on, then lay off. Laying on means applying the paint first in long strokes in one direction. Laying off means crossing your first strokes. By using the recommended method, the paint is distributed evenly over the surface, the surface is covered completely, and a minimum amount of paint is used.

Always paint overhead first, working from the corner that is farthest from compartment access. By painting the overhead first, you can wipe drippings off the bulkhead without smearing the bulkhead paint.

When painting overhead surfaces, coats on the panels normally should be applied in a fore-and-aft direction; those on the beams, athwartships. But where panels contain many pipes running parallel with the beams, it is often difficult to lay off the panels fore-and-aft. In such situations, lay off the panels parallel with the beams.

To avoid brush marks when finishing up a square, use strokes directed toward the last square finished, gradually lifting the brush near the end of the stroke while the brush still is in motion. Every time the brush touches the painted surface at the start of a stroke, it leaves a mark. For this reason, never finish a square by brushing toward the unpainted area. Instead, always end up by brushing back toward the area already painted.

When painting pipes and stanchions and narrow straps, beams, and angles, lay the paint on diagonally. Lay off along the long dimension.

Always carry a rag for wiping up dripped or smeared paint. Carefully remove loose bristles sticking to the painted surface.

Cutting in: After you master the art of using a paint brush properly, you should learn to cut in. Cutting in is a simple procedure, and anyone with a fairly steady hand can learn it quickly.

Film thickness: For interior painting, paint must be applied in the lightest possible coat that will cover the surface. The paint should be applied lightly for several reasons. Heavy layers of paint are a fire hazard—the thicker the paint film, the faster it will burn. If paint is applied heavily, it is likely to entrap solvents and thinners that burn rapidly. Thick coats of paint have a greater tendency to crack and peel. They undoubtedly will be uneven, and may show marks and scratches more readily than thinner coats. Thick coats of paint do not penetrate as well as thinner ones, and do not dry to as hard a surface. Moreover, heavy layers of paint add noticeably to the weight of the ship, and may cut its speed.

Paint rollers: The dip type of paint roller used in the Navy is equipped with a replaceable cylinder of knitted plush fabric over a solvent-resistant paper core. It rotates on the shaft of a corrosion-resistant steel frame.

Large areas, such as decks and ship's sides (free of rivets, bolts, cables, pipes, and so on), can be covered with paint quickly by the roller method. The paint should be laid on and laid off the same way as with brushes. A moderate amount of pressure must be applied to the roller to ensure that the paint is worked into the surface. If pressure is not exerted, the paint will not adhere and soon will peel off. With the proper amount of pressure applied, a roller will apply a more even coat and use less paint than is possible with a brush.

394

CARE OF BRUSHES AND ROLLERS

Unfortunately, far too many good paint brushes are ruined simply because painters have little or no idea how to care for them. They should pay particular attention to the following hints, and heed them at all times. Treat brushes as though you paid for them yourself and must replace them when they no longer are usable.

Do not let a brush stand on its bristles in a pot of paint for more than a few minutes. The weight of the brush bends the bristles, making it almost impossible to do a good paint job. Never allow paint to dry on a brush. If you intend to leave a paint-filled brush for long periods, as over the noon hour, fold wax paper or other heavy paper around the bristles in such a way that air is kept out. Twist the paper around the handle and secure it with rope yarn or sail twine. Cover your pot of paint, and place both it and the brush in a safe place. Before starting to paint again, stir the paint thoroughly with a paddle—not with the brush. At the end of the day, before turning in your paint and brush to the paint locker, clean as much paint from the brush as possible by wiping it across the edge of the paint pot or mixing paddle.

Ordinarily, those working in the paint locker will clean and stow the brushes turned in. Occasionally, though, they require help, and you may be detailed to the job. If so, follow instructions carefully, and thoroughly clean the brushes.

Paint lockers usually have containers with divided compartments for stowing different types of brushes (paint, varnish, shellac, etc.) for short periods of time. These containers normally have tight covers and are equipped for hanging brushes so that the entire length of the bristles and the lower part of the ferrule are covered by the thinner or linseed oil kept in the container. Brushes are suspended so that the bristles do not touch the bottom, thus preventing them from becoming permanently misshaped.

Brushes to be used the following day should be cleaned in the proper thinner and place in the proper compartment of the container. Those not to be used again soon should be cleaned in thinner, washed in soap or detergent and water, rinsed thoroughly in fresh water, and hung to dry. After drying, they should be wrapped in waxed paper and stowed flat. Do not leave a brush soaking in water. Water causes the bristles to separate into bunches, flare, and become bushy.

Paint rollers are cleaned differently. After use, the fabric cylinder should be stripped from the core, cleaned in the solvent recommended for the paint used, washed in soap and water, rinsed thoroughly in fresh water, and replaced on the core to dry. Combing the pile of the fabric while it is damp prevents matting.

The following items must not be painted:

1. Start-stop mechanisms of electrical safety devices and control switchboards on machinery elevators.

2. Bell pulls, sheaves, annunciator chains, and other mechanical communication devices.

3. Composition metal water ends of pumps.

4. Condenser heads and outside surfaces of condenser made of composition metal.

5. Dry sprinkling piping within magazines.

6. Exposed composition metal parts of any machinery.

7. Glands, stems, yokes, toggle gear, and all machined external parts of the valves.

8. Heat exchange surfaces of heating or cooling equipment.

9. Identification plates.

10. Joint faces of gaskets and packing surfaces.

11. Lubricating gear, such as oil holes, oil or grease cups, zerk-fittings, lubricators, and surfaces in contact with lubricating oil.

12. Lubricating oil reservoirs.

13. Machined metal surfaces of reciprocating engines or pumps.

14. Metal lagging.

15. Rods, gears, universal joints, and couplings of valve operating gear.

16. Rubber elements of isolation mounts.

17. Ground plates.

18. Springs.

19. Strainers.

20. Threaded parts.

21. Zincs.
22. Working surfaces.
23. Hose and applicator nozzles.
24. Knife edges, rubber gaskets, dogs, drop bolts, wedges, and operating gear of watertight doors, hatches, and scuttles.
25. Electrical contact points and insulators.
26. The original enamel, lacquer, or crackle finish on all radio, electrical, and sound equipment, unless damage makes refinishing essential.
27. Decorative plastic, such as table tops.

V. Seamanship, Navigation, and Communication

21. Marlinespiking and Use of Ground Tackle

Marlinespike Seamanship

This is the art of handling and working with line or rope. The name comes from the marlinespike, an instrument used in working with rope.

Rope is manufactured from wire, fiber, and combinations of the two. Fiber rope—or line, as it is commonly called—is fashioned from natural or synthetic fibers. Lines made from a variety of natural fibers, such as cotton, agave, jute, hemp, sisal, and abaca, have seen service in the Navy in the past. Some are still in use. For example, tarred hemp is known as marline and ratline. On the other hand, sisal has been dropped from the supply system, and manila serves in its place—for lashings, frapping lines, steadying lines, etc. Synthetic lines have been substituted for manila in most other uses.

Line currently used in the Navy is three-strand line which has been twisted, braided, or plaited. In three-strand line, fibers are twisted into yarns or threads, the yarns are twisted in the opposite

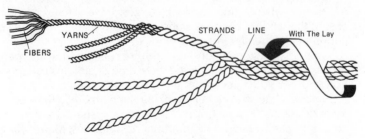

Figure 21–1 The method of twisting to form yarn, strands, and rope.

directions into strands, and the strands are twisted back in the first direction, into ropes. Taking the process further, ropes are twisted into cable. Rope can be either three- or four-strand, and the direction the strands are twisted determines the lay of the rope. That is, if the strands are twisted to the right, the rope is said to be "right laid."

Braided lines have certain advantages over twisted ropes. They will not kink or cockle (terms which are explained later), nor will they flex open to admit dirt or abrasives. The construction of

some braids, however, makes it impossible to inspect the inner
yarns for damage. The more common braided lines are hollow
braided, stuffer braided, solid braided, and double braided.

Synthetic-Fiber Lines

The synthetic fibers used in making line are nylon, polyester
(dacron), polypropylene, and polyethylene (in descending order
of strength). The characteristics of synthetic line differ from those
of manila line.

Synthetic line has nearly replaced natural-fiber line and is used
in all sizes—ranging from ⁵/₈ inch to 12 inches in circumference.
Nylon is over twice as strong as manila, lasts five times as long,
and will stand seven times the shock load. Its big disadvantage is
that it will stretch. Dacron is even stronger when wet than when
dry, and polypropylene is so light it floats.

When using synthetic line, safety precautions more exacting
than those for manila must be observed. A complete list of the
precautions is contained in the NAVSHIPSTECHMAN, but the
most important ones are listed here:

Due to the low friction of synthetic line, exercise extreme care
when a line is being payed out or eased from securing devices—
bitts, capstans, bollards, cleats, gipsy heads, etc. For control in
easing out, fill bitt barrels with round turns and avoid using more
than 2 figure-eight bends.

To minimize the hazard of pulling a line handler into a securing device when a line suddenly surges, have safety observers
ensure that all line handlers stand as far as possible from the securing device being tended or worked.

Since a snapback action inevitably occurs when a line parts
under tension, never stand in the direct line of pull. Instead, position yourself 90 degrees from the direction of the tension force.

Synthetic line has higher breaking strengths (BS) than equal
sizes of manila. Failures of blocks, padeyes, shackles, and line
couplings can be caused by improper substitutions. Many fittings
in common use in the fleet are designed for natural-fiber line. For
this reason, determine the identification and capacity of all gear
and fittings used with synthetic line, to ensure that strength exceeds the minimum BS of the rope.

Synthetic line has poor knot-holding characteristics. Some
knots which are good for securing manila, such as the square
knot, are not adequate for synthetic. The bowline is one knot
known to offer reasonable security when bending together or securing synthetic line.

Normally, synthetic-fiber line is furnished on reels and is
unreeled in the same fashion as wire rope (discussed on page

405). Before using new, three-strand synthetic, it should be faked down on deck and allowed to relax for 24 hours. The period can be shortened to about two hours by hosing down the line with fresh water.

When wet, synthetic line shrinks slightly but does not swell or stiffen. When the line is put under tension the water squeezes out; and under working loads, it appears as vapor.

Oil and grease do not cause synthetics to deteriorate, but they make them slippery. When this happens, the line should be scrubbed down. Spots may be removed by cleaning the line with light oils, such as kerosene or diesel oil.

LINE CHARACTERISTICS

Every line used in the Navy is manufactured to certain specifications devised to produce the best lines for particular types of jobs. To ensure longest life, a line must be used within its safe working load (SWL). The SWL of the line ranges from $1/15$ to $1/5$ of its breaking strength (BS), depending on the type of line, the condition of the line, the weather, and the blocks and other gear the line is being used with.

Sailors who work with natural-fiber line soon learn how to judge the tension in such lines by the sounds they produce. Unfortunately, although synthetic lines under heavy strain thin down considerably, they give no audible indication of stress—even when they are about to part. For this reason, a tattletale cord should be attached to synthetic lines when they are to be subjected to loads that may exceed their SWLs. A tattletail cord is a bight of heavy cord or light small stuff hanging from two measure points on the working line. The line, when tensioned to its SWL, will stretch to a certain percentage of its length. When this point is reached, the small stuff becomes taut, warning that there is danger of exceeding the line's SWL.

Natural-Fiber Line

Although synthetic-fiber line is rapidly becoming the standard in today's Navy, there is still some use of natural-fiber line. Such line requires special care and handling.

Coils of line should always be stowed on shelves or platforms clear of the deck. They should never be allowed to become covered with an accumulation of junk which may prevent the evaporation of moisture. Natural-fiber line is susceptible to mildew and rotting.

Coils of small stuff should be arranged along a shelf in order of size, and each coil should be set up in the way in which it opens properly—that is, with the inside end at the bottom of the center tunnel. The burlap wrapper should be left on each coil. The stops

which secure the coil are inside the wrapper. These should be
cut and drawn up the inside end so that the line is started properly. It is a common custom, and a good idea, to set up a narrow,
flat strip of wood horizontally over the shelf containing the small
stuff, with a hole bored in the strip over each coil. The starting
end of the line is drawn up through the hole and is prevented
from dropping back by an overhand knot. This ensures that anyone coming down for small stuff need not grope around inside
the tunnel for the end, with the resulting possibility of getting
hold of the wrong one when the coil is almost depleted.

Coils of large line should be stowed with their proper side up
for opening. Line from 2 to 4 inches, which will be needed in
various lengths on deck, should be opened, and a few feet of the
end led out. Mooring lines should not be opened until needed.

Figure 21–2 A deck sailor tries to untangle line for proper care.

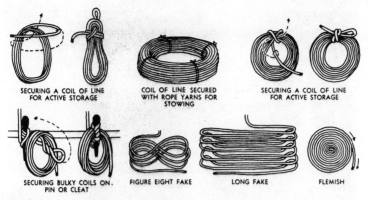

| SECURING A COIL OF LINE FOR ACTIVE STORAGE | COIL OF LINE SECURED WITH ROPE YARNS FOR STOWING | SECURING A COIL OF LINE FOR ACTIVE STORAGE |
| SECURING BULKY COILS ON. PIN OR CLEAT | FIGURE EIGHT FAKE | LONG FAKE | FLEMISH |

Figure 21–3 Details on coiling, faking, and flemishing line.

When a new coil of line is opened, give it your personal attention. Five minutes of your time here may save hours later trying to work kinks out of an improperly opened coil.

Whenever possible, line which has become wet in use should be dried before stowing. Sometimes this is impossible, as with mooring lines, which must be sent below before the ship gets outside in heavy weather. If line must be stowed wet, it should be laid up on gratings in long fakes or suspended in some other way so that it may dry as quickly as possible. It should never be covered until it is dry.

DISTORTIONS, KINKS, AND TWISTS

If a line doesn't lead easily to a winch drum (gipsy head), it will be badly distorted when heaved in. Frequently, therefore, it is necessary to put on inside turns to obtain a fairlead. Because the outside end is attached to the load and unavailable, enough slack must be hauled up in the hauling part to make the necessary number of turns. The turns should be started from inboard.

Whenever possible, a right-laid line should be put on a winch drum or capstan right-handed, or in clockwise turns. Heaving on a right-laid line with left-handed turns will eventually kink the line. About the only time left-handed turns can't be avoided is when a winch is heaving on two lines at once, with one of them on either drum.

A line that has a kink in it, or a tackle which is twisted from having a dip in it, should never be heaved hard while that condition exists. A strong strain on a kinked or twisted line will put a permanent distortion in the line.

DETERIORATION

The following are some pointers on the use and care of natural-fiber line. Remember them.

Figure 21–4 Caution must be used in handling wire rope to keep it from bending, twisting, or kinking.

Coil right-laid line right-handed or clockwise.

Keep line from touching stays, guys, or other standing rigging.

When surging line around bitts or capstans, take off enough turns so that the line will not jerk but surge smoothly.

If line becomes chafed or damaged, cut and splice. A good splice is safer than a damaged section.

Do not lubricate the line.

Whip all line ends.

Inspect frequently for deterioration. Open the lay and inspect the fibers. White powdery residue indicates internal wear.

Do not drag a line over sharp or rough objects which can cut or break the outer fibers. When line is dragged on the ground, dirt and other particles are picked up and eventually work into the line, cutting the inner strands.

The strength of line exposed to the atmosphere deteriorates about 30 percent in two years from weathering alone.

Line loaded in excess of 75 percent of its breaking strength (BS) will be damaged permanently. Inspect the inside threads to see if all or a portion of the fibers in the threads are broken.

Keep bitts, chocks and cleats in smooth condition to minimize abrasion.

Use chafing gear on rough, hard surfaces and sharp metal edges.

Apply loads slowly and carefully.

Wire Rope

The basic unit of wire-rope construction is the individual wire, made of steel or other metal in various sizes. These wires are laid together to form strands. The number of wires in a strand varies according to the purpose for which the rope is intended. A number of strands are laid together to form the wire rope itself. Wire rope is designated by the number of strands per rope and the number of wires per strand. Thus, a 6 × 19 rope has six strands with a total of 19 wires per strand, but has the same outside diameter as a 6 × 37 wire rope, which has six strands with a total of 37 wires of much smaller size per strand.

Wire rope made up of a large number of small wires is flexible, but the small wires break so easily that the rope is not resistant to external abrasion. Wire rope made up of smaller number of larger wires is more resistant to abrasion, but less flexible.

Wire rope is layed up in various ways:

Right regular lay: Wires in the strands are twisted to the left; strands in the rope are twisted to the right.

Left regular lay: Wires in the strands are twisted to the right; strands are twisted to the left.

Right lang lay: Both wires in the strands and strands in the rope are twisted to the right.

Left lang lay: Both wires in the strands and strands in the rope are twisted to the left.

Reverse lay: Wires of alternate strands are twisted to the right; those in the other strands are twisted to the left. Strands are twisted to the right.

USES OF WIRE ROPE

The NAVSHIPSTECHMAN specifies the uses that may be made of wire rope of various constructions. A few of the common ones and some of their uses follow:

6 × 7: Only the galvanized type is specified. It is not suitable for general hoisting, but is applicable for permanent standing rigging.

6 × 19: Size for size, this type of construction is the strongest of all the wire ropes. When made of galvanized wire, it is used principally for heavy hoisting and is particularly useful on derricks and dredges. Standing rigging, guys, boat slings, and topping lifts for booms are often made of 6 × 19 galvanized wire rope. Where either noncorrosive or nonmagnetic properties are needed, phosphor bronze 6 × 19 wire rope is used; for example, in lifelines, wheelropes, radio antennas, antenna downloads, etc.

6 × 37: When made of ungalvanized steel wire, this construction is flexible, making it suitable for cranes and similar machinery; it may also be used for heavy hoisting. When made of galvanized steel, it may be used for steering gear, boatcrane falls, towing hawsers, bridles, torpedo slings, and heavy running rigging.

CARE OF WIRE ROPE

If a wire rope becomes kinked, never try to pull it out by putting a strain on either part. As soon as you notice a kink, uncross the ends by pushing them apart; this reverses the process that started the kink. Then turn the bent portion over, place it on your knee or some firm object, and push downward until the kink straightens out somewhat. Then lay it on a flat surface and pound it smooth with a wooden mallet.

If a heavy strain is put on a wire rope with a kink in it, the rope no longer can be trusted. Cut out the kinked part and splice the ends together.

Frequently abrasions, reverse bends, or sharp bends cause individual wires to break and bend back. These are known as fishhooks. If several occur at a point near each other, or several along the rope's length, the safe working load is reduced. When 4 percent of the total number of wires in the rope are found to have breaks within the length of one wire rope lay, the rope is unsafe.

Wire rope should be inspected frequently, checking for fishhooks, kinks, and worn corroded spots. Worn spots show up as shiny flattened surfaces.

Wire rope should never be stored in places where acid is or has been kept. Prior to storage, wire rope should always be cleaned and lubricated.

WIRE ROPE FAILURE

Here are some common causes of wire rope failure:

1. Using incorrect size, construction, or heavy grade.
2. Dragging over obstacles.
3. Lubricating improperly.
4. Operating over sheaves and drums of inadequate size.
5. Overriding or crosswinding on drums.
6. Operating over misaligned sheaves and drums.
7. Operating over sheaves and drums with improperly fitted grooves or broken flanges.
8. Jumping off sheaves.
9. Subjecting to moisture or acid fumes.
10. Attaching fittings improperly.
11. Subjecting to excessive heat.
12. Permitting to untwist.
13. Promoting internal wear by allowing grit to penetrate between the strands.
14. Subjecting to severe or continuing overloads.
15. Kinking.

Making Ready Line and Splicing

Once a line has been removed from the coil, it may be made up for storage or ready use, either by winding it on a reel or in one of these ways:

Coiling down: Lay the line down in circles, roughly one on top of the other. Right-laid line is always coiled down right-handed, or clockwise. When a line has been coiled down, the end that went down last on top is ready to run off. If you try to walk away with the bottom end, a foul-up will result. If for some reason the bottom end must go out first, turn the entire coil upside down to free it for running.

Faking down: The line is laid down as in coiling down, except that it is laid out in long, flat bights, one forward of the other, instead of a round coil. This saves space a large coil might occupy. Faking down a heavy line is easier than coiling it down. A faked line runs more easily than a coiled line.

Flemishing down: Coil the line down first, then wind it tight from the bottom end, counterclockwise, so that it forms a close mat. Slack ends of boat painters, boat falls, boat boom guys, or any other short lines not in constant use should be flemished down for neatness.

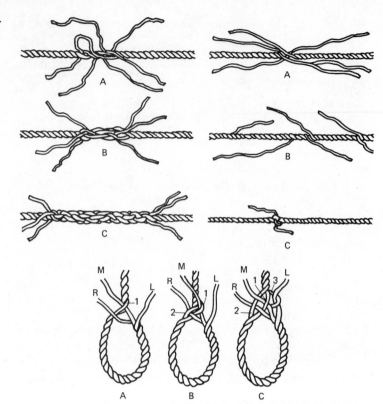

Figure 21–5 Three types of splice are the short splice, long splice, and eye splice.

Securing ends: Never leave the end of a line without a whipping. This prevents unlaying, which it'll do on its own. Use tape to whip nylon line ends, then singe each strand.

A temporary plain whipping can be made with anything, even a rope yarn. Lay the whipping along the line and bind it down with a couple of turns. Then lay the other end on the opposite way, bind it with a couple of turns from the bight of the whipping and pull the end tight.

A permanent whipping is put on with a palm and needle, threaded with sail twine, doubled. Shove the needle through the middle of a strand so that it comes out between two strands on the other side. Bind the end down with six to eight turns, wound on from inboard toward the end, and again push the needle through the middle of a strand near the end so that it comes out between two strands. Then work it up and down between strands, with a cross-seizing good and tight. The needle comes cut in the middle of a strand on the last shove, so the strand will hold the end after you cut the sail twine.

Seizings (pronounced "seezings") are used when two lines, or two parts of a single line, are to be married permanently. This should be done with "seizing stuff"—generally rope-laid, tarred American hemp of 6, 9, or 12 threads. For seizing small stuff, however, marline is adequate.

Many types of seizings were used for special purposes in old sailing ships, but the four described here should suffice for seamen in modern ships.

Flat seizing: This is a light seizing and is used where strain is not too great.

Round seizing: Stronger than the flat type, it is used where strain is greater.

Racking seizing: Use this type where there is an unequal strain on the two parts of the line.

Throat seizing: Throat seizing is actually a round seizing and is used whenever a permanent eye is needed in the middle of a line. Sometimes this seizing is used to keep mooring spring lines from chafing where they cross.

SPLICING

Splicing means permanently joining the ends of two lines or bending a line back on itself to form a permanent loop. If properly done, it does not weaken the line. A splice between two lines will run over a sheave or other object much easier than a knot.

Short splice: For a short splice, both ends of line are unlaid for a short distance and the strands are interlaced. One strand is tucked through the lay of the other line, which has been opened by a marlinespike or wooden fid. The other strands are similarly tucked. Threads are then cut away from the ends of each tucked strand until they are two-thirds their original size, and then they are again tucked. Again the strands are similarly cut away until they are one-third their original size, and a third and last tuck is taken. This produces a neat, tapered splice.

In splicing a four-strand line, the first strand is tucked under two parts of the first tucking only.

Long splice: For a long splice, the ends are unlaid further than for a short splice and then are similarly interlaced. Then a strand of one piece is unlaid for quite a distance, and the corresponding strand is laid in the opening. The remaining ends of the two strands are twisted together for convenience, the line is turned end for end, and the first operation is repeated with two other corresponding strands.

The remaining strands of each part are left at the original position. This leaves pairs of strands at three positions along the line. Each strand is halved. Two of these halves at each position are tied together with an overhand knot. And the remaining two halves are tucked over one and under one of the full remaining strands of the line. After all strands have been tucked, the loose ends are trimmed off smooth. This splice will run over a sheave easily and is hardly noticeable. In splicing nylon line, make several extra tucks to be certain the splice holds.

Eye splice: An eye splice is made the same way, except that the line is first brought back on itself enough to give the desired size of eye, and the strands are then tucked into the body of the line.

Worming, parceling, and serving: This is done to protect wire rope that must be exposed to the weather or to hard use.

Worming consists of following the lay of the rope between the strands with tarred small stuff. This keeps moisture from penetrating to the interior of the rope and fills out the rope, giving it a smooth surface for the parceling and serving.

Parceling consists of wrapping the rope spirally with long narrow strips of canvas, following the lay of the rope and overlapping turns to shed moisture.

Serving consists of wrapping small stuff snugly over the parceling, pulling each turn as taut as possible so that the whole forms a stiff protecting cover for the rope. A serving mallet is used for passing the turns in serving, and each turn is pulled taut by the leverage of the handle. Remember: Worm and parcel with the lay, turn and serve the other way.

Knots, Bends, and Hitches

According to a seaman's use of the term, in a knot the line usually is bent to itself. The knot forms an eye or a knob, or secures a cord or line around something. A bend ordinarily is used to join two lines together.

There are four classes of knots: (1) Knots at the end of a line, used in fastening it upon itself or around an object, (2) Knots for bending two lines together, (3) Knots that secure a line to a ring or spar (hitches or bends), (4) Knots used to give finish to the end of a line, to prevent unreeving, or for ornamentation. This last one is called MacNamara lace. Some of the more common knots are described here and illustrated in Figure 21–6.

Reeving line bend: Frequently it is necessary to bend together two lines that must reeve around a capstan or winch drum. This is the best knot for it.

Double Matthew Walker: This knot has many uses in fancy work, but it also has practical applications, such as keeping the end of a line from coming unlaid. This should be considered a temporary measure because a proper whipping should be put on the line at the earliest opportunity and the knot cut off.

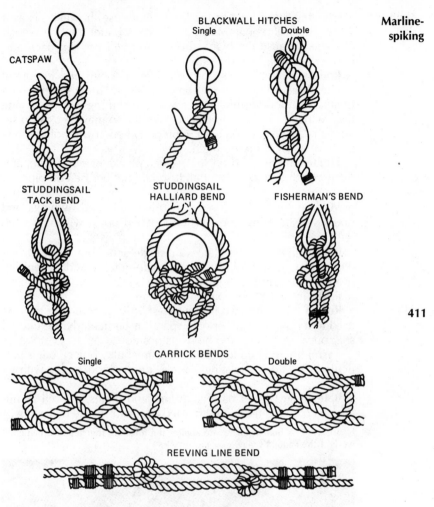

CATSPAW

BLACKWALL HITCHES
Single   Double

STUDDINGSAIL
TACK BEND

STUDDINGSAIL
HALLIARD BEND

FISHERMAN'S BEND

CARRICK BENDS
Single   Double

REEVING LINE BEND

Figure 21–6 Completed knots, bends, and hitches.

Fisherman's bend: This knot is used to bend a line to a becket
or eye, as a messenger to a mooring line. It can also be used to
secure a rope to a buoy, or a hawser to the ring of an anchor.

Bowline: This is a temporary eye in the end of a line. It will not
slip or jam. A bowline on a bight is used to sling a man over the
side since it will not slip and constrict him.

Masthead knot: Although this knot is usually seen in fancy-
work, it also has a practical purpose. In the days of sailing ships,
these knots were set at the top of the masts, and the stays and
shrouds were secured to the knots. It's a good knot to remember
if you ever have to rig a jury mast.

Spanish bowline: Whenever it is desirable to have two eyes in a line, this is the knot to use. Its primary use, however, is as a substitute for the boatswain's chair. Many prefer it to the French bowline because the bights are set and will not slip back and forth when weight is shifted.

Rolling hitch: This is one of the most useful and important hitches used on deck. It can be used for passing a stopper on a boatfall or mooring line, when you are shifting the fall or line from winch or capstan to cleat or bitt. It also may be used to secure a taut line back on itself. If properly tied, it will hold as long as there is strain on the hitch.

Timber hitch: Used on logs, spars, planks or other comparatively rough-surfaced material. It should not be used on pipes or other metal.

Marline hitch: It is used on furled sails and awnings and double-up mooring lines. When cinched up, it will hold itself tight.

Blackwall hitch: The Blackwall, single or double, is used to secure a rope to a hook. It can be made quickly and, when tied properly, is secure. Except when there is insufficient rope end remaining to make a bowline, it seldom is used.

Round turn with two half hitches: This combination may be used in a ring, padeye, or on a spar. It is particularly useful on a spar because it grips and holds its position.

Barrel hitch: Used to hoist almost any bulky object, but is particularly useful in hoisting barrels, drums, and boxes without tops.

Bale sling: Closed barrels, drums, and boxes, as well as numerous other items, can be hoisted by means of the bale sling. A

Figure 21–7 A boatswain's mate applies the finishing touches to ornamental work of the captain's gig.

temporary sling may be fashioned simply by knotting the ends of a line together with a square knot or a becket bend.

Square knot: Also called a reef knot. This knot is used for bending lines together. If not tied properly (both knots should be tied right- or left-handed, instead of one right and one left), it becomes a granny knot, which will slip under strain. A square knot will jam under heavy tension.

Figure eight: This knot is used to prevent the end of a line from unreeving through a block or eyebolt.

Catspaw: This is used to secure a sling to a cargo hook. It cannot slip or jam.

Carrick bend: Used to bend two hawsers together. It will not slip or jam. No matter how long the hawsers are in the water, it can be easily untied.

Ornamental Work

Ornamental work can be constructed using various materials and serves the purpose of safety, habitability, coverings, completions of work, and appearances. Only a few of the common ones appear here; there are many encyclopedias on the subject that can be obtained through shipboard or local libraries.

Turk's heads: Usually thought of as strictly ornamental, but they serve many useful purposes, such as keeping the leathers on lifelines, and the looms of oars in position.

Coxcombing: Used to cover boat tillers, bucket bails, handrails for ladders, etc. It looks smart and affords a more secure grip.

Cross pointing: Generally used on stanchions, but can also be employed in many other places where a round core is covered. It looks best on cores of fairly large diameter. Strips of canvas, leather, or small stuff, are often used in multiples of four for cross pointing.

Fox and geese: This is a simple and fast way of covering a handrail or stanchion. It can be used any place coxcombing or cross pointing can be used.

Sennit or braid: Made of small cord, such as codline or Belfast cord and is used to form ornamental lines or lanyards. A well-known book of knots describes and illustrates close to 400 sennits, so don't be misled into believing the examples in Figure 21–7 are the only ones, or even the basic ones.

Ground Tackle

Ground tackle includes all the equipment used in anchoring a ship: anchors, anchor cables (or chains), connecting fittings, anchor windlass, and miscellaneous items such as shackles, de-

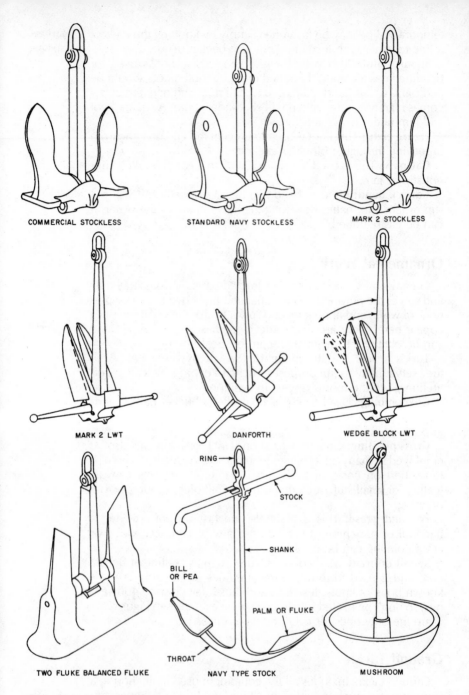

COMMERCIAL STOCKLESS

STANDARD NAVY STOCKLESS

MARK 2 STOCKLESS

MARK 2 LWT

DANFORTH

WEDGE BLOCK LWT

TWO FLUKE BALANCED FLUKE

RING

STOCK

SHANK

BILL
OR PEA

PALM OR FLUKE

THROAT

NAVY TYPE STOCK

MUSHROOM

Figure 21–8 Types of anchors.

tachable links, mooring swivels, dip ropes, chain stoppers, chain
cable jacks, mooring hooks, and anchor bars.

ANCHORS

There are various types of anchors and different methods of
anchoring. When a ship has one anchor down, she is anchored.
When she has two anchors down and swings from a mooring
swivel connected to both, she is moored. (A ship secured to a
dock with lines or to a buoy with an anchor chain is also
moored.) In a Mediterranean moor, a ship usually has the stern
moored to a pier, and an anchor out on each bow. A ship's biggest anchor is her sheet anchor. An anchor carried aft and used
by amphibious ships to pull themselves off the beach (retract) is
called a stern anchor. A stream anchor, now seldom used, is a
small anchor dropped off the stern or quarter of a ship to prevent
her swinging to a current.

Stockless anchors: Stockless anchors are easy to stow and
were adopted by the Navy for this reason, despite the fact that
they do not have the holding power of the old-fashioned anchor.
Three designs of stockless anchors are in use on naval ships:
commercial, the Mk 2, and the standard Navy stockless. Of the
three, the Mk 2 with its long flukes has the greatest holding
power; it is made only in the 60,000-pound size for use aboard
aircraft carriers.

Mushroom anchor: Used to anchor buoys and torpedo testing
barges.

Lightweight (LWT) anchors: There are two types of LWT anchors used on Navy ships: The Mk 2 LWT and the wedge block
LWT. These, as well as the commercially made Danforth anchor,
are shown in Figure 21-8, for comparison. Both types have
holding power for their weights. For example, both 10,000-
pound LWT anchors are designed to have a holding power in a
sand bottom approximately equal to the 22,500-pound standard
Navy stockless. Sizes below 150 pounds are used as boat anchors.

Two-fluke balanced-fluke anchor: This anchor is used for anchoring some surface ships and the newest submarines and is
normally housed in the bottom of the ship. This anchor is used
on surface ships in place of a bow anchor, which would interfere
with the ship's bow sonar dome.

Old-fashioned anchors: They are no longer used. You will
probably see them only on the lawns of some naval station.

CHAINS AND RELATED EQUIPMENT

Anchor chains: These are made of steel. Their sizes vary according to the size of the ship and its anchors. Chain comes in
15-fathom lengths (90 feet) called shots. A destroyer will have

one eight-shot chain and one seven-shot chain. Shots are connected by detachable links. These and their adjacent links are
painted red, white or blue to let the anchor detail know how
much chain has run out. Each link of the next-to-last shot is
painted yellow. The entire last shot is red. This is to warn that the
bitter end of the chain is coming up. When an anchor is hoisted,
the chain comes off the anchor windlass and into the chain
locker.

Shot Number	Color of Detachable Link	Number of Adjacent Links Painted White	Turns of Wire on Last White Links
1 (15 fathoms)	Red	1	1
2 (30 fathoms)	White	2	2
3 (45 fathoms)	Blue	3	3
4 (60 fathoms)	Red	4	4
5 (75 fathoms)	White	5	5
6 (90 fathoms)	Blue	6	6

Outboard swivel shots: On most ships, standard outboard
swivel shots also called "bending shots," attach the anchor
chain to the anchor. They make it possible to stop off the anchor
and break the chain between the windlass and the anchor. Outboard swivel shots consist of detachable links, regular chain
links, a swivel, end link, and a bending shackle. They vary in
length up to approximately 14 fathoms. The taper pins in the detachable links in the outboard swivel shot are secured with a
wire locking clip (sometimes called a "hairpin").

Bending shackles: These are used for attaching the anchor to
the chains.

Riding and housing chain stoppers: These consist of a turn-
buckle inserted in a short section of chain, with a slip or pelican
hook attached to one end of the chain and a shackle at the other.
The housing stopper is the one nearest the hawsepipe. Any
others are riding stoppers. They're used for holding the anchor
taut in the hawsepipe, for riding to an anchor, or for holding an
anchor when it is disconnected for any reason. When in use, a
stopper is attached to the chain by straddling a link with the
tongue and strongback of the pelican hook.

Mooring shackles: These forged steel shackles are used for attaching the anchor chain to mooring buoys. Forged steel mooring swivels with two links attached at each end are inserted in
the chain outboard of the hawsepipe, to keep the chain from
twisting as the ship swings.

Anchor windlass: This machine is used to hoist the bow anchor. A ship with a stern anchor has a stern-anchor winch to
hoist it. On combatant ships the anchor windlass is a vertical
type with controls, friction brake handwheel, capstan and wild-

Figure 21–9 A 30-ton aircraft carrier anchor dwarfs the sailor painting it.

cat above deck, and an electric and hydraulic drive for the wildcat and capstan below deck. On auxiliary ships the anchor windlass is a horizontal type, all above deck, with two wildcats, one
for each anchor. The wildcat is fitted with ridges called whelps,
which engage the links of the chain and prevent it from slipping.
The wildcat may be disengaged from the shaft so that it turns
freely when the anchors are dropped, and it is fitted with a brake
to stop the chain at the desired length or scope.

Anchor detail: On most ships, the first lieutenant is in charge
on the forecastle, with a boatswain's mate assisting and men detailed to duties by the WQ&S bill. "Heave around" from the
bridge is the order to the anchor windlass to take a strain on the
chain and start bringing it in. "Anchors aweigh" from the forecastle means that the anchor is clear of the bottom and the ship is
underway, whether the propellers are turning or not.

Scope of chain: Scope means the amount of chain in use from

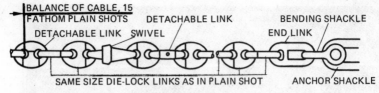

Figure 21–10 Parts of a standard outboard swivel shot assembly.

the ship to the anchor. In 10 to 15 fathoms, the length of chain used is equal to six times the depth of water. In 15 to 20 fathoms, the length of chain is five times the depth. In 20 to 30 fathoms, the length is three times the depth.

Why the lesser scope in deeper water? Because if a ship puts heavy strain on her chain in bad weather, more of the length lifts off the bottom and the anchor will break out and drag. With too long a scope, the chain may part before its entire length lifts off the bottom.

MOORING

Mooring a ship to a pier, buoy, or another ship, and unmooring, are the most basic jobs of the deck department. These tasks involve skillful use of mooring lines (called line handling), winches, and such fittings as cleats, bitts, bollards, chocks, and towing pads. Quick, efficient line handling, when coming along-side or getting underway, is one of the marks of a smart ship.

MOORING LINES

Mooring lines are numbered from forward aft in the order that they are run out from the ship, but their names describe their lo-cation, their use, and the direction they tend as they leave the ship. See Figure 21–13.

The *bow line* (1) runs through the bull-nose or chock nearest the eyes of the ship and is led well up the pier to reduce after motion of the ship.

The corresponding line used to reduce stern motion of the ship is the *stern line* (7). A *breast line* (4) leads nearly at right angles to the center of the line of the ship. Amidships, more than one breast line may be used, in which case they are named from forward aft: *bow breast, waist breast,* and *quarter breast.* Spring lines lead out from the ship in pairs, at sharp angles and cross each other. Those forward are called *after bow spring* (2) and *forward bow spring* (3). Those aft are called *after quarter spring* (5) and *forward quarter spring* (6). Men who work with mooring lines are called line handlers.

DECK FITTINGS

A *cleat* consists of a pair of projecting horns used for belaying a line. *Bitts* are cylindrical shapes of cast iron or steel, arranged

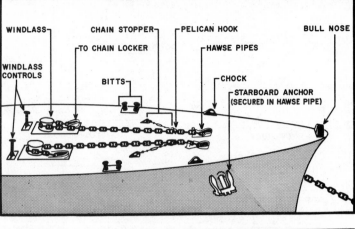

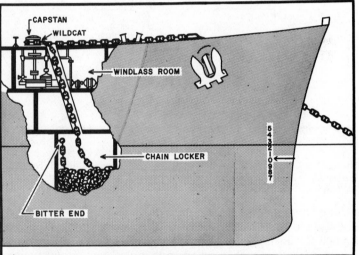

Figure 21-11 Ground tackle installation on a typical ship is arranged on the forecastle and below decks.

in pairs on deck, forward and aft of each chock. They are used for delaying mooring lines. A *chock* is a heavy fitting through which mooring lines are led; the lines run from bitts on deck through chocks to bollards on the pier. The three types of chocks are open, closed, and roller. A *bollard* looks somewhat like half a bit, but it's larger. It is on the dock or pier where the bight of a line is placed over it. A *towing pad* is a large padeye that is welded to the deck. It is used in towing operations.

Mooring may often involve putting out fenders, handling camels, and placing rat guards. Fenders are shock absorbers of

Ground
Tackle

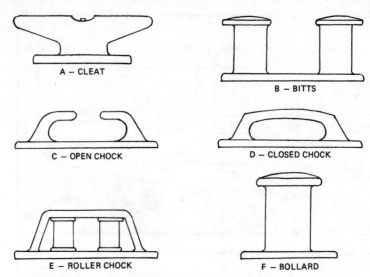

Figure 21–12 Deck fittings on a ship are the cleat, bitts, open chock, closed chock, and roller chock. The bollard is found on a pier or dock.

420

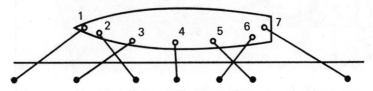

Figure 21–13 Mooring lines are: 1. Bow line, 2. After bow spring, 3. Forward bow spring, 4. Waist breast, 5. After quarter spring, 6. Forward quarter spring, 7. Stern line.

various types placed between ships or between a ship and a pier. They are dropped over the side and tended from on deck. Camels are floats used to keep a ship, particularly an aircraft carrier, away from a pier or wharf so that elevators or other overhanging structures will not strike objects on the pier. Rat guards are circular metal discs lashed to mooring lines to keep rats from coming aboard.

In mooring, the messenger (a light line) is first sent over by heaving line, bolo, or a line-throwing gun. Then it is hauled in with the attached mooring line. A heaving line is a light line with a weight, called a monkey fist, on one end; a bolo line is a nylon line with a padded lead weight or a monkey fist on it. A .45-caliber line-throwing gun looks like a small shotgun. It fires a projectile about the size of a pencil that carries a light nylon line. It will reach farther than a heaving line but is dangerous to use where many people are on deck. With practice, a good seaman can heave a bolo more than 100 yards.

When the ship is secured, the mooring lines are normally doubled up. A bight of line is passed to the pier or other ship, giving
three parts of line each taking an equal strain, instead of only one
part. The size of mooring line used depends on the type of line
and type of ship. Destroyers generally use 6-inch manila or 5-
inch nylon. Smaller ships use 5-inch manila or 4-inch nylon, and
aircraft carriers use 10-inch manila or 8-inch nylon.

COMMANDS TO LINE HANDLERS

Commands to line handlers are listed here, with the precise
meaning following each command.

Stand by your lines. Man the lines, ready to cast off or let go.

Let go, or *Let go all lines.* Slack off smartly to permit those tending lines on the pier or another ship to cast off.

Send the lines over. Pass the lines to the pier, place the eye
over the appropriate bollard, but take no strain.

Take (name of line) *to the capstan.* Lead the end of the line to
the capstan, take the slack out of the line, but take no strain.

Heave around on (name of line). Apply tension on line with
the capstan.

Avast heaving. Stop the capstan.

Hold what you've got. Hold the line as it is.

Hold. Do not allow any more line to go out. Caution: this risks
parting the line.

Check. Hold heavy tension on line but render it (let it slip) as
necessary to prevent parting the line.

Surge. Hold moderate tension on the line, but render it enough
to permit movement of the ship (used when moving along the
pier to adjacent position).

Double up. Pass an additional bight on all mooring lines so
that there are three parts of each line to the pier.

Single up. Take in all bights and extra lines so that there remains only a single part of each of the normal mooring lines.

Take in all lines. Used when secured with your own lines.
Have the ends of all lines cast off from the pier and brought on
board.

Cast off all lines. Used when secured with another ship's lines
in a nest. Cast off the ends of the lines and allow the other ship to
retrieve her lines.

Shift. Used when moving a line along a pier. Followed by a
designation of which line should be moved: *Shift number three
from the bollard to the cleat.*

If auxiliary deck machinery is to be used to haul in on a line,
the command is given, *Take one* (number one) *to the winch* (capstan). This may be followed by, *Heave around on one* (number
one) and then, *Avast heaving on one* (number one).

After a ship has completed mooring to another ship or a pier, rat guards are put out on all mooring lines. Putting out rat guards is a tiresome job, especially on a cold rainy night, but it is essential. Rats carry contagious diseases, and once they get aboard, it is almost impossible to get rid of them.

Towing

Most routine towing jobs in the Navy are handled by harbor tugs, fleet tugs, salvage vessels, and submarine rescue vessels—all ships which are especially fitted for the work. Some ships used in ocean towing have automatic tension towing machines, powerful electric-drive winches mounted in the stern, that automatically heave in or pay out the towing hausers and maintain proper tension at all times. Tugs working in harbors usually use the alongside method because there is no room in crowded areas for a long stern tow, and with barges properly secured alongside, the tug has greatly increased maneuverability.

Combatant vessels—carriers, cruisers, and destroyers—can tow another vessel or can be towed, but such operations are usually done only in an emergency and involve what is called the fixed towing method. The towing rig varies among classes and types of ships, but includes these items in one form or another:

On the stern of the towing vessel, a *towing pad* eye, usually on the centerline.

A *towing assembly*, chiefly a large pelican hook, which is shackled to the towing pad and made fast to a towing hawser.

The *hawser* itself, a wire rope varying in length from 100 fathoms for a destroyer to 150 fathoms for a larger ship. The hawser is attached to one of the towed ship's anchor chains, which is disconnected from the outboard shot, let out through the bull-nose, and veered to 20 to 45 fathoms.

The length of the towline—hawser and chain—is adjusted to hang in a deep underwater curve called a *catenary*, which helps to relieve surges on the line caused by movements of the two ships. Proper towing technique, whether with two motor launches or two cruisers, requires that the towline be of such a scope (or length) that the two craft are in "step." Both must reach the crest of a wave at the same time, or the towline will be whipped out of the water under terrific strain and may do great damage.

Once a towing hawser is properly rigged, it is necessary for the towing vessel to get way on very slowly as the towed vessel commences to move. Otherwise, the line may part. Course changes also must be made slowly, as the towed vessel will flounder at the end of the line and may have difficulty steering a course.

Figure 21–14 A deck hand rigs the vang line, which supports a boom.

Every naval ship is furnished with a plan (explained in the Standard Organization and Regulations of the U.S. Navy) showing the proper method of rigging for towing or being towed. Towing requires skillful seamanship, proficiency in shiphandling, and perfect communications between the towing craft and the one being towed.

Cargo Handling

Cargo is loaded or off-loaded by ship's gear or dockside or floating cranes when in port, by ship's gear in underway replenishment (UNREP), and by helicopters in vertical replenishment (VERTREP) operations. Combatant ships have limited cargo-handling equipment, except for UNREP operations. Amphibious warfare ships and service ships are fitted with heavy-lift cargo systems. One of our LKAs can lift a 70-ton boat, and one of our new AOEs can transfer cargo or pump fuel through 15 replenishment stations at once.

Aboard such ships, deck seamanship is primarily concerned with heavy-cargo handling. A knowledge of the principal parts of all cargo gear and the various "rigs" or methods of handling cargo is essential for seamen aboard such ships. For a better understanding of the terms used in the following discussion, see Figure 21–15.

RIGGING

This is a general term for all wires, ropes, and chains supporting masts or kingposts, and operating booms and cargo hooks. *Standing rigging* includes all lines that support but do not move, such as stays and shrouds. *Running rigging* includes all movable lines rove (running) through blocks, such as lifts, whips and vangs.

RUNNING RIGGING

Booms are moved into position and cargo is moved into and out of holds by running rigging. Topping lifts working on topping lift blocks move the boom vertically and hold it at the required height. Inboard and outboard guys, or vangs, move the boom horizontally or hold it in working position over hatch or dock. The cargo hook is raised or lowered by cargo whips running from winches over heel blocks near the gooseneck and head blocks at the top of the boom.

BOOMS

A boom is a long pole built of steel. The lower end is fitted with a gooseneck, which supports the boom in a boom step bracket. The upper end is raised or lowered and held in position by a topping lift. Booms range in capacity from 5 tons to 75 tons. When they are used in pairs, the boom lifting cargo from a hold is called the hatch boom. The boom that positions cargo over the side to lower it to a dock or boat is called the yard boom. Booms are used singly, or in combination as follows:

Single swinging boom: This arrangement is generally used to hoist or lower landing craft on LPDs and LKAs. The topping lift is led to a winch that can raise or lower the boom with a full load. The boom is swung over the side by vangs and the cargo hook is attached to the boat's lifting bridle. Another winch takes up the cargo hoist leadline to raise the load. The boom is swung over the side by the vangs, and the boat is hooked on. Then the hoist winch raises the boat clear of the railing, after which the vang on the side opposite the boat swings it on deck. Cargo, in nets or pallets, can be handled the same way.

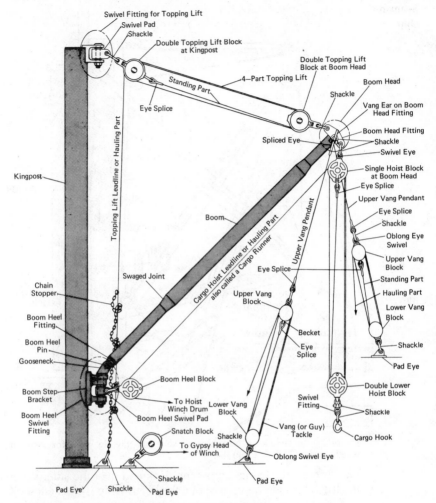

Figure 21-15 Rigging detail for single swinging boom.

Yard and stay (or burtoning): Two booms are used, a hatch boom and a cargo boom (Figure 21–16). The hatch boom is centered over the working hatch. The yard boom is rigged out with its head over the pier or receiving boat. There are two cargo whips—a hatch whip and yard whip—rove through their respective heel and head blocks on the hatch and yard booms and both shackled to the same cargo hook. Each whip has its own winch. With the hatch boom secured above the center of the open hatch and the yard boom rigged out over the side of the ship, the cargo hook is dropped into the hold for a load. The yard whip hangs slack while the hatch whip hoists the load clear. Then the yard whip heaves around and the hatch whip is payed out, and the

Cargo Handling

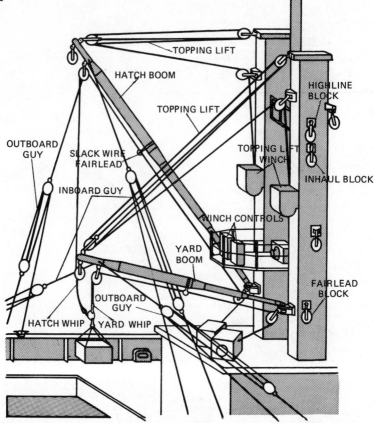

Figure 21–16 Details of burtoning or yard-and-stay rig, used for medium-weight cargo of up to 3,500 lbs.

load is racked (swung) across the deck and over the side. When the load is under the yard boom, the hatch whip is slackened off, and the yard whip lowers away. In loading cargo, the procedure is reversed.

INSPECTING RIGGING

A weekly inspection of all booms and their rigging and associated fittings is conducted by the responsible officer of the weapons or deck department, in accordance with the requirements of the planned maintenance system (PMS).

Whenever a boom is to hoist or lower a load equal to its rated capacity as shown on the label plate, the first lieutenant or an officer he designates must make a thorough inspection of the boom, fitting, and rigging before the lift is made. Details about the use, care, and testing of cranes, booms, and rigging is contained in NAVSHIPSTECHMAN.

Underway Replenishment

Underway replenishment (UNREP) refers to all methods of transferring fuel, munitions, supplies, and men from one ship to another while at sea. The term "replenishment at sea," formerly used in this sense, now applies to all methods except for fueling at sea.

Before the techniques of UNREP were developed, a ship that ran low on fuel, supplies, or ammunition had to return to port, or the fleet had to lie to while she was replenished by means of small boats. Consequently, the effectiveness of the fleet was reduced by the ships that had to leave; moreover, a fleet lying to in order to replenish was more vulnerable to attack. With UNREP, an entire fleet can be resupplied, rearmed, and refueled within hours, while the fleet is proceeding on its mission.

Two general methods of UNREP are used: connected and vertical. They may be used separately or simultaneously. In connected replenishment (CONREP), two or more ships steam side by side, their hoses and lines being used to connect the ships. Vertical replenishment (VERTREP) is done by helicopters, with the ships in close proximity or miles apart, depending on the tactical situation and the amount of cargo to be transferred.

Connected replenishment involves two processes—refueling and resupply. In refueling at sea (FAS), fuel is pumped from a delivery ship, which may be a replenishment tanker (AOR), oiler (AO), fast combat support ship (AOE), or a large combat ship. Other replenishment ships, such as the combat store ship (AFS)

Figure 21–17 Burton rig for underway replenishment has a maximum load of 3,500 lbs.

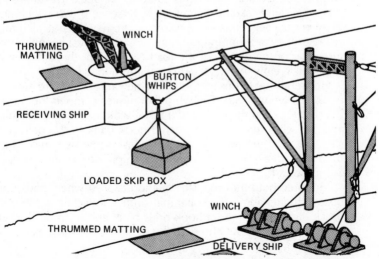

THRUMMED MATTING

WINCH

BURTON WHIPS

RECEIVING SHIP

LOADED SKIP BOX

WINCH

THRUMMED MATTING

DELIVERY SHIP

and the ammunition ship (AE), can deliver lesser amounts of fuel. But their primary purpose is to deliver solid cargo—that is, supplies and ammunition—by methods now referred to as replenishment at sea (RAS).

The most common methods of refueling are the span wire and the close-in. The span wire method has several variations—single hose, double hose and probe. The span wire may be either tensioned or untensioned. The tensioned span wire or highline, as it is called in RAS, also is used in the standard tensioned replenishment alongside method (STREAM) of transfer, described on page 432.

Other common methods of replenishment at sea include manila highline, wire highline, burton, housefall, modified housefall, and double housefall.

The illustrations in this chapter and the procedures described are meant to be representative only. For the sake of clarity, many of the variations have been omitted from illustrations. The naval warfare publication Replenishment at Sea (NWP-14 [Rev. A]) should be consulted for more precise information, rigging details, and the personnel and tools required.

CARGO RIGS

Here's a brief description of each rig or system:

Burton rig: The cargo is moved from delivering ship to receiving ship by two burton whips, which correspond to the hatch whip and cargo whip. A winch on each ship handles one whip. The delivering ship hoists the load clear, then the receiving ship takes in her burton whip as the delivering ship slacks hers off. When the load is spotted over the deck of the receiving ship, her whip is slacked and the load is eased to the deck. The entire operation requires skillful teamwork between the two winchmen. They must keep constant tension on both whips at all times, whether they are running in or out, and they must keep the load just clear of the water—if the load is too high, the strain on all rigging is greatly increased. The maximum load is 3,500 pounds.

Housefall rig: In this method both the cargo whips are handled by the delivering ship. The whip that moves cargo to the receiving ship is called the outboard transfer whip (same as yardwhip), and the whip that hauls the cargo hook back to the delivering ship is called the inboard transfer whip (same as cargo whip). Both winchmen are on the delivering ship. The maximum load is 2,500 pounds.

Modified housefall rig: This method is used when loads must be kept higher above the water than with a housefall rig. A trolley block carrying the cargo hook rides back and forth on the outboard transfer whip. Otherwise the rigging is the same as that for the housefall rig.

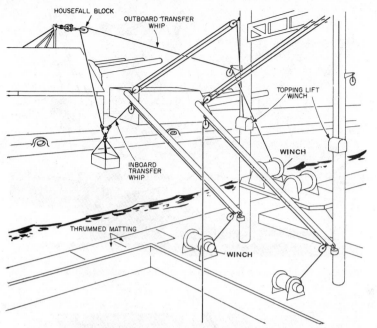

HOUSEFALL BLOCK

OUTBOARD TRANSFER
WHIP

TOPPING LIFT
WINCH

WINCH

INBOARD
TRANSFER
WHIP

THRUMMED MATTING

WINCH

Figure 21–18 The housefall rig has a maximum load of 2,500 lbs.

Double housefall rig: This is used to speed transfers to ships that cannot handle more than one housefall rig. It is slower than housefalling to two separate receiving stations, but faster than housefalling to one station. In this method, the delivering ship uses two adjacent housefall rigs attached to a single point on the receiving ship. In handling cargo with this method, the delivering ship sends over a loaded net with one rig at the same time the other brings back an empty net from the receiving ship. The two nets pass each other in opposite directions each time a load is transferred.

Wire highline rig: This method involves a trolley moving on a highline that extends from a winch on the delivering ship through a block on a boom head and across to a pad eye on the receiving ship. An outhaul line (same as yard whip) is heaved in by hand on the receiving ship to move the load over. A winch-operated inhaul line (same as hatch whip) on the delivering ship returns the trolley for another load. The wire highline is the standard procedure in transferring cargo to destroyers and other small ships, and at times is the best means of transfer to large ships. In order to use this method, the receiving ship must have a place in her superstructure high enough to attach the line for good working conditions and strong enough to handle the load.

Manila highline rig: This is the same as the wire highline rig,

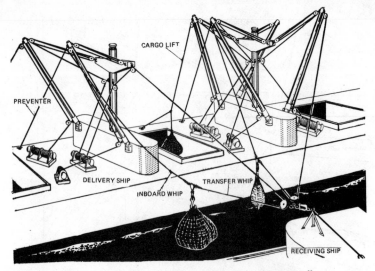

Figure 21–19 The double housefall rig's maximum load is 2,500 lbs.

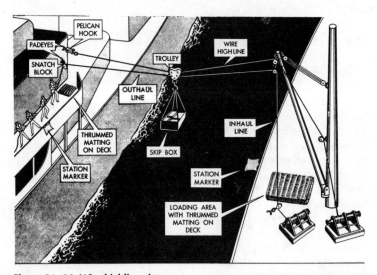

Figure 21–20 Wire highline rig.

except that manila is used instead of wire. Only light cargo can be handled. No boom is needed on the delivery ship. The receiving ship needs only a 12-inch snatch block attached to a padeye. The highline is kept taut during transfer either by 25 men or a capstan. The capstan cannot be used if men are being transferred. The trolley that rides the highline is moved by inhaul and outhaul lines, both handled by men on deck. The rig is easily and quickly set up and is the safest method of transferring men from ship to ship. The maximum load is 600 pounds.

Personnel transfer: Besides the manila highline rig, men can be transferred by the burton rig and by helicopter. With the burton rig, used particularly when many men must transfer quickly and time does not allow the use of a highline, a ship box is used to send over four or five men at a time. The danger in the burton system is in having the transfer controlled by winchmen on two different ships. The only approved rig for transferring men ship-to-ship is the manila highline. This is because the line must be tended constantly to prevent parting if the ships roll away from each other, and manila can be tended by hand. Wire cannot, however. The maximum load is 600 pounds.

FUELING AT SEA

The two basic systems are close-in and span wire rigs. The system used depends on the types of ships involved, the kind of fuel being transferred, and weather and operating conditions. The two rigs differ mainly in the method by which the delivering ship sends the hose over to the receiving ship. For fuel, a six-inch, 230-foot hose is used. Fleet oilers and many major combatant ships have equipment for the span wire method. Other ships use the close-in method.

Close-in method: In this system the hose is supported by inboard and outboard saddle whips attached to the inboard and outboard saddles and running to booms or other high points on the delivery ship. If an outer bight line is used, it runs from the outboard saddle to the receiving ship. The ships steam about 60 feet apart.

Span wire method: The fuel hose is sent across by a single span wire stretched between the two ships. The hose is suspended by a trolley that rides along the span wire. This system lets the ships keep 140 to 180 feet apart, which makes shiphandling easier and allows use of antiaircraft batteries. The span wire method, because it carries the hose higher above the sea, gives it better protection in rough weather. The hose may be rigged out by the all-wire or the manila rig. The all-wire span method involves a span wire on which a trolley carries the outboard saddle and a retrieving wire line. This method can be used only if there are enough winches at the stations to be rigged. Generally, at least three winches are required. Of the two span wire methods, the all-wire rig is most used.

Manila rig: This rig is simpler than the all-wire one, but it requires more men at each station to handle the inboard and outboard saddle whips.

Probe fueling system: This system has been developed to reduce fueling time by eliminating the need for connecting and disconnecting fuel lines. Its basic parts are a fueling probe at the delivery end of a 7-inch fueling hose and a probe receiver suspended between the bitter end of the span wire and the padeye on the receiving ship. The receiver is mounted on a swivel fitting and so is always lined up with the span wire and the probe.

Robb coupling: This is a combined quick-release coupling and valve used by some ships. It consists of a male end attached to the fueling manifold on the receiving ship, and a female end on the hose sent over by the delivering ship. A spring-loaded valve in the female end is held closed until a lever on the male end moves a cam and opens the valve.

Trunk refueling connection: Many old ships can use neither the probe nor Robb couplings. Such ships have an open trunk on deck, leading to the fuel tanks, and the delivering ship sends over a standard hose with a soft rubber hose, called a pig tail, on its end. The pig tail goes into the trunk, the hose is lashed in place and on signal the delivering ship commences pumping.

STANDARD TENSIONED REPLENISHMENT
ALONGSIDE METHOD (STREAM)

STREAM is actually not a single method of replenishment but several methods and rigging combinations. They can be broadly grouped under the headings missile STREAM and cargo STREAM. The missile method is a high-speed, automated, heavy-weather system of transferring uncrated missiles under precise, full-load control. Cargo STREAM in various modifications can transfer almost any cargo that can be transferred by conventional methods, and it can do it safer and faster.

VERTICAL REPLENISHMENT (VERTREP)

VERTREP uses a helicopter to transport solid cargo from the deck of an underway replenishment ship to the deck of the receiving ship. Vertical replenishment augments or, in some cases, replaces connected replenishment. It can be conducted with the receiving ship alongside during connected replenishment, though it can also be done over the horizon, anywhere within range. Range depends on the helicopter, flying conditions, and the load.

Cargo can be carried internally, but the preferred method is to sling it from a hook installed in the rescue hatch in the bottom of the cabin. Internal cargo is restricted to what can be handled by an internal winch with a capacity of 600 pounds. External cargo, depending on the helicopter and flying conditions, can be up to 7,000 pounds.

Almost any ship can be replenished by helo if she has a small open area for landing the cargo, a larger unobstructed area overhead in which the helo can hover, and unobstructed access to

the hover area. Ships are specified by class according to their fa- spiking
cilities for conducting VERTREP.

FAST AUTOMATIC SHUTTLE TRANSFER (FAST)

This is a completely mechanized system for transferring missiles from the hold of the delivery ship to the magazine of the
receiving ship. FAST can also be used to transfer conventional
cargo to frigates and aircraft carriers.

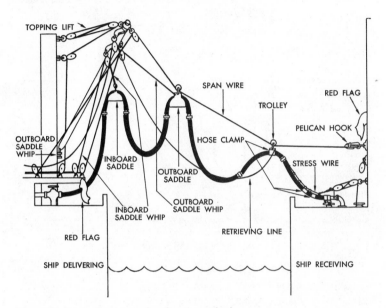

Figure 21–21 Fueling at sea by close-in method.

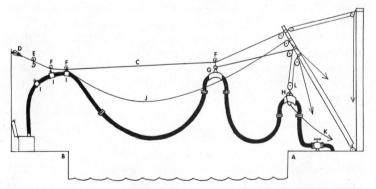

Figure 21–22 Fueling at sea by all-wire-span method: A. Delivering ship, B. Receiving ship, C. Wire span, D. Pelican hook, E. Free trolley, F. Trolley, G. Outboard saddle, H. Inboard saddle, I. Hose clamps, J. Retrieving wire, K. Wire
pendant, L. Wire saddle whip.

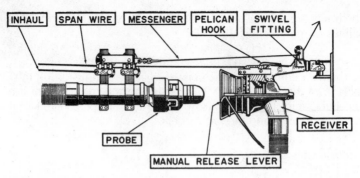

Figure 21–23 Details of fueling probe.

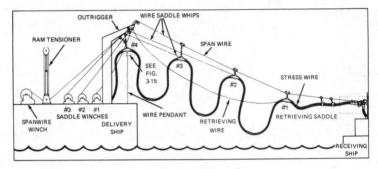

Figure 21–24 Fuel STREAM, single hose with probe.

COMMON FEATURES OF
REPLENISHMENT TECHNIQUES

Many features are common in all replenishment operations.
First, it is the responsibility of the officer in tactical command
(OTC) to select a suitable course and speed, taking into consideration the mission of the group and the condition of the sea. Generally, the delivering ship takes station, and the receiving ship
maneuvers to come alongside and adjusts course and speed as
necessary to maintain position during operations. When replenishing large aircraft carriers, however, replenishment ships may
complete the final phase of the approach, because of obstructions to the view from the bridge of the carrier during this phase
of the maneuver.

Except for gear actually rigged on the receiving ship, and the
distance line and burton whips, the delivering ship furnishes all
the equipment. There's one exception—when carriers and
cruisers are alongside replenishment ships and personnel are to
be transferred, the combatants must furnish and tend the manila
highline. All stations involved in the evolution are in communication with one another via sound-powered telephone line. This

includes a communication link between the bridges of both ships.

Persons assigned to replenishment stations must be thoroughly schooled in safety precautions and should be so well trained that they observe them almost automatically. Unfortunately, people tend to be careless, particularly when doing familiar tasks. For this reason, all personnel are rebriefed before each exercise. If you don't know what you're doing, or if you have a doubt as to where you're supposed to be, ask. It might save your life or the life of a shipmate.

22. Small Boats

The Navy uses thousands of boats, ranging from 9-foot dinghies to 135-foot landing craft. They're powered by diesels, outboard motors, gas turbines, and underwater jets. Most boats are built of aluminum, plastic, or fiberglass. Landing craft are built of steel. A few boats are still made of wood. The term "boat" refers to small craft that are limited in their use by size. Usually they are not capable of making regular, independent voyages of any length on the high seas.

Standard Boats

A standard boat is a small vessel carried aboard a ship to perform various ship's tasks and evolutions.

LANDING CRAFT

These boats, carried by various amphibious ships, are usually referred to by their designations rather than by full names. All landing craft are designed to carry troops, vehicles, or cargo from ship to shore under combat conditions, to unload, to retract from the beach, and to return to the ship. They are especially rugged, with powerful engines, and are armed.

Principal types are LCVPs (landing craft, vehicle and personnel); LCP(L)s (landing craft, personnel [large]); LCP(R)s (landing craft, personnel [ramped]); LCMs (landing craft, medium); and LCUs (landing craft, utility). The LCVPs and LCMs are generally used in today's fleet. A brief description of each follows.

The LCVP is a single-engine 36-foot boat with a hand-operated bow ramp. It is used for vehicles and personnel, although frequently it is used to land liberty parties, handle stores, and the like. When run up on the beach, the forward ramp is lowered, and vehicles and personnel disembark across the lowered ramp. It can carry 36 men, 4 tons of cargo, or a combination of jeeps, trucks, or other equipment.

There are two types of the LCM, both larger versions of the LCVP. They have twin engines, power-operated bow ramps and after structures with enginerooms, pilot houses, and storage compartment. The LCM-8, called Mike 8, is 73 feet long, has a 21-foot beam, and carries a heavy tank or 60 tons of cargo. The LCM-6, Mike 6, was produced in a variety of configurations for use in river warfare in Vietnam. One version, the monitor (MON)

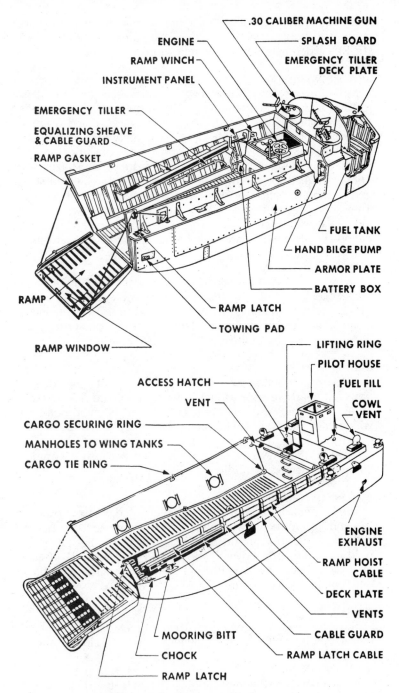

Figure 22–1 Landing craft LCVP (above) and LCM.

was fitted with heavy armor for shore bombardment and gunfire support to troops. Another version, the command control boat (CCB), carried extensive communications equipment.

MOTORBOATS (MBs)

MBs are fast decked-over boats with closed compartments forward and aft, and open cockpits amidships, where coxswains steer by wheel. The closed compartments are roofed over by rounded metal canopies. MBs are used mainly for carrying officers. Enlisted passengers, when aboard, occupy the forward cabin. Those designed for carrying officers are painted haze gray. Those assigned for use by commanding officers, chiefs of staff, and squadron, patrol, or division commanders are called gigs. They are also painted haze gray. MBs assigned to flag officers (admirals) are called barges. They have black hulls and white canopies. MBs are 35 and 40 feet long, and are diesel-powered.

MOTOR LAUNCHES (MLs)

These are heavy-duty, square-sterned boats. They are 40 and 50 feet long, diesel-powered, with removable seats (thwarts).

MLs are used for hauling liberty parties and stores. The engine is aft and the coxswain steers with a tiller bar from a platform called the coxswain's flat, at the very stern of the boat.

MOTOR WHALEBOATS (MWBs)

These round-bottomed, double-ended, 26-foot long, diesel-powered boats are used as lifeboats and shipboard utility boats. Many small ships use them as gigs and officers' motorboats, in which case they have metal or canvas canopies. MWBs are divided into forward, engine, and after compartments. Not very seaworthy, the MWB is never overloaded because it swamps easily. It is steered by a tiller.

PERSONNEL BOATS (PERS)

These are fast, V-bottomed, double-ended, diesel-powered 28- and 40-foot boats with enclosed passenger spaces, specifically designed to transport officers, although smaller types are used for shore party boats, lifeboats, and mail boats. A 40-foot boat will carry a maximum of 43 persons. Smaller types have only one closed compartment.

PUNTS

These are open square-enders, 10 or 14 feet long. They are either rowed or sculled, and are generally used by side cleaners.

UTILITY BOATS (UBs)

Standard
Boats

These boats, varying in length 22 to 65 feet, are generally used as cargo and personnel carriers or as heavy-duty work boats.

Figure 22–2 A whaleboat is lowered for a man-overboard drill.

Many have been modified for survey work, tending divers, and
minesweeping operations. A 50-foot UB will, under ideal
weather conditions, carry 146 men, plus crew. The largest UB, a
general-purpose work boat with a 24,000-pound carrying capacity, is steered from a pilot house.

WHERRIES

These are also open and are 12, 14 and 16 feet long with
square sterns. Wherries are rowed or may be powered by outboard motors.

Figure 22–3 Current Navy fleet boats.

A 26-foot whale boat

A 26-foot personnel boat

A 33-foot personnel boat

A 40-foot personnel boat

A 40-foot utility boat

A 50-foot utility boat

Special Boats

These boats are used by shore activities and are seldom seen in the fleet. They include line-handling boats, buoy boats, aircraft rescue boats, torpedo retrievers, and various patrol and picket boats.

LANDING CRAFT SWIMMER RECONNAISSANCE (LCSR)

This 23-ton, 52-foot fiberglass boat, powered by two 1,000-horsepower gas turbines, has a top speed of 38 knots. It is designed to speed into enemy territory and drop sea-air-land teams (SEALs), underwater demolition teams (UDTs), and other special operations personnel.

PATROL CRAFT, FAST (PCF)

This twin-diesel, 25-knot, radar-equipped patrol boat, with only a 4½-foot draft, was designed to operate, intercept, and search native craft in shallow rivers in Southeast Asia.

PATROL BOAT, RIVER (PBR)

This is a 31-foot, 25-knot twin-diesel boat with a fiberglass hull and water-jet pump propulsion that permits it to operate in 15 inches of water. The PBR is highly maneuverable and can reverse course in its own length. It carries radar, communications equipment, and machine guns.

PATROL AIR CUSHION VEHICLE (PACV)

This boat is the Navy's smallest fast craft. It rides about a foot above the surface on a cushion of air, at a speed of 60 knots over water and 40 over land.

FAST PATROL BOAT (PTF)

This is a modern version of the famous World War II PT boats. PTFs are 80 feet long, displace 82 tons and can make 45 knots with twin diesel engines. They're known as the "Nasty class."

MISCELLANEOUS BOATS

These include experimental, commercial, and obsolete types used when others are in short supply. Landing craft no longer fit for amphibious use, and others not classified as standard boats, along with small landing craft or special boats, are all in this category. Some miscellaneous boats are: the 9-foot dinghy, 12-foot punt, 22-foot motorboat, 26-, 30-, and 36-foot motor launch and a 33-foot plane rearming boat.

Boat Crews

Most boats have permanently assigned crews. The size varies, depending on type of boat, but it always includes the coxswain, engineer, bowhook, and sternhook. All must be qualified swimmers.

COXSWAIN

The coxswain and his crew are in charge of the lives and property of the passengers and equipment in their care. Subject to the orders of the OOD and the senior line officer embarked, a coxswain has full charge and is responsible for the appearance, safety, and efficient operation of the boat. The crew and passengers are required to fully cooperate with him. In fulfilling his responsibilities, the coxswain must be familiar with all details relating to the care and handling of his boat. Equally important, he must be able to instruct his crew in all aspects of general service and drills. He is also responsible for the appearance and behavior of his crew.

Coxswains and boat crews represent their ship and should, for that reason, take pride in their own appearance and in the "image" presented by their boat. The efficiency and smartness of a ship's boats and boat crew reflect the standards of their ship. Often, clean white uniforms can be a problem on some ships, but custom dictates that every day the ship's laundry wash and press a uniform for each member of the duty boats' crews. Ships' regulations frequently require that crew members wear sneakers. This is a safety factor, but it also keeps boats looking good.

The coxswain must always obey the rules of the road. Taxiing planes and ships underway do not maneuver as readily as small boats, so he should keep clear of them. He should avoid cutting

442

Figure 22–4 The coxswain and boat crew must take pride in their appearances, which reflect on the ship they represent.

close across the bow or stern of a moored or anchored ship, and should not pass close around the corner of a pier. And he should run dead slow when passing other boats alongside ships or landings, when in narrow or crowded waters, or when passing heavily loaded boats.

The coxswain is also responsible for recording all courses to and from all landings and the length of time on each course. Entries are kept in the compass course book for use in low-visibility conditions. In an LCVP or LCM, the coxswain sees that the engineer and deckhands perform their duties smartly. He also has authority over troops while they are being carried in the craft. He directs and controls the operation of the ramp. He is also responsible for the boat checks before getting underway and while securing.

In gigs, barges, and motorboats, the coxswain controls engine speed. In motor launches and motor whaleboats, he signals the engineer by the standard bell codes:

1 bell	Ahead slow.
2 bells	Engine idling, clutch out.
3 bells	Back slow.
4 bells	Full speed in direction propeller is turning.

ENGINEER

In an open boat the engineer sits abaft the power plant, facing forward. In a decked-over craft, he is stationed in the engine room. He must see that the engine is in good condition and ready to run. Only the engineer should work on the engine. In the LCVP his station is to starboard of the engine, and he operates the hand winch to raise or lower the ramp. In the LCM he stands by the port engine, which powers the ramp while it is operated.

BOWHOOK

The bowhook mans the bow boathook, painter, and the bow line. He also tends fenders and forward weather cloths (canvases spread for protection against the wind). In an open boat the bowhook usually sits on the starboard side, outboard, on the forward thwart. In storms he may move to the lee side. He faces the bow and serves as a lookout. If the boat is decked over, the bowhook stands on the starboard after deck facing forward.

The LCVP bowhook serves as forward lookout, releases the ramp latch when the coxswain directs, and handles fenders, bow line, and other lines; in combat, he mans the starboard machine gun.

On approaching the landing, the bowhook should be ready to spring ashore smartly with the painter, and take a turn on the nearest cleat. Also, he should be in the bow with his boathook when approaching a ship's gangway, ready to snag the boat line and make it fast. He should always have a fender ready to drop over at the proper spot if a bump is unavoidable.

STERNHOOK

The sternhook, likewise, should be ready to jump ashore at once with the stern fast. Frequently the stern is somewhat off the landing and occasionally the sternhook has to make quite a leap. (He should never try a leap that's going to take two jumps, though.) In an open boat the sternhook normally sits on the starboard side, outboard on the after thwart, facing aft. On decked-over craft he would probably stand on the port side on the after deck, facing forward. The LCVP sternhook serves as a signalman, besides tending the stern line, fenders, and other gear. He mans the port machine gun and assists the engineer in handling the winch when the ramp is raised. Duties and stations of the LCM crew are similar to those on the LCVP. The third deck hand, however, remains at the ramp during the run to the beach, while the other two man the guns.

BOAT OFFICER

During heavy weather and other times as deemed necessary an officer (sometimes a CPO) is assigned to each duty boat. A boat officer naturally has authority over the coxswain. He does not assume the coxswain's responsibilities nor relieve the coxswain of his normal duties. The situation is somewhat like the relationship between the OOD and the commanding officer on the bridge. The coxswain and boat officer are responsible for the boat and the safety and welfare of the crew and passengers.

Care of Boats and Equipment

A boat crew is responsible for the boat's care and all equipment. Proper maintenance greatly increases the service life of the boat and assures its operational readiness.

In wooden-hull boats every effort should be made to provide thorough ventilation and drainage, and to prevent fresh-water leakage. To this end, all ventilation terminals should be kept open.

Deck seams, especially in the plank sheer area, must be carefully calked and maintained. Decks must be sanded carefully to retain the proper camber and to eliminate low areas that might accumulate water. Hatches and deck plates should be opened during fair weather to increase air circulation. Wet dunnage, rope, and lifejackets in lockers and forepeak spaces should be removed and aired out.

Wooden boats should be washed down with salt water, not

fresh water. Varnished surfaces, chrome and brass fittings, and

Figure 22–5 Proper stowage of a motor launch requires secure lashings of the canvas cover.

windows should have salt removed by a sponge or chamois dipped in fresh water. On wooden boats, the stem, stern and bilge areas are purposely left unpainted. Wood preservative solutions should be used there.

Great care must be taken to prevent corrosion of steel-hulled boats. Proper upkeep of all paint and preservation coatings is necessary. The proper number of zincs must be installed in the

Care

stern area on steel (and some wooden hulls) to prevent electro-
lytic corrosion.

Maintenance and repair of these plastic and fiberglass hulls involve the same materials and techniques used on sports cars. Do
not use laminates, resins, or hardeners without fully reading instructions. They're in the training courses for hull maintenance
technicians.

Repair minor damage, tighten loose bolts, and fix or replace
leaking gaskets as soon as possible, to avoid more difficult repairs later. Secure all loose gear to avoid damage. Keep the boat
and its equipment free of dirt, corrosion, and accumulated
grease.

The propeller shaft alignment should be checked monthly, and
crankcase oil should be changed after every 100 hours of running. Gear housings, steering mechanisms, and other moving
parts must be well lubricated. Fenders should be placed between
boats when tied up. When a boat is hoisted out, the struts, propeller, sea suctions, and shaft bearings should be checked. Dog-
eared propellers or worn shaft bearings cause heavy vibration,
resulting in severe damage to hull and engine.

All rubber exhaust couplings should be checked for tightness
and condition. Batteries being charged must be ventilated to
avoid a hydrogen explosion.

Oil-soaked bottom planking on wooden boats can't be successfully painted or calked. In steel or plastic hulls, oil-soaked
bilges are a fire hazard. When draining or filling fuel tanks or engine crankcases, avoid spilling diesel fuel or engine oil.

Improper stowage of boats results in hogging of the keel, mis-
alignment of shafts, and distortion of the hull so the boat cannot
be operated. Boats must have a full-length keel rest for support
while in stowage. Overhang at the stem and stern should be supported by wooden blocking and wedges. Chocks should be located opposite frames or bulkheads. Loads imposed by gripe
pads on a hull should be distributed over as wide an area as possible to prevent hull damage. Take-up devices on the gripes
should be marked at the limit of tightening required, and that
limit should not be exceeded.

Boat Markings, Identification

The national ensign is displayed from Navy boats when:

Underway during daylight in a foreign port.
Ships are required to be dressed or full dressed.
Going alongside a foreign vessel.
An officer or official is embarked on an official occasion.

A flag or general officer, a unit commander, a commanding officer, or a chief of staff is embarked in a boat of his command or in one assigned to his personal use, and is in uniform.

Prescribed by the senior officer present (SOP). Since small boats are a part of a vessel, they follow the motions of the parent ship regarding the half-masting of colors.

PERSONAL FLAGS, PENNANTS, AND BOW INSIGNIA

When embarked in a Navy boat on official occasions, an officer in command (or a chief of staff when acting for him) displays from the bow of the boat his personal flag or command pennant —or, if not entitled to either, a commission pennant. An officer entitled to display a personal flag or command pennant may display a minature of his flag or pennant near the coxswain's station when embarked on any unofficial occasion.

In a boat assigned to the personal use of a flag or general officer, unit commander, chief of staff, or commanding officer, on which a civil official is embarked, these flagstaff insignia are fitted at the peak:

Spread eagle: For an official whose authorized salute is 19 or more guns (Secretaries of the Navy, Army, Air Force, and above).

Halberd: For flag and general officers whose official salute is fewer than 19 guns and for civil official whose salute is 11 or more, but fewer than 19 guns (Assistant Secretaries of Defense down to and including consul generals).

Ball: For an officer of the grade or relative grade of captain in the Navy and for a career minister, a counselor, or first secretary of an embassy, legation, or consul.

Star: For an officer of the grade or relative grade of commander in the Navy.

Flat truck: For an officer below the grade or relative grade of commander in the Navy and for a civil official not listed in this section, for whom honors are prescribed for an official visit.

The head of the spread eagle and cutting edges of the halberd must face forward. The points of the star must face fore and aft.

Barges are marked with chrome stars on the bow, arranged as on the admiral's flag. The official abbreviated title of the flag officer's command appears on the stern in gold leaf decal letters— CINCPACFLT, for example. On gigs assigned for the personal use of unit commanders not of flag rank, the insignia is a broad or burgee replica of the command pennant with the squadron or division numbers superimposed. The official abbreviated title of the command appears on the stern in gold leaf letters, such as DESRON NINE.

The gig for a chief of staff not of flag rank is marked with the official abbreviated title of the command in chrome letters, with an arrow running through the letters. Other boats assigned for staff use have brass letters but no arrows. Boats assigned to commanding officers of ships are marked on the bow with the ship type or name, and the ship's hull number in chrome letters and numerals; there is a chrome arrow running fore and aft through the markings. On officers' boats the arrow is omitted. Letters are brass. The ship's full name, abbreviated name, or initials may be used instead of the ship's type designation. An assigned boat number is sometimes used instead of the ship's hull number.

Amphibious ships' boats carry identification markings on their sterns and transoms, consisting of the ship-type abbreviation (KA, PD, LSD, etc), the hull number, and the boat's shipboard number. Landing craft assigned to amphibious ships, except for LST boats, also carry a two-letter abbreviation of the ships' name on the bow ramp. LCVPs assigned to LSTs carry the hull number of the parent ship on the bow ramp.

Other ships' boats are marked on the bow with either the ship's type and name or initials, followed by a dash and the boat number; for example, ENTERPRISE-1. These markings also appear on the stern of all boats, except whaleboats. Letters and numbers are brass, painted black. Numerals are painted on miscellaneous small boats such as line-handling boats, punts, and wherries.

Boat Equipment

Every Navy boat in active service is required to have a complete outfit of equipment necessary to meet an ordinary situation. Formerly, these outfits were issued with the boat, but now it is necessary to requisition part of the outfit. The coordinated shipboard allowance list (COSAL) lists all items allowed for each boat. Items for a 26-foot motor whaleboat, for instance, would consist of an anchor, bucket, life rings, fenders, grapnel hook, boathook, anchor line, grapnel line, bow painter, stern fast, and a portable fire extinguisher.

When a boat is turned in, her outfit also must be turned in, unless the boat is to be replaced by another of the same type. In that event, the outfit is retained on board. If a boat is to be replaced by one of a different type, the only items that may be retained are those allowed for the new boat.

HOISTING AND LAUNCHING BOATS

The process of hoisting and lowering boats with a crane is fairly simple. It entails handling the slings by the safety runner. The safety runner, a short wire pendant, is attached to the bill of the hook on a boat crane and is connected to a tripping line. A pull on the tripping line causes the safety runner to dump the ring of the boat slings off the hook.

When a boat comes alongside an underway ship to be hoisted in, she first secures the end of the sea painter—a long, strong

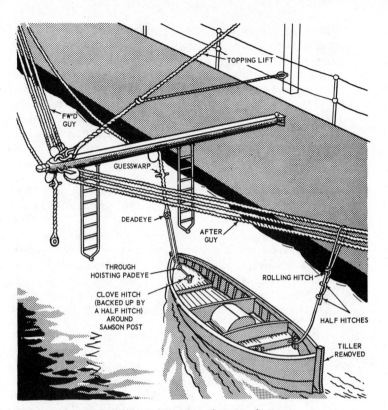

FW'D
GUY

TOPPING LIFT

GUESSWARP

DEADEYE

AFTER
GUY

THROUGH
HOISTING PADEYE

ROLLING HITCH

CLOVE HITCH
(BACKED UP BY
A HALF HITCH)
AROUND
SAMSON POST

HALF HITCHES

TILLER
REMOVED

Figure 22–6 The proper way of securing a boat at a boom.

manila line that hangs over the side of the ship and is forward of the spot where the boat will be hoisted. The shipboard end of the line is bent securely to a cleat or a set of bitts. The boat end is lowered by a light line and tied to the inboard end of the forward thwart or on an inboard cleat.

The sea painter is never bent to the boat's stern nor to the side of the bow away from the ship. If it is, when the boat rides to the painter she will dive against the ship's side and perhaps capsize. It is also important that the boat be driven ahead and allowed to drop back on the sea painter in order to be exactly under the crane before lifting. Otherwise, she may broach to and capsize as she starts to leave the water.

Once she rides to the painter, her engine is secured and the slings are attached. Steadying lines are secured to the cleats on the outboard side of the boat and brought back on deck to hold the boat steady as she rises. The bowhooks and sternhooks must fend her off the side. When the boat is in the air, the plugs should be removed so the bilges will drain before the boat reaches the deck.

Hoisting boats with davits is somewhat more complicated than lifting them with a crane. In using a davit, the boat is attached to the sea painter in the same manner as with a crane—particularly if the ship has headway, and must therefore take the same precautions against broaching to when the boat is lifted. The lower block of the forward fall is slacked down to the bowhook first, and is always attached before the after block. Before he hooks on, the bowhook must rotate the block until all the twists are out of the falls. Otherwise a dangerous jam will occur as the blocks draw together. Once the forward block is hooked on (hook pointing aft), and the slack in the falls is taken up, the sternhook removes the twists in the after fall and attaches the after block (hook pointing forward). Both then stand by to hold the releasing hooks by their lanyards.

Lifelines from the span are lowered to the boat, and each man aboard must keep one of them in hand as she rises, to be ready in any emergency. Frapping lines are passed around the falls. Then the order "set taut" is given. With this order, power is applied to the hauling part of the falls—either by man-hauling or winches. When the falls are taut and the boat is just about to rise, the boatswain's mate in charge sings out: "Vast heaving." Heaving is stopped while he checks everything. When satisfied, he calls out, "Hoist away," and the steady heave up begins.

When the boat is high enough to swing in, the order "vast heaving" is given again, and heaving stops. Men in the boat now come aboard. The falls are held taut while the stoppers are passed. These short lines, usually braided, are called rattail stoppers; they are fastened to strong points on the davits, above the cleats where the falls are to be belayed (fastened).

A rolling hitch is passed around the fall; a short distance above that, a half hitch. Spiral turns then are taken in the reverse direction, and the end of the stopper joined securely to the fall by hand.

When all stoppers are passed, the order "walk back" is given. If the falls are hoisted by hand, the men holding them walk back slowly, and the stoppers gradually take up the strain. If the falls are catheads or capstans, they are slackened by slowly working the turns back so as to slacken the lines. No turns are thrown off, because it is possible for a stopper to slip, resulting in the boat dropping.

When the BM is satisfied that the stoppers have taken hold, he orders, "Up behind," which means to run back the slack. Until the falls are belayed on the cleats, only the stoppers are holding up the boat. Men at catheads or capstans rapidly throw off their turns, grab up a handful of slack, and run with it toward the cleat.

The next order is, "Belay!" which means the boat falls are secured on a cleat. Because the boat must be lowered from the cleat, the falls must be belayed in such a way as to make the lowering without dropping the boat. For belaying, two round turns and several figure-eights are taken.

Before swinging out a boat to be lowered, you first must make sure that the plugs are in. With quadrantal (quarter of a circle) davits, your falls must be good and taut; otherwise your boat won't lift off the chocks. With any type of davit, the falls must be belayed securely. Each man in the boat must wear his lifejacket and must have a lifeline in hand. Run your sea painter outboard of everything on the ship, to the ship side of the bow, and belay with a toggle, so you can let it go without difficulty. If there are any preventer wires on the falls, they must be released before you start to swing out. After swinging out over the water, pass the frapping lines. Gripes must be let go, and the hinged half of the chocks must be dropped on boats' quadrantal davits.

Only experienced sailors should be stationed at the cleats to slack the falls. Slowly and carefully, they take off all but the two round turns. At "Lower away!" they carefully start to slack, making sure they don't allow the hauling part to ride off the cleat. The boatswain's mate watches to keep the boat level, or slightly by the stern, and, if one end starts to get ahead of the other, orders: "Hold her forward (aft)!" Keep your eye on the BM, and be sure you know which end of the boat you are lowering.

When the boat reaches the water and tows to the painter, the order "Up behind!" is given, and the falls are thrown off the cleats. In releasing, the after block is always unhooked first. The boat's engine is started while the boat is in the air, but the clutch is never engaged until the falls are unhooked and hauled clear. Before starting ahead, take care that no trailing lines are astern that might foul the screw. When the boat runs ahead and the painter slackens, it is thrown off by pulling out the toggle. The sea painter is hauled back to the ship by the light line attached to it.

TYPES OF DAVITS

Radial davits, sometimes called round-bar davits, usually are used for motor whaleboats. When the boat is stowed, the davit arms point inboard. To get the boat out to the lowering position, it is necessary to hoist the boat high enough for the keel to clear the forward davit. Next, it must be swung out, forward, and then aft to the lowering position.

Quadrantal davits are used chiefly on merchant vessels. The boat rests in chocks under the davits. Outboard sections of the chocks usually are hinged so that, once the weight of the boat is off them, they can be laid flat on the deck, making it unnecessary to raise the boat high enough to clear them in their normal positions. Turning the crank that operates the worm gear raises the

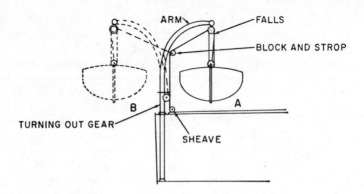

Figure 22–7 Types of davits include radial or round-bar.

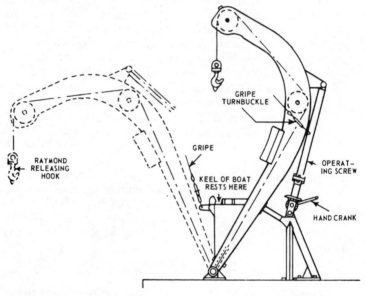

Figure 22–8 The crescent davit.

boat high enough to clear the flattened chocks. Continued crank-
ing racks the boat out to the lowering position. The boat is
lowered away, as with the radial davit.

Crescent davits and other makes of hinging-out davits (which
have largely superseded radial and quadrantal mechanical
davits) have been used in all classes of Navy vessels, including
combatant ships. They generally handle boats that are 26 to 30
feet long and weigh up to 13,500 pounds. In this type of davit,
the arms usually are crescent-shaped and are racked in and out
by means of a sheath screw.

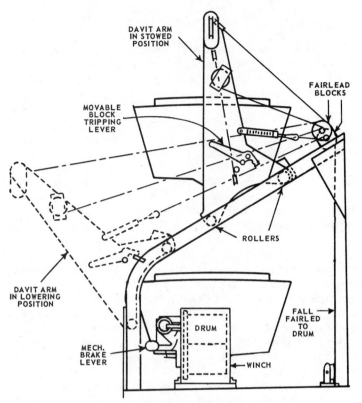

DAVIT ARM
IN STOWED
POSITION

FAIRLEAD
BLOCKS

MOVABLE
BLOCK
TRIPPING
LEVER

ROLLERS

DAVIT ARM
IN LOWERING
POSITION

FALL
FAIRLED
TO
DRUM

DRUM

MECH.
BRAKE
LEVER

WINCH

Figure 22-9 The Welin trackway gravity davit.

Gravity davits are usually found on newer ships. They are the trackway pivoted boom or the double-linked pivoted type. Gravity davits that handle the larger boats, such as LCPLs and LCVPs, are generally equipped with a strongback between the davit arms. An electric-powered two-drum winch, located near the davits, provides power to hoist the boats. Cranks can be attached to the winch for manual hoisting. Power is not required to lower boats. The boat lowers by gravity as it is suspended from the falls, and the descent speed is controlled with the boat davit winch manual brake.

Several types of gravity davits are used. Depending on design, a pair of modified davits may handle one to four boats and are designated as single-, double-, or quadruple-bank davits. These are used mainly with amphibious craft.

A single-arm gravity davit, being introduced on DD, CGN and FFG type ships, will allow superior boat-handling operations. It also allows rescue-boat handling in higher sea states than are considered safe with conventional double-arm davits.

Ready Lifeboat

Regulations require that a ship at sea have at least one boat rigged and ready to be lowered for use as a lifeboat. The ship's boat bill (discussed on page 342) states the exact specifications which the lifeboat must meet, and the equipment that must be in it.

At the start of each watch, the lifeboat coxswain musters the crew, checks the boat and gear, has the engine tested, and reports to the OOD. On some ships the crew always remains near the boat. The boatswain's mate of the watch (BMOW) is in charge of lowering the boat. When a man goes overboard and a boat must be used to recover him, everyone must know the recovery procedures. This is vital because a man can only last a few minutes overboard. Don't lose time trying to get the boat in the water.

The ready lifeboat, usually a motor whaleboat, is secured for sea in the davits, and swung out ready for lowering. As a safety measure, wire preventers connected to the davit heads may be attached to the boat's hoisting eyes. Preventers must be removed before lowering. The lifeboat has her sea painter already rigged and the lifelines from the span are coiled down clear for running. To keep the boat from swinging, it is held against a pair of soft paddings on a heavy spar called a strongback, securely lashed between the davits.

The boat also should have a full tank of fuel, and the lubricating oil reservoir should be full. An extra can of oil should be onboard. The bilge should be clean and dry and the boat plug in place. Lifejackets should be ready nearby or in the boat so the crew may don them before lowering away.

23. Navigation and Electronics

All navigational methods depend on exact measurement of distance, speed, direction, and time. Marine navigation also sometimes requires measurements of water depth; these are called soundings. The final result, in any method, is a position or location—usually called a "fix."

Location

The location of any place on earth is determined by its latitude, the distance north or south of the equator, and longitude, the distance east or west of the prime meridian, which runs from the North Pole to the South Pole through Greenwich, England. Latitude is measured in degrees north or south of the equator, with 0 degrees at the equator and 90 degrees at each pole. Longitude is measured in degrees from Greenwich—180 degrees east and 180 degrees west. The place where 180 degrees east and 180 degrees west meet, halfway around the world from Greenwich, is called the International Date Line.

CHARTS

Charts, which show ocean areas and shore lines, and maps, which show land masses, are marked off in parallels of latitude (degrees north or south) and meridians of longitude (degrees east or west). Each degree (°) is divided into 60 minutes (') or nautical miles. A nautical mile measured along the equator is 6076.11549 feet, or roughly 2,000 yards. Any position at sea or place ashore is stated in degrees and minutes north or south and east or west. For example, Cleveland, Ohio, is 41° 30'N. and 81° 45'W.; the island of Funafuti in the South Pacific is 8° 30'S. and 178° 30'E.

DISTANCE

Distance at sea is measured in nautical miles. A nautical mile is one minute, or one sixtieth of a degree. Speed is measured in knots, a seaman's term meaning nautical miles per hour. A ship makes 27 knots, never 27 knots per hour. (In electronic navigation, distance measured by radar is called "range.")

DIRECTION

This is determined by a compass, either magnetic or gyro. The four cardinal directions are north, east, south, and west. All di-

rections are measured from north on a system of 360 degrees, in
which east is 090 degrees, south is 180 degrees, west is 270 degrees, and north is either 360 or 000 degrees, whichever designation is most convenient.

TIME

Two kinds of time are used at sea: local apparent time as determined by the passage of the sun across the sky, and Greenwich
mean time (GMT), which is mean time (time based on the sun) at
the prime meridian in Greenwich, England. All standard time is
also measured from that meridian. GMT is used for observations
in celestial navigation and is shown by chronometers—highly
accurate clocks. (GMT is also used in communications, as described in Chapter 24.)

Each standard time zone bears a number, a plus (+) or minus
(−) sign, and a letter. The number refers to the difference in time
between that zone and the Greenwich zone. The sign tells
whether the time is earlier (+) or later (−) than the Greenwich
zone time; the sign shows how to find Greenwich time from the
standard time in any zone. If a ship is in zone + 4, and the clock
showed the time to be 1300 aboard the ship, it would be 1300
+ 4 or 1700 in the Greenwich zone. In radio traffic, when the
time of origin of a dispatch is expressed in GMT, that fact is indicated by stating "ZULU" after the date-time group. (For example, 1700 ZULU.)

SOUNDINGS

Soundings are made with an electronic device, usually a fathometer. A ship is said to be "on soundings" when she is in water
shallow enough that a lead line can be used to determine depth.
Deep-sea soundings will indicate when a ship crosses a submarine canyon, sea mount, or other bottom feature. When a
chart shows bottom contours, soundings may be used to establish an actual fix.

Methods of Determining Position

PILOTING

This is the oldest method of navigation, used before men ven-
tured beyond sight of land and across the seas. It is a method of
determining position and directing the movements of a ship by
reference to landmarks, navigational aids, or soundings. Ordinarily, piloting is used as a primary means of navigation when
entering or leaving port and in coastal navigation. It may be used
at sea when the bottom contour makes it possible to establish a
fix. In piloting, the navigator obtains warnings of danger, fixes
the position frequently and accurately and determines the proper
course of immediate action.

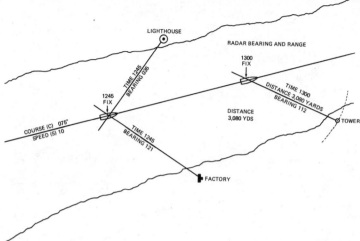

LIGHTHOUSE

RADAR BEARING AND RANGE

1300
FIX

TIME 1245
BEARING 035

1245
FIX

DISTANCE 3,080 YARDS
TIME 1300
BEARING 112

COURSE (C) 075°
SPEED (S) 10

DISTANCE
3,080 YDS

TIME 1245
BEARING 121

TOWER

FACTORY

Figure 23–1 Fixes established by gyro compass (1245 Fix) and by radar bearing and range (1300 Fix).

Piloting aids: Navigational aids used in piloting include: the compass, used to determine ship's heading; the bearing circle, used to determine direction of objects on land, buoys, ships, etc.; charts, which depict the outlines of the shore, as well as the positions of land and seamarks and the standard depths of water at many locations; and buoys and navigational lights. Also used is the echo sounder or fathometer, which determines the depth of the water under the ship's keel by measuring the time it takes a sound signal to reach the bottom and return to the ship; and the lead line, which determines the depth of the water by actual physical measurement.

Special publications: Some special publications are also used: *Coast Pilot* and *Sailing Directions* are books containing detailed information on coastal waters, harbor facilities, etc., for use in conjunction with charts of the area. Tide tables, which predict the times and heights of the tide, and current tables, which predict the times, direction of flow, and velocity of tides are also used.

Bearing, range, and fixes: In clear weather piloting, the ship's position is usually determined by taking simultaneous gyrocompass bearings on two objects of fixed position. Radar may be used for ranges and bearings.

Figure 23–1 shows how the ship's position can be fixed by simultaneous visual bearings of two known objects, and also by a radar bearing and range on a single object, which is plotted or drawn on the chart. The lighthouse bears 035°, below the line as shown.

457

Methods

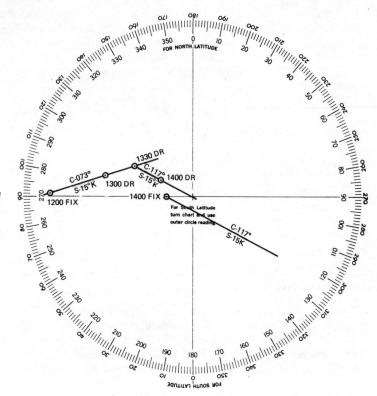

l

Figure 23–2 Dead-reckoning plot, showing 1200 fix, 1300, 1330, and 1400 DR position. At 1400 a new fix is taken and the ship's position on the chart is changed accordingly.

The intersection of these two lines represents the actual position of the ship on the chart. A position that has been accurately established is called a fix, and is so labeled, together with the time that it was established.

A line drawn from the fix in the direction in which the ship is steaming is called a course line. The direction or course is labeled above the line; speed in knots is indicated below the line.

The manner of obtaining a fix by radar bearing and range or distance is also shown in Figure 23–1. Radar gives a bearing of 112° on a prominent tower and a range of 3,080 yards. The navigator again plots a line from the tower, uses dividers to measure 3,080 yards on the chart scale, then puts one leg of the dividers on the tower location on the chart, and marks the bearing line with the other end. This establishes the fix by bearing and range.

DEAD RECKONING (DR)

This is a method of navigation in which position is determined by plotting the direction and distance traveled from a known point of departure. A ship underway is moving through water, which is a very unstable element. She might leave point A, steer an exact course according to the true bearing between point A and point B, and still wind up a long distance from B, depending on how much leeway she makes. Likewise, estimating the distance traveled seldom produces an exact result. The DR position, therefore, is only an estimated position, calculated from values that rarely are exact. A fix, on the other hand, is a relatively exact location derived from the intersection of two or more lines of position (LOPs). A DR position is not a fix, but is a calculation from the last fix obtained.

Figure 23–2 shows the DR plot on the chart. The 1200 fix is plotted and labeled. A course line is drawn from the fix on the ship's course of 073°. Course is labeled above the line and the speed of 15 knots below the line. At 15 knots, in one hour the ship will cover one-quarter degree, or 15 minutes on the chart. To determine the 1300 position, the navigator uses dividers to measure 15 minutes of latitude on the vertical latitude scale printed on either side of the chart. (One degree of latitude equals 60 nautical miles; one minute of latitude equals one mile.) This distance is marked off from the fix along the course line, and the resulting spot is labeled "1300 DR," as shown.

459

The captain orders the OOD to put the ship on a new course, 117° at 1330. Using his dividers, the navigator marks a spot seven and one-half miles from the 1300 DR position along the direction in which the ship is steaming, labels it "1300 DR," and draws in a new course line in the direction of 117°.

Figure 23–3 One of the miniaturized components used in electronic navigation.

When properly maintained, the DR plot permits the ship's approximate position to be quickly determined.

ELECTRONIC NAVIGATION

Basically, electronic navigation is a form of piloting, the branch of navigation in which a ship's position is obtained by refering to visible objects on the earth whose locations are known. This reference usually consists of bearing and distance of a single object, cross bearings on two or more objects, or two bearings on the same object with an interval between them. Position is determined in electronic navigation much as it is in piloting, but there is one important difference: the objects by which a ship's position is determined need not be visible from the ship. Instead, bearings (and sometimes ranges) of the objects are obtained by electronic means, usually in the form of radio waves.

There are currently a half-dozen different systems in operation throughout the Navy, and many other electronic navigation systems that are available but less widely used.

Loran systems: There are currently two types of loran (long-range navigation) systems in use today: loran-A and loran-C. They both provide a means of obtaining accurate navigational positions from pulsed radio signals radiating from land-based transmitters. Depending on the mode of loran operations, atmospheric conditions, and the time of day or night—which affect radio frequency transmission—fixes are possible at a distance up to 1,400 nautical miles from the transmitting station.

The loran-A system depends on two transmitting stations, a master and a secondary (called a slave), to give a signal line position. The master station starts the cycle of transmission by sending out a pulse of radio energy that is radiated in all directions. After traveling over the distance between the two transmitting stations (known as the baseline), the pulse arrives at the secondary. The time of its arrival is used by the secondary as a reference for the transmission of its own signal. After the signal is transmitted, the entire cycle is repeated constantly at the same definite time intervals. By measuring the time difference between the transmitted pulses of the master station and slave station, ship position can be determined.

Under almost any kind of weather conditions, lines of position by loran-A are as accurate as those obtained from good celestial observations. The U.S. Coast Guard operates approximately 39 loran-A transmitting stations throughout the world. Other nations operate 40 additional stations.

Loran-C is a pulsed low-frequency (LF) radio navigation system that derives its high accuracy from time-difference measurements of the pulsed signals, and from the inherent stability of low-frequency propagation. Ranges of 800–1,200 nautical miles

Figure 23–4 An electronics expert searches for a bad circuit in the wiring used for satellite navigation.

are typical, depending on transmitter power, receiver sensitivity, and losses over the signal path. Loran-C chains are composed of a master transmitting station, two or more secondary transmitting stations, and, if necessary, system area monitor (SAM) stations.

The transmitting stations are so located that the signals from the master and at least two secondary stations can be received throughout the desired coverage area. Hyperbolic navigation systems operate on the principle that the difference in time of arrival of signals from two stations, observed at a point in the coverage area, is a measure of the difference in distance from the point of observation to each of the stations.

The Coast Guard is currently responsible for the operation of seven loran-C chains using 27 transmitting stations to provide coverage over 16 million square miles. Thirteen additional stations are planned to complete the coverage.

Satellite navigation: The navigational satellite system is a global all-weather system. Using it, navigators in ships on or below the ocean surface can obtain a fix to within a fraction of a mile, night or day, in all parts of the world. Although it can be used worldwide, fix information is available only during a satellite pass, which may occur every 45 to 150 minutes. Passes occur more often at high latitudes than on the equator.

The system operates on the doppler principle. Doppler can best be described by example. Suppose, as you stand at a railroad crossing, a train approaches with its whistle sounding. As the train comes nearer, the pitch of the whistle becomes higher until the train passes you. At the time the pitch drops and, as the train goes off into the distance, the pitch of the whistle gradually grows lower. The signal from a satellite approaching and passing over a ship likewise has a change in pitch, or a doppler shift. Analysis of the doppler shift enables the navigator to calculate his position relative to the satellite so that the navigator can take the doppler information, along with the satellite position information, and determine the ship's position.

Shoran: Shoran (short-range navigation) was developed during World War II to allow accurate bombing through undercast. Employed principally in surveying, shoran uses ranges rather than bearings, and is accurate to within 50 feet. Signals from a ship's radar automatically trigger two fixed transmitters ashore. The signals emitted by these transmitters are in the form of pips and are received simultaneously. You measure the ranges of these pips in the same manner as you would any contact and then plot the ranges on a chart. The point where these two ranges intersect is your position.

Omega: Omega is an expansion of loran. It is a very low-frequency (VLF) navigation system which enables navigators to obtain reliable positions comparable in accuracy to loran-A, on a worldwide and nearly continuous basis. When omega is in full operation it will have eight stations, located in North Dakota, Liberia, Norway, Argentina, Ile de la Reunion (in the Indian Ocean), Hawaii, Japan, and Australia. With the transmission stations so situated, the extremely long-range VLF signals will ensure that the user will be able to receive at least three stations. Depending upon his location, he may be able to receive as many as six stations.

The measurement performed by the receiver is a comparison of the relative phase angles of the VLF signals. The navigator can determine the line of position by any convenient pair of transmitting stations, and then cross it with one or more lines derived from another pair of transmitting stations.

Radar: Radar was developed in World War II as a means for detecting and ranging on targets in warfare, but it has been developed into a valuable electronic navigational aid. Its great advantage over loran is that it does not require shore transmitting stations. Its disadvantage is that its maximum range, for a surface vessel, is limited to slightly more than the line-of-sight (LOS) of the horizon. Despite its limitations, radar remains an important navigational aid. The Navy now uses several types of radar, designed especially for surface search, air search, fire control, missile guidance, and airborne early warning.

Radar involves sending out a narrow beam of very high frequency (VHF) radio waves (from 60 to 4,000 cycles per second). Upon striking any object in their path, they are reflected and return to the transmitter as "echoes." Exact measurement of the time of return of each—based on the fact that radio waves travel at 186,000 miles a second—gives the distance (or range) to the object or target. The bearing of a target can be determined by the

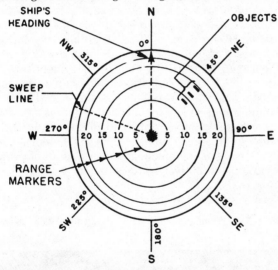

Figure 23–5 Drawing of a PPI presentation. The ship is at the center of the scope and the sweep has just passed 045 degrees.

position of the antenna, which is indicated by a bright line on an oscilloscope. Targets appear as bright spots of light, called "pips."

The scope may be marked with a scale of miles, yards, or degrees, or with a combination of miles and yards, so that from the position of a single echo on the scope, an observer can tell the range, bearing, and, depending on the kind of equipment used, the altitude of the target.

The form of oscilloscope most often used is the plan position indicator (PPI; Figure 23–5), which provides a bird's-eye view of the area covered by the radar, with your ship in the center. The

sweep originates in the center of the scope and moves to the outside edge. This straight-line sweep is synchronized with the radar
antenna and rotates 360°. This type of scope shows surface targets, and navigational features such as islands, lighthouses, and
buoys.

Radars designed to track aircraft also show altitude, by use of a
range height indicator (RHI) presentation. The RHI scope cannot
show range, so it has to be used with a PPI.

Sonar: Sonar uses the pulsed transmission of sound waves in
water to detect and track a target, and to determine the range and
bearing of underwater objects. Sonar is similar in principle to
radar. Where radar employs electromagnetic waves traveling
through space, sonar uses sound waves traveling through water.
Sonar can be used to detect submarines and surface ships, to
measure depth, and to serve as an aid to navigation.

Sonar equipment is classed as active or passive. Active sonar
involves transmission of sound energy into the water; the range
and bearing of the target will be determined by the reflected
sound waves. Passive sonar depends on the sound originating
from the target, such as propeller or machinery noise. Active
sonar normally is used on surface ships and is a transmitting
(called "pinging") and receiving system. The device used to
transmit the sound energy in an active system is a transducer; it
contains a diaphragm that is made to vibrate at a frequency corresponding to an applied voltage from the system's transmitter.
The vibration of the diaphragm produces a series of compression
waves. Compression waves, propagated through water, are
sound waves.

The wave generated by the transducer moves outward in a cir-

**Figure 23–6 RHI presentation, showing an aircraft about 25 miles out from the
tracking ship.**

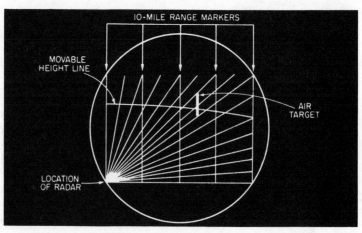

cle. When it strikes an object, a small portion is reflected back to the transducer, just as in radar. The transducer converts outgoing electrical signals from the transmitter into sound waves and converts the returning sound echoes to electrical signals for use by the receiver. The receiver amplifies the extremely small signals resulting from the sound echo and converts them to signals which can be heard over a loudspeaker or headphone.

Passive sonar is used primarily by submarines which must remain undetected. These subs transmit no sound, but depend entirely on the target's noise as the sound source. The passive sonar designed for modern submarines is so efficient that a skilled operator can identify and track targets miles away.

In active sonar systems the signals are presented by azimuth-range indicators, which give a visual indication of target bearing, the range, and the audio response from targets.

Other systems: Several other electronic navigation systems that are available but less widely used are decca, consol, star tracker, SINS, and NAVDAC.

Decca is a British system, which, like loran, requires special receiving equipment. The receiving unit measures phase differences between a master and a group of three slave stations, all of which are transmitting at different frequencies. Fixes are obtained by plotting the phase differences directly on a chart printed with decca hyperbolic lines.

Consol is a long-range, short-baseline system whose signals may be received by ordinary radio equipment. The signals consist of a series of dots and dashes, which are counted by the receiving operator.

Star tracker is an extremely sensitive optical telescope with radio or infrared components that calculate elevation (altitude) and azimuth date from celestial bodies, including the sun. The system may be used even during periods of poor visibility.

Ship's internal navigation system (*SINS*) is, at present, chiefly a navigational aid for submarines and aircraft carriers. Eventually it will be operational on most surface vessels. SINS provides ships with an accurate and continuous dead-reckoning position. Because SINS is a self-contained system, it is a valuable wartime navigational aid. When the loran and similar systems are knocked out, SINS remains operable. SINS operates on an arrangement of gyros and accelerometers.

NAVDAC is among the most advanced navigational systems. NAVDAC (navigation data assimilation computer) combines, evaluates, and stores data received from navigational systems— for example, loran-C, SINS, and star tracker. In effect, it is a memory bank of highly accurate navigational data, capable of rejecting solutions of poor quality and accepting only those with a high degree of probable accuracy.

CELESTIAL NAVIGATION
Piloting, including its electronic phases, and dead reckoning compose that branch of navigation that determines position by reference to objects or localities on earth. Another branch, in which position is determined by reference to heavenly bodies—such as the sun, moon, stars, and planets—is called celestial navigation. An accurately measured and properly corrected altitude on any navigational body can give an accurate line of position.

This is the most widely used offshore navigation method. Observations, made with a sextant, involve measuring the altitude above the horizon of navigational stars or other bodies. These observations are called "sights." When the navigator and quartermaster take a sight, they are said to be "shooting a star."

Many of the navigational aids used in piloting are also used in celestial navigation. Some additional equipment is required, such as chronometers and sextants; these are discussed below. A DR plot is always maintained; on some ships this is done automatically by a dead reckoning tracer (DRT).

Instruments and Equipment

The following presentation lists and explains the basic functioning of the major instruments and equipment used in navigation.

SEXTANT

The sextant is a precision instrument that can measure angles in degrees, minutes, and seconds. Through a system of mirrors, the image of a star is brought down to the horizon; the scales allow the navigator to read the exact angle between the actual star and the horizon. This angle is called the altitude and is the basis of all celestial navigation.

In establishing a position by star sight, several observations are taken. Each one is reduced or worked out by means of the Nautical Almanac and the reduction tables, to produce a single line of position—a line that passes through the ship's position. The ship's location is represented by the point at which the various lines of position intersect on the chart. This is the ship's location at the time of observation and is marked "2000 posit," "0530 posit," etc.

STADIMETER

The stadimeter measures the distance of an object of known height, such as a masthead light, between heights of 50 to 200 feet, at distances of 200 to 10,000 yards. Like a sextant, the stadimeter measures an angle. The height of an object is set on a scale, and then the reflecting image is made to coincide with the actual direct image. The distance is read off another scale.

AZIMUTH CIRCLE AND BEARING CIRCLE

An azimuth circle is a metal ring which fits over a compass bowl. It measures bearings of objects on the surface of the earth, and azimuths (or bearings) of celestial bodies.

PLOTTING EQUIPMENT

Position plotting on a chart is usually done with a universal drafting machine, also called a parallel motion protractor (PMP), which is clamped to a chart table and allows both distance and bearing to be plotted at once. Sometimes a simple plastic protractor and straight edge is used.

CHRONOMETER

This is a highly accurate clock, mounted in a brass case, which is supported in gimbals in a wooden case, in order to counteract the ship's motion. The chronometers are kept in a cabinet in the chart room, usually on the centerline of the ship, where they are protected against shock and temperature changes. Chronometers are set to show GMT and they are wound every day at exactly the same time. Once a chronometer is started, it is never allowed to stop, and it is not reset while it is aboard ship. A record is kept of whether it is running fast or slow; however, a good chronometer will never deviate more than a hundredth of a second from its average daily rate. Chronometers are checked against radio time signals, which are broadcast all over the world. To do this, a quartermaster uses a comparing watch, or hack watch; he calls the process "getting a time tick." The exact GMT time, as determined by radio, is never used to change the chronometer, but only to show whether it is running fast or slow.

Celestial navigation requires an exact measure of time, since it is based on tables using GMT. The time of a celestial observation, anywhere in the world, must be converted to GMT before the navigator can work out his position.

467

MAGNETIC COMPASS

The magnetized compass needles align themselves with the earth's magnetic field and are fastened to either a disc or a cylinder marked with the cardinal points of the compass: North, East, South, and West. North, on the magnetic compass, points to the magnetic North Pole, which is several hundred miles from the geographic North Pole.

The card and needles are supported on a pivot. No matter how the ship, aircraft, or boat swings, the card is free to rotate until it has realigned itself to the magnetic north.

The moving parts are contained in a bowl or housing provided with a window through which the compass card may be seen. Ship's compasses usually have a flat glass top for all-around visibility and for taking bearings.

The lubber's line, a mark in the window of the compass or on the compass bowl, indicates the fore-and-aft line of the ship or boat (Figure 23–7).

The compass direction under the lubber's line tells the ship's heading. Attached to the binnacle—the stand in which the compass is housed—or nearby, is a "deviation card." It gives the deviation for various headings, in this form:

Ship's Heading (Magnetic)	Dev	Ship's Heading (Magnetic)	Dev	Ship's Heading (Magnetic)	Dev
000°(360°)	14°W	120°	15°E	240°	4°E
015°	10°W	135°	16°E	255°	1°W
030°	5°W	150°	12°E	270°	7°W
045°	1°W	165°	12°E	285°	12°W
060°	2°E	180°	13°E	300°	15°W
075°	5°E	195°	14°E	315°	19°W
090°	7°E	210°	12°E	330°	19°W
105°	9°E	225°	9°E	345°	17°W

Variation: This is the difference between geographic north and magnetic north (Figure 23–8). Variation for any given locality, together with the amount of yearly increase or decrease, is shown on the compass rose of the chart for that particular locality. Figure 23–9 shows a compass rose on a chart dated 1945, which indicates a 14° 45′ westerly variation in that area, increasing 1′ yearly.

To find the amount of variation in that same place, figure out how many years have passed since 1945 and multiply that number by the amount of yearly increase; then add the result to the variation in 1945. In this case the number should be added, because it is a yearly increase. If the chart showed a decrease, the result would be subtracted from the variation given for 1945. Variation remains the same for any heading of the ship at a given position.

Deviation: This error is caused by the magnetic effect of any metal near the compass. It is different for different headings of the ship. Periodically the navigator and quartermaster perform an operation called "swinging ship." The ship steams in a complete circle from 0° to 360°, and the amount of her compass deviation is noted at every 15°. The results are compiled in a deviation table that is kept near the compass. There is a similar table near the magnetic compass in every aircraft. *Compass error* for any

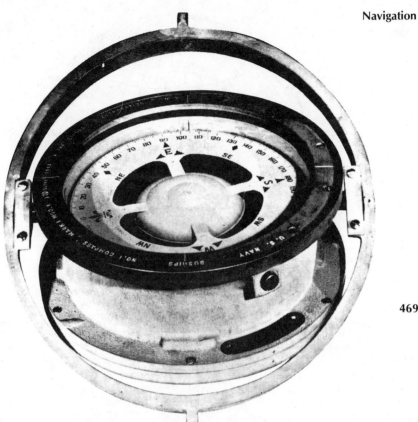

Figure 23–7 The lubber's line on the Navy's standard magnetic compass shows the heading as 104½ degrees.

compass is the combination of the variation of the locality and deviation of the ship's heading. In some cases these must be added; in other cases one is subtracted from the other, as explained above.

True course: This is the heading of the ship in degrees measured clockwise from true north.

Magnetic course: This course is the heading of the ship in degrees measured clockwise from magnetic north.

Compass course: The reading of a particular magnetic compass, that is, the course that the compass actually indicates, is called the compass course.

Correcting for compass error: Combining variation and deviation gives what is known as *magnetic compass error*. The course on which the ship is to head is the true course, worked out from the chart, on which only true courses and bearings are given. Given the true course, you must find the compass course

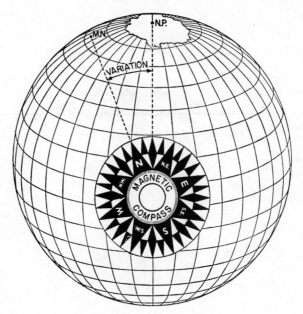

Figure 23–8 The diagram shows how variation affects the compass. The magnetic needle points to the magnetic north pole (MN) instead of the geographic
north pole (NP).

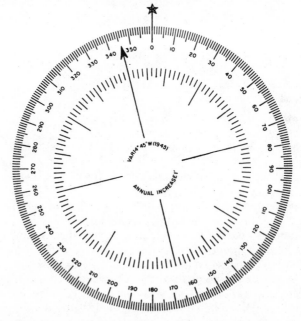

Figure 23–9 The compass rose shows a variation of 14 degrees, 45 minutes
west, the year observed (1945), and the annual increase (1).

that you must steer in order to make good the true course. Do this by applying variation and deviation to the true course. This is done by a simple rule, remembered as a nonsense statement: *Can Dead Men Vote Twice?*

In order to change from true to compass course, or vice versa, set up the columns as follows:

Can	Compass
Dead	Deviation
Men	Magnetic
Vote	Variation
Twice	True

Going up, or changing from true to compass, is called *uncorrecting*. Coming down, or changing from compass to true, is called *correcting*. Just remember this rule:

When correcting, add easterly error and subtract westerly error.

When uncorrecting, subtract easterly error and add westerly error.

All compass errors are either easterly or westerly; there are no northerly or southerly errors. To correct a compass course of 270° to the true course, first correct the deviation; then correct for variation. An example is given below. The deviation table described earlier shows that the deviation for 270° is 7° West. Assume that the chart shows the variation to be 12° East. Make a table as follows:

Compass	270°	Compass	270°
Deviation	7°W	Deviation	7°W
Magnetic		Magnetic	263°
Variation	12°E	Variation	12°E
True		True	275°
Total error		Total error	5°E

To find true course, the 7°W deviation is subtracted from the compass course of 270° (column two), which gives a magnetic course of 263°. The variation, 12°E, is then added to the magnetic course, giving the true course of 275°. The total compass error is 5°E, which is the difference between the 7°W and the 12°E.

But how do you decide whether to add or subtract the deviation or variation? Remember: when correcting—going from compass course to true course—add easterly errors and subtract westerly errors.

Note that true differs from magnetic by the amount of variation, and that magnetic differs from compass by the amount of deviation.

Uncorrecting: The process of finding the compass course from
the true course is called uncorrecting. Suppose that the given
true course is 180° and variation is 10°W.

Compass		Compass	176°
Deviation		Deviation	14°E
Magnetic	190°	Magnetic	190°
Variation	10°W	Variation	10°W
True	180°	True	180°
Total error		Total error	4°E

This is uncorrecting, so reverse the rule and add westerly variation, giving a magnetic course of 190°.

Refer to the deviation table previously discussed. Take the deviation nearest the heading you are on. In this case the nearest
deviation is 14°E, or that shown for 195°. Remember: when uncorrecting—going from true to compass—add westerly errors
and subtract easterly errors.

GYROCOMPASS (GYRO)

This instrument is essentially a heavy flywheel driven at high
speed by an electric motor and mounted on gimbals so that it is
free to move in all directions. It is usually located in a well-protected place below deck. Repeaters—compass cards electrically
connected to the gyrocompass and placed on the bridge and in
other parts of the ship—show the same readings as the master
gyrocompass.

Gyro error: The gyrocompass is not affected by variation or
deviation. The motion of the earth will cause the rotor to move so
that its axis lies in a north-south direction. For mechanical reasons and because of the vibrations of the ship, even the best gyrocompass will sometimes vary from true north. This gyro error is
rarely more than a few degrees, and normally it is constant over a
long period of time and on any heading of the ship.

Correcting for gyro error: Gyro error is determined by taking
an azimuth, or bearing, on a celestial body where the exact bearing can be determined. This error is applied every time the compass is used, and the rule for the magnetic compass is followed:
when *correcting*, add easterly errors and subtract westerly errors.

Bearings

Bearings are lines drawn, pointed, or sighted from one object
to another. For accurate navigation, a system of true and relative
bearings has been worked out so that all directions at sea are
given in bearings that are measured in degrees.

True bearings are based on a circle of degrees with true north
as 000° (or 360°), east as 090°, south as 180°, and west as 270°.

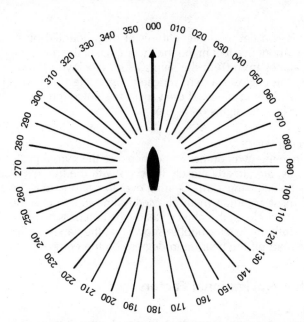

Figure 23–10 Relative bearings, measured clockwise from the ship's head, locate an object in relation to the ship. They have nothing to do with geographical directions.

Relative bearings are based on a circle drawn around the ship itself, with the bow as 000°, the starboard beam as 090°, the stern as 180°, and the port beam as 270° (Figure 23–10). Thus, if a ship is on a course true north (000°), another ship sighted dead ahead would bear 000° true and 000° relative. But if the ship were on a course true east and sighted a ship dead ahead, the sighted ship would bear 090° true but would still be dead ahead or 000° relative.

RELATIVE BEARINGS
Relative bearings are used wherever there is no compass. Lookouts cannot have accurate compasses on hand, nor can they be expected to know the course of the ship and the true directions that lie about it. They need a way to point out where objects lie, and this method must be fast, accurate, and unmistakable. By using the Navy system of relative bearings measured in degrees from the bow of the ship, a man can soon learn to report objects in such a way that anyone can locate them immediately.

TRUE BEARINGS
True bearings can be obtained directly from a gyro repeater, from a magnetic compass situated so as to make bearings on outside objects possible (and with the appropriate corrections applied), or by calculation from a relative bearing.

Bearings

PELORUS
This is a flat, nonmagnetic metal ring mounted on a vertical stand about five feet high. The inner edge of the ring is graduated in degrees from 0° at the ship's head, clockwise through 360°. This ring encloses a gyro repeater. Upon the ring is mounted a pair of sighting vanes. These vanes are sighted through an object much like the sights on a rifle.

GYRO BEARINGS
Since the gyrocompass, and therefore the gyro repeater in the pelorus, are already closely lined up with the true geographical directions, taking a true bearing over the gyro card is the easiest and most common method. Merely line the vane sights of the bearing circle on the object, steady the compass bowl in its gimbals until the leveler bubble shows that the vanes are level, and then read off the bearing in degrees on the compass card.

Other Navigational Factors

TIDES
Tides are very important in naval operations. Amphibious landings are scheduled for high tide so that troops and equipment can land well up on a beach. In some harbors, deep-draft ships may be able to enter only at high tide. Large ships are usually launched, or drydocked, at high tide. Ships going alongside piers in channels subject to strong tide and currents will usually wait for slack water, when the tide is neither ebbing nor flooding. Every Navy man who is concerned with the handling of a vessel must understand what causes tides and the meaning of different tidal conditions.

The term "tide" describes the regular rise and fall of the water level along a sea coast or in an ocean port. The gravitational attraction of the moon is the primary cause of tides; it exerts a very

Figure 23–11 Relation of positions of the sun and moon to the tides.

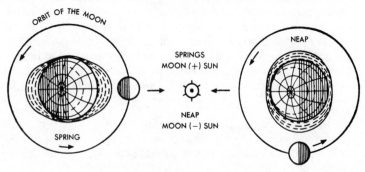

considerable attraction or pull on the sea, pulling the water away from the earth. There is an almost equal bulge of water on the opposite side of the earth, as shown in Figure 23–11, because the centrifugal force of the earth's motion piles the water up where the pull of the moon is weakest.

Since the moon orbits the earth every 24 hours and 50 minutes, there are two low and two high tides at any place during that period. The low and high tides each are 12 hours and 25 minutes apart. The sun also affects the tide, but it is so much farther away than the moon that its pull is not nearly so great. A tide rising or moving from low to high water is said to be flooding. When the tide is falling, after high tide, it is said to be ebbing.

The difference in depth between a high and the next low tide is considerable in many harbors; areas that are safe for a power-boat at high tide may be completely dry at low water.

CURRENTS

In most harbors and inlets, the tides are the chief causes of currents; however, if the port is situated on a large river, its flow may have a marked effect on tidal currents. The flow of such a river will prolong the duration of the ebb current as compared to that of the flood, and the velocity of the ebb current will be considerably greater than that of the flood.

475

Where the currents are chiefly caused by the rise and fall of the tide, their direction and speed are largely governed by the shape of the shore lines and the contour of the bottom. Where there is a long beach, or straight section of waterway, the current will tend to flow most rapidly in the center and much more slowly in the shallower water near either shore. If a boat goes with the current, the coxswain will generally want to stay near the center of the waterway. If the boat goes against the current, he will stay as near to shore as the prevailing water depth will allow.

In many wide inlets, near the time of slack water, when the current is at the end of the ebb or flood, the current may actually reverse itself in part of the inlet; while the ebb is still moving out in the main channel, a gentle flood current may start near one shore. This condition, where it exists, can be very helpful to a small-boat operator.

Where there is a bend in the channel, the current will flow strongest on the outside of the bend. This effect is very marked, particularly with a strong current.

In some areas, a strong current can create areas of very rough water, called tide rips. These are usually shown on charts, and should be avoided.

Every vessel, regardless of her size, must make some allowance for the set and drift of the current, for it may affect the course to be steered.

One more thing to bear in mind about currents is that only on the sea coast does the turn of the current occur at the same time as high water. At many ports, owing to the effect of the shape of the land on the water flow, there may be a very considerable difference between the time of high (or low) water and the time that the current starts to ebb (or flood).

WINDS

Modern naval vessels are not dependent on the wind for power, as sailing ships were; but, at times, the wind's effect must be considered. During flight operations, a carrier usually steams into the wind, because the increased *apparent wind* speed helps aircraft take off and land. A strong wind blowing across a ship from side to side makes steering more difficult, and ships with high superstructures may list, or lean away from the wind.

When a ship is underway, the wind usually seems to blow from straight ahead to straight astern. This is *apparent wind,* the combination of the real wind, and the "wind" created by the ship's motion. If there is no real wind at all and a ship is making 25 knots, the apparent wind will be 25 knots from dead ahead. If the real wind is 25 knots and the ship makes 25 knots upwind (straight into it), the apparent wind will be 50 knots. If the ship turns around and makes 25 knots downwind (with the wind), the speed of the wind and the ship cancel each other out and there will appear to be no wind.

A wind takes the name of the direction it blows from; a north wind comes from the north, a west wind comes from the west. Windward means toward the wind, leeward means away from the wind; the side of the ship toward the wind is the windward side, away from the wind is the leeward side. When the wind changes direction to the right, or clockwise, it veers; when it changes in the other direction, it backs. At sea, the true wind is indicated by streaks of foam down the back sides of waves, while the apparent wind is shown by the way the commission pennant or stack gas blows.

Lookouts

Radars and sonars may fail to detect such things as smoke, small navigational markers, objects close to the ship, flares, or men in the water. These must be reported by the lookouts—the eyes of the ship. Upon their alertness rests a large part of the safety of their ship and their shipmates.

A lookout must do much more than keep his eyes open. He must learn how to search in a way that will cover every inch of his sector, and how to report the location of an object so that the OOD will know how to look for it. A lookout must watch for ships, planes, land, rocks, shoals, periscopes, discolored water, buoys, beacons, lighthouses, distress signals, floating objects of all kinds, and anything else of interest to the OOD. He also reports sounds of objects heard but not sighted—such as fog horns, ships' bells, whistle buoys, airplanes, and surf.

The number of lookouts and how they are assigned depends upon the ship's organization and duties. Small ships will have only the bridge (port and starboard) lookouts and one after lookout (life buoy watch). Each is stationed where he can best cover the surface and sky within his zone. In fog or thick weather, special lookouts are stationed immediately in the "eyes of the ship" and on the bridge wings.

The forward lookouts keep a sharp watch on either bow. The men on the bridge wings watch from ahead to astern and the after lookout scans for anything which might overhaul the ship from astern.

Sound carries much farther in a fog than on clear days, so a lookout must listen closely, especially if he is in the bow, for whistles, bells, buoys, and even the wash of water against a ship's stem. For this reason, fog lookouts do not wear sound-powered phones. Another sailor is required to man the phones at each fog lookout station.

NIGHT VISION

If you were to go on night watch directly from a lighted compartment, you would seem to be almost blind for a few minutes. This reaction is the same experience as walking from a lighted theater lobby into the darkened theater. As your eyes become accustomed to the weak light, your vision gradually improves. After 10 minutes you can see fairly well and after 30 minutes you reach your best night vision. This improvement of vision in dim light is called "dark adaptation."

Specially designed red goggles will be provided you before you go on night lookout duty. They prepare your eyes for darkness while you wear them, without affecting your ability to write letters or to get ready for your watch. You should wear them without interruption for at least a half hour before going on watch. Even then, it will still take you at least five minutes more in darkness to develop your best night vision.

After your eyes are dark-adapted, you still must learn to use your "night eyes." In the daytime, you look directly at an object to see it best. In the dark, however, you may look to one side of an object to see it best.

At night it is easier to locate a moving object than one standing still. Because most objects on or in the water move relatively slowly, we move our eyes instead, and the effect is nearly as good. Thus, while scanning at night, a lookout moves his eyes in slow sweeps across his area, instead of stopping his eyes to search a section at a time.

BINOCULARS

Contrary to widespread opinion, it is not always better to search with binoculars instead of using the naked eye. Several factors govern when and how they should be used. In fog, for instance, they should not be used at all. At night, however, they should be used quite often. Another factor is the field of view, which is only about 7° with binoculars. Such a narrow field hampers proper scanning techniques for certain types of search.

SCANNING PROCEDURE

In good weather, lookouts can easily spot planes at 15 miles with the naked eye. With binoculars and in unusually clear weather, lookouts have detected planes at 50 miles. At night, skilled lookouts will detect objects that the untrained lookout would never suspect were there.

The lookout's technique of searching is called "scanning," which is a step-by-step method of looking. It is the only efficient and sure way of doing the job. Scanning does not come naturally —you must learn to scan through practice. In the daytime your eyes must stop on an object to see it. Try moving your eyes around the room or across the water rapidly, and note that as long as your eyes are in motion, you see almost nothing. Allow

Figure 23–12 Step-by-step method of scanning.

your eyes to move in short steps from object to object. Now you can really see what is there.

Figure 23–12 shows how you should search along the horizon. (You also must cover the surface between your ship and the horizon.) Search your sector in 5° steps, pausing between steps for approximately 5 seconds to scan the field of view. At the end of your sector, lower the glasses and rest your eyes for a few seconds, then search back across the sector with the naked eye.

A sky lookout searchs from the horizon to the zenith (overhead), using binoculars only to identify a contact. Move your eyes in quick steps—also about 5°—across your sector just above the horizon, shift your gaze upward about 10°, and search

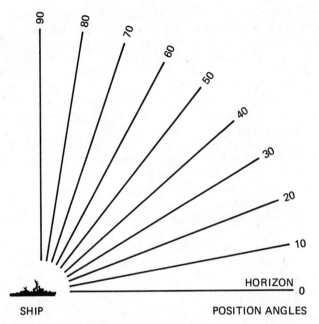

SHIP   POSITION ANGLES

Figure 23–13 Position angles locate an object in the sky. They measure up, not down.

back to the starting point. Repeat this process until the zenith is reached, then rest your eyes for a few seconds before starting over.

When searching at night, keep your eyes moving. Try to adhere to the sector scan (and upward shift) even though the horizon may not be visible. If you spot a target (or even think you have), don't stare at it. Instead, look about 10° to either side.

REPORTS

Every object sighted should be reported, no matter how insignificant it may seem to you. The initial report consists of two basic parts: what you see, and its bearing (direction) from the ship. Aircraft sighting reports also include altitude (position angle). Report the contact to the OOD immediately. Amplifying reports will include the object's identity—destroyer, periscope, log, etc.—and its direction.

Bearings: Lookouts report objects in degrees of relative bearing. (Figure 23–10, page 473, shows the relative bearings around a ship.) To prevent confusion, the Navy has established a definite procedure for reporting bearings, ranges, etc. (A pronunciation guide is found on page 504.)

Bearings are always reported in three digits, and spoken digit-by-digit. Objects that are dead ahead or astern (000° or 180°), on either beam (090° or 270°), or on either bow (045° or 315°) or quarter (135° or 225°) may be indicated as such. For example, a ship bearing 315° could be reported as being on the port bow, although the bearing itself can also be used.

A sky object is located by its relative bearing and position angle. The position angle of an aircraft is its height in degrees above the horizon, as seen from the ship. The horizon is 0° and directly overhead is 90°. The position angle can never be more than 90°. (See Figure 23–13.)

Position angles are given in one or two digits, and spoken as a whole number, not digit-by-digit. The reference "position angle" is always spoken before the numerals.

Ranges: Range estimates take practice. A lookout has to learn how a certain type of ship looks a mile away, and two miles away, etc. Knowing your height above water will help you in estimating ranges. At a height of 50 feet, for example, the distance to the horizon is about 16,000 yards (8 miles); at a height of 100 feet, the distance is about 23,000 yards (11½ miles).

24. Communications

When you mention communications in the Navy, most sailors think of a radioman copying a radio message or a signalman handling flaghoists during fleet operations. But it is much more than that, and everyone is involved. The bow lookout using a sound-powered telephone to report to the bridge is communicating; so is the officer of the deck (OOD) using the talk-between-ships (TBS) link to advise another ship of a course change. The lookout is using internal communications; the OOD is using external communications. All naval communications can be classified as one or the other.

Internal Communications

Internal communications are those that take place aboard a single ship. Internal communications are carried out using both sound and visual methods. Communication by messenger, probably the oldest of all methods, is still the most reliable system. Other methods can include everything from "passing the word" over the MC circuits, to using "squawk boxes," the sound-powered telephone system, regular dial phones, bell and buzzer systems, or boat gongs.

Internal communications also mean printed or written material such as the plan of the day (POD), visual display systems such as the rudder angle indicator and engine order telegraph on the bridge, the CIC plot, and even the "on-board/ashore" board for officers at the quarterdeck. Everyone aboard ship must be aware of the internal communications system at all times.

PASSING THE WORD

In the old Navy, before the days of loudspeaker systems, the boatswain's mate passed any orders for the crew by word of mouth. The boatswain or BM of the watch sounded "Call mates" on his pipe to get the BMs together and they answered repeatedly with the same call as they converged on the bridge or quarterdeck. When they heard the word, they dispersed fore and aft to sing it out at every hatch.

While this procedure was very colorful, it took a lot of time. Today a single BM can quickly pass the word over the intercommunications voice (MC) network, while the others stay where they are. The basic MC circuit is the 1MC, the general announcing system, over which the word can be passed to every space in the ship. The general alarm system is also tied into it. Transmitters are located on the bridge, quarterdeck, and central station; additional transmitters may be installed at other points.

An announcement is generally preceded with "Now hear this," or "Now hear there," unless a boatswain's call is used. When a boatswain's call (or pipe) is used, "All hands" is piped before any word concerning drills and emergencies. "Attention" is piped before the passing of routine messages.

Common shipboard events are listed here, with the appropriate words following each one:

Air bedding: "All divisions, air bedding."

Arrivals and departures: (Title of officer, preceded by proper number of boat gongs.) For example, "CNO, arriving (departing)."

Boats: "Away, the motor whaleboat (gig, barge), away."

Church call: "Divine services are now being held in (location). Maintain silence about the decks during divine services."

Eight o'clock reports: "On deck all eight o'clock reports."

Extra duty men: "Lay up to the quarterdeck for muster, all extra duty men (or other special groups)."

Fire: "Fire! Fire! compartment A-205-L (or other location, including deck, frame, and side)."

Flight quarters: "Flight quarters. Flight quarters. Man all flight quarters stations to launch (recover) aircraft (helicopters)."

General quarters: "General quarters! General quarters! All hands man your battle stations."

Hoist boats: "First division stand by to hoist in (out) number _____ motor launch (gig)."

Idlers: "Up all idlers."

Inspection (personnel): "All hands to quarters for captain's personnel inspection."

Inspection (material): "Stand by all lower deck and topside spaces for inspection."

Knock off work (before evening meal): "Knock off all ship's work. Shift into the uniform of the day." (First pipe "All hands.")

Late bunks: "Up all late bunks."

Liberty: "Liberty to commence for the (first) and (third) sections at 1600; to expire on board at (hour, date, month)."

Mail: "Mail call."

Meals: "All hands, pipe to breakfast (noon meal or dinner; evening meal or supper)." (First pipe "Mess call.")

Mess gear (call): "Mess gear (call). Clear the (all) mess decks." (First pipe "Mess call.")

Mistake or error: "Belay that last word."

Muster on stations: "All divisions muster on stations."

Pay: "The crew is now being paid in the mess hall."

Preparations for getting underway: "Make all preparations for getting underway."

Quarters for muster: "All hands to quarters for muster."

Quarters for muster (inclement weather): "All hands to quarters for muster. Foul weather parade." (First pipe "All hands.")

Rain squall: "Haul over all hatch hoods and gun covers."

Readiness for getting underway reports: "All departments, make readiness for getting underway reports to the officer of the deck on the bridge."

Relieving the watch: "Relieve the watch. On deck the _____ section. Lifeboat crew on deck to muster. Relieve the wheel and lookouts." (First pipe "Attention.")

Rescue and assistance: "Away rescue and assistance party, _____ section."

Reveille: "Reveille. Reveille, all hands heave out and trice (lash) up." Or, "Reveille. Up all hands, trice up all bunks." (First pipe "All hands.")

Shifting the watch: "The officer of the deck is shifting his watch to the bridge (quarterdeck)."

Side boys: "Lay up on the quarterdeck, the side boys."

Smoking: "The smoking lamp is lighted (out)." (Unless the word applies to the whole ship, the location should be specified.)

Special sea detail: "Go to (man) your stations, all the special sea detail." Or, "Station the special sea detail."

Sweepers: "Sweepers, start (man) your brooms. Make a clean sweep down fore and aft." (First pipe "Sweepers.")

Taps: "Taps, lights out. All hands turn in to your bunks and keep silence about the decks. Smoking lamp is out in all living spaces." (First pipe "Pipe down.")

Turn to: "Turn to (scrub down all weather decks, scrub all canvas, sweep down compartments, dump trash)."

The OOD is in charge of the 1MC. No call can be passed over it unless it is authorized by him, the executive officer, or the captain, except for a possible emergency call by the damage control officer.

Normally, the 1MC is equipped with switches that make it possible for certain spaces to be cut off from announcements which are of no concern to them. The captain, for instance, does not want his cabin blasted with calls for individuals to lay down to the spud locker. If the BMOW is absent, and you are required to pass the word yourself, be sure you know which circuits should be left open. Some parts of the ship have independent MC circuits of their own, such as the engineers' announcing system (2MC) and the hangar-deck announcing system (3MC).

The bull horn (6MC) is the intership announcing system, but is seldom used for actual communication between vessels. It is, however, a convenient means of passing orders to boats and tugs alongside, or to line-handling parties beyond the range of the speaking trumpet. If the transmitter switch is located on the 1MC control panel, you must be careful to avoid accidentally cutting the bull horn when you are passing a routine word.

The 1MC, 2MC, 3MC, and 6MC are all one-way systems. A full list of loudspeaker systems is given below:

One-way systems		Two-way systems	
1MC	Battles and general	19MC	Readyroom
2MC	Engineers	20MC	Combat information
3MC	Hangar deck	21MC	Captain's command
4MC	Damage control	22MC	Radio room
5MC	Flight deck	23MC	Distribution control
6MC	Boat control	24MC	Flag officer's command
7MC	Submarine control	25MC	Wardroom
10MC	Docking control	26MC	Machinery control
11MC	Turret	27MC	Sonar control
16MC	Turret	28MC	Squadron
17MC	Antiaircraft	29MC	Sonar information
18MC	Bridge	30MC	Bomb shop
		31MC	Escape trunk

SQUAWK BOXES

Such MC circuits as the 21MC, familiarly known as "squawk boxes," differ from the public address systems in that they provide for two-way communication. Each unit has a number of selector switches. In order to talk to one or more stations, it is only necessary for you to throw the proper switches and operate the press-to-talk button. A red signal light mounted above each selector switch shows whether the station called is busy. If it is busy the light flashes; if it burns with a steady light, you know that the station is ready to receive.

Following is an example of how to operate the intercom. You're on the signal bridge, at the 24MC transmitter, and you want to call conn. First you throw the selector switch marked "conn." We'll assume the line is clear for your message, which means that a steady red light appears over the signal bridge selector switch at the conn transmitter. When the operator at conn throws on the signal bridge switch, the signal lights at both stations begin to flash. Now you can operate the press-to-talk button and start your message. Any other station attempting to cut in gets the flashing busy signal.

The chief disadvantage of the intercom is that it raises the noise level in any space in which is is located. For this reason, it is seldom used when telephone circuits are available.

You probably will stand some sort of watch aboard ship as a telephone talker. A ship at sea requires many talkers, even during a peacetime cruising watch. In addition to the lookouts, there are talkers on the bridge, in firerooms, and in enginerooms, to mention only a few. To do your job properly, you must learn proper telephone-talking procedures.

These phones are used on all ships, and some ships have hundreds of them. They do not require outside electrical power; the user's voice acts on a carbon-filled cell and diaphragm to generate enough current to power the circuit.

The headset phone consists of a headband which holds the receivers over the ears, a breastplate supported by a cloth neckstrap, and a yoke that holds the transmitter in front of the mouth. The phone has a lead, which may be up to 50 feet long, with a jack on the end. The jack plugs into a jackbox which is connected to the circuit.

The headset is delicate and can be easily damaged. When you pick up the set to put it on, hold the entire unit in your left hand. You will find the headpiece is hung over the transmitter's supporting yoke and the lead wires are coiled.

485

To put the gear on, first unhook the right side of the neckstrap from the breastplate. Second, put on the earphones and adjust the headband so that the center of the earpiece is directly over your ear. Last, insert the plug into the jackbox and screw the collar on firmly.

Adjust the mouthpiece so that it is directly in front of your mouth when you stand erect. When you speak into the transmitter, it should be about ½ to 1 inch from your mouth. In making this adjustment, remember that the fine wire that goes to the transmitter can be broken easily. Be sure there are no sharp bends in it, and do not allow it to get caught between the transmitter and the yoke.

When you are wearing the headset, always keep some slack in the lead cord, and be sure it is flat on deck. If you have the cord stretched taut, someone may trip over it and damage the wires, injure themselves, or injure you. Do not allow objects to roll over or rest upon the cord.

After plugging in the phones, test them with someone on the circuit. If the phones are not in order, report the fact to the person in charge of your station and don a spare set; don't attempt to repair the set yourself.

If you are on lookout and should be listening as well as searching, cover only one ear with an earpiece so that you can also hear outside noises. Keep the unused earpiece flat against the side of your head so that noises will not be picked up by the transmitter.

Internal

Never secure the phones until you have permission to do so. When permission is given, make up the phones for stowage in accordance with the following instructions:

Remove the plug from the jackbox by holding the plug in one hand and unscrewing the collar with the other. When the collar is loose, grasp the plug and pull it out. (Pulling by the lead will weaken, and eventually break, the connection.) When the plug is out, lay it carefully on the deck. Immediately screw the cover on the jackbox, as dust and dirt will soon cause a short circuit in a jackbox that has been left uncovered. (If you see an uncovered jackbox, cover it, even though you were not responsible for the carelessness.)

Remove the headpiece and hang it over the transmitter yoke.

Coil the lead cord, starting from the end at the phone. Coil the lead in a clockwise direction, holding the loops in one hand. The loops should be 8 to 10 inches across, depending on the size of the space where the phones are stowed. When you are coiling the lead, be careful not to bang the plug against the bulkhead or deck.

When the lead is coiled, remove the headpiece from the transmitter yoke, and put the headband in the same hand with the coil. Use this same hand to hold the transmitter while you unhook one end of the neckstrap from the chestplate. Fold the transmitter yoke flat, being careful not to put a sharp bend in the transmitter cord.

Wrap the neckstrap around the coil and headband two or three times and snap the end back on the breastplate, then fold the mouthpiece up again against the junction box. You then have a neat, compact package to be stowed.

Put the phones into the box, or hang them on the hook provided. Be careful not to crowd or jam the leads.

Headset phones should always be unplugged when not in use. If they are left plugged in, the earpieces will pick up noise and carry it into the circuit. Never place the phones on deck. Not only is it possible that someone may step on them, but decks are good conductors of noise, which can be picked up by the phones.

THE J CIRCUITS

It is possible that not all of the circuits listed here may be installed in your ship; for this reason, you should learn them all.

JA	Captain's battle circuit	61JS	Sonar information
JC	Weapons control	1JV	Maneuvering and docking
JL	Lookouts		
21JS	Surface search and radar	2JZ	Damage control
22JS	Air search radar	X8J	Replenishment at sea

Every one of the circuits listed, if it is in the ship at all, has an outlet on the bridge. Some of them are manned at all times; most of them are manned during general quarters. You must know where the outlet for each circuit is, when the circuit should be manned, and the type of traffic it handles. Circuits fall into three categories: primary, auxiliary, and supplementary systems.

The primary system includes all circuits necessary for controlling armament, engineering, damage control, maneuvering, and surveillance functions during battle. These circuits are designated JA through JZ.

The auxiliary system duplicates many of the primary circuits. It maintains vital communications in the event of damage to the primary system. Auxiliary circuits are separated as much as possible from primary circuits. Circuit designations are the same as the primary system, preceded by the letter X, as in the XJA, X1JV, etc.

The supplementary system, S1J through X61J, consists of several short, direct circuits—such as those from the bridge to the quarterdeck, quarterdeck to wardroom, etc. Circuits in the primary and auxiliary systems can be tied together at various switchboards, or individual stations may be cut out of the circuits. The supplementary system, however, does not have these provisions. Because circuits in the supplementary system are not manned, most circuits contain a buzzer system so that one station can alert another station that communications between the two are desired.

The following explains the standard purpose of each J circuit.

The JA circuit is used by the commanding officer to communicate with his department heads and their assistants.

The JC is the weapons officer's command circuit on ships having a single-purpose main battery. The circuit is controlled by the weapons officer, but has a bridge outlet for use by the commanding officer and the OOD.

The JL is the circuit over which the lookouts report. It is an important channel of vital information to the bridge, CIC, and gun control. In wartime the JL circuit is manned under all cruising conditions. In peacetime it is manned when circumstances require extra lookout precautions, but it may then be combined with other circuits. The controlling JL station is on the bridge, and the bridge talker is often designated the lookout supervisor.

On a ship with a dual-purpose main battery, the 2JC circuit serves the same purpose as the JC on a ship having a single-purpose main battery and a separate secondary battery. Ships having both use the 2JC as the air defense officer's circuit.

The 1JS is used as an ASW command circuit and also as a CIC dissemination circuit. When the 1JS is used as an ASW command circuit, there are communication links to sonar control, CIC, underwater battery (UB) plot, and the bridge. This circuit enables stations on the communication link to exchange information without interrupting the constant flow of information on other circuits. On some ships the 1JS is used to disseminate CIC information to the conning, gunnery, and aircraft control stations. The 1JS is usually controlled by the CIC evaluator.

The 1JV, called the primary maneuvering circuit, is the one with which the quartermasters are chiefly concerned. It connects the bridge and other conning stations with main engine control, after steering, and other emergency steering stations. Also, it has outlets on the main deck for control of the anchor detail and line-handling parties fore and aft. This circuit is always manned in CIC; other control stations may do likewise when advisable. The conning officer controls the 1JV, and the circuit is always manned—or at least ready for instant use—whenever the ship is underway.

The JW is the navigator's circuit, by which quartermasters stationed at peloruses and navigational rangefinders may report directly to the navigator at the chart table. During piloting, the JW is especially useful.

The JX is the crcuit by which the communication officer, at his battle station on the bridge, is connected with communication spaces.

The JZ circuit is a damage control circuit.

Some of the foregoing circuits may vary slightly on different ships. As soon as you report aboard a new ship for duty, you must learn the details of any possible variance.

TELEPHONE TECHNIQUE

The way you talk in ordinary conversation is not the way you should talk on a telephone. The person on the other end of the line cannot see you, he may not know you, and he may be unfamiliar with the things you say. Telephone talkers must speak clearly, be specific, and act businesslike; they are not on the circuit for social chitchat. When using the phones, follow these suggestions:

Use a strong, calm voice. Speak slowly, pronounce words carefully.

Don't mumble, run things together, or talk with gum or a cigarette in your mouth.

Use standard terms and phraseology. Avoid slang or "in" words.

When transmitting numbers and letters, use approved communication procedure. The expression "Item 5C" may sound like "Item 9D," but "Fife Charlie" will not be mistaken for "Nin-er Delta."

Circuit discipline: Circuits are like a "party line"—everyone can talk and listen at the same time. To prevent confusion, strict circuit discipline must be maintained.

Send only official messages.

Keep the button on the off position except when you're actually talking.

Do not leave your station or engage in other work or activities without permission.

Use only standard phraseology.

Never show anger, impatience, or excitement.

Each phone talker is a key link in the ship's interior communications chain. Unauthorized talking means that the chain is weakened. Don't do it, and don't permit others to.

Circuit testing: To find out if stations on the circuit are manned and ready, the control station talker says: "All stations, control, testing." Each talker then acknowledges in the assigned order (or sequence). Here's how it would go on a gun circuit:

Gun one: "One, aye, aye."
Gun two: "Two, aye, aye."
Gun three: "Three, aye, aye."

Normally each station answers up in order, but does not wait more than a few seconds if the station ahead of it fails to acknowledge. If you are on gun three, and gun two fails to answer up, acknowledge for your gun. Gun two then can come in at the end.

The test is not complete until each station has answered and any equipment faults have been checked.

Message form: Most messages have three parts: the name of the station being called, the name of the station calling, and the information to be sent. This format must always be followed. Call the station the message is for, identify your own station, then transmit the message. Remember this order: who to, who from, what about. If you are on the anchor detail and want to call the bridge, the message is "Bridge (who to), forecastle (who from); anchor secured (what about)."

Messages are acknowledged when understood by the station identifying itself and adding "Aye, aye." This lets the sender know the message has been received by the station it was intended for, and is understood. If you don't understand, ask for a repeat. If the sender wants to make certain an important message has been received correctly, he may ask you to repeat it back.

Sending a message: First name the station being called. Next name the station doing the calling. Then the message:

"Bridge, forecastle; anchor ready for letting go."

Receiving a message: First identify your own station; then acknowledge for the message. If your station is the forecastle, and the bridge has just ordered the anchor "let go," acknowledge with "Forecastle, aye, aye."

Sometimes there are three or four steps involved. For example: "Forecastle, bridge; how many lines are to the pier?" If you don't know, you say, "Forecastle, aye, aye; wait." After getting the information, call the bridge: "Bridge, forecastle; five lines to the pier." The bridge will acknowledge: "Bridge, aye, aye."

Requesting repeats: If an incoming message is not clear, the receiving station says, "Repeat." When the message is repeated and understood, the receiving station acknowledges by repeating the name of the sending station and adding "Aye, aye."

Spelling words: Difficult or little-known words are spelled out, using phonetic alphabet: "Stand by to receive officer from CHINFO. I spell Charlie, Hotel, India, November, Foxtrot, Oscar —CHINFO."

Securing the phones: Never secure until you have permission from the control station:

Forecastle: "Bridge, forecastle; permission to secure?"

Bridge: "Bridge, aye, aye; wait."

After the bridge talker learns that the forecastle may secure; he

says:

"Forecastle, bridge; you may secure."

"Forecastle, aye, aye; securing."

Remember to make the phones up properly and stow them before leaving your station.

VOICE TUBE

On most minecraft, patrol boats, and the like, the voice tube is still the primary means of interior communications, although some have sound-powered telephone circuits. A voice tube requires neither electrical nor sound power; but its effectiveness decreases in direct ratio to the length of the tube. On large ships, the voice tube is for short-distance communications only, as between open conning stations and the pilothouse.

External Communications

External communications involve two or more ships, stations, or commands. A ship's external communications are made by physical delivery, telecommunication, or any combination of the two. Physical delivery includes the use of messengers and mail delivery. Telecommunication means communication over a distance, and includes any transmission or reception using visual, electrical, or sound systems.

Visual signals include the flaghoist, semaphore, and signal searchlight or blinker. Whistles, bells, foghorns, or even a gun (for distress signal) may be part of the sound system. Electrical

Figure 24–1 Signalmen hoist flags, one of several external means of communication from ships.

and electronic communication is accomplished through radiotelegraph (CW), radiotelephone (RT), radioteletype (RATT), facsimile (FAX), and voice radio.

In delivering each communication, transmitting stations must
take into account the precedence (urgency), security requirement, and limitations of the available equipment. From a security

Figure 24–2 A flashing light enables a signalman to send a Morse code message when distance or darkness make flag messages impractical.

standpoint, the order of desirability of the various methods is: (1) messenger, (2) registered mail, (3) approved wire circuit, (4) ordinary mail, (5) non-approved wire circuit, (6) visual, (7) sound system and (8) radio.

With ships operating 24 hours a day around the world, the Navy must have rapid, accurate communications, not only for tactical and strategic control of the fleets in war, but also for administrative and logistic purposes. No ship is ever out of touch with its base of operations or its tactical, type, or administrative commander.

VISUAL SIGNALS

The three main sysems of visual signals are: flashing light, semaphore, and flaghoist.

Flashing-light signaling: This system uses short and long flashes of light to spell out dot-and-dash messages. The transmitting signalman sends one word at a time, with a slight pause between each letter. The receiving signalman flashes a dash after each word, meaning that it was received and he is ready for another.

With the directional method, the sender aims his light directly at the receiving ship or installation. Other types of directional gear are the blinker tube (or blinker gun) and the multipurpose lamp; both are battery operated, with trigger switches to control the light flashes.

The non-directional method is also called "all-around" signaling. Most of it is done by yardarm blinkers, lights mounted high on a mast and controlled by a signal key on the signal bridge. This method is best for sending a message to several ships at once.

While the other two signal systems use "white" light, a system called Nancy uses invisible infrared light. Messages sent by this system can be seen only by those who have a special Nancy receiver, which gathers the infrared rays and converts them to visible light. Nancy, with a range of from 10,000 to 15,000 yards, can be used only at night and is a very secure method of communication.

Semaphore signaling: Semaphore is much faster than flashing light for short-distance transmissions in clear daylight. Semaphore may be used to send messages to several ships at once if they are in suitable positions. Because of its speed, semaphore is better adapted than the other visual methods for long messages. When radio silence is imposed, semaphore is considered the best substitute for the handling of administrative traffic.

Although semaphore's usefulness is limited somewhat by its short range, it is more secure than flashing light or radio because there is less chance of interception by an enemy or unauthorized persons. Speed and security, therefore, are the two factors favoring the use of semaphore.

Semaphore requires little in the way of equipment. The two hand flags attached to staffs are all you need. Usually the standard semaphore flags are 15 to 18 inches square and each staff is long enough to enable the sender to grasp it firmly. Most semaphore flags issued to the fleet today are fluorescent and are made of sharkskin. (When sender and receiver are very close to each other, as when ships are alongside for underway replenishment, no special equipment is necessary. The semaphore characters are made simply by moving the hands to the proper positions.)

When you are using fluorescent flags, your background is relatively unimportant. With cotton flags, however, you must have a good background to enable the receiving operator to see your flags clearly.

A good signalman can send or receive about 25 five-letter groups a minute. Only 30 positions need to be learned; they are shown in Figure 24–3.

Flaghoist signaling: This is the most rapid system of visual signaling, but like semaphore it can be used only in daytime. It is generally used for tactical orders. The meanings of each signal must be looked up in a signal book. There is a signal flag for each letter of the alphabet, one for each numeral from 0 through 9, and others with special uses. A complete set of signal flags will have 68 flags and pennants; with them, thousands of different

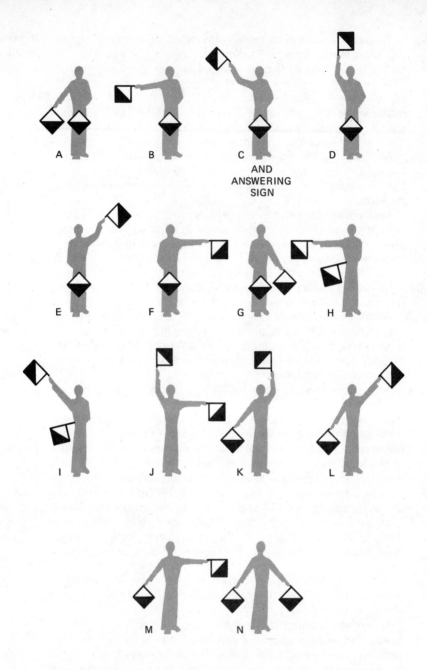

AND
ANSWERING
SIGN

Figure 24–3 The semaphore alphabet is fast, but useful only for short-range visual transmission.

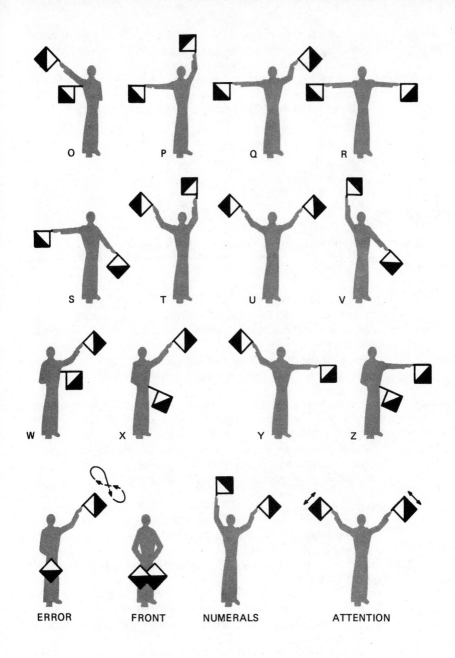

O   P   Q   R

S   T   U   V

W   X   Y   Z

ERROR   FRONT   NUMERALS   ATTENTION

signals can be sent. Most ships carry only two or three complete sets of flags, and substitutes are used when particular flags are already flying: the first substitute repeats the first flag or pennant in the same hoist, the second substitute repeats the second flag or pennant, and so on.

Other important flags: The following six flags and their meanings should be known by every sailor:

BRAVO: Ship is handling explosives or fuel oil.
CODE-ALPHA: Divers in water
FIVE FLAG: Breakdown.
OSCAR: Man overboard.
PAPA: All hands return to ship.
QUEBEC: All boats return to ship.

Absentee pennants, flown when the commanding officer or senior officer is absent from his command, are described on page 81.

OTHER VISUAL SIGNAL SYSTEMS

Other visual signaling systems involve special methods for special and emergency occasions. Here are some commonly used systems.

Speed indicators: These are flags and pennants, or red and white lights flashing in combinations, which are used to show a ship's speed.

Pyrotechnics: These are colored smoke and flare signals, usually used for distress and emergency purposes. (See Distress Signals, page 506.)

Panels: These are large strips of colored cloth, laid out in various designs on the ground or the deck of a ship to signal aircraft; they are also used in an emergency situation.

INTERNATIONAL MORSE CODE

International Morse code is standard for all naval communications transmitted by flashing light or radiotelegraph. The code is a dot-dash system in which letters, numerals, and punctuation marks are signified by various combinations of dots or dashes. A skilled radioman or signalman sends code in evenly timed dots and dashes, in which a dot is one unit long, a dash three units long. There is a one unit interval between dots and dashes in a letter, three units between letters of a word, and seven units between words.

The following chart lists the International Morse Code signal for each letter of the alphabet, along with a phonetic-alphabet equivalent and a pronunciation guide. (The Morse Code signals for numbers are given on page 504, along with a pronunciation guide.

Letter	Phonetic Alphabet	Pronunciation Guide	International Morse Code	Commu-nications
A	Alfa	**Al**-fah	· —	`
B	Bravo	**Brah**-voh	— · · ·	
C	Charlie	**Char**-lee	— · — ·	
D	Delta	**Dell**-tah	— · ·	
E	Echo	**Eck**-oh	·	
F	Foxtrot	**Foks**-trot	· · — ·	
G	Golf	Golf	— — ·	
H	Hotel	Hoh-**tell**	· · · ·	
I	India	**In**-dee-ah	· ·	
J	Juliett	**Jew**-lee-ett	· — — —	
K	Kilo	**Key**-loh	— · —	
L	Lima	**Lee**-mah	· — · ·	
M	Mike	Mike	— —	
N	November	No-**vem**-ber	— ·	
O	Oscar	**Oss**-cah	— — —	
P	Papa	Pah-**pah**	· — — ·	
Q	Quebec	Keh-**beck**	— — · —	
R	Romeo	**Row**-me-oh	· — ·	497
S	Sierra	See-**air**-rah	· · ·	
T	Tango	**Tang**-go	—	
U	Uniform	**You**-nee-form	· · —	
V	Victor	**Vik**-tah	· · · —	
W	Whiskey	**Wiss**-key	· — —	
X	X ray	**Ecks**-ray	— · · —	
Y	Yankee	**Yang**-key	— · — —	
Z	Zulu	**Zoo**-loo	— — · ·	

ELECTRONIC COMMUNICATIONS

Electronic communications include radio, wire, or telegraph. Wire communications go directly from sender to receiver and cannot be intercepted except by physically cutting into the circuit. Radio uses electromagnetic waves which are broadcast through the atmosphere in all directions. It includes radiotelegraph (CW), radiotelephone (RT), radioteletype (RATT) and facsimile (FAX).

Radiotelegraph (CW): Radiotelegraph uses International Morse Code. If the transmission is in plain language, anyone can intercept and read it. Important messages may be encrypted and sent in code or cipher systems known only to the sender and receiver. *Codes* are word-for-word substitutions, and both sender and receiver must use the same code book. *Ciphers* are letter-for-letter substitutions, which may require a machine to encode and decode the message. A coded message may be copied by anyone, but without the code system it is difficult (but not impossible) to read.

Radio telegraph messages are called "traffic," and are sent to the fleet in two ways. In the broadcast method, one station transmits traffic for many ships, and every ship copies all traffic. Ships do not acknowledge, so an enemy cannot determine how many ships are listening or where they are positioned.

In the receipt method, each station acknowledges its traffic. This way there is no doubt that it has been received. The disadvantage of this system is obvious: it allows the enemy, through use of radio direction-finding equipment, to locate stations acknowledging receipt of traffic.

Radiotelephone (RT): The radiotelephone, commonly known as the voice radio, is an effective and convenient method of communication. It is used extensively for ship-to-ship tactical communication, for convoy work, for the control of airborne aircraft, and for countless tasks requiring rapid, short-range communications. Small vessels, such as district craft, rely almost entirely on voice radio.

Voice radio supplements both radiotelegraph and visual methods of communications—it does not replace either form. It has the advantages of simplicity of operation and direct transmission of the spoken word; but its ease of operations has lead to abuse. Careless use of voice procedure, plus overloading of circuits, has created confusion at times when good communication was imperative.

RT is considered the least secure means of electronic communication. Anyone who has the necessary receiving equipment and is within reception range can copy messages.

Radioteletype (RATT): This is an electrically operated typewriter which, by either radio or telegraph line, can operate another similar typewriter elsewhere. RATT is used extensively both at sea and ashore. A typewriter keyboard produces printed letters simultaneously at both sending and receiving machines, no matter how many machines are on the circuit. RATT perforated tapes may also be prepared in advance, for use in later transmissions.

Facsimile (FAX): Facsimile is a method for transmitting pictorial and graphic information electronically by wire or radio. The information is reproduced in its original form at the receiving station. The image to be sent is scanned by a photoelectric cell; electrical variations, corresponding to the light and dark areas being scanned, are transmitted to the receiving unit. The process is similar to television, but is much slower and cannot produce a moving picture. FAX signals may be transmitted by wire or radio. FAX is often used to transmit complete weather charts and data.

TRANSMITTING TECHNIQUES

Because radiotelephone is used so widely, in ships, aircraft, and motor vehicles, everyone must understand the basics of cir-

cuit discipline. Under most circumstances, the following practices are specifically forbidden:

Violation of radio silence.
Unofficial conversation between operators.
Transmitting in a directed net without permission.
Excessive tuning and testing.
Unauthorized use of plain language.
Transmission of an operator's name or personal sign.
Use of unauthorized prowords.
Linkage or compromise of classified call signs and address
groups by plain language disclosures or association with unclas-
sified call signs.
Unauthorized use of plain language in place of applicable
prowords.
Use of profane, indecent, or obscene language.

Listen before transmitting, for break-ins cause confusion.
Speak clearly and distinctly; slurred syllables and clipped speech
are difficult to understand. Speak slowly, so that the recorder has
a chance to understand the entire message the first time. This
way, you'll save time and avoid repetitions. Avoid extremes of
pitch in voice modulation.

Be natural, and maintain a normal speaking rhythm. This is a
form of essential communication, not "big-time" radio. Send
your message phrase-by-phrase instead of word-by-word.

Use standard pronunciation, avoiding regional dialects. Keep
correct distance (about 2 inches) between your lips and the microphone. Speak in a moderately strong voice to override background noises. Shield your microphone. While transmitting,
keep your head and body between sources of noise and the microphone.

Keep the volume of the headset earphone low. Also keep
speaker volume down to a moderate level. Give an accurate
evaluation in response to a request for a radio check. Pause mo-
mentarily, when possible, during your transmission; pausing
allows any other station with higher-precedence traffic to break
in.

Follow closely prescribed procedures. Transact your business
and get off the air. Preliminary calls are unnecessary when communications are good and the message is short. Do not hold the
microphone button in the push-to-talk position until you're ready
to transmit. Apply firm pressure to the microphone button to prevent an unintentional release, which may cause a signal interruption.

PROCEDURE WORDS AND PROCEDURE SIGNS

Procedure words (prowords) and procedure signs (prosigns)
are words and phrases used to speed up radio traffic. They both

provide, in brief form, certain orders, requests, and instructions that are frequently used in communications. Prosigns may be sent by radiotelegraph, radioteletype, semaphore, and flashing light. Signs with a line above them are sent without the usual pause between letters.

Proword	Explanation	Prosign
ADDRESS GROUP	The group that follows is an address group.	
ALL AFTER	The portion of the message to which I refer is all that follows ____.	AA
ALL BEFORE	The portion of the message to which I refer is all that precedes ____.	AB
AUTHENTI-CATE	The station called is to reply to the challenge which follows.	
AUTHENTICA-TION IS	The transmission authentication of this message is ____.	
BREAK	I hereby indicate the separation of the text from other portions of the message.	BT
CALL SIGN	The group that follows is a call sign.	
CORRECT	You are correct, or what you have transmitted is correct.	C
CORRECTION	An error has been made in this transmission. Transmission will continue with the last word correctly transmitted. An error has been made in this transmission (or message indicated). The correct version is ____.	EEEEEEEE
DISREGARD THIS TRANS-MISSION— OUT	This transmission is in error. Disregard it. (This proword shall not be used to cancel any message that has been completely transmitted and for which receipt or acknowledgement has been received.)	EEEEEEEE $\overline{AR}$
DO NOT AN-SWER	Stations called are not to answer this call, acknowledge receipt of this message, or otherwise transmit in connec-	F

tion with this transmission.
(When this proword is em-
ployed, the transmission shall
be ended with the proword
OUT.)

EXECUTE | Carry out the purport of the | $\overline{IX}$ (5 sec.
message or signal to which | dash)
this applies. (To be used only
with the Executive Method.)

EXECUTE TO | Action on the message or sig- | $\overline{IX}$
FOLLOW | nal which follows is to be
carried out upon receipt of
the proword EXECUTE. (To be
used only with the Delayed
Executive Method.)

EXEMPT | The addresses immediately | XMT
following are exempted from
the collective call.

FIGURES | Numerals or numbers follow.

FLASH | Precedence FLASH. | Z

FROM | The originator of this message | FM
is indicated by the address
designator immediately following.

GROUPS | This message contains the | GR
number of groups indicated
by the numeral following.

GROUP NO | The groups in this message | GRNC
COUNT | have not been counted.

I AUTHENTI- | The group that follows is the
CATE | reply to your challenge to au-
thenticate.

IMMEDIATE | Precedence IMMEDIATE. | $\overline{O}$

IMMEDIATE EX- | Action on the message or sig- | $\overline{IX}$
ECUTE | nal following is to be carried
out on receipt of the word
EXECUTE. (To be used with
the Immediate Executive
Method.)

INFO | The addresses immediately | INFO
following are addressed for
information.

I READ BACK | The following is my response
to your instruction to read
back.

I SAY AGAIN | I am repeating transmission or | $\overline{IMI}$
portion indicated.

501

External

I SPELL	I shall spell the next word phonetically.	
I VERIFY	That which follows has been verified at your request and is repeated. (To be used only as a reply to VERIFY.)	
MESSAGE	A message which requires recording is about to follow. (Transmitted immediately after the call.)	
NET NOW	All stations are to net their radios on the unmodulated carrier wave which I am about to transmit.	
NUMBER	Station serial number.	NR
OUT	This is the end of my transmission to you and no answer is required or expected.	
OVER	This is the end of my transmission to you and a response is necessary. Go ahead; transmit.	K
PRIORITY	Precedence PRIORITY.	P
READ BACK	Repeat this entire transmission back to me exactly as received.	G
REBROADCAST YOUR NET	Link the two nets under your control for automatic rebroadcast.	
RELAY (TO)	Transmit this message to all addressees immediately following.	T
ROGER	I have received your last transmission satisfactorily.	R
ROUTINE	Precedence ROUTINE.	R
SAY AGAIN	Repeat all of your last transmission. Followed by identification data means "Repeat ____ (portion indicated)."	
SERVICE	The message that follows is a service message.	SVC
SIGNALS	The group which follows is taken from a signal book. (This proword is not used on nets primarily employed for conveying signals; it's intended for use when tactical	

	signals are passed on nontactical nets.)	
SILENCE (Repeated three or more times)	Cease transmissions on this net immediately. Silence will be maintained until lifted.	$\overline{HM}$ $\overline{HM}$ $\overline{HM}$
SILENCE LIFTED	Silence is lifted.	
SPEAK SLOWER	Your transmission is at too fast a speed. Reduce speed of transmission.	
STOP RE-BROADCAST-ING	Cut the automatic link between the two nets that are being rebroadcast, and revert to normal working.	
THIS IS	This transmission is from the station whose designator immediately follows.	DE
TIME	That which immediately follows is the time or date-time group of the message.	
TO	The addressees immediately following are addressed for action.	TO
UNKNOWN STATION	The identity of the station with whom I am attempting to establish communications is unknown.	$\overline{AA}$
VERIFY	Verify the entire message (or portion indicated) with the originator and send correct version. To be used at the discretion of or by the addressee to which the questioned message is directed.	
WAIT	I must pause for a few seconds.	$\overline{AS}$
WAIT-OUT	I must pause for longer than a few seconds.	$\overline{AS}$ $\overline{AR}$
WILCO	I have received your signal, understand it, and will comply. (To be used only by addressee. Since the meaning of ROGER is included in that of WILCO, the two prowords are never used together.)	
WORD AFTER	The word of the message to which I refer is that which follows _____.	WA

WORD BEFORE   The word of the message to   WB
which I refer is that which
precedes _____.

WORDS TWICE   Communication is difficult.
Transmit(ting) each phrase (or
each code group) twice. (This
proword may be used as an
order, request, or as information.)

WRONG   Your last transmission was incorrect. The correct version is

_____.

PRONOUNCING LETTERS AND NUMBERS

When necessary to identify any letter of the alphabet, use the
standard phonetic alphabet. (See page 497.) Take care to distinguish numbers from similarly pronounced words. Before numbers, you may use the proword "figures." The numeral 0 is always spoken as "ze-ro," never as "oh." It is written as 0.
Decimal points are spoken as "day-see-mal." Example: 123.4 is
spoken as "Wun too tree day-see-mal fow-er." Numbers will be
transmitted digit-by-digit, except that exact multiples of thousands may be spoken as such.

Numbers	Pronunciation	International Morse Code
1	Wun	· _ _ _ _
2	Too	· · _ _ _
3	Tree	· · · _ _
4	Fow-er	· · · · _
5	Fife	_ · · · ·
6	Six	_ · · · · ·
7	Sev-en	_ _ · · ·
8	Ait	_ _ _ · ·
9	Nin-er	_ _ _ _ ·
0	Ze-ro	_ _ _ _ _
44	Fow-er fow-er	
90	Nin-er ze-ro	
136	Wun-tree six	
500	Fife ze-ro ze-ro	
1,478	Wun fow-er sev-en ait	
7,000	Sev-en tou-sand	
16,000	Wun six tou-sand	
812,681	Ait wun too six ait wun	

Some special instances require procedures different from the
normal digit-by-digit pronunciation. Ranges and distances given
in mile units and speed given in knots, for instance, are always

transmitted as cardinal (whole) numbers. Examples: 10 is spoken as "ten;" 13 as "thur-teen;" 25 as "twen-ty fife;" 50 as "fif-ty;" 110 as "wun hun-dred ten;" 300 as "tree hun-dred."

Bearings are always given in three digits and are transmitted digit-by-digit. For example: Bearing 090 is spoken as "ze-ro nin-er ze-ro;" 180 as "wun ait ze-ro;" 295 as "too nin-er fife."

SOUND SIGNALING

Owing to the nature of the device used—a whistle, siren, or foghorn—sound signaling is necessarily slow. Moreover, the misuse of sound signaling can create serious confusion at sea. Sound signaling in fog should, therefore, be reduced to a minimum. Signals other than the single-letter signals should be used only in extreme emergency and never in heavily travelled waters.

The signals should be made slowly and clearly. They may, if necessary, be repeated, but at sufficiently long intervals to ensure that no confusion can arise and that one-letter signals cannot be mistaken as two-letter groups.

MAIL SYSTEMS

A vast amount of administrative detail concerning personnel, supplies, logistics, and operations is handled by official mail, which is carried through the U.S. postal system. Official mail between ships in the same port is carried by guard mail. Ships and stations have guard mail petty officers designated to log and receive this type of correspondence. Classified mail is carried by designated couriers.

Personal mail in the Navy is handled much as it is in a civilian community. Every ship has a post office and men specially designated to handle U.S. mail—postal clerks (PCs). Every ship also has a fleet post office (FPO) number to enable the New York and San Francisco FPOs to better direct mail for ships at sea or overseas.

In time of war, all letters written by personnel on ships or at overseas bases must be examined by official Navy censors before they are sent.

When censorship is in effect, censors must delete such information as: location, identity, and actual or prospective movements of ships or aircraft; information on the forces, weapons, military installations, or plans of the United States or her allies; information regarding the employment of any naval or military unit of the United States or her allies; effects of enemy operations, including casualties to personnel or material of the United States or her allies; and criticism of equipment or morale of U.S. or allied forces.

Distress Signals

Distress signals may be made either separately or together. There is no basis for the popular notion that the national ensign, hoisted upside down, is a recognized signal of distress. No man-of-war would ever subject the colors to this indignity. But if you should see a private craft with her insignia hoisted upside down, she probably is in distress, and you should go to her assistance without delay.

Distress signals are as follows:

A gun or other explosive fired at intervals of about 1 minute.

A continuous sounding with any fog-signal apparatus.

Rockets or shells, throwing red stars, fired one at a time at short intervals.

The signal group · · · – – – · · · (SOS) in Morse Code.

The radio-telephone signal "Mayday."

The international signal of distress indicated by the letters NC.

The distress signal, a square flag having above or below it a ball or anything resembling a ball.

Flames on a vessel, as from a burning tar barrel or oil barrel.

A rocket parachute flare or a hand flare showing a red light.

A smoke signal giving off a volume of orange-colored smoke.

Slowly and repeatedly raising and lowering arms outstretched to each side.

The following signals are prescribed for submerged submarines in emergency situations involving rising to periscope depth or surfacing.

A yellow smoke flare fired into the air from a submarine indicates that the submarine is coming to periscope depth, in preparation for surfacing. Ships should clear the immediate vicinity, but should not stop propellers.

A red smoke flare fired into the air from a submarine is a signal that the submarine is in serious trouble and will surface immediately if possible. Smoke flares of any color, fired into the air at short intervals, mean that the submarine requires assistance. All ships in the vicinity should stand by to give aid.

506

Appendices

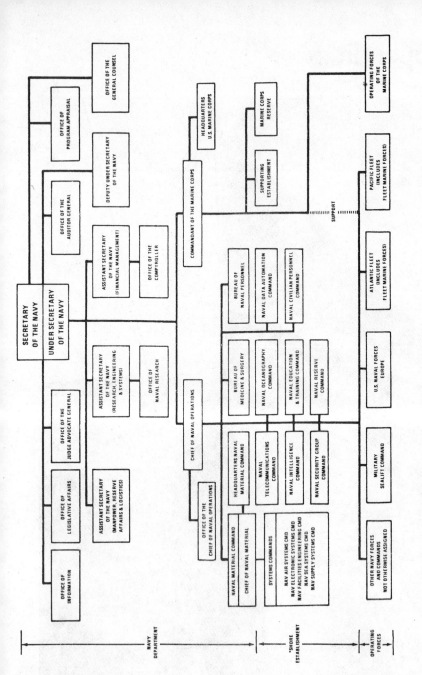

* Also Includes Other Designated Shore Activities, Not Shown On The Chart. Which Are Under The Command Or Supervision Of The Organizations Depicted.

A. Navy Organization

The Navy is part of the Defense Department, along with the Army and Air Force. Until 1947, the Navy was a separate department of the government as was the Army. The National Security Act of 1947 created the National Military Establishment (NME) which in 1949 became the Department of Defense (DOD) headed by the Secretary of Defense (SECDEF), a cabinet officer and a civilian.

The Navy Department was created in 1798 when Benjamin Stoddert, the first Navy secretary, was appointed. The first executive organization in the Navy came in 1815 when a three-man board of naval commissioners was created. In 1842 a system of bureaus was set up, and the structure lasted—with minor changes—until 1966. The position and title of Chief of Naval Operations (CNO) was created in 1915. The establishment of the Naval Material Command (NMC) in 1966, with its functional systems commands, resulted in the organizational structure under which the Navy operates today.

Department of Defense

The Department of Defense is the largest government agency in the United States. It spends over 30 percent of the national budget and employs nearly 4 million persons (including 950,000 civilians).

The Defense Department is composed of the Office of the Secretary of Defense (OSD); the Joint Chiefs of Staff (JCS) and their supporting establishment; the Departments of the Army, Navy, and Air Force; and various unified and specified commands. It provides for our military security and supports our national policies and interests. The National Security Act of 1947, as amended, is the controlling military law of the United States.

OFFICE OF THE SECRETARY

The Secretary of Defense is the principal assistant to the President in all matters relating to the Department of Defense and exercises direction, authority, and control over the department.

The Deputy Secretary of Defense supervises and coordinates the activities of the department and takes the place of the Secretary during his absence or disability.

The Armed Forces Policy Council (AFPC) advises the Secretary of Defense on matters of broad armed forces policy.

THE JOINT CHIEFS OF STAFF

The JCS consists of the chairman and the chiefs of staff of the Army and Air Force, and the Chief of Naval Operations (CNO). When Marine Corps matters are under consideration, the Commandant of the Marine Corps (CMC) also sits with the Joint Chiefs.

The JCS prepares strategic plans and provides strategic direction for the military forces. It prepares joint logistic plans and establishes unified commands in strategic areas. It formulates policies for joint training of the military forces, coordinates the education of members of the military forces, and reviews major material and personnel requirements. The JCS is assisted by a Joint Staff of 400 officers from the four services.

UNIFIED AND SPECIFIED COMMANDS

A unified command, composed of components of two or more services, has a broad continuing mission, and has a single commander.

The unified commands are: Atlantic Command, Pacific Command, U.S. European Command, U.S. Southern Command, and Readiness Command.

A specified command, like a unified command, has a broad continuing mission but is normally composed of forces from one service. There are three specified commands: Strategic Air Command (SAC); Aerospace Defense Command (ADCOM); and Military Airlift Command (MAC).

The Naval Establishment

The Department of the Navy (DON) includes more than the Navy Department, the central executive authority of the Navy in Washington; it also includes Headquarters, Marine Corps; all active and reserve forces, including Naval Aviation and the Marine Corps; and all shore (field) activities, headquarters, forces, bases, installations, and functions under the control or supervision of the Secretary of the Navy (SECNAV). The Coast Guard is also under the jurisdiction of DON operating as part of the Navy (in war, or when the President so directs).

SECRETARY OF THE NAVY

The Secretary of the Navy, a civilian, is in charge of the Department of the Navy. Under the direction, authority, and control of the Secretary of Defense (SECDEF), he is responsible for the policies and control of the DON, including its organization, administration, operation, and efficiency.

The civilian executive assistants to SECNAV are the Under Secretary of the Navy, the Assistant Secretaries of the Navy, the Deputy Under Secretary of the Navy, and the General Counsel of the Navy.

Staff assistants to the Secretary of the Navy include the Director of Civilian Personnel, the Chief of Information, the Chief of Legislative Affairs, and the Director, Office of Program Appraisal.

UNDER SECRETARY OF THE NAVY

The Under Secretary is the deputy and principal assistant to the Secretary and the general manager of the Department of the Navy. He is responsible for supervising, among other things, the Office of Program Appraisal, the Office of General Counsel, the Office of Information, the Office of the Judge Advocate General, and the Office of Legislative Affairs.

ASSISTANT SECRETARIES OF THE NAVY

There are three Assistant Secretaries of the Navy. They are in charge of Financial Management (ASN(F&M)); Manpower, Reserve Affairs and Logistics (ASN(M,RA&L)); and Research, Engineering and Systems (ASN(R,E&S)).

SECNAV Staff Offices

OFFICE OF THE COMPTROLLER

The Office of the Comptroller sets the financial policies of the Navy and prescribes budget, accounting, and auditing procedures which enable the Navy to meet operating and planning requirements.

OFFICE OF THE JUDGE ADVOCATE GENERAL (JAG)

JAG is involved in all phases of law other than business and commercial law. The chief concerns of this office are military law, international law, admiralty law, law suits, administrative law, and civil law. JAG is the principal adviser to the Chief of Naval Operations (CNO) and the Chief of Naval Personnel on military legal matters.

OFFICE OF NAVAL RESEARCH (ONR)

ONR is charged with promoting, planning, initiating, and coordinating naval research. The Chief of Naval Research reports to the ASN(R,E&S). He is also the Assistant Oceanographer of the Navy for ocean science matters.

OFFICE OF INFORMATION (CHINFO)

The Chief of the Office of Information (CHINFO) develops and disseminates information to the public on the operations of the

Navy. He also makes sure that all appropriate information about DON policies and programs is available to naval personnel.

OTHER STAFF OFFICES

Besides those described, other staff offices of SECNAV are the Office of General Counsel, the Office of Civilian Manpower Management, the Office of Legislative Affairs, the Office of Naval Petroleum and Oil Shale Reserves, and the Office of Program Appraisal.

Chief of Naval Operations (CNO)

The CNO is the senior military officer of the Department of the Navy. As such he outranks all naval officers (unless a naval officer is serving as chairman of the Joint Chiefs of Staff). He is the principal naval adviser to the President and SECNAV on matters of war and the principal adviser and executive to SECNAV on DON activities. The CNO represents the Navy on the JCS, and keeps SECNAV informed on the activities of the JCS. He is responsible to SECNAV for the use and administration of the operating forces in wartime and is charged with the preparation, readiness, and logistical support of the forces and also with the coordination and direction of the Naval Material Command (NMC) and the bureaus and offices of the Navy Department.

OFFICE OF THE CHIEF OF NAVAL OPERATIONS (OPNAV)

The CNO is assisted by a large organization, formally known as OPNAV, in executing his duties. The principal assistant and adviser to the CNO is the Vice Chief of Naval Operations (VCNO), who exercises executive authority as delegated by the CNO and performs the duties of CNO in that officer's absence. He directs the activities of the Navy Program Planning Group and coordinates the efforts of the Deputy Chiefs of Naval Operations (DCNOs) and the Office of Naval Intelligence, Office of Naval Communications, and Office of Antisubmarine Warfare.

The VCNO's chief assistant, responsible for the general administration of OPNAV, is the Assistant Vice Chief of Naval Operations (AVCNO). He controls the Office of the Oceanographer of the Navy and the Naval Observatory.

Other major officers in the CNO organization are the Deputy Chiefs of Naval Operations: DCNO (Manpower, Personnel and Training), CHNAVPERS; DCNO (Submarine Warfare); DCNO (Surface Warfare); DCNO (Logistics); DCNO (Air Warfare); and DCNO (Plans, Policy and Operations).

Other Commands

CHIEF OF NAVAL MATERIAL (CNM)

CNM runs the Naval Material Command (NMC) which supplies the material needed by the operating forces and the Marine Corps. The NMC consists of a headquarters and the following five principal subordinate commands, each with a headquarters and various shore activities: NAVAIRSYSCOM, NAVELECSYSCOM, NAVFAC, NAVSEASYSCOM, and NAVSUPSYSCOM.

NAVAL AIR SYSTEMS COMMAND (NAVAIRSYSCOM)

NAVAIR is responsible for Navy and Marine Corps aircraft, airborne weapons systems, and other aviation-related equipment; and for photographic and meteorological equipment.

NAVAL ELECTRONIC SYSTEMS COMMAND (NAVELECSYSCOM)

This command is responsible for airborne and shipboard electronic equipment as well as navigational, communication, and test gear. NAVELEX is the central authority on electronic standards.

NAVAL FACILITIES ENGINEERING COMMAND (NAVFAC)

NAVFAC runs the Navy's construction program, plans and maintains facilities, and operates all utilities. It manages real estate owned by the Navy and runs programs on natural resources and pollution control. It supplies material, such as floating cranes, pontoons, moorings, and ocean structures. NAVFAC also provides transportation and construction equipment, as well as engineering and technical services to nuclear shore power and radioisotope-power devices.

NAVAL SEA SYSTEMS COMMAND (NAVSEASYSCOM)

NAVSEA is responsible for ships, their components, and their weapons systems. It coordinates shipboard subsystems and supervises salvage operations, such as raising sunken ships and rescuing stranded ones. NAVSEA is responsible for all shipboard ordnance safety, including nuclear power.

NAVAL SUPPLY SYSTEMS COMMAND (NAVSUPSYSCOM)

Responsibilities here include managing the Navy's supply system, publications and printing, the resale program, the Navy stock fund, the field purchasing service, and the transportation of Navy property. NAVSUP also oversees food and clothing services.

CHIEF OF THE BUREAU OF MEDICINE AND SURGERY (BUMED)

BUMED safeguards the health of Navy personnel, cares for and treats those sick or injured (including Marines and dependents). BUMED supervises medical and dental training, research, and programs aimed at preventing and controlling diseases, injuries, and occupational illnesses.

NAVAL MILITARY PERSONNEL COMMAND (NMPC)

This command is responsible for just about everything that pertains to Navy personnel—promotions, discipline, retirement, religious guidance, welfare, morale, uniforms, regulations, ceremonies and etiquette.

For 36 years this command was known as the Bureau of Naval Personnel (BUPERS). On 31 October 1978, the bureau was divided into a policy-making command (DCNO (MPT)) and a policy-executing command (NMPC). Some of the details of this division are still being resolved; therefore, you may see and hear the name BUPERS for some time to come. Until these details are resolved, you will still be governed by BUPERS instructions, notices, and the BUPERSMAN referred to in this manual and throughout Appendix J.

CHIEF OF NAVAL EDUCATION AND TRAINING (CNET)

514

CNET is in charge of the Navy's education and training programs. He manages the funds that pay for education, the facilities that house the classrooms, and the curricula. CNET supervises all training except some aspects of fleet training and those that are BUMED's responsibility. Technical training at shore stations, air stations, and at sea comes under his jurisdiction. Under CNET are the Chief of Naval Air Training and the Chief of Naval Education and Training Support.

COMMANDANT OF THE MARINE CORPS (CMC)

He is responsible, under the Secretary of the Navy, for the administration, discipline, internal organization, training requirements, efficiency, and readiness of the Marine Corps. His command includes the headquarters, the operating forces of the Corps, the Marine Corps support establishment, and the Marine Corps Reserve. CMC is not a part of the command structure of the CNO; there is, however, close cooperation between the two military heads.

Other advisers to SECNAV and CNO include the Naval Inspector General (NIG), the Special Studies and Presentation Group, and the Marine Corps Liaison Officer.

The Operating Forces

The CNO answers to SECNAV for the command, use, and administration of the Navy's operating forces. These forces consist of the fleets, the seagoing forces, the Military Sealift Command (MSC), the district forces, the Coast Guard (when operating as a service of the Navy), Fleet Marine Forces (FMF) and other assigned Marine Corps forces, and other forces and activities assigned to the CNO.

Pacific and Atlantic Fleets include ships and craft classified and organized into commands by types, the titles of which are: training commands, surface forces, fleet marine forces, naval air forces, and submarine forces.

Commander-in-Chief, Pacific Fleet (CINCPACFLT), commands the Third and Seventh Fleets; the Commander-in-Chief, Atlantic Fleet (CINCLANTFLT), the Second Fleet; and the Commander-in-Chief, U.S. Naval Forces, Europe (CINCUSNAVEUR), the Sixth Fleet. CINCUSNAVEUR commands the naval component of the unified command under the U.S. Commander-in-Chief, Europe (CINCEUR). Ships that make up the operational (numbered) fleets are provided by type commanders. Thus, an aircraft carrier might be under the administrative command of Commander Naval Air Force, Pacific (COMNAVAIRPAC). Fleet Marine Forces are type commands under the administrative control of the Commandant of the Marine Corps. These forces operate under the respective commanders-in-chief as do other type commands.

The Military Sealift Command (MSC), operated by the Navy for all armed services, consists of ships and commercial vessels manned by civil service personnel employed on a contract basis. These ships transport servicemen, their dependents, combat troops, and material throughout the world. MSC's prime mission is to provide immediate sealift capability in an emergency. MSC also operates the ships used for scientific projects and various programs run by U.S. agencies.

A shore activity may be placed under the command of the operating forces if it is outside a naval district or if it provides support only to units of operating forces. Some of the activities so assigned include naval air facilities, communication facilities, naval and submarine bases, ship repair facilities, and supply depots.

TASK FORCE ORGANIZATION

This system, developed during World War II, further divides fleets into forces, groups, units, and elements. Each subdivision has a numbered designation and an appropriate communication call sign.

Under the fleet numbering system, the Commander Sixth Fleet, for instance, would assign certain numbered task forces. A task force (TF) breakdown could include: a striking force, TF 60; an amphibious force, TF 61; a service force, TF 62; etc. Within each force there could be further subdivisions, called task groups (TGs). For example, within TF 60 there might be a carrier group, TG 60.1, and a heavy support group, TG 60.2.

Task groups may be further subdivided, into task units (TUs). For example, TG 60.1—the carrier group—may have a carrier unit, designated TU 60.1.1. A destroyer screen—considered to be part of that unit—would be a task element; its new designation would be TE 60.1.11. Another element, perhaps an advanced screen, would be designated TE 60.1.12; and so on.

With this system, the task commander has a task force that is adaptable to any change in size.

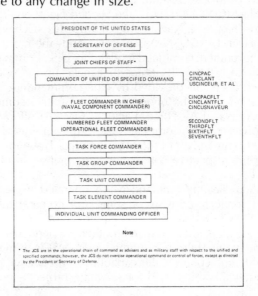

Shore Activities

Although many shore activities exist at the Navy Department level (e.g., systems commands under CNM, the Naval Weather Service Command under CNO), this section concerns those shore activities which have the primary function of supplying, maintaining, and supporting the operating forces with material, services, and personnel.

A typical list of such activities might include naval bases, air facilities and stations, reserve training units, ammunition depots, communication stations, fleet intelligence centers, fuel depots, naval hospitals, laboratories, medical centers, recruiting stations, shipyards, supply centers, and schools.

Many shore activities are at strategic points along the U.S. coasts and overseas where they can most directly serve the needs of the operating forces. Activities for which nearness to the forces afloat is not essential or practical, however, are distributed at various interior points within the United States. Among these activities are the finance offices, recruiting stations, research and development activities, and training centers.

AREA COORDINATION

Area coordinators are responsible to the Chief of Naval Operations for the coordination of all shore activities. Although an area coordinator has no authority over the internal affairs of specific field activities, he must ensure that there is ready support for the fleet within his area.

Area coordinators may delegate some of their responsibilities to commands and activities within their jurisdictions.

NAVAL DISTRICTS

Commandants of naval districts are regional representatives of the CNO and SECNAV. The naval districts, which once numbered up to seventeen, have been reorganized. Today, only Naval District Washington, D.C., remains.

NAVAL BASES

A naval base includes all naval shore activities in a given place. The primary purpose of a naval base is to coordinate all services provided to the fleet by the nearest naval shore activities. Each base commander has jurisdiction over such activities, including air stations in some cases. These activities may also include a shipyard which provides direct support to the fleet. A naval base commander exercises military command over the component activities, unless command relationships are otherwise prescribed.

Regular Navy

The United States Navy consists of the Regular Navy and the Naval Reserve. Each element has its own important functions, and each must work closely with the other branches of the military. The Regular Navy consists of officers, either in the line or in a staff corps, and enlisted men and women. As of the end of 1980, the Navy budgeted for approximately 524,000 officers and enlisted personnel.

Line and Staff Corps: The names of the various ranks and charts showing sleeve and shoulder insignia are on pages 42–45. All officers serve either in the regular line or in a special staff corps, according to their specialties. An officer wears the device of his specialty on his sleeve above the stripes, or on shoulder boards or collar, depending on the uniform worn. Line officers exercise military command; only line officers command at sea, and, in general, only line officers exercise command on shore. Members of certain staff corps, such as Medical, Supply, and the Civil Engineer Corps command shore activities and units (such as Seabees) under the control of their respective bureaus.

Medical Corps (MC): Commissioned doctors provide medical services and administer the hospitals, dispensaries, sickbays, and other medical units in the Navy.

Dental Corps (DC): Commissioned dentists provide dental services and run dispensaries on board larger ships. The Dental Corps, like the Medical Corps, Nurse Corps, and Medical Service Corps, comes under the Bureau of Medicine and Surgery.

Medical Service Corps (MSC): This corps has specialists in optometry, pharmacy, bacteriology, biochemistry, psychology, sanitation engineering, and medical statistics.

Nurse Corps (NC): Navy nurses are commissioned officers in the Nurse Corps. They serve in hospitals and dispensaries in the United States and on foreign stations, aboard hospital ships, and on transports at sea. The first woman to become an admiral in the Navy was promoted to that rank in the Nurse Corps in 1971.

518

Supply Corps (SC): This is the business branch of the Navy; it receives and disburses funds for supply and pay, subsistence, and transportation.

Chaplain Corps (CHC): Officers of the Chaplain Corps are ordained ministers of various denominations; they conduct religious services and promote the spiritual and moral welfare of the Navy and Marine Corps.

Civil Engineer Corps (CEC): This corps is composed of graduate civil engineers, who are normally restricted to shore duty. The CEC supervises the buildings, grounds, and plants, as well as all construction, on shore stations.

Judge Advocate General's Corps (JAG): Established in 1967, this staff corps is composed of graduate lawyers certified for legal duties within the Navy.

WARRANT OFFICERS

Commissioned warrant officers have advanced through the enlisted ranks in various technical specialties and probably possess the most detailed practical knowledge of the modern Navy. For the various warrant specialties, see page 45.

WOMEN IN THE NAVY

Women have served in the Navy since 1908, when the Navy Nurse Corps was established as part of the Medical Department by an act of Congress. Nurses were given military rank in 1942. In April 1947 the Nurse Corps was established as a staff corps within the Medical Department. Nurses appointed to the Navy now hold permanent commissions in the Regular Navy.

Congress authorized the Women's Reserve of the Navy on 30 July 1942, with 1,000 officers and 10,000 enlisted women. The first enlisted women in the Navy were rated as female yeomen, nicknamed "yeomanettes," who served during World War I. The Women's Armed Services Integration Act of 1948 provided that laws which authorize commissioned and warrant officers in the Regular Navy also include authority to enlist and appoint women to the Regular Navy and Naval Reserve.

Today women are an integral part of the Navy. They are recruited, trained, and assigned under the same regulations as men and are entitled to the same benefits. On 28 October 1978, the president signed a law allowing provisions for women to be permanently assigned to duty in hospital ships, transports, training ships, and vessels of a similar classification—auxiliaries and service craft. They also may be assigned temporary duty—not to exceed 180 days—to any Navy ship or squadron. The law does not permit them to be assigned to any Navy ship or aircraft expected to be engaged in a combat mission. Long-range plans call for 190 women officers and 5,000 enlisted women to be on sea duty by FY85.

Approximately 28,500 women are on active duty in the Navy, serving interchangeably with men in a full spectrum of assignments. Training for both officers and enlisted women has been integrated with the training for men.

Women officers may be selected for senior service schools and the war colleges; they serve in a variety of challenging staff positions, and as commanding and executive officers of naval facilities and stations.

Women unrestricted line (URL) officers work in career fields such as administration, data processing, communications, and geophysics. In February 1976, Captain Fran McKee became the first woman URL officer selected for promotion to flag rank. Eight URL women entered aviation training in 1973. Since then many URL women have been designated as naval aviators. Some women officers also serve in the staff corps—such as supply, medical, chaplain, civil engineering, and Judge Advocate General.

Eligible for 85 percent of the Navy technical schools and for all non-seagoing jobs, enlisted women work in some of the Navy's most specialized ratings, such as electronics, data systems, and aviation fire control.

Women have earned a distinguished reputation as vital members of the Navy Medical Department, which provide health care for Navy and Marine personnel. Officers in the Navy Nurse Corps serve all over the world in a variety of nursing specialties; two have been named administrators of Navy health-care facilities. Although male nurses joined the Corps in 1965, women still make up 75 percent of the 2,600 Navy nurses. In the Hospital Corps, enlisted women provide essential health-care services, working as laboratory, dermatology, pharmacy, and physical therapy technicians and in other technical specialties.

Naval Reserve

An important part of the Navy is the Naval Reserve, which provides qualified individuals and trained ships' crews for active duty in wartime, national emergency, or whenever national security requires.

The Naval Reserve is administered by the regular naval establishment, and all agencies in the Navy function for and provide for the Naval Reserve just as they do for the regular Navy. The Chief of Naval Reserve (CHNAVRES), headquartered in New Orleans, is in charge of about 87,000 selected reservists, about 10,000 of whom are on full-time active duty in training and administrative jobs. There are more than 2,400 Naval Reserve units located throughout the country.

Surface, construction, and submarine-oriented units generally train at Naval Reserve centers. Aviation units train principally at Naval Reserve air activities.

Whatever your rating, you can be almost certain there is a need for you in the Naval Reserve, since the Reserve operates major combatant ships, tenders, construction forces, amphibious ships and units, special warfare units, service force ships, and aviation squadrons.

Naval Reservists are placed in one of these categories:

Ready Reserve (USNR–R): Members of the Ready Reserve are eligible for assignment to paying billets; they receive pay and allowances for duly authorized active duty in training (ACDUTRA) periods, and are eligible for promotion. All Ready Reserves have active status and can be recalled to active duty in a national emergency, or when otherwise authorized by law. Reserve personnel on active duty are also considered members of the Ready Reserve.

Standby Reserve–Active (USNR–S1): The only reservists who may be retained in this category are those who are eligible to participate in the NAVRES training program for retirement point credit. They are: reservists still under military obligation; those being retained in an active status with at least 18 but less than 20 years of qualifying service for retirement on their transfer to the

Standby Reserve–Active; key employees of the U.S. government who are screened from the Ready Reserve; and those temporarily assigned for hardship or other reasons with the expectation of being returned to the Ready Reserve. Members can be recalled to active duty in time of war or national emergency and are eligible for promotion.

Standby Reserve–Inactive (USNR–S2): Members of this category are not eligible to participate in the NAVRES training program or to be assigned to any unit or mobilization position, nor are they eligible for promotion.

Retired Reserve (USNR–Retired): All members of the Retired Reserve are liable for active duty (under the same provisions as those of the Ready Reserve and Standby Reserve–Active categories). This category includes both retired with pay and without pay. These reservists may not receive any retirement point credit for the performance of any duty, except extended active duty. All members are in an inactive status.

Naval Reservists train by drilling with organized units, by going on active duty for periods of two or more weeks annually, and through correspondence courses. Reserve programs are divided into paying or non-paying billets. The latter programs are primarily for officer training.

United States Marine Corps

The Marine Corps was established by an act of Congress on 11 July 1798, although the Marines celebrate their birthday on 10 November, the date in 1775 when the Continental Marines were established by the Continental Congress. The authorized strength of the Corps is set at 20 percent of that authorized for the Navy. The Marine Corps consists of two Fleet Marine Forces (FMF), one in the Atlantic and one in the Pacific. The Corps's mission is: to provide FMFs, with supporting air components, for service with the fleet; to develop tactics, techniques, and equipment; to provide detachments and organizations for service on board naval vessels; and to provide security detachments for the protection of naval stations and bases.

The Navy and Marine Corps together are responsible for developing and maintaining an effective amphibious warfare capability. This team is unique because its mobility and versatility enables it to fight on both land and sea, as well as in the air. Individual Marines serve with Navy men in Navy commands and vice versa, and units are likewise freely interchanged. Most Navy staffs include Marine officers and men, while Marine units and stations have Navy doctors, dentists, chaplains, and hospital corpsmen.

Women Marines in the Regular Marine Corps were authorized

by the Women's Armed Services Integration Act of 1948. Enlisted women recruits are trained at Parris Island. Women candidates for commissions in the Regular Marine Corps, selected from qualified college graduates and undergraduates and from enlisted women Marines, are trained at Quantico, Va. Their training closely parallels that of male officer candidates, except that the women are not given combat training.

U.S. Coast Guard

The Coast Guard is another military service within the armed forces although in peacetime it is under the jurisdiction of the Department of Transportation. Coast Guard personnel receive the same pay as those under the Department of Defense and are subject to the Uniform Code of Military Justice. On declaration of war or when the President directs, the Coast Guard operates within the Naval Establishment.

The Coast Guard's peacetime duties include protecting lives and property on the seas and along the coasts, including Alaska and Hawaii; and manning lifeboat stations, search and rescue centers, lighthouses, lightships, and Loran stations. The USCG is responsible for locating icebergs and recommending safe sea lanes in northern waters. It enforces maritime safety regulations and mans ocean "stations" that gather weather data and assist aircraft navigation; it also helps planes and ships in trouble. In wartime the Coast Guard escorts ships, engages in antisubmarine warfare, mans transports, maintains port security, and operates landing craft.

The Women's Reserve of the Coast Guard Reserve, called SPARS, from the Coast Guard motto "Semper Paratus," was established by the same amendment to the Naval Reserve Act of 1938, passed July 1942, that authorized the WAVES and Women Marines. Identical to the WAVES in composition and basic duties, the SPARS served the Coast Guard and the Navy with distinction during World War II. In 1973, the restriction that women could only serve in the Reserve was abolished, and women now serve in the regular Coast Guard.

The Coast Guard has been in operation since 1790, when it was organized by Secretary of the Treasury Alexander Hamilton as the Revenue Marine Service. The name was later changed to Revenue Cutter Service and, in 1915, to Coast Guard. It consists of about 30,000 officers and enlisted personnel, as well as civilian employees. Appointments to the Coast Guard Academy at New London, Connecticut, are by competitive examination, open to civilians and enlisted men eighteen to twenty-two years of age from any armed service. Graduates receive B.S. degrees and are commissioned as ensigns in the Coast Guard.

B. Navy History

Why History?

History, some say, is "dry" and "dull." It can be. But a quick look at the history of an organization can give you a pretty good picture of what that organization is like, and what it has done. Knowing that, you can more easily figure out your place in it. History can show you where mistakes were made before, and if enough people are aware of those mistakes, we can avoid making them again.

So what follows is a "bare-bones" record of the accomplishments—and some of the failures—of our Navy, to help you find out more about this organization of which you are now a member. Remember, today is tomorrow's history. You are helping to make it.

The Earliest Years

America was born of the sea. The people who made this nation came here over the sea, and they were sustained by goods exchanged by the shipload. This trade had been going on for 150 years before the desire to be master of their own destiny led the colonists to strike for independence. These first efforts at sea power were often feeble and fruitless, and yet they had their impact on the course of events. And at the critical juncture, it was the timely actions of the French Navy that resulted in the isolation of British General Cornwallis, and his subsequent surrender.

12 Jun 1775	First engagement at sea in the Revolution. Citizens of Machias, Maine, under the command of Jeremiah O'Brien, seized a cargo sloop taking lumber to Boston and with it captured the cutter HMS *Margaretta*. (TB 30 and DDs 51, 415, and 725 were named O'Brien.)
6 Sep 1775	Schooner *Hannah* sails as first unit of "George Washington's Navy" of converted merchantmen.
13 Oct 1775	The Continental Congress authorized the outfitting of a 10-gun warship "for intercepting such transports as may be laden with stores for the enemy"—the start of the Continental Navy.
3 Dec 1775	Lt. John Paul Jones hoisted the first official

American flag on a ship (*Alfred*) for the first
time.

3–4 Mar 1776   A Continental squadron under the command
of Como. Esek Hopkins, composed of the
Alfred (24 guns), *Columbus* (20), *Andrea
Doria* (14), *Cabot* (14), *Providence* (12), *Hornet* (10), *Wasp* (8), and *Fly* (8), successfully
attacked the British at Nassau in the Ba-
hamas. Captured were 71 cannon and 15
mortars. This was also the first amphibious
assault by American Marines, under the
command of Capt. Samuel Nicholas. (DDs
311 and 449 were named for him.)

4 Apr 1776   Make-do brig *Lexington* (16), under John
Barry, defeated HMS *Edward* (8) in lower
Delaware Bay. This was the earliest of
Barry's successes. (DDs 2, 248, and 933
have been named for him.)

11 Oct 1776   Continental squadron, under Gen. Benedict
Arnold, defeated a British force on Lake
Champlain in the Battle of Valcour Island.
This caused the British to delay the invasion
of the Hudson River Valley for a year, by
which time the Continental Army was ready
to turn it back.

16 Nov 1776   U.S. flag saluted for the first time by the
Dutch governor of St. Eustatius Island in the
West Indies.

24 Apr 1778   John Paul Jones, in command of the sloop
Ranger (20), defeated the sloop HMS *Drake*
(2) off Belfast, Ireland. The *Drake* became the
first major British warship to be taken by the
new Navy.

23 Sep 1780   John Paul Jones, now commanding the converted merchantman *Bon Homme Richard*
(42), defeated the frigate HMS *Serapis* (50) in
a night fight off Flamborough Head, England.
His ship badly battered (it would sink after
the fight), Jones rejected the British surrender
question with his defiant, "I have not yet
begun to fight!" (DDs 10 and 230, and DDG
32 were named in honor of Jones, and DDs
4, 290, and 353, and CG 19 in honor of his
gallant first lieutenant, Richard Dale.)

17 Oct 1781   Gen. Cornwallis surrendered at Yorktown,
Virginia, effectively ending the Revolutionary War.

19 Apr 1783	George Washington proclaimed the Revolution officially ended.	
2 Aug 1785	The frigate *Alliance*, last survivor of the Continental Navy, sold out of service.	

Rebirth and the Second War of Independence

The United States did without a Navy, or even the authorization for one, for nine years. It had been hoped that the world would leave the new country alone. But that was not to be. Barbary pirate states on Africa's north coast captured our defenseless shipping and demanded ransom. And then, when we finally began reacting to that problem, war broke out between France and Great Britain and our neutral shipping (we had one of the largest merchant fleets in the world then) became a target for both sides.

With our miniscule new Navy, whose first units were launched in 1797, we first settled the French problem, then the Barbary pirates, and finally fought the British. And when the last war was over, the United States found itself a recognized major sea power.

27 Mar 1794	President Washington signed into law "an act to provide a naval armament," which provided for the building of six frigates: the *Constitution, United States, Constellation, Congress, Chesapeake,* and *President.* The captains were to be paid $75 a month and ordinary seamen, $10. Rations were valued at 28 cents a day.
May–Oct 1797	The frigates *United States, Constellation,* and *Constitution* were launched, beginning the modern U.S. Navy.
30 Apr 1798	The Navy Department was established.
18 Jun 1798	Benjamin Stoddert, first Secretary of the Navy, took office. His salary was $3,000 a year. First actions in quasi-war (undeclared) with France occured in June. (DD 302 and DDG 22 have honored Stoddert.)
9 Feb 1799	The *Constellation* (38), under Thomas Truxton, defeated the French frigate *L'Insurgente* (36) in 30 minutes. The Frenchmen had 100 casualties; the Americans, 4.
1 Feb 1800	The *Constellation,* still under Truxton, battered the French ship *La Vengeance* (52 guns) for five hours; but nightfall and damage to the American vessel combined to let the Frenchman get away. Midshipman James C.

Jarvis was lost when the *Constellation's* mainmast went by the board. (DDs 14, 229, and CGN 35 have been named for Truxton; and DDs 38, 393, and 799 for Jarvis.)

7 Feb 1800   The 32-gun frigate *Essex* became the first U.S. man-of-war to cross the equator.

31 Oct 1803   The frigate *Philadelphia* (36), under Capt. William Bainbridge ran aground on a reef off Tripoli (Libya) while pursuing Barbary pirate craft; he was captured. The American crew spent 20 months in a Tripolitan prison before being freed.

14 Feb 1804   Lt. Stephen Decatur, with 83 volunteers from the frigate *Constitution* and the schooner *Enterprise,* entered Tripoli harbor at night in the ketch *Intrepid* and succeeded in destroying the *Philadelphia* without a single loss. English Admiral Lord Nelson termed it "the most daring act of the age." (DDs 5 and 341 and DDG 31 have been named for Decatur.)

3 Aug 1804   Como. Edward Preble in the *Constitution* led the U.S. Mediterranean Squadron in the first of a series of attacks against Tripoli that ultimately ended the Barbary Wars and freed Bainbridge and other Americans. The peace treaty was signed 5 Jun 1805. (DDs 12 and 345, and DDG 46 were named Preble.)

16 May 1811   In the mistaken belief he was attacking the frigate HMS *Guerriere* (38), which had been conducting some high-handed operations off our east coast, Capt. John Rodgers in the *President* (44) blasted the sloop HMS *Little Belt* (22) in a night encounter begun by the smaller ship. (TB 4, DDs 254 and 574 remembered him.)

18 Jun 1812   President Madison declared war on Great Britain over "free trade and sailors' rights." The U.S. Navy then had but 17 warships; the British, over 600!

16–18 Jun 1812   The *Constitution,* under Capt. Isaac Hull, escaped a five-ship British squadron in a classic 69-hour chase.

3 Aug 1812   The *Essex,* commanded by David Porter, captured the sloop HMS *Albert* (16) after a single broadside.

19 Aug 1812   Isaac Hull and the *Constitution* defeated the frigate HMS *Guerriere* in a 35-minute slugfest that left the Britisher a hulk. This was the

first time an American frigate had defeated a British frigate, and greatly cheered the nation. At this time the United States became a major sea power in the world. As a result of the battle, the *Constitution* received her famous nickname "Old Ironsides." (Hull has been remembered by DDs 7, 330, 350, and 945.)

18 Oct 1812   Jacob Jones, commanding the sloop *Wasp* (18), smashed the brig HMS *Frolic* (22) off the Chesapeake Capes. (Jacob Jones was honored by DDs 61 and 130, and DE 130.)

25 Oct 1812   The frigate *United States*, sister ship to the *Constitution*, with Stephen Decatur in command, defeated the frigate HMS *Macedonian* (38) in a two-hour combat that left over 100 British casualties to 12 American. Taken into our Navy, the USS *Macedonian* served until 1828.

29 Dec 1812   The *Constitution*, now commanded by William Bainbridge, left the HMS *Java* (38) a shambles in a hard two and one-half hour fight off Brazil. With this third loss in three frigate-to-frigate actions in five months, the Royal Navy received orders not to take on the American 44s like the *Constitution* and *United States* with less than squadron strength. (Bainbridge has been remembered in DDs 1 and 246, and CGN 25.)

14 Feb 1813   The *Essex* became the first U.S. man-of-war to round Cape Horn and enter the Pacific Ocean.

24 Feb 1813   The sloop *Hornet* (18), under James Lawrence, ruined the brig HMS *Peacock* (2) in two broadsides off Guyana.

30 Mar 1813   Lt. John M. Gamble, USMC, took command of the *Greenwich* (10). He was the only Marine ever to command a Navy ship.

1 Jun 1813   Rashly responding to a British captain's challenge, newly promoted Capt. Lawrence, now commanding the frigate *Chesapeake* (36) and a green crew, was defeated and killed off Boston in a fight with the frigate HMS *Shannon* (38). Lawrence's dying words "Don't give up the ship!" have lived on as one of the slogans of our Navy. (Lawrence has been memorialized in TB 8, DD 250, and DDG 4.)

13 Aug 1813	The brig *Argus* (20), under William Allen, was captured by the brig HMS *Pelican* (20) in the Irish Sea after her raiding operations had taken 20 British merchantmen. (DD 66 was later named the *Allen*.)
5 Sep 1813	In a bloody engagement, William Burrows' brig the *Enterprise* (14) overcame the brig HMS *Boxer* (14) off the coast of Maine. Both captains were killed and were buried side-by-side in Portland, Me. (DD 29 and DE 105 honored Burrows.)
10 Sep 1813	The Battle of Lake Erie. Oliver Hazard Perry, commanding a U.S. squadron of nine ships, defeated a British six-ship squadron to ensure U.S. control of the Great Lakes and the Northwest Territory. Perry carried Lawrence's dying command "Don't Give Up the Ship" on his battle flag, and the opening phrase of his victory report is still remembered today: "We have met the enemy, and they are ours . . ." (Perry's name has been carried by DDs 11, 340, and 844, and FFG 7.)
28 Mar 1814	The *Essex*, still under Porter, after cruising Pacific waters in a highly successful operation against British whalers, was trapped and defeated at Valparaiso, Chile, by the frigate HMS *Phoebe* (36) and the sloop HMS *Cherub* (18). (David Porter has been remembered by TB 6, and DDs 59, 356, and 800.)
29 Apr 1814	The new American sloop *Peacock* (22), named after the British unit defeated by the *Hornet* the previous year, defeated the brig HMS *Epervier* (18) off the Florida coast. The Britisher was found to be carrying $25,000 in gold bullion! (Lewis Warrington, *Peacock's* captain, was memorialized in DDs 30, 383 and 843.)
22 Jun 1814	The *Independence* (74), first ship-of-the-line in the U.S. Navy, was launched. She served in one capacity or another until 1912.
28 Jun 1814	The second *Wasp* of the War of 1812, a 22-gun sloop commanded by Johnston R.Y. Blakeley, bested the brig HMS *Reindeer* (22) in just 19 minutes, in the English Channel. (TB 27, DD 150, and DE 140 have been named for Blakeley.)

24 Aug 1814	British invaders burn Washington, D.C. The only defense of the nation's capital was by sailors under Capt. Joshua Barney at Bladensburg, Md. (TB 25 and DD 149 bore his name.)
11 Sep 1814	Battle of Lake Champlain. A bloody engagement between Como. Thomas MacDonough's 16-ship squadron and a British one of like number ended in defeat for the invaders, much as in the Battle of Valcour Island in the Revolution (11 Oct 1776). (MacDonough has been honored by DDs 9, 331, and 351, and DDG 39.)
23 Oct 1814	The *Demologos*, a "floating steam battery" designed by Robert Fulton, was launched for the Navy. Carrying its paddlewheel between twin hulls joined fore and aft, it had 20 guns and made 5 knots. Never actively used, the *Demologos* was demolished by explosion and fire in 1829.
24 Dec 1814	The Treaty of Ghent formally ended the War of 1812. Because of poor communications of the day, all the following events occurred because one or both sides hadn't been so informed.
8 Jan 1815	The Battle of New Orleans. Gen. Andrew Jackson and a largely militia army defeated a British regular army invasion force. Jackson's defenses had time to organize because a Navy gunboat force under Como. Daniel T. Patterson and Lt. Thomas C. Jones had fought a successful delaying action along the way north from the Gulf of Mexico at Lake Borgne. (Patterson's name has been carried by DDs 36 and 392, and FF 1061.)
15 Jan 1815	The frigate *President* (44) was run down and captured by a British four-ship squadron. She was the only American heavy frigate ever lost to an enemy.
7 Feb 1815	Board of Naval Commissioners established to oversee the maintenance and operation of the Navy, under the direction of the Secretary.
20 Feb 1815	In a stunning night fight, Charles Stewart in the *Constitution* defeated both the frigate HMS *Cyane* (34) and corvette *Levant* (21) off Madeira Island. The *Levant* was later recap-

tured by the British, but the *Cyane* served actively in the U.S. Navy until 1827. (DD 13 and 224, and DE 238 have borne the name of Stewart.)

23 Mar 1815   James Biddle in the *Hornet* (18) took the brig HMS *Penguin*, also 18 guns, in 22 minutes. (Biddle has been honored by TB 26, DD 151, DDG 5, and CG 34.)

30 Jun 1815   In the final naval action of the War of 1812, the sloop *Peacock* captured the brig HMS *Nautilus* (14) off Java, while under the command of Lewis Warrington.

Until The Civil War

In these 45 years, the Navy fought in a small war with Mexico, that gave it experience in amphibious and riverine operations. The Navy also helped pacify Indians, suppress piracy, explore, and experiment. Steam propulsion, iron hulls, exploding shells, rifled guns—all appeared in this period. Our men-of-war appeared in all corners of the world, showing the flag and protecting the rights of our overseas citizens.

22 Mar 1820   Capt. James Barron killed the popular Como. Stephen Decatur in a duel at Bladensburg, Md. The resulting public outrage spelled the beginning of the end for duels.

23 Apr 1821   In an experiment typical of this time, the *Constitution* was propelled at three knots in Boston Harbor by hand-cranked paddlewheels! The experiment, seeking a way to power sailing ships in close quarters, was not repeated.

16 May 1821   The frigate *Congress* (36) became first U.S. warship to visit China.

31 Aug 1826–
8 Jun 1830   The sloop *Vincennes* (18), under Capt. W.B. Finch, became first U.S. Navy warship to go around the world.

2 Apr 1827   Construction of the first naval hospital was begun at Portsmouth, Va.

6 Dec 1830   The U.S. Naval Observatory, the first in the country, was established.

17 Jun 1833   The ship-of-the-line *Delaware* (74) drydocked in Gosport (now Portsmouth, Va.) Navy Yard, the first warship to be drydocked in the United States.

12 Jul 1836   Charles H. Haswell became the first "chief

	engineer" (of the steam frigate *Fulton II*) in the U.S. Navy.
3 Mar 1837	The rank of commander was created, formalizing the hitherto temporary grade of master commandant.
1838–1842	Commander Charles Wilkes took a six-ship naval expedition around the world, exploring Antarctica and many places in the Pacific. (TB 35, and DDs 67 and 441 have borne the name *Wilkes*.)
Feb 1841	First regulations providing details for enlisted uniforms are issued. These regs included the first specifics on rating insignia.
1 Sep 1842	The Board of Naval Commissioners was superseded by five technical bureaus, subordinates to the Secretary of the Navy. With variations in number and titles, they continue in existence today as the naval systems commands.
5–6 Dec 1843	The *Michigan,* the Navy's first iron-hulled warship, launched herself during this night with no one present! She finally left naval service 105 years later.
10 Dec 1843	The *Princeton,* the Navy's first screw-propelled steam frigate, was launched.
29 Mar 1844	Uriah Levy, the Navy's first Jewish officer, was promoted to captain. (DE 162 recalled his service.)
1845	A captain's annual pay was a maximum of $4,500. The highest enlisted monthly pay was $40 (for a yeoman) and a ship's boy received $6–8 monthly. The rum ration was valued at 20 cents a day.
10 Oct 1845	U.S. Naval Academy was established at Annapolis, Md.
18 Feb 1846	"Larboard and starboard" became "port and starboard" by general order.
11 May 1846	War declared on Mexico.
11 Jul 1846	The Naval Academy commissioned its first ship's officer, Passed Midshipman Richard Aulick.
20 Jul 1846	The *Columbus* (74) became the first U.S. man-of-war to visit Japan.
1847	"The Kedge-Anchor," by Sailing Master William Brady, USN, was first published. This book was an ancestor to *The Bluejackets' Manual.*

9 May 1847 Army troops (12,000) under Gen. Winfield
Scott make amphibious assault against Vera
Cruz, Mexico. The city surrendered 20 days
later.

Jun 1847 A squadron under Como. Matthew C. Perry
captured the Mexican city of Tabasco after
fighting its way 70 miles upriver.

1848 The Treaty of Guadelupe Hidalgo ended the
Mexican War, with the United States gaining
most of its present southwestern territory.

1850 Flogging—whipping with a cat-o'-nine tails
—was ended as a punishment in the Navy.

31 Mar 1854 Como. Matthew C. Perry signed a treaty with
the Japanese at Yokohama, opening that
country to western trade.

2 Mar 1859 The first Navy ship to be built on the west
coast, the paddlewheel gunboat *Saginaw*,
was launched at Mare Island, Calif.

The Civil War

The Navy's principal role in this struggle was to blockade the
South's coastline to prevent the export of cotton and the entry of
munitions. On the Western rivers, the Navy developed specialized craft used to dominate the Mississippi and its tributaries, and
thus cut the Confederacy off from other supply sources via Texas.
In this war, revolving turrets, ironclads, steam power, observation balloons, submersibles, and mines were tried, often for the
first time in battle. This was done despite the fact that about one-
third of the Navy's officers "went south" as the war began.

9 Jan 1861 The steamer *Star of the West* was fired upon
by South Carolinians while attempting to resupply Fort Sumter in Charleston Harbor.
This was the first in a chain of events resulting in the Civil War.

27 Aug 1861 A squadron under Flag Officer Silas Stringham bombarded Forts Hatteras and Clark in
North Carolina into submission. (*Stringham*
was the name of TB 19 and DD 83.)

7 Nov 1861 Flag Officer Samuel DuPont led his squadron
to victory over Port Royal, S.C. (TB 7, and
DDs 152 and 941 have been named *Du-
Pont.*)

21 Dec 1861 The Medal of Honor was authorized by Congress. (It wasn't authorized for award to officers until 1915.)

6 Feb 1862 A squadron under Flag Officer Andrew H.

	Foote helped take Fort Henry on the Tennessee River.
7 Feb 1862	A squadron under Flag Officer Louis M. Goldsborough captured Roanoke Island, N.C. (TB 20, DD 188, and DDG 20 have honored Goldsborough.)
14–16 Feb 1862	Foote's squadron again participated in the assault on a Confederate fort, this time helping to take Fort Donelson on the Cumberland River. (TB 3 and DDs 169 and 511 were named for Foote.)
9 Mar 1862	The *Monitor* (Capt. John L. Worden), first warship with a revolving gun turret, met the Confederate *Virginia* (ex-*Merrimack*) in world's first battle of ironclads. The battle ended in a draw, but the *Virginia* never fought again. (DDs 16, 288, 352 and CG 18 have been named *Worden*.)
14 Mar 1862	Flag Officer Goldsborough's squadron captured New Berne, N.C.
24 Apr 1862	Flag Officer David G. Farragut led his squadron past Forts St. Phillip and Jackson up the Mississippi River to a commanding position above New Orleans, which surrendered the next day. (TB 11, DDs 300 and 348, and DDG 37 honor Farragut.)
10 Jun 1862	The *Red Rover*, the Navy's first hospital ship, went into operation on the Mississippi River.
16 Jul 1862	David Glasgow Farragut was appointed the first rear admiral in the Navy. In 1864, he became our first vice admiral; and on 25 Jul 1866, our first admiral. The act creating the rank of rear admiral also created the ranks of commodore, lieutenant commander, master, and ensign.
21 Aug 1862	The *New Ironsides*, the Navy's first armored ship, was completed.
31 Aug 1862	The issuance of grog to ship's companies was ended, a year after being terminated for officers and warrant officers.
16 Feb 1864	Confederate submarine the *Hunley*, commanded by Infantry Lieutenant G.E. Dixon, sank the Union steam sloop *Housatonic* with a spar torpedo, the first sinking of a warship by a submarine. The *Hunley* also was lost in the blast. (AS 31 recalls the builder of this craft, H.L. Hunley.)

19 Jun 1864	The Union steam sloop *Kearsarge* (Capt. John A. Winslow) sank the famed Confederate raider *Alabama* (Capt. Raphael Semmes) off Cherbourgh, France. (Winslow has been honored by TB 5, and DDs 53 and 359.)
5 Aug 1864	A Union squadron under Vice Adm. Farragut assaulted Confederate forces in Mobile Bay and won a decisive victory. It was here, when mines (then called torpedoes) endangered his forces, that Farragut ordered, "Capt. Drayton, go ahead! Damn the torpedoes! Go on!"
27 Oct 1864	A steam launch, commanded by Lt. William B. Cushing, sank the large Confederate ironclad *Albemarle* with a spar torpedo. (Cushing was remembered by TB 1, and DDs 55, 376 and 797.)
15 Jan 1865	A squadron under Rear Adm. David D. Porter cooperated with an Army force under Maj. Gen. A.H. Terry in capturing Fort Fisher, N.C. (LSD 40 recalls the event.)

Decline and Rebirth

After the Civil War, a combination of war-weariness and the westward expansion resulted in the Navy being allowed to decline. For nearly 20 years, the Navy languished. Finally, in the mid-1880s, as a nationalistic urge swept over the country, the Navy once again received attention. On this wave of enthusiasm, the nation was swept into the Spanish-American War, the development of the Great White Fleet, and the building of the Panama Canal.

17 Apr 1866	Congress appropriated $5,000 to test the use of "petroleum oil" as fuel for ships' boilers.
1869	New regulations provided an enlisted working uniform for the first time. (Before, old dress uniforms were used.)
28 Jun 1869	William M. Wood was appointed first Surgeon General of the Navy. (DD 715 was named for him.)
10 Jun 1871	A Navy-Marine Corps assault force made a landing in Korea in a punitive operation against a Korean fort that had fired on a peaceful American ship. Lt. Hugh W. McKee was killed in the attack and honored by TB 18 and DDs 87 and 575.

11 Sep 1872	James Henry Conyers became the first black to enter the Naval Academy.
9 Oct 1873	A meeting held by a group of naval officers resulted in the formation of the U.S. Naval Institute, publisher of *The Bluejackets' Manual*.
28 Jun 1874	The *Jeanette*, a supply ship, received the first Navy shipboard electrical system. While proceeding on a mission to the Arctic she was crushed in the ice pack on 13 Jun 1881.
31 Jul 1874	The *Intrepid*, first Navy torpedo boat to carry self-propelled torpedoes, was commissioned.
3 Mar 1883	The rank of master became lieutenant (junior grade).
6 Oct 1884	Naval War College established.
1885	Distinctive first, second, and third class rates were provided in new uniform regulations.
14 Feb 1885	Congress approved a military retirement act, the first formal retirement program for our armed forces. But an oversight omitted the Navy, and it wasn't until 1899 that sailors were included.
8 Dec 1885	The gunboat *Dolphin*, first steel warship for the U.S. Navy, was commissioned.
1 Apr 1893	New regulations provided for chief petty officers (rating insignia developed from the masters-at-arms petty officers.)
15 Feb 1898	The battleship *Maine* was sunk by internal explosion (due to spontaneous combustion) in Havana harbor. Belief that she had been attacked by Spaniards, encouraged by the press of the day, inflamed American public opinion and resulted in a declaration of war on 25 Apr 1898.
1 May 1898	Como. George Dewey's Asiatic Squadron defeated the Spanish in Manila Bay. The battle had been begun by Dewey's order to his flagship captain, "You may fire when ready, Gridley." Dewey later was promoted to Admiral of the Navy as a result of the publicity given his victory. (DD 349 and DDG 45 have been named for him; and DDs 92 and 380 and CG 21 for Gridley.)
3 Jul 1898	Rear Adm. William T. Sampson's squadron defeated a fleeing Spanish force near Santiago, Cuba. Every Spanish ship was sunk or

run ashore. (Sampson has been honored by DDs 63 and 394 and DDG 10.)

13 Aug 1898	Spain asked for peace.
2 Mar 1899	George Dewey was promoted to Admiral of the Navy, a rank held by him alone. The act creating this rank also abolished the rank of commodore.
11 Apr 1900	The *Holland,* the Navy's first submarine, was commissioned.
11 Nov 1902	The *Bainbridge,* the Navy's first destroyer, was commissioned. It was 250 feet long, and carried two 3-inch guns and two 18-inch torpedo tubes.
16 Dec 1907	The Great White Fleet, the modern U.S. battle squadron, began its round-the-world tour, which ended on 22 Feb 1908.

The Twentieth Century

In the last 70 years, we have been involved in two world wars, two Asiatic wars and a variety of lesser incidents. At the end of World War II, the United States Navy was the mightiest the world had ever seen. Since then, other calls for national resources have resulted in the Navy "living" on its accumulated resources until nearly all have been spent; nevertheless, the Navy has been adequate to accomplish its missions and to be a leader in many areas of science and technology.

8 Jan 1907	By executive order, President Theodore Roosevelt directed that all American commissioned ships be titled "United States Ship" (USS).
6 Apr 1909	Comdr. Robert E. Peary became the first man to reach the North Pole. (DE 132 and FF 1073 have honored him.)
1910	The *Paulding* (DD 22) became the first Navy ship to operate on fuel oil.
14 Nov 1910	Eugene Ely, a civilian contract pilot, flew a plane off a 57-foot wooden deck built over the bow of the cruiser *Birmingham*—the first takeoff from a ship.
18 Jan 1911	Ely landed on a platform built over the stern of the *Pennsylvania* in San Francisco Bay—the first shipboard landing.
Oct 1911	The Navy received its first aircraft. One was built by the Wright Brothers and two by Glen Curtiss.
26 Jul 1912	The letter "D," in Morse code, was sent by a

	plane to the destroyer *Stringham* a mile away —the first radio message received from an aircraft.
1 Jul 1914	Liquor prohibited on all ships and stations.
6 May 1916	The first ship-to-shore radiotelephone conversation took place between the *New Hampshire* (BB 25) and Washington D.C.
2 Apr 1917	The United States entered World War I.
4 May 1917	The first U.S. destroyer squadron arrived in Queenstown, Ireland, to help the British in escorting convoys. When asked by the English admiral when his ships would be prepared for duty, Comdr. Joseph K. Taussig replied, in a manner characteristic of "tin can" sailors, "We will be ready when fueled, sir".
17 Nov 1917	German *U-58* became the first submarine sunk by the U.S. Navy, done in by the destroyers *Fanning* (DD 37) and *Nicholson* (DD 52).
28 Feb 1919	*Osmond Ingram* (DD 255) the first Navy ship named for an enlisted man, launched. Ingram was the first enlisted man killed in action in World War I, lost when the destroyer *Cassin* (DD 43) was torpedoed in Oct 1917.
31 May 1919	Navy flying boat NC-4, under Lt. Comdr. Albert C. Read, became the first aircraft to fly across the Atlantic Ocean.
17 Jul 1920	General Order No. 541 established the present system of ship designation (DD 963, FF 1052, etc.)
21 Aug 1920	The first radio message heard around the world was broadcast from a Navy radio station near Bordeaux, France.
20 Mar 1922	The *Jupiter*, a collier (coal-carrier), was recommissioned after conversion to the Navy's first aircraft carrier, the *Langley* (CV 1).
8 Aug 1925	The first night carrier landing took place aboard the *Langley*.
27 Feb 1928	Comdr. T.G. Ellyson, the Navy's Aviator #1, was killed in an air crash.
28 Nov 1929	Lt. Comdr. Richard E. Byrd flew over the South Pole. He previously flew over the North Pole in 1926. (DDG 23 bears his name.)
Apr 1937	The first sea trials of radar were conducted on a U.S. destroyer.
7 Dec 1941	In a surprise attack on Pearl Harbor, the Japa-

537

nese inflicted severe damage on major units of the U.S. Pacific Fleet and killed 2,008 Navymen.

13 Dec 1941	Guam was captured by the Japanese.
23 Dec 1941	The Marines on Wake Island finally surrendered to vastly superior Japanese forces.
26 Jan 1942	Japanese submarine *I-173* sunk by the *Gudgeon* (SS 211), the first enemy naval vessel sunk by a U.S. submarine.
27 Feb 1942	A combined American-British-Dutch-Australian naval force was defeated by a Japanese force in the Battle of the Java Sea.
1 Mar 1942	Bataan surrendered.
4–5 May 1942	The Battle of the Coral Sea was fought, resulting in the end of Japanese advances in the southwest Pacific. The *Lexington* (CV 2) was lost, as was the Japanese light carrier *Shoho*. This was the first battle fought solely by air groups—the fleets never saw each other.
6 May 1942	Corregidor surrendered.
4–6 Jun 1942	The Battle of Midway resulted in four Japanese carriers being sunk, as opposed to one American (the *Yorktown*), and turned the Pacific war in favor of the United States.
3 Aug 1942	Mildred McAfee was commissioned as the first woman naval (line) officer.
9 Aug 1942	U.S. Marines landed on Guadalcanal in Solomons in the first American offensive action in the Pacific.
9 Aug 1942	A Japanese cruiser force smashed a similar United States–Australian force in the Battle of Savo Island, sinking four cruisers in a half-hour night action.
11–12 Oct 1942	The Americans won a night action in the Battle of Cape Esperance, sinking two Japanese warships and damaging two more without loss.
8 Nov 1942	The U.S. Navy and Army participated in simultaneous amphibious landings in North Africa—at Algiers and Oran, Algeria, and Fedala, Morocco.
13–15 Nov 1942	In a series of furious night actions, U.S. naval forces slugged it out with the Japanese in the Battle of Guadalcanal. The Japanese lost two cruisers and six destroyers—and the U.S. Navy had begun receiving new units at an increasing rate, and so had more "muscle" left

than the Japanese. The five Sullivan brothers who died in one of the American cruisers lost were honored by *The Sullivans* (DD 537), first destroyer named for more than one person.

30 Nov 1942 The Battle of Tassafaronga was the last Japanese try to save Guadalcanal. The *Northampton* was lost and so was a Japanese destroyer. The *Rogers* (DD 876) was named for three brothers lost with the cruiser.

9 Apr 1943 Rank of commodore reestablished (but discontinued again after the war).

May 1943 The first antisubmarine "hunter-killer" group was formed under Capt. Arnold J. Isbell with the *Card* (CV 11), *Bristol* (DD 453), *Ludlow* (DD 438) and *Woolsey* (DD 437). It was an almost immediate success. (DD 869 recalls Capt. Isbell.)

1943 Hunter-killer groups of escort carriers, destroyers and destroyer escorts went into widespread operation, and made a major contribution to defeating the U-boats.

10 Jul 1943 The U.S. Navy participated in the invasion of Sicily.

13 Jul 1943 The Second Battle of Kula Gulf resulted in the sinking of a Japanese light cruiser and the loss of the *Gwin* (DD 433).

25 Jul 1943 The *Harmon* (DE 678) was launched, the first ship to be named for a black.

6 Aug 1943 The Japanese lost three destroyers in the Battle of Vella Gulf. There were no U.S. Navy losses.

2 Nov 1943 At Empress Augusta Bay, U.S. Navy forces defeated a Japanese attack, sinking a cruiser and a destroyer.

21 Nov 1943 Three Japanese destroyers went down in the Battle of St. George, New Ireland Island.

21 Jan 1944 The assault at Anzio was the last amphibious attack on Italy.

2 Feb 1944 Amphibious assaults conducted against Kwajalein, Roi, and Namur Islands in the Marshalls; the islands were conquered quickly despite fierce resistance.

18 Feb 1944 Further landings secured Eniwetok and Engebi Islands.

29 Feb 1944 The Navy landed occupation forces in the Admiralty Islands.

22 Apr 1944	U.S. landings at Hollandia, New Guinea, met little opposition.
19 May–1 Jun 1944	The *England* (DE 635) sank a record six Japanese submarines during this period. Three were killed in the first four days, and five of the six were downed without assistance! CG 22 is also the *England*.
4 Jun 1944	*U-505* captured by a hunter-killer group led by the *Guadalcanal* (CVE 60)—the only time the order "Boarders away!" has been passed in this century.
6 Jun 1944	The Allies invade Europe at Normandy. Nearly 2,500 U.S. Navy ships and craft were involved in the largest amphibious assault ever. At one beach alone, 21,328 troops, 1,742 vehicles and 1,695 tons of supplies were landed in 12 hours.
15 Jun 1944	The 2nd and 4th Marine Divisions were landed on Saipan and completed operations three weeks later.
19–20 Jun 1944	In the Battle of the Philippine Sea, also called the "Marianas Turkey Shoot," naval aviators downed 426 Japanese aircraft while losing only 95 planes.
21 Jul 1944	Marines and Army troopers were landed on Guam and took complete control of the island by 10 Aug 1944.
24 Jul 1944	The Marines landed on Tinian Island against light resistance.
15 Aug 1944	The Navy participated in amphibious landings in Southern France, the last ones conducted in Europe.
15 Sep 1944	The Navy-Marine team combined again to assault Peleliu Island, getting closer to the Philippines.
20 Oct 1944	U.S. forces returned to the Philippines in an amphibious assault of Leyte Island.
23–25 Oct 1944	In three connected battles, known collectively as the Battle of Leyte Gulf, the Imperial Japanese Navy was virtually destroyed. Lost to the Japanese were three battleships, one attack carrier, three light carriers, six heavy cruisers, four light cruisers, eight destroyers, and a submarine. U.S. Navy losses: one light carrier, two escort carriers, two destroyers, one destroyer escort, a submarine, and a torpedo boat.

Twentieth Century

14 Dec 1944	The rank of fleet admiral was created. It was terminated in late 1952.	**Navy History**
15 Dec 1944	The U.S. Army landed on Mincoro Island in the Philippines.	
9 Jan 1945	Army forces landed at Lingayen Gulf, Luzon.	
19 Feb 1945	The Marines were landed on Iwo Jima. It took 26 days of bitter fighting to secure the island.	
1 Apr 1945	In the final major amphibious assault of World War II, Army units were landed on Okinawa this Easter Sunday. Navy units were subjected repeatedly to Japanese suicide (kamikaze) attacks. Thirty-four ships were lost, 288 others were damaged. The Japanese lost 1,228 planes and pilots in the kamikaze effort. Resistance finally ended on 21 Jun.	
7 May 1945	Germany surrendered. She had lost over 800 submarines to Allied action in the Battle of the Atlantic.	
6 Aug 1945	The first atomic bomb was detonated over Hiroshima, Japan. Weaponeer on the bomber, "Enola Gay," was Navy Capt. W.S. Parson. (DDG 33 bears his name.)	**541**
9 Aug 1945	The second atomic bomb was dropped on Nagasaki, Japan.	
2 Sep 1945	Japan formally surrendered on board the *Missouri* (BB 63).	
Oct 1945	The *Stewart* (DD 224) was returned to the U.S. Navy. Damaged early in the war and supposedly scuttled beyond salvage at Soerabaja (Indonesia), she had been out in Japanese service as a patrol boat (P 102) and had been active throughout the war.	
2 Jul 1946	A jet aircraft operated from an aircraft carrier for the first time.	
29 Sep 1946	The Navy's first supersonic aircraft, the Douglas D-558-1, broke the sound barrier for the first time.	
3 Jun 1949	John Wesley Brown became the first black to graduate from the Naval Academy.	
26 Jun 1950	U.S. forces are ordered to support South Korean troops against invading North Korean troops.	
3 Jul 1950	F9F-2 Panthers from the *Valley Forge* (CV 45) attacked Pyongyang, the North Korean capital, in the first strike by carrier-launched jet aircraft.	Twentieth Century

15 Sep 1950	Marines were landed at Inchon, near Seoul, Korea, in a surprise thrust deep behind the front lines. This attack caused the Communist invaders to fall back northward.
9 Nov 1950	First dogfight involving a Navy jet and an enemy jet. Lt. Comdr. W.T. Amen, in a Panther, shot down a MiG-15, Russian-built fighter.
28 Aug 1952	First use of carrier-launched guided missiles. Pilotless, radio-controlled (via a TV guidance system) F6F5 Hellcat fighters with high explosives were used against land targets from the *Boxer* (CV 21).
3 Nov 1952	Marine Maj. W. Stratton, in an F3D-2 Skyknight, scored the first "kill" by an airborne intercept radar-equipped fighter. He got a Russian-built YAK-15.
27 Jul 1953	The Korean Armistice went into effect.
3 Dec 1954	The *Gyatt* (DD 712) recommissioned as DDG 1, was the first combatant Navy ship with antiaircraft missiles.
17 Jan 1955	The *Nautilus* (SSN 571), the world's first nuclear-powered submarine, began operations.
17 Mar 1958	The Navy's "Vanguard I" satellite was placed in orbit, where it should remain for 2,000 years! It is the oldest man-made object in orbit today.
3 Aug 1958	The *Nautilus* became the first ship in history to reach the North Pole.
16 Nov 1958	Proficiency (pro) pay went into effect.
14 Jul 1959	The *Long Beach* (CGN 9), the world's first nuclear-powered surface warship, was launched at Quincy, Mass.
1960	The *Triton* (SSN 586) became the first submarine to circumnavigate the world submerged. The voyage covered 41,500 miles in 83 days at an average speed of 18 knots.
20 Jul 1960	The *George Washington* (SSBN 598) made the first submerged launching of a Polaris ballistic missile, off Cape Canaveral.
15 Nov 1960	The first deterrent Polaris patrol was begun by the *George Washington*. It lasted 66 days, 10 hours.
5 May 1961	Comdr. Alan B. Shepard became the first American in space, riding Mercury capsule *Freedom 7* on a 15-minute suborbital flight.
20 Feb 1962	Marine Maj. John Glenn became the first

American to orbit the earth in Friendship 7. Other Navy and Marine Corps officers to explore outer space have included "Gus" Grisson, Walter Schirra, James Lovell, Scott Carpenter, "Pete" Conrad, Richard Gordon, and Alan Bean.

Oct 1962　President Kennedy gave the Russians a lesson in the use of sea power when he "quarantined" Cuba with air, surface, and subsurface units and caused the Russians to stop sending in shiploads of strategic nuclear missiles.

10 Apr 1963　The *Thresher* (SSN 593) was lost east of Portsmouth, N.H., due to material failure during a test dive, the first nuclear submarine to be lost from any cause.

20 Jul 1969　Lunar module *Eagle* landed on the Sea of Tranquillity on the moon, after detaching from Apollo 11. Commander of the mission and first man to set foot on the moon was Neil Armstrong, who had been a Navy fighter pilot in the Korean War.

17 Dec 1969　The *New Jersey* (BB 62), the last active U.S. battleship, was decommissioned. She and her sisters, the *Missouri, Iowa,* and *Wisconsin,* remain in reserve.

22 Jun 1973　The Skylab I team, operating the world's first orbiting space laboratory, completed a 30-day operation. Its members were all naval aviators.

1 Jul 1973　The traditional sailor's white hat, broad collar, and bell-bottomed trousers were superseded by a more conventional "suit" type uniform.

1 Jan 1978　Navy returns to traditional bell-bottom uniform for sailors in grades E-1 through E-4.

7 Apr 1979　*Ohio,* the first of the Trident submarines, was christened and is expected to be commissioned in late 1980.

1 May 1980　The Navy began issuing traditional jumper, bell-bottom uniform to all male recruits.

9 May 1980　The *Coral Sea* pulled into Subic Bay concluding 102 consecutive days at sea.

26 May 1980　The *Nimitz* completed 144 consecutive days at sea, a longer underway period than any ship since World War II.

C. Uniform Code of Military Justice

Congress and the Navy have taken steps to ensure that you will know the disciplinary laws and regulations most likely to affect your station in the Navy. Article 137 of the Uniform Code of Military Justice (UCMJ) states that Articles 2, 3, 7–15, 25, 27, 31, 37, 38, 55, 77–134 and 137–139 of the code must be fully and carefully explained to every enlisted person. This is done at the time of entering active duty, after six months of active service, and at the time of reenlistment.

In addition, Article 137 requires a complete copy of the UCMJ be made available to every person covered by those regulations. Navy Regulations further spell out this provision by requiring that the text of the UCMJ be posted in a conspicious place. You will find in every naval activity a copy of the UCMJ on the bulletin board or some other prominent place.

Outline of UCMJ, Articles 1–140

546

Article 134, properly known as the "general article," is designed to cover all disorders and neglects detrimental to good order and discipline in the armed forces and crimes and offenses not capital in nature.

Outline

D. Beaufort Scale

Beaufort Number	Wind Speed in Knots	Seaman's Term	Appearance of Sea
0	Below 1	Calm	Surface like a mirror.
1	1–3	Light air	Ripples that look like fish scales; but without foam crests.
2	4–6	Light breeze	Small wavelets, still short but more pronounced; crests look glassy and do not break.
3	7–10	Gentle breeze	Large wavelets. Crests begin to break. Glassy-looking foam. Perhaps scattered white horses.
4	11–16	Moderate breeze	Small waves, becoming longer; fairly frequent white horses.
5	17–21	Fresh breeze	Moderate waves, taking a more pronounced long form; many white horses are formed. (Chance of some spray.)
6	22–27	Strong breeze	Large waves begin to form; white foam crests are more extensive everywhere. (Probably some spray.)
7	28–33	Moderate gale (high wind)	Sea heaps up and white foam from breaking waves begins to be blown in streaks along the direction of the wind. Spindrift begins.
8	34–40	Fresh gale	Moderately high waves of greater length; edges of crests break into spindrift. The foam is blown in well-marked streaks along

				the direction of the wind.
9	41–47	Strong gale		High waves. Dense streaks of foam along the direction of the wind. Sea begins to roll. Spray may affect visibility.
10	48–55	Whole gale		Very high waves with long overhanging crests. The resulting foam in great patches is blown in dense white streaks along the direction of the wind. The whole surface of the sea looks white. The rolling of the sea becomes heavy and shocklike. Visibility is affected.
11	56–63	Storm		Exceptionally high waves. (Small and medium-sized ships might for a long time be lost to view behind the waves.) The sea is completely covered with long white patches of foam lying along the direction of the wind. Everywhere the edges of the wave crests are blown into froth. Visibility is affected.
12	64–71	Hurricane		The air is filled with foam and spray. Sea completely white with driving spray; visibility very seriously affected.
13	72–80			
14	81–89			
15	90–99			
16	100–108			
17	109–118			

E. Navigational Aids

Aids to navigation are lighthouses, lightships, minor lights, buoys, and day beacons. Aids are placed so that they provide a nearly continuous and unbroken chain of charted marks for coast and channel piloting.

Buoys

Navigational buoys are moored floating markers (Figure E–1), placed to guide ships in and out of channels, warn them of hidden dangers, lead them to anchorage areas, and the like. Their location usually is shown on the area navigational chart, which makes them invaluable aids in piloting. Buoys may be of various sizes and shapes. Regardless of their shapes, however, their distinctive coloring is the chief indication of their purpose.

Although a buoy's shape generally has no special navigational significance, it may help toward its identification from the description given on the chart. The following are the principal types of buoys.

Spar: Large logs, trimmed, shaped, and appropriately painted. They also may be of metal, constructed in the familiar spar shape.

Can and nun: Cylindrical and conical, respectively.

Bell: Flat top, surmounted by a framework supporting a bell. Older bell buoys are sounded by the restless motion of the sea. Newer types are operated automatically by gas or electricity.

Gong: Similar to bell buoy, except that it has a series of gongs, each with a different tone.

Whistle: Usually cone-shaped, it carries a whistle sounded by the sea's motion, or horns that are sounded at regular intervals by mechanical or electrical means.

Lighted: Carries batteries or gas tanks and is surmounted by a framework supporting a light.

Combination: One in which a light and sound signal are combined, such as a lighted bell, gong, or whistle buoy.

Examples of *special purpose buoys* are quarantine buoys, which are yellow, and dredging and survey operations buoys, which are white with green tops.

In the United States, red buoys mark the right side, and black buoys mark the left side of the channel, coming from seaward. Remember: "Red–right–returning."

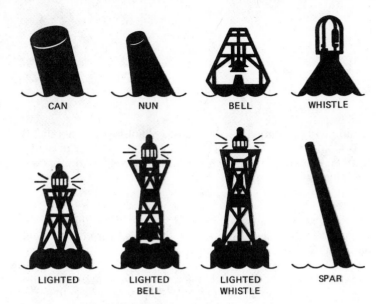

CAN NUN BELL WHISTLE

LIGHTED LIGHTED
BELL LIGHTED
WHISTLE SPAR

550 Figure E–1 Principal types of buoys.

Normally, red channel buoys are cone-shaped nun buoys, and black channel markers are cylindrical can buoys; but this is not always true. It is the color that is most important. Sometimes red and black buoys are painted white on top to enable them to be located more easily at night. Black and red horizontally banded buoys mark obstructions. They may be passed on either side, but, unless you know the dimensions of the obstructions, it is best to give such buoys a wide berth.

If the top band is red, the preferred channel is to the left of the buoy, coming from seaward; if the top band is black, the preferred channel is to the right. Buoys with black and white vertical stripes mark the middle of a channel or fairway.

Buoys painted all white have no special significance; they are used for purposes not concerned with navigation, such as the marking of ordinary anchorage areas. Buoys with black and white horizontal stripes mark fishing areas in some locales. A white buoy with a green top usually means dredging area.

Buoys are valuable aids to navigation, but they must never be depended upon exclusively. Buoys frequently drag their moorings or they may go adrift. Lights on buoys may go out of commission. Whistles, bells, and gongs usually sounded by the sea's motion may fail to function in smooth water. Anyone navigating by buoy's must be alert to these possibilities.

Numbering: The red buoys marking the right side of a channel bear even numbers starting with the first buoy from seaward. This

Buoys

is perhaps the only time you'll find anything to starboard having an even number. Black channel buoys, to the left of the channel coming from seaward, have odd numbers. Banded or striped buoys are not numbered but some have letters for identification.

Lights: Red lights are used only on red buoys or on ones that are horizontally banded in red and black, with the topmost band red. Green lights are only for black buoys, or for black and red horizontally banded buoys with the topmost band black. A white light may be (and frequently is) substituted for either the green or the red light. White lights are the only lights used on the black and white vertically striped buoys which mark the middle of a channel or fairway.

Lighting characteristics vary:

Fixed (steady) light means either a black or a red channel buoy.

Flashing light at regular intervals of not more than 30 flashes per minute may also mean either a black or red buoy.

Quick-flashing light with no fewer than 60 flashes per minute is also on either a black or red buoy, but at a turning point or junction where special caution is required.

Interrupted quick-flashing light with a series of repeated quick flashes, separated by about four-second dark intervals, indicates a red and black horizontally banded obstruction buoy.

Short-long flashing light, whose flash recurs at the rate of about eight per minute, is placed on a black and white vertically striped midchannel buoy.

DAY BEACONS

Unlighted aids to navigation (except unlighted buoys) are called day beacons. Like lighthouses and light structures, day beacons usually are colored to distinguish them from their surroundings and make them easy to identify. Day beacons marking channels are colored and numbered like channel buoys. Many are fitted with reflectors that show the same colors a lighted buoy would show at night in the same position.

Two day beacons, located some distance apart on a specific true bearing, constitute a day-beacon range. When a ship reaches a position where the two lights or beacons are seen exactly in line, she is "on the range." Ranges are especially valuable for guiding ships through narrow channels. Much steering through the Panama Canal is accomplished on ranges.

Storm-Warning Information

In the United States, information regarding weather and the approach of storms is furnished by the Weather Bureau. This information is disseminated by means of bulletins, reports furnished by newspapers, radio broadcasts, and in certain seaports, by flags during the day and with lanterns at night. Some storm-warning flags are 8 feet square, and the pennants have a hoist of 8 feet, and fly of 15 feet. Smaller ones are half this size.

SMALL CRAFT WARNING

One red pennant displayed by day, and a red light over a white light at night, indicate winds up to 38 miles an hour (33 knots) and sea conditions dangerous to small craft in the area.

GALE WARNING

Two red pennants displayed by day, and a white light above a red light at night, indicate that winds ranging from 39 to 54 miles an hour (34 to 47 knots) are forecast for the area.

STORM WARNING

A single square red flag with a black center displayed by day, and two red lights at night, indicate that winds of 55 miles an hour (48 knots) and higher are forecast for the area. (If winds are associated with a tropical cyclone or hurricane, the storm warning display indicates that winds with the range 55 to 73 miles an hour [48 to 63 knots] are forecast.)

552

HURRICANE WARNING

Two square red flags with black centers displayed by day, and a white light between two red lights at night, indicate that winds 74 miles an hour (64 knots) and above are forecast.

F. Running Lights

Running lights for steam or other power-driven vessels.

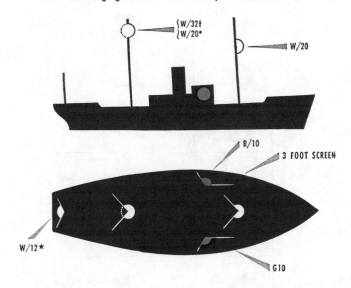

{ W/32†
{ W/20*

W/20

R/10

3 FOOT SCREEN

W/12★

G 10

† REQUIRED UNDER INLAND RULES FOR NON-SEAGOING VESSELS
* REQUIRED UNDER INTERNATIONAL RULES FOR SEA-GOING VESSELS OF OR OVER 150'
★ REQUIRED UNDER INTERNATIONAL RULES FOR ALL VESSELS UNDER WAY AND BY INLAND RULES IN CASES WHERE NO OTHER LIGHT IS VISIBLE AFT.

THE NUMBER LISTED AFTER THE INITIAL DESIGNATING COLOR (W FOR WHITE, ETC.) IS THE NUMBER OF POINTS OVER WHICH THE LIGHT MUST SHOW. A POINT IS 11¼ DEGREES.

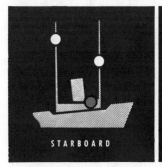

STARBOARD

HEAD-ON

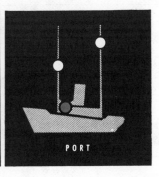

PORT

G. Signal Pennants and Flags

Pennant	Spoken	Pennant	Spoken	Pennant	Spoken
	PENNANT ONE "WUN"		CODE		SQUAD
	PENNANT TWO "TOO"		SCREEN		STARBOARD
	PENNANT THREE "THUH-REE"		CORPEN		STATION
	PENNANT FOUR "FO-WER"		DESIG		SUBDIV
	PENNANT FIVE "FI-YIV"		DIV		TURN
	PENNANT SIX "SIX"		EMER-GENCY		FIRST SUB
	PENNANT SEVEN "SEVEN"		FLOT		SECOND SUB
	PENNANT EIGHT "ATE"		FORMA-TION		THIRD SUB
	PENNANT NINE "NINER"		INTER-ROGATIVE		FOURTH SUB
	PENNANT ZERO "ZERO"		NEGAT		PORT
	ANSWER		PREP		SPEED

Flag	Name — Written / Spoken	Flag	Name — Written / Spoken	Flag	Name — Written / Spoken
	A ALFA "AL-FA"		M MIKE "MIKE"		Y YANKEE "YANG-KEY"
	B BRAVO "BRAH-VOH"		N NOVEMBER "NO-VEM-BER"		Z ZULU "ZOO-LOO"
	C CHARLIE "CHAR-LEE"		O OSCAR "OSS-CAH"		ONE - 1 "WUN"
	D DELTA "DEL-TAH"		P PAPA "PAH-PAH"		TWO - 2 "TOO"
	E ECHO "ECK-OH"		Q QUEBEC "KAY-BECK"		THREE - 3 "THUH-REE"
	F FOXTROT "FOKS-TROT"		R ROMEO "ROW-ME-OH"		FOUR - 4 "FO-WER"
	G GOLF "GOLF"		S SIERRA "SEE-AIR-RAH"		FIVE - 5 "FI-YIV"
	H HOTEL "HOH-TEL"		T TANGO "TANG-GO"		SIX - 6 "SIX"
	I INDIA "IN-DEE-AH"		U UNIFORM "YOU-NEE-FORM"		SEVEN - 7 "SEVEN"
	J JULIETT "JEW-LEE-ETT"		V VICTOR "VIK-TAH"		EIGHT - 8 "ATE"
	K KILO "KEY-LOH"		W WHISKEY "WISS-KEY"		NINE - 9 "NINER"
	L LIMA "LEE-MAH"		X XRAY "ECKS-RAY"		ZERO - 0 "ZERO"

H. Decoration and Award Ribbons

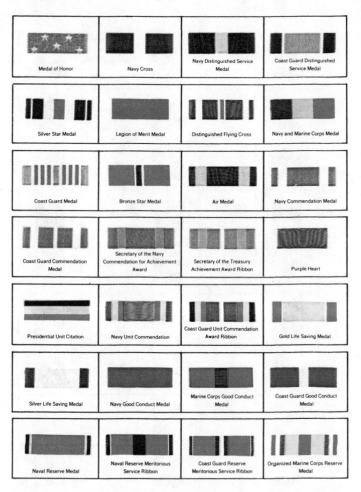

A decoration is conferred on an individual by name for exceptional courage, bravery, skill, or performance of duty. The Purple Heart is given to members of all military services who are wounded in action. Some minor decorations are not included. Service Awards are given for participation in designated wars, campaigns, or expeditions, or for service in various military theaters. There are more than three dozen such awards, which are not shown here.

Ribbons

I. Notes on Sources

The following list contains the principal sources used to prepare this edition. All of the official publications will be found aboard every ship and station, and most of the Naval Institute Press publications named will be found in ship or station libraries.

All Hands magazine
Bibliography for Advancement Study (NAVEDTRA 10052)
Bureau of Naval Personnel Manual (BUPERSMAN, NAVPERS 15791)
Catalog of Navy Training Courses (CANTRAC, NAVEDTRA 10500)
Enlisted Transfer Manual (TRANSMAN, NAVPERS 15909)
Flags, Pennants, and Customs (DNC 27 [B])
General Military Training (GMT, OPNAVINST 1500.22)
Information Security Program Regulation (OPNAVINST 5510.1)
List of Training Manuals and Correspondence Courses (NAVEDTRA 10061)
Manual of Enlisted Classification Procedures (NAVPERS 15812)
Manual of Advancements (NAVPERS 15989)
Naval Orientation (NAVPERS 10900-83)
Navy Pay and Personnel Procedures Manual (PAYPERSMAN, NAVSO P-3050)
Navy Recruiting Manual—Enlisted (CRUITMAN-ENL, COMNAVCRUITCOMINST 1130.8)
Naval Reserve Indoctrination Guide (RAD 716-0257)
Organization of the U.S. Navy (NWP 2)
Rate Training Manuals (RTMs):
  Airman (NAVPERS 10307-C)
  Basic Military Requirements (NAVEDTRA 10054-D)
  Boatswain's Mate 3 & 2 (NAVEDTRA 10121-F)
  Disbursing Clerk 3 & 2 (NAVEDTRA 10274-G)
  Electrician's Mate 3 & 2 (NAVEDTRA 10546-D)
  Engineman 3 & 2 (NAVPERS 10541-B)
  Fireman (NAVEDTRA 10520-E)
  Gunner's Mate 3 & 2 (NAVEDTRA 10573)
  Hull Maintenance Technician (NAVEDTRA 10573)
  Personnelman 3 & 2 (NAVEDTRA 10254-C)
  Quartermaster 3 & 2 (NAVEDTRA 10149-F)
  Seaman (NAVPERS 10120-F)
  Signalman 3 & 2 (NAVEDTRA 10135-D)
  Yeoman 3 & 2 (NAVEDTRA 10240-G)
Replenishment at Sea (NWP 14 [A])

Retention Team Manual (NAVPERS 15878)
Standard Organization and Regulations of the U.S. Navy (OP-NAVINST 3120.32)
Uniform Code of Military Justice (UCMJ)
Uniformed Services Almanac 1977, Lee E. Sharff, Uniformed Services Almanac, Inc., Washington D.C., 1977.
United States Navy Regulations, 1973 (change 2)
United States Navy Uniform Regulations, 1978
Weapon Systems of the U.S. Navy 1977 (NAVSO P-3564 Rev.)

Publications by the Naval Institute Press, Annapolis, MD

A Mariner's Guide to the Rules of the Road, William H. Tate, 1976.
Combat Fleets of the World 1980/81, Jean Labayle Couhat, 1978.
Dictionary of Naval Abbreviations, Bill Wedertz, 2nd ed., 1977.
Division Officer's Guide, Capt. John V. Noel (USN Ret.) and Comdr. Frank E. Bassett, USN, 7th ed., 1976.
Engineering for the OOD, Cdr. Dan Felger, USN, 1980.
Introduction to Shipboard Weapons, (Fundamentals of Naval Science Series), Lt. Comdr. Carl D. Corse Jr., 1975.
Mariner's Pocket Companion Wallace E. Tobin III, 1976.
The Naval Aviation Guide, Vice Adm. Malcolm W. Cagle (USN Ret.) 3rd ed., 1976.
Naval Ceremonies, Customs, and Traditions, Vice Adm. W.P. Mack USN (Ret.) and LCdr. R.W. Connell, USN, 5th ed., 1980.
Naval Shiphandling, Capt. R.S. Crenshaw Jr. (USN Ret.) 4th ed., 1975.
Naval Terms Dictionary, Capt. John V. Noel Jr. (USN Ret.) and Capt. Edward L. Beach (USN Ret.), 4th ed., 1978.
Navigation and Operations, (Fundamentals of Naval Science Series), 1972.
Ops Officer's Manual, Cdr. P.T. Deutermann, USN, 1980.
Shipboard Damage Control, A.M. Bissell, E.J. Oertel and D.J. Livingston, 1976.
Ship Organization and Personnel, (Fundamentals of Naval Science Series), 1972.
The Ships and Aircraft of the U.S. Fleet, Norman Polmar, 11th ed., 1978.
Watch Officer's Guide, Cdr. Kenneth C. Jacobson, USN, 11th ed., 1979.

J. Official Publications and Directives

While the Constitution, various treaties, and the laws passed by the Congress make up the fundamental laws governing the Navy, they are really only broad outlines. The Navy has various publications and official directives expressly setting forth specific procedures for the day-to-day operations of the Navy Department and for the administration of personnel.

Although a complete knowledge of these publications and directives is required for the yeoman (YN) and personnelman (PN) ratings, a basic working knowledge of them will help you determine important policies and programs affecting your Navy career, regardless of your rating.

Perhaps the single most important publication, which affects nearly everything you do—including applications for various educational programs, transfers, discharges and separations—is the *Bureau of Naval Personnel Manual* (BUPERSMAN) (NAVPERS 15791). Other important, general-interest publications include pamphlets and brochures distributed by the Bureau of Naval Personnel. The title of this bureau has been changed to the Naval Military Personnel Command (NMPC). (See page 514.) They are identified as NAVPERS publications and forms.

A list of the major publications follows:

Navy Regulations (NAVREGS) is an important official publication. It outlines the organizational structure of the Department of the Navy and provides the principles and policies by which the Navy is governed. Its chapters, among many other things, define the responsibility, purpose, authority, and relationship of each bureau and office of the Navy Department.

Manual for Courts-Martial, United States, 1969 (Rev.) (MCM) describes the types of courts-martial established by the UCMJ, defines their jurisdiction, and prescribes their membership and procedures. It also covers such matters as nonjudicial punishment (NJP), reviews court-martial proceedings, new trials, and limitations on punishment.

Manual of the Medical Department (MANMED) (NAVMED P-117) contains material on the following subjects: general instructions for medical care of personnel, directions for procurement, storage, issue, and accounting of medical supplies and for training medical and dental personnel; procedures for keeping health records and submitting reports; and special instructions for procedures and reports in case of death.

559

Manual of the Judge Advocate General (JAGMAN) (JAGINST 5800.7) covers legal and judicial matters that apply only to the naval service. Included among these are instructions regarding boards of investigation and examining boards—their composition, authority, and procedures.

United States Navy Uniform Regulations (NAVPERS 15665), or "Uniform Regs" for short, describes the various uniforms for personnel in all categories, lists the uniforms required, and contains lists of articles worn or used together. It describes occasions when the various uniforms should be worn; methods of wearing medals, decorations, ribbons, rating badges, and special markings; and gives notes on the care of the uniform.

Joint Travel Regulations (JTR) is issued in two volumes; only the first volume deals with travel of members of the uniformed services. JTR interprets the laws and regulations concerning: travel, the manner in which transportation is furnished, provisions for travel of dependents, transportation of household goods (HHGs), reimbursement for travel expenses, and similar information.

U.S. Naval Travel Instructions (NAVSO P-1459) amplifies the rules laid down in Vol. 1 of the JTR.

Department of Defense Military Pay and Allowance Entitlements Manual (DODPM) covers statutory provisions for entitlements, deductions, and collections on military pay and allowances.

Navy Pay and Personnel Procedures Manual (PAYPERSMAN) (NAVSO P-3050) contains detailed pay and personnel procedures for maintaining the joint uniform military pay system (JUMPS) for members of the Navy. (The JUMPS system is described on pages 177–80.)

Enlisted Transfer Manual (TRANSMAN) (NAVPERS 15909) is the official manual for the distribution and assignment of enlisted personnel; it supplements the BUPERSMAN. The purpose of the TRANSMAN is to provide a quick reference of instructional and informational material relative to all facets of enlisted distribution.

Navy and Marine Corps Awards Manual, usually known simply as the "Awards Manual," is issued by the Secretary of the Navy (SECNAVINST 1650.1) for guidance in all matters pertaining to decorations, medals, and awards. Detailed information on the manner of wearing them is contained in Uniform Regs.

Manual of Advancement, published by the Bureau of Naval Personnel (BUPERSINST 1430.16), provides for the administration of the advancement system. It supports and enlarges on the basic policies outlined in BUPERSMAN and further provides for determining eligibility requirements for advancement; preparations of necessary forms; ordering, custody, and disposition of

Navy-wide exams; administration of all examinations for advancement; changes in rate or rating; and procedures for effecting advancements.

**Publica-
tions and
Directives**

Directives System

In addition to the publications already described, there are certain others which will affect your Navy life. The following commands produce instructional materials governing transfers, educational programs, financial and medical benefits, etc. They are listed as short titles first, since this is the way you will normally hear them described. The full title appears in the right-hand column.

BUMED	Bureau of Medicine and Surgery
BUPERS	Bureau of Naval Personnel
CNET	Chief of Naval Education and Training
COMNAVCRUITCOM	Commander, Navy Recruiting Command
COMNAVAIRLANT	Commander, Naval Air Force, Atlantic Fleet
COMNAVAIRPAC	Commander, Naval Air Force, Pacific Fleet
DOD	Department of Defense
GPO	Government Printing Office
JAG	Judge Advocate General
NAVAIR	Naval Air Systems Command
NAVCOMP	Comptroller of the Navy
NAVEDTRA	Chief of Navy Education and Training (Command)
NAVMILPERSCOM	Navy Military Personnel Command
NAVSUP	Naval Supply Systems Command
NAVTRA	Chief of Naval Training
NAVMAT	Naval Material Command
NAVSO	Executive Offices of the Secretary of the Navy
OPNAV	Office of the Chief of Naval Operations
SECNAV	Secretary of the Navy
VA	Veterans Administration

A directive—prepared as either an instruction, notice, or change transmittal—prescribes or establishes policy, organization, conduct, methods, or procedures. They either require some specific action or report or supply detailed information that is essential.

Directives

An instruction (abbreviated INST) contains authority or information that has a continuing reference value or that requires a continuing action. It remains in effect until superseded or cancelled, by its originator or by a higher authority. A notice (abbreviated NOTE) is a directive of a one-time or brief nature, which has a self-cancelling provision.

Here's an example of how the system works:

Let's take a hypothetical example using the Bureau of Naval Personnel (BUPERS). The reference may require you to look up a certain BUPERS instruction, such as BUPERSINST 1560. You may discover that there is no BUPERSINST 1560, but there is a 1560.1. The latter indicates an update of the basic instruction, and is the most current information available on your desired subject. It may also appear as BUPERSINST 1560.1C, which indicates that the previous instructions—1560, 1560.1, 1560.1A and 1560.1B—have been superseded by the new 1560.1C.

If you cannot find the reference, BUPERSINST 1560, do not mistakenly think that 1561 is the newest reference. It is not— 1561 will apply to a different subject entirely. If BUPERSINST 1560 is not listed, it probably means that the program has been disestablished . . . and you'll probably have to seek the advice of your resident personnelman to track down a new reference.

One other factor should also be considered. Again, using our hypothetical example, you may find, once you've consulted the reference (BUPERSINST 1560), that certain pages appear as BUPERSINST 1560 CH 1. This indicates that a change transmittal— which has provided specific updated information—has been added. Normally a change transmittal will only affect certain pages of an instruction; the remainder of the "original" instruction is still effective in its current form.

If there is some slight—usually temporary—modification in the program covered by BUPERSINST 1560, you can locate that information by consulting the current BUPERS notice (BUPERS-NOTE 1560), which covers the same program.

These same basic rules can be applied to the following command references which should prove useful during your career:

"A" schools	NAVEDTRA 10500
	TRANSMAN, Chap. 7,8
Abbreviations	BUPERSINST 2340.1
Accelerated advancement program	BUPERSMAN, Art. 2230150
Active duty agreements	BUPERSMAN, Art. 1050200
Active duty service date	BUPERSMAN, Art. 5030460
Advance, leave	BUPERSMAN, Art. 3020320

**Publica-
tions and
Directives**

563

Directives

	BUPERSMAN, Art. 6610300
Personnel reliability program	BUPERSINST 5510.11
Obesity	BUPERSMAN, Art. 3410150
	BUPERSMAN, Art. 3420440
Officer candidate school	
(OCS) program	BUPERSINST 1120.35
	NAVPERS 15878
Open rates/skills list	BUPERSINST 1133.25
Orders	
Proceed time	BUPERSMAN, Art. 1810300
Reimbursement	BUPERSMAN, Art. 1810280
Standard transfer orders (STOs)	TRANSMAN, Chap. 23
Travel time	BUPERSMAN, Art. 1810320
Overseas assignments	TRANSMAN, Chap. 4
	BUPERSINST 1300.26
	BUPERSINST 1300.40
	NAVPERS 15878
Overseas diplomacy	OPNAVINST 5400.36
Passports	BUPERSMAN, Art. 3020420
	BUPERSMAN, Art. 4640100
	BUPERSINST 4650.14
Pay and allowances	BUPERSMAN, Art. 2610100
	PAYPERSMAN
Pay entry base date (PEBD)	BUPERSMAN, Art. 2610150
Paygrades	NAVPERS 15812
	BUPERSMAN, Art. 2210200
Personal affairs	NAVEDTRA 46600
Personal services centers	NAVEDTRA 10119
	BUPERSMAN, Art. 1810580
	OPNAVINST 1740.1
Personal staff duty performance	BUPERSMAN, Art. 3410150
Personnel advancement	
requirements (PAR) program	BUPERSINST 1418.10
Personnel exchange program (PEP)	NAVPERS 15878
	OPNAVINST 5700.7
Physical fitness	OPNAVINST 1500.22
	BUPERSMAN, Art. 3420440
Place of separation	BUPERSMAN, Art. 3810260
Preferred overseas duty	TRANSMAN, Chap. 4
Pregnancy status	
Maternity care	BUPERSMAN, Art. 3810180
Separation request	BUPERSMAN, Art. 3810170
PREP (predischarge	
education program)	OPNAVINST 1560.5
	CNETINST 1560.1
Preparatory schools	
BOOST	BUPERSMAN, Art. 1020360
Military/Air Force academies	BUPERSMAN, Art. 6620120

Photo Credits

8, 10: Bill Wedertz
19: JOCS John Burlage
111, 200, 212, 232, 303: PHC Milt Putnam
39: PH1 Terry Mitchell
ii, 56, 343: PHC Charles L. Wright
62: JOC Dave Garrison
63: PH1 A.J. Riguette
66: PH2 Felimon Barbante
72, 116, 167, 247, 265, 371, 459, 461, 491: PH2 Dwain Patton
82: PHAA Jason J. Jorgensen
107, 163, 346: PH1 Harold D. Phillips
113: PH1 J.A. Davidson
143, 189: PH1 William Fair
149: PH1 Jim Preston
152: PH1 Jon P. Sagester
153: JOC Warren W. Grass
157: JO2 Art Robb
162: PHC Donald F. Grantham
170, 297: PH1 William J. Galligan
173: PH2 Nush Grabouski
184, 349: PHC Ken Markham
190: PH2 Dave Longstreath
203: JO1 Jerry Atchison
222: JOC Robert D. Moser
245: PH1 Arthur Legare
250, 372, 402: PH1 John R. Sheppard
255: PH2 George D. Lloyd
263: Lt. D.V. Orgill
273: PH1 R.H. Green
282, 351: Ens. Carl R. Begy
284: PHCS Chuck Bassi
299, 442: JO1 Rick Miller
300: CDR Tony DeMarco
325: PH1 Randy Emmons
335: PH1 Robert E. Woods
344: JOCS Ernie Filtz
360: PHAN Thomas McAuliffe
374, 378, 404: PH2 Harry Diffenbaugh
389: PH3 Bob Collins
412: PHAN Glenn M. Souther
423: JOCS James F. Falk
439: PHC Lonnie McKay
445: JO2 George Webb
492: PH1 John P. Francavillo
507: Robert de Gast

The cover design for this edition was adapted from a photograph by JO2 Art Robb.

All other uncredited photos are official U.S. Navy.

577

Index

578

591